T0214275

Lecture Notes in Computer Science 12122

Founding Editors

Gerhard Goos
Karlsruhe Institute of Technology, Karlsruhe, Germany
Juris Hartmanis
Cornell University, Ithaca, NY, USA

Editorial Board Members

Elisa Bertino
Purdue University, West Lafayette, IN, USA
Wen Gao
Peking University, Beijing, China
Bernhard Steffen
TU Dortmund University, Dortmund, Germany
Gerhard Woeginger
RWTH Aachen, Aachen, Germany
Moti Yung
Columbia University, New York, NY, USA

More information about this series at http://www.springer.com/series/7409

Anoop Singhal · Jaideep Vaidya (Eds.)

Data and Applications Security and Privacy XXXIV

34th Annual IFIP WG 11.3 Conference, DBSec 2020
Regensburg, Germany, June 25–26, 2020
Proceedings

 Springer

Editors
Anoop Singhal
National Institute of Standards
and Technology
Gaithersburg, MD, USA

Jaideep Vaidya (iD)
Rutgers University
Newark, NJ, USA

ISSN 0302-9743   ISSN 1611-3349   (electronic)
Lecture Notes in Computer Science
ISBN 978-3-030-49668-5   ISBN 978-3-030-49669-2   (eBook)
https://doi.org/10.1007/978-3-030-49669-2

LNCS Sublibrary: SL3 – Information Systems and Applications, incl. Internet/Web, and HCI

This Springer imprint is published by the registered company Springer Nature Switzerland AG
The registered company address is: Gewerbestrasse 11, 6330 Cham, Switzerland

Preface

This volume contains the papers selected for presentation at the 34th Annual IFIP WG11.3 Conference on Data and Applications Security and Privacy (DBSec 2020), that was supposed to be during June 25–26, 2020, in Regensburg. While the conference was held on the dates as scheduled, due to the COVID-19 situation it was held virtually (for the first time in the history of DBSec), instead of physically in Regensburg.

In response to the call for papers of this edition, 41 submissions were received, and all submissions were evaluated on the basis of their significance, novelty, and technical quality. The Program Committee, comprising 40 members, performed an excellent job, with the help of additional reviewers, of reviewing all submissions through a careful anonymous process (three or more reviews per submission). The Program Committee's work was carried out electronically, yielding intensive discussions. Of the submitted papers, 14 full papers and 8 short papers were selected for presentation at the conference.

The success of DBSec 2020 depended on the volunteering effort of many individuals, and there is a long list of people who deserve special thanks. We would like to thank all the members of the Program Committee and all the external reviewers, for all their hard work in evaluating the papers and for their active participation in the discussion and selection process. We are very grateful to all people who readily assisted and ensured a smooth organization process, in particular Günther Pernul for his efforts as DBSec 2020 general chair; Sara Foresti (IFIP WG11.3 chair) for her guidance and support; Yuan Hong and Benedikt Putz (publicity chairs) for helping with publicity; and Petra Sauer for helping with other arrangements for the conference. EasyChair made the conference review and proceedings process run very smoothly.

Last but certainly not least, thanks to all the authors who submitted papers and all the conference attendees. We hope you find the proceedings of DBSec 2020 interesting, stimulating, and inspiring for your future research.

April 2020

Anoop Singhal
Jaideep Vaidya

Organization

Program Committee

Ayesha Afzal	Air University, USA
Vijay Atluri	Rutgers University, USA
Frédéric Cuppens	Télécom Bretagne, France
Nora Cuppens-Boulahia	IMT Atlantique, France
Sabrina De Capitani di Vimercati	Università degli Studi di Milano, Italy
Giovanni Di Crescenzo	Perspecta Labs, USA
Csilla Farkas	USC, USA
Barbara Fila	INSA Rennes, IRISA, France
Sara Foresti	Università degli Studi di Milano, Italy
Steven Furnell	Plymouth University, UK
Ehud Gudes	Ben-Gurion University, Israel
Yuan Hong	Illinois Institute of Technology, USA
Sokratis Katsikas	Open University of Cyprus, Cyprus
Costas Lambrinoudakis	University of Piraeus, Greece
Adam J. Lee	University of Pittsburgh, USA
Yingjiu Li	University of Oregon, USA
Giovanni Livraga	University of Milan, Italy
Javier Lopez	UMA, Spain
Brad Malin	Vanderbilt University, USA
Fabio Martinelli	IIT-CNR, Italy
Sjouke Mauw	University of Luxembourg, Luxembourg
Catherine Meadows	NRL, USA
Charles Morisset	Newcastle University, UK
Martin Olivier	University of Pretoria, South Africa
Stefano Paraboschi	Università di Bergamo, Italy
Günther Pernul	Universität Regensburg, Germany
Silvio Ranise	FBK-Irst, Italy
Indrajit Ray	Colorado State University, USA
Indrakshi Ray	Colorado State University, USA
Kui Ren	State University of New York at Buffalo, USA
Pierangela Samarati	Università degli Studi di Milano, Italy
Andreas Schaad	WIBU-Systems, Germany
Anoop Singhal	NIST, USA
Scott Stoller	Stony Brook University, USA
Shamik Sural	IIT Kharagpur, India
Jaideep Vaidya	Rutgers University, Australia
Vijay Varadharajan	The University of Newcastle, Australia

Lingyu Wang	Concordia University, Canada
Wendy Hui Wang	Stevens Institute of Technology, USA
Edgar Weippl	University of Vienna, Austria
Attila A. Yavuz	University of South Florida, USA
Nicola Zannone	Eindhoven University of Technology, The Netherlands

Additional Reviewers

Alcaraz, Cristina	Mohamady, Meisam
Berlato, Stefano	Mykoniati, Maria
Binder, Dominik	Nieto, Ana
Bursuc, Sergiu	Roman, Rodrigo
Chen, Xihui	Sascha, Kern
Clark, Stanley	Schlette, Daniel
Derbeko, Philip	Sciarretta, Giada
Georgiopoulou, Zafeiroula	Shafiq, Basit
Groll, Sebastian	Thang, Hoang
Haefner, Kyle	Voloch, Nadav
Liu, Bingyu	Wan, Zhiyu
Liu, Yongtai	Wang, Han
Lyvas, Christos	Yan, Chao

Contents

Visualization and Analytics for Security

Spatial Systems and Crowdsourcing Security

Secure Outsourcing and Privacy

Network and Cyber-physical Systems Security

Modeling and Mitigating Security Threats in Network Functions Virtualization (NFV)

Nawaf Alhebaishi[1,2(✉)], Lingyu Wang[1], and Sushil Jajodia[3]

[1] Concordia Institute for Information Systems Engineering, Concordia University, Montreal, Canada
{n_alheb,wang}@ciise.concordia.ca
[2] Faculty of Computing and Information Technology, King Abdulaziz University, Jeddah, Saudi Arabia
[3] Center for Secure Information Systems, George Mason University, Fairfax, US
jajodia@gmu.edu

Abstract. By virtualizing proprietary hardware networking devices, Network Functions Virtualization (NFV) allows agile and cost-effective deployment of diverse network services for multiple tenants on top of the same physical infrastructure. As NFV relies on virtualization, and as an NFV stack typically involves several levels of abstraction and multiple co-resident tenants, this new technology also unavoidably leads to new security threats. In this paper, we take the first step toward modeling and mitigating security threats unique to NFV. Specifically, we model both cross-layer and co-residency attacks on the NFV stack. Additionally, we mitigate such threats through optimizing the virtual machine (VM) placement with respect to given constraints. The simulation results demonstrate the effectiveness of our solution.

1 Introduction

As a cornerstone of cloud computing, virtualization has enabled providers to deliver various cloud services to different tenants using shared resources in a cost-efficient way. The trend of virtualization has also led to many innovations in networking in and outside clouds. In particular, traditional networks heavily rely on vendor specific hardware devices with integrated software, such as routers, switches, firewalls, IDSs, etc., which lacks sufficient flexibility demanded by today's businesses. Consequently, the need for decoupling software from hardware in network devices has led to Network Functions Virtualization (NFV) [14], which basically virtualizes proprietary hardware networking devices. As a key enabling technology of 5G, NFV has seen an increased adoption among cloud service providers, especially in the telecommunication industry [22].

However, the reliance on virtualization and the increased complexity together imply that NFV may unavoidably introduce new security concerns. First, as an NFV stack involves several abstraction levels covering the physical and virtual

© IFIP International Federation for Information Processing 2020
Published by Springer Nature Switzerland AG 2020
A. Singhal and J. Vaidya (Eds.): DBSec 2020, LNCS 12122, pp. 3–23, 2020.
https://doi.org/10.1007/978-3-030-49669-2_1

infrastructures as well as the virtual network functions [14], it naturally has a larger attack surface, opening doors to new security threats such as cross-layer attacks. Second, as one of the main advantages of NFV is to provide diverse network services to different tenants using the same hardware infrastructure, NFV would also share similar cross-tenant attacks as those seen in clouds (e.g., [44]). Therefore, security threats introduced by the multi-layer and multi-tenant nature of NFV need to be better understood and mitigated.

Attack modeling and mitigation in NFV has only received limited attention (a more detailed review of related work will be given in Sect. 6). Existing works have focused on specific vulnerabilities caused by orchestration and management complexities [43] and vulnerabilities resulting from the lack of interoperability [15] or the lack of proper synchronization between different abstraction levels [24]. There also exist works on dynamically managing security functions in NFV [41] and verifying Service Function Chaining (SFC)-related properties [17,28,38,45]. Existing works on co-residency attacks mostly focus on clouds [4,6] instead of NFV. To the best of our knowledge, there lack a general approach to modeling and mitigating NFV attacks.

In this paper, we take the first step toward modeling and mitigating security attacks in NFV. Our key ideas are threefold. First, we propose a multi-layer resource graph model for NFV in order to capture the co-existence of network services, VMs, and physical resources at different abstraction levels inside an NFV stack, and how those could potentially be exploited by attackers. This model allows us to capture not only attacks that target each layer of the NFV stack, but also attacks that go across different layers by exploiting the inter-dependencies between corresponding resources at those layers. Second, we also model the insider threats posed by malicious or compromised users of co-resident tenants inside the same NFV stack. The model allows us to captures how a co-residency attack may allow insiders to satisfy certain initial security conditions, such as privileges or connectivity, which are normally not accessible to external attackers. Third, we propose a solution to mitigate security attacks in NFV through VM placement and migration, which is a low cost option already available in NFV. The aforementioned model allows us to formulate the attack mitigation in NFV as an optimization problem and solve it using standard optimization techniques. We evaluate our approach through simulations to demonstrate its effectiveness under various situations. In summary, the main contribution of this paper is twofold:

- To the best of our knowledge, this is the first study on the modeling of security threats in an NFV stack. Our multi-layer resource graph model demonstrates the possibility of novel security threats in NFV, such as cross-layer and co-residency attacks, and also provides a systematic way to capture and quantify such threats.
- By formulating the optimization problem of mitigating attacks on NFV through optimal VM placement and migration, we provide an effective solution, as evidenced by our simulation results, for achieving a better trade-off between security and other constraints using standard optimization techniques.

The remainder of this paper is organized as follows; Sect. 2 presents background information on NFV and co-residency in NFV, and provides a motivating example. In Sect. 3, we present our multi-layer resource graph and insider attack model, and describe the application of a security metric. Section 4 formulates the optimization problem and discusses several use cases. Section 5 gives the simulation results. Section 6 reviews related works. Section 7 concludes the paper.

2 Preliminaries

This section first provides background information on NFV and co-residency in NFV, and then gives a motivating example.

2.1 Background on NFV

As a main technology pillar of network softwarization and 5G, NFV provides network functions through software running on standard hardware. NFV enables network service providers to deploy dynamic, agile and scalable Network Services (NS). Such benefits come from the fact that an NFV deployment stack is usually an integration of various virtualization technologies including cloud and SDN together with various network orchestration and automation tools.

Specifically, the left side of Fig. 1 shows the European Telecommunications Standards Institute (ETSI) NFV reference architecture [14]. The architecture builds on three main blocks, i.e., virtual network function (VNF), NFV infrastructure (NFVI), and NFV management and orchestration (MANO). First, the VNF provides network functions, such as router, switch, firewall, and load balancer, running on top of VMs through software. Second, NFVI represents the cloud infrastructure that provides basic computations, network, and storage needs for the execution of VNFs. Lastly, MANO has three management components, virtual infrastructure manager (VIM), virtual Network function manager (VNFM), and network function virtualization orchestrator (NFVO), which together manage and orchestrate the lifecycle of physical and virtual resources.

In addition, the right side of Fig. 1 shows a multi-layer NFV deployment model [24] which complements the aforementioned ETSI architecture with deployment details, and divides an NFV stack into four layers, i.e., service orchestration (layer 1), resource management (layer 2), virtual infrastructure (layer 3), and physical infrastructure (layer 4).

2.2 Co-Residency in NFV

As an NFV stack is multi-layer and multi-tenant in nature, placing and migrating a VM or VNF can be a challenging task for the provider due to the issue of co-residency. It is well known that co-residency may lead to various security issues, such as side-channel attacks, and additionally the tenant may have specific requirements in terms of (the lack of) co-residency. Co-residency may occur in an NFV environment when a new VM or VNF is first placed, or when an

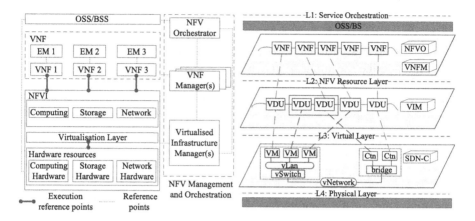

Fig. 1. ETSI reference architecture [14] (left) and multi-layer NFV model [24] (right)

existing VM or VNF is migrated. The tenant requirements may specify that certain VNFs are to be placed on a dedicated host, or a VM needs to have the auto-scaling feature such that its need for more space can be quickly fulfilled. In terms of security, co-resident VMs or VNFs may belong to tenants with conflicting interests, and the co-residency may enable an insider attack with increased privileges and connectivity not available to regular attackers.

A unique aspect of co-residency in NFV is that, in an NFV stack, co-residency can happen between more layers, such as between VNFs and physical hosts, between VNFs and VMs, or between VMs and physical hosts. The co-residency of VNFs or VMs on the same physical host can occur due to placement or migration, which is known to lead to side-channel or resource depletion attacks due to the shared physical resources such as CPU, memory, or cache. The co-residency of VNFs on the same VM can also occur when different tenants employ the same VM to run similar network functions, such as virtual firewall or virtual IDS [21,23,32].

2.3 Motivating Example

In the following, we present a concrete example of NFV stack to demonstrate the challenges in modeling and mitigating security threats for NFV. First of all, as NFV is a relatively new concept, there lack public access to information regarding the detailed hardware and software configurations used in real NFV environments. As can be seen in Fig. 1, both the ETSI architecture [14] and the multi-layer deployment model [24] are quite high level, and lack such details. Most other existing works either focus on high-level frameworks and guidelines for risk and impact assessment [26,29,33], or very specific vulnerabilities [25,30, 31], with a clear gap in between.

To address such limitations, we design a concrete example of NFV stack, as shown in Fig. 2, based on both the ETSI architecture [14] and the multi-layer

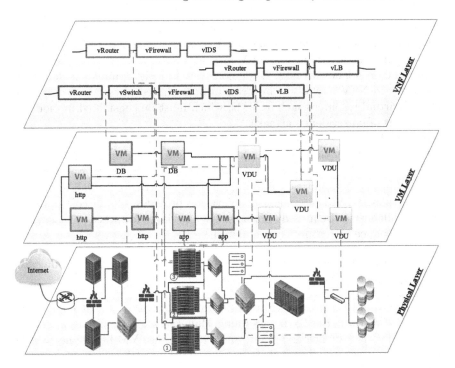

Fig. 2. A concrete example of NFV stack (vFirewall: virtual firewall, LB: load balancer, DB: database, VM: virtual machine, VDU: virtual deployment unit)

deployment model [24], as well as other public available information gathered from various providers and vendors. As shown in Fig. 2, the NFV stack is depicted on three layers where the VNF layer shows three service function chains (SFCs), and the VM and physical layers show the corresponding virtual and physical infrastructures used to implement those SFCs, respectively. The dashed lines between layers demonstrate the correspondence between the services and the virtual or physical resources. We assume there are three tenants, shown in Fig. 2 through different colors, i.e., Alice (blue), Bob (green), and Mallory (red)), that are hosted on this NFV stack.

In such a scenario, both the NFV provider and each tenant may want to understand and mitigate potential security threats. While existing threat models such as various attack trees and attack graphs may be applied, there are some unique challenges and opportunities as follows.

– First, as can be seen in Fig. 2, the NFV stack is composed of different layers, and the inter-dependencies between resources on those layers may lead to novel cross-layer attacks. The NFV tenant and provider need to consider all layers and the inter-dependencies between layers when analyzing potential security threats because of the possibility of such cross-layer attacks.

- Second, the fact that multiple tenants are sharing both virtual and physical resources in the same NFV stack poses another challenge, i.e., co-residency attacks. In contrast to clouds, NFV may have an increased attack surface in terms of co-residency attacks. As demonstrated in Fig. 2, unlike in clouds, co-residency in NFV may occur in terms of both shared physical resources and shared virtual resources such as VMs, which must be considered in modeling the threat of co-residency attacks.
- On the other hand, virtualization in NFV also provides an opportunity for mitigating security threats through a unique hardening option, i.e., through VM placement or migration. In contrast to other hardening options, such as patching vulnerabilities, disabling services, or stricter firewall and access control rules [8], VM placement or migration provides a lower cost option as it is a built-in feature already employed by providers for other purposes such as maintenance or resource consolidation.

More specifically, we consider concrete problems of threat modeling and attack mitigation based on Fig. 2 as follows.

- First, we would like to model potential multi-step attacks that could occur in this NFV stack (Fig. 2), by assuming Mallory (whose resources are shown in red color) is a malicious tenant, and the database VM belonging to Alice (whose resources are shown in blue color) is the critical asset in question. The modeling process must consider the multi-layer and multi-tenant nature of NFV and its many security implications, e.g., an attacker's VM placed on the database server (node # 1) or on the *http* server (node # 3) would certainly incur very different security threats, and an attacker co-residing with the target tenant on the VM level could have a better chance of compromising the target than one co-residing on the physical host level.
- Second, we would like to mitigate the modeled threats posed by Mallory to Alice's database VM, through optimal placement or migration of virtual resources in this NFV stack. The solution must quantify the security threats before and after the hardening process in order to show the amount of improvement in terms of security, and the solution should be able to accommodate other considerations or constraints, e.g., limiting the scope to one layer or multiple layers, supporting different VM placement policies (such as those used in CloudSim [11]), and limiting the cost of placement or migration (such as the maximum number of VM migrations).

To this end, we will present our threat modeling solution in Sect. 3 and our attack mitigation solution in Sect. 4.

3   Modeling Security Threats in NFV

This section presents our solutions for modeling potential multi-step attacks on an NFV stack (Sect. 3.1), for modeling insider attacks from co-residing tenants (Sect. 3.2), and for quantifying the threats using a security metric (Sect. 3.3).

3.1   Multi-layer Resource Graph

Threat Model: Our goal is to help the NFV provider or tenants to better understand and mitigate the security threats from an external attacker, a dishonest or compromised user or tenant, or a tenant administrator or cloud operator with limited privileges. We assume the NFV provider and its administrators are trusted and consequently the inputs to our threat modeling process are intact. Our in-scope threats are security attacks used to escalate privileges or gain remote accesses through exploiting known or zero day vulnerabilities in the physical or virtual entities inside an NFV stack. Out-of-scope threats include attacks which do not involve exploiting vulnerabilities (e.g., phishing or social engineering attacks) or do not propagate through networks (e.g., flash drive-based malware).

To model the security threats in an NFV stack, our key idea is to apply the resource graph concept [34] (which is syntactically similar to attack graphs, but focuses on modeling zero day attacks exploiting unknown vulnerabilities) while considering the multi-layer nature of NFV (as explained in Sect. 2.1). Specifically, based on a model of the NFV stack with three layers, i.e., the VNF layer, VM layer, and physical layer, as previously demonstrated in Fig. 2, we propose the concept of *cross-layer resource graph* to represent the causal relationships between different resources both inside each layer, and across different layers, in a given NFV stack.

We first illustrate the concept through an example, before giving the formal definitions. Figure 3 shows an example of a cross-layer resource graph for our running example (only a portion of the cross-layer resource graph is shown here due to space limitations). The VNF layer maps to layer 1 and layer 2 in the multi-layer NFV deployment model [24], which depicts exploits of various virtual network functions, such as virtual firewalls, load-balancers, switches, etc. The VM layer corresponds to layer 3 in the NFV deployment model, which includes exploits of the VMs that are used to implement the virtual network functions in the cloud layer. Finally, the physical layer includes exploits of the physical hosts. The left-hand side of Fig. 3 shows the cross-layer resource graph for one tenant, whereas the right-hand side shows co-residency attacks from other tenants (which will be explained in next section).

Each triple inside an oval indicates a potential zero day exploit (in which case the unknown vulnerability is represented by the exploited service itself) or an exploit of known vulnerabilities, in the form of <service or vulnerability, source host, destination host>. For example, <Xen, 3, h3> indicates an exploit of Xen coming from a VM on physical host 3 to that physical host itself, and the plaintext pairs indicate the pre- or post-conditions of those exploits in the form of <condition, host>, where a condition can be a privilege on the host, e.g., <root,3> means that the root privilege on the VM runs on host 3, and <user,vFW> means the user privilege is on the VNF layer for the virtual firewall. Additionally, conditions may include the existence of a service on the host (e.g., <Xen,3>), or a connectivity (e.g., <0,3> means that attackers can connect to a VM on host 3 from host 0, and <2,h2> means a local exploit is occurring

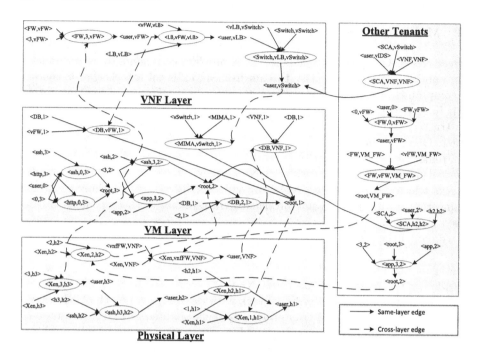

Fig. 3. An example of cross-layer resource graph (FW: firewall, LB: load balancer, DB: database, MIMA: man in the middle attack, SCA: side-channel attack)

on host 2). The edges point from pre-conditions to an exploit and then to its post-conditions, which indicate that any exploit can be executed if and only if all of its pre-conditions are satisfied, whereas executing an exploit is enough to satisfy all of its post-conditions. The following provides formal definitions of those concepts.

Definition 1 (Same-layer Resource Graph). *Given a collection of hosts (physical hosts or VMs) H and the set of resources HR (services or VNFs running on a physical host or a VM) with the resource mapping $rm(.) : H \rightarrow 2^{HR}$, and also given a set of zero day exploits $E = \{< r, h_s, h_d > | h_s \in H, h_d \in H, h_r \in rm(h_d)\}$ and the set of their pre- and post-condition C, a same-layer resource graph is a directed graph $G(E \cup C, HR_r \cup HR_i)$ where $pre \subseteq C \times E$ and $post \subseteq E \times C$ are the pre- and post-condition relations, respectively.*

Definition 2 (Cross-layer Resource Graph). *Given the same-layer resource graph for the three layers, $G_i(E_i \cup C_i, pre_i \cup post_i)(1 \leq i \leq 3)$, and given the cross-layer edges $pre_c \subseteq \bigcup_1^3 C_i \times \bigcup_1^3 E_i$ and $post_c \subseteq \bigcup_1^3 E_i \times \bigcup_1^3 C_i$, a cross-layer resource graph is a directed graph $G(\bigcup_1^3 (E_i \cup C_i), \bigcup_1^3 (pre_i \cup post_i) \cup pre_c \cup post_c)$.*

3.2 Modeling Co-Residency Attacks

In modeling co-residency attacks, our main idea is to capture the consequences of such attacks as satisfying certain conditions inside the cross-layer resource graph of the targeted tenant. For example, in Fig. 3, the left-hand side shows the cross-layer resource graph of the targeted tenant, which depicts what an external attacker may do to compromise the critical asset <user, h1>. On the other hand, the right-hand side of the figure depicts the insider threat coming from potential co-residency attacks launched by other tenants. The (dashed) lines pointing from the right to the left side of the figure show that, as the consequence of the co-residency attacks (right), some conditions inside the targeted tenant's resource graph (left) may be satisfied, either within the same layer or across different layers. The co-residency could occur w.r.t. the physical layer, which is similar to the co-residency in clouds (when tenants share the same physical host). The co-residency could also occur w.r.t. the VMs when tenants employ the same VM to run their VNFs, which is unique to NFV.

For example, as shown on the right-hand side of Fig. 3, a malicious co-resident tenant can potentially gain a user privilege on the vSwitch service of the targeted tenant through a local exploit <SCA, VNF, VNF>, or he/she can gain a root privilege on a VM on host 2 through a similar attack (<SCA, h3, h3>) (where <user, 3'> means the privilege of the malicious tenant on a VM on host 3). A malicious tenant who shares VNFs running on the same VM may attack the virtual firewall VNF and subsequently the corresponding VM to eventually be able to control the firewall (<root, VM_FW>) and modify its rules in order to gain access to the critical asset. A malicious tenant can also exploit an application running on VM 2 to gain control of that VM, and subsequently attack the co-residing host h2. These examples show how our model can capture co-residency attacks between different layers of the NFV stack.

3.3 Applying the Security Metric

Before we could mitigate the modeled security threats, we need to first quantify them such that we could evaluate the level of threats before and after we apply a hardening option. For this purpose, we apply the k-zero day safety security metric [39,40] originally proposed for traditional networks. The metric basically counts how many distinct unknown vulnerabilities must be exploited in order to compromise a given critical asset. A larger k value will indicate a relatively more secure network because the possibility of having more unknown vulnerabilities occurring at the same time, inside the same network, and exploitable by the same attacker would be significantly lower. The metric can be evaluated on the resource graph of a network, which basically gives the length of the shortest path (in terms of the number of distinct zero day exploits). The exploits of known vulnerabilities can be either regarded as a shortcut (i.e., they do not count toward k) or assigned with a significantly lower weight in the calculation of k.

On the basis of the cross-layer resource graph model introduced in previous sections, the k-zero day safety metric ($k0d$) can be applied in several ways. First, we could evaluate the metric on the cross-layer resource graph of the targeted tenant, without considering others tenants, whose result provides an estimation for the threat coming from external attackers. Second, we could also evaluate the metric on the cross-layer resource graph including co-resident attacks from others tenants, and we could consider one particular malicious tenant, or multiple such tenants either separately (assuming they do not collude) or collectively (as one, assuming they may collude). Third, we could evaluate the metric before, and after applying a placement or migration-based hardening option, and the difference in the results will indicate the effectiveness of such a hardening option (which we will further investigate in next section).

For example, in Fig. 3, by considering a malicious tenant sharing the same physical host with the targeted tenant (indicated by privilege <root, VM_FW>) would yield a $k0d$ value of 2 since two zero day exploits <Xen, vnfFW, NFV>, and <DB, VNF, 1> are needed to reach the critical asset. Whereas considering a malicious tenant with privilege <user, 2'> (here 2' indicates the privilege belongs to a tenant different from the targeted one) would yield a k value of 3 since three zero day exploits, <SCA, h2, h2>, <DB, 2, 1>, and <Xen, 1, h1> are needed.

4   Attack Mitigation

In this section, we present the optimization-based mitigation through placement and migration of VNFs and VMs, and demonstrate its applicability through discussing several use cases.

4.1   Optimization-Based Mitigation

Based on our previous definition of cross-layer resource graph model and the discussions on modeling co-residency and applying the $k0d$ metric, we can define the problem of optimal placement and migration of VMs and VNFs. As shown in Definition 3, hosts and resources are defined in a way such that the placement and migration may apply to both VMs (on physical hosts) and VNFs (on VMs) through the resource mapping function. The objective function is the application of the $k0d$ metric to the cross-layer resource graph (which can under a value assignment of the resource mapping function. Note that the application of the $k0d$ metric could take several forms for different purposes, as discussed in Sect. 3.3), which gives different variations of the optimization problem. Although not specified in the definition, constraints may be given in terms of possible value assignments to the resource mapping function, e.g., which VM (or VNF) may be placed or migrated to which physical host (or VM), or a threshold for the maximum number of migrated VMs.

Definition 3 (The optimal NFV co-residency problem). *Given a collection of hosts (physical hosts or VMs) H, the set of resources HR (services* *or VNFs running on a physical host or a VM), and the collection of tenants T with the tenant mapping function $tm(.) : HR \rightarrow T$, the optimal NFV co-residency problem is to find a resource mapping function $rm(.) : H \rightarrow 2^{HR}$ to maximize $k0d(G)$ where G is the cross-layer resource graph, and $k0d(G)$ denotes the application of the $k0d$ metric to G.*

The optimal NFV co-residency problem we have defined is intractable, since it can be easily reduced to the NP-hard problem of network hardening through diversity in traditional networks [7]. Specifically, the goal in the diversity problem is to maximize the $k0d$ metric by changing the instance of services (e.g., from IIS to Apache for web service), assuming that different instances of the same service along the shortest path would both count toward the k value (conversely, two identical instances would only count as one). Our problem can be reduced to this since, for any given resource graph G under the diversity problem, we can construct a special case of our problem by regarding G as the VM-layer resource graph, and regarding the instance of a service as the physical host on which that service resides (such that identical instances of a service are always co-resident). By further assuming that the attacker can always trivially exploit all co-resident services as long as he/she can exploit one (i.e., co-resident services only count as one toward the k value), the two problems then become equivalent.

In our study, we use the genetic algorithm (GA) [18] to optimize the VM (VNF) placement and migration for maximizing k. Our choice of GA is inspired by [13] and based on the fact that GA provides a simple way to encode candidate solutions and requires little information to search effectively in a large search space [18]. Specifically, the cross-layer resource graph is taken as input to the optimization algorithm, with k (averaged between tenants) as the fitness function. We try to find the best VM placement within a reasonable number of generations. The constraints we have considered include defining the resource mapping function in the case that specific VMs can be assigned to each host (e.g., firewall only), enforcing a given placement policy (e.g., CloudSim [11] placement policy), or satisfying a maximum number of migrating VMs. In our simulations, we choose the probability of 0.8 for crossover and 0.2 for mutation based on our experiences.

4.2   Use Cases

We demonstrate the applicability of our solution through several use cases with different types of attackers and while considering different layers. The first use case contrasts an external attacker to an insider launching cross-tenant attacks. The second use case compares a same-layer attack versus a cross-layer attack. The last use case is based on the motivating example shown in Sect. 2.3.

- Use Case A: In this case, we have an external attacker using a victim tenant's resources, and an insider malicious tenant co-residing with the victim tenant. Figure 4 shows the cross-layer resource graph for the external attacker (AE) and the insider attacker (AI). The figure shows the shortest path (dashed

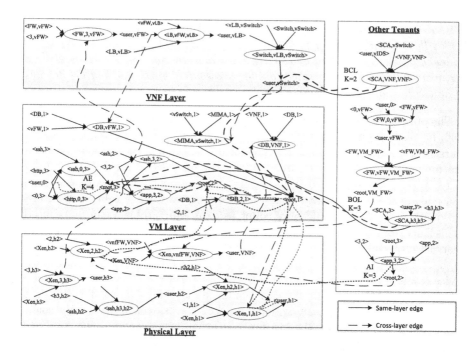

Fig. 4. Use Cases A and B (FW: firewall, LB: load balancer, DB: database, MIMA: man in the middle attack, SCA: side-channel attack, AE: external attacker, AI: insider attacker, BCL: cross-layer attack, BOL: one-layer attack)

lines) for calculating the $k0d$ metric, and the critical asset is represented as $< user, h1 >$. After optimization, the value of k for the external attacker (AE) is 4, and for the insider attacker (AI) is 3 (which means there is less room to mitigate the insider threat).

– Use Case B: In this case, we compare a one-layer attack (BOL) to a cross-layer attack (BCL) for an insider malicious tenant. The BOL and BCL dashed lines shown in Fig. 4 show the shortest paths for the malicious tenant using his/her co-residency with the victim tenant to reach the target $< root, 1 >$. After optimization, the value $k = 3$ for BOL and $k = 2$ for BCL show that there is less room to mitigate the insider threat when the attack may go across layers.

– Use Case C: This case shows the optimal placement result for our motivating example discussed in Sect. 2.3. We consider three tenants (Alice (A), Bob (B), and Mallory (M)) and three servers each of which can host four VMs. We consider Mallory a malicious tenant and the database VM belonging to Alice a target. Table 1 shows three different placements. The upper left table shows the placement before applying our optimization solution and the value of $k = 2$. The right upper table and the bottom table show the optimal placement after we apply our solution by the victim tenant (where the migration is limited to the tenant's resource) and the provider (where the

Table 1. The optimal solution to the motivating example (Sect. 2.3)

Host	VM / VDU				VM / VDU				
1	app A	app B	DB A	DB B	app A	app B	DB A	DB B	
2	LB A / Switch A	Router A	http B	http A	LB A / Switch A	FW A / IDS A	http B	http A	
3	FW A / IDS A	FW B / IDS B	http M	Router B	Router A	FW B / IDS B	http M	Router B	
	Before mitigation $k = 2$				After mitigation by tenant $k = 4$				

Host	VM / VDU			
1	app A	app B	DB A	FW A / IDS A
2	LB A / Switch A	Router A	http B	http A
3	DB B	FW B / IDS B	http M	Router B
	After mitigation by provider $k = 5$			

migration is applied to all resources), respectively. The value of k increases to $k = 4$ and $k = 5$ for mitigation by the tenant and provider, respectively. The result of mitigation by the provider is slightly better than by the tenant because more VMs may be migrated.

5   Simulations

This section shows the simulation results of applying our mitigation solution under various constraints. All VM placement in the simulations are based on CloudSim [9,11,20]. We applied the three placement policies in CloudSim (i.e., the random, least, and most policies) to our NFV environment. We have 300 hosts and 7,000 VMs, and the following shows the default configurations for the host and VMs from CloudSim.

- For the physical machine, we specify the capacity of the hosts as having 16 GB of RAM, 1000 GB of storage space and a 10,000 MB/s bandwidth
- The virtual machine's resource requirements are 512 MB of RAM, 10 GB of storage space and a 1,000 MB/s bandwidth

Moreover, we use a virtual machine equipped with a 3.4 GHz CPU and 8 GB RAM in the Python 2.7.10 environment under Ubuntu 12.04 LTS and the MATLAB R2017b's GA toolbox. To generate a large number of resource graphs for simulations, we start with seed graphs with realistic configurations similar to Fig. 2 and the cloud infrastructure configurations presented in [1,2], and then generate random resource graphs by injecting new nodes and edges into those seed graphs based on the VM placement results of CloudSim. Those resource graphs were used as the input to the optimization toolbox where the fitness function maximizes the average insider threat value k under various constraints. The parameters and constraints used in our simulations include the VMs placement policy, size of the network, type and number of attackers, and maximum number of VMs migrating to malicious users. We repeat each simulation on 400 different resource graphs to obtain the average result.

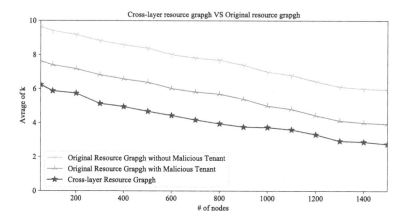

Fig. 5. Comparing the original resource graph and cross-layer resource graph

The objective of the first simulation is to study how cross-layer attacks may affect the security of the NFV stack. We compare the $k0d$ metric on the original resource graph (without any cross-layer attacks), and cross-layer resource graphs. In Fig. 5, the number of malicious users (external attackers or insider tenants) is between 5 and 15, while the size of the network varies between 50 and 1,500 along the X-axis. The Y-axis shows the average of k among all malicious users. The red line represents the results of the original resource graph without considering malicious tenants in this particular case. The green line represents the results of the original resource graph while considering malicious tenants. The blue line shows the result of cross-layer resource graph (with both malicious tenants and cross-layer attacks considered).

Results and Implications: From the results, we can make the following observations. First, the value of k decreases in all cases almost linearly; this is expected because, as the size of the network increases, there is a higher chance for the length of the shortest path to decrease, which means attackers may require less attack steps. Second, the value of k drops on the original resource graph (without considering cross-layer attacks) after considering the presence of malicious tenants (i.e., co-residency attacks), which is as expected. Third, the value of k drops by approximately 55% between the original resource graph without considering the malicious tenant, and the cross-layer resource graph, which shows the additional threat of cross-layer attacks.

In Fig. 6 the objective is to show how different placement policies can affect the value of k. In this simulation, we employ the cross-layer resource graph to measure the value of k for three types of attackers (external, malicious tenant, and lower-layer provider who has access to all the hosts) under three different placement policies used in CloudSim (i.e., the most, least, and random policies). The three figures show how the three placement policies can slightly affect the value of k. Each trend on the figure shows a different type of attackers, while the

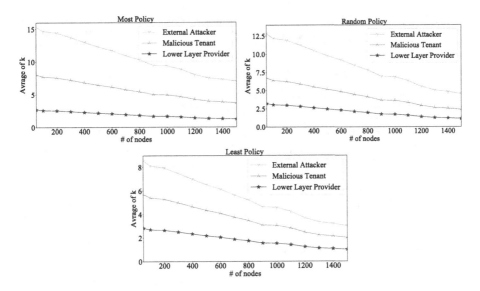

Fig. 6. Comparing the three placement policies in CloudSim

total number of attackers stays between 5 and 20. The X-axis depicts the size of the network and the Y-axis shows the average value of k among all attackers.

Results and Implications: From the three figures, we can make the following observations. First, similar as in previous results, the value of k in all trends decreases almost linearly as the size of the network increases. Second, the trends of external attackers and malicious tenants decrease faster than the lower-layer provider. This is expected because the lower-layer provider already has access to all the hosts, which enables him/her to either use his/her privileges to attack higher layers, which means much lower k values and hence less room for further decrease as the network size increases. Finally, the most placement policy has the highest value of k both external attackers and malicious tenants and the lowest k for lower layer provider. This is because, under the most policy, the target tenant's VMs tend to stay closer to each other, which renders them less vulnerable to external attackers or malicious tenants, but more so to a lower-layer provider managing the hosts of such VMs.

The objective of the next three simulations is to study how the different types of attackers behave under our attack mitigation solution. Figure 7 shows the simulation of applying the mitigation solution on the least placement policy for external attackers and malicious tenants, and the placement policy for the lower-layer provider. The three simulations are based on similar X and Y axis as in previous simulations. The solid lines represent the results after applying our mitigation solution under the constraints of the maximum number of VMs migration. The dashed lines represent the results before applying the mitigation solution.

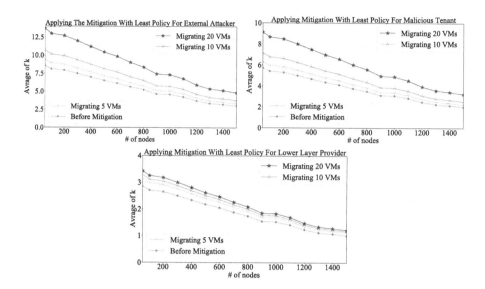

Fig. 7. Applying mitigation solution with the maximum number of VMs migrating

Results and Implications: From the simulation results, we can make the following observations. First, our solution is improving the value of k in all cases. Second, all three simulations follow the same trend and the value of k improves when we increase the maximum number of VMs that are allowed to migrate, i.e., the cost of migration. Finally, improving the result for the lower-layer provider is difficult to attain because the low-layer provider already is assumed to have the power to access more than one host (based on the privilege he/she has) so migration has less effect.

The objective of the last simulation is to study how the number of malicious tenants can increase insider threat under different placement policies, and how the mitigation solution may improve the value of k in each case. In Fig. 8, the size of the network is fixed at 700 nodes, while the number of malicious tenants is varied between 0 and 25 along the X-axis. The Y-axis shows the average value of k among all malicious tenants. The solid lines represent the results after applying the mitigation solution, and the dashed lines are for the corresponding results before applying the solution.

Results and Implications: From the results, we can make the following observations. First, the mitigation solution successfully reduces the insider threat (increasing the average of k values) in all cases. Second, the results before and after applying the solution start with a sharp decrease prior to following similar linear trends (meaning increased insider threat) as the number of malicious tenants increase from zero. Finally, the result of the random placement policy after applying the solution is slightly better than the result of the most placement policy before applying the solution, which means that the mitigation solution may improve the placement algorithm w.r.t. the co-residency attack.

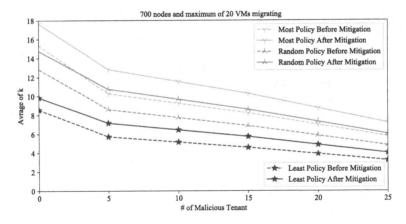

Fig. 8. The results of the mitigation solution under different placement policies

6   Related Work

To the best of our knowledge, this is the first work proposing a threat model specifically for NFV environments. On the other hand, many exists works focus on clouds. In particular, our previous work applies different threat modeling techniques to cloud data center infrastructures for different types of attackers [2]. Gruschka and Jensen devise a high level attack surface framework to show from where the attack can start [19]. The NIST emphasizes the importance of security measuring and metrics for cloud providers in [29]. A framework is propose by Luna et al. for cloud security metrics using basic building blocks [26]. There exist other works focusing on insider threats in clouds [1,10]. Chinchani et al. proposed a graph-based model for insider attacks and measure the threat [10]. There are many works that focus on the co-residency attacks by improving the placement policy. Han et al. introduces a new strategy to prevent attackers from achieving co-residency by modifying the placement policy on CloudSim [20]. Madi et al. propose a quantitative model and security metric for multi-tenancy in the cloud at different layers [27]. Atya et al. study co-residency in clouds and suggest solutions for the victim tenant to avoid co-residency with malicious users [4].

Unlike our work which focuses on the cross-layer and co-resident threats and the application of threat models and security metric, existing studies on NFV security [16,25,31,42] mostly focus on issues related to virtualization. Lal et al. [25] propose to adapt several well-known best practices like VM separation, hypervisor introspection, and remote attestation to NFV. Pattaranantakul et al. [31] adapt best practices like access control to address virtualization-related threats in NFV. Our cross-layer resource graph model is partially inspired by existing works [35,36] in which Sun et al. use a cross-layer Bayesian network to measure security threats for enterprise networks [35] and additionally they employ a multi-layer attack graph to measure security in clouds [36].

There also exist related works on other aspects of NFV security. Firoozjaei et al. [16] show how multi-tenancy and live migration can affect the security on NFV by using a side-channel and shared resource misuse attack. Alnaim et al. [3] uses architectural modeling to analyze security threats and the possible mitigating solution for NFV; their model is relatively abstract and only considers a malicious tenant to exploit vulnerability when he/she co-resides with the target VM on the same physical machine. Tian et al. propose a framework that uses a hierarchical attack and defense model which divides the 5G network to four layers (physical layer, virtual layer, service layer, and application layer) [37]. Basile et al. [5] propose to add a new policy manager component to enforce security policies during deployment and configuration of security functions. Coughlin et al. [12] integrate trusted computing solution based on Intel SGX to enforce privacy with secure packet processing.

7   Conclusion

In this paper, we have modeled cross-level and co-residency attacks in the NFV stack. We have also formulated the optimal VNF/VM placement problem to mitigate the security threats through standard optimization algorithm. Furthermore, we conducted simulations whose results showed that our solution could significantly reduce the level security threats in NFV. Our future work will focus on following directions. First, we will make our solution incremental and more efficient in order to handle more dynamics in terms of VM placement and immigration. Second, we will consider weighing different exploits and asset values to optimally choose among those different options for a given NFV application. Finally, we will study the integration of our solution with existing deployment policies based on an NFV testbed.

Acknowledgements. The authors thank the anonymous reviewers for their valuable comments. This work was partially supported by the National Science Foundation under grant number IIP-1266147, by the Army Research Office grant W911NF-13-1-042, and by the Natural Sciences and Engineering Research Council of Canada under Discovery Grant N01035.

References

1. Alhebaishi, N., Wang, L., Jajodia, S., Singhal, A.: Mitigating the insider threat of remote administrators in clouds through maintenance task assignments. J. Comput. Secur. **27**(4), 427–458 (2019)
2. Alhebaishi, N., Wang, L., Singhal, A.: Threat modeling for cloud infrastructures. ICST Trans. Secur. Saf. **5**(17), e5 (2019)
3. Alnaim, A.K., Alwakeel, A.M., Fernandez, E.B.: Threats against the virtual machine environment of NFV. In: 2019 2nd International Conference on Computer Applications Information Security (ICCAIS), pp. 1–5, May 2019
4. Atya, A.O.F., Qian, Z., Krishnamurthy, S.V., Porta, T.F.L., McDaniel, P.D., Marvel, L.M.: Catch me if you can: a closer look at malicious co-residency on the cloud. IEEE/ACM Trans. Netw. **27**(2), 560–576 (2019)

5. Basile, C., Lioy, A., Pitscheider, C., Valenza, F., Vallini, M.: A novel approach for integrating security policy enforcement with dynamic network virtualization. In: NetSoft 2015, pp. 1–5 (2015)
6. Bates, A., Mood, B., Pletcher, J., Pruse, H., Valafar, M., Butler, K.: Detecting co-residency with active traffic analysis techniques. In: Proceedings of the 2012 ACM Workshop on Cloud Computing Security Workshop, CCSW 2012, pp. 1–12, Association for Computing Machinery, New York (2012)
7. Borbor, D., Wang, L., Jajodia, S., Singhal, A.: Diversifying network services under cost constraints for better resilience against unknown attacks. In: Proceedings of the 30th Annual IFIP WG 11.3 Conference on Data and Applications Security and Privacy XXX, DBSec 2016, Trento, Italy, 18–20 July 2016, pp. 295–312 (2016). https://doi.org/10.1007/978-3-319-41483-6_21
8. Borbor, D., Wang, L., Jajodia, S., Singhal, A.: Securing networks against unpatchable and unknown vulnerabilities using heterogeneous hardening options. In: Livraga, G., Zhu, S. (eds.) DBSec 2017. LNCS, vol. 10359, pp. 509–528. Springer, Cham (2017). https://doi.org/10.1007/978-3-319-61176-1_28
9. Calheiros, R.N., Ranjan, R., Beloglazov, A., Rose, C.A.F.D., Buyya, R.: CloudSim: a toolkit for modeling and simulation of cloud computing environments and evaluation of resource provisioning algorithms. Softw. Pract. Exp. **41**(1), 23–50 (2011)
10. Chinchani, R., Iyer, A., Ngo, H.Q., Upadhyaya, S.: Towards a theory of insider threat assessment. In: 2005 International Conference on Dependable Systems and Networks (DSN 2005), pp. 108–117, June 2005
11. CloudSim. CloudSim: a framework for modeling and simulation of cloud computing infrastructures and services (2020). http://www.cloudbus.org/cloudsim/. Accessed 27 Jan 2020
12. Coughlin, M., Keller, E., Wustrow, E.; Trusted click: overcoming security issues of NFV in the cloud. In: SDN-NFV@CODASPY 2017, pp. 31–36 (2017)
13. Dewri, R., Poolsappasit, N., Ray, I., Whitley, L.D.: Optimal security hardening using multi-objective optimization on attack tree models of networks. In: Ning, P., di Vimercati, S.D.C., Syverson, P.F. (eds.) Proceedings of the 2007 ACM Conference on Computer and Communications Security, CCS 2007, Alexandria, Virginia, USA, 28–31 October 2007, pp. 204–213. ACM (2007)
14. ETSI: ETSI-Welcome to the World of Standards. https://www.etsi.org
15. Fayazbakhsh, S.K., Reiter, M.K., Sekar, V.: Verifiable network function outsourcing: requirements, challenges, and roadmap. In: Workshop on Hot Topics in Middleboxes and Network Function Virtualization (HotMiddlebox 2013), pp. 25–30 (2013)
16. Firoozjaei, M.D., Jeong, J.P., Ko, H., Kim, H.: Security challenges with network functions virtualization. Future Gener. Comput. Syst. **67**, 315–324 (2017)
17. Flittner, M., Scheuermann, J.M., Bauer, R.: ChainGuard: controller-independent verification of service function chaining in cloud computing. In: NFV-SDN 2017, pp. 1–7 (2017)
18. Golberg, D.E.: Genetic Algorithms in Search, Optimization, and Machine Learning. Addion wesley, Boston (1989)
19. Gruschka, N., Jensen, M.: Attack surfaces: a taxonomy for attacks on cloud services. In: 2010 IEEE 3rd International Conference on Cloud Computing, pp. 276–279. IEEE (2010)
20. Han, Y., Chan, J., Alpcan, T., Leckie, C.: Virtual machine allocation policies against co-resident attacks in cloud computing. In: IEEE International Conference on Communications, ICC 2014, Sydney, Australia, 10–14 June 2014, pp. 786–792 (2014)

21. Huang, W., Zhu, H., Qian, Z.: AutoVNF: an automatic resource sharing schema for VNF requests. J. Internet Serv. Inf. Secur. **7**(3), 34–47 (2017)

22. Intel. Realising the benefits of network functions virtualisation in telecoms network. https://www.intel.com/content/dam/www/public/us/en/documents/white-papers/benefits-network-functions-virtualization-telecoms-paper.pdf./

23. Ixia, A.K.B.: Network Function Virtualization (NFV): 5 Major Risks. https://www.ixiacom.com/resources/network-function-virtualization-nfv-5-major-risks/

24. Lakshmanan, S., et al.: Modeling NFV deployment to identify the cross-level inconsistency vulnerabilities. In: 2019 11th IEEE International Conference on Cloud Computing Technology and Science (CloudCom), pp. 167–174, December 2019

25. Lal, S., Taleb, T., Dutta, A.: NFV: security threats and best practices. IEEE Commun. Mag. **55**(8), 211–217 (2017)

26. Luna, J., Ghani, H., Germanus, D., Suri, N.: A security metrics framework for the cloud. In: 2011 Proceedings of the International Conference on Security and Cryptography (SECRYPT), pp. 245–250, July 2011

27. Madi, T., et al.: QuantiC: distance metrics for evaluating multi-tenancy threats in public cloud. In: 2018 IEEE International Conference on Cloud Computing Technology and Science, CloudCom 2018, Nicosia, Cyprus, 10–13 December 2018, pp. 163–170 (2018)

28. Marchetto, G., Sisto, R., Yusupov, J., Ksentini, A.: Virtual network embedding with formal reachability assurance. In: CNSM 2018, pp. 368–372 (2018)

29. National Institute of Standards and Technology. Cloud Computing Service Metrics Description. http://www.nist.gov/itl/cloud/upload/RATAX-CloudServiceMetricsDescription-DRAFT-20141111.pdf

30. Pattaranantakul, M., He, R., Meddahi, A., Zhang, Z.: SecMANO: towards network functions virtualization (NFV) based security management and orchestration. In: 2016 IEEE Trustcom/BigDataSE/ISPA, pp. 598–605, August 2016

31. Pattaranantakul, M., He, R., Song, Q., Zhang, Z., Meddahi, A.: NFV security survey: from use case driven threat analysis to state-of-the-art countermeasures. IEEE Commun. Surv. Tutor. **20**(4), 3330–3368 (2018)

32. Rates Crippa, M., et al.: Resource sharing for a 5g multi-tenant and multi-service architecture. In: 23th European Wireless Conference on European Wireless 2017, pp. 1–6, May 2017

33. Saripalli, P., Walters, B.: QUIRC: a quantitative impact and risk assessment framework for cloud security. In: 2010 IEEE 3rd International Conference on Cloud Computing, pp. 280–288, July 2010

34. Sheyner, O., Haines, J., Jha, S., Lippmann, R., Wing, J.M.: Automated generation and analysis of attack graphs. In: Proceedings of the 2002 IEEE Symposium on Security and Privacy 2002, pp. 273–284 (2002)

35. Sun, X., Dai, J., Singhal, A., Liu, P.: Inferring the stealthy bridges between enterprise network islands in cloud using cross-layer bayesian networks. In: Tian, J., Jing, J., Srivatsa, M. (eds.) SecureComm 2014. LNICSSITE, vol. 152, pp. 3–23. Springer, Cham (2015). https://doi.org/10.1007/978-3-319-23829-6_1

36. Sun, X., Singhal, A., Liu, P.: Towards actionable mission impact assessment in the context of cloud computing. In: Proceedings of the 31st Annual IFIP WG 11.3 Conference on Data and Applications Security and Privacy XXXI, DBSec 2017, Philadelphia, PA, USA, 19–21 July 2017, pp. 259–274 (2017)

37. Tian, Z., Sun, Y., Su, S., Li, M., Du, X., Guizani, M.: Automated attack and defense framework for 5G security on physical and logical layers. CoRR, abs/1902.04009 (2019)

38. Tschaen, B., Zhang, Y., Benson, T., Banerjee, S., Lee, J., Kang, J.-M.: SFC-checker: checking the correct forwarding behavior of service function chaining. In: NFV-SDN 2016, pp. 134–140 (2016)
39. Wang, L., Jajodia, S., Singhal, A., Cheng, P., Noel, S.: k-zero day safety: a network security metric for measuring the risk of unknown vulnerabilities. IEEE Trans. Dependable Secure Comput. **11**(1), 30–44 (2014)
40. Wang, L., Jajodia, S., Singhal, A., Noel, S.: k-zero day safety: measuring the security risk of networks against unknown attacks. In: Gritzalis, D., Preneel, B., Theoharidou, M. (eds.) ESORICS 2010. LNCS, vol. 6345, pp. 573–587. Springer, Heidelberg (2010). https://doi.org/10.1007/978-3-642-15497-3_35
41. Wang, Y., Li, Z., Xie, G., Salamatian, K.: Enabling automatic composition and verification of service function chain. In: IWQoS 2017, pp. 1–5 (2017)
42. Yang, W., Fung, C.: A survey on security in network functions virtualization. In: NetSoft 2016, pp. 15–19 (2016)
43. Zhang, X., Li, Q., Wu, J., Yang, J.: Generic and agile service function chain verification on cloud. In: IWQoS 2017, pp. 1–10 (2017)
44. Zhang, Y., Juels, A., Oprea, A., Reiter, M.K.: HomeAlone: co-residency detection in the cloud via side-channel analysis. In: 2011 IEEE Symposium on Security and Privacy, pp. 313–328, May 2011
45. Zhang, Y., Wu, W., Banerjee, S., Kang, J.-M., Sanchez, M.A.: SLA-verifier: stateful and quantitative verification for service chaining. In: INFOCOM 2017, pp. 1–9 (2017)

Managing Secure Inter-slice Communication in 5G Network Slice Chains

Luis Suárez$^{(\boxtimes)}$ (ID), David Espes, Frédéric Cuppens, Cao-Thanh Phan,
Philippe Bertin, and Philippe Le Parc

IRT b<>com, Cesson-Sévigné, France
{Luis.Suarez,David.Espes,Frederic.Cuppens,Cao-Thanh.Phan,
Philippe.Bertin,Philippe.Le-Parc}@b-com.com

Abstract. Network Slicing is one of the cornerstones for network operators to provide communication services. It is envisioned that in order to provide richer communication services, network slices need to be connected to each other in an orderly fashion, interlacing their functionalities. The challenge is to manage inter-slice communication securely, leveraging on security attributes inherent to the communication service and the constituting network slices.

To solve this inter-slice communication problem, we present a mathematical model based on the concept of Network Slice Chains. This concept helps to specify the end-to-end path of network slices that data must follow for the achievement of the communication service. We propose basic attributes and properties that the Network Slice Chain must comply with in order to be chosen as a valid path for the traffic to flow through. This way, it respects security constraints and assures inter-slice communication obeying the rules stated in the policy.

Keywords: Inter-slice communication · Network Slice Chain · Security · 5G

1 Introduction

Network slicing is one of the key enablers for the use cases that are proposed for 5G [16]. Along with Software Defined Network (SDN), Network Functions Virtualization (NFV) and cloud computing, they provide a novel partitioning scheme to instantiate a Communication Service (CS) on top of network slices. They will use resources that belong to the same Communication Service Provider (CSP) that offers the service or to different operators, organizations and stakeholders [5].

Interactions between network slices will become commonplace, because the CSP can provide common functions through a network slice that is accessible for consumption by other dedicated slices. As network slice interconnection brings

© IFIP International Federation for Information Processing 2020
Published by Springer Nature Switzerland AG 2020
A. Singhal and J. Vaidya (Eds.): DBSec 2020, LNCS 12122, pp. 24–41, 2020.
https://doi.org/10.1007/978-3-030-49669-2_2

the risk of exposure to threats from other players, a secure interaction should be guaranteed to minimize security risks. In order to do so, the CSP has to set up different rules and measures to guarantee secure inter-slice communication, knowing beforehand that slices have different security levels, according to their nature and purpose.

An interesting challenge is: how to manage the interactions between network slices when each one has different security attributes and different security requirements? How to bring this to a next level when a chain of slices is considered?

According to our research, as it will be presented in Sect. 2, no work has been made regarding the formal model of a communication service that uses network slices, taking into account their inherent security attributes. Moreover, there is no study about the evaluation of these attributes when inter-slice communication is considered, specially in the case where successive network slices need to be connected. The presented new concepts contribute to go beyond the access control models that already exist (which are more focused on the user or the resources), by adding an end-to-end view of the communication service considering the security needs for its deployment.

Our contribution is three-fold: (i) model the network slicing structure mathematically using graph theory, leveraging on the definitions given by Standard Developing Organizations; (ii) deduce a general concept called Network Slice Chain, which describes the sequence of network slices that data must flow through in order to provide a Communication Service; and (iii) provide properties and policy rules to validate whether the Network Slice Chain can be used, according to the security constraints that are specified in the policy.

The document is organized as follows: Sect. 2 presents works related to inter-slice communication. Section 3 presents an example of a common network slice set-up from a CSP, who will experience challenges regarding the secure composition of a communication service. Section 4 describes the mathematical model, definitions and properties of a Network Slice and Network Slice Chain. Section 5 describes the different components used on the communication model. Section 6 describes the rules and policy validation steps that govern communication in the Network Slice Chain, which are applied to a use case in Sect. 7. After putting into practice these ideas in Sect. 8, Sect. 9 draws concluding remarks.

2   Related Work

Inter-slice access control has attracted few research works. In [4], the 5G-ENSURE project focuses on the access control from end-users to the resources offered by a network slice in a 5G network. They provide a set of countermeasures and enablers for this purpose. The inter-slice communication and access control are not addressed.

In a different perspective, authors in [7] address the inter-slice communication regarding the need to guarantee isolation. They point out that improper inter-slice isolation leads to threats in network slicing. They include the suggestion to use a fine-grained access control to limit access from a tenant to the entire infrastructure.

In [6] the 5G-Monarch project works on providing end-to-end slicing support via enablers pertaining to inter-slice control and management, which are some of the proposed innovations of their work in order to provide slice admission control. The inter-slice management still resides into the Network Slice Management Function (NSMF), as a way to assure that the resources assigned to the network slice instance are optimal, used wisely, at the same time guaranteeing Service Level Agreement (SLA). In the same fashion, authors in [8] propose an inter-slice management mechanism to control events in a 5G network. Using queue and graph theory, they create a reference model that captures events from the network and according to their importance or impact on metrics, classifies the events for resolution, avoiding network congestion. The projects do not provide information about access control mechanisms.

Authors in [14] present how authentication and authorization was integrated in the SONATA Service Platform, in order to manage the authentication, identity management and authorization of users and microservices in a 5G network. Their approach is generic, supplying these security features for the users and the networks functions inside 5G. The slice use case is not mentioned, neither inter-slice communication management.

In [18] authors propose to enhance the Topology and Orchestration Specification for Cloud Applications (TOSCA) modeling language with security parameters. They leverage on the SDN paradigm to use these parameters and, via an access control model, deploy services on Virtual Network Function (VNF) with embedded security countermeasures. In a similar fashion in [11] authors propose an enhancement of the TOSCA language to model the protection of clouds, represented as resources in unikernel system instantiated in virtual machines. Both approaches provide a way to specify and build secured network functions, nonetheless, their approach can be improved by considering a top layer approach from a Communication Service point of view and considering a chain of those VNF of kernels in order to build richer services.

Other authors address the interactions between network functions that are inside a network slice. Leveraging of SDN capabilities, all the required VNF are linked together in a chain in order to manage the traffic as desired. In [10], authors apply this concept to map network slice attributes into the infrastructure of datacenters. Their approach does not cover security attributes or a mathematical modelization. A similar approach is proposed in [20], where a traffic steering solution is implemented for various use cases, keeping in mind a consisted throughput, packet loss, latency and jitter to guarantee quality of service. No slicing consideration or security model is proposed. In [17] authors explore the modelization of network slices considering the allocation of a service instance to a slice instance, according to availability, resources, quality of service and isolation. Even though their model work over the slice instance abstraction, does not consider the interconnection of slices to provide a service.

These works point out challenges, focus on the isolation problem, on how an end user or tenant access to resources, on resource assignment to guarantee a performance rating, and how to perform the inter-slice management and orchestration via a broker mechanism [5]. No formal model of the network slice environment is provided, neither security considerations for inter-slice communication when several network slices need to be connected to provide composite services. This is a central issue for a CSP that is deploying services via network slices.

3   Motivating Example

In order to better understand the properties and different elements that are inside the proposed model, a use-case scenario is presented. Even though it does not depict a specific service, it is generic enough to fit into any communication service offered by a CSP. The architecture is presented in Fig. 1, which contains a set of Network Slices, connected arbitrarily according to the needs of the CSP. Each Network Slice (NSlice) is configured according to a *service type* to perform a

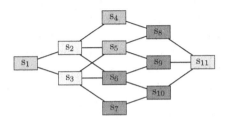

Fig. 1. Topology of the network slices and corresponding types for a CSP. (Color figure online)

specific function, as specified by 3rd Generation Partnership Project (3GPP) [1]: Enhanced Mobile Broadband (eMBB), Ultra-Reliable and Low Latency Communications (URLLC), and Massive Machine Type Communications (mMTC). These service types are represented by a different color: orange, yellow, green, blue, red and grey.

For example, the orange NSlice could be an aggregation service slice for an enterprise; the yellow slice an IoT slice; green and blue slices constitute added value services (built from network functions to provide services such as traffic filtering, IDS/IPS); the red slice a 5G network slice to provide final connectivity; and the grey slice a data network that provides a concrete service. A more concrete use case illustrating a similar setup is provided in Sect. 7.

All network slices are connected together in an ordered sequence to provide a service. For example, assume the presence of a communication service that we name CS_1. It considers the orange, yellow, green, red and grey service types. Similarly, another communication service named CS_2 has orange, yellow, blue, red and grey service types.

Each Communication Service CS_1 and CS_2 can be set up according to the needs from the CSP by connecting NSlices creating a Communication Service

Graph (CSG). For example, regarding CS_1, it can be considered as two CSG: CSG_{11} (Fig. 2a) and CSG_{12} (Fig. 2b). The key message is that, even though the nature of the CS is the same, each slice can have a different configuration and different resources, enabling to provide options of deployment according to the needs. The same approach can be made with CS_2, in which two CSG are

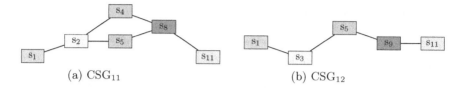

(a) CSG_{11} (b) CSG_{12}

Fig. 2. Communication service graphs for CS_1 and CS_2. (Color figure online)

presented: CSG_{21} (Fig. 3a) and CSG_{22} (Fig. 3b). Other arrangements of CSG can be made, enriching the exercise. The advantage of considering the service as a CSG is that the operators can configure the routing of the system in order to forward the traffic through the slices according to a certain policy. With this, traffic can exploit the characteristics of the network topology and then be treated according to the specification of each slice. The traffic will follow a chain of slices that comply with a use-case for the customer. Concretely for CSG_{11},

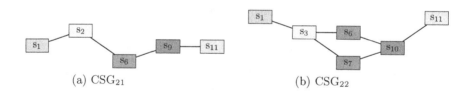

(a) CSG_{21} (b) CSG_{22}

Fig. 3. Communication service graphs for CS_2

the provider can set up two network slice chains specified by blue and red dotted lines. As presented in Fig. 4a, the blue Network Slice Chain (going through s_1, s_2, s_4, s_8 and s_{11}) covers a green slice with an IDS that detects a certain type of traffic. Similarly, the red Network Slice Chain (going through s_1, s_2, s_5, s_8 and s_{11}) can contain a green slice that has an IDS with a different detection policy. The same approach can be made for CSG_{22}, as shown in Fig. 4b. The presented topology is complex even though the number of network slices is small. As the number of network slices increase, their management becomes a challenge. This manageability has to do with the way to connect the network slices (must ensure the proper authentication and security between them) and how to keep the guarantees of the service offerings to the customer. This implies that the set-up and configuration of the communication service must follow certain rules

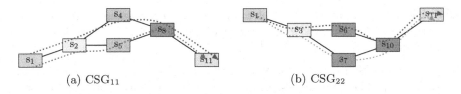

(a) CSG_{11} (b) CSG_{22}

Fig. 4. Example of two CSG with two network slice chains. (Color figure online)

and constraints expressed in the policy, which specifies its security requirements and the type of traffic that is allowed to flow. Moreover, as the network is a dynamic entity, the topology can change, so the CSP must perform validation that a path, represented by a Network Slice Chain, can be used for the service required by the customer. Not addressing the needs regarding management and security validation, makes difficult the secure deployment of rich communication services using several connected network slices.

With this setup, the next section elaborates on the properties of Network Slice and Network Slice Chains, whose specification constitutes the major contribution of this work.

4   Network Slice and Network Slice Chain

This Section provides the mathematical background to describe the novel concept called Network Slice Chains. To do so, it evolves from its basic building blocks to then state its key properties.

4.1   Network Service (NS)

The network slicing model relies for its realization on the European Telecommunications Standards Institute (ETSI) NFV concept of Network Service (NS), detailed in [12]. A NS is a composition of network functions arranged as a set of functions with either unspecified connectivity between them or connectivity specified according to one or more forwarding graphs [13]. It is deduced that key components of a NS are Virtual Network Function (VNF), Virtual Link (VL), and VNF Forwarding Graph (VNFFG). All these elements provide a specific functionality and resource requirements for network slices, which will be presented in the next subsection.

4.2   Network Slice (NSlice)

3GPP [2] defines that a CS is offered by a set of Network Slices, being each NSlice composed by an ordered set of NS. This notion of "interconnection" leads us to represent the NSlice as a connected graph.

Definition 1. *The NSlice is a graph composed of: (**i**) a non-empty set of vertices (V), which are the NS; and (**ii**) a set of edges (E), which are the VL. For a Network Slice $\mathcal{A}$: NSlice$_\mathcal{A}$ = (NS($\mathcal{A}$), VL($\mathcal{A}$)).* □

Property 1. Let $\mathcal{S}$ be the set of NSlices that belong to a CSP. $\mathcal{S} = \{$ s_1, s_2, ..., s_i, ..., $s_m\}$. The CSP uses s_i to provide a service to its customers and the disposition of the NSlices obeys the CSP's internal rules and policies. □

Property 2. Each Network Slice has one *service type* that describes its function. The set of types is called $\mathcal{T}_\mathcal{S}$. $|\mathcal{T}_\mathcal{S}|$ represents the number of *service types* that are provided by the CSP as defined by 3GPP [1]. □

Property 3. The function **type** is used to know the *service type* that the NSlice has. A NSlice can have only one type. The function **type** is defined as **type**: $\mathcal{S} \rightarrow \mathcal{T}_\mathcal{S}$. □

Going back to the example in Sect. 3, Fig. 1 helps to represent a set $\mathcal{S}$ of NSlices with its types, identified by a different color.

The CSP uses several interconnected Network Slices to provide a complete service to the customer: this constitutes what is called a Communication Service. Next subsection defines analytically this concept and the inference of the Communication Service Graph.

4.3 Communication Service Graph (CSG)

A CS is defined as an ordered set of types of Network Slices, whose services are offered to different market segments, obeying a business purpose [3]. These Network Slices are connected via Network Slice Links (NSL).

Definition 2. *A type of CS is defined as $\mathcal{T}_{CS} = \langle \mathcal{T}_{CS_1}, \mathcal{T}_{CS_2}, ..., \mathcal{T}_{CS_m} \rangle$, i.e., the traffic of a CS is going to flow through an ordered set of NSlices. $\mathcal{T}_{CS} = \langle \mathcal{T}_{CS_1}, \mathcal{T}_{CS_2}, ..., \mathcal{T}_{CS_k} \rangle \mid \forall i \in [1; k], \mathcal{T}_{CS_i} \in \mathcal{T}_\mathcal{S}$.* □

There can exist several NSlices deployed by a CSP for a type $\mathcal{T}_{CS_i}$. In fact, there exist a set $\mathcal{S}_{\mathcal{T}_{CS_i}} = \{s \mid \textbf{type(s)} = \mathcal{T}_{CS_i}\} \in \mathcal{S}$. The interconnection of successive $\mathcal{S}_{\mathcal{T}_{CS_i}}$, $\mathcal{S}_{\mathcal{T}_{CS_{i+1}}}$ creates an ordered graph.

Definition 3. *The CSG $\mathcal{C}$ is a directed weighted graph such as: $\mathcal{C} = (\mathcal{S}', NSL)$ where: $\mathcal{S}' = \{s \mid s \in \mathcal{S} \wedge \textbf{type(s)} \in \mathcal{T}_{CS}\}$ and $NSL = \{(u,v) \mid u, v \in \mathcal{S} \wedge u \neq v\}$.* □

Property 4. Each link $(u, v) \in NSL$ has a set of attributes $\{a_1, a_2, ..., a_m\}$. (u, v) inherits a quality from graph theory called weight $\mathcal{W}_{(u,v)}$ that is a function which, using the values of the attributes, computes an unified metric for (u, v). $\mathcal{W}_{(u,v)} = \mathcal{F}(a_1, a_2, ..., a_m)$. The definition of $\mathcal{F}$ and the presentation of the attributes are explained in Sect. 5.1. □

These aforementioned definitions and properties help to define a CSG, which provides a way to deploy a concrete communication service and permit the flow of data among a subset to those Network Slices. That is where the concept of Network Slice Chain comes to play, as is shown in the next subsection.

4.4 Network Slice Chain

The Network Slice Chain (NSliceCh) is conceived as a concrete path in the CSG that a flow of data follows, which complies with certain requirements related to the Communication Service purpose, the nature of the traffic and security attributes. The NSliceCh leverages on Definition 3, which defines the CSG as a set of NSlices whose type respects $\mathcal{T_{CS}}$ over which the traffic will flow. For readability of the definition, $\mathcal{P}$ represents a NSliceCh.

Definition 4. *The CSG $\mathcal{C} = (\mathcal{S'}, NSL)$ contains a set of Network Slice Chains $\mathcal{P_C}$, which comply with the sequence of types of Network slices $\mathcal{T_{CS}}$ and do not form a loop.*

$$\mathcal{P_C} = \{\langle \mathcal{S}_{\mathcal{P}_1}, ... \mathcal{S}_{\mathcal{P}_i}, ... \mathcal{S}_{\mathcal{P}_m}\rangle \mid \forall\, i \in [1, m], \mathcal{S}_{\mathcal{P}_i} \in \mathcal{S'}\, \wedge$$
$$\boldsymbol{type}(\mathcal{S}_{\mathcal{P}_i}) = \mathcal{T}_{\mathcal{CS}_i} \wedge \nexists\, \mathcal{S}_{\mathcal{P}_i} \in \langle \mathcal{S}_{\mathcal{P}_{i+1}}, ..., \mathcal{S}_{\mathcal{P}_m}\rangle \}$$

□

A *security constraint* refers to the factors that impose restrictions and limitations on the system or actual limitations associated with the use of the system [19]. Applied to the subject under consideration, a security constraint refers to the requirements that a system should comply with in relation to security parameters. Examples could be the encryption level of a Virtual Private Network, or the protocol that must be used in a communication. These requirements are stated in the policy, which, as a system, makes sure it is enforced as needed.

In Fig. 4a two different NSliceCh are shown: one in red and the other in blue dotted line. It is supposed that they comply with the demands from the CS and its security constraints.

With all the previous definitions, all the elements are provided in order to use the tools to assess inter-slice communication.

5 Operators and Elements Involved in Inter-slice Communication

From the mathematical representations, definitions and properties shown in Sect. 4, we define operators and elements needed to manage inter-slice communication. These are the *attributes* of Network Slices and their corresponding measurement using *metrics*.

5.1 Attributes

Attributes refer to a feature or property of an entity [15]. Since entities are diverse in nature and functionality, it is difficult to have a complete list of attributes, specially for security requirements. For this proposal, attributes that are considered important from a security perspective are Affinity (Af), Trust (T) and

Security Level (SL). In this subsection, operations are proposed among them, being these operations a particular case of the function $\mathcal{F}$ stated in Property 4.

Let $\mathcal{C} = (\mathcal{S}', \text{NSL})$. Each NSlice $s \in \mathcal{S}'$ has a set of attributes defined as $\mathcal{A}(s) = \{(a_i, v_i) \mid a_i \in \{\text{Af, T, SL}\}, v_i \in \mathbb{R} \wedge \forall j \in [1, |\mathcal{A}|] \backslash \{i\}\ a_j \neq a_i\}$.

Each attribute is defined and specified according to formulas and properties as follows:

Affinity (Af): It is used to avoid conflicts regarding the nature of the offered slices, helping to determine whether they can be connected or can coexist.

Affinity has a nominal type of data, specified by the network administrator. Considered values are the basic *service types* for 5G established by 3GPP with the addition of a *common service type* that contains regular functionality and aids to connect dissimilar NSlices.

Property 5. Affinity for a link $(s_i, s_j) \in \text{NSL}$ is achieved if the (s_i, s_j) that make it up have the same affinity parameter. We call $\mathcal{F}_{\text{Af}}$ the function that finds the affinity for a link $(s_i, s_j) \in \text{NSL}$.

$$\mathcal{F}_{\text{Af}} : \mathcal{S} \times \mathcal{S} \to \mathbb{R}$$

$$\forall s_i, s_j \in \mathcal{S}'\ \text{NSL}, \exists\ (a_{i_p}, v_{i_p}) \in \mathcal{A}(s_i) \wedge (a_{j_k}, v_{j_k}) \in \mathcal{A}(s_j) \mid a_{i_p} = a_{j_k} = \text{Af} \Rightarrow$$

$$\mathcal{F}_{\text{Af}}(s_i, s_j) = \begin{cases} 1, \text{if } v_{ip} = v_{jk} \\ 0, \text{otherwise} \end{cases}$$

This means that if the services belong to the same *service type*, their affinities are the same and the function will have 1 as a result. □

Property 6. Affinity for a NSliceCh $\mathcal{P}$:

Let $\mathcal{C} = (\mathcal{S}', \text{NSL})$. $\forall\ \mathcal{P} = \langle s_1, s_2, ..., s_n \rangle \in \mathcal{P}_C \wedge \forall\ s_i \in \mathcal{S}' \wedge (s_i, s_{i+1}) \in \text{NSL}$: $\mathcal{G}_{\text{Af}} : \mathcal{P}_C \to \mathbb{R}$ with: $\mathcal{G}_{\text{Af}}(\mathcal{P}) = \prod_{i=1}^{n-1} \mathcal{F}_{\text{Af}}(s_i, s_{i+1})$

This means that for a chain of network slices, the result for affinity is the product of values of this attribute for each of the links that belongs to the NSliceCh. □

Corollary 1. *Affinity for a NSliceCh is achieved as a consequence of Property 5, since the NSliceCh is a subset of the CSG.*

Trust (T): It denotes the confidence to establish a business relation, enabled by the acknowledgement of the identity of the other party. Trust has an ordinal type of data, enabling to have levels of trust, for example, {trusted, not-trusted}, or equivalently, {1, 0}.

Property 7. Intuitively, the trust level of the destination NSlice has to be at least greater or equal to the trust level of the source NSlice.

We call $\mathcal{F}_T$ the function that finds the trust for a link $s_i, s_j \in$ NSL.

$$\mathcal{F}_T : \mathcal{S} \times \mathcal{S} \to \mathbb{R}$$
$$\forall s_i, s_j \in \mathcal{S}', \exists \, (a_{i_p}, v_{i_p}) \in \mathcal{A}(s_i) \wedge (a_{j_k}, v_{j_k}) \in \mathcal{A}(s_j) \mid a_{i_p} = a_{j_k} = \mathrm{T} \Rightarrow$$
$$\mathcal{F}_T(s_i, s_j) = \begin{cases} 1, \text{if } v_{ip} \geq v_{jk} \\ 0, \text{otherwise} \end{cases}$$

This means that if the trust of the links are at least the same, the function will have 1 as a result. □

Property 8. Trust level for a NSliceCh $\mathcal{P}$:

Let $\mathcal{C} = (\,\mathcal{S}', \text{NSL})$. $\forall \, \mathcal{P} = \langle s_1, s_2, ..., s_n \rangle \in \mathcal{P}_C \wedge \forall \; s_i \in \mathcal{S}' \wedge (s_i, s_{i+1}) \in$ NSL:
$\mathcal{G}_T : \mathcal{P}_C \to \mathbb{R}$ with: $\mathcal{G}_T(\mathcal{P}) = \prod_{i=1}^{n-1} \mathcal{F}_T(s_i, s_{i+1})$
This means that for a chain of network slices, the result for trust is the product of values of this attribute for each of the links that belongs to the NSliceCh. □

Corollary 2. *The trust in a NSliceCh is obtained as an extension of the trust value in the links which embed it.*

Security Level (SL). It shows the rating of the slice in terms of security, for example its confidentiality, integrity or other criteria that can be measured for the slice internal components. SL has an ordinal type of data, making possible to create, as its name implies, security levels to classify NSlices and manage their communication. The quantity of levels depends on the use case and need, as well as the criteria used to find its rating. For example, {high, medium, low}, or equivalently {3, 2, 1}.

Property 9. The intuition is that the SL of the destination NSlice has to be at least as high as the SL of origin NSlice:

We call $\mathcal{F}_{SL}$ the function that finds the Security Level for a link $s_i, s_j \in$ NSL.

$$\mathcal{F}_{SL} : \mathcal{S} \times \mathcal{S} \to \mathbb{R}$$
$$\forall s_i, s_j \in \mathcal{S}', \exists \, (a_{i_p}, v_{i_p}) \in \mathcal{A}(s_i) \wedge (a_{j_k}, v_{j_k}) \in \mathcal{A}(s_j) \mid a_{i_p} = a_{j_k} = \mathrm{SL} \Rightarrow$$
$$\mathcal{F}_{SL}(s_i, s_j) = min(s_i, s_j)$$

The outcome of this function is the minimum value of SL for the considered links. □

Property 10. Security Level for a NSliceCh $\mathcal{P}$:

Let $\mathcal{C} = (\,\mathcal{S}', \text{NSL})$. $\forall \, \mathcal{P} = \langle s_1, s_2, ..., s_n \rangle \in \mathcal{P}_C \wedge \forall \; s_i \in \mathcal{S}' \wedge (s_i, s_{i+1}) \in$ NSL:
$\mathcal{G}_{SL} : \mathcal{P}_C \to \mathbb{R}$ with: $\mathcal{G}_{SL}(\mathcal{P}) = min_{i=1}^{n-1} \mathcal{F}_{SL}(s_i, s_{i+1})$
This means that for the NSliceCh the minimum value is used as a way to portray the lowest security level admitted on the path. □

5.2   Metrics

According to [21], a metric is a standard of measurement that describes the conditions and the rules for performing a measurement of a property and for understanding the results of a measurement. A metric provides knowledge about an entity via its properties and the measured values obtained for that property. In our case, metrics are associated to links. For every link $(s_i, s_j) \in$ NSL, it exists a metric vector m.

It is defined as: $m_{(s_i,s_j)} = \{(\text{Af}, \mathcal{F}_{\text{Af}_{(s_i,s_j)}}), (\text{T}, \mathcal{F}_{\text{T}_{(s_i,s_j)}}), (\text{SL}, \mathcal{F}_{\text{SL}_{(s_i,s_j)}})\}$.

5.3   Final Remarks

After stating the attributes for Network Slices, the metrics and the functions to perform operations on them, the set of tools needed to validate a Network Slice Chain is complete. This compliance with a security policy is presented in the next Section.

6   Policy Validation for Network Slice Chains

The inter-slice communication depends on the use case and the service type of the NSliceCh. Somehow, the communication should be regulated according to certain *rules* r_i that are grouped in a policy Π. Specifically, rules are expressed as a vector $\langle$ Subject $\mathcal{SU}$, Object $\mathcal{O}$, Security Constraint SC, Permission $\rangle$ and its components specify the conditions for communication. This Section presents these components along with a *compliance operator* and the mechanisms to *validate the compliance* with the policy.

6.1   Entities: Subjects and Objects

Entities indicate the name of the actors that interact in the topology. Specifically, the entity called **subject**, denotes the active entity, refers to the NSlice that requests a service. The passive entity, the **object**, refers to the NSlice that receives the request. Subjects $\mathcal{SU}$ and objects $\mathcal{O}$ are represented as sets:
$\mathcal{SU} = \{su_1, su_2, ..., su_n\}$; $\mathcal{O} = \{o_1, o_2, ..., o_n\}$.

6.2   Security Constraint

Security Constraint, denoted by SC, represents the security conditions that the path has to comply with i.e., each link of the path must guarantee a security attribute superior or equal to the one specified in the rule. It is defined as follows:

$$\text{SC} = \{(a_i, v_{i_{min}}) \mid a_i \in \{\text{Af, T, SL}\}, \ v_{i_{min}} \in \mathbb{R} \wedge \forall j \in [1, |\mathcal{A}|] \setminus \{i\} \ a_j \neq a_i.$$

6.3   Permission

Describes the ability to perform an operation on a protected object or resource. Considered actions for can be to *allow* or *deny* the operation after its evaluation.

6.4   Compliance Operator

Denoted by $\cong$, its purpose is to validate if the metrics of a link $(s_i, s_j) \in$ NSL complies with the security constraints SC_i of the rule r_i. It is defined as:

$$\forall (a_k, v_k) \in m_{(s_i, s_j)}, \exists\, (a_p, v_p) \in \mathrm{SC}_i \mid a_k = a_p \land v_k \geq v_p) \Leftrightarrow m_{(s_i, s_j)} \cong \mathrm{SC}_i$$

This means that for each set of attributes specified for a subject, it needs to exist a pair of the same name of attributes for the object. Subject and object refer to Network Slices, that is, the link between them that complies with the security constraint.

The $\geq$ symbol, the *greater or equal to* operator, provides a way to compare quantitatively the values of the attributes. It specifies the preference to communicate with an object that has a security attribute having a greater or equal value. This is clarified better with an example in Sect. 7.

6.5   Rule for Policy Validation

It is necessary to verify that at least one NSliceCh, represented by $\mathcal{P}$, exists and complies with the metric in the policy.

SC corresponds to the constraints that must be respected, that is to say, that a path $\mathcal{P} \in \mathcal{P}_C$ in a CSG C matches the criteria if: $\mathcal{G}_{\mathrm{Af}}(\mathcal{P}) \geq \mathrm{SC}_{\mathrm{Af}} \land \mathcal{G}_{\mathrm{T}}(\mathcal{P}) \geq \mathrm{SC}_{\mathrm{T}} \land \mathcal{G}_{\mathrm{SL}}(\mathcal{P}) \geq \mathrm{SC}_{\mathrm{SL}}$. This means that not only the evaluation of each one of the attributes should be greater than the ones specified by the constraints in SC, but also that all those evaluations should agree.

Property 11. A path $\mathcal{P} = \langle s_1, s_2, ..., s_n \rangle$ complies with a rule r_i if each link of $\mathcal{P}$ complies with the security constraints SC_i of r_i such as:

$$\mathcal{P} \cong \mathrm{SC}_i \Leftrightarrow \forall\, j \in [1, n-1],\ m_{(o_j, o_{j+1})} \cong \mathrm{SC}_i$$

$\square$

Property 12. A CSG $\mathcal{C}$ complies with the policy if at least a path exists that fulfils the constraints for each rule of the policy. $\square$

Property 13. For an end-to-end NSliceCh, trust and affinity compliance are enforced if the product of all the computed trust values of the NSL that constitute the NSliceCh has a result of 1. This can be inferred from Property 7 and Property 5 respectively.

Property 14. For an end-to-end NSliceCh, security level compliance is achieved if the SL values of the NSL that conform the NSliceCh are superior to the minimum value established by the policy.

Corollary 3. *The compliance with the SL for a NSliceCh is guaranteed since the NSliceCh is a subgraph of the CSG.*

After this verification of the policy, the CSP can be warned about rules that are not satisfied because the deployed Network Slices do not meet a security criteria. In consequence, the CSP can either add other network slices that meet the security constraints or soften the security policy.

6.6 Discussion

The rules presented in this Section provide assurance that the components of a NSliceCh comply with the constraints expressed in the policy. Moreover, they enforce not only compliance but that the metric meets a certain level stated in the policy. At the same time, special care has to be taken when including a high number of attributes, which can render difficult the task to find a NSliceCh due to the fact that the problem cannot be solved in polynomial time (it is exponential). This approach gives way to think about a more complex scenario, where there could be a possibility that two NSliceCh exist, and the policy helps to choose the best one according to the security requirement. This will be shown via a concrete use case in the following Section.

7 Use Case

This section describes with a use case the way in which the rules stated in Sect. 6 are applied. The topology is shown in Fig. 5, which leverages on the CSG_{11} from Fig. 4a.

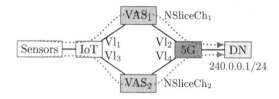

Fig. 5. Topology of a use-case scenario involving inter-slice interactions.

7.1 Description

The CSP has four network slices, one for a 5G network, another used by a customer (a tenant) that is configured for an IoT service, and two intermediate network slices that provide value-added services (VAS), such as analytics, traffic filtering or monitoring.

The sensors operating under the IoT slice use the services provided by the IoT network slice. Nonetheless, there could be some special devices that need to have access to a specific server on the Internet. To this end, the idea is to allow this specific connectivity using the 5G Core (5GC) slice as a bridge to reach the server hosted in a Data Network (DN) in the Internet. The attributes and corresponding metrics for the entities involved in this interaction are specified in Table 1. Similarly, the policy Π states that communication is allowed only if the proposed NSliceCh has a minimum SL of medium (numeric value 2). The objective is to check the validity of coherence of policy: verify the existence of the NSliceCh that complies with the policy, so the communication is authorized.

Table 1. Parameters for the elements in the example scenario

	IoT slice	VAS$_1$ slice	VAS$_2$ slice	5G slice
Af	mIoT	Common	Common	eMBB
SL	Medium:2	Low:1	Medium:2	High:3
T	Y	Y	Y	Y

7.2   Validation of Compliance of the NSliceCh

It is assumed that the topology represented in Fig. 5 represents a CSG from a CSP that provides a CS and it is possible to find a NSliceCh as a sequence of NSlices and NSL. Considering the concept of connectivity and directed-graph characteristics of the outbound traffic, there exist two NSliceCh:

NSliceCh$_1$ = ⟨IoT, VAS$_1$, 5G⟩

NSliceCh$_2$ = ⟨IoT, VAS$_2$, 5G⟩

Compliance for Affinity. The need is to connect an IoT slice to a 5G Slice (which are dissimilar) via an intermediary slice that has a common functionality. $\mathcal{G}_{Af}(NSliceCh_1) = 1$, because IoT-VAS$_1$ and VAS$_1$-5G have compliant affinity values. Similarly, $\mathcal{G}_{Af}(NSliceCh_2) = 1$, because IoT-VAS$_2$ and VAS$_2$-5G have compliant affinity values. Both Network Slice Chains are compliant with this requirement.

Compliance for Trust. From Table 1, it is inferred that the CSP trusts its tenant, its services and they have good business relationship. $\mathcal{G}_T(NSliceCh_1) = \mathcal{G}_T(NSliceCh_2) = 1$, because the trust level of the source and destination Network Slices are equal.

Compliance for Security Level. This attribute obeys Property 9, 14 and Corollary 3. $\mathcal{G}_{SL}(NSliceCh_1) = 1$, since it is the lowest SL on this path. $\mathcal{G}_{SL}(NSliceCh_2) = 2$, since it is the lowest SL on this path.

NSliceCh$_2$ complies with the requirement by traversing two consecutive network slices with medium security level to then go into a high security level network slice. From the evaluation of the attributes, it can be concluded that NSliceCh$_2$ is the one that complies with what is stated in the policy Π.

7.3   Discussion

The example depicts a use case that will become usual inside a CSP network. The CSP can have an orchestrator that automatically chooses the NSliceCh that complies with the policy. If there exists a NSliceCh that respects the constraint, it will be selected. If it is not the case, the CSP will know and can adjust the configuration of the NSlices or the policy to comply with the policy. This enables a CSP to have tools to compare different NSliceCh according to their security characteristics and choose the best one. This approach is extensible to other type of metrics such as latency, performance or cost.

8 Implementation

A test-bed was set up in order to verify the proposed approach to manage inter-slice communication. It uses:

- TOSCA as a specification to describe service components, their relationships and its orchestration, in order to create a Service Template that can be implemented in diverse cloud environments [9].
- Tacker as Generic VNF Manager (VNFM) and an NFV Orchestrator (NFVO) to deploy and operate Network Services and VNF on a NFV infrastructure platform as Openstack.
- Openstack Heat as orchestration engine to launch multiple composite cloud applications based on templates.
- Openstack Neutron and Nova as orchestrators for network connectivity and compute capabilities towards the infrastructure.

The architecture is shown in Fig. 6, where the process to setup the CSP environment is specified by six steps: **(1)** VNF, NS, VNFFG TOSCA templates are

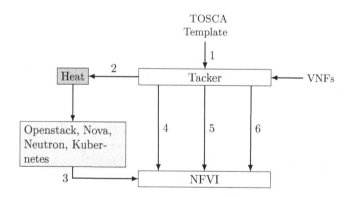

Fig. 6. Topology of a use-case scenario involving inter-slice interactions.

deployed into Tacker; **(2)** Tacker instructs Heat to perform VNF onboarding, orchestration and LCM; **(3)** Openstack Nova and Neutron triggers deployment into the NFVI; **(4)** the service is configured; **(5)** the VNFFG is installed on Open vSwitch (OVS) via an SDN Controller; and **(6)** deploy the set-up of the monitoring scheme for the service.

The architecture shown in Fig. 6 is used to deploy CSG consisting of 20, 40, 60 and 100 network slices. Each one has connections with a security level constraint (low, medium or high). A single policy is implemented, which dictates that connectivity between slices is allowed only if the security level of the next network slice is equal or higher than the origin network slice.

The algorithm proceeds to scan all possible paths from source to destination slice, and evaluates whether the found paths comply with the policy. Figure 7 shows with a blue line the results for the experiment, conceived to tell the time spent to find the first valid path that complies with the policy. For instance, for a CSG composed of 100 network slices, 1318 valid paths were found and only 0.22 ms were needed to find the first valid path.

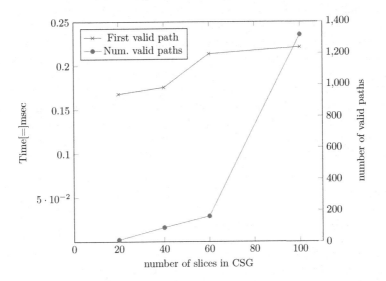

Fig. 7. Time to obtain the first valid path according to policy (in blue) and the number of valid paths (in red) for a CSG of 20, 40, 60 and 100 network slices (Color figure online)

From Fig. 7 it can also be inferred that as the number of network slices increases, the time that is needed to calculate one valid path that satisfies the policy increases as well. This is related with the increment in the number of valid paths that are found, shown with a red line in the same Figure. Nonetheless, a duration of up to 0.22 ms for the case with 100 network slices is valuable, because it is low enough to be used in real-time to find a path that satisfies a policy.

9 Conclusions

The utilisation of network slices as a mechanism to provide communication services to customers and tenants will become commonplace, as technology becomes mature and adoption of enabling technologies such as NFV and SDN increases. Since the nature of a network slice is conceived as a unit specially assembled for a certain use case, the creation of rich end-to-end communication services necessarily involves the communication between several network slices. From a security perspective, the interconnection of the slices must obey policies that guarantee secure interactions and enable just the required traffic between them. In this paper the concept of Network Slice Chain is defined, leveraging from the definitions provided by ETSI and 3GPP and empowered by graph theory.

These elements are used in the communication model that **(1)** assures that there is a Network Slice Chain connecting the required network slices; **(2)** that the Network Slice Chain complies with the constraints expressed in the policy; and **(3)** assures that beyond compliance, it has a minimum rating level compared to what is needed in the policy. These three elements provide a secure environment for the CSP and its tenants.

Regarding the experimental results, the execution time to find a compliant path for a CSG is low, which permits to use our proposition to compute the validation of a security policy in real-time. The objectives for the future will be to find the best path among all the paths that respect the security policy.

The proposed inter-slice communication model is extensible for application in any service and for the inclusion of other security attributes, so security requirements can be expressed more richly. It complies with any access control model, ensuring a straightforward implementation.

References

1. 3GPP: Specification # 23.501 (2018)
2. 3GPP: Specification # 28.531 (2018)
3. 3GPP: Specification # 28.801 (2018)
4. 5G-ENSURE: Deliverable D2.7 - Security Architecture (2016)
5. 5G-PPP: View on 5G Architecture (Version 2.0) (2017)
6. 5G-PPP: D2.3, 5G Mobile Network Architecture, Final overall architecture (2019)
7. Americas, G.: The Evolution of Security in 5G (2019)
8. Bordel, B., Alcarria, R., Sánchez-de-Rivera, D., Sánchez, Á.: An inter-slice management solution for future virtualization-based 5G systems. In: Barolli, L., Takizawa, M., Xhafa, F., Enokido, T. (eds.) AINA 2019. AISC, vol. 926, pp. 1059–1070. Springer, Cham (2020). https://doi.org/10.1007/978-3-030-15032-7_89
9. Brogi, A.: TOSCA in a nutshell: promises and perspectives (2014)
10. Clayman, S., Tusa, F., Galis, A.: Extending slices into data centers: the VIM on-demand model. In: 2018 9th International Conference on the Network of the Future (NOF), pp. 31–38 (2018)
11. Compastié, M., Badonnel, R., Festor, O., He, R.: A TOSCA-oriented software-defined security approach for unikernel-based protected clouds. In: 2019 IEEE Conference on Network Softwarization (NetSoft) (2019)
12. ETSI: ETSI GR NFV-EVE 012 V3.1.1 (2017–12) (2017)
13. ETSI: ETSI GS NFV-IFA 014 V2.3.1 (2017–08) (2017)
14. Guija, D., Siddiqui, M.S.: Identity and access control for micro-services based 5G NFV platforms. In: Proceedings of the 13th International Conference on Availability, Reliability and Security. ACM (2018)

15. Herrmann, D.: Complete Guide to Security and Privacy Metrics: Measuring Regulatory Compliance, Operational Resilience, and ROI. CRC Press, Boca Raton (2007)
16. Marsch, P., Bulakci, O., Queseth, O., Boldi, M.: 5G System Design: Architectural and Functional Considerations and Long Term Research, 1st edn. Wiley, Hoboken (2018)
17. Nowak, T.: Matematyczny model izolacji usług w sieciach plastrowych. Przeglkad Telekomunikacyjny + Wiadomości Telekomunikacyjne (2017)
18. Pattaranantakul, M., He, R., Zhang, Z., Meddahi, A., Wang, P.: Leveraging network functions virtualization orchestrators to achieve software-defined access control in the clouds. IEEE Trans. Dependable Secure Comput., 1 (2018)
19. Ross, R., McEvilley, M., Oren, J.: Systems Security Engineering: Considerations for a Multidisciplinary Approach in the Engineering of Trustworthy Secure Systems. Technical report, NIST Special Publication (SP) 800–160, vol. 1, National Institute of Standards and Technology (2018)
20. Trajkovska, I., et al.: SDN-based service function chaining mechanism and service prototype implementation in NFV scenario. Comput. Stand. Interfaces **54**, 247–265 (2017)
21. de Vaulx, F.J., Simmon, E.D., Bohn, R.B.: Cloud Computing Service Metrics Description. Special Publication (NIST SP) - 500–307 (2018)

Proactively Extracting IoT Device Capabilities: An Application to Smart Homes

Andy Dolan[1], Indrakshi Ray[1], and Suryadipta Majumdar[2(✉)]

[1] Computer Science, Colorado State University, Fort Collins, USA
adolan5@rams.colostate.edu, Indrakshi.Ray@colostate.edu
[2] Information Security and Digital Forensics, University at Albany, Albany, USA
smajumdar@albany.edu

Abstract. Internet of Things (IoT) device adoption is on the rise. Such devices are mostly self-operated and require minimum user interventions. This is achieved by abstracting away their design complexities and functionalities from the users. However, this abstraction significantly limits a user's insights on evaluating the true *capabilities* (i.e., what actions a device can perform) of a device and hence, its potential security and privacy threats. Most existing works evaluate the security of those devices by analyzing the environment data (e.g., network traffic, sensor data, etc.). However, such approaches entail collecting data from encrypted traffic, relying on the quality of the collected data for their accuracy, and facing difficulties in preserving both utility and privacy of the data. We overcome the above-mentioned challenges and propose a proactive approach to extract IoT device capabilities from their informational specifications to verify their potential threats, even before a device is installed. We apply our approach to the context of a smart home and evaluate its accuracy and efficiency on the devices from three different vendors.

1 Introduction

The popularity of IoT devices is gaining momentum (e.g., projections of 75.44 billion devices worldwide by 2025 [18]). This large ecosystem is comprised of a variety of devices that are being used in diverse environments including healthcare, industrial control, and homes. Manufacturers emphasize certain features and characteristics of the IoT devices and often abstract away their actual design complexity and functionalities from the user. Many IoT devices are equipped with an extended set of sensors and actuators which allows them to perform different functionalities. For example, a smart light with a microphone and motion detector can possibly perform far more than just light sensing.

Such abstraction and extended (and in many cases hidden) functionalities of an IoT device result in a blind spot for the consumers and leave an IoT system vulnerable to various security and privacy threats. Installing the above-mentioned smart light necessitates that the consumer understand its potential

A. Singhal and J. Vaidya (Eds.): DBSec 2020, LNCS 12122, pp. 42–63, 2020.
https://doi.org/10.1007/978-3-030-49669-2_3

security and privacy consequences. This requires the consumer to study its design specifications to find out what sensors it possess. Furthermore, she must have the insights to realize the security and privacy consequences of having a microphone and motion detector in a light, and determine if any of those consequences violate the policies of the household or organization. Performing all these steps is infeasible for most IoT users due to either their time constraints or lack of knowledge. Therefore, IoT consumers need assistance to properly interpret the underlying security and privacy threats from these devices. Our work aims to fill this gap by providing consumers information on IoT device capabilities.

A comprehensive knowledge of device capabilities can be used in various security applications, including security verification, monitoring, risk analysis, and digital forensics. One example application is proactively verifying the security and privacy of IoT devices in a smart home or in an organization. Specifically, once we know the capabilities of a device, we can check if any of those capabilities violate any of the security and privacy policies in an organization or a household. We can also ensure that the deployment of an IoT device in some location or under some configuration does not cause any security or privacy breaches and can take adaptive measures to mitigate that risk.

Several works [12, 14, 21–25, 33, 35] that profile IoT devices and their behaviors to detect security breaches and/or monitor an IoT environment pose two limitations: (i) Collecting and interpreting data from an IoT system is extremely challenging. Existing solutions [12, 35] either perform entropy analysis of encrypted traffic or use only the unencrypted features of network traffic (e.g., TCP headers and flow metadata). Due to its great reliance on data inference, false positives/negatives are a legitimate concern. Providing better accuracy in these security solutions is a critical challenge. (ii) Such approaches may reveal sensitive information (e.g., daily routines of smart home users [14]) about an IoT system and its users, threatening their privacy. Preserving privacy while sharing sensitive data for security analysis is another challenge.

We overcome these limitations and propose an approach to proactively extract IoT device capabilities from their design specifications. We first define the notion of device capability in the context of IoT. Second, we extract the transducer (e.g., sensors and actuators) information for each device using vendor-provided specification materials. Third, we identify the capabilities of a device by deriving the capabilities of each sensor and actuator of that device. We discuss our approach in the context of smart homes, an important IoT domain (with projections of 505 million active smart home devices worldwide by this year [19]) and evaluate its efficiency and accuracy. The main contributions of this paper are as follows.

- We propose a new approach to proactively extract the device capabilities from design specifications. The key advantages of this approach over existing works are: (i) this approach does not rely on environment data and is therefore not directly affected by the difficulties of collecting and interpreting IoT data, and further is free from the privacy concerns of data sharing; and (ii) this approach enables proactive security verification of an IoT device even before it is installed or deployed.

- We are the first to define this concept of device capability in IoT, which can potentially be applied in the future security solutions for various IoT applications (e.g., smart grid, autonomous vehicle, smart health, etc.) to offer proactive security guarantee.
- As a proof of concept, we apply our approach in the context of smart homes. We demonstrate the applicability of our approach by applying it to devices from various vendors (e.g., Google, Ring, and Alro), and we evaluate it in terms of its efficiency and accuracy.

The remainder of the paper is organized as follows. Section 2 summarizes related work. Section 3 provides background on vendor materials. Section 4 presents our methodology. Section 5 describes its implementation. Section 6 presents the evaluation results. Section 7 concludes the paper.

2 Related Work

Research on IoT security has gained significant interest. These studies [12,13, 16,17,21–25,27,28,33–36]) are categorized into device fingerprinting, application monitoring, intrusion detection, and access control.

The existing device fingerprinting techniques [12,21–25,35] monitor and analyze network traffic in IoT. More specifically, [21,24] automatically discover and profile device behaviors by building machine learning models trained on network traffic according to their service (e.g., DNS, HTTP) and the semantic behaviors of devices (e.g., detected motion), respectively. Similar analysis is performed in Zhang et al. [35], where the fingerprints of a particular smart home device are built using its network traffic. Other works (e.g., [12,22,23,25]) use similar techniques to automatically determine device identity or typical aggregate behaviors (as opposed to specific behavior). Bezawada et al. [12] utilize machine learning to build behavior profiles based on network traffic for devices using the device category and device type. IoTSentinel [23], AuDI [22] and DeviceMien [25] use unsupervised learning to build models for individual device-types based on network traffic captured during a device connection.

There exist several other security solutions (e.g., [16,20,32,36]) for smart homes. The existing application monitoring techniques (e.g., [20,32]) run on source code of IoT applications and analyze these applications. More specifically, ContextIoT [20] and SmartAuth [32] offer permission-based systems to monitor an individual app. ProvThings [33] builds provenance graphs using security-critical APIs for IoT forensics. Soteria [15] and IoTGuard [16] verify security and safety policies by performing static and dynamic code analysis, respectively. Zhang et al. [36] monitor isolation-related properties among IoT devices through a virtual channel. Yang et al. [34] protect IoT devices from remote attacks by hiding them inside onion gateways.

Limitations of Existing Work. First, most of the solutions above rely on a great amount of inference, especially when considering encrypted network traffic.

Many solutions either perform entropy analysis of encrypted traffic [12] or use only the unencrypted features of network traffic such as TCP headers and other packet and flow metadata [21–25,35]. Because of this inference, false positives and false negatives are a legitimate concern of these solutions. Second, as most of the existing works rely on the application of inferential models (machine learning or otherwise), they are vulnerable to deceptive attacks, where an adversary may craft an attack that conforms to the model's expectation of legitimate traffic or behavior, thereby circumventing the model. An attack at the other end of this spectrum would be to simply conduct a denial-of-service attack by, for example, inundating the system with purposefully malicious traffic to overwhelm the model and prevent the processing of any legitimate traffic. Third, these related works cannot detect/prevent the critical safety or privacy implications that are not observable from the network traffic.

Our paper, on the other hand, is complementary to those existing works, and targets a different threat model where we extract IoT device capabilities from their design specifications that will facilitate evaluating potential security threats even before a device is installed.

3   Vendor Materials

3.1   Vendor Material Description

We consider vendor materials including product webpages, technical specifications, and developer documentations which are publicly available and contain aspects of the specifications (sensors, actuators, or related features) of a device.

Product Webpages. Product webpages are official marketing pages from which a consumer can purchase the product, and contain the summary information about a device. For instance, Google has an online store for its smart home products (e.g., [4]). These pages can be an initial source of information about a smart home device and its specifications.

Technical Specifications. Technical specification pages provide details about a device and its hardware specifications. For instance, Google has a technical specification page for its smart home products (e.g., [5]). This work considers these technical specification pages as one of the most significant sources of information about a device's hardware components.

Developer Documentations. Developer documentations provide information to developers who create applications for the smart home devices. Even though these materials are intended for application developers, they can be used as a source for the extraction of information about the hardware and capabilities of a device.

3.2   Investigation on the Real-World Vendor Materials

Analysis of the Vendor Materials. We analyze the contents of several vendor materials by leveraging natural language processing techniques. These analyses result in insights on the challenges that come with the extraction of vendor materials, which is illustrated through the following examples.

Figure 1a shows the term frequency distribution for the Google Nest Cam Indoor's vendor materials as a word cloud, where the larger terms appear more frequently across the corpus. This particular corpus is constructed from the Nest Cam Indoor main product page, technical specifications page, technical specifications support page, and the Nest Cam Developer API documentation [2,4,5,10]. The full corpus contains 4,175 words after pre-processing. The word cloud suggests that terms that would intuitively be assumed to appear frequently, such as "camera" and "nest" appear often, as these terms are directly related to the primary functionality of the device. However, terms that are indicative of other transducers and their capabilities appear less often, and even appear less often than terms that are unrelated or potentially indicative of transducers that the device does not have. Figure 1b illustrates the frequency distribution of only a subset of notable terms.

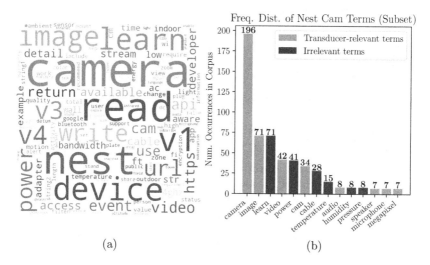

(a)   (b)

Fig. 1. (a) The term frequencies for the corpus of vendor materials on the Nest Cam Indoor, visualized as a word cloud. (b) The term frequencies for a subset of terms from vendor materials on the Nest Cam Indoor. Terms that are more directly related to the transducer they refer to appear in blue, while other terms appear in red. (Color figure online)

Additionally, term frequency-inverse document frequency (TF-IDF) calculations are also performed within individual corpora for a device. Specifically, each separate vendor material for a device is treated as an article in the corpus, and the TF-IDF metric is computed for an individual corpus. Overall, TF-IDF fails to find terms that are most indicative of a device's transducers and capabilities due to their infrequent appearances. We also apply TF-IDF on each section of a vendor material as an individual document. However, this technique also does not produce any conclusive results.

Challenges in Extracting Capabilities from Vendor Materials. Based on the outcome of the analysis above, we enumerate the major challenges in extracting capabilities from vendor materials as follows.

- *No Standaridized Template.* Each vendor follows different templates for their materials and furthermore, different materials of the same vendor follow different formats. There is no standard template or specification for how to describe different generic features or hardware components. This implies significant effort to learn those different templates to enable their extraction.
- *Brevity of the Materials.* Vendor materials are usually expressed in a brief manner and do not include all explicit specifications of a device. Therefore, extracting device information from them requires more interpretation of the contents. Additionally, terms that are indicative of particular hardware components may only appear a limited number of times within the materials, especially if they are not related to the primary function of the device.
- *Vendor-Specific Jargons.* Each vendor tends to use their own set of terminologies for their devices. Mainly due to their business policy, vendors craft languages around what information they believe is the most useful to or well-received by the consumer, and include terminology that may be unique to only their line of products. Accordingly, learning the vocabularies used for various vendors and then normalizing them to infer their capabilities presents additional challenges.
- *Interpreting Visual Contents.* Several contexts (e.g. device type) of a material is visually represented and is therefore very difficult to encode automatically. An interesting aspect of the marketing and technical specification pages for IoT devices is the way that page layout and structure provide contextual information in the form of visual cues and hierarchical organization. Therefore, text processing alone becomes insufficient in those cases.
- *Distributed Materials.* The information about a device is distributed over various materials (e.g., product webpage, technical specifications, user manual, and developer documentation), and it is essential to obtain information from as many different materials as possible, normalize their formats, and extract capabilities for the most thorough extraction.

4   Methodology

We first present our threat model and the assumptions of our approach, followed by the overview, and finally the details.

4.1   Threat Model

We focus on smart homes, an IoT application, in this work. We assume that the sensors and actuators in a smart home device may be used to conduct various security and privacy attacks. Our approach, therefore, builds the device capabilities (i.e., the actions that a device can perform) which can later be used to detect/prevent the adversaries that exploit these sensors or actuators. Our approach does not consider the threats from a malicious or vulnerable trans-ducer; which includes misbehavior and malfunction. Also, any network attack that does not involve the transducers is beyond the scope of this paper. In this work, we derive the device capabilities from the vendor-provided materials that are publicly available. In this paper, the impact of negation in the language of this materials is not considered in extracting capabilities. Therefore, any missing information about a device in those materials may affect the effectiveness of our approach.

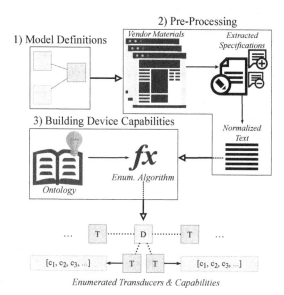

Fig. 2. An overview of our methodology, including 1) development of the model, 2) pre-processing of vendor materials, and 3) applying an ontology to extracted specifications by way of an automatic enumeration function.

4.2   Overview

Figure 2 illustrates an overview of our approach to extract the capabilities of a smart home device from its specifications. The three steps are described below, and we provide the example of a motion-activated smart camera throughout.

[**Step 1: Defining Capability Model for IoT Devices**] We first define IoT devices, then define their transducers (e.g., sensors and actuators), and finally define the capability models that map transducers to their set of capabilities (See Sect. 4.3).

[**Step 2: Normalizing Specifications from Vendor Materials**] We first extract the device specifications from various vendor materials, then prune the extracted data to eliminate irrelevant contents (e.g., stop words and site navigation links), and finally normalize the pruned contents to refer to the transducer information (See Sect. 4.4).

[**Step 3: Building IoT Device Capabilities**] We first build the ontology of the device specifications, then derive an enumeration of transducers for a device by applying this ontology on the processed vendor materials, and finally map these transducers to their capabilities (See Sect. 4.5).

4.3   Defining Capability Models for IoT Devices

This work defines a *transducer* as a sensor or actuator (partly inspired by the definitions in NIST 8228 [29]). A *sensor* holds the core functionality of sensing or measuring various aspects of a physical environment and converting it to a digital signal. For example, image sensors, motion sensors, and microphones sense light, motion, and sound from a physical environment, respectively. An *actuator* converts a digital signal to various physical actions (e.g., emitting light, producing sound, actuating a lock to toggle its state).

The set of all transducers T is partitioned into two sets, where S is the set of all sensors and A is the set of all actuators, where $T = S \cup A$ and $S \cap A = \emptyset$. A capability of a sensor is denoted as c_{si} and the capability of an actuator is denoted as c_{aj}. Note that, $\forall i, j, c_{si} \neq c_{aj}$. However, for any two sensors s_m and s_n, where $m \neq n$ and $s_m, s_n \in S$, their set of capabilities may overlap.

Definition 1. [**Transducer**]: *A transducer t_i is either a sensor s_i or an actuator a_i. That is, if $t_i = s_i$, then $t_i \neq a_i$. Also, if $t_i = a_i$, then $t_i \neq s_i$. Each sensor s_i and each actuator a_i consists of a non-zero finite set of capabilities, denoted as $s_i = \{c_{s1}, c_{s2}, \ldots, c_{sp}\}$ and $a_i = \{c_{a1}, c_{a2}, \ldots, c_{aq}\}$. Also $s_i \neq \{\}$ and $a_i \neq \{\}$.*

Definition 2. [**Device:**] *A device is an embedded system that consists of a set of transducers. A device D_i consists of a set of sensors S_i and actuators A_i where $S_i \subseteq S$ and $A_i \subseteq A$ and $S_i = \{s_1, s_2, \ldots, s_n\}$ and $A_i = \{a_1, a_2, \ldots a_m\}$. The number of transducers in D_i equals $n + m$.*

Multiple devices may have common sensors or actuators. For example, smart cameras and smart video doorbells both have a camera sensor. Two devices D_r and D_s shown below have common sensor s_3 and common actuator a_2.
$D_r = S_1 \cup A_1 = \{s_1, s_2, s_3, a_1, a_2\}; D_s = S_2 \cup A_2 = \{s_3, s_4, a_2, a_3\}$.

Definition 3. [**Device Capability**]: *A capability of device D_i is a function the device can perform. The set of capabilities for D_i is computed as the union of the set of capabilities of the transducers comprising the device.*

Multiple devices can have common capabilities. For example, a smart camera has an image sensor and therefore holds the capability of capturing an image.

On the other hand, a smart light has both light and motion sensors; therefore it holds the capabilities of sensing lights and detecting motion. In the following, the two devices D_p and D_q have common capabilities c_{s3} and c_{a2}:
$D_p = \{c_{s1}, c_{s2}, c_{s3}, c_{a2}, c_{a3}\}$; $D_q = \{c_{s3}, c_{s4}, c_{s5}, c_{a1}, c_{a2}\}$.

4.4   Normalizing Specifications from Vendor Materials

To prepare the vendor materials for building device capabilities, we first extract the device specifications from the vendor materials, then remove irrelevant information (e.g., external navigation links or copyright information) from those extracted specifications, and finally refine them into a more homogeneous, and machine-friendly format.

Selective Extractions of Device Specifications. The initial extraction of the device specification is a process that operates on the input vendor materials. The vendor materials must be parsed for their contents, which can be defined in terms of semantics as well as more abstract information such as document structures and page layouts. This work extracts the vendor materials in HTML and/or text formats.

For HTML documents, we first remove the non-HTML contents from each web page, such as style and script blocks. We then extract the raw text from the resulting HTML elements. We parameterize this step so that specific sections of a page can be extracted. For example, the technical specifications page for a smart camera may contain page elements unrelated to the device, such as navigation links, or even additional specification information for similar products (e.g., video doorbells). With our parameterized method, we are able to extract only the specification information for the smart camera. We also tailor the parameters to specific vendor pages; these parameters are often reusable, as web design under a single vendor is often homogeneous.

Normalizing the Data. To ensure that the contents extracted from the vendor materials are best suited for the transducer enumeration technique, our approach normalizes those contents by removing elements that are not critical to the enumeration process, including punctuation, non-alphanumeric, and non-white-space characters, as well as "stop words" (i.e., common articles and prepositions in English). The term case and plurality are also normalized through lemmatization, a process of linguistics that simply involves homogenizing different inflections of the same term to the dictionary form of the term. The content output by the normalization step contains a more homogeneous sequence of terms in the original order that they appeared in the vendor materials.

For example, a motion activated camera's marketing page may contain the following text: *"with the camera's array of motion sensors, video will be recorded automatically"*. After this step, the same string will read *"camera array motion sensor video record automatically"*.

4.5   Building IoT Device Capabilities

We now describe how to derive the device capabilities after pre-processing.

Building the Ontology. Our approach understands the language and structure of the vendor materials, and then builds an ontology. The ontology will contain an understanding of the terminologies used to refer to specific components of a device. It is possible to include other information as well that can be derived from the vendor products.

Enumerating Transducers. To enumerate device transducers using the above-mentioned ontology, we devise three algorithms, namely, ranked key term set matching (rKTSM), unranked key term set matching (KTSM), and unguided key term set matching, where *key terms* are one or more words related to a transducer. These algorithms use two types of key terms: indicative terms and related terms. The *indicative terms* are unambiguously indicative of the presence of a transducer. The *related terms* are related to a transducer, but may be more ambiguous, and hence are not sufficient in drawing conclusions about its presence. In the case of a motion-activated camera, the term "camera" is considered indicative of an image sensor, while the term "video" is considered related to an image sensor. We describe each algorithm below, in which the notation "x[y]" indicates the mapping or membership of a field y in x.

– *Ranked Key Term Set Matching (rKTSM) Algorithm:* Algorithm 1 first filters the key term sets for different abstract device types, and then performs key term matching based on the most relevant set of indicative terms. Specifically, Lines 1–11 outline the first matching step, which uses both indicative and related terms to determine which abstract device type is most likely being represented by the corpus of vendor materials. The "get_matches" function extracts any matching key terms in the provided set that are contained within the input corpus. The indicative terms of the device type that is ranked as the best match candidate are considered to be the terms that refer to the transducers of the device. A reverse-mapping step is then performed on Line 12, where only these indicative terms are used to determine which transducers are present. Note that the output of the first matching step is a subset of indicative terms for the selected abstract device type. The reverse mapping step determines which transducer each indicative term refers to, where some transducers may be referred to by more than one indicative term. The final results contain an enumeration of transducer identifiers, which are returned at Line 12.

Algorithm 1: Ranked Key Term Set Matching (rKTSM)

---

1 best_score ← 0
2 best_indicative ← **null**
3 **for** *d in Ontology[Devices]* **do**
4   indicative_terms ← d[transducers][indicative_terms]
5   related_terms ← d[transducers][related_terms]
6   ind_matches ← get_matches(indicative_terms, corpus)
7   rel_matches ← get_matches(related_terms, corpus)
8   match_score ← |rel_matches| + |ind_matches|
9   **if** *match_score > best_score* **then**
10   best_score ← match_score
11   best_indicative ← ind_matches

12 transducer_identifiers ← reverse_map(best_indicative)

The rKTSM algorithm is able to better exploit context clues found in the related terms while avoiding erroneous matches that can be introduced by their ambiguity. Additionally, the approach accounts for the fact that terms that are most directly indicative of the presence of a transducer may have a frequency that is much lower than that of other terms. For example, even if the indicative term "microphone" appears only twice within the entire corpus, the presence of related terms such as "audio" or "voice" can help bolster confidence when concluding that a microphone transducer is present.

– *Unranked Key Term Set Matching (KTSM) Algorithm:* Algorithm 2 uses only the indicative terms without ranking term sets. Specifically, it evaluates the corpus for any matching indicative terms of any transducer, and identifies the transducers through the same reverse-mapping process (as in Algorithm 1).

Algorithm 2: Unranked Key Term Set Matching (KTSM)

---

1 all_indicative_terms ← $\bigcup_d$ d[transducers][indicative_terms]
2 ind_matches ← get_matches(all_indicative_terms, corpus)
3 transducer_identifiers ← reverse_map(ind_matches)

– *Unguided Key Term Set Matching:* Additionally, we consider a completely unguided KTSM alrogithm, shown in Algorithm 3, that performs the same matching as unranked KTSM, but also matches on the related terms. We consider this algorithm to be the least focused and exact, as it attempts to match using an entire vocabulary.

Algorithm 3: Unguided Key Term Set Matching

1 all_indicative_terms ← $\bigcup_{d}$ d[transducers][indicative_terms]

2 all_related_terms ← $\bigcup_{d}$ d[transducers][related_terms]

3 all_terms ← all_indicative_terms + all_related_terms

4 all_matches ← get_matches(all_terms, corpus)

5 transducer_identifiers ← reverse_map(all_matches)

The transducers that are enumerated from the extraction step must be represented in a standardized way, (e.g., using the same identifier for the transducer type), where each extracted transducer is completely decoupled from the device instance it was extracted from. This is to ensure that the transducers fit into the model that is described in Sect. 4.3.

Mapping to Device Capabilities. Capabilities of a device are enumerated from its constituent transducers. This work assumes that transducers are associated with a static, finite set of capabilities that are established during the creation of the ontology. Each transducer can be directly mapped to its set of capabilities as per Sect. 4.3. The capabilities contained in the final output set represent a device's functionality unambiguously. Table 1 provides examples of the outputs of our methodology.

5   Implementation

We build the ontology of vendor materials for seven smart home products: Arlo Ultra Camera, Nest Cam Indoor, Nest Hello Doorbell, Nest Protect, Nest Learning Thermostat, Nest X Yale Lock, and Ring Indoor Camera [1,3,4,6–9].

Our pre-processing step is implemented (in Python) to fetch the product web pages directly over the network via the requests library [26] by way of their URI, or to read pages fetched previously and saved locally. To extract the textual content from those pages, we utilize the BeautifulSoup package [11] which allows us to extract only specific sections of vendor material pages by providing parameters with specific HTML tags and attributes used to identify page portions. Our current implementation supports the static elements in web pages (i.e., HTML), which is the current format for most vendor materials. However, if some vendor materials only display the content dynamically, a simple workaround would be to use a web engine to first internally render any dynamic content before processing the resulting HTML. To normalize the text, a separate Python function replaces stop words and non-alphanumeric characters via regular expressions. For the normalization of term plurality, lemmatization is performed using the Spacy natural language processing package [31].

The KTSM algorithms described in Sect. 4.5 are also implemented as Python functions that take a corpus as input from which to enumerate transducers. To encode the ontology created during the manual review process (as described

Table 1. An excerpt of outputs from our approach.

Device	Category	Transducer	Atomic capabilities
Arlo Ultra [1]	**Sensors**	Image sensor	Capture image, Capture video, Detect light
		Microphone	Capture sound
		Motion sensor	Detect motion
	Actuators	Speaker	Produce sound
		LED light	Produce light
		Infrared light	Produce IR light (enabling night vision)
		Siren	Produce high-volume siren
Nest Cam Indoor [5]	**Sensors**	Image sensor	Capture image (take photo), Capture video, Detect light
		Microphone	Capture sound
	Actuators	Speaker	Produce sound
		LED light	Produce light
		Infrared light	Produce IR light (enabling night vision)
Nest Protect 2nd Gen [8]	**Sensors**	Smoke sensor	Detect smoke
		Carbon monoxide sensor	Detect carbon monoxide
		Temperature sensor	Measure temperature
		Humidity sensor	Measure humidity, detect steam
		Microphone	Capture sound
		Motion sensor	Detect motion
		Light sensor	Detect light
	Actuators	Speaker	Produce sound
		LED light	Produce light
Nest X Yale Lock [9]	**Sensors**	Light sensor	Detect light
		Touch sensor	Detect (capacitive) contact
	Actuators	Lock	Lock and unlock door
		Speaker	Produce sound
		LED light	Produce light

in Appendix A), a data model is created to represent abstract device types, transducers, their capabilities, and key term sets. Each transducer is represented in the data model as having a static set of capabilities, a set of indicative terms, and a set of related terms. These data models act as additional parameters to our KTSM functions. Given the corpus of a device's vendor materials and the data model, the implemented KTSM functions utilize the tree-based flashtext algorithm [30] to perform key term matching. In the case of ranked KTSM, the number of matches is used to determine the best abstract device type. In unranked and unguided KTSM, only the matching step takes place with all indicative terms, and with all indicative and related terms, respectively. Any matches are mapped to their associated transducer's identifier automatically (enabled by the Python implementation of flashtext).

6   Evaluation

This section discusses the performance of our implemented solution, which is used to extract enumerations of transducers for the seven devices. All extractions are performed on a system with an Intel Core i7-8550U processor @ 1.80 GHz and 8 GB of memory. We evaluate the performance of our implementation in terms of its efficiency, the enumeration accuracy for each device, and the proportion of incorrect transducer matches for each device.

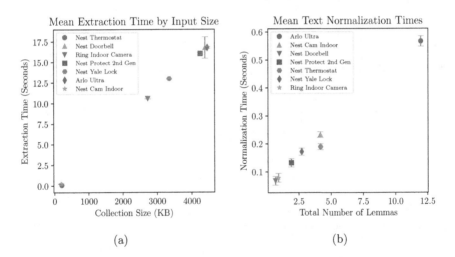

Fig. 3. (a) Average text extraction time of the vendor materials for different devices by their size on disk, computed over 5 trials. (b) Average text normalization time by the total number of lemmas in a corpus, computed over 5 trials.

Efficiency. The goal of the first set of our experiments is to measure the efficiency of our approach. The efficiency of our implementation refers to the total time required to perform the pre-processing step on the input vendor materials for a particular device. Displayed in Fig. 3a, the extraction step is the most significant source of processing time in our methodology, ranging from less than a second to nearly 20 s.

The time required for the extraction step depends on the size of the vendor materials that are used as input. HTML files for devices may exhibit a large range of sizes; for example, pages on Google Nest devices have the largest range of sizes on disk, from 38 KB to 2.6 MB. The HTML extraction portion of the pre-processing step takes the largest amount of time, between 15 and 18 s, for the largest collections of web pages (over 4 MB total). Comparatively, smaller collections of pages (totalling 200 KB or less) take less than a second for extraction. Figure 3a indicates that extraction time scales with the size linearly.

For most evaluated devices, the times required to perform the text normalization step, displayed in Fig. 3b, are negligible when compared to those of the extraction step. Consistently, across all devices, the text normalization step is performed in less than a second, increasing slightly with the total number of lemmas extracted.

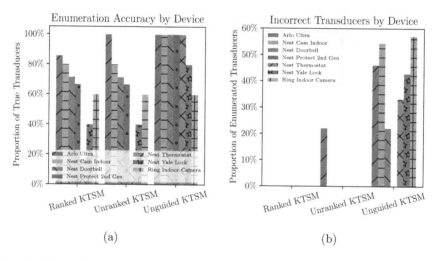

Fig. 4. For each device, grouped by KTSM algorithm (a) the proportion of ground truth transducers that are correctly enumerated, and (b) the proportion of matching transducers that are incorrectly identified.

We do not analyze the impact of the automatic enumeration of device transducers from normalized texts, due to the efficiency of the tree-based flashtext algorithm for keyword extraction which we use. Additionally, we do not consider the mapping from enumerated transducers to their capabilities as having any impact on efficiency, due to the fact that this mapping is statically defined in the ontology. That is, once the transducers have been enumerated, establishing their corresponding capabilities requires a trivial lookup in the ontology.

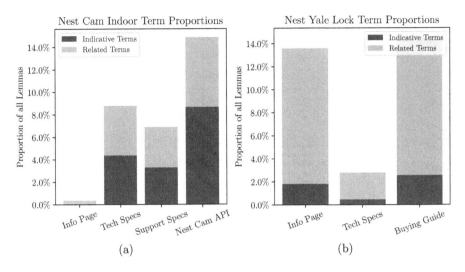

Fig. 5. A comparison of the proportions of indicative and related terms per document for (a) the Nest Cam Indoor [5] and (b) the Nest X Yale Lock [9].

Enumeration Accuracy. For the purposes of evaluation, a sample set of transducers for the evaluated devices are enumerated manually as ground truth. Enumeration accuracy is computed as the ratio between the number of these ground truth transducers that were correctly identified by an extraction approach to the total number of ground truth transducers. Figure 4a displays the results of our enumerations on the seven different devices from three different vendors, grouped by the enumeration algorithms.

Figure 4a shows that both the ranked and unranked KTSM algorithms provide similar proportions of correctly identified transducers, averaging about 60% and 62%, respectively, of ground truth transducers identified among all devices with a standard deviation of 24% and 27%, respectively.

For each extraction approach, there is a large disparity between the transducer enumeration rate for the Nest Cam Indoor and the Nest Yale Lock. We present a comparison of these two devices in Fig. 5, showing the proportion of indicative and related terms for each document per device. An interesting property that follows from this comparison is the correlation between this property and the enumeration accuracy for each device. As can be seen in Fig. 6a, as the proportion of indicative terms grows larger, the overall enumeration accuracy of the rKTSM algorithm generally does as well. This is fairly intuitive, in that a set of vendor materials with a larger number of terms that more explicitly reference a particular transducer will better inform a reader of the association of that transducer with the device. This means that a more refined ontology will contribute to an increased number of indicative terms and improve the enumeration accuracy.

Similarly, Fig. 6b displays the negative relationship between proportion of lemmas that are related terms and the transducer enumeration rate. This rela-

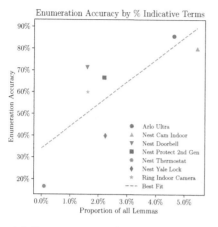
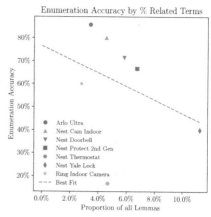

(a) By proportion of indicative terms   (b) By proportion of related terms

Fig. 6. The proportion of corpus terms that are (a) indicative and (b) related correlated with transducer enumeration rate of ranked KTSM.

tionship follows from that of indicative terms and transducer enumeration rate, as a higher proportion of related terms in a corpus is likely accompanied by a lower proportion of indicative terms in the corpus.

Proportion of Incorrect Transducer Matches. To evaluate the tendencies of our algorithms to incorrectly identify transducers, we also measure the proportion of matched transducers that are not within the ground truth set. In other words, we measure the rates at which our algorithms enumerate transducers that are not actually associated with the device.

Figure 4b shows the proportion of incorrect matches. The unguided KTSM approach suffers from the highest proportions of incorrect matches across all devices, with an average of 36% of all transducer matches for each device. Unranked KTSM, on the other hand, averages only 3% incorrect transducers, and ranked KTSM does not incorrectly attribute any transducers to any of the new evaluated devices.

The advantage that comes from applying ranked KTSM on texts extracted from vendor materials is the fact that only the indicative terms that are associated with certain devices as defined in the ontology are applied for matching. This ensures that only the most relevant terms with the least ambiguity will be used to draw conclusions about the device's transducers. If ranked KTSM behaves in a way that is too restrictive and fails to enumerate transducers that unranked or unguided KTSM can enumerate, it may be the case that the term sets used for matching are not thorough enough, or a sign that the ontology's representation of the device in question should be improved.

7   Conclusion and Future Work

With the growing popularity of IoT, the necessity of ensuring its security becomes important than ever. We proposed a proactive approach to extract IoT device capabilities from their design specifications to verify their potential threats even before a device is installed. More specifically, we defined the notion of device capability in the context of IoT, extracted the transducer information for each device using vendor-provided design specifications and finally identified the capabilities of a device.

Our current work relies only on vendor provided materials that are publicly available and may be missing some information. In future, we plan to augment our approach with information from software specifications, device configurations, and firmware versions. Our future work also includes adapting our methodology to other IoT applications including smart grid, smart health, and autonomous vehicle.

Acknowledgement. The authors thank the anonymous reviewers for their comments. This work was funded in part by NIST under Contract Number 60NANB18D204, by funds from NSF under Award Number CNS 1650573, CNS 1822118, and funds from AFRL, SecureNok, Furuno Electric Company, and CableLabs. We would also like to thank Upakar Paudel for help with code development.

A   Study on Vendor materials

Reviewing vendor materials manually is important for understanding any inferences required in drawing conclusions about a device's transducers and capabilities. The goal of the manual review step is to enumerate the different hardware components and capabilities of a device for a baseline of ground truth, and also to enumerate and analyze the inferences and assumptions that are required for the reader to draw these conclusions. These results are captured and become the basis for the ontology that will be used as a parameter for the automated enumeration process.

The process of manually reviewing vendor materials is the same for all devices. This process involves reading through different documents that are associated with each device and interpreting from them the set of transducers (and capabilities) on the device. During this process, any insights, inferences, or context clues that are used to make this interpretation are also captured. The most important of these features that are key terms that act as indicators of the presence of a particular transducer or capability. In some cases, key terms are only indicative of a transducer or capability when considered in conjunction with another key term.

For example, during the manual review of the Nest Cam Indoor's technical specifications on the Google Nest support forums [10], simple terms such as "camera" are indicative of the presence of an image sensor. On the other hand, a term like "video" is more ambiguous, and could refer to the video captured by the image sensor, or video displayed on some kind of screen. In this case, it

Table 2. Obtained ontology for the Nest Cam Indoor

Category	Transducer	Capabilities
Sensors	Image sensor	Capture image, Capture video, Detect light
	Microphone	Capture sound
Actuators	Speaker	Produce sound
	LED light	Produce light
	Infrared light	Produce infrared light

can be "inferred" that this term refers to an image sensor because of context clues provided by additional related terms such as "1080p," which refers to the resolution of the video captured by the sensor, and "lens," which refers to the lens of the camera. On their own, these additional terms do not necessarily suggest the presence of an image sensor, but they can provide context when considered in conjunction with other camera-related terms to suggest with higher confidence the presence of the sensor. The understanding of these terms as context clues carries an assumed level of prerequisite knowledge of camera-related terminology. A sample outcome for the Google Nest Cam Indoor is summarized in Table 2.

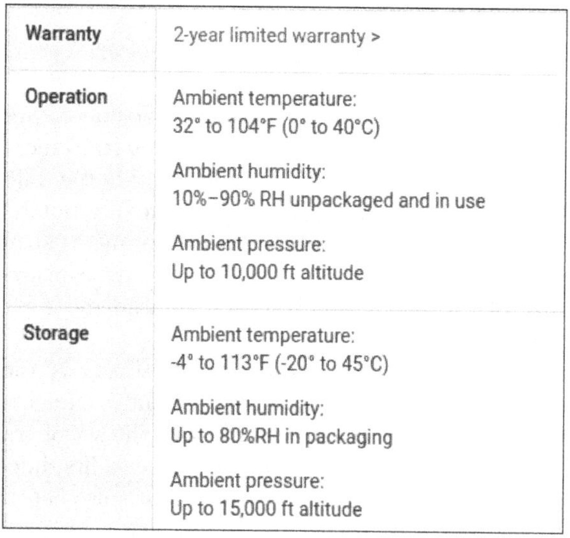

Warranty	2-year limited warranty >
Operation	Ambient temperature: 32° to 104°F (0° to 40°C) Ambient humidity: 10%–90% RH unpackaged and in use Ambient pressure: Up to 10,000 ft altitude
Storage	Ambient temperature: -4° to 113°F (-20° to 45°C) Ambient humidity: Up to 80%RH in packaging Ambient pressure: Up to 15,000 ft altitude

Fig. 7. Different sections of the Nest Cam Indoor technical specifications page [10], where the terms "temperature" and "humidity" can be seen multiple times, but only in reference to the theoretical temperature range in which the device can regularly operate and be stored.

The visual cues provided by page structure can also help a reader understand the context around the terms. For the Nest family of products, it is common for the term "temperature" to appear on technical specification pages for devices that have no sensors or actuators related to the measurement or alteration of any temperature. Instead, these instances of the term are used to describe the "operating" constraints of the device (the theoretical range of temperature in which it can operate). The only real indicator of this difference is in the table layout of the Nest Cam Indoor's technical specifications page, where a reader can see by way of the row's label "operation" that the temperature in this case refers to the device's operating temperature and not any sensor. This part of the page is illustrated in Fig. 7.

Perhaps the most abstract feature that is considered during manual review, which is largely dependent on the individual reviewer, is the use of technical background knowledge to infer, from a described concept, how a certain feature of a device may be implemented. The term "motion detection," for example, could indicate the presence of a motion sensor or of software that enables an image sensor to perform motion detection. Regardless, the ability for the reviewer to conceive of these possibilities is dependent on their technical background knowledge.

References

1. Arlo ultra — hd security camera — wireless camera system. https://www.arlo.com/en-us/products/arlo-ultra/default.aspx
2. Camera API — nest developers. https://developers.nest.com/reference/api-camera
3. Indoor cam — indoor security cameras — ring. https://shop.ring.com/products/mini-indoor-security-camera
4. Nest cam indoor - home security camera - google store. https://store.google.com/us/product/nest_cam
5. Nest cam indoor - installation and tech specs - google store. https://store.google.com/us/product/nest_cam_specs
6. Nest hello video doorbell - know who's knocking - google store. https://store.google.com/us/product/nest_hello_doorbell
7. Nest learning thermostat - installation and tech specs - google store. https://store.google.com/us/product/nest_learning_thermostat_3rd_gen_specs
8. Nest protect 2ng gen - installation and tech specs - google store. https://store.google.com/us/product/nest_protect_2nd_gen_specs
9. Nest x yale lock - key-free smart deadbolt - google store. https://store.google.com/us/product/nest_x_yale_lock
10. Technical specifications for nest cameras and video doorbells - google nest help. https://support.google.com/googlenest/answer/9259110
11. beautifulsoup: beautifulsoup4 4.8.2. https://pypi.org/project/beautifulsoup4/
12. Bezawada, B., Bachani, M., Peterson, J., Shirazi, H., Ray, I., Ray, I.: Behavioral fingerprinting of IoT devices. In: Proceedings of ASHES, pp. 41–50 (2018)
13. Bhatt, S., Patwa, F., Sandhu, R.: An access control framework for cloud-enabled wearable Internet of Things. In: CIC (2017)
14. Birnbach, S., Eberz, S., Martinovic, I.: Peeves: physical event verification in smart homes. In: Proceedings of CCS, pp. 1455–1467. ACM (2019)

15. Celik, Z.B., McDaniel, P., Tan, G.: SOTERIA: automated IoT safety and security analysis. In: USENIX ATC (2018)
16. Celik, Z.B., Tan, G., McDaniel, P.D.: IoTGuard: dynamic enforcement of security and safety policy in commodity IoT. In: NDSS (2019)
17. Choi, J., et al.: Detecting and identifying faulty IoT devices in smart home with context extraction. In: IEEE DSN (2018)
18. market forecast, S.: Internet of Things (IoT) connected devices installed base worldwide from 2015 to 2025 (2016). https://www.statista.com/statistics/471264/iot-number-of-connected-devices-worldwide/
19. market forecast, S.: Smart home - United States (2019). https://www.statista.com/outlook/279/109/smart-home/united-states
20. Jia, Y.J., et al.: ContexIoT: towards providing contextual integrity to appified iot platforms. In: NDSS (2017)
21. Lopez-Martin, M., Carro, B., Sanchez-Esguevillas, A., Lloret, J.: Network traffic classifier with convolutional and recurrent neural networks for Internet of Things. IEEE Access 5, 18042–18050 (2017)
22. Marchal, S., Miettinen, M., Nguyen, T.D., Sadeghi, A., Asokan, N.: AuDI: toward autonomous IoT device-type identification using periodic communication. IEEE J. Sel. Areas Commun. 37(6), 1402–1412 (2019)
23. Miettinen, M., Marchal, S., Hafeez, I., Asokan, N., Sadeghi, A., Tarkoma, S.: IoT SENTINEL: automated device-type identification for security enforcement in IoT. In: Proceedings of ICDCS, pp. 2177–2184, June 2017
24. OConnor, T., Mohamed, R., Miettinen, M., Enck, W., Reaves, B., Sadeghi, A.R.: HomeSnitch: behavior transparency and control for smart home IoT devices. In: Proceedings of WiSec, pp. 128–138 (2019)
25. Ortiz, J., Crawford, C., Le, F.: DeviceMien: network device behavior modeling for identifying unknown IoT devices. In: Proceedings of IoTDI, pp. 106–117. Montreal (2019)
26. Requests: Requests: HTTP for humans. https://requests.readthedocs.io/en/master/
27. Román-Castro, R., López, J., Gritzalis, S.: Evolution and trends in IoT security. Computer 51(7), 16–25 (2018)
28. Serror, M., Henze, M., Hack, S., Schuba, M., Wehrle, K.: Towards in-network security for smart homes. In: ARES (2018)
29. Shen, V., Siderius, D., Krekelberg, W., Hatch, H.: Considerations for managing Internet of Things (IoT) cybersecurity and privacy risks. Technical Report, National Institute of Standards and Technology, June 2019. https://doi.org/10.6028/NIST.IR.8228
30. Singh, V.: Replace or retrieve keywords in documents at scale. ArXiv e-prints October 2017. http://adsabs.harvard.edu/abs/2017arXiv171100046S, provided by the SAO/NASA Astrophysics Data System
31. spaCy: spaCy: Industrial-strength natural language processing in Python. https://spacy.io/
32. Tian, Y., et al.: SmartAuth: user-centered authorization for the Internet of Things. In: USENIX Security (2017)
33. Wang, Q., Hassan, W.U., Bates, A., Gunter, C.: Fear and logging in the Internet of Things. In: NDSS (2018)
34. Yang, L., Seasholtz, C., Luo, B., Li, F.: Hide your hackable smart home from remote attacks: the multipath onion IoT Gateways. In: ESORICS (2018)

35. Zhang, W., Meng, Y., Liu, Y., Zhang, X., Zhang, Y., Zhu, H.: HoMonit: monitoring smart home apps from encrypted traffic. In: Proceedings of CCS, pp. 1074–1088 (2018)
36. Zhang, Y., Chen, J.l.: Modeling virtual channel to enforce runtime properties for IoT services. In: ICC (2017)

Security Enumerations for Cyber-Physical Systems

Daniel Schlette[(⊠)] [iD], Florian Menges [iD], Thomas Baumer [iD],
and Günther Pernul

University of Regensburg, 93053 Regensburg, Germany
{daniel.schlette,florian.menges,thomas.baumer,guenther.pernul}@ur.de

Abstract. Enumerations constitute a pivotal element of Cyber Threat
Intelligence (CTI). References to enumerated artifacts support a universal understanding and integrate threat information. While traditional
IT systems and vulnerabilities are covered by security enumerations,
this does not apply to Cyber-Physical Systems (CPS). In particular,
complexity and interdependencies of components within these systems
demand for an extension of current enumerations. Taking on a CPS security management perspective this work identifies deficiencies within the
Common Platform Enumeration (CPE) and the Common Vulnerabilities
and Exposures (CVE) enumeration. Models for CPS are thus proposed
to cover comprehensiveness and usability. A prototype is used to evaluate
the feasibility by demonstrating key features of security enumerations for
CPS.

1 Motivation

At present we are experiencing an encompassing transition of our daily life and
environment caused by the availability of technology and the efficient processing
of information. Formerly separate domains such as physical processes and IT systems become interconnected and can now be remotely controlled. The resulting
Cyber-Physical Systems (CPS) allow for exciting new applications. Since this
development is accompanied by a continuous increase in complexity, it is also
an essential factor for the emergence of many vulnerabilities of CPS. Even for
security experts it is a challenging task to keep track of all vulnerabilities that
may cause an issue for their organization and require quick countermeasures.

It is evident that a reduction of the given complexity is necessary to solve
this issue. Security enumerations are suitable to make complexity manageable as
they cover various Cyber Threat Intelligence (CTI) artifacts such as platforms,
vulnerabilities or even natural hazards. In general, they are designed to enhance
the information flow between organizations by setting up a common and usable
reference for considered objects. CTI makes use of security enumerations not
only to describe cyber attacks but also to share and collaboratively improve
valuable threat information via dedicated platforms and data formats [12,14].

© IFIP International Federation for Information Processing 2020
Published by Springer Nature Switzerland AG 2020
A. Singhal and J. Vaidya (Eds.): DBSec 2020, LNCS 12122, pp. 64–76, 2020.
https://doi.org/10.1007/978-3-030-49669-2_4

Two of the most notable enumerations are the Common Vulnerabilities and Exposures (CVE) enumeration and the Common Platform Enumeration (CPE). They are, for example, used to describe different properties of the TRITON malware which we will use in our case study. More specifically, *CVE-2018-7522* provides a standardized identifier, an additional description and further references about the leveraged TRITON vulnerability found in Cyber-Physical Systems. Besides, the firmware component "Schneider Electric - Triconex Tricon MP 3008" affected by the aforementioned CVE entry is encoded as CPE name *cpe:2.3:o:schneider-electric:triconex_tricon_mp_3008_firmware:10.0*. This name covers key characteristics of the platform including vendor, product and version.

While CVE and CPE provide guidance for communicating about vulnerabilities and platforms, the US National Vulnerability Database (NVD) goes one step further. By collecting and linking entries of both security enumerations a connected CPE and CVE search engine is realized. Ultimately, this search engine allows to check whether a vulnerability affects a specific device or vice versa.

However, in appreciation for the NVD and its community there are still improvements targeting complexity as well as the search engine possible. Focusing on CPS, one issue while working with the NVD is the requirement imposed on the user to know the CPE names of her own assets prior to searching for related vulnerabilities. The complexity and heterogeneity of CPS make a comprehensive overview of the deployed components already a challenging task [19,20]. Additionally, CPS introduce novel components for the enumerations such as Supervisory Control And Data Acquisition (SCADA) systems, Programmable Logic Controllers (PLC), actuators and sensors which need to be managed alongside existing components. Security management of CPS also requires highly specific knowledge about CPS as well as cyber security which combined may constitute an obstacle to recognize vulnerabilities and to act quickly according to them.

This culminates in the three following research questions tackled in this paper addressing the reduction of complexity within security management of CPS:

1. How can the overview of numerous and heterogeneous CPS components in a given organization be improved?
2. How can novel classes of CPS components be added to CPE?
3. How can usability of CPE and CVE for users without specific domain knowledge be enhanced?

The remainder of this paper proceeds as follows: First a review of background information on CPS and security enumerations is given in Sect. 2. We then describe our conceptual approach and perform a detailed analysis of CPS characteristics in Sect. 3. Deficiencies found in the two security enumerations CPE and CVE lead towards extensions proposed in our concept. Our prototypical implementation is demonstrated based on a use case in Sect. 4. Subsequently, we give an overview on related work in the areas of CPS and enumerations in Sect. 5 and conclude the paper in Sect. 6.

2   Background

In this section we briefly introduce Cyber-Physical Systems, Common Platform Enumeration (CPE) as well as Common Vulnerabilities and Exposures (CVE).

2.1   Cyber-Physical Systems (CPS)

Digital transformation has reached areas from industrial production to medical applications and household sectors. Accordingly, the concept of CPS is applied to describe the deep integration of physical elements into computing and control processes of the cyber domain [10]. The cyber domain categorizes traditional IT, such as servers or workstations, while the physical domain describes physical entities, such as mechanical or chemical processes and components. CPS also cover advanced functionalities and scenarios based on spatial proximity, such as real-time data processing or feedback loops. While these characteristics are desirable from a functionality perspective they introduce complexity as it is often the case for highly connected systems containing multiple components [1].

2.2   Common Platform Enumeration (CPE)

In the context of cyber security, enumerations define a naming schema for standardization purposes. They provide unique names to cyber threat intelligence (CTI) artifacts and support, for instance, the identification of IT assets, vulnerabilities, attack patterns as well as quality aspects [21].

The Common Platform Enumeration (CPE) describes IT assets and is maintained by the National Institute of Standards and Technology (NIST). It fulfills two main objectives. First, it allows to assign unique names to classes of applications, operating systems and hardware devices [3]. Secondly, it provides matching mechanisms, including details on how to search and compare CPE names [18].

The naming specification includes three distinct naming methods. A given CPE name is either described as *well-formed CPE name (WFN)*, *formatted string (FS)* or *Uniform Resource Identifier (URI)*, allowing to define product classes [3]. While WFN is an abstract set of attribute-value pairs, both FS and URI names are machine-readable encodings [3]. Listing 1 shows the structure and the individual components of a FS encoding. The values for the listed attributes are implemented as strings. In case values are unspecified (ANY) or there is no meaningful value (NA) these are encoded respectively.

```
CPE:2.3:{PART}:{VENDOR}:{PRODUCT}:{VERSION}:
    {UPDATE}:{EDITION}:{LANGUAGE}:{SW_EDITION}:
    {TARGET_SW}:{TARGET_HW}:{OTHER}
```

Listing 1. CPE – FS name structure

CPE is in particular useful to link classes of IT assets to vulnerabilities. It is easy to infer that based on CPE entries, context relevant threat information can be retrieved and information security workflows realized. As a result CPE and CVE are oftentimes applied together [23]. Decision making, the creation of information security policies adapted to the prevalent IT infrastructure and the configuration of platforms are additional use case scenarios of CPE.

2.3   Common Vulnerabilities and Exposures (CVE)

Enumerations not only focus on platforms found in CPE but also target security artifacts directly. The Common Vulnerabilities and Exposures (CVE) enumeration describes vulnerabilities that may lead to exploitation of systems or violations of security policies[1]. Central element to the CVE enumeration are CVE entries, which serve as unique, common identifiers for publicly known information security vulnerabilities. Essentially, each CVE entry consists of the three main components: **CVE ID**, **description** and **references**.

However, these only show an excerpt of the CVE data model capabilities. The CVE automation working group maintains a repository[2] with the specification of a CVE JavaScript Object Notation (JSON) schema with additional elements. Figure 1 provides a simplified overview of the CVE JSON 4.0 data model. The hierarchy of CVE JSON elements is thereby indicated by different tones of gray.

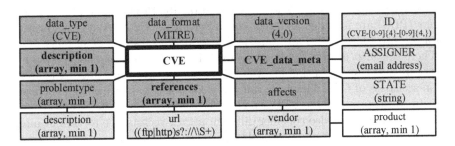

Fig. 1. CVE simplified JSON data schema

The CVE features are integrated in security products based on the CVE data format. CVE entries are also enhanced by metrics like the Common Vulnerability Scoring System (CVSS). Linking CVE entries to CPE entries can further be of value to organizations trying to protect their IT assets.

3   Conceptual Approach

To introduce essential characteristics of CPS into security enumerations our work follows a conceptual approach. First, based on formal CPS specifications we examine common characteristics to derive relevant requirements and deficiencies within existing security enumerations. Then, extensions to the data models

---

[1] https://cve.mitre.org/about/terminology.html.
[2] https://github.com/CVEProject/automation-working-group.

of CPE and CVE are proposed. Here, the perspective of a domain expert is incorporated to put focus on complexity and usability aspects. Finally, the approach is implemented in a prototypical search engine to evaluate the previous findings.

3.1 Requirements

Our twofold requirements analysis addresses CPS and security issues in CPS as well as the two security enumerations CPE and CVE in the following.

Assumption 1 (Secure CPS). *The security of CPS is a positive property.*

Common characteristics of CPS go beyond of traditional IT systems. CPS leverage reactive computation and concurrency. Feedback control via designated controllers, real-time computation and utilization in safety-critical scenarios are part of CPS [1]. The characteristics are realized with sensing, actuating and control components and lead to interdependencies [19]. However, this opens various attack vectors. As prior analysis shows, attacks on nuclear facilities and other critical infrastructures do occur and can have far-reaching consequences [13].

Besides that, most CPS include a multitude of different components like sensors and actuators on the field level. Additionally, Programmable Logic Controllers (PLC) are included as direct control elements. SCADA systems provide another control layer. CPS are thus best described as *systems of systems*.

There are also diverse application areas for CPS, such as energy systems, healthcare and transportation [9]. While security experts know about the application scenarios of CPS, they have much less knowledge about procedures inside CPS. In consequence, these CPS are black boxes from a security perspective.

CPS security must also consider different attack vectors due to various interfaces, operating systems and protocols [11]. Since security assessments and measures require a thorough understanding, formal attack detection, security testing and threat modelling [2,6] have received the researchers' attention. Although, guidelines and tools for CPS security management exist [22], usability for component and vulnerability identification can be improved.

Assumption 2 (Enumerations). *Security enumerations support security management through identification and searchability of artifacts.*

In an organizational setting, information security workflows are aligned to structured data formats. Security management based on CPE is of great importance in the asset management domain and permits risk analyses. CVE further allows to pinpoint security flaws and vulnerabilities of managed IT assets.

Mapping CPS characteristics to the data models of CPE and CVE reveals a number of deficiencies. While there are security products (e.g. NVD) that combine and link CVE and CPE data there is no properly maintained direct reference. This generic deficiency is further accompanied by deficiencies broadly categorized as *component-based* and *system-based*.

Component-Based Deficiencies: Currently, CPE supports traditional IT assets but CPS specifics are missing. This is mainly because CPS components contain specific programming languages or protocols. With a focus on multiple elements contained within CPS the CPE data model also neglects various technical aspects. The embedded nature of components and their interfaces are aspects left aside. As these properties implicate possible attack vectors and allow the identification of CPS, integration into CPE is deemed necessary.

System-Based Deficiencies: From a system perspective CPS represent a new concept of highly-connected components. Grouping multiple components described by their CPE names and linking related vulnerabilities is not supported by CPE and CVE data models. System-based deficiencies are thus related to the usability of the enumerations by security analysts with minor CPS knowledge.

Combining the assumptions it can be concluded that there is a need to support a more comprehensive presentation of the CPS, as this is key to enable the search for vulnerabilities. Our extensions to CPE and CVE aim to foster a better understanding of CPS and a reduction of complexity. Integrating enumerations and making security of CPS manageable is a first step towards secure CPS.

3.2   Conceptual Meta Model

Our proposed model is built upon the findings of the requirements phase and describes a formal structure and relationships between entities of CPE and CVE. In our enhancements we explicitly take into account compatibility with earlier versions. To achieve this, new attributes are added while the existing ones remain unchanged. Following the identified CPS characteristics as well as CPE and CVE deficiencies we group extensions into four categories. The applied naming convention of these categories documents central features that are addressed by our proposal. Extensions relating to CPS characteristics missing in CPE are specified within *technically exhaustive security enumerations*. Bundling CPS components leads to *recursive security enumerations*. *Application-oriented security enumerations* include extensions with usability focus. Last but not least, *coupled security enumerations* address extensions connecting CPE and CVE directly.

Technically exhaustive security enumerations streamline representation of the various components within CPS. We include new elementary attributes and change attribute values as shown in Table 1 to provide a detailed technical description. In this context, the CPS architecture hints at the importance and embedded nature (inseparable software and hardware) of some CPS components [11]. Thus, we introduce *embedded* as a new possible attribute value that covers components within the *part* attribute of CPE names. Interdependencies of CPS are targeted by the new attributes *protocol* and *interface* added to CPE as these allow to express means of communication and connection. Applications used in CPS oftentimes rely on specific programming languages. CPE is extended by a *programming language* attribute to cover this CPS property.

Recursive security enumerations address the *system of systems* concept which is inherent to CPS. We therefore propose the extension of CPE with an additional *CPS Bundle* entity type. As a result, multiple connected components of a CPS can be referenced within the model and build a self-contained unit. The attributes of a *CPS Bundle* reflect the recursive nature of CPS and are specified as *ID*, *description* and *references* shown in Table 1. Due to the fact, that CPS are different and contextually dependent we envision a customization option to describe CPS with a *CPS Bundle*. It is thus possible to provide a brief description of a CPS according to a given situation. The purpose of the *description* attribute is to facilitate a first understanding of these systems on a higher level of abstraction. Also, recursive reference to another CPS Bundle in the *references* attribute is possible and supports hierarchical structuring.

Table 1. Conceptual meta model entity extensions

	Attribute	Description	Examples
CPE Extension	part	The part attribute shall have a new value: "e" - embedded component	e
	sector	The sector attribute should capture areas where systems are typically deployed	energy; healthcare; transportation
	capability	The capability attribute should capture physical functionalities	pressure; viscosity; acceleration
	protocol	The protocol attribute should capture means of communication	Profinet; OPC-UA; DNP3; Modbus; IP
	programming language	The programming language attribute should capture notations for computer programs	Ladder Diagram; C; Java; Instruction List
	interface	The interface attribute should capture means of connection	USB; PCI; SCSI; SATA; RJ-45
	Attribute	**Description**	
CPS Bundle	ID	The ID attribute should capture unique IDs for a CPS bundle	
	description	The description attribute should capture essential CPS information	
	references	The reference attribute should capture CPE names of the CPS components and different CPS bundle IDs	
CVE Ext.	CVE_ID	The CVE_ID attribute should capture assigned CVE IDs	
	description	The description attribute should capture vulnerability information	
	references	The references attribute should capture external data sources describing the given vulnerability as well as CPE name representations	

Application-oriented security enumerations include requirements imposed by security experts without detailed knowledge about CPS. Extensions to CPE with focus on application areas of CPS are aimed to make their security manageable regardless of technical background. Our approach captures usability from a security management perspective through the new *sector* and *capability* attributes shown in Table 1. We thereby assume that some knowledge about CPS in the form of capabilities or application area is present at all times.

Coupled security enumerations introduce a closer tie between CVE and CPE. Focusing on the JSON data schema for CVE we propose an extension for the attribute values captured with the *references* attribute. Besides references to external data sources documenting the vulnerability, the *references* attribute is able to capture CPE names shown in Table 1. In consequence, CVE and CPE are coupled and vulnerabilities affecting a given CPS can be retrieved more easily.

The meta model for our CPS security enumerations search engine is shown in Fig. 2. First, to cover *coupled security enumerations* multiple vulnerabilities (CVE) can be associated with an IT asset (CPE). In addition, Fig. 2 describes *recursive security enumerations* as CPE entities can be part of an individual CPS Bundle entity. Any CPS bundle can also contain other CPS bundles.

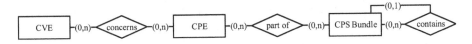

Fig. 2. Meta model of CPS security enumerations search engine

At last, note that migration of data previously described with either CPE or CVE and integration with our model is feasible. Also, CPE entries do not need to contain values for all (new) attributes. Our model is explicitly designed to capture CPS, as these are currently neglected by security enumerations.

4 Use Case

In this section we outline a use case to evaluate our concept. A CPS security enumerations search engine analogous to the generic NVD is central to security management in an organizational setting. Related security processes and common associations are schematically depicted in Fig. 3. In general, a security enumerations search engine proves viable by allowing vulnerabilities and IT assets to be identified and eventually patched. The reduction of complexity and improved usability for security management experts without detailed CPS knowledge is the aim of our concept and prototype. Ultimately, if fulfilled this can lead to a better security posture. In the following, the applied technology of our CPS security enumerations search engine and a case study are presented.

Fig. 3. Simplified use case for a CPS security enumerations search engine

4.1 Case Study

To demonstrate our concept we refer to the TRITON malware used for attacks on oil and gas production facilities in 2017. The malware manipulates *Safety Instrumented Systems (SIS)* that aim to prevent incidents causing severe damage to assets, environment or even humans. Instead of extreme and uncontrollable events, SIS initiate a safe shut down of industrial processes as a last line of automated defence [5]. Since the attackers behind TRITON were able to interact with SIS controllers, there was a risk of unforeseeable disasters, which the SIS was supposed to prevent. Although, TRITON has not yet destroyed physical assets, it has halted production causing financial losses.

Considering the enumerations CPE and CVE, two aspects of the TRITON malware are of relevance. First, it concerns both hardware and operating systems in multiple versions. A standardized description with CPE names is thus an necessity to avoid miscommunication. Despite of its significance for industrial facilities, relevant elements of the TRITON attacks are not yet properly described by CPE and CVE. While NVD lists related CVE entries and mentions affected components[3], CPE names cannot be found in the dictionary.

In our concept for CPS security enumerations we provide relevant extensions to improve the representation of e.g. cyber attacks using the TRITON malware. We allow the grouping of multiple CPS components within a CPS Bundle as our concept includes *recursive security enumerations*. Despite the fact, that the malware itself mainly targets the "Triconex Tricon MP 3008" controller and its firmware, other CPS components are also affected. To conduct their attack, the attackers leveraged further vulnerabilities of networks, operating systems and workstations prior to infecting the SIS. A comprehensive representation capturing these additional elements is supported by the CPS Bundle and part of the *recursive security enumerations* we designed. Table 2 shows an exemplary **Petrochemical CPS Bundle** related to TRITON with multiple components.

An extension to CPE names addressing technical details of CPS components is part of our concept. We propose *technical exhaustive security enumerations* that cover the "NCM" network modules of hardware affected by the TRITON malware. Listing 2 shows an exemplary CPE name adhering to the extended model. Furthermore, our model can recognize embedded components like SIS.

---

[3] https://nvd.nist.gov/vuln/detail/CVE-2018-7522.

Table 2. Exemplary CPS composed of multiple components

ID	Description	References (abbreviated)
1	**Petrochemical CPS:** Interconnected components deployed in an industrial setting to refine oil and gas	`cpe:2.3:h:schneider-electric:triconex_tricon_mp_3008 [...];` `cpe:2.3:e:weatherford:maximizer [...];` `[...]`

```
cpe:2.3:h:schneider-electric:triconex_tricon_mp_3008:*:*:*:*:*:*:*:*
    :Oil_Gas_Production:Safety_Instrument:*:*:NCM
```

Listing 2. Exemplary extended CPE name

Application oriented security enumerations ensure complexity reduction and usability through CPS properties known to security experts without detailed CPS knowledge. This is achieved by capturing the "oil and gas production" sector as well as "safety instrument" capabilities within a CPE name as shown in Listing 2. These rather generic CPS properties lead to further described information about an entire petrochemical CPS and potential vulnerabilities.

When CPE and CVE are not properly linked it is an impediment for usability and effective security workflows. Integration of both security enumerations is the focal point of *coupled security enumerations*. Within our CPS security enumerations search engine we provide the option to relate entries of CPE and CVE. E.g., the missing link between the "Triconex Tricon MP 3008" firmware and CVE-2018-7522 is established and persisted in the database.

4.2   Prototypical Implementation

In order to demonstrate the practical applicability of our concept, we have implemented a prototypical CPS search engine for our enumeration concept. The source code of the prototype is available online[4]. It consists of two main components. The conceptual model is implemented using a MySQL database and the application was created with JavaEE 6. The database contains *CPE*, *CVE* and *CPS Bundle* as central entity tables. The references within the database and the functional scope of the application are based on the NVD and extend it to the components presented in this work. As this is a prototype application, additional tools are available for editing the data inventory and creating new CPE, CVE and CPS Bundle objects. The application also offers functionalities to search for CPE and CVE entries and to display the available links between them. The search for CPS bundles also displays the relationships within the bundles.

The data building the basis for our prototypical implementation reflects the state of CPE and CVE from February 2020. In addition, we provide two small sample CPS containing multiple components as exemplary data for CPS bundles.

---

[4] https://github.com/tarnschaf/cyberphysical

5   Related Work

Information security and CTI [8,12,14] use security enumerations to describe relevant artifacts [15,25]. To the best of our knowledge, there is no academic literature on extending security enumerations although security enumerations evolved and raised their version numbers. It is therefore reasonable to assume, that extensions to security enumerations are driven by dedicated communities.

A multitude of work focuses on CPS due to their prominent role in critical infrastructures [1,10]. Related work on security of CPS approached the topic through the Internet of Things [20]. From there on, the various different areas of security are applied to CPS research. While a number of surveys and overview articles aim to cover CPS security at large [7], attack detection [16], vulnerability analysis [4,24] and formal approaches [6,26] are extensively considered.

Work about both, security enumerations and CPS, is rare. Closest to our research is the work by Upadhyay and Sampalli [24]. It discusses vulnerabilities within SCADA systems, highlighting the necessity of awareness about vulnerabilities within SCADA software and protocols. Here, a strong focus is placed on a review of existing vulnerabilities partially described by CVE. Similar, Nicholson et al. [17] point to unpatched software as a major flaw in SCADA systems.

Maidl et al. [11] provide interesting research results by defining a pattern to structure CPS and classifying the individual components. In addition, the authors outline security considerations about attack vectors for these systems.

McLaughlin et al. [13] present a methodology for security assessment of industrial control systems. They are characterizing parts and features of these systems as a starting point for a more comprehensive description with security enumerations. In a more general perspective Takahashi et al. [23] show the use of security enumerations for security management.

6   Conclusion and Future Work

With our work we aim to make security of CPS more accessible for security experts. Our analysis showed that CPS and their interdependent components are not yet completely covered by security enumerations. To remediate the identified deficiencies, we propose an extension of CPE and CVE enabling a comprehensive description of CPS. Effective security management also relies on the integration of data from CPE and CVE to attribute vulnerabilities to the affected IT assets.

The meta model we propose extends the security enumerations and provides an overview of the numerous and heterogeneous CPS components. Our search engine realizes the adaptation of CPS to a organization setting and addresses the 1st research question outlined in Sect. 1 of this paper. Our work extends the CPE data model with technical features to capture the embedded nature of CPS components. This allows us to address the 2nd research question. Comprehensiveness and usability aspects relevant for security management are incorporated in our extended CPE. To respond to the 3rd research question we introduce sector and capability attributes lowering entry knowledge to CPS. The concept is evaluated through a prototype using TRITON as use case.

Although, our work's results are a first step towards security enumerations for CPS several topics demanding further research remain.

First, future work should address the alignment with other standardization efforts and products. While we propose a concept for a CPS security enumerations search engine the usage may be within existing products such as NVD. Other standards for IT asset identification and their integration or conversion to CPE should also be considered. Moreover, management processes related to an IT asset inventory and vulnerabilities will be future points of reference.

Second, further extensions to our proposed meta model might become necessary due to additional user requirements and CPS development. It will be favourable to conduct a user study to determine precise requirements of security management experts beyond the ones described in academic literature. The results can then be used to trigger further improvements and might either culminate in a stand-alone security product or lead towards additional modifications.

A third topic of interest is the collection of data for CPS Bundles. Gathering and maintaining the data can include vendors and operators of CPS. The model can also be complemented by predefined vocabularies for specific attributes to avoid ambiguity and ease usability.

References

1. Alur, R.: Principles of Cyber-Physical Systems. The MIT Press, Cambridge (2015)
2. Caselli, M., Kargl, F.: A security assessment methodology for critical infrastructures. In: Panayiotou, C.G.G., Ellinas, G., Kyriakides, E., Polycarpou, M.M.M. (eds.) CRITIS 2014. LNCS, vol. 8985, pp. 332–343. Springer, Cham (2016). https://doi.org/10.1007/978-3-319-31664-2_34
3. Cheikes, B.A., Waltermire, D., Scarfone, K.: Common Platform Enumeration: Naming Specification Version 2.3. NIST, Maryland, USA (2011)
4. Coffey, K., Smith, R., Maglaras, L., Janicke, H.: Vulnerability analysis of network scanning on SCADA systems. Secur. Commun. Netw. **2018**, 1–21 (2018)
5. Di Pinto, A.A., Dragoni, Y., Carcano, A.: TRITON: the first ICS cyber attack on safety instrument systems. In: Proceedings of the Black Hat USA, pp. 1–26 (2018)
6. Fernandez, E.B.: Threat modeling in cyber-physical systems. In: 2016 IEEE 14th International Conference on Dependable, Autonomic and Secure Computing, pp. 448–453 (2016)
7. Humayed, A., Lin, J., Li, F., Luo, B.: Cyber-physical systems security—a survey. IEEE Internet of Things J. **4**(6), 1802–1831 (2017)
8. Kampanakis, P.: Security automation and threat information-sharing options. IEEE Secur. Priv. **12**(5), 42–51 (2014)
9. Khaitan, S.K., McCalley, J.D.: Design techniques and applications of cyberphysical systems: a survey. IEEE Syst. J. **9**(2), 350–365 (2014)
10. Lee, E.A.: Cyber-physical systems-are computing foundations adequate. In: Position Paper for NSF Workshop on Cyber-Physical Systems, vol. 2, pp. 1–9 (2006)
11. Maidl, M., Wirtz, R., Zhao, T., Heisel, M., Wagner, M.: Pattern-based modeling of cyber-physical systems for analyzing security. In: Proceedings of the 24th European Conference on Pattern Languages of Programs, pp. 1–10 (2019)

12. Mavroeidis, V., Bromander, S.: Cyber threat intelligence model: an evaluation of taxonomies, sharing standards, and ontologies within cyber threat intelligence. In: European Intelligence and Security Informatics Conference (EISIC), pp. 91–98 (2017)
13. McLaughlin, S., et al.: The cybersecurity landscape in industrial control systems. Proc. IEEE **104**(5), 1039–1057 (2016)
14. Menges, F., Pernul, G.: A comparative analysis of incident reporting formats. Comput. Secur. **73**, 87–101 (2018)
15. Menges, F., Sperl, C., Pernul, G.: Unifying cyber threat intelligence. In: Gritzalis, S., Weippl, E.R., Katsikas, S.K., Anderst-Kotsis, G., Tjoa, A.M., Khalil, I. (eds.) TrustBus 2019. LNCS, vol. 11711, pp. 161–175. Springer, Cham (2019). https://doi.org/10.1007/978-3-030-27813-7_11
16. Mitchell, R., Chen, I.R.: A survey of intrusion detection techniques for cyber-physical systems. ACM Comput. Surv. **46**(4), 1–29 (2014)
17. Nicholson, A., Webber, S., Dyer, S., Patel, T., Janicke, H.: Scada security in the light of cyber-warfare. Comput. Secur. **31**(4), 418–436 (2012)
18. Parmelee, M.C., Booth, H., Waltermire, D., Scarfone, K.: Common Platform Enumeration: Name Matching Specification Version 2.3. NIST, Maryland, USA (2011)
19. Rinaldi, S.M., Peerenboom, J.P., Kelly, T.K.: Identifying, understanding, and analyzing critical infrastructure interdependencies. IEEE Control Syst. **21**(6), 11–25 (2001)
20. Roman, R., Zhou, J., Lopez, J.: On the features and challenges of security and privacy in distributed internet of things. Comput. Netw. **57**(10), 2266–2279 (2013)
21. Schlette, D., Böhm, F., Caselli, M., Günther, P.: Measuring and visualizing cyber-threat intelligence quality. Int. J. Inf. Secur. **19**(2), 1–18 (2020)
22. Stouffer, K., Falco, J., Scarfone, K.: Guide to industrial control systems (ICS) security. NIST Spec. Publ. **800**(82), 16 (2014)
23. Takahashi, T., Miyamoto, D., Nakao, K.: Toward automated vulnerability monitoring using open information and standardized tools. In: 2016 IEEE International Conference on Pervasive Computer and Communications Workshops (PerCom Workshops). IEEE (2016)
24. Upadhyay, D., Sampalli, S.: SCADA (supervisory control and data acquisition) systems: vulnerability assessment and security recommendations. Comput. Secur. **89**, 101666 (2020)
25. Vielberth, M.: Human-as-a-security-sensor for harvesting threat intelligence. Cybersecurity **2**(1), 1–15 (2019). https://doi.org/10.1186/s42400-019-0040-0
26. Yampolskiy, M., Horváth, P., Koutsoukos, X.D., Xue, Y., Sztipanovits, J.: A language for describing attacks on cyber-physical systems. Int. J. Crit. Infrastruct. Prot. **8**, 40–52 (2015)

Information Flow and Access Control

Inference-Proof Monotonic Query Evaluation and View Generation Reconsidered

Joachim Biskup[✉]

Fakultät für Informatik, Technische Universität Dortmund, Dortmund, Germany
`joachim.biskup@cs.tu-dortmund.de`

Abstract. The concept of inference-proofness has been introduced for capturing strong confidentiality requirements—including privacy concerns—of an information owner, communicating with a semi-honest partner by means of their message exchanging computing agents according to some agreed interaction protocols. Such protocols include closed-query evaluation and view generation by the information system agent under the control of the information owner, and the corresponding request preparation by the client agent. The information owner employs a security mechanism for controlled interactions, shielding the epistemic state of the information system agent and suitably altering messages sent to the client agent. The alterings provably guarantee that the partner cannot infer the validity of any piece of information that the information owner has declared as being prohibited. Based on selected previous work, we carefully describe and inspect the underlying function and attack scenario and summarize and analyze basic approaches for controlled interactions within an abstract framework for epistemic states.

Keywords: Abstract data source · A priori knowledge · Best current view · Closed-query evaluation · Confidentiality · Epistemic state · Inference-proofness · Interaction protocol · Lying · Prohibition · Security invariant · Simulated current view · View generation

1 Introduction

High level security requirements like availability, integrity and confidentiality have been refined in sophisticated guidelines for constructing and evaluating secure computing systems of various kinds and, correspondingly, a rich variety of specific security mechanisms have been developed. Accordingly, for each concrete class of applications, in the spirit of computing engineering in general, a comprehensive range of considerations is due, from a precise specification of the wanted system functionality and the explicit description of the in most cases conflicting security interests of the expected user as well as of further "attackers" over mathematical models and their formal verification to final actual implementations and their ongoing multi-literal inspections.

© IFIP International Federation for Information Processing 2020
Published by Springer Nature Switzerland AG 2020
A. Singhal and J. Vaidya (Eds.): DBSec 2020, LNCS 12122, pp. 79–99, 2020.
https://doi.org/10.1007/978-3-030-49669-2_5

This work is devoted to contribute to such a comprehensive view of security by reconsidering a specific kind of security mechanisms proposed to support the *confidentiality* interests as *exceptions* of the *availability* interests of an information owner while using an *information system* for *query evaluation* and *view generation* to communicate with some cooperation partner. Clearly, within this short article we again have to focus on aspects held to be particularly important, including the followings ones. What precisely is the object of protection? Who precisely is seen as an attacker and which precise means are exploited by him for violations? How to formally model the wanted kind of confidentiality? What kind of enforcing security mechanisms have been designed? How to mathematically verify their actual achievements? More concretely, we treat these concern by reconsidering a specific fraction of the in the meantime highly ramified line of research about confidentiality-preserving query–response interactions of a logic-oriented information system like a suitably restricted relational database system.

Even more specifically, our contributions can be summarized as follows, while the overall achievements and limitations are discussed in the conclusions:

- On the layer of social cooperation mediated by computing agents, in Sect. 2, we identify the "epistemic state of an information system agent" as the actual object in need of protection against a class of most powerful attackers.
- On the layer of computing agents, in Sect. 3, we further elaborate a formal model of abstract data sources, which captures the relevant features of monotonic and complete information systems.
- On the layer of security specification, in Sect. 4, we adapt inference-proofness as strong confidentiality to the model of abstract data sources.
- On the layer of security enforcement, in Sect. 5, we present unified expositions and verification of security mechanisms in terms of that model.

These contributions are—unifying and partly extending—extracted from the seminal work [7,13] and further specific refinements [2–6], which are part of larger efforts [1]. Moreover, we note that our treatment of confidentiality is in the spirit of various other work, e.g., already early ones on statistical database security [8] and about non-interference of general program execution [9], together with the rich elaborations of follow-up studies, which for example are concisely surveyed in [10]. In contrast to some other work, we do not aim at "total confidentiality" but see confidentiality as an exception from availability and, thus, allow specifically declared information flows like for declassification [11] and, additionally, we want to construct enforcing mechanism in the sense of [12].

2   Function and Attack Scenario

Since ever, among many other activities, and in a closely intertwined manner, people reason as individuals by acquiring, structuring, keeping and exploiting *information* to make up their respective minds and behave as social creatures by *communicating* with others. With the advent of computing technologies, both individually dealing with information and socially communicating have been partly delegated to *computing agents*. On the one hand, the delegation should facilitate routine task or even enhance human capabilities. On the other hand, depending on the context, as delegators, individuals at their discretion or groups of them according to some socially accepted norm aim to still control the computing agents executing protocols as their delegatees, or at least the human delegators should appropriately configure the computing delegatees.

Being aware of the resulting reduction, we can simplifying map concepts of human reasoning and communication to the inference protocols and interaction protocols of their computing agents and, correspondingly, actually performed human activities to protocol-complying computing process executions. Under such a reduction, and even more simplifying, a group of human individuals is modeled to be complemented by a *multi-agent* computing configuration. In this model, each *human individual* controls a dedicated computing agent that, at least partly and by means of *protocol executions*, both deals with the information owned by that individual, in particular by internally deriving an epistemic state from a chosen information representation, and mediates the communications of that individual, in particular by sending and receiving *messages* according to one or more agreed interaction protocols.

Though, in principle, each individual can act in diverse roles and, correspondingly, each controlled computing agent can execute diverse protocols, we further specialize the model sketched above in focusing on only two individuals with their computing agents. One individual is seen as an *information owner* controlling an *information system agent*, and the other individual is treated as a cooperating *communication partner* employing a *client agent*. Moreover, to enable *cooperation*, in principle the information owner is willing to *share information* with the communication partner. However, complying with *privacy issues* or pursuing other *confidentiality requirements*, as an exception from sharing, the information owner might want to hide some specific *pieces of information*.

Summarizing the simplified model, we assume an overall *framework* with the eight *features* outlined in the following and visualized in Fig. 1.

1. [Epistemic state of information system agent as single object of protection.]
   The human information owner does not deal with information processing and reasoning by himself but only provides the inputs to the information system agent under his *control*. At each point in time, that agent is internally deriving a formally defined *epistemic state*.
2. [Mediation of human communications by interacting computing agents.]
   Once having agreed on cooperation, the human information owner and his human communication partner do not communicate directly with each other, but only mediated by the computing agents under their respective control.
3. [Dedicated access permissions for information sharing.]
   As a normally initial input to his information system agent, independently of the actual epistemic state, the information owner has granted dedicated *access permissions* to his communication partner. That permissions declare that over the time the client agent of the partner may *interact* with the information system agent of the owner following some explicitly chosen *interaction*

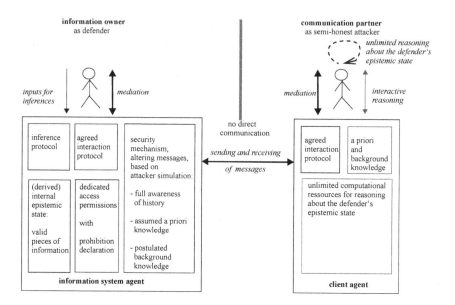

Fig. 1. The framework of a defending information owner with his information system agent and an attacking communication partner with his client agent

protocols that exclusively refer to the internal epistemic state of the information system agent (but, e.g., not to the physical mind of the information owner or any "real world" besides the multi-agent model).

4. [Exceptions by explicit prohibitions designating pieces of information.]
   However, as a further normally initial input to his information system agent, also independently of the actual epistemic state, the information owner explicitly *declares* exceptions from the dedicated access permissions in the form of prohibitions. Each *prohibition* specifies a piece of information that the communication partner should not be able to learn. More precisely, each prohibition being expressed in terms of the information system agent and thus referring to possible epistemic states, the communication partner should never be able to become sure about the actual *validity* in the epistemic state of the information system agent. In other words, from the partner's point of view it should always appear to be *possible* that the prohibited piece of information is *not valid* in the epistemic state of the information system.

5. [Partner suspected to reason about validity of prohibitions.]
   Though the client agent is restricted to exactly follow the interaction protocols mentioned in the dedicated access permissions, the human communication partner can choose any sequence of permitted commands. Moreover, the communication partner is assumed to have unlimited computational resources when rationally reasoning about the validity or non-validity of a prohibited piece of information, whether employing the client agent under his control or any other means.

6. [Security mechanism implanted in owner's information system agent.]
   To enforce the confidentiality requirements of the information owner, the information system agent is enhanced by some *security mechanism* that should shield the underlying information processing from a direct contact with the client agent. That security mechanism first inspects each message to be sent by the information system agent to the client agent according to the pertinent interaction protocol whether a *violation* of the information owner's confidentiality requirements would be enabled on the side of the communication partner. If this is the case, the security mechanism then *alters* the message such that the message is still as informative as possible on the one hand but all options for a violation are blocked on the other hand.

7. [Reasoning supported by a priori knowledge and background knowledge.]
   First of all, the communication partner's rational reasoning about the internal epistemic state of the information system agent is based on the messages exchanged by the respective computing agents and, thus, completely known to both agents. Additionally, the partner's rational reasoning is presumed to be supported by some *a priori knowledge* about the application dealt with in the cooperation between the two individuals involved and additional *background knowledge* comprising both a complete specification of the *interaction semantics* and the full *awareness of the security mechanism* (possibly even including the prohibition declaration) and, most notably, nothing else.

8. [Principle inaccessibility of the partner.]
   The internals of both the human communication partner and his client agent are considered to be principally inaccessible for the information owner and his system agent. This implies that the latter ones can only rely on *assumptions* about the details of the a priori knowledge and a *postulation* about the background knowledge available to the former ones.

We follow a somehow martial but common terminology of security in computing, which ignores that in many scenarios an individual involved as communication partner will primarily treated as cooperating in a friendly manner.

- Partially trusted for consciously sharing information in principle and correctly executing the agreed interaction protocols, the *communication partner* with the *client agent* is denoted as a *semi-honest attacker*, suspected to potentially aiming to maliciously infer the actual validity of pieces of information that the information owner has declared to be kept confidential.
- Accordingly, the *information owner*—together with the *information system agent* controlled by him—is denoted as the *defender*.

The security mechanism implanted in the defending information system agent has to invariantly enforce a suitable version of the following still informally expressed *security policy* of *inference-proofness*, which also specifies the *attacker model*: For each prohibited piece of information ψ, the information content of messages sent to the attacking client agent will never enable the attacking receiver to rationally infer that ψ is valid in the epistemic state, even when

– inspecting the complete *history* of preceding *interactions*,
– considering some *a priori knowledge* about the possible *epistemic states*,
– applying the *semantics* of the agreed *interaction protocols* and
– being *aware* of the *functionality* of the *security mechanism* (possibly even including the prohibition declaration).

The concept of *rationality* on the side of the attacker is then captured by the following rephrasement of the still to be suitably versioned security policy of *inference-proofness* in terms of *indistinguishability*:

> For each prohibited piece of information ψ, for each epistemic state d satisfying the a priori knowledge, for each sequence of messages exchanged during an interaction history and complying with the agreed interaction protocols but potentially altered by the security mechanism, there exists an "*alternative*" epistemic state d' such that (i) the same sequence of messages would be generated, in compliance with the agreed interaction protocols and subjected to the alterations by the security mechanism, but (ii) ψ is not valid in d'.

The epistemic state d is thought as actually be derived (or "stored") by the information system agent and might satisfy the prohibited piece of information ψ or not. The former case implies that the alternative state d' required to exist is different from d; in the latter case, the actually stored state d and the alternative state d' might be the same. Accordingly, declaring ψ as a prohibition does not intent to block any option to infer the non-validity of ψ.

Confidentiality as inference-proofness could be trivially achieved by granting no access permissions at all or altering the information content of all messages sent to the attacker to nothing, violating any conflicting *availability requirements* and, thus, making the whole thing useless. Accordingly, confidentiality requirements and availability requirements always have to be suitably balanced. We focus on the following three-level *conflict resolution* strategy, which leads to a combination of a *constraint solving problem* and an *optimization problem*:

1. As a general rule, for the sake of *availability*, some dedicated access permissions are granted, as far as not conflicting with level 2 of the strategy.
2. As exceptions, for the sake of *confidentiality* specific prohibitions are declared that have to be enforced by alterations made by the security mechanism, but to comply with level 3 of the strategy only as far as definitely necessary.
3. Again for the sake of *availability*, as limitation for the effect of exceptions, the alterations made have to be minimal.

3   Abstract Data Sources as Epistemic States

The notion of an *abstract information system* is intended to capture common important features of information contents like at least *semi-structured* and *logic-oriented knowledge bases*, including *relational databases* under suitable restrictions, and as far as they are *complete* regarding query answering under *monotonic reasoning*. A possibly occurring information content of such an abstract information system is seen as an *epistemic state*, though it is formally just an element of a pertinent finite or countably infinite set. We call such an element an *"abstract data source"*, not assuming any internal properties.

However, we impose a set-algebraic structure with natural properties on the considered *universe* of all abstract data sources. These properties should reflect the *model-theoretic* approach of various monotonic logics to define *semantics* for the underlying syntax of a formal language by assigning *truth-values* to atomic sentences and then, by induction, to all sentences. In fact, if on the syntactic side the language provides means to express negation, conjunction and disjunction, then on the semantic side the corresponding *sets* of satisfying *truth-value assignments* (*models*, *interpretations*) are treated by (set) *complement*, (set) *intersection* and (set) *union*, respectively. So, using sentences to syntactically express *closed queries* whose semantics are the respective sets of satisfying truth-value assignments, we may identify a syntactic query expression with its semantic evaluation. Accordingly, totally refraining from any syntax for abstract information systems, we define queries as a particular sort of subsets of the universe.

For the case of an *infinite* universe with countably infinitely many queries, to deal with iteratively determined *fixpoints*, we even consider countably infinite intersections which, however, do not need to generate a query. Instead, we require *compactness* of the set of queries, which captures a straightforward corollary to the existence of a correct and complete proof system for classical first-order logic, roughly saying that any (possibly infinite) logical entailment implies a finite entailment (since formal proofs are finite by definition). Note that for the finite case this property trivially holds.

A (set) *inclusion* of the form $q_1 \subseteq q_2$ corresponds to a *logical entailment* in the logics that motivated our abstract settings. In fact, thinking of q_1 and q_2 as the satisfying sets of truth-value assignments for some sentences χ_1 and χ_2, respectively, then $q_1 \subseteq q_2$ says that each truth-value assignment that makes χ_1 true also does so for χ_2; this is just the classical definition of logical entailment.

Definition 1 (abstract data sources and closed queries).
A universe of data sources is a (finite or infinite) set U.
A query set Q for a universe U satisfies the following properties:

1. *$\{\varnothing, U\} \subseteq Q \subseteq \wp U$ with Q being finite or countably infinite;*
2. *Q is closed under complement, finite intersection and finite union;*
3. *Q is compact, i.e., for all $Q' \subseteq Q$, for all $q \in Q$,*
   if $\bigcap Q' \subseteq q$, then there exists a finite $Q'' \subseteq Q'$ such that $\bigcap Q'' \subseteq q$.

Moreover, $Seq(Q)$ is the set of all (possibly) infinite sequences of queries and $Int(Q)$ is the set of all (possibly) infinite intersections of queries.

Following the explanations and the common intuitive understanding, *query evaluation* could be defined for a query $q \in Q$ and a data source $d \in U$ by the expression IF $d \in q$ THEN *true* ELSE [IF $d \in U \setminus q$] *false*. However, for our formal investigations the following equivalent definition is more convenient.

Definition 2 (abstract (stepwise) query evaluation). *Let Q be a query set for a universe U. Then the* query evaluation *function is defined by*

$$quer : Q \times U \longrightarrow Q \quad \text{with} \quad quer(q,d) = \text{ IF } d \in q \text{ THEN } q \text{ ELSE } U \setminus q. \quad (1)$$

The stepwise extension $\quad quer : Seq(Q) \times U \longrightarrow Seq(Q) \quad$ *is defined by*

$$quer(\langle q_1, q_2, \dots \rangle, d) = \langle quer(q_1, d), quer(q_2, d), \dots \rangle. \quad (2)$$

Equation (1) immediately implies that for all data sources $d \in U$ and $d' \in U$, for all queries $q \in Q$ and $\tilde{q} \in Q$ the following assertions hold:

$$d \in quer(q, d), \quad (3)$$

$$d' \in quer(q, d) \text{ iff } quer(q, d') = quer(q, d), \quad (4)$$

$$\text{if } d \in q \text{ and } d' \in q \text{ ,then } q \subseteq quer(\tilde{q}, d) \text{ iff } q \subseteq quer(\tilde{q}, d'). \quad (5)$$

Besides being an element of the universe, the properties of a data source $d \in U$ are only determined by its query evaluations. In particular, two data sources are *indistinguishable* if they are contained in exactly the same queries. Hence, imagining an enumeration $q_1, q_2, \dots$, of all queries in Q, we can characterize a data source d as being in the intersection of its query evaluations. In this sense, the *best view* of d "from outside" is just this intersection, which always includes d itself but might also contain many further "indistinguishable" data sources. If the best view of d is a singleton, then it represents *complete* knowledge of d.

Definition 3 (abstract best view generation). *Let Q be a query set for a universe U. Then the* view generation *function is defined by*

$$view : U \longrightarrow Int(Q) \quad \text{with} \quad view(d) = \bigcap_{q \in Q} quer(q, d). \quad (6)$$

4   Inference-Proofness for Known Prohibition Declaration

As explained and motivated in Sect. 2 we imagine an owner of the abstract information system who implants a security mechanism into the defending information system agent under his control, aiming to enforce inference-proofness of interactions as a sophisticated kind of confidentiality regarding the message-based interactions with an attacking client agent operated by some only semi-honest communication partner. We study two interactions:

– *closed-query evaluation* with *response* preparation: we see the queries as request messages sent from the attacking client agent and the corresponding responses as reaction messages returned by the defending system agent;
– *view generation:* we image a (formally not represented) request message from the attacking client agent to obtain a best view and we see the generation result as the respond message returned by the defending system agent.

Besides the request messages and the respond messages, the formal notions of inference-proofness depend on two further parameters, to be declared by the information system owner specifically for the attacking client agent: (i) a set of *prohibitions*, i.e., pieces of information that the rationally reasoning attacker should not be able to learn; (ii) the *a priori knowledge* held by the attacker about the actually stored abstract data source, as assumed by the defender. The attacker is also implicitly postulated to be fully aware of the security mechanism employed by the defender and to even know the declared prohibitions. The notion of the attacker's rationality is implicitly related to the semantics of query evaluation and view generation. Finally, our notions of inference-proofness include the following natural *security preconditions*:

- The stored data source complies with the (assumed) a priori knowledge.
- The (assumed) a priori knowledge does not violate the pertinent confidentiality requirement expressed by the prohibition declaration.

Definition 4 (abstract prohibitions and abstract a priori knowledge).

1. *A prohibition is a query $p \in Q$, and a set of* enforceable[1] *prohibitions is denoted by $P \subseteq Q$. A prohibition declaration is a finite set $proh \subseteq P$.*
2. *An assumed a priori knowledge is a query $prior \in Q$, and a set of* tolerable[1] *(pieces of) assumed a priori knowledge is denoted by $A \subseteq Q$.*

The following four versions of inference-proofness formally reflect the intuitive assumption that the attacker *knows the prohibition declaration* by treating it being invariant under alternative data sources. Regarding controlled query evaluation, the wanted security mechanisms are naturally intended to operate *stepwise* and *history-dependent* but *without a look-ahead*.

Definition 5 (inference-proofness for closed-query evaluation).

1. $con\_quer : Seq(Q) \times U \times A \times \wp P \longrightarrow Seq(Q)$ *is a stepwise controlled query evaluation function iff for each (point in time) $t = 1, 2, \ldots$ the result value $con\_quer(\langle q_1, q_2, \ldots \rangle, d_{st}, prior, proh)_t$ depends in addition to d_{st}, prior and proh only on the finite prefix $q_1, q_2, \ldots, q_t$ of the argument sequence and, thus, implicitly, also on the finite prefix $r_1, r_2, \ldots, r_{t-1}$ of the result sequence with $r_i = con\_quer(\langle q_1, q_2, \ldots \rangle, d_{st}, prior, proh)_i$, such that we can define $con\_quer(\langle q_1, q_2, \ldots, q_t \rangle, d_{st}, prior, proh) = \langle r_1, r_2, \ldots, r_t \rangle$.*
2. *The function is* inference-proof *iff for each prohibition declaration $proh \in \wp P$, for each a priori knowledge $prior \in A$ such that $prior \not\subseteq p$ for all $p \in proh$, for each prohibition $p \in proh$, for each ("stored") data source $d_{st} \in prior$, for each sequence $\langle q_1, q_2, \ldots \rangle$ of closed queries $q_i \in Q$, there exists an ("alternative") data source $d_{al}^p \in prior$ such that*
   - *indistinguishability of d_{st} and d_{al}^p (w.r.t. the prohibition p): $con\_quer(\langle q_1, q_2, \ldots \rangle, d_{st}, prior, proh) = con\_quer(\langle q_1, q_2, \ldots \rangle, d_{al}^p, prior, proh);$*

---

[1] For each practical framework, the notions of "enforceable" and "tolerable" have to be appropriately defined to capture application needs and complexity issues.

– harmlessness *of d_{al} (w.r.t. the prohibition p):* $d_{al}^p \notin p$.
3. *The function is* strongly inference-proof *iff it is inference-proof for proh substituted by* $\{\bigcup proh\}$.

Definition 6 (inference-proofness for view generation).

1. $con\_view : U \times A \times \wp P \longrightarrow Int(Q)$ *is a* controlled view generation *function.*
2. *The function is* inference-proof *or* strongly inference-proof, *respectively, iff the corresponding condition, but without the clause for the sequence of queries, of Definition 5, part 2 or part 3, respectively, holds.*

5   Controlled Interactions

We study three fundamental approaches to provably achieve inference-proofness for interaction sequences of unlimited length only consisting of closed-query evaluations together with the respective response preparations for the case of abstract data sources as epistemic states. The achievement of inference-proofness for sequences of stepwise *closed-query evaluations* will be based on enforcing a pertinent *security invariant* for all points in time t, starting with some pertinent *security precondition*. In the definitions of inference-proofness, the latter assertions are already formally stated and the former assertions are suggested by requiring the existence of a harmless data source. In fact, the attacker's *best current view bestcv* on the defender's actual data source d_{st} always consists of all those data sources d' that are *indistinguishable* from the actual one and, thus, constitutes the *least uncertainty* left to the attacker so far. Accordingly, the harmless data source d_{al} required to exist has to be an element of the attacker's best current view.

Conceptually, at each point in time t, the best current view is determined as a kind of an *inverse image* of the interaction history performed so far, i.e., of the submitted queries $q_1, q_2, \ldots, q_t$ under the a priori knowledge *prior* and the prohibition declaration *proh* together with the returned responses $con\_quer(\langle q_1, q_2, \ldots, q_t \rangle, d_{st}, prior, proh) = \langle r_1, r_2, \ldots, r_t \rangle$. More formally, for the *best current view* we have the following:

$$bestcv_t = \{ d \mid d \in U \cap prior, \text{ and } con\_quer(\langle q_1, q_2, \ldots, q_t \rangle, d_{st}, prior, proh)$$
$$= con\_quer(\langle q_1, q_2, \ldots, q_t \rangle, d, prior, proh) \}$$
$$= con\_quer^{-1}[con\_quer(\langle q_1, q_2, \ldots, q_t \rangle, d_{st}, prior, proh)] \cap prior ;$$

$$bestcv_\infty = \{ d \mid d \in U \cap prior, \text{ and } con\_quer(\langle q_1, q_2, \ldots \rangle, d_{st}, prior, proh)$$
$$= con\_quer(\langle q_1, q_2, \ldots \rangle, d, prior, proh) \}$$
$$= con\_quer^{-1}[con\_quer(\langle q_1, q_2, \ldots \rangle, d_{st}, prior, proh)] \cap prior.$$

As a technical means, however, a *security mechanism* might only maintain a *simulated current view simcv* still invariantly containing a harmless data source, which is employed for checking tentative updates of the attacker's uncertainty for violations of the security invariant. For studying abstract information systems refraining from representing syntax at all, we will use such a simulated current view directly as a kind of *log file* to keep the *essence* of the interaction history.

Though we are literally speaking about technical means having machine-executable programs in mind, we deal with abstract information systems as purely mathematical objects and, accordingly, do not actually care about computability. Nevertheless, by abuse of language, we will denote purely mathematical methods for controlled interactions as algorithms, since we have come up with even efficiently computable procedures for suitable refinements based on appropriate syntactic representations of the mathematical items.

5.1   Controlled Query Evaluation by Refusing

For the approach to alterations of a harmful query evaluation by *refusing*, the existence of an *"alternative" harmless data source* will explicitly be monitored by inspecting the assertion "for all $p \in proh$: $simcv \nsubseteq p$" as part of the security invariant enforced for each response to a submitted query. In fact, if a (previously unknown) *correct response* is returned to the attacker, then the invariance of the assertion after updating *simcv* accordingly has been confirmed explicitly by a tentative update before.

However, to additionally enforce the *indistinguishability* property to avoid meta-inferences from the fact of observing a refusal, we have to strengthen the invariant such that it becomes *independent* of the actual results of the query evaluations. In fact, if a (previously unknown) *correct response* is returned and the simulated current view *simcv* has actually been updated accordingly, then not only the tentative update with that response but also with its complement has been inspected for harmlessness explicitly before. Consequently, if at least one alternative has been found to be harmful, the resulting refusal might be caused by the correct response or its complement, such that the attacker cannot find out which alternative has actually occurred. For convenience, here *refusing* is signified be returning the universe U, which provides no new information, and, accordingly, no update of the simulated current view *simcv* is necessary.

As a special case, the correct response might *already be known* from the a priori knowledge together with the responses to previously inspected queries, as summarized in the value of the simulated current view *simcv*. To avoid an unnecessary refusal, this case is dealt with separately, by just confirming the correct query evaluation and, consequently, leaving *simcv* unchanged.

Theorem 1 (inference-proofness by refusing).   *The stepwise controlled query evaluation function with alterations by refusing for a known prohibition declaration, as computed by Algorithm 1, is* inference-proof *(and strongly inference-proof under the substitution of proh by* $\{\bigcup proh\}$*).*

Input: $\langle q_1, q_2, \dots \rangle$ queue of closed queries, submitted by attacker
　　　　　d_{st} stored abstract data source
　　　　　prior   a priori knowledge as query
　　　　　proh   prohibition declaration as finite set of queries
Output: $\langle r_1, r_2, \dots \rangle$ list of (possibly) altered responses, returned to attacker

```
 1  time ← 0                    //initialize counter for discrete points in time;
 2  simcv ← prior               //initialize simulated current view;
 3  repeat
 4  │   time ← time + 1;
 5  │   query ← receive next query q_time from input queue;
 6  │   correct ← quer(query, d_st)       //determine correct query evaluation;
 7  │   if simcv ⊆ correct then
 8  │   │   return correct to output list
 9  │   │       //confirm correct response; leave simcv unchanged
    │   else
10  │   │   if for all p ∈ proh: simcv ∩ query ⊈ p  and  simcv ∩ (U \ query) ⊈ p
    │   │      then
11  │   │   │   return correct to output list    //respond correctly;
12  │   │   │   simcv ← simcv ∩ correct
    │   │   │       //update simulated current view accordingly
13  │   │   else
14  │   │   │   return U to output list
    │   │   │       //signify refusing; leave simcv unchanged
15  │   │   end
16  │   end
17  until input queue has externally been closed, if ever;
```

Algorithm 1: Stepwise controlled query evaluation with alterations by refusing for a known prohibition declaration

Proof. A full proof is given in the appendix. Here we only sketch the overall structure of the proof. An execution of Algorithm 1 determines a sequence of values for the simulated current view *simcv* with a fixpoint, such that

$$prior = simcv_0 \supseteq simcv_1 \supseteq simcv_2 \supseteq \dots \; with \; simcv_\infty = \bigcap_{t=0,1,2,\dots} simcv_t.$$

By the construction and by assertion (3), $d_{st} \in simcv_\infty$. By an inductive argument based on the compactness, and because of the explicit check of the security invariant in step 10, we have $simcv_\infty \nsubseteq p$ for all $p \in proh$. Thus, for each $p \in proh$ there exists a data source $d_{al}^p \in simcv_\infty \setminus p$, which satisfies the precondition and is harmless by the construction.

Moreover, d_{al}^p is also *indistinguishable* (of the "stored" data source d_{st}), as is even any data source $\tilde{d} \in simcv_\infty$. Basically, this claim follows from the inductive procedure to decide whether the value of *simcv* should be changed, based on the *instance independent* security invariant enforced by step 10.   □

Theorem 2 (refusing provides best current view directly). *Algorithm 1 executed for inputs* $\langle q_1, q_2, \ldots \rangle$, d_{st}, *prior and proh satisfying the preconditions* $d_{st} \in prior$ *and* $prior \nsubseteq p$ *for all* $p \in proh$ *for inference-proofness provides the best current view* $bestcv_\infty$ *by the fixpoint* $simcv_\infty$ *of the simulated current view* $simcv$, *i.e., we have* $bestcv_\infty = simcv_\infty$.

Proof. In the proof of Theorem 1 we show that $bestcv_\infty \supseteq simcv_\infty$. Conversely, assume $\tilde{d} \in prior$ but $\tilde{d} \notin simcv_\infty$. Then executing the Algorithm 1 for d_{st} and $\tilde{d}$, respectively, yields the same value for $simcv$ at time 0 according to step 2 but different values for some later point in time. Consider the point in time $min > 0$ such that for the first time the executions differ for the value $simcv$. Accordingly, at time min for at least one of the data sources there was no refusing and, by the independence of the guarding expression in step 10, for both of them there was no refusing. Moreover, by the minimality of min, the query evaluations have been different, i.e., $quer(query_{min}, d_{st}) \neq quer(query_{min}, \tilde{d})$, such that the executions can be distinguished. Hence $\tilde{d} \notin bestcv_\infty$. □

5.2   Controlled Query Evaluation by Lying

For alterations by *lying*, the existence of an *"alternative" harmless data source* has to be ensured regarding a strengthen version of harmlessness that requires non-elementship in the *union over the prohibition declaration*. This version avoids the *hopeless situation* arising from lies on both that union and all its contributing prohibitions. The existence of such a data source will only partly explicitly be monitored, aiming to make the assertion "$simcv \nsubseteq \bigcup proh$" part of the security invariant. In fact, if a *correct response* is returned to the attacker, then the invariance of the assertion after updating $simcv$ accordingly has been checked explicitly by a tentative update before. Otherwise, if a *lied response* is returned to the attacker, then no explicit additional inspection is necessary. Moreover, the *indistinguishability* property is also already implicitly be enforced, since a data source that satisfies each of the responses generated for the actual data source—whether correct or lied—turns out to generate the same reactions.

Theorem 3 (strong inference-proofness by lying). *The stepwise controlled query evaluation function with alterations by lying, as computed by Algorithm 2, is strongly inference-proof.*

Proof. Structurally as for refusing, by an inductive argument that the correct response and the lied response are not both harmful for a single prohibition. □

Input: $\langle q_1, q_2, \dots \rangle$ queue of queries, submitted by attacker
          d_{st} stored abstract data source
          prior   a priori knowledge as query
          proh   prohibition declaration as finite set of queries
Output: $\langle r_1, r_2, \dots \rangle$ list of (possibly) altered responses, returned to attacker

```
1  time ← 0                    //initialize counter for discrete points in time;
2  simcv ← prior               //initialize simulated current view;
3  repeat
4  │  time ← time + 1;
5  │  query ← receive next query q_time from input queue;
6  │  correct ← quer(query, d_st)        //determine correct query evaluation;
7  │  lied ← U\correct                   //prepare the lie;
8  │  if simcv ∩ correct ⊈ ⋃proh then
9  │  │  return correct to output list    //respond correctly;
10 │  │  simcv ← simcv ∩ correct
   │  │  //update simulated current view accordingly
11 │  else
12 │  │  return lied to output list        //respond by the lie;
13 │  │  simcv ← simcv ∩ lied
   │  │  //update simulated current view accordingly
14 │  end
15 until input queue has externally been closed, if ever;
```

Algorithm 2: Stepwise controlled query evaluation with alterations by lying for a known prohibition declaration

5.3   Controlled Query Evaluation by Combination

For alterations by a *combination of refusing and lying*, the existence of an *"alternative" harmless data source* will explicitly be monitored by inspecting the assertion "for all $p \in proh$: $simcv \not\subseteq p$" as the security invariant. In fact, first the *correct response* is explicitly inspected for harmlessness by a tentative update of *simcv*, and only in case of a failure, subsequently the *lied response* is also explicitly inspected for harmlessness. If both inspections fails, i.e., both the correct response and the lied response are harmful, then refusing is due. No further means are necessary to achieve the *indistinguishability* property as well.

Theorem 4 (inference-proofness by combination). *The stepwise controlled query evaluation function with alterations by a combination of refusing and lying, as computed by Algorithm 3, is* inference-proof *(and strongly inference-proof under the substitution of proh by* $\{\bigcup proh\}$ *).*

Proof. Similar as for the proof of Theorem 1, following its overall structure.   □

Input: $\langle q_1, q_2, \dots \rangle$ queue of queries, submitted by attacker
$\phantom{\textbf{Input:}}$ d_{st} stored abstract data source
$\phantom{\textbf{Input:}}$ $prior$ a priori knowledge as query
$\phantom{\textbf{Input:}}$ $proh$ prohibition declaration as finite set of queries
Output: $\langle r_1, r_2, \dots \rangle$ list of (possibly) altered responses, returned to attacker

```
 1  time ← 1                        //initialize counter for discrete points in time;
 2  simcv ← prior                   //initialize simulated current view;
 3  repeat
 4  │   time ← time + 1;
 5  │   query ← receive next query q_time from input queue;
 6  │   correct ← quer(query, d_st)          //determine correct query evaluation;
 7  │   lied ← U \ correct                    //prepare the lie;
 8  │   if for all p ∈ proh: simcv ∩ correct ⊈ p then
 9  │   │   return correct to output list      //respond correctly;
10  │   │   simcv ← simcv ∩ correct
    │   │       //update simulated current view accordingly
11  │   else
12  │   │   if for all p ∈ proh: simcv ∩ lied ⊈ p then
13  │   │   │   return lied to output list      //respond by the lie;
14  │   │   │   simcv ← simcv ∩ lied
    │   │   │       //update simulated current view accordingly
15  │   │   else
16  │   │   │   return U to output list
    │   │   │       //signify refusing and leave simcv unchanged
17  │   │   end
18  │   end
19  until input queue has externally been closed, if ever;
```

Algorithm 3: Stepwise controlled query evaluation with alterations by a combination of refusing and lying for a known prohibition declaration

5.4 Controlled View Generation

So far, we have studied stepwise controlled query evaluation functions for abstract data sources as epistemic states, employing refusing or lying or the combination of refusing and lying, respectively, as alterations of a harmful query evaluation. These functions are proven to be inference-proof for any sequence of closed-query evaluation with response preparation. Each proof has been based on investigating the properties of the sequence of the *simulated current views* maintained by the pertinent algorithm to keep track of the *interaction history* and to enforce a suitable *security invariant*, together with the fictitious fixpoint of that sequence. Essentially, this fixpoint is the intersection of the (possibly) altered query responses.

We further exploit the three fundamental approaches for such an algorithm to deal with the interaction of *view generation*. A *best view* is abstractly defined as the intersection of the query evaluations of *all* queries in the considered query set. Then, roughly outlined, we can form a queue of *all* such queries, or a suitably *exhaustive* part of it, submit it to the pertinent algorithm, and will (at least conceptually) obtain the fixpoint as a (possibly) altered inference-proof view. In an interaction of *controlled view generation*, that fixpoint can be returned to the communication partner suspected to be only semi-honest and attacking the dedicated prohibition declaration.

Theorem 5 (inference-proofness by refusing, lying and the combination). *The controlled view generation functions with alterations by refusing or lying or the combination of refusing and lying, respectively, for a known prohibition declaration, as computed by Algorithm 4, are weakly or strongly or weakly inference-proof, respectively.*

Proof. The claim straightforwardly follows from the inference-proofness of the imported algorithms.   □

Input:	d_{st}	stored abstract data source
	prior	a priori knowledge as query
	proh	prohibition declaration as finite set of queries
Output:	*view*	returned to attacker as controlled view

1 **Import:** Algorithm i for
  either $i = 1$: refusing or $i = 2$: lying or $i = 3$: combination

2 form *exhaustive* queue $\langle q_1, q_2, \ldots \rangle$ of closed queries;
3 apply Algorithm i to $\langle q_1, q_2, \ldots \rangle$ and the inputs, using local variable *simcv*;
4 **on exit** from the repeat-loop (actually or fictitiously) **do**
5 $view \leftarrow \bigcap simcv$;
6 return *view* as output

Algorithm 4: Controlled view generation with alterations by refusing, lying or the combination of refusing and lying based on Algorithm 1, Algorithm 2 or Algorithm 3, respectively, for a known prohibition declaration

5.5   Some Comparisons

For refusing, we have $d_{st} \in simcv$ and $simcv = bestcv$. Basically, this intuitively means that the literal claims of returned controlled responses are a correct and complete disjunctive weakening of the best view. In contrast, for lying and the combination, whenever a lied response has actually occurred, we have $d_{st} \notin simcv$ and, consequently, $simcv \neq bestcv$, in particular saying that literal claims do not directly reflect the actual situation. The following theorem shows that this difference disappears under the substitution of *proh* by $\{\bigcup proh\}$, since then the occurrence of a refusal corresponds to a potential lie.

Theorem 6 (best current views for aggregated policy declaration). *Under the substitution of proh by $\{\bigcup proh\}$, the inverse functions of the controlled view generation functions with alterations by refusing or lying or the combination of refusing and lying, respectively, as computed by Algorithm 4, yield the same best current views.*

Proof. The full proof, given in the appendix, shows that for the single aggregated prohibition in $\{\bigcup proh\}$, the effect of the instance-independent check for harmfulness by refusing corresponds to the effect of instance-independently always returning a harmless response by lying.   □

6   Conclusions

Enforcing inference-proofness as a sophisticated version of confidentiality relies on crucial assumptions about the a priori knowledge of the specific attacker and further postulations about the overall attack scenario. Furthermore, the notion of a defender or an attacker, respectively, refers to both human individuals and the computing agents under their control. Accordingly, for coming up with formally provable assertions about confidentiality the precise specification of the object to be protected by a security mechanism on the defender side as well as a precise specification of the capabilities on the attacker side are mandatory.

Our main contributions are complying with these requirements. On the defender side the epistemic state of the information system agent is identified as the basic protection object, independently of the actual syntactic representation and of any additional knowledge held by the human information owner. On the attacker side, our characterization of the attacker as a rational reasoner about message observations, a priori knowledge, the semantics of the agreed interactions and the functionality of the security mechanism refers to both the client agent and the human communication partner. Accordingly, the defender side is restricted by the possibilities of efficient algorithms, whereas the attacker side might employ unlimited resources. However, as far as the attacker relies on the computing resources of the client agent, refusing and lying essentially differ in determining the best current view: while for refusing the best current view is directly delivered by the returned accumulated information represented by the simulated current view, for lying the best current view has to be generated by a sophisticated function inversion procedure.

We have focused on conceptual and computational foundations rather than on specific applications. Regarding usability, our foundational results suggest that in each concrete practical situation we might be forced to admit relaxations and approximations. Regarding computational complexity, view generation as an off-line procedure might be preferred to closed-query evaluations as a dynamic and often time-constrained protocol. Moreover, in practice we are faced with structured epistemic states which allow more sophisticated interactions, e.g., open (SQL-like) queries and update transactions for relational databases. Interactions might also refer to non-monotonic operations regarding a structured epistemic state seen as "belief", e.g., a revision under suitable postulates. So far, these and further issues have already been preliminarily studied for specific frameworks, as discussed in [1]. It would be worthwhile to unify and further elaborate all these studies as an enhancement and extension of the present work.

Acknowledgements. I would like to sincerely thank Piero Bonatti very much for fruitful cooperation on the works underlying this article.

Appendix 1: Proof of Theorem 1

Consider the execution of Algorithm 1 for some inputs $\langle q_1, q_2, \ldots \rangle$, d_{st}, $prior$ and $proh$ satisfying the preconditions $d_{st} \in prior$ and $prior \not\subseteq p$ for all $p \in proh$. Let $\langle simcv_0, simcv_1, simcv_2, \ldots \rangle$ be the sequence of values obtained by the simulated current view $simcv$, with $simcv_0 = prior$ according to step 2, and with $simcv_{time}$ being the updated value at the end of the $time$-th iteration of the repeat-loop for $time > 0$, according to either step 12, 14 or 8, respectively. Then we have

$$simcv_0 \supseteq simcv_1 \supseteq simcv_2 \supseteq \ldots . \tag{7}$$

Define the fixpoint of this chain as

$$simcv_\infty = \bigcap_{time=0,1,2,\ldots} simcv_{time}. \tag{8}$$

This fixpoint has the following properties:

1. $simcv_\infty \in Int(Q)$, according to Definition 1.
2. $d_{st} \in simcv_\infty$, by the *construction* during the execution of Algorithm 1, since for each $time = 0, 1, 2, \ldots$ one of the following alternatives apply: $d_{st} \in prior$ in step 2; $d_{st} \in correct$ in step 8 or 12 by assertion (3); $d_{st} \in U$ in step 14.
3. $simcv_\infty \not\subseteq p$ for all $p \in proh$, based on the *compactness* of the query set Q according to Definition 1, as verified below.

Let $p \in proh$. Assume indirectly that $simcv_\infty \subseteq p$. Then, by the compactness of the query set Q, there would exist a finite set F of values in the sequence (7) having a minimal element $simcv_F$ (with maximum index of time) such that $simcv_F = \bigcap F \subseteq p$. Let then min be the first time such that $simcv_{min} \subseteq p$. By the precondition, min > 0. Then, depending on the evaluation of the guarding expressions in step 7 and step 10, respectively, either $simcv_{min} = simcv_{min-1} \cap correct_{min}$ according to step 12 in the inner if-branch or $simcv_{min} = simcv_{min-1}$ according to step 14 in the inner else-branch or $simcv_{min} = simcv_{min-1}$ according to step 8 in the outer if-branch. However, the first case contradicts the value of the inner guarding expression and the second case and third case contradict the definition of min.

So, by $simcv_\infty \not\subseteq p$ there exists a data source $d_{al}^p \in simcv_\infty \setminus p$. We claim that d_{al}^p is the "alternative" data source required to exist:

4. d_{al}^p *satisfies the a priori knowledge*, since $d_{al}^p \in simcv_\infty \setminus p \subseteq simcv_\infty \subseteq simcv_0 = prior$.
5. d_{al}^p *is harmless* (w.r.t. the prohibition p), i.e., $d_{al}^p \notin p$, by the construction.
6. d_{al}^p *is indistinguishable* (of the "stored" data source d_{st}), since below we can show by induction that for each $time = 1, 2, \ldots$ the repeat-loop of Algorithm 1 takes the same actions, in fact not only for d_{al}^p but even for all data sources $\tilde{d} \in simcv_\infty$.

So, consider any $\tilde{d} \in simcv_\infty$ and suppose inductively that the value $simcv_{time-1}$ of the simulated current view $simcv$ is the same for the stored data source d_{st} and the considered data source $\tilde{d}$.

Case 1: $simcv_{time-1} \subseteq quer(query_{time}, d_{st})$.
Then, the outer guarding expression at step 7 is true for d_{st} and, thus, the response $quer(query_{time}, d_{st})$ is returned in step 8. Then we have

$$\tilde{d} \in simcv_\infty \subseteq simcv_{time-1} \subseteq quer(q_{time}, d_{st})$$

and thus, by assertion (4), $quer(q_{time}, \tilde{d}) = quer(q_{time}, d_{st})$. This equality implies that also $simcv_{time-1} \subseteq quer(query_{time}, \tilde{d})$ and, accordingly, that the outer guarding expression at step 7 is also true for $\tilde{d}$ such that $quer(query_{time}, \tilde{d})$ is returned in step 8 as the same response.

Case 2: $simcv_{time-1} \nsubseteq quer(query_{time}, d_{st})$.
Case 2.1: For all $p' \in proh$: $simcv_{time-1} \cap query_{time} \nsubseteq p'$ and $simcv_{time-1} \cap (U \setminus query_{time}) \nsubseteq p'$.

Then $quer(query_{time}, d_{st})$ is returned in step 11 and $simcv$ is updated accordingly in step 12, and we have

$$\tilde{d} \in simcv_\infty \subseteq simcv_{time} = simcv_{time-1} \cap quer(q_{time}, d_{st}) \subseteq quer(q_{time}, d_{st})$$

and thus, by assertion (4), $quer(q_{time}, \tilde{d}) = quer(q_{time}, d_{st})$. This equality implies that also $simcv_{time-1} \nsubseteq quer(query_{time}, \tilde{d})$ and, accordingly, that the outer guarding expression at step 7 is also false for $\tilde{d}$ and the inner guarding expression is checked in line 10. Being independent of the query evaluation, this expression is also true for $\tilde{d}$ by the assumption of Case 2.1, such that $quer(query_{time}, \tilde{d})$ is returned in step 11 as the same response and the same update of $simcv$ occurs in step 12.

Case 2.2: For some $p' \in proh$: $simcv_{time-1} \cap query_{time} \subseteq p'$ or $simcv_{time-1} \cap (U \setminus query_{time}) \subseteq [4]p'$.

Then the universe U is returned in step 14, signifying a refusal for d_{st}. Regarding $\tilde{d}$, since both $d_{st} \in simcv_{time-1}$ and $\tilde{d} \in simcv_{time-1}$, we have $simcv_{time-1} \nsubseteq quer(query_{time}, \tilde{d})$ by the assumption of Case 2 and assertion (5). So, the outer guarding expression in step 7 is also false for $\tilde{d}$ and the inner guarding expression is checked in line 10. Being independent of the query evaluation, this expression is also false for $\tilde{d}$ by the assumption of Case 2.2, such that the universe U is returned in step 14, signifying a refusal as the same response.   □

Appendix 2: Proof of Theorem 6

By Theorem 2, we already know that for refusing with suitable inputs the simulated current view $simcv_\infty$ equals the best current view $bestcv_\infty$. Thus it suffices to show the following claim by induction:

For a single aggregated prohibition $\bigcup proh$, the simulated current view $simcv_{time}$ of refusing equals the best current views $bestcv_{time}$ of lying and the combination, respectively.

At $time = 0$, for all of the three approaches we have $simcv_0 = bestcv_0$. At $time > 0$, assume inductively that $simcv_{time-1}$ for refusing equals $bestcv_{time-1}$ for lying and the combination, respectively.

Case 1: Refusing returns the correct response $quer(query_{time}, d_{st})$.

Case 1.1: $simcv_{time-1} \subseteq quer(query_{time}, d_{st})$, i.e., refusing confirms the correct response. This response is harmless, for otherwise $simcv_{time-1}$ would already be harmful, contradicting the security invariant. Then, for refusing,

$$simcv_{time} = simcv_{time-1} = simcv_{time-1} \cap quer(query_{time}, d_{st}). \tag{9}$$

Case 1.2: Otherwise, we have for all $p \in proh$: $simcv \cap query \not\subseteq p$ and $simcv \cap (U \setminus query) \not\subseteq p$ and, again, for refusing,

$$simcv_{time} = simcv_{time-1} \cap quer(query_{time}, d_{st}). \tag{10}$$

In both subcases, regarding lying, the correct response $quer(query_{time}, d_{st})$ is returned for d_{st}, as exactly for all $d' \in quer(query_{time}, d_{st})$, for each of which we $quer(query_{time}, d') = quer(query_{time}, d_{st})$ by (4). The same reasoning applies for the combination. Accordingly, we have for both lying and the combination

$$bestcv_{time} = bestcv_{time-1} \cap quer(query_{time}, d_{st}), \tag{11}$$

together with (9), (10) and the induction assumption implying the claim.

Case 2: Refusing returns U to signify a refusal and, thus, for refusing,

$$simcv_{time} = simcv_{time-1} \cap U = simcv_{time-1}. \tag{12}$$

Then, according to the instance-independent guarding expression for refusing, there exists $p' \in \{\bigcup proh\}$ such that $simcv_{time-1} \cap query_{time} \subseteq p'$ or $simcv_{time-1} \cap (U \setminus query_{time}) \subseteq p'$. This implies that we have

either $simcv_{time-1} \cap query_{time} \subseteq \bigcup proh$
or $simcv_{time-1} \cap (U \setminus query_{time}) \subseteq \bigcup proh$
but not both.

For assume otherwise that both inclusions hold, then

$$\begin{aligned}
&simcv_{time-1}\\
&= simcv_{time-1} \cap U\\
&= simcv_{time-1} \cap (query_{time} \cup (U \setminus query_{time}))\\
&= (simcv_{time-1} \cap query_{time}) \cup (simcv_{time-1} \cap (U \setminus query_{time}))\\
&\subseteq \bigcup proh,
\end{aligned}$$

contradicting that the security invariant for refusing has been enforced at time $time - 1$.

Now, regarding lying, the strict alternative given above means that for all $d' \in U$ the uniquely determined harmless version in the set $\{query_{time}, U \setminus query_{time}\}$ is returned, independently of whether it is correct or lied. The same observation applies for the combination. Accordingly, for both approaches we have

$$bestcv_{time} = bestcv_{time-1} \cap U = bestcv_{time-1}, \qquad (13)$$

together with (12) and the induction assumption implying the claim. $\square$

References

1. Biskup, J.: Selected results and related issues of confidentiality-preserving controlled interaction execution. In: Gyssens, M., Simari, G. (eds.) FoIKS 2016. LNCS, vol. 9616, pp. 211–234. Springer, Cham (2016). https://doi.org/10.1007/978-3-319-30024-5_12

2. Biskup, J., Bonatti, P.A.: Lying versus refusal for known potential secrets. Data Knowl. Eng. **38**(2), 199–222 (2001)

3. Biskup, J., Bonatti, P.: Controlled query evaluation for enforcing confidentiality in complete information systems. Int. J. Inf. Secur. **3**(1), 14–27 (2004). https://doi.org/10.1007/s10207-004-0032-1

4. Biskup, J., Bonatti, P.A.: Controlled query evaluation for known policies by combining lying and refusal. Ann. Math. Artif. Intell. **40**(1–2), 37–62 (2004). https://doi.org/10.1023/A:1026106029043

5. Biskup, J., Bonatti, P.A., Galdi, C., Sauro, L.: Optimality and complexity of inference-proof data filtering and CQE. In: Kutyłowski, M., Vaidya, J. (eds.) ESORICS 2014. LNCS, vol. 8713, pp. 165–181. Springer, Cham (2014). https://doi.org/10.1007/978-3-319-11212-1_10

6. Biskup, J., Bonatti, P.A., Galdi, C., Sauro, L.: Inference-proof data filtering for a probabilistic setting. In: Brewster, C., Cheatham, M., d'Aquin, M., Decker, S., Kirrane, S. (eds.) 5th Workshop on Society, Privacy and the Semantic Web - Policy and Technology, PrivOn 2017. CEUR Workshop Proceedings, vol. 1951. CEUR-WS.org (2017). http://ceur-ws.org/Vol-1951/PrivOn2017_paper_2.pdf

7. Bonatti, P.A., Kraus, S., Subrahmanian, V.S.: Foundations of secure deductive databases. IEEE Trans. Knowl. Data Eng. **7**(3), 406–422 (1995)

8. Denning, D.E.: Cryptography and Data Security. Addison-Wesley, Reading (1982)

9. Goguen, J.A., Meseguer, J.: Unwinding and inference control. In: IEEE Symposium on Security and Privacy, pp. 75–87 (1984)

10. Halpern, J.Y., O'Neill, K.R.: Secrecy in multiagent systems. ACM Trans. Inf. Syst. Secur. **12**(1), 5.1–5.47 (2008)

11. Sabelfeld, A., Sands, D.: Declassification: dimensions and principles. J. Comput. Secur. **17**(5), 517–548 (2009)

12. Schneider, F.B.: Enforceable security policies. ACM Trans. Inf. Syst. Secur. **3**(1), 30–50 (2000)

13. Sicherman, G.L., de Jonge, W., van de Riet, R.P.: Answering queries without revealing secrets. ACM Trans. Database Syst. **8**(1), 41–59 (1983)

Network Functions Virtualization Access Control as a Service

Manel Smine[1][(✉)], David Espes[2], Nora Cuppens-Boulahia[1,3],
and Frédéric Cuppens[1,3]

[1] IMT Atlantique, Rennes, France
`manel.smine@imt-atlantique.fr`, {`nora.cuppens`,`frederic.cuppens`}`@polymtl.ca`
[2] University of Western Brittany, Brest, France
`david.espes@univ-brest.fr`
[3] Polytechnique Montréal, Montreal, Canada

Abstract. NFV is an important innovation in networking. It has many advantages such as saving investment cost, optimizing resource consumption, improving operational efficiency and simplifying network service lifecycle management. NFV environments introduce new security challenges and issues since new types of threats and vulnerabilities are inevitably introduced (e.g. security policy and regular compliance failure, vulnerabilities in VNF softwares, malicious insiders, etc.). The impact of these threats can be mitigated by enforcing security policies over deployed network services. In this paper, we introduce an access control as a service model for NFV services. The proposed approach can deploy several kinds of access control model policies (e.g. RBAC, ORBAC, ABAC, etc.) for NFV services and can be easily scaled.

Keywords: Network Functions Virtualization (NFV) · Access control · Policy enforcement · Domain type enforcement (DTE)

1 Introduction

Network Functions Virtualization (NFV) is a network architecture concept which virtualises network functions (firewalling, DNS, intrusion detection, etc.). It creates a Virtualized Network Function (VNF) instance that is deployed over a Virtualized infrastructure. Usually, a Virtualized infrastructure is able to host many VNFs of different types. These VNFs can be chained to provide virtual network services. NFV promises a number of advantages to network operators such as reducing hardware costs, deployment in fast time and scalability. Despite advantages, security concerns are an important obstacle for a wide adoption of NFV. New threats and vulnerabilities are inevitably introduced such as security policy violation [12], VNF softwares vulnerable to different kinds of software flaws [18], and malicious insiders that can be a serious threat for user privacy and can lead to data confidentiality exposure [12]. Solutions to enhance the security of VNF network services are (1) to control the access to the different

© IFIP International Federation for Information Processing 2020
Published by Springer Nature Switzerland AG 2020
A. Singhal and J. Vaidya (Eds.): DBSec 2020, LNCS 12122, pp. 100–117, 2020.
https://doi.org/10.1007/978-3-030-49669-2_6

components of the VNF network service and (2) to control what information is authorized to be transferred between the different components of the VNF network service.

In this paper we propose a formal model that provides a software-defined access control as a service capability for network services. First, it allows to specify high-level access control requirements to be enforced over network services. Second, it uses a provably correct method for transforming the high-level access control requirement towards a domain type enforcement (DTE) specification. Finally, our model defines an efficient enforcement method, as illustrated by the different conducted experimental evaluations in Sect. 5. Compared to existing models, our model is: (1) generic since it takes into consideration any type of access control policy such as RBAC [20], ORBAC [11], ABAC [9], etc., (2) compliant with the ETSI-NFV infrastructure in the sense that it does not require any modification of the latter for policy deployment, (3) and scalable thanks to our enforcement method that allows to add as many enforcement points as needed (e.g., for load balancing purposes) without impacting the functioning of the network services.

The paper is organized as follows. Section 2 reviews previous related research on existing security orchestrators and access control models for NFV infrastructure. Section 3 provides some background knowledge for understanding the proposed architecture. Section 4 defines our proposed model. Section 5 provides an overview of the implementation of our model and presents the evaluation results. Finally, Sect. 6 concludes the paper and outlines future work.

2   Related Work

Policy management and deployment in NFV architecture have recently been the topic of several researches. Many approaches have been proposed to define and enforce security policies over NFV architecture to ensure their security. Basile et al. propose in [4] an approach aiming to provide specific security properties over Virtualized networks. This approach relies on a new software component called Policy Manager to handle high-level security policies specified by the users and refine them into configurations for specific VNF. Unfortunately, this approach does not specify what kind of properties can be handled and how these required security property are refined to deployable configurations. In [14], Montero et al. propose a user-centric model named SECURED, allowing to express and deploy security policies to protect users' security in NFV. Due to its user-centric characteristic, the proposed model is completely oriented to protect users' security when interacting with NFV network services and cannot be used to secure NFV network services themselves. In FlowIdentity [24], a Virtualized network access control function using OpenFlow protocol is proposed. It is a solution for network access control in SDN architectures with policy enforcement over a stateful role-based firewall on OpenFlow switches. Unfortunately, the proposed approach is deeply dependent on the SDN architecture and thus cannot be directly used in an NFV architecture. To overcome the previous limitations,

Leopoldo, et al. propose ACLFLOW [13] that is a Network Functions Virtualization (NFV)/Software-Defined Networking (SDN) security framework allowing to translate regular ACL rules into OpenFlow filter rules. ACLFLOW optimizes the evaluation of ACL rules by prioritizing the most popular rules to accelerate switching operations. Unfortunately, ACLFLOW cannot be used to enforce more advanced access control policy models such as Role Based Access Control (RBAC), Organization-Based Access Control (ORBAC), Attribute-Based Access Control (ABAC), etc.

To solve multi-propagation problems of the concept of NFV such as verification and authorisation issues, Guija and Siddiqui [7] use the NFV-based SONATA Service Platform for authentication and authorisation mechanisms, specifically for Identity and Access control of micro-services in 5G platforms for services Virtualization, orchestration and management. This solution relies mainly on OAuth 2 [8] and OpenID Connect [19] to form the implementation of the user management module allowing Role Based Access Control and Identity management to follow the centralized authorization approach. However, This dependency on OAuth 2 and OpenID Connect makes this solution applicable only on services where a HTTP-based communication is used between their different components.

The model proposed in the standard ETSI-NFV [6] describes the NFV Security Monitoring and Management architecture. The proposed architecture introduces two components: The NFV Security Controller that orchestrates system wide security policies and acts as a trusted third party and the NFV Security Monitoring Analytics System which performs secure Telemetry acquisition from the NFV system and can derive threats and anomalies from the telemetry. However, only the model is defined and no specification of how all this work is done. In addition, several interfaces that the architecture defines are not specified (e.g. the connection between the controller and the Operating Support System/Business Support System (OSS/BSS).

In the literature, several security orchestrators have been defined to control the access in NFV infrastructure. In [10], Jaeger et al. propose an SDN based security orchestrator which improves the ETSI NFV reference architecture with an extensive management of trust and offer a global view for fast and efficient topology validation. Unfortunately, no concrete use case and implementation of the provided security requirements are given. The authors of [23] present an architecture for NFV environments focusing on the automation of access control management deployment. Unfortunately, the authors do not provide any information about how access control policies are deployed in a VNF network service. In [15], Montida et al. develop a security orchestrator as an extension of the MANO NFV orchestrator to manage the security properties of network services in their entire lifecycles. They extend the Topology and Orchestration Specification for Cloud Applications (TOSCA) model [5] with particular security attributes that are required to create access control policies and finally enforced in the cloud infrastructure. They instantiate the proposed security orchestrator in [16,17] through the implementation of an access control model which consists of deploying an access control policy over a network service. However, the proposed approach suffers from several limitations. First, it requires the modification of the NFV infrastructure since specific agents has to be deployed on the NFV that compose the considered network service to enforce the access control policy. Second, the proposed access control model is not generic enough since it can only handle policies specified using the RBAC model. Finally, it is not clear how the high level access control policy is transformed into a concrete deployable policy.

Compared to existing access control models, our model offers several advantages. First, it is a generic model as it can handle most kind of access control policy models such as RBAC, ORBAC, ABAC, etc. Second, it offers formal and efficient methods for deploying access control policies at the concrete level. Third, the deployment method proposed in our model does not require any modification at the NFV infrastructure level.

3   Background

This section provides background material about all main technologies to enable the deployment of our security policy.

VNF Forwarding Graph: ETSI defined the notion of a VNF forwarding graph (VNFFG) [3] known also as Service Function Chaining (SFC). It is used to manage a traffic through a sequence of network functions (NF) that should be traversed in an order list of VNFs. VNFFG are described by VNF Forwarding Graph Descriptors (VNFFGD). Each forwarding graph is composed of a set of forwarding paths.

Network Service: A VNF service is composed of a set of VNFs that are represented using a deployment template VNF descriptor (VNFD) which define their properties and a set of forwarding graphs that are defined using a deployment template VNF FG Descriptor (VNFFGD).

Domain and Type enforcement (DTE): The technique Domain and Type Enforcement (DTE) protects the integrity of military computer systems. It was designed to be used in combination with other access control techniques. As with many access control schemes, DTE views a system as a collection of active entities (subjects) accessing a collection of passive entities (objects) based on rules defined in an attached security context and groups processes into domains, files into types and restricts access from domains to types as well as from domains to other domains.

4   The Proposed Model

4.1   Adversary Model

To understand the scope of the problem and assess the risks, we have to develop an adversary model. The adversary model considered in this paper is composed of an attacker, a NFV infrastructure hosting the multiple VNFs that compose the network services to be deployed, and an access control engine that is used to deploy the access control policy. In our model, the objective is to allow users including the likely attacker to perform operations that a normal VNF infrastructure user can do. It means that the attacker can generate and modify a flow, attack to try to compromise a VNF. We suppose that the adversary will be able to interact with the VNF composing the deployed network service but he cannot control or modify the behavior of the access control engine as well as the VNF that will be used to enforce the access control policy. This later is supposed to be hardened, i.e., keeping the operating system up to date, minimising the installed packages to minimize vulnerabilities, enable and correctly configure a firewall, etc.

4.2 New Enforcement Model

In this section, a formal modelization of the security policy to be deployed is proposed. The proposed model defines what is an access query and how it can be evaluated. Since DTE has made its evidence for the enforcement of access control policies at operating system level, a method for transforming an access control policy towards a DTE specification is proposed. The proposed transformation allows us to benefit from the advantages of DTE. In particular, it allows entities having the same access requirements to be collected into domains and types which allows to find an appropriate balance between security and policy deployment complexity. We prove that the proposed transformation method is correct and we show how the DTE policy is enforced.

Security Policy Specification

Definition 1 (Security Policy). *A security policy SP is composed of a set of access control rules $\{r_1, \cdots, r_i\}$. Each rule r_i comprises:*

- *A subject S_i that represents one or many entities that want to access the object, these entities are characterized by a set of properties $\mathcal{P}_i^S = \{p_1^s, \cdots, p_n^s\}$.*
- *An action A_i that represents the operation that is going to be performed by S_i on O_i, each action is characterized by a set of properties $\mathcal{P}_i^A = \{p_1^a, \cdots, p_l^a\}$.*
- *An object O_i represents one or many resources over which the action A_i is going to be performed. O_i are characterized using two types of properties: (1) a set of properties $\mathcal{P}_i^E$ that characterises the entities (e.g., VNF) and (2) a set of properties $\mathcal{P}_i^R$ that characterises the resources inside those entities and over which the action A_i will be performed.*
- *A context C_i under which the rule can be invoked.*
- *A decision D_i indicating whether it is a permission or denial rule.*

In our model, each rule r_i in the security policy will be represented as follows:

$$r_i = \langle S_i, A_i, O_i, C_i, D_i \rangle$$

We note that the properties that characterize the entities representing the subject S_i (resp. the object O_i) may include: attributes of S_i (resp. O_i) in the considered system (e.g., the IP address of a network to which the subject belongs, etc.), functional attributes representing the provided functionalities (e.g., routing, deep packet inspection, firewalling, etc.), and security attributes that represent the security properties that is associated to S_i (resp. O_i) (e.g., the security level, trust level, etc.). These properties are to be retrieved from the VNF descriptors that compose the service to be deployed. For instance, the rule saying that any VNF providing web client functionalities and having a high security level can read the content of any web page on a VNF providing a web server functionality and having a high security level if the client is using *https*, can be specified using the following notation:

$$\langle S = \{func : web\_client, sec\_level : high\}, A = Action : read, proto = https, O =$$
$$\{\mathcal{P}^E = \{func : web\_server, sec\_level : high\}, \mathcal{P}^R = file\_name : any\},$$
$$C = \{\text{between 8am and 8pm}\}, D = allow\rangle$$

Our specification of the security policy represented in Definition 1 can be used to represent many access control model policies such as RBAC and ABAC. First, RBAC is based on the notion of *subject, permission* that is represented by a relation between an *action* and an *object*, and a specific attribute representing a *role*. The first three notions (i.e., subject, object and action) can be straightforwardly translated to our model. The notion of *role* can be seen in our model as a specific property of the subject. Similarly, the attributes used in the ABAC model can be translated in our model to properties that characterize a subject, an object, a context, or an action.

Definition 2 (Access Query). *An access query $\mathcal{AQ}$ is represented by the quadruplet $\langle S^q, O^q, A^q, C^q \rangle$ where S^q represents the subject performing the query, O^q the object over which the query is performed, A^q the action performed by the query, and C^q the request context under which the query is performed. Given a security policy $\mathcal{SP}$, $\mathcal{AQ}$ is allowed by $\mathcal{SP}$ if and only if the following condition holds:*

(i) *$\exists r_i \in \mathcal{SP}$ such that $S^q \in S_i, O^q \in O_i, A^q \in A_i$, C^q satisfies C_i, and $D_i = allow$.*

$\mathcal{AQ}$ is denied by $\mathcal{SP}$ if and only if one of the following conditions hold:

(ii) *$\nexists r_i \in \mathcal{SP}$ such that $S^q \in S_i, O^q \in O_i, A^q \in A_i$, C^q satisfies C_i, and $D_i = allow$.*

(iii) *$\exists r_i \in \mathcal{SP}$ such that $S^q \in S_i, O^q \in O_i, A^q \in A_i$, C^q satisfies C_i, and $D_i = deny$.*

Policy Transformation. In this section, we propose a method for transforming an access control policy as defined in Definition 3 towards a DTE specification. Then, we prove that the transformation we propose is correct.

Definition 3. *Given a security policy $\mathcal{SP}$ composed of n rules $r_1, \cdots, r_n$. $\mathcal{SP}$ is transformed to a DTE policy by performing, for each rule $r_i \in \mathcal{SP}$ the following steps:*

- **step 1:** *If there exist no $j < i$ such that $\mathcal{P}_i^S = \mathcal{P}_j^S$, define the domain $s\_\mathcal{P}_i^S\_d$ which will contain all entities of the considered system (i.e., the network service to be deployed) that have the set of properties $\mathcal{P}_i^S$ used to characterize the subject S_i. Otherwise, use the same domain $s\_\mathcal{P}_j^S\_d$ (i.e., $s\_\mathcal{P}_i^S\_d = s\_\mathcal{P}_j^S\_d$) defined for the subject S_j of the rule r_j.*
- **step 2:** *If there exist no $k < i$ such that $C_i = C_k$, define new type c_i_t. Otherwise, use the same type c_k_t defined for the context of the rule r_k (i.e., $c_i\_t = c_k\_t$).*
- **step 3:** *If there exist no $l < i$ such that $\mathcal{P}_i^R = \mathcal{P}_l^R$ define new type $o\_\mathcal{P}_i^R\_t$ which will be associated to all resources of the considered system that have the set of properties $\mathcal{P}_i^R$. Otherwise, use the same type $o\_\mathcal{P}_l^R\_t$ (i.e., $o\_\mathcal{P}_i^R\_t = o\_\mathcal{P}_i^R\_t$). In addition, if there exist no $l' < i$ such that $\mathcal{P}_i^E = \mathcal{P}_l^E$, define new domain $o\_\mathcal{P}_i^E\_d$ that will contain all entities of the considered system that have the set of properties $\mathcal{P}_i^E$. Otherwise, use the same domain $o\_\mathcal{P}_{l'}^E\_d$ (i.e., $o\_\mathcal{P}_{l'}^E\_d = o\_\mathcal{P}_i^E\_d$) defined for the object of the rule r_l.*
- **Step 4:** *When associated to the request context C^q of an access query $\mathcal{AQ}$ (i.e., the context of the rule r_i is satisfied by the context C^q of $\mathcal{AQ}$), allow the type c_i_t to be an entry point allowing to transit $\mathcal{AQ}$ from domain $s\_\mathcal{P}_i^S\_d$ to the domain $o\_\mathcal{P}_i^O\_d$.*
- **Step 5:** *Authorize access queries that transit from $s\_\mathcal{P}_i^S\_d$ to $o\_\mathcal{P}_i^E\_d$ to perform the actions A_i on any objects having the type $o\_\mathcal{P}_i^R\_t$.*

Finally, we denote $\mathcal{C}$ to be the set containing the set of DTE type c_i_t and their respective context of the rule C_i created in step 2 ($\mathcal{C} = \{(c_i\_t, C_i)\}$).

We note here that only the rules having an *allow* decision are considered in the previous definition. This choice is due to the fact that DTE is using by default closed policies.

In our model, when an access query is created by the system, the query inherits all the types associated to the subject S^q and belongs to the DTE domains of S^q. In addition, we suppose that the system associates types to C^q as follows. $\forall (c_i\_t, C_i) \in \mathcal{C}$: if C_i is satisfied in C^q, then associate the type c_i_t to the request context C^q of the access query.

Example 1. This example illustrate the security policy transformation method we defined in Definition 3. Let us consider that we have a security policy $\mathcal{SP}$ that is composed of three rules r_1, r_2 and r_3 such that:

- $r_1 = \langle S_1 = \{func : web\_server, sec\_level : high\}, A_1 = read, O_1 = \{\mathcal{P}_1^E = \{func : ftp\_server, sec\_level : high\}, \mathcal{P}_1^R = \{file\_name : any\}\}, C_1 = \{between\ 8am\ and\ 8pm\}, D_1 = allow\rangle$
- $r_2 = \langle S_2 = \{func : web\_server, sec\_level : high\}, A_2 = write, O_2 = \{\mathcal{P}_2^E = func : database\_server, sec\_level : low\}, \mathcal{P}_2^R = db\_name : service\_db\}, C_2 = \{between\ 8am\ and\ 8pm\}, D_2 = allow\rangle$

– $r_3 = \langle S_3 = \{func : web\_client, sec\_level : high\}, A_3 = access, O_3 = \{\mathcal{P}_3^E = func : ftp\_server, sec\_level : high, \mathcal{P}_3^R = file\_name : web\_config\}, C_3 = \{between \ 8am \ and \ 8pm\}, D_3 = allow \rangle$

According to Definition 3, the transformation of the policy $\mathcal{SP}$ to a DTE specification is illustrated using the schema in Fig. 1. Subjects $S_1, S_2,$ of rules r_1, r_2 are respectively represented in the transformation by the DTE domain $s\_web\_server\_high\_d$ while the subject S_3 of r_3 is represented by the domain $s\_web\_client\_high\_d$. The entities of objects O_1 and O_3 of r_1 and r_3 (described using the set of properties P_1^E and P_3^E) are represented in the DTE transformation by the DTE domain $o\_ftp\_server\_high\_d$ and the resources of the objects O_1 and O_3 (described using the set of properties P_1^R and P_3^R). In the case of O_2, the entities described using the set of properties P_2^E and the resources are described using the set of properties P_2^R. The DTE domains $o\_ftp\_server\_high\_d$ and $o\_db\_server\_low\_d$ are respectively created by the transformation of the rules r_1 and r_3. After the transformation, $o\_ftp\_server\_high\_d$ contains the ftp server having the security level high while $o\_db\_server\_low\_d$ contains the database servers having the security level low. Finally, c_t is a DTE type that will be associated to any access query satisfying the context C_1, C_2, and C_3 of the rules r_1, r_2, and r_3. Let us consider the access query $\mathcal{AQ}$:$\langle S^q = web\_client, O^q = ftp\_server, A^q = read, C^q = \{query \ time = 12 \ am\}\rangle$ to be evaluated and performed on the considered system. According to our

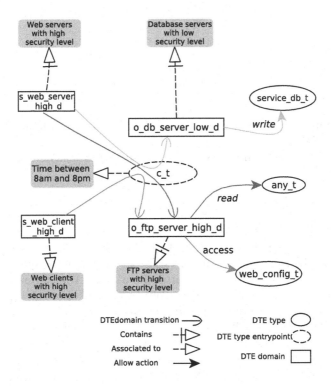

Fig. 1. Transformation from a specific policy to a DTE policy

transformation method, $\mathcal{AQ}$ will inherit the domain of its subject, so it will initially belongs to the domain $s\_web\_client\_high\_d$. Moreover, the context C^q of $\mathcal{AQ}$ satisfies the contexts C_1, C_2 and C_3 of the three rules r_1, r_2, and r_3. Hence, the type c_t will be associated to the query $\mathcal{AQ}$. According to the step 4 of our transformation method, the DTE type c_t will allow the access query $\mathcal{AQ}$ to transit from the domain $s\_web\_client\_high\_d$ to the domain $o\_ftp\_server\_high\_d$. Furthermore, according to the transformation shown in Fig. 1, the action $access$ is authorized to be performed by access queries belonging to the domain $o\_ftp\_server\_high\_d$ over objects associated to the DTE type $o\_ftp\_server\_high\_t$. So, we conclude that the query $\mathcal{AQ}$ is to be authorized by the transformation of $\mathcal{SP}$.

Policy Transformation Correctness. A security policy transformation method is correct if, for any access query, no rule in the transformed security policy is violated when the transformation resulting policy is deployed. This is formalized using the following definition.

Definition 4. *Given a security policy $\mathcal{SP} = \{r_1, \cdots, r_n\}$ and its corresponding DTE transformation $\mathcal{SP}_{DTE}$ (as described in Definition 3). The transformation from $\mathcal{SP}$ to $\mathcal{SP}_{DTE}$ is correct if and only if for any access query $\mathcal{AQ}$: if $\mathcal{AQ}$ is allowed (resp. denied) by $\mathcal{SP}$, then it is allowed (resp. denied) by $\mathcal{SP}_{DTE}$.*

Theorem 1. *The policy transformation method proposed in Definition 3 is correct.*

Proof. We prove the previous theorem by contradiction. Let us denote by $\mathcal{SP}$ the transformed policy and $\mathcal{SP}_{DTE}$ the transformation resulting policy. According to Definition 4, the policy transformation method is not correct if one of the following cases hold:

- **case 1:** There exists an access query $\mathcal{AQ}$ such that it is allowed by $\mathcal{SP}$ and denied by $\mathcal{SP}_{DTE}$.
- **case 2:** There exists an access query $\mathcal{AQ}$ such that it is denied by $\mathcal{SP}$ and allowed by $\mathcal{SP}_{DTE}$.

For both cases, a contradiction is shown in the following.

Case 1: Formally, this case implies that $\exists r_i \in \mathcal{SP}, \exists \mathcal{AQ}$ such that: $S^q \in S_i, O^q \in O_i, A^q \in A_i$, C_i is satisfied in C^q, and $D_i = $ allow. $S^q \in S_i$ means that S^q will belong to the same domain as S_i ($s\_\mathcal{P}^{S_i}\_d$) and that the query itself will belong to $s\_\mathcal{P}^{S_i}\_d$. According to the step 3 of our policy transformation method (Definition 3), $O^q \in O_i$ implies that the object O^q will have the type $o\_\mathcal{P}^{R_i}\_t$. In addition, according to the query initialization rules, C_i is satisfied in C^q means that the type c_i_t will be assigned to C^q. Then, according to the step 4 of Definition 3, when executed, $\mathcal{AQ}$ will transit from the domain $s\_\mathcal{P}^{S_i}\_d$ to the domain $o\_\mathcal{P}^{E_i}\_d$. Subsequently, and according to the step 5 of Definition 3, since $\mathcal{AQ}$ transited to $o\_\mathcal{P}^{E_i}\_d$, it will have the permission to perform the set of actions

A_i on all entities having the type $o\_\mathcal{P}^{R_i}\_t$. Finally, since $O^q \in O_i$ and $A^q \in A_i$, then $\mathcal{AQ}$ will have the permission to perform the action A^q on the object O^q which contradicts the hypothesis of the case 1.

Case 2: This case happens if one of the following conditions hold:

case 2.1: Given the access query $\mathcal{AQ}$, there exists no rule in the policy $\mathcal{SP}$ that allow $\mathcal{AQ}$. Formally, $\nexists r_i \in \mathcal{SP}$ such that $S^q \in S_i, O^q \in O_i, A^q \in A_i$, C^q satisfies C_i, and $D_i = $ allow. Let us suppose that the $\mathcal{AQ}$ is allowed by $\mathcal{SP}_{DTE}$. According to the transformation method, action permission is only specified in step 5 of Definition 3. This step means that if $\mathcal{AQ}$ is allowed by $\mathcal{SP}_{DTE}$, then there exist a domain $s\_\mathcal{P}^{S_i}\_d$ and a type $o\_\mathcal{P}^{R_i}\_t$ such that $\mathcal{AQ}$ belongs to $s\_\mathcal{P}^{S_i}\_d$ and O^q has the type $o\_\mathcal{P}^{R_i}\_t$. This means that there exists $r_i \in \mathcal{SP}$ such that $A_q \in A_i$ and $O^q \in O_i$. In addition, according to step 3 of Definition 3, $o\_\mathcal{P}^{R_i}\_d$ ($i \in [1, n]$) does not contain any access query when created. These domains are only accessible for access queries thought the transformation rule defined in step 4 of Definition 3. Since we already showed that $\mathcal{AQ}$ belongs to $s\_\mathcal{P}^{S_i}\_d$, then there exits an entrypoint type c_i_t that allow $\mathcal{AQ}$ to transit to the domain $o\_\mathcal{P}^{E_i}\_d$ which allow us to deduce that C_i is satisfied in C^q and that both S_i and S^q belongs to the same domain $s\_\mathcal{P}^{S_i}\_d$ (since $S^q \in S_i$). Then, we deduce that $\exists r_i \in \mathcal{SP}$ such that $S^q \in S_i$, $O^q \in O_i$, $A^q \in A_i$, C_i satisfied in C^q and $D_i = allow$ which contradicts the case 2.1.

case 2.2: This case implies that given the access query $\mathcal{AQ}$, in one hand $\exists r_i \in \mathcal{SP}, \exists \mathcal{AQ}$ such that: $S^q \in S_i, O^q \in O_i, A^q \in A_i$, C_i is satisfied in C^q, and $D_i = $ deny and in the other hand $\mathcal{AQ}$ is allowed by $\mathcal{SP}_{DTE}$. $S^q \in S_i$ means that S^q will belong to the same domain as S_i ($s\_\mathcal{P}^{S_i}\_d$) and that the query itself will belongs to $s\_\mathcal{P}^{S_i}\_d$, since $\mathcal{AQ}$ inherit the domain of its subject then $\mathcal{AQ}$ belongs also to $s\_\mathcal{P}^{S_i}\_d$. Since the rule r_i is transformed using our transformation method, then there exists the type c_i_t that represents an entrypoint to the domain $o\_\mathcal{P}^{E_i}\_d$. Since C_i is satisfied in C^q, the type c_i_t will be associated to the C^q of $\mathcal{AQ}$, as a result, when executed, $\mathcal{AQ}$ will transit from $s\_\mathcal{P}^{S_i}\_d$ to $o\_\mathcal{P}^{E_i}\_d$. However, based on the transformation of r_i, the domain $o\_\mathcal{P}^{E_i}\_d$ will be denied to perform the action A_i on the type $o\_\mathcal{P}^{R_i}\_t$. Finally, since $O^q \in O_i$ and $A^q \in A_i$ then the query $\mathcal{AQ}$ will be denied by the $\mathcal{SP}_{DTE}$ which contradicts the case 2.2.

Service Requirements Specification

In our model, a security policy is going to be deployed on a VNF service. A VNF service S is composed of a set of VNFs $\{vnf_1, \cdots, vnf_n\}$ and a set of forwarding graphs $\{fg_1, \cdots, fg_m\}$. Each forwarding graph fg_i is composed of a set of forwarding paths $\{fp_1, \cdots, fp_d\}$, each fp_i can be represented using the following couple $\langle\langle vnf_1^i, vnf_2^i, \cdots, vnf_{n_i}^i\rangle, fp\_m_i\rangle$, where vnf_1^i is the VNF that is forwarding the traffic, vnf_n^i is the VNF to which the traffic is forwarded, and fp_m_i is the match policy that will be used to distinguish which traffic should traverse the path.

In our model, a traffic $\mathcal{T}$ is used to represent each exchange between two consecutive VNFs in the considered forwarding path. It is modeled as the quadruple $\langle vnf\_src, vnf\_dst, t\_context, t\_content \rangle$ where vnf_src, vnf_dst, $t\_context$, and $t\_content$ represent respectively, the VNF that is sending the traffic, the VNF destination of the traffic, the context and the content of the traffic. Formally, a forwarding path $fp = \langle \langle vnf_1, vnf_2, \cdots, vnf_n \rangle, fp\_m \rangle$ is represented using $n-1$ traffics $\mathcal{T}_i = \langle vnf_i, vnf_{i+1}, fp_m, t\_content \rangle$, $1 \leq i < n$.

It is worth highlighting that the action involved in the security policy to be deployed can be implemented in the content of a traffic. For example, the "write" action can be implemented according to the protocol that is used. If the FTP protocol is used, a traffic containing the "post" ftp command implements the action "writ" used in the security policy. Thanks to the previous observation, a traffic can be modelled as an access query as defined in the following.

Definition 5. *A traffic $\mathcal{T} = \langle vnf\_src, vnf\_dst, t\_context, t\_content \rangle$ will be modeled as an access query $\mathcal{AQ} = \langle S^q, O^q, \mathcal{A}^q, C^q \rangle$ where vnf_src equals to S^q, vnf_dst equals to O^q, $\mathcal{A}^q$ are the actions that can be implemented by the traffic content $t\_content$, and $C^q = t\_context$.*

To ensure a proper functioning of the VNF service to be deployed, the traffics that represent each forwarding path should be allowed to flow according to the latter. To meet the previous objective, for each traffic $\mathcal{T}_i = \langle vnf_i, vnf_{i+1}, t_i\_context, t_i\_content \rangle$ that is modeled as the access query $\mathcal{AQ}_i = \langle vnf_i, vnf_{i+1}, \mathcal{A}_i^q, C_i^q \rangle$, we define the following policy rule:

$$r_{\mathcal{T}_i} = \langle S = vnf_i, O = vnf_{i+1}, A = A_i^q, C = C_i^q, D = allow \rangle$$

The previous rule states that vnf_i is allowed to perform the action A_i^q (implemented by the content of the traffic $\mathcal{T}_i$) over vnf_{i+1} if the context C_i^q is satisfied in the considered system. Finally, The previous rule is transformed to a DTE specification as described in Definition 1.

DTE Policy Enforcement. The DTE policy obtained from the transformation of the access control policy to be enforced and the network service to be deployed is enforced using a special VNF that we called VNF_Filter. VNF_Filter will basically analyze the traffics exchanged between the different VNF that compose the deployed network service to evaluate the authorization of each access query. In order to allow this, we should modify (as described in Definition 6) the forwarding graphs used to orchestrate and manage traffic through the VNFs that compose the deployed network service to make sure that these traffics pass certainly through the VNF_Filter.

Definition 6 (Forwarding graph modification). *Given a network service $\mathcal{S}$ composed of a set of forwarding graphs $\{fg_1, \cdots, fg_m\}$. Each forwarding graph fg_i is composed of a set of forwarding paths $\{fp_1, \cdots, fp_d\}$, and each fp_i is represented by a sequence $sq_i = \langle vnf_1^i, vnf_2^i, \cdots, vnf_{n_i}^i \rangle$ of the VNF that represents* the path that should be traversed by a traffic. Each $sq_i = \langle vnf_1^i, vnf_2^i, \cdots, vnf_{n_i}^i \rangle$ of a forwarding path fp_i will be modified as following:

$$sq_i = \langle vnf_1^i, \boldsymbol{vnf\_filter}, vnf_2^i, \boldsymbol{vnf\_filter}, \cdots, \boldsymbol{vnf\_filter}, vnf_{n_i}^i \rangle$$

To illustrate, let us consider a forwarding path fp composed of a sequence of three VNFs $\langle vnf1, vnf2, vnf3 \rangle$. The modification of fp according to Definition 6 makes sure that the traffic managed by fp will pass through the VNF_Filter as shown in Fig. 2.

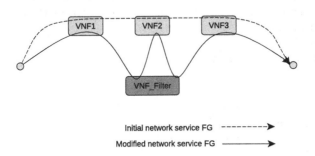

Fig. 2. Network Service forwarding graph modification

The observation of all traffics exchanged between the VNF that compose the considered network service gives VNF_Filter the ability to analyze those traffics and authorize only the ones that are allowed by the considered DTE policy. The pseudo-code in Algorithm 1 outlines the procedure used by the VNF_Filter to authorize a traffic exchanged between two VNF. It takes as inputs the traffic to be authorized, the sets $\mathcal{C}$ of types and their respective contexts created in the policy transformation process (Definition 3). It outputs a value (*allow_traffic* or *deny_traffic*) indicating whether or not the traffic is allowed by the DTE policy. The function *parse_traffic* allow to model the traffic $\mathcal{T}$ into an access query as defined in Definition 5. The functions *get_domains*, *get_types*, *get_transition_src*, and *get_transition_dst* are used to retrieve respectively, the set of domains to which the subject of the access query belong, the set of types associated with the object of the access query, the source domain of the domain transition, and the destination domain of the transition. The function *assign_types* assigns to the access query $\mathcal{AQ}$ the types used in $\mathcal{C}$ if their respective context matches the context of $\mathcal{AQ}$. Finally, the function *check_permission* check whether a DTE domain is allowed or denied to perform the actions in $\mathcal{A}^q$ on a given DTE type.

Input: $\mathcal{T}$ /* the traffic to be authorized */
$\quad\quad \mathcal{C} = \{(c\_r_i\_t, C_i)\})$ /* Definition 3 (step 2) */

$\mathcal{AQ} : \langle S^q, O^q, \mathcal{A}^q, C^q \rangle = \textbf{parse\_traffic}(\mathcal{T})$
$subject\_domains = \textbf{get\_domains}(S^q)$
$object\_types = \textbf{get\_types}(O^q)$
$\mathcal{AQ}\_types = \textbf{assign\_types}(\mathcal{AQ}, \mathcal{C})$
$possible\_domains = \emptyset$
foreach $\mathcal{AQ}\_type \in \mathcal{AQ}\_types$ **do**
$\quad$ **if** $\mathcal{AQ}\_type$ *is not a DTE entrypoint* **then continue** ;
$\quad$ **if** $\textbf{get\_transition\_src}(\mathcal{AQ}\_type) \notin subject\_domains$ **then**
$\quad\quad$ **continue** ;
$\quad$ $possible\_domains = possible\_domains \cup$
$\quad\quad$ $\textbf{get\_transition\_dst}(\mathcal{AQ}\_type)$
end
is_allowed = false
foreach $type \in object\_types$ **do**
$\quad$ **foreach** $domain \in possible\_domains$ **do**
$\quad\quad$ **if** $\textbf{check\_permission}(domain, type, \mathcal{A}^q) = allow$ **then**
$\quad\quad$ $\mid$ is_allowed = true;
$\quad\quad$ **else if** $\textbf{check\_permission}(domain, type, \mathcal{A}^q) = deny$ **then**
$\quad\quad$ $\mid$ **return** deny_traffic;
$\quad$ **end**
end
if *is_allowed* **then return** allow_traffic ;

Algorithm 1: Access query authorization

5   Implementation and Experimental Evaluations

This section presents the implementation details of a prototype of our proposed access control model. The design architecture of the prototype implementing the proposed model is illustrated in Fig. 3. The major functional components are described in the following.

- **OpenStack Tacker** [22]: it is an official OpenStack project that orchestrates and manages infrastructure resources and maintain the lifecycle management of network services and VNF instances over the OpenStack infrastructure.
- **Access control engine (ACE):** it works together with the VNF orchestrator (Taker) security policy enforcement to the deployed VNF service components (e.g., VMs, VNFs.)
- **OpenFlow Manager of OpenDaylight** (ODL) [1] is an open-source application development and delivery platform. OpenFlow Manager (OFM) [2] is an application that runs on top of ODL allowing to visualize OpenFlow topologies, program network traffic flow paths and gather network traffic stats.

– **OpenStack Infrastructure:** OpenStack as a virtual infrastructure manager (VIM) layer is used to give a standardized interface for managing, monitoring and assessing all resources within VNF infrastructure.

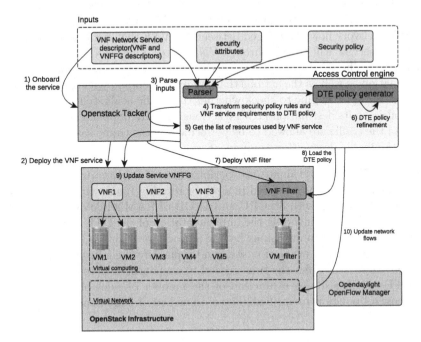

Fig. 3. Design architecture of the implementation of the proposed model and the operational flow of an access control policy deployment

In addition, Fig. 3 illustrates the different steps that are implemented in order to deploy an access control policy on a VNF network service. In the following, more details on each step are given.

– Onboard and deploy the network service (Steps 1 and 2): In these steps, Tacker uses the network service descriptor provided as an input to onboard and deploy the network service on the OpenStack infrastructure.
– Access control policy parsing and transformation (Steps 3 and 4): In these steps, the access policy engine parses the VNF service descriptor, the security properties associated which the different VNF that compose the network service (e.g., security level, trust level, etc.), and the access control policy to be deployed. Then, it transforms the access control policy to a DTE policy as described in Definition 3.
– DTE policy refinement (Steps 5 and 6): The ACE engine queries Tacker to get the set of resources (e.g., VMs, Connection points, networks, etc.) that are used to deploy the different VNF that compose the deployed service. Then it refines the DTE-policy at the resources level of the VNF service.

– Policy enforcement (Steps 7, 8, 9 and 10): To enforce the DTE policy, the ACE
first uses Tacker to deploy VNF_Filter which is a special VNF that implements a DTE engine we developed in python [21]. Second, it loads the refined
DTE policy to be enforced over the deployed VNF service on VNF_Filter.
Third, ACE updates the forwarding graphs of the deployed network service
(as illustrated in Fig. 2) and uses OpenFlow Manager of ODL to make sure
that all network flows exchanged between the VNF that compose the deployed
network service will transit through VNF_Filter. Once VNF_Filter receives a
network traffic, it starts by parsing the traffic to extract its source and its
destination as well as the actions that are implemented by its content. Finally
it uses the DTE engine to check whether the traffic is allowed to transit from
its source to its destination i.e., the actions that are implemented by the content of the traffic are allowed to be performed by the traffic source component
over the traffic destination component.

We experimentally evaluate the performance of our approach. Our access
control engine prototype is hosted in a server running Linux with an Intel Xeon
E5-2680 v4 Processor with 8 vCPU and 16 GB of RAM while our implementation of the VNF filter including the implementation of the DTE engine is hosted
in a virtual machine running Linux having a processor with 2 vCPU and 2 GB of
RAM. In our empirical evaluation, we aim to quantify the following characteristics of our approach. First, the time needed to transform an access control policy
to a DTE specification as a function of the number of rules of the considered
access control policy is quantified. The obtained results are depicted in Fig. 4.

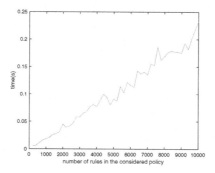

Fig. 4. Policy transformation time

They show that transformation method we are proposing is quite efficient
since it takes around 230 ms to transform an access control policy composed
of 10^4 rules to a DTE specification. The time needed to transform a security
policy to a DTE specification grows linearly in function of the number of rules
in policy. Second, we quantify the round-trip time (RTT) required for a packet
as a function of the activation of our VNF_Filter (i.e., we aim to compare the

RTT when our VNF_filter is used and when it is not) and the number of rules in the considered access control policy.

Figure 5 reports a linear growth of the measured RTT in function of the number of rules in the policy to be deployed. It shows that our implementation introduces less than 2 ms delay when a policy composed of 500 rules is considered.

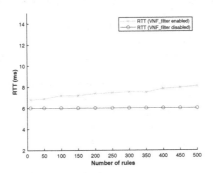

Fig. 5. RTT as a function of the number of rules in the access policy to be deployed

6   Conclusion

This paper proposes an access control as a service model to improve security management in the context of NFV. We firstly investigated several existing NFV orchestrators and several existing access control model in NFV infrastructure and observed that (1) none of them provides a generic model and (2) they are often not fully compliant with the ETSI NFV infrastructure in the sense that the deployment of the access control policies requires often the modification of the NFVI infrastructure. The previous observations motivate us to define a new software-defined access control as a service model. Compared to existing models, our proposition offers several advantages to VNF users. First, it is generic in the sense that they can deploy most types of access control policy such as RBAC, ORBAC, ABAC, etc. Second, it complies with the ETSI-NFV infrastructure because it does not require any modification of the latter for policy deployment. The conducted experimentations show that the implementation of the proposed model is quite efficient. The deployment of a security policy composed of 500 rules introduces less than 2 ms delay for the round-trip time of a network packet. As a future work, we aim to extend our proposed model to allow to check whether a given network service deployment satisfies the requirements of a given security policy.

References

1. The OpenDaylight Platform. https://www.opendaylight.org/. Accessed 30 Jan 2019

2. Openflow Manager. https://github.com/CiscoDevNet/OpenDaylight-Openflow-App. Accessed 30 Jan 2019
3. VNFFG. https://docs.openstack.org/tacker/latest/user/vnffg_usage_guide.html. Accessed 1 Jan 2019
4. Basile, C., Lioy, A., Pitscheider, C., Valenza, F., Vallini, M.: A novel approach for integrating security policy enforcement with dynamic network Virtualization. In: Proceedings of the 2015 1st IEEE Conference on Network Softwarization (NetSoft), pp. 1–5. IEEE (2015)
5. Binz, T., Breitenbücher, U., Kopp, O., Leymann, F.: TOSCA: portable automated deployment and management of cloud applications. In: Bouguettaya, A., Sheng, Q., Daniel, F. (eds.) Advanced Web Services, pp. 527–549. Springer, New York (2014). https://doi.org/10.1007/978-1-4614-7535-4_22
6. ETSI NFV: Management and orchestration; VNF packaging specification. Technical report, DGS/NFV-IFA011
7. Guija, D., Siddiqui, M.S.: Identity and access control for micro-services based 5G NFV platforms. In: Proceedings of the 13th International Conference on Availability, Reliability and Security, pp. 1–10 (2018)
8. Hardt, D.: The OAuth 2.0 Authorization Framework. RFC 6749, October 2012. https://doi.org/10.17487/RFC6749. https://rfc-editor.org/rfc/rfc6749.txt
9. Hu, V.C., Kuhn, D.R., Ferraiolo, D.F., Voas, J.: Attribute-based access control. Computer 48(2), 85–88 (2015)
10. Jaeger, B.: Security orchestrator: introducing a security orchestrator in the context of the ETSI NFV reference architecture. In: 2015 IEEE Trustcom/BigDataSE/ISPA, vol. 1, pp. 1255–1260. IEEE (2015)
11. Kalam, A.A.E., et al.: Organization based access control. In: Proceedings of the IEEE 4th International Workshop on Policies for Distributed Systems and Networks, POLICY 2003, pp. 120–131. IEEE (2003)
12. Lal, S., Taleb, T., Dutta, A.: NFV: security threats and best practices. IEEE Commun. Mag. 55(8), 211–217 (2017)
13. Mauricio, L.A., Rubinstein, M.G., Duarte, O.C.M.: ACLFLOW: an NFV/SDN security framework for provisioning and managing access control lists. In: 2018 9th International Conference on the Network of the Future (NOF), pp. 44–51. IEEE (2018)
14. Montero, D., et al.: Virtualized security at the network edge: a user-centric approach. IEEE Commun. Mag. 53(4), 176–186 (2015)
15. Pattaranantakul, M., He, R., Meddahi, A., Zhang, Z.: SecMANO: towards Network Functions Virtualization (NFV) based security management and orchestration. In: 2016 IEEE Trustcom/BigDataSE/ISPA, pp. 598–605. IEEE (2016)
16. Pattaranantakul, M., He, R., Zhang, Z., Meddahi, A., Wang, P.: Leveraging Network Functions Virtualization orchestrators to achieve software-defined access control in the clouds. IEEE Trans. Depend. Secure Comput. (2018)
17. Pattaranantakul, M., Tseng, Y., He, R., Zhang, Z., Meddahi, A.: A first step towards security extension for NFV orchestrator. In: Proceedings of the ACM International Workshop on Security in Software Defined Networks & Network Function Virtualization, pp. 25–30 (2017)
18. Reynaud, F., Aguessy, F.X., Bettan, O., Bouet, M., Conan, V.: Attacks against Network Functions Virtualization and software-defined networking: state-of-the-art. In: 2016 IEEE NetSoft Conference and Workshops (NetSoft), pp. 471–476. IEEE (2016)
19. Sakimura, N., Bradley, J., Jones, M.B., de Medeiros, B., Mortimore, C.: OpenID connect core 1.0. https://openid.net/specs/openid-connect-core-1_0.html

20. Sandhu, R.S., Coyne, E.J., Feinstein, H.L., Youman, C.E.: Role-based access control models. Computer **29**(2), 38–47 (1996)
21. Smine, M.: DTE engine. https://github.com/msmine/vnf-access-control-as-a-service
22. Tacker, O.: Tacker-openstack NFV orchestration (2017)
23. Thanh, T.Q., Covaci, S., Corici, M., Magedanz, T.: Access control management and orchestration in NFV environment. In: 2017 IFIP Networking Conference (IFIP Networking) and Workshops, pp. 1–2. IEEE (2017)
24. Yakasai, S.T., Guy, C.G.: FlowIdentity: software-defined network access control. In: 2015 IEEE Conference on Network Function Virtualization and Software Defined Network (NFV-SDN), pp. 115–120. IEEE (2015)

Effective Access Control
in Shared-Operator Multi-tenant Data
Stream Management Systems

Marian Zaki[1]([⊠]), Adam J. Lee[2], and Panos K. Chrysanthis[2]

[1] College of Science and Engineering, Computer Science,
Houston Baptist University, Houston, TX, USA
mzaki@hbu.edu
[2] Department of Computer Science,
University of Pittsburgh, Pittsburgh, PA, USA
{adamlee,panos}@cs.pitt.edu

Abstract. The proliferation of stream-based applications has led to the widespread use of Data Stream Management Systems (DSMSs), which can support the real-time requirements of these applications. DSMSs were developed to efficiently execute continuous queries (CQs) over incoming data. Multiple CQs can be optimized together to form a query network by sharing operators across CQs. DSMSs are also required to enforce access controls over operators according to data providers' policies. In this paper, we propose the first solution to satisfy access control policies at run-time in shared-operator networks in an non-disruptive, efficient manner. Specifically, we propose a new set of low overhead streaming operators, coined as Privacy Switches (PrSs), which are strategically placed in the operator network to dynamically allow or deny the flow of data in certain branches of the network based upon the current state of access control permissions. Our experimental evaluation confirms that our approach introduces low overheads in the shared operator networks while achieving high savings in the overall network performance.

Keywords: Access control · Operator networks · Stream processing engines

1 Introduction

Nowadays, an increasing amount of data is produced in the form of high velocity data streams. This has led to the proliferation of *stream-based applications* such as sensor-based monitoring (surveillance, car traffic, air quality), financial applications (stock markets, fraud detection), and health care applications. At the same time, it has led to the widespread use of *Data Stream Management Systems* (DSMSs) [1,4,5,8,10,15], developed to efficiently execute *continuous queries* (CQs) over streaming data to support these classes of applications.

© IFIP International Federation for Information Processing 2020
Published by Springer Nature Switzerland AG 2020
A. Singhal and J. Vaidya (Eds.): DBSec 2020, LNCS 12122, pp. 118–136, 2020.
https://doi.org/10.1007/978-3-030-49669-2_7

DSMSs are also referred to as Stream Processing Engines (SPEs) and stream processing systems.

CQs are stored queries that execute continuously over data streams as data arrives, on the fly. Since CQs are long-running, multiple CQs can be optimized together to form a query (operator) network, in which multiple queries may share one or more physical operators. The intermediate tuples produced by a shared operator are placed in a shared input queue for the downstream operators of the individual queries involved in the sharing. These optimizations increase the throughput of processing multiple CQs simultaneously and minimize the memory usage and computation times.

In DSMSs that host sensitive data, e.g., patient monitoring data, financial data, etc., data providers restrict data accesses via access control policies that describe the conditions under which users are permitted access to specific data streams. Accordingly, the CQs registered by the system users may be granted or denied access to specific data streams during the execution of these queries.

The most commonly used ways of applying access control over operators in query networks enforce access control either before (pre-filtering) or after (post-filtering) the execution of the network [17]. In both techniques, the fixed placement of the access control filters may considerably limit query performance. Pre-filtering means cutting off the streams in case any of the users lose access, which will affect the input streams feeding into downstream shared-operator networks. Post-filtering on the other hand, causes all operators to execute until the end and then denying access to the query results for the users who lost access. This wastes resources by processing query results that are never accessed.

An alternative solution is to isolate the queries that have temporarily lost access from the rest of the shared-operator network. This requires modifying the shared-operator network at runtime whenever access control changes are encountered. This can cause extensive overheads on the system that can potentially affect the system throughput and overall performance.

Under these challenges, it is vital for DSMSs to satisfy the access control policies at run-time in shared-operator networks in a non-disruptive and efficient manner, reinforcing both the *need to share* and *need to protect* design models. To balance these properties, we propose a cost-effective way for shared-operator networks to enforce access control within the network, thereby eliminating the need to perform any changes to the structure of the shared-operator networks in case of intermittent changes in the access control.

Specifically, in this paper we make the following contributions:

- We propose a new set of low overhead streaming operators that we refer to as *Privacy Switches* (PrSs). These switches dynamically allow or deny the flow of data streams in shared-operator networks based upon the current state of the access control permissions. Accordingly, certain branches of the query operator networks can be halted and spared execution to accommodate intermittent loss of access to different users.
- We propose a placement algorithm to identify the best placement points for PrSs in an optimized shared-operator network. The strategic placement of

the switches ensures seamless execution of CQs and reduces overheads in the networks while honoring all changes in access permissions.

– We experimentally evaluate our approach by generating shared-operator networks with a controlled set of generation rules and input parameters. Our experiments show that PrSs introduce low overheads in shared-operator networks and achieving high savings in overall network performance.

The remainder of the paper is organized as follows. Section 3 describes prior work on access control in DSMSs and introduces the concept of security punctuations. Section 4 presents our system model, assumptions, and preliminaries. Section 5 describes our proposed approach, which is evaluated in Sect. 6. Section 7 concludes the paper.

2   Motivating Example

In the smart healthcare industry [9,13], wearable smart devices are equipped with various bio sensors that are used to measure and monitor diverse health data of individuals such as blood glucose levels, blood pressure, oxygen saturation, heart rate, etc. This data makes it possible for different health care applications to continuously query these data stream and provide an alarm service, notifying in the risk of health issues based on individual activities of daily living.

Even though a large collection of health data is a valuable asset to the smart healthcare field, serious concerns of data privacy are being raised. That is, indiscriminate collection of personal health data can cause significant privacy issues. Hence, most users do not agree to their health data being collected for the purposes of data analysis which presents a major obstacle for the development of smart healthcare services.

The following listing demonstrates three different data streams and Fig. 1 illustrates two example CQs that can be used in smart healthcare applications.

```
Stream1:  streamid , location , heartRate , timestamp
Stream2:  streamid , location , speed
Stream3:  streamid , location , screentime , category
```

Listing 1.1. Data streams generated by smart devices

```
SELECT s1.streamid, s1.heartRate
  FROM Stream1 as s1 [RANGE 5 min, SLIDE 1 min],
       Stream2 as s2 [RANGE 5 min, SLIDE 1 min]
 WHERE s1.location = s2.location
   AND s1.timestamp > 6:00am
   AND s1.timestamp < 7:00pm
   AND s2.speed < 30;
```

```
SELECT s1.streamid, s1.heartRate
  FROM Stream1 as s1 [RANGE 10 min, SLIDE 1 min],
       Stream2 as s2 [RANGE 10 min, SLIDE 1 min],
       Stream3 as s3 [RANGE 10 min, SLIDE 1 min]
 WHERE s1.location = s2.location
   AND s2.location = s3.location
   AND s1.timestamp > 8:00am
   AND s1.timestamp < 7:00pm
   AND s2.speed < 0
   AND s3.screentime > 5h;
```

Fig. 1. Continuous queries $CQ1$ and $CQ2$

When executing these CQs in DSMSs, the queries optimizer will be able to identify the common sub-expressions (both **SELECT** timestamps within the same

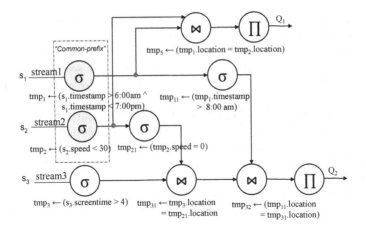

Fig. 2. Shared-operators network for $Q1$ and $Q2$

interval and have the same JOIN conditions on the input streams) found in the queries and accordingly construct a shared-operator network as shown in Fig. 2. The figure excludes the window specifications, for clarity since they are the same for all three data streams. Furthermore, in the figure, the highlighted vertices are annotated as "common-prefix" operators since those are the shared operators between both queries CQ_1 and CQ_2 (i.e., the output of these operators feed into two different operators belonging to the two queries).

3   Related Work

Prior work on access control enforcement in DSMSs can be divided into two different categories: *cryptographic* solutions and *non-cryptographic* solutions. Cryptographic solutions such as those presented in Streamforce [2], utilize Attribute-Based Encryption (ABE) to enforce access control which requires the data provider to be directly involved in the querying process. PolyStream [21] allows untrusted third-party infrastructure to compute on encrypted data, allowing in-network query processing and access control enforcement. PolyStream uses a combination of security punctuations, ABE, and hybrid cryptography to enable flexible (ABAC) access control policy management. Sanctuary [20] uses Intel's SGX as a trusted computing base for executing streaming operations on untrusted cloud providers.

Non-cryptographic solutions such as those presented by Carminati et al. [6,7], provide access control via enforcing Role Based Access Control (RBAC) and replacing the operators with secure versions which determine whether a client can access a stream by referencing an RBAC policy. Lindner et al. [14] utilize limited disclosure by using filtering operators and applying them to the stream query processing results to filter the output based on relevant access control policies. Ng et al. [18] also use the principles of limited disclosure to limit who can access and operate on data streams, requiring queries to be rewritten to match the level at which they can access the data.

Most non-cryptographic solutions require changing the underlying DSMS either by modifying the traditional operators to become security aware or by rewriting the queries, and therefore they are not globally applicable. Limited disclosure applies basic filtering to the query outputs which means that query operators execute at all times regardless of whether the output is used or not.

Unfortunately, all the cryptographic and non-cryptographic solutions that have been proposed to maintain privacy through access control focused mainly on independently executing queries. There has been no research to date that allows access control policies on the input data streams and queries to be applied over shared-operator networks to maintain both privacy and high performance. Our proposed privacy switches approach is the first work in this context.

4   Preliminaries and System Model

In this section we will introduce our system model, assumptions and the preliminaries used in our proposed solution.

4.1   System Model

The system consists of the following four main classes (entities) as shown in Fig. 3):

- *Data Providers* generate and distribute data streams to DSMSs. They have the choice of creating and updating the access control policies for the data streams that they emit.
- *Data Consumers* can be individuals or applications who submit CQs to the DSMSs Data consumers must submit credentials to satisfy the policies protecting access to their registered queries.
- *DSMSs* handle all the incoming data streams and submitted queries. They execute query optimizers to generate shared-operator networks for the interleaved execution of queries and schedule the operators' execution. They enforce the access control policies on the data streams and the corresponding query results.
- *Authorization Servers* can be separate entities or an integral part of the DSMSs. They validate users' credentials to check authorizations, and inject relevant SPs into the incoming data streams. They keep track of system state changes such as new data consumers signing up, changes in access control policies, and changes in the users' credentials (e.g., revoked or expired). These changes can trigger the injection of new SPs into impacted data streams to alter which users are able to see the results of CQs.

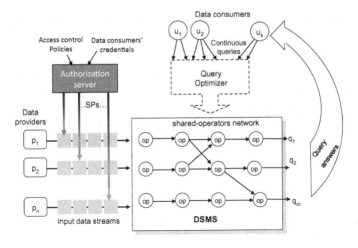

Fig. 3. DSMS system model

4.2 Operators and Operator Networks

The following are the main defining elements of data streams, CQs, and operator networks that will be used throughout the remainder of this paper:

- DSMSs are capable of processing long running set of continuous queries $\mathcal{CQ}s = q_1, q_2, \ldots, q_n$ executing over data streams in the system.
- $\mathcal{S}$ denotes the set of all input data streams in the system, while a continuous data stream $s \in \mathcal{S}$ is a potentially unbounded sequence of tuples that arrive over time.
- Tuples in a data stream are of the form $t = [sid, tid, A]$, where sid is the stream identifier, tid is the tuple identifier, and A is the set of attribute values of the tuple.
- Queries are comprised of a set of relational query operators $o_1, o_2, \ldots, o_n$.

A relational operator o_i is presented as $operator_{predicate}$ with an associated predicate. This may be a **SELECT** operator σ over one data stream, a **JOIN** operator $\bowtie$ between multiple data streams, a **PROJECT** operator Π that reduces the number of attributes included in a single data stream, or a **GROUP AGGREGATE** operator with predicate over a single attribute of a data stream to perform some algebraic aggregate function (e.g., **MAX**, **COUNT**, **SUM**, etc.).

For example, the following are valid query operators

$expr_1$: $o_1 = \sigma_{s_2.speed<30}$

$expr_2$: $o_2 = \bowtie_{s_1.location=s_2.location \ \& \ s_1.timestamp>6:00am \ \& \ s_1.timestamp<7:00pm}$

The query optimizer takes as input a set of continuous queries $\mathcal{CQ}$ and identifies groups of queries that share sub-expressions. The optimizer then generates a shared-operator network, arranged in a Directed Acyclic Graph (DAG) format, for each group of queries.

Definition 1. *An interleaved execution plan for a group of queries is a DAG network $\mathcal{N} = (V, E, L)$. V, E, and L being the set of vertices, edges and set of labels, respectively, and are defined as follows:*

- *A vertex v_i is introduced for every operator o_i in query q_i. If the results of o_i are used by more than one operator belonging to different queries, then the vertex v_i will be annotated as "Common-prefix"*
- *If the results of o_i are used in o_j, an edge $(v_i \rightarrow v_j)$ is introduced*
- *The label $L(v_i)$ is the processing done by the corresponding operator o_i (i.e., $operator_{predicate}$).*

4.3 Access Control

We assume that DSMSs can enforce *query-based* access restrictions that can be specified by both the data stream providers and/or the DSMSs over the entire data stream. For example, if a user does not renew his subscription to access certain query results in a DSMS, then this user could be temporarily denied access to any of his registered queries—by denying access to their corresponding data streams—until the subscription is renewed. Similarly, stream data providers can define policies to identify the different data consumers who are allowed to query those data streams. The work presented in this paper is very generic in that it can accommodate a wide range of access control models (e.g., RBAC [11], ABAC [12], or DAC [19]).

In general, let $\mathcal{P}$ denote the set of all authorization policies, each authorization policy $P : P \in \mathcal{P}$ enforced by a DSMS is defined as: $P \subseteq \mathcal{CQ} \times U$, where U is the set of users or user roles/attributes. Let function m be a mapping such that $m : \mathcal{CQ} \rightarrow S$, that is, m identifies the set of data streams that are being accessed by a continuous query.

For each policy P, the authorization server will perform the following:

1. evaluate the proofs of authorization for each (q_i, u_i) pair in P
2. execute the mapping function m to identify the set of streams S that are involved in each query q_i in the case of query-based policies
3. construct the necessary SPs to identify the access privileges of each user or group of users and inject them in the corresponding streams

According to the outcome of the proofs of authorizations, the *Sign* field in the SP will be set to $Sign = \text{`+'}$, if a user may access the data stream tuples for a given query at any time $ts_{access} \geq ts$ or $Sign = \text{`--'}$ if a user is denied access to the data stream at any time $ts_{access} \geq ts$. Accordingly, the injected SPs are used by our proposed algorithms to trigger the PrSs to turn *on* or *off* in the shared-operator networks to enforce access control.

4.4 Security Punctuations

We adopt the notion of *Security Punctuations* (SPs) [16,17] proposed to enforce access control in operator networks. SPs are considered meta-data in the form of

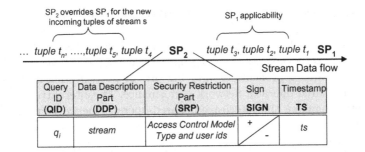

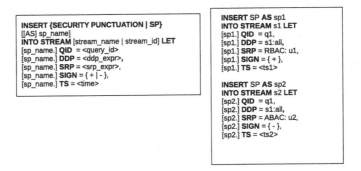

Fig. 4. Security Punctuations injected in a data stream

```
INSERT {SECURITY PUNCTUATION | SP}
[[AS] sp_name]
INTO STREAM [stream_name | stream_id] LET
[sp_name.] QID  = <query_id>
[sp_name.] DDP = <ddp_expr>,
[sp_name.] SRP = <srp_expr>,
[sp_name.] SIGN = { + | - },
[sp_name.] TS = <time>
```

```
INSERT SP AS sp1
INTO STREAM s1 LET
[sp1.] QID  = q1,
[sp1.] DDP = s1:all,
[sp1.] SRP = RBAC: u1,
[sp1.] SIGN = { + },
[sp1.] TS = <ts1>

INSERT SP AS sp2
INTO STREAM s2 LET
[sp2.] QID  = q1,
[sp2.] DDP = s1:all,
[sp2.] SRP = ABAC: u2,
[sp2.] SIGN = { - },
[sp2.] TS = <ts2>
```

Fig. 5. SP syntax (right) and sample SPs injected in two separate data streams (left)

predicates that are injected into data streams in the order of their timestamps and describe the access control privileges of each query. SPs are comprised of the following fields (see Fig. 4):

- *Query ID:* the identifier of the query that the SP is defining access for.
- *Data Description Part:* indicates the schema fields of a data stream tuple that are protected by the policy. This can be at the granularity of an entire stream, or specific tuples or attributes within the tuples.
- *Security Restriction Part:* defines the access control model type and the data user(s) authorized by the policy.
- *Sign:* specifies if the authorization is positive $(+)$ or negative $(-)$.
- *Timestamp:* the time at which the SP is generated.

Figure 4 shows an example input data stream with two SPs. Figure 5 shows an extension to the CQL syntax [3] to support the specification of SPs in data streams. The figure illustrates the syntax of an SP as well as an example of two SPs injected into two data streams. Each SP indicates the access privileges of a separate user over the tuples of the input data stream.

5   Privacy-Aware Shared Operator Networks

We now present the details of our proposed approach to achieve a cost-effective way of handling access control in shared-operator networks. As mentioned earlier in Sect. 1, the naive approaches of applying pre- or post-filtering may considerably limit the shared-operator network performance. The alternative approaches of constantly changing the interleaved shared-operator networks to isolate the queries that are no longer accessible by any of the users, or even maintaining different copies of shared-operator networks are both considered very costly approaches for handling access control.

To overcome these limitations, our proposed solution involves embedding a new set of operators called *Privacy Switches*(PrSs) in the networks. At a high level, the main idea is to strategically place these switches in the network to shut off branches of operators in the case of total access loss to certain query outputs or by filtering out the query results in the case of partial access loss to queries. By doing so, the shared-operator networks can execute disruptively and efficiently.

5.1   Privacy Switches

Privacy Switches (PrSs) are the novel set of operators that will be integrated within the shared-operator networks. These switches allow shared-operator networks to execute the queries impeccably while performing access control-based filtering. For this purpose, three different types of PrSs are introduced:

- **initial-switches:** placed at some of the input streams to each operator network and perform the traditional pre-filtering operations.
- **in-network switches:** embedded within the operator network and are capable of temporarily shutting off certain branches in the network to save the unnecessary execution of some operators in certain access permission cases.
- **terminal-switches:** placed at the query outputs and they act as multiplexers that can selectively filter query output to multiple users.

All three types of PrSs operate just like any other conditional query operator. They are similar to SELECT or PROJECT operators' that filters data input streams based on the security predicates determined by the SPs injected in the streams.

To better understand how the PrSs operate, assume there is a shared-operator network that interleaves the execution of multiple queries and each query could possibly be shared by multiple users in the DSMS. The three different types of the PrSs cover the following access scenarios:

- *Case I: partial loss of access:* In this case, only a subset of users lose access to the data streams processed by one or more of the interleaved queries in the shared-operator network. In this case, terminal switches will be in charge of granting access of the query results to the subset of users who did not lose their access privileges.

Algorithm 1: PrS execution algorithm

---

input: Stream

```
1  set PrS.AccessCounter = 0;
2  new SPs_batch arrives;
3  foreach SP ∈ SPs_batch do
4  |   if SP.TS < ts_access then
5  |   |   discard SP;
6  |   else
7  |   |   if PrS.Type = "in-network" OR "initial" then
8  |   |   |   if SP.Sign = '+' AND PrS.QueryID = SP.QID then
9  |   |   |   |   increment PrS.AccessCounter;
10 |   |   |   if SP.Sign = '-' AND PrS.QueryID = SP.QID AND PrS.AccessCounter
   |   |   |      != 0 then
11 |   |   |   |   decrement PrS.AccessCounter;
12 |   |   |   if PrS.AccessCounter > 0 then
13 |   |   |   |   send stream to PrS output;
14 |   |   |   else
15 |   |   |   |   discard stream;
16 |   |   else
17 |   |   |   if PrS.Type = "terminal" then
18 |   |   |   |   if SP.Sign = '+' AND PrS.QueryID = SP.QID then
19 |   |   |   |   |   add SP.SRP.u_id to PrS.U;
20 |   |   |   |   |   discard SP;
21 |   |   |   |   |   send stream to output of SP.SRP.u_id;
22 |   |   |   |   else
23 |   |   |   |   |   if SP.Sign = '-' AND PrS.QueryID = SP.QID then
24 |   |   |   |   |   |   remove SP.SRP.u_id from PrS.U;
25 |   |   |   |   |   |   discard stream;
```

– *Case II: total loss of access:* In this case, all users lose access to one or more of the interleaved queries in the shared-operator network. Accordingly, instead of operating terminal switches and having possibly unnecessary operators executing, both initial and in-network switches will shut off the isolated branches of operators in the network that are not shared by any other queries. In this case, a considerable amount of unnecessary work will be saved and performance gains will be achieved.

Initial and in-network PrSs are defined as: $PrS = <Type, QueryID, AccessCounter>$, where $Type$ defines whether this is an initial or in-network PrS, $QueryID$ is the query that the PrS is governing access to, and $AccessCounter$ is a counter that changes during the execution of the PrS to identify the number of users who have access to that particular query. The counter will have a value greater than zero in the case of partial loss of access, and will be set to zero in the case of total loss. Terminal switches are defined as: $PrS = <Type, QueryID, U>$, where U is the set of users that have access to the query $QueryID$ governed by this switch.

Algorithm 1 shows the pseudocode for executing the different types of PrSs. The input to each PrS is a data stream with embedded SPs. The PrSs execute this algorithm only when new SPs arrive in the data streams. The algorithm shows how the PrSs will allow or prevent the data streams from flowing through the network based on the output of the authorization predicates indicated by the *Sign* value in each SP.

Both initial and in-network PrSs operate in a similar manner. Each of these PrSs increment their *AccessCounter* whenever an SP with a matching QueryID and a '+' sign is encountered in the input stream and decremented each time a matching SP with a '−' sign shows up. In the case of partial access loss, the *AccessCounter* will be greater than zero (i.e., there is at least one SP in a stream that grants access to any user). In this case, the PrS will be switched *on* and the data stream tuples will flow normally through the network (lines 14 and 15). Note that the assumption made here is that the authorization server will re-inject SPs for the same user or set of users only if there are changes in the access control permissions for those users.

In the case of total loss of access, the *AccessCounter* will decrement down to zero (i.e., the last user who had access to the query lost that access). Accordingly, the PrS will be switched *off* and the flow of the tuples will halt temporarily (lines 16 and 17) until new SPs show up with positive access signs.

Terminal switches operate slightly different. They multiplex the final query output tuples to the users that have positive access as defined by their SPs (lines 20–24). Note that for privacy preservation, the default setup of terminal switches is deny the output to all users and only grant access when explicitly granted by an SP (i.e., they start by an empty set of users U). Similarly, initial and in-network switches have their *AccessCounter* initialized to zeros, which by default will deny any access to the query outputs.

The operation of the PrSs is very similar to the well known notion of counting semaphores that are typically used by many systems to coordinate access to different resources. By looking at the status and counter of each PrS, the DSMSs can collect statistics about how many users in the system are currently allowed access to a certain query output. The PrSs present an effective and simple solution for enforcing access control in shared-operator networks. They allow the on-the-fly adjustment of the network status as changes in access control take place without the need to re-direct the input streams to different networks or the need to restructure the operator network.

5.2 Placement of Privacy Switches

Algorithm 2 shows the pseudo-code for the PrSs placement algorithm. This algorithm extends the query optimizer, i.e., after a query optimizer constructs a shared-operator network strategically embedding the switches in the network.

The input to the algorithm is a shared-operator network pre-computed by the queries optimizer in the DSMSs. The placement of terminal switches is straightforward, at the end of each query output a terminal-switch will be inserted (line 2). In-network switches placement requires some analysis of the network graph. The main idea is to find the operators that are shared by multiple queries. Those shared-operators annotated are the ones annotated as "Common-Prefixes". The in-network switches will be placed along the outgoing edges of the last set of operators that belong to the common-prefixes (line 15). Finally, the initial-switches are placed at the input streams (lines 7 and 8) to apply pre-filtering of the input streams in the case of total access loss.

Algorithm 2: PrSs placement algorithm

input: A shared-operator network $\mathcal{N} = (V, E, L)$
Data: s defines a stack

1 **foreach** *query q_i output traverse $\mathcal{N}$ backwards (DFS-search)* **do**
2 | insert $PrS = \; <Type = \text{"terminal"}, QueryID = q_i, U = null>$ at the output of q_i;
3 | $s.push(v)$;
4 | **while** *s is not empty* **do**
5 | | $v = s.pop()$;
6 | | **if** *v is NOT annotated "Common-prefix"* **then**
7 | | | **if** *$\mathcal{N}.adjacentEdges(v) == \phi$* **then**
8 | | | | insert $PrS = \; <Type = \text{"inital"}, QueryID = q_i, AccessCounter = 0>$ at the input stream;
9 | | | **else**
10 | | | | **foreach** *edge from v to $w \in \mathcal{N}.adjacentEdges(v)$* **do**
11 | | | | | $s.push(w)$;
12 | | **else**
13 | | | insert $PrS = \; <Type = \text{"in - network"}, QueryID = q_i, AccessCounter = 0>$ at outgoing edge from v;

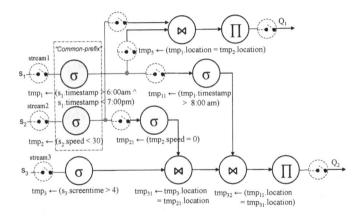

Fig. 6. Example of a privacy-aware shared-operators network

5.3   Example Execution of Privacy Switches

Figure 6 shows the same shared-operator network as that of the motivating example from Sect. 4 with the PrSs embedded in the network according to the proposed placement algorithm.

Assume that this shared-operator network is being executed by multiple users who initially have access granted to all three data streams, hence all users can view the output of both queries. From the figure, the dotted box highlights the "Common-prefix" zone of the operators shared by both executing queries. According to the switches placement Algorithm 2, the in-network privacy switches are placed right after those operators. Also at the output of both queries, terminal switches are placed, and at the front of the streams initial PrSs are placed.

In this particular example, if all users accessing $Q2$ lose access to the input streams feeding into this query, the PrSs will shut off six out of the ten operators in the network saving unnecessary processing and bandwidth. When any of these users gain their access back, the PrSs will resume operating all the nodes. This shows that the different switches orchestrated together are capable of enforcing the access control policies in shared-operator networks in a cost-effective way.

6 Evaluation

In the following sections we will present the details of the shared-operator networks simulator we implemented to evaluate the performance of our proposed privacy-aware shared-operator networks, as well as the experimental results.

6.1 Configurations and Experimental Setup

Generating synthetic shared-operator networks gave us control over the input parameters and the different scenarios of access control. The simulator takes as input the following parameters: *number of input streams, number of interleaved queries, number of users executing those queries, number of query operators,* and *degree of sharing.* The degree of sharing input parameter indicates the percentage of the query operators that will be included in the "common-prefix" of the network (i.e., how many query operators will be shared across the executing queries). An assumption is made that all shared operators are defined over the same window specifications which are omitted for simplicity of the analysis. Given these parameters the simulator generates shared-operator networks arranged as DAGs.

Some heuristics were enforced to assure the correctness and validity of the generated networks. For example, the "join-push-down" approach of operators was enforced (i.e., SELECT and shared SELECT nodes appear before JOIN and shared JOIN nodes). This is a common practice for queries optimizer to execute the SELECT operators first to filter out the tuples as early as possible and improve queries processing times. SELECT and PROJECT operators take one input stream and produce a filtered output stream, while JOIN operators take two different input streams and produce a single joined output stream.

After the random shared-operator networks are generated, our placement Algorithm 2 executes to identify the locations of the PrSs. The number of PrSs is dependent on the topology of the generated network. Finally, the users are randomly assigned to the query outputs of each generated graph. Figure 7 illustrates two randomly generated shared-operator networks by the simulator. Note that the final total number of query operators generated could be slightly higher than the initial input parameter.

In the experiments, the average processing time per tuple for each SELECT and PROJECT operator in the network was set to 0.1ms, and the average processing time per SP for each PrS to 0.1 ms as well. JOIN operators average processing time per tuple was set to 0.3 ms. Since these simulations are intended to compare

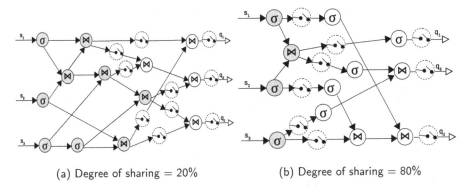

(a) Degree of sharing = 20%   (b) Degree of sharing = 80%

Fig. 7. Samples of randomly generated shared-operator networks [input streams = 3, queries = 3, total operators = 12]

and contrast the performance of different operator networks, these values were chosen as rough estimates and defined as constants throughout the execution of the networks. In reality, the processing times of operators would be different from one another. The upper bound on the processing time of each network to process 1000 input tuples was computed. Note that the reported times are upper bound since not every single operator in the network will process all 1000 tuples, as the input tuples get filtered by the SELECT operators, fewer tuples will be processed in the network. The arrival rate of SPs was set to be 100 tuples (i.e., for every 100 tuples, new SPs will show up in the input streams for each user in the system). The PrSs will process all SPs but will only take action for those SPs that match with the $SP.QID = PrS.QueryID$.

To better understand the security enforcement overheads in different shared-operator networks, the upper bound of the network execution times were compared for the following three cases: i) *no-sharing* – each user is executing a separate operator network for each submitted query (base case), ii) *shared without PrSs* – shared-operator network with only post-filtering applied, iii) *shared with PrSs* – shared-operator network with security enforcement using PrSs.

6.2 Experiment 1: Varying Degree of Sharing

These set of experiments attempt to answer the following question: *Q1: what are the security enforcement overheads in the shared-operator networks induced by the PrSs?*

To answer this question, the experiments computed the average processing times of 1000 input tuples for different degrees of sharing. Two different experiment settings were used, once for 3 interleaved queries with 15 operators and another for 5 interleaved queries with 25 operators. For each degree of sharing the network execution times were averaged for 10,000 randomly generated operator networks.

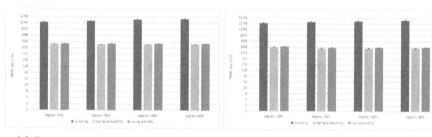

(a) Execution time for a network with 15 operators

(b) Execution time for a network with 25 operators

Fig. 8. Experiment 1 results

Figures 8a and 8b show the reported execution times (in log_2 ms) of the networks. The figures show that the average execution time of shared-operator network outperforms the non-shared networks with approximately 92%. This validates the benefits of executing shared-operator networks in DSMSs. The experiments show that the PrSs add negligible overheads to the network performance (an average of 0.5% increase in the execution time). This behavior is justified by the fact that PrSs execute infrequently (only when they encounter a new SPs in the streams that match the query id). The experiments also show that both the number of PrSs inserted in the networks by the placement algorithm and the execution times were insensitive to the degree of sharing.

6.3   Experiment 2: Varying Access Control

These experiments were designed to answer the following two questions: *Q2: how much cost savings in the networks can be achieved as users start losing access to queries?* and *Q3: how much does the overlap between queries affect the execution times as users start losing access to queries?*

To answer both questions, the experiments measured the execution times of the networks as users start losing access to query outputs. To cover all cases, all different possible combinations of access loss were examined. For each degree of sharing examined, the network execution times were averaged for 10,000 randomly generated shared-operator networks. For each generated network, the execution times were measured in the following scenarios: shared network without PrSs and only post-filtering, shared network with PrSs and full access to all queries and all possible combinations of queries' losses. Figure 9 shows the results for networks generated with 3 input streams and 3 interleaved queries with an average total of 20 operators. On average 11 PrSs were inserted in the generated graphs.

From Fig. 9, and consistent with the previous experiments, the difference in execution times between shared networks with and without PrSs was minimal. As the queries start losing access, the savings in the execution times were noticeable when compared to the cases of shared with only post-filtering of query

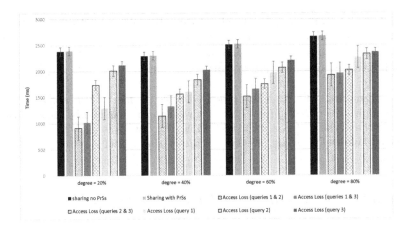

Fig. 9. Network execution time for varying degrees of sharing and access loss patterns

outputs and shared with PrSs and full access. The average execution time savings between the shared with PrSs and shared without PrSs was approximately 38% in the case of two out of three queries lose access, and 19% in the case of one query access loss.

Another observation is that PrSs improve the network performance when the queries have lower degrees of sharing (i.e., less common subexpressions). The reason is, with fewer shared-operators, the in-network switches can shut off more isolated (unshared) query operators in the case of total users loss of some query outputs. This behavior of the privacy-aware shared operator networks show that even with low degrees of sharing, the performance benefits would be even bigger when intermittent total access control loss is encountered.

7   Conclusions

In this paper we presented a novel solution for enforcing access control over shared-operator networks in DSMSs. The solution presented allows DSMSs to interleave the execution of multiple overlapping queries shared by multiple users while applying access control restrictions on a per user or group of users basis without disrupting the operation of the shared-operator networks. The solution introduces a new set of operators, Privacy Switches (PrS), that are capable of seamlessly configuring the network to allow or deny access to certain query results complying with the access control policies defined in the system. The experimental evaluations showed that the proposed technique induces minimal overheads on the shared-operator networks while achieving great gains in the network performance in the cases of intermittent access loss to some streams and queries. The technique proved to perform better in the case of total access loss with queries that have less common subexpressions, which shows greater benefits of the privacy-aware shared-operator networks even in lower degrees of sharing. A dynamically configurable shared-operator network saves not only time, but also bandwidth consumption, and several consequential monetary costs associated with configuring and executing shared-operator networks in DSMSs that could possibly be operating in cloud environments.

Acknowledgments. This work was produced while the first author was a PhD student at the University of Pittsburgh. This work was supported in part by the NSF award CNS–1253204 and the NIH award U01HL137159. The content is solely the responsibility of the authors and does not necessarily represent the official views of the NSF and NIH.

Appendix A Correctness of Privacy Switches

In this appendix we will present proof of correctness of the PrSs operation to ensure that the data streams privacy are enforced at all times. The proof will show that the PrSs will only allow tuples of a particular stream to be accessed by the users that are specified in the SPs, otherwise they will enforce denial-by-default.

Theorem 1 (PrSs Correctness). *During the execution of the PrSS as described by Algorithm 1, for any tuple t, PrS will allow the flow of t only if its preceding SP has a '+' access sign, otherwise PrS will block the flow of t.*

Proof. To prove this claim, the following must be asserted:

(i) terminal PrSs will only allow users specified by the SPs to access the tuples.
(ii) in-network and initial PrSs only allow tuples to flow through the network if there is at least one user that has access granted.

Note that the terminal PrSs are the switches that have the ultimate control of which users can access the tuples of a particular data stream, even if the initial and in-network PrSs allow all the tuples to flow through the network. As such, proving the privacy of a shared-operators network is only dependent on proving that assertion (i) is true. Yet, to prove that a shared-operators network not only denies access to the data streams to those users who are not allowed access, but also ensures that access is granted to those users who are allowed access, then both assertions (i) and (ii) need to be true.

For the base case, assume that $\exists$ authorization policy P that specifies that u_1 can access q_1 and SP is used to encode this policy and is injected in all data streams used in processing q_1. Let $t \in T$, where T is a set of tuples, be a tuple that belongs to the data stream used in processing q_1. There are two cases to be considered to assert both (i) and (ii):

1. SP arrives prior to tuple t,
2. tuple t arrives prior to SP.

Case 1: if $SP.q_1$ is '+', then all initial and in-network PrSs processing this SP will increment their $PrS.AccessCounter$ and allow the following data tuple t and $SP.q_1$ to reach to the terminal switches. Terminal switches will in turn add $SP.SRP.u_{id}$ to the list $PrS.U$ and open up the access channel for this user to allow tuple t to flow into query output.

If $SP.q_1$ is '−', then all initial and in-network PrSs will decrement their counters. If the counter value goes down to zero, this means this user was the last user to have access and the PrSs will not allow the tuples to flow to the output (total loss case). If the counter is greater than zero, then the tuples will flow to the terminal switches. For each terminal switch, if $SP.SRP.u_{id} \in PrS.U$, then this user will be removed from the list, and the access channel to this user will be blocked.

Case 2: tuple t will only flow to the channel assigned to user u_1 iff $u_1 \in PrS.U$. Since users are only added to the PrS users list and given access if an explicit SP with a '+' sign is encountered at time $SP.TS < ts_{access}$, then if t arrives prior to the SP, the denial-by-default will be enforced.

The above cases account for the possible scenarios of a set of tuples T and their equivalent SPs showing up in the data streams. By proving that both assertions (i) and (ii) are true, it is shown that Theorem 1 holds in the base case.

Observe that an argument similar to that used in the base case shows that the same behavior of PrSs would apply to all policies. Furthermore, the inductive hypothesis can be used to prove that the value of the $SP.Sign$ is in charge of activating or deactivating the users channels of the terminal PrSs. As such, only those tuples that are preceded with a positive SP sign will flow to the users specified by the SPs, and Theorem 1 holds for all policies.

References

1. Abadi, D.J., et al.: Aurora: a new model and architecture for data stream management. VLDB J. **12**, 120–139 (2003). https://doi.org/10.1007/s00778-003-0095-z
2. Anh, D.T.T., Datta, A.: StreamForce: outsourcing access control enforcement for stream data to the clouds. In: Proceedings of the 4th ACM Conference on Data and Application Security and Privacy, CODASPY 2014, pp. 13–24. ACM, New York (2014)
3. Arasu, A., Babu, S., Widom, J.: The CQL continuous query language: semantic foundations and query execution. VLDB J. **15**, 121–142 (2006). https://doi.org/10.1007/s00778-004-0147-z
4. Cangialosi, F.J., et al.: The design of the Borealis stream processing engine. In: Second Biennial Conference on Innovative Data Systems Research, CIDR 2005, January 2005
5. Carbone, P., Katsifodimos, A., Ewen, S., Markl, V., Haridi, S., Tzoumas, K.: Apache flink^{TM}: stream and batch processing in a single engine. IEEE Data Eng. Bull. **38**, 28–38 (2015)
6. Carminati, B., Ferrari, E., Tan, K.: Enforcing access control over data streams. In: Proceedings of the 12th ACM Symposium on Access Control Models and Technologies, SACMAT 2007, pp. 21–30. ACM, New York (2007)

7. Carminati, B., Ferrari, E., Tan, K.L.: Specifying access control policies on data streams. In: Kotagiri, R., Krishna, P.R., Mohania, M., Nantajeewarawat, E. (eds.) DASFAA 2007. LNCS, vol. 4443, pp. 410–421. Springer, Heidelberg (2007). https://doi.org/10.1007/978-3-540-71703-4_36

8. Çetintemel, U., et al.: The Aurora and Borealis stream processing engines. In: Garofalakis, M., Gehrke, J., Rastogi, R. (eds.) Data Stream Management. DSA, pp. 337–359. Springer, Heidelberg (2016). https://doi.org/10.1007/978-3-540-28608-0_17

9. Chen, C.M., Agrawal, H., Cochinwala, M., Rosenbluth, D.: Stream query processing for healthcare bio-sensor applications. In: Proceedings. 20th International Conference on Data Engineering, pp. 791–794, April 2004

10. Chen, J., DeWitt, D.J., Tian, F., Wang, Y.: NiagaraCQ: a scalable continuous query system for internet databases. In: Proceedings of the 2000 ACM SIGMOD International Conference on Management of Data, pp. 379–390. SIGMOD, ACM (2000)

11. Ferraiolo, D.F., Barkley, J.F., Kuhn, D.R.: A role-based access control model and reference implementation within a corporate intranet. ACM Trans. Inf. Syst. Secur. **2**, 34–64 (1999)

12. Hu, V.C., Kuhn, R., Ferraiolo, D.F., Voas, J.: Attribute-based access control. Computer **48**, 85–88 (2015)

13. Kim, J.W., Jang, B., Yoo, H.: Privacy-preserving aggregation of personal health data streams. PLOS ONE **13**, 1–15 (2018)

14. Lindner, W., Meier, J.: Securing the borealis data stream engine. In: 2006 10th International Database Engineering and Applications Symposium, IDEAS 2006, pp. 137–147, December 2006

15. Liu, X., Buyya, R.: D-Storm: dynamic resource-efficient scheduling of stream processing applications. In: 2017 IEEE 23rd International Conference on Parallel and Distributed Systems (ICPADS), pp. 485–492, December 2017

16. Nehme, R.V., Lim, H.S., Bertino, E.: Fence: continuous access control enforcement in dynamic data stream environments. In: Proceedings of the Third ACM Conference on Data and Application Security and Privacy, CODASPY 2013, pp. 243–254. ACM, New York (2013)

17. Nehme, R.V., Rundensteiner, E.A., Bertino, E.: A security punctuation framework for enforcing access control on streaming data. In: Proceedings of the 2008 IEEE 24th International Conference on Data Engineering, ICDE 2008, pp. 406–415. IEEE Computer Society, Washington, DC (2008). https://doi.org/10.1109/ICDE.2008.4497449

18. Ng, W.S., Wu, H., Wu, W., Xiang, S., Tan, K.L.: Privacy preservation in streaming data collection. In: 2012 IEEE 18th International Conference on Parallel and Distributed Systems, pp. 810–815, December 2012

19. Sandhu, R.S., Samarati, P.: Access control: principle and practice. IEEE Commun. Mag. **32**(9), 40–48 (1994)

20. Thoma, C., Lee, A., Labrinidis, A.: Behind enemy lines: exploring trusted data stream processing on untrusted systems. In: Proceedings of the Ninth ACM Conference on Data and Application Security and Privacy, CODASPY 2019, pp. 243–254. ACM, New York (2019)

21. Thoma, C., Lee, A.J., Labrinidis, A.: PolyStream: cryptographically enforced access controls for outsourced data stream processing. In: Proceedings of the 21st ACM on Symposium on Access Control Models and Technologies, SACMAT 2016, pp. 227–238. ACM, New York (2016)

Information Flow Security Certification for SPARK Programs

Sandip Ghosal and R. K. Shyamasundar[(⊠)]

Department of Computer Science and Engineering, Indian Institute of Technology,
Bombay, Mumbai 400076, India
sandipsmit@gmail.com, shyamasundar@gmail.com

Abstract. SPARK 2014 (SPARK hereafter) is a programming language designed for building highly-reliable applications where safety and security are key requirements. SPARK platform performs a rigorous data/information flow analysis to ensure the safety and reliability of a program. However, the flow analysis is oriented towards establishing functional correctness and does not analyze for flow security of the program. Thus, there is a need to augment the analysis that would enable us to certify SPARK programs for security. In this paper, we propose an analysis to find information flow leaks in a SPARK program using a *Dynamic Labelling* (DL) approach for multi-level security (MLS) programs and describe an effective algorithm for detecting information leaks in SPARK programs, including classes of *termination/progress-sensitive* computations. Further, we illustrate the application of our approach for overcoming information leaks through unsanitized sensitive data. We also show how SPARK can be extended for realizing MLS systems that invariably need *declassification* through the illustration of an application of the method for security analysis of Needham-Schroeder public-key protocol.

1 Introduction

SPARK [1] is a programming language built on Ada 2012. While the SPARK data flow analysis [4,5] primarily emphasizes on establishing functional correctness, the flow security aspect remains neglected. Thus, certifying a program for flow security [8] is crucial for building reliable and secure applications.

A security property, often referred to as *information-flow policy* (IFP), governs the flow security certification mechanisms. One of the widely used policies for security certification first advocated in [8] says: if there is information flow from object x to y, denoted by $x \rightarrow y$, then the flow is secure if $\lambda(x)$ *can-flow-to* $\lambda(y)$, where λ is a labelling function that maps subjects (stakeholders of a program in execution) and objects (variables, files) of a program to the respective security *label* or *class* which describe the confidentiality and integrity of program values. The security labels together form a security lattice. In this paper, we are concerned with algorithmic techniques for security certifications of SPARK programs that comply with the IFP over a security lattice.

© IFIP International Federation for Information Processing 2020
Published by Springer Nature Switzerland AG 2020
A. Singhal and J. Vaidya (Eds.): DBSec 2020, LNCS 12122, pp. 137–150, 2020.
https://doi.org/10.1007/978-3-030-49669-2_8

First, we highlight the security aspects of information flow and sanitization of sensitive data in SPARK programs following an assessment of proposed solutions in the literature.

1. Role of Implicit Flows: Two principle flows of information in a program are *direct* and *indirect* or *implicit* flows. A typical example of direct information flow is an explicit assignment of a secret value. Implicit flows arise when the control flow of a program is affected by secret values. Note that often secret information could be encoded in terms of differences in side effects of control flow. Such a property leads to various further classifications, such as termination-sensitive/insensitive or progress-sensitive/insensitive.

The work by Rafnsson *et al.* [17] was the first exploration towards the flow security in SPARK programs with the focus on termination-and progress-sensitive information leaks. We shall briefly describe the evidence of information leaks as shown in [17].

a. Termination-insensitive flow analysis in **SPARK** [17]:

A *termination-sensitive* flow analysis can track an instance that depends on the program termination. However, it is evident from the example shown in Table 1 that SPARK follows a *termination-insensitive* flow analysis. Note that the program outputs a character '!' depending on the termination of if block, which eventually terminates if the variable H is an odd number. If H is secret, then the program leaks one bit of sensitive information.

Table 1. SPARK program leaking information through a non-terminating loop.

```
procedure Leak (H:in out Byte) is
begin
  H:=H;
  if H mod 2 = 0 then
    while True loop
      H := H;
    end loop;
  end if;
  Write(Standard_Output,
    Character'Pos('!'));
end Leak;
```

Table 2. SPARK program leaking information progressively.

```
procedure Leak (H:in out Byte) is
  K: Byte := 0;
begin
  H:=H;
  while True loop
    Write(Standard_Output, K);
    if K >= H then
      while True loop
        H:=H;
      end loop;
    end if;
    K := K + 1;
  end loop;
end Leak;
```

b. Progress-insensitive flow analysis in **SPARK** [17]:

A *progress-sensitive* analysis can track the completion of an instance through the continuous progress of a program. The program shown in Table 2 outputs all the numbers up to H through an intermediate variable K, thus progressively reveals the sensitive information in H. The program passes through the SPARK examiner, proving the flow analysis is *progress-insensitive*.

The solution proposed in [17] identifies the terminating loops using *termination oracles* [14] and performs a graph transformation by introducing additional edges going out from potentially infinite loops to the end of the program. Therefore, it extends the dependency in the program and lets SPARK to perform dependency analysis on control flow graphs. While the approach avoids explicit exceptions, it needs to instrument the code from a global understanding, and further, there is no concrete feedback on the reasons for insecurity to the programmer. The main shortcomings of the above solutions are: (i) the transformations are not algorithmic (automatic), (ii) difficult to detect the issues of information leak. Nonetheless, the source-to-source transformation approach of [17] connects the theory of progress-sensitive non-interference with the practice, the SPARK data flow analysis together with the above approach is insufficient to enforce the classic notion of non-interference [6,11,20] while building MLS systems. Thus, it would be nice if an algorithmic strategy could be established that would enable us to overcome the above problems.

2. Sanitizing Data: Another aspect of security in SPARK, as highlighted by Chapman [7], concerns *sanitizing sensitive* local data in Ada-SPARK programs for building secure applications. The author elaborates potential leaks due to access to "unsanitized" sensitive temporary data, e.g., OS page files or core dump of a running process. For instance, in the simple decryption program shown in Table 3, the local variables N and D become sensitive and, if not sanitized, could leak secret information in S. Chapman demonstrates the issue of Ada language, where an attempt to sanitize sensitive data is suppressed by the compiler while performing optimization. In SPARK, the sanitization step is *ineffective* as it does not influence the final exported value. The discussion arises questions like:

How do we define 'sensitive'? What objects in the program are 'sensitive'? How are they identified?

The author prescribes one possible solution, i.e., adopting coding policies to sanitize sensitive local data in the Ada-SPARK project, e.g., use of **pragma Inspection_ Point**. Further, following the naming convention for the sensitive data, e.g., adding prefixes "Sensitive_", "_SAN" to the names of types, variables, would aid the programmer to handle it appropriately. Thus, it must be evident that there is a need to

Table 3. A simple decryption program written in SPARK.

```
procedure Decrypt(C: in Integer; S: in
      Private_Key; M: out Integer) is
   N,D:Integer;
begin
   N := Get_N(S);
   D := Get_D(S);
   M := (C**D) mod N;
   -- Sanitize N and D
   N := 0;
   D := 0;
end Decrypt;
```

build a succinct definition of "sensitive" data and provide an algorithmic analysis for the compiler/runtime monitor for appropriate treatment.

In this paper, we propose a single alternative solution to the above problems using a dynamic labelling algorithm [9,10] that not only helps to identify the sensitive local objects but also detects potential information leaks in SPARK programs, thus alleviate the burden of manual intervention in the source program. The automation receives a list of immutable security labels of global variables as input and generates mutable labels for the local variables while following the IFP throughout the computation. Primarily, objects sensitive to the outside world are considered as global, but the programmer may use her discretion to choose any variable as a global object.

Further, developing a secure application that involves objects with security labels from a multi-point general lattice often demands the need for *declassification*. We introduce the construct `Declassify` borrowing the notion of declassification from the security model RWFM [12,13] as an briefed in the later section.

The main contributions of our work are summarized below:

1. Propose an algorithmic solution for SPARK statements using information flow policies and establish its capability to detect program points that could plausibly leak information.
2. Illustrate the efficacy of our approach in detecting information leaks primarily through termination channels [19] or progress channels [3] and discuss the advantages, such as localizing possible leaking points, identifying sensitive objects automatically.
3. Introduce "Declassify" construct for SPARK programming language based on the model proposed in [12] and illustrated its usage through an application on a cryptographic protocol.

The rest of the paper is organized as follows. Section 2 provides the necessary background for dynamic labelling algorithm and RWFM flow security model. Section 3 presents a single alternative solution to overcome the shortcoming of SPARK flow analysis using security labels and dynamic labelling algorithm. Section 4 discusses the necessity of *declassification* as an extension in the SPARK language and illustrate the `Declassify` construct with an application of Needham-Schroeder (NS) public key protocol. Finally, implementation highlights are given in Sect. 5 followed by conclusions in Sect. 6.

2   Background

In this section, we briefly discuss the dynamic labelling algorithm and provide an overview of a recently proposed flow security model RWFM that is used for labelling subjects and objects and governing information flow transitions while developing an MLS system in SPARK.

2.1 Dynamic Labelling Algorithm (DL) [9, 10]

Let G and L be the sets of global and local variables of a program, and λ is a projection from subjects, objects, and program counter pc to its' respective security label from the lattice. Function var returns the set of variables appearing in expression e and SV, TV provide the set of source and target variables respectively for a given statement S. The algorithm DL takes three parameters as inputs: basic SPARK statements such as assignment, selection, iteration, or sequence denoted by S; the highest security label cl of the executing subject referred to as *clearance*; and a labelling function λ where the global variables are mapped to their given immutable labels. If all the local variables are successfully labelled, the algorithm returns a new map λ' otherwise flags a message

Table 4. Description of Algorithm DL for basic SPARK statements such as assignment, selection, iteration and sequence

1. S : null:: $SV(S)=\{\emptyset\}$; $TV(S)=\{\emptyset\}$; $DL(S, cl, \lambda)$: return λ	
2. S : x := e:: $SV(S)=var(e)$; $TV(S)=\{x\}$; $DL(S, cl, \lambda)$: $\quad tmp = \bigoplus_{v \in var(e) \cap G} \lambda(v)$ $\quad$ if $(tmp \not\leqslant cl)$ then $\quad\quad$ exit 'UNABLE TO LABEL' $\quad \lambda_1 = \lambda$ $\quad \lambda_1(pc) = \lambda(pc) \oplus tmp$ $\quad$ if $x \in L$: $\quad\quad \lambda_1(x) = \lambda(x) \oplus \lambda(pc) \oplus tmp$ $\quad\quad$ return λ_1 $\quad$ if $x \in G$: $\quad\quad$ if $\big([\lambda(pc) \oplus tmp \oplus cl] \leqslant \lambda(x)\big)$ then $\quad\quad\quad$ return λ_1 $\quad\quad$ else exit 'UNABLE TO LABEL'	**3. S :** if e then S_1[else S_2] end if:: $SV(S)=SV(S_1) \cup SV(S_2) \cup var(e)$; $TV(S)=TV(S_1) \cup TV(S_2)$ $DL(S, cl, \lambda)$: $\quad tmp = \bigoplus_{v \in var(e) \cap G} \lambda(v)$ $\quad$ if $(tmp \not\leqslant cl)$ then $\quad\quad$ exit 'UNABLE TO LABEL' $\quad \lambda' = \lambda$ $\quad \lambda'(pc) = \lambda(pc) \oplus tmp$ $\quad \lambda_1 = DL(S_1, cl, \lambda')$ $\quad \lambda_2 = DL(S_2, cl, \lambda')$ $\quad \lambda_3(pc) = \lambda_1(pc) \oplus \lambda_2(pc)$ $\quad \forall x \in L : \lambda_3(x) = \lambda_1(x) \oplus \lambda_2(x)$ $\quad$ return λ_3
4. S : while e then S_1 end loop:: $SV(S)=SV(S_1) \cup var(e)$; $TV(S)=TV(S_1)$; $DL(S, cl, \lambda)$: $\quad tmp = \bigoplus_{v \in var(e) \cap G} \lambda(v)$ $\quad$ if $(tmp \not\leqslant cl)$ then $\quad\quad$ exit 'UNABLE TO LABEL' $\quad \lambda_1 = \lambda$ $\quad \lambda_1(pc) = \lambda(pc) \oplus tmp$ $\quad \lambda_2 = DL(S_1, cl, \lambda_1)$ $\quad$ if $(\lambda_2 \neq \lambda_1)$ $\quad\quad \lambda_1 = \lambda_2$ $\quad\quad \lambda_2 = DL($while e then S_1 end loop, $\quad\quad\quad$ cl$, \lambda_1)$ $\quad$ return λ_2	**5. S :** $S_1; S_2;$:: $SV(S)=SV(S_1) \cup SV(S_2)$; $TV(S)=TV(S_1) \cup TV(S_2)$; $DL(S, cl, \lambda)$: $\quad$ return $DL(S_2, cl, DL(S_1, cl, \lambda))$; Here, problem of "insecurity" will be indicated by one of the recursive calls.

Note that "UNABLE TO LABEL" yields the control point where a certain object fails to satisfy the information flow policy.

"UNABLE TO LABEL" on detecting a possible flow leak. Note that, initially, the mutable labels of all the local variables, including pc are labelled as *public* ($\bot$). The algorithm DL for basic control statements of SPARK language is described in Table 4.

2.2   Readers-Writers Flow Model (RWFM) [12,13,15]: An overview

We provide a brief overview of the Readers-Writers Flow Model (RWFM) for information flow control.

Definition 1 (RWFM Label). *A RWFM label is a three-tuple (s, R, W) $(s, R, W \in$ set of principals/subjects $P)$, where s represents the owner of the information and policy, R denotes the set of readers allowed to read the information, and W identifies the set of writers who have influenced the information so far.*

Definition 2 (can-flow-to relation ($\leqslant$)). *Given any two RWFM labels $L_1 = (s_1, R_1, W_1)$ and $L_2 = (s_2, R_2, W_2)$, the can-flow-to relation is defined as:*

$$\frac{R_1 \supseteq R_2 \quad W_1 \subseteq W_2}{L_1 \leqslant L_2}$$

Definition 3 (Join and meet for RWFM Labels). *The join ($\oplus$) and meet ($\otimes$) of any two RWFM labels $L_1 = (s_1, R_1, W_1)$ and $L_2 = (s_2, R_2, W_2)$ are respectively defined as*

$$L_1 \oplus L_2 = (-, R_1 \cap R_2, W_1 \cup W_2) \quad L_1 \otimes L_2 = (-, R_1 \cup R_2, W_1 \cap W_2)$$

The set of RWFM labels $SC = P \times 2^P \times 2^P$ forms a bounded lattice $(SC, \leqslant, \oplus, \otimes, \top, \bot)$, where $(SC, \leqslant)$ is a partially ordered set and $\top = (-, \emptyset, P)$, and $\bot = (-, P, \emptyset)$ are respectively the maximum and minimum elements.

Definition 4 (Declassification in RWFM). *The declassification of an object o from its current label (s_2, R_2, W_2) to (s_3, R_3, W_3) as performed by the subject s with label (s_1, R_1, W_1) is defined as*

$$\frac{s \in R_2 \quad s_1 = s_2 = s_3 \quad R_1 = R_2 \quad W_1 = W_2 = W_3 \quad R_2 \subseteq R_3}{(W_1 = \{s_1\} \vee (R_3 - R_2 \subseteq W_2))}{(s_2, R_2, W_2) \text{ may be declassified to } (s_3, R_3, W_3)}$$

This says, *the owner of an object can declassify the content to a subject(s) only if the owner is the sole writer of the information or that subject(s) had influenced the information earlier.*

3   Our Approach Using Dynamic Labelling Algorithm

Our approach relies on the application of dynamic labelling for the SPARK program. We first extend the set of rules given earlier with the labelling rules for the SPARK procedures as described below.

Extended Labelling Algorithm (DL^+) for SPARK Procedure:

Consider a procedure call, say $p(a_1, \ldots, a_m; b_1, \ldots, b_n)$ where, $a_1, \ldots, a_m$ are the actual input arguments and $b_1, \ldots, b_n$ are the actual input/output arguments corresponding to the formal input parameters (mode IN) $x_1, \ldots, x_m$ and formal input/output parameters (mode OUT or IN OUT) $y_1, \ldots, y_n$. The dynamic labelling algorithm for SPARK procedure call is shown in Table 5. Once given a procedure call, the DL algorithm first computes the procedure body before returning the control to the caller. The algorithm adheres to the parameters passing mechanisms while transferring the control. Following are the operations the algorithm performs at entry & exit points of the procedure: (i) at the entry point it initializes the labels of formal input parameters with the corresponding labels of the actual input arguments; (ii) creates an instance pc local to the procedure; (iii) initializes the pc and local variables with the mutable label $\bot$; (iv) evaluates the procedure body; and (v) finally resets the pc label on exiting from the procedure and returns the final labels to the caller.

Note that, the intrinsic property of the labelling algorithm automatically enforces the required security constraints for a procedure call given in [18].

With the extended dynamic labelling algorithm for SPARK statements are in place (Tables 4, 5), certifying information flow security for a given SPARK program consists of the following steps:

Table 5. DL algorithm for a procedure call.

6. $S : p(a_1, \ldots, a_m; b_1, \ldots, b_n) ::$
$DL(S, \text{cl}, \lambda):$
//Initialize the label of the parameters
$\lambda' = \lambda_{\text{init}}$
forall $i \in 1 \ldots m, \lambda'(x_i) = \lambda(a_i)$
// Evaluate the body of the procedure
$\lambda_1 = DL(p - body, cl, \lambda')$
return λ_1

1. Initialize the labels of global variables for the given SPARK program.
2. Apply the labelling algorithm DL^+, for the SPARK program.
3. If the labelling succeeds, then the program has no information leak; if the labelling algorithm outputs the message "UNABLE TO LABEL" it implies there is a possibility of information leak.

Illustration:

First, we apply the algorithm to the programs shown in Table 1, 2, and demonstrate solutions to issues 1(a)–(b) of Sect. 1. Consider H and Standard_Output are the global objects initialized with the immutable labels $\underline{H}$ and $\bot$ (i.e., public) respectively, such that information *cannot flow* from H to Standard_Output, i.e., $\lambda(H) = \underline{H} \not\leq \lambda(Standard\_Output) = \bot$. Also, we assume that the executing subject has the clearance label $\underline{H}$. Then the derived labels of local variables as well as *program counter* (pc) are shown in the Tables 6, 7.

(i) Detecting *termination-sensitive* information leaks:

In Table 6, it can be observed that since pc reads the variable H its label is raised to $\underline{H}$. Now execution of the procedure call Write(Standard_Output, Character'Pos('!')) causes a flow from pc to Standard_Output, therefore, the label of Standard_Output must be at least equal to the label of pc. Since the

Table 6. SPARK program leaking information through a non-terminating loop. Clearance: $cl = \underline{H}$. Initial labels of global objects: $\lambda(H) = \underline{H}$, $\lambda(Standard\_Output) = \bot$.

Program	pc Label
`procedure Leak (`H`:in out Byte) is`	
`begin`	$\bot$
$\quad H$`:=`H`;`	$\underline{H}$
`  if `H` mod `$2 = 0$` then`	
`    while True loop`	
`      `$H := H$`;`	
`    end loop;`	
`  end if;`	$\underline{H}$
`  Write(Standard_Output,`	
`      Character'Pos('!'));`	`UNABLE TO LABEL`
`end Leak;`	

Table 7. SPARK program leaking information progressively. Clearance: $cl = \underline{H}$. Initial labels of global objects: $\lambda(H) = \underline{H}$, $\lambda(Standard\_Output) = \bot$.

Program	Derived Labels
`procedure Leak (`H`:in out Byte) is`	
`  `K`: Byte := 0;`	$\underline{K} = \bot$
`begin`	$pc = \bot$
`  `$H := H$`;`	$\underline{pc} = \underline{H}$
`  while True loop`	
`    Write(Standard_Output, `K`);`	`UNABLE TO LABEL`
`    if `$K >= H$` then`	
`      while True loop`	
`        `$H := H$`;`	
`      end loop;`	
`    end if;`	
`    `$K := K + 1$`;`	
`  end loop;`	
`end Leak;`	

label of `Standard_Output` is immutable, the algorithm fails to update the label, hence exits by throwing the message "`UNABLE TO LABEL`". The point of failure detects the location and objects responsible for flow policy violation.

(ii) Detecting *progress-sensitive* information leaks:
Similarly, since the procedure `Write(Standard_Output, K)` causes information flow from both K and pc to `Standard_Output` it needs to satisfy the constraint $\lambda(K) \oplus \lambda(PC) \leqslant \lambda(Standard\_Output)$. But, the algorithm fails to continue as $\lambda(pc) \nleqslant \bot$.

(iii) Identifying sensitive data for sanitization:

Here, we shall address the questions and solution related to handling "sensitive" data discussed in Sect. 1. Note that the labelling algorithm takes the initial classification of sensitive/non-sensitive data and transfer the sensitivity to local variables automatically during computation. Since the algorithm generates the labels of local variables from the given set of sensitive global variables, any attempt to access unsanitized sensitive local objects must satisfy the IFP, thus restrict access as required.

Consider the program shown in Table 3 where global objects C, S and M are sensitive data with the label given $\underline{H}$. Then applying the dynamic labelling algorithm would compute the labels of local variables N and D as $\underline{H}$ transferring the sensitivity label of global variables. Thus any attempt to read the sensitive data by a less-sensitive user (or process) would indicate misuse of information flow.

Remarks: One can write statements like $H = H$ followed by $L = L$ (H and L are global and denote a *high* and *low* variables respectively) somewhere in the program. In such cases, the platform would indicate "UNABLE TO LABEL" as it fails to satisfy the constraint $\underline{H} \oplus \underline{pc} \leqslant \underline{L}$. We ignore such corner cases and leave the onus of correcting the code on the programmer.

3.1 Comparison with Rafnsson *et al.* [17] and SPARK Analysis

Table 8 provides a comparison of DL^+ with the SPARK analysis and approach proposed in [17] in terms of common objectives that are generally sought in the information flow analysis tools. From the comparison it is evident that our approach subsumes the advantages of other two approaches.

Table 8. Comparison of DL^+ with SPARK analysis and approach proposed in [17]

Objectives	SPARK flow analysis	Approach by [17]	DL^+ algorithm
Termination-and progress-sensitive flow analysis	✗	✓	✓
Recurring backward information flow analysis in loop statements	✓	✗	✓
Precisely localize the program point violating flow policy	✗	✗	✓
Identify unauthorized access to unsanitized sensitive data	✗	✗	✓

4   Need of Declassification in MLS Systems

Quite often, in a decentralized labelling environment, it is required to relax the confidentiality level and reveal some level of information to specific stakeholders for the successful completion of the transaction. For this purpose, the notion of *Declassification* or *Downgrading* needs to be captured either implicitly or explicitly. We shall understand the context from the classic password update problem shown in Table 9.

Consider a function `Password_Update` that updates password database by a new password (*new_pwd*) only if the guess password (*guess_pwd*) provided by the user matches with the old password and updates the result accordingly. Note that there is a need to convey the *result* as an acceptance of the new password so that the user can use it further.

Table 9 shows that the *result* becomes sensitive data by the time the function returns its value. In the context of the MLS system, passing this sensitive data (i.e., *result*) to a less-sensitive entity (i.e., user) may violate the information flow policy. Therefore, it demands controlled declassification. There are two possibilities for introducing declassification at the point of returning the value: (i) Have an assertion that ensures declassification explicitly, or (ii) Perform declassification implicitly at the function return.

Table 9. Labelling password update program using DL. Initial labels of global variables: $pwd\_db = \underline{a} \oplus \underline{b}$, $guess\_pwd = new\_pwd = \underline{b}$. *result* is a local variable and $cl = \underline{a} \oplus \underline{b}$.

Program	Derived Labels
`function Password_Update(`*pwd_db*`,`*guess_pwd*`,`*new_pwd*`: Boolean)`	
`return Boolean is`	
`begin`	$pc = \bot$
`if` *pwd_db* $=$ *guess_pwd* `then`	$pc = \underline{a} \oplus \underline{b}$
pwd_db $:=$ *new_pwd*;	$pc = \underline{a} \oplus \underline{b}$
result $:= True$;	$result = \underline{a} \oplus \underline{b}$
`else`	
result $:= False$;	
`end if;`	
`return result;`	$result = \underline{a} \oplus \underline{b}$
`end Password_Update;`	

Declassification in SPARK: We adopt an explicit declassification mechanism for SPARK. The programmer may localize the program point that needs a declassification and place the construct `Declassify` to add specific readers. However, the addition needs to be robust as otherwise, the declassification may appear to be a mere discretionary that would have serious consequences in a decentralized model. For this reason, we shall borrow the "Declassification" rule from the RWFM model [12] as briefed in the Sect. 2.2.

Consider $p, p_1, \ldots$ range over the set of principals P, and x ranges over the set of objects/variables. Functions A, R and W have the form $f : L \to P$ which map to owner, readers and writers fields respectively for a given security label in the lattice L. Now let us assume principal p executes the statement `Declassify(x,` $\{p_1, \ldots, p_n\})$ to add $p_1, \ldots, p_n$ into the readers set of a variable x. Then we define the algorithm DL^+ for the `Declassify` statement as below:

$\mathbf{S} : \mathrm{DL}(\texttt{Declassify}(\mathbf{x}, \{\mathbf{p_1}, \ldots, \mathbf{p_n}\}), \mathbf{cl}, \lambda) ::$
$\mathrm{DL}(S, cl, \lambda) :$
  if $(\lambda(x) \nleq cl)$ then
    exit 'UNABLE TO LABEL'
  if $x \in G$ and $\lambda(pc) \nleq \lambda(x)$:
    exit 'UNABLE TO LABEL'
  $\lambda_1 = \lambda$
  $tmp = \lambda(pc) \oplus \lambda(x)$
  $\lambda_1(pc) = tmp$
  if $A(\lambda(tmp)) = \{p\}$ and $(W(\lambda(tmp)) = \{p\}$ or $\{p_1, \ldots, p_n\} \subseteq W(\lambda(tmp)))$:
    $R(\lambda_1(x)) = R(\lambda(tmp)) \cup \{p_1, \ldots, p_n\}$
    return λ_1
  else
    exit 'UNABLE TO LABEL'

A Look at the Fragment of N-S Public-Key Protocol [16]:

Table 10 shows an abstract program in SPARK demonstrating the N-S public-key protocol. The global variables are as follows: Aid represents the identity of the subject A; Na and Nb denote the fresh nonces created by the subject A and B respectively; Pub_a and Pub_b represent individual *public-key* of subjects A and B; Pri_a and Pri_b denote the *private-key* of A and B respectively. Initially, the local variables are readable by all the stakeholders (denoted by '*'), and nobody has influenced at this point. The functions `Encrypt`, `Decrypt` are executed by each of the subject A and B with the clearance level $\underline{a}$ and $\underline{b}$ respectively. Note that the program is self-explanatory, with the step numbers given in the comments depict the execution flow. Further, the generated labels for each variable are shown in the superscript.

A creates Pri_a that is accessible to A only, therefore labelled as $(A, \{A\}, \{A\})$. Similarly, Pri_b obtains a label $(B, \{B\}, \{B\})$. Further, A and B create the nonces Na, Nb respectively, that are readable by both the subjects, hence labelled as $(A, \{A, B\}, \{A\})$, $(B, \{A, B\}, \{B\})$. The public keys and identities of A and B are given identical labels as Na and Nb respectively. The clearance labels of the subjects A, B executing the programs are given as $\underline{a} = (A, \{A\}, \{A, B, S\})$ and $\underline{b} = (B, \{B\}, \{A, B, S\})$ respectively.

Note that the encrypted message, at step 2.2 obtains a label inaccessible to A, therefore, explicitly declassified by B so that A can decrypt the message for further use. Similarly, A also performs a declassification at step 3.3 so that B can access the data.

Table 10. A prototype of a program for N-S public-key protocol [16]

Program	Derived Labels
`procedure NS_Protocol_A(- - list of parameters) is`	
`- - Declarations of local objects` Ma	$Ma^{(A,\{*\},\{\})}$
`begin`	$pc^{(S,\{*\},\{S\})}$
`- - 1) A encrypts` $Na,\ Aid$ `using B's key` Pub_b	$pc^{(S,\{A,B\},\{A,B,S\})}$
Ma`:=Encrypt(`Aid,Na,Pub_b`);`	$Ma^{(A,\{A,B\},\{A,B,S\})}$
`- - 3.1) A decrypts` Mb `using A's key` Pri_a	$pc^{(S,\{A\},\{A,B,S\})}$
Ma`:=Decrypt(`Mb,Pri_a`);`	$Ma^{(A,\{A\},\{A,B,S\})}$
`- - 3.2) A encrypts` $Na,\ Nb$ `using B's key` Pub_b	$pc^{(S,\{A\},\{A,B,S\})}$
Ma`:=Encrypt(`Na,Nb,Pub_b`);`	$Ma^{(A,\{A\},\{A,B,S\})}$
`- - 3.3) A declassifies` Ma	$pc^{(S,\{A\},\{A,B,S\})}$
`Declassify(`$Ma,\{B\}$`)`	$Ma^{(A,\{A,B\},\{A,B,S\})}$
`end NS_Protocol_A;`	

Program	Derived Labels
`procedure NS_Protocol_B(- - list of parameters) is`	
`- - Declarations of local objects` Mb	$Mb^{(B,\{*\},\{\})}$
`begin`	$pc^{(S,\{*\},\{S\})}$
`- - 2.1) B decrypts` Ma `using B's key` Pri_b	$pc^{(S,\{B\},\{A,B,S\})}$
Mb`:=Decrypt(`Ma,Pri_b`);`	$Mb^{(B,\{B\},\{A,B,S\})}$
`- - 2.2) B encrypts` $Na,\ Nb$ `using A's key` Pub_a	$pc^{(S,\{B\},\{A,B,S\})}$
Mb`:=Encrypt(`Na,Nb,Pub_a`);`	$Mb^{(B,\{B\},\{A,B,S\})}$
`- - 2.3) B declassifies` Mb	$pc^{(S,\{B\},\{A,B,S\})}$
`Declassify(`$Mb,\{A\}$`)`	$Mb^{(B,\{A,B\},\{A,B,S\})}$
`- - 4) B decrypts` Ma `using B's key` Pri_b	$pc^{(S,\{B\},\{A,B,S\})}$
Mb`:=Decrypt(`Ma,Pri_b`);`	$Mb^{(B,\{B\},\{A,B,S\})}$
`end NS_Protocol_B;`	

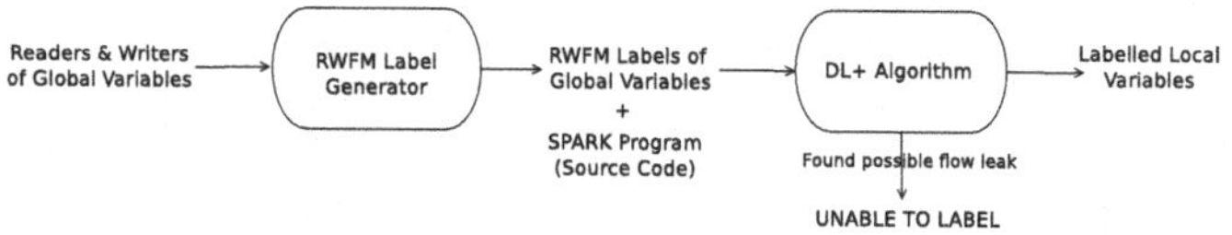

Fig. 1. A schematic diagram of our implementation.

It follows from the above illustrations that declassification for MLS is essential, and the DL algorithm, along with the RWFM model, ensures appropriate automatic labelling to ensure security properties.

5   Implementation of DL$^+$ for SPARK

The implementation of our approach first generates RWFM labels for the global variables of a SPARK program from the given readers and writers set of respective variables. Once the labels are generated, the set of global variables annotated with the corresponding RWFM labels and the SPARK program are given as input to the dynamic labelling algorithm. The algorithm either outputs the labels of all the intermediate variables or throws the message "UNABLE TO LABEL" in the presence of possible flow leaks. Figure 1 presents a schematic diagram of the implementation. We have analyzed the programs discussed in this paper and tested in a security workbench for Python language under development using the dynamic labelling approach.

6   Conclusions

In this paper, we have illustrated how an extended form of dynamic labelling algorithm integrated with RWFM provides an effective platform for flow security certification of SPARK programs, including termination- and progress-sensitive flows. The approach enables us to use an automatic compile-time labelling algorithm for data that aids in detecting information leaks due to termination and progress sensitivity, and unsanitized data. Also, the programmer gets feedback on the reasons for the misuse of information at the specific program point, enables him to refine the program only to realize flow security. These features add to the usability of the program. The approach provides a natural stepping stone for direct/implicit introduction of declassification for programming MLS systems in SPARK, thus preserve end-to-end confidentiality properties. So far, we have experimented on these aspects on our security workbench developed for Python programs. One can further develop an axiomatic proof system that follows naturally on similar lines as proposed in [2,18]. One of the distinct advantages of our approach is keeping the SPARK analysis and security analysis orthogonal – thus, enabling technology adaptation easily to the SPARK platform.

References

1. Spark 2014. http://www.spark-2014.org/about
2. Andrews, G.R., Reitman, R.P.: An axiomatic approach to information flow in programs. ACM Trans. Program. Lang. Syst. (TOPLAS) **2**(1), 56–76 (1980)
3. Askarov, A., Hunt, S., Sabelfeld, A., Sands, D.: Termination-insensitive noninterference leaks more than just a bit. In: Jajodia, S., Lopez, J. (eds.) ESORICS 2008. LNCS, vol. 5283, pp. 333–348. Springer, Heidelberg (2008). https://doi.org/10.1007/978-3-540-88313-5_22
4. Barnes, J.G.P.: High Integrity Software: The Spark Approach to Safety and Security. Pearson Education, London (2003)
5. Bergeretti, J.F., Carré, B.A.: Information-flow and data-flow analysis of while-programs. ACM Trans. Program. Lang. Syst. (TOPLAS) **7**(1), 37–61 (1985)
6. Boudol, G.: On typing information flow. In: Van Hung, D., Wirsing, M. (eds.) ICTAC 2005. LNCS, vol. 3722, pp. 366–380. Springer, Heidelberg (2005). https://doi.org/10.1007/11560647_24
7. Chapman, R.: Sanitizing sensitive data: how to get it right (or at least less wrong...). In: Blieberger, J., Bader, M. (eds.) Ada-Europe 2017. LNCS, vol. 10300, pp. 37–52. Springer, Cham (2017). https://doi.org/10.1007/978-3-319-60588-3_3

8. Denning, D.E., Denning, P.J.: Certification of programs for secure information flow. CACM **20**(7), 504–513 (1977)
9. Ghosal, S., Shyamasundar, R.K., Kumar, N.V.N.: Static security certification of programs via dynamic labelling. In: Proceedings of the 15th International Joint Conference on e-Business and Telecommunications, ICETE 2018 - Volume 2: SECRYPT, Porto, Portugal, 26–28 July 2018, pp. 400–411 (2018)
10. Ghosal, S., Shyamasundar, R.K., Narendra Kumar, N.V.: Compile-time security certification of imperative programming languages. In: Obaidat, M.S. (ed.) ICETE 2018. CCIS, vol. 1118, pp. 159–182. Springer, Cham (2019). https://doi.org/10. 1007/978-3-030-34866-3_8
11. Goguen, J.A., Meseguer, J.: Security policies and security models. In: IEEE Symposium on SP, p. 11 (1982)
12. Kumar, N.V.N., Shyamasundar, R.K.: Realizing purpose-based privacy policies succinctly via information-flow labels. In: IEEE 4th International Conference on Big Data and Cloud Computing (BdCloud), pp. 753–760 (2014)
13. Kumar, N.V.N., Shyamasundar, R.K.: A complete generative label model for lattice-based access control models. In: Cimatti, A., Sirjani, M. (eds.) SEFM 2017. LNCS, vol. 10469, pp. 35–53. Springer, Cham (2017). https://doi.org/10.1007/978-3-319-66197-1_3
14. Moore, S., Askarov, A., Chong, S.: Precise enforcement of progress-sensitive security. In: Proceedings of the 2012 ACM Conference on Computer and Communications Security, pp. 881–893. ACM (2012)
15. Narendra Kumar, N., Shyamasundar, R.: Poster: dynamic labelling for analyzing security protocols. In: Proceedings of the 22nd ACM SIGSAC Conference on Computer and Communications Security, pp. 1665–1667. ACM (2015)
16. Needham, R.M., Schroeder, M.D.: Using encryption for authentication in large networks of computers. Commun. ACM **21**(12), 993–999 (1978)
17. Rafnsson, W., Garg, D., Sabelfeld, A.: Progress-sensitive security for SPARK. In: Caballero, J., Bodden, E., Athanasopoulos, E. (eds.) ESSoS 2016. LNCS, vol. 9639, pp. 20–37. Springer, Cham (2016). https://doi.org/10.1007/978-3-319-30806-7_2
18. Robling Denning, D.E.: Cryptography and Data Security. Addison-Wesley Longman Publishing Co., Boston (1982)
19. Volpano, D., Smith, G.: Eliminating covert flows with minimum typings. In: Proceedings 10th Computer Security Foundations Workshop. pp. 156–168. IEEE (1997)
20. Volpano, D.M., Irvine, C.E., Smith, G.: A sound type system for secure flow analysis. J. Comput. Secur. **4**(2/3), 167–188 (1996)

Privacy-Preserving Computation

Provably Privacy-Preserving Distributed Data Aggregation in Smart Grids

Marius Stübs[1]([✉]), Tobias Mueller[1], Kai Bavendiek[2], Manuel Loesch[3], Sibylle Schupp[2], and Hannes Federrath[1]

[1] University of Hamburg, Hamburg, Germany
`{stuebs,mueller,federrath}@informatik.uni-hamburg.de`
[2] Hamburg University of Technology, Hamburg, Germany
`{kai.bavendiek,schupp}@tuhh.de`
[3] FZI Research Center for Information Technology, Karlsruhe, Germany
`loesch@fzi.de`

Abstract. The digitalization of power systems leads to a significant increase of energy consumers and generators with communication capabilities. Using data of such devices allows for a more efficient grid operation, e.g., by improving the balancing of power demand and supply. Fog Computing is a paradigm that enables efficient aggregation and processing of the measurements provided by energy consumers and generators. However, the introduction of these techniques is hindered by missing trust in the data protection, especially for personal-related data such as electric consumption. To resolve this conflict, we propose a privacy-preserving concept for the hierarchical aggregation of distributed data based on additive secret-sharing. To increase the trust towards the system, we model the concept and provide a formal proof of its confidentiality properties. We discuss the attacker models of colluding and non-colluding adversaries on the data flow and show how our scheme mitigates these attacks.

Keywords: Smart grid security · Smart metering · Formal model · Automated proof · Additive secret sharing · Distributed and decentralized security

1 Introduction

The electricity consumption of private households is usually not monitored nor managed in real-time. Traditionally, the power meter aggregates the electricity flow over the year and the aggregated value is only read for billing. However, the continuing increase in the share of renewable energies will require small-scale consumers and producers to actively participate in the demand-supply matching process. In order to gain more insight in the power flows within their grids, grid operators have strong interests in obtaining additional measurements from their customers. Power suppliers also want to allow their customers to benefit from

© IFIP International Federation for Information Processing 2020
Published by Springer Nature Switzerland AG 2020
A. Singhal and J. Vaidya (Eds.): DBSec 2020, LNCS 12122, pp. 153–173, 2020.
https://doi.org/10.1007/978-3-030-49669-2_9

price fluctuations at wholesale electricity markets. The roll-out of smart meters sets the foundation for Smart Grid services such as selective data aggregation and distributed power balancing [48]. For the grid operators, an important use case is power system state estimation, where measurements from different sources are aggregated to provide a more precise overview of the respective distribution grid.

In the context of Smart Grid, privacy is a major concern for consumers and prosumers [37]. Depending on the precision of the measurement data, researchers were even able to distinguish between TV channels and thereby identify the movie that was being displayed on a specific type of home TV screens [1]. This can also reveal other personal information and daily routines, such as how many inhabitants are home and when they leave or return. In Europe, the legislator demands data to be processed in ways that have been designed to respect the privacy of the users ("Privacy by Design and Default") [24, §25]. Whether households agree to participate in local market schemes or choose to demand cloud-based Smart Grid services therefore heavily depends on the perception of these services as serious and trustworthy. One way to increase the plausibility and transparency of cloud-based applications is to incorporate security measures already in an early stage and explain as well as verify these measures. This is where formal modeling and automated proofs come into play to back the security-related claims of the service providers.

1.1 Fog Computing in Power Grids

In power grids, the control of consumers and generators can be hierarchically aggregated for provisioning of smart grid services at different grid levels. Smart grid services are, e.g., power adjustments required in the demand-supply matching process. Technically, they are realized by Energy Management Systems (EMSs). The aggregation of control options and data allows for improved decisions as further information such as the grid structure can be considered at higher aggregation levels.

At the lowest aggregation level, Nano Grids can be recognized. Examples for Nano Grids are buildings with an EMS that locally processes data and balances power demand and supply within the building. They also may provide grid services and data to external Smart Grid Service Providers or higher-level aggregators. Nano Grids are always dependent on the connection to the main grid [39]. At a higher aggregation level Micro Grids can be recognized. Micro Grids are often defined to be self-sufficient in the sense that they can support islanding and that they, in case of emergency, can encapsulate themselves from the higher-level distribution grid. Examples for Micro Grids are districts with an EMS that processes data of multiple buildings for balancing the district's power demand and supply. Control options and data provided by multiple Micro Grids can be aggregated by an EMS at the level of the corresponding distribution grid which is operated by a Distribution System Operator (DSO). Finally, control options and data of multiple distribution grids can be aggregated by an EMS on the level of the transmission grid which is operated by a Transmission System

Operator (TSO). EMSs at different aggregation levels allow for different smart grid services. In particular DSOs and TSOs are highly regulated regarding the smart grid services they have to provide. DSOs are responsible for voltage control and TSOs are responsible for frequency control.

The hierarchical structure of Fog Computing is visualized in Fig. 1. It fits well to the structure of electric grids, especially when extending the fog node layer to a multi-layer architecture. In this paper we propose to extend previous approaches that aggregate values in Fog nodes and to implement a hierarchical aggregation scheme for sensor data that resembles the structure of the power lines. Aggregated sensor data (such as aggregated power values of multiple districts within a distribution grid) set the foundation for the realization of Smart Grid services that are ensuring grid stability.

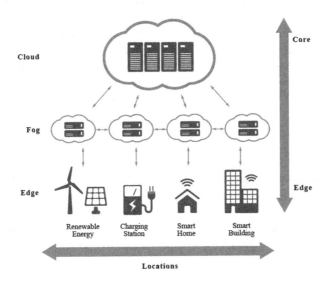

Fig. 1. The edge computing schematic.

1.2 Smart Metering and Data Security

In order to facilitate the integration of fluctuating renewable energy resources and to improve the demand-supply matching, the European Union directive 2009/72/EG requires member states to install smart metering infrastructures. As a consequence, it can be expected that a large share of households will deploy EMSs in the near future [48]. In this context, Smart Meter Gateways (SMGWs) provide a communication link between Nano Grids such as Smart Buildings and external parties. This communication link offers access to smart meter data and hence sets the foundation for the provisioning of grid services to Smart Grid Service Providers or higher-level aggregators.

The aggregation of data is a security critical function that needs to maintain the users' privacy by keeping the data as confidential as possible. Data about electricity consumption contains information about the user's habits. The more fine-grained the data, the better can the attacker infer details about the subject. Not only has it been shown that it is possible to detect the appliances a consumer is using [33], it is also possible to infer what TV program the consumer is watching [25]. The aggregation of data must thus be private in that the parties involved learn as little as possible.

1.3 Data Flow Modeling and Automated Proofs

Several approaches exist to show that a system works as intended. Testing is a well known technique, which, however, cannot demonstrate the absence but only the presence of errors. Formal methods on the other hand follow another approach by formalizing the system in way such that certain properties can be proven. One example of a formal method is model checking where a formal model is verified to follow a certain specification. The specification can be expressed using formal properties. To actually verify formal properties of a system, one has to make a formal description of the system. The complexity of real-life systems might be neither beneficial nor necessary for the verification of certain properties. Therefore, a formal model can be a good abstraction of, for instance, the data flow of a system.

1.4 Structure of the Paper

Section 2 comprises a comparative review of related work. In Sect. 3 the fundamental design decisions and goals are elaborated. The general data flow privacy validation scheme is described in Sect. 4. The concept of hierarchical data aggregation is elaborated in Sect. 5 and is then evaluated in the security discussion in Sect. 6. We conclude the paper with a short summary in Sect. 7.

2 Related Work

The proposed concept combines two areas of research, namely Fog Computing based privacy-preserving data aggregation and modeling of privacy-respecting data flows. In this section, we present the work related to each field.

The transition to smart metering and the Smart Grid evoked a lively scientific discussion about the impacts on privacy the transition entails [5,41,47]. With the discussion, several approaches, mitigations, and solutions have been proposed ranging from adding noise to the actual usage pattern to make analysis harder [31] to privacy-preserving data aggregation techniques to be used in Smart Grids [19,20]. A different approach on private data protection is using batteries to add noise to hide usage pattern [31]. Over the course of the last decade, the use of secret-sharing, additive or otherwise, for aggregating smart meter readings has been proposed [12,15,35], as have other privacy preserving mechanisms [21,29], such as ensuring ϵ-differential private aggregation [8,18].

Due to the recent interest on Cloud and Fog Computing, several publications (e.g. [4,16,42–44]) that apply cloud-based solutions to deal with the data explosion challenge in a Smart Grid. Especially when it comes to reducing the communication bandwidth between the smart meter and cloud in cloud computing, regional [45] or hierarchical [46] aggregation schemes based on Fog Computing are still not fully researched. Moreover, data security and privacy are also critical issues when sensitive smart meter data is aggregated in only partially trusted environments such as Fog nodes and cloud applications.

In the field of privacy-respecting data flow verification different approaches exist to model data flow and verify privacy properties. A survey paper by Gürses, Troncoso, and Diaz shows different privacy properties and case studies including homomorphic encryption in an automated toll pricing system [26]. A Smart Grid case study with focus on smart metering is described in [17]. It has the same research question but makes a distinction between accountable and private readings. Application-specific approaches range from e-government [28,30] over e-healthcare [32,36] and medical registers [10] to cloud computing [11,49]. Approaches based on the applied pi-calculus [6,13,34] are popular for protocol-oriented applications with focus on data integrity (often in e-voting systems). ProVerif is one of the few tools in this field, which implements a typed version of the applied pi-calculus. Another category of formal methods are approaches based on type systems [22,23,38]. These papers usually aim at achieving differential privacy by using typing rules. Other approaches, like this paper, base their modeling on software architectures. Some of these employ modal logics like modified epistemic logic [2,3,9,27] or temporal logic for reasoning about data minimization [7]. Of the former ones CAPRIV [2] and CAPVerDE [9] are tools that support the modeling and verification of data minimization properties in software architectures. However, to the best of our knowledge, the tool CAPRIV and its source are not openly accessible. The open source tool CAPVerDE is a very similar tool that operates on software architectures and a modified epistemic logic with focus on data minimization and access control.

3   Models and Design Goals

We consider the electricity supply and demand in a Micro Grid. We assume that the Micro Grid is properly designed such that a portion of the electricity demand related to basic living usage (e.g., lighting) from the residents, termed basic usage, can be guaranteed by the minimum capacity of the Micro Grid. There is randomness in both electricity supply (due to, e.g., weather change) and demand (e.g., entertainment usage in weekends). To cope with the randomness, the Micro Grid works in the grid-connected mode and is equipped with energy storage systems (ESSs), such as an electrochemical battery, superconducting magnetic energy storage, flywheel energy storage, etc. The ESSs store excess electricity for future use.

3.1 Modeling of Privacy-Respecting Data Flows

For this paper we make use of a logic and tool called *CAPVerDE* [9]. The logic consists of a formal description language for software architectures, a data flow property language, and a rule-based verification system. With these building blocks we can describe the data flow of a software system, express properties like "Actor A should have access to Data d", and verify whether the specified model satisfies said properties. The tool aids us by automatically solving the inference-rule based satisfaction problem.

The process of using this technique is to first identify the relevant data flow, actors, and data dependencies of the system. Then use a formal description language to describe the data flow. Setting up a formal model is already a big step because one decides which details are important and where to abstract. Once the system is modeled, one has to formalize the design goals for the system. This is done using a logic that allows for certain statements about the model. The verification rules allow for checking whether such a property holds for the provided model. If the verification returns that the model satisfies all properties, the model meets the design goals.

For the specific use case of this paper, we want to look at privacy design goals. These are usually expressed by properties that state that an 'untrustworthy' actor should **not** have access to data that is considered personal or worth of protection. For a Smart Grid architecture this means, for instance, protecting measurements of smart meters against curious intermediate aggregators. To verify such a property, we have to model the data flow from smart meters to service providers, including the implicit data flow, i.e., dependencies between data.

In order to achieve the goals that we have modeled, we make use of an additive secret-sharing-based multi-party computation as suggested in the past [12,15,35]. With that technique, we can achieve the private aggregation of values and prevent disclosure of single measurements. However, we are also interested in hiding the aggregated values from unauthorized intermediary nodes, so we additionally share a secret with the intended receiver of the aggregated result. With this approach we can have the values aggregated by any number of nodes in the Fog, but only the intended recipient can remove the blinding and obtain the actual result.

3.2 Network Model

The roles of the proposed encryption scheme are depicted in Fig. 2. Actors in the distribution grid are a) Smart Meter Gateways (SMGWs) that collect and disseminate measurement data, b) Intelligent Energy Devices (IEDs) that are controllable via a interface and consume electricity or in case of distributed energy resources inject power into the distribution grid, c) data aggregators that operate on Fog nodes to collect, aggregate and redirect measurement data, and d) Smart Grid Service Providers who receive the aggregated measurements. The e) key management authority enables confidential end-to-end connections between the other actors.

a) **Smart Meter Gateway (SMGW):** The measurements from the IEDs are encrypted and disseminated by the SMGW. The data is encrypted using secret-sharing, so that is can be aggregated without decryption.

b) **Intelligent Energy Devices (IED):** For our scheme, the readings from the IED are communicated to local SMGWs. The produced data is then encrypted by the SMGW and disseminated to the correct data aggregators.

c) **Data Aggregators (DA):** The DAs receive encrypted data that are then aggregated for the use either by authorized Smart Grid Service Provider, or by the next level data aggregators.

d) **Smart Grid Service Providers (SGSP):** Each Smart Grid Service Provider is associated with an aggregation layer. The authorization to read the aggregated measurements is expressed in a "layer key" which allows them to decrypt respective data sets.

e) **Key Management Authority (KMA):** The KMA provides a central trust infrastructure for the data flow. To establish a trusted link between the SMGWs, the DAs and the Smart Grid Service Providers, the KMA distributes secrets for each hierarchical aggregation layer.

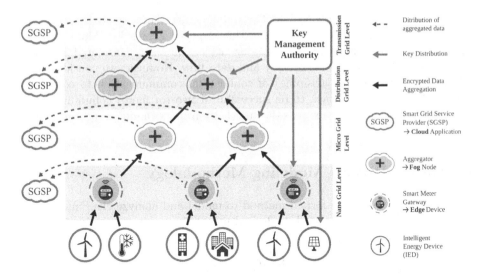

Fig. 2. The lowest layer includes the consumers and generators. In the higher layers, only aggregators reside. Aggregators can not decrypt the aggregated values. Possible data flow is indicated by the arrows. Only the Smart Grid Service Providers have access to the aggregated data. Authorization is based on the aggregation level.

3.3 Threat Model

The presented scheme is designed to provide the confidentiality of data with respect to hierarchical layers in the aggregation architecture. Following the formal modeling approach, we can distinguish between two types of adversaries: Colluding and non-colluding attackers.

Non-colluding Attackers. For the non-colluding attacker, we consider the honest-but-curious attacker model [14], where the respective node complies to the protocol in such that they are only collecting and analyzing the data that they lawfully receive. This type of adversary does not forget any data once received. They try to computationally and statistically break any obfuscation on the received data to break confidentiality where possible. The attacker model is called honest-but-curious because they do not actively request data if not obliged to by the protocol.

For the evaluation, we consider all individual actors – that is edge nodes, Fog nodes and cloud services – as potential attackers and formally model the requirement that the proposed scheme has to protect the personal data from unauthorized access.

Colluding Attackers. In extension of the previous model, we also formally describe that nodes communicate their knowledge among each other to collaborate on breaking the confidentiality. The colluding attacker actively shares information with other nodes and combines this acquired knowledge. Manipulation of data, selective forwarding and forging attacks are not considered because the focus of this paper is on privacy and data flow. However, we consider out-of-band forwarding (via gossiping) of confidential communication to colluding nodes. We assume an attack to be successful, if two (or more) colluding nodes can derive knowledge that exceeds the knowledge from both (all) respective nodes individually.

4   Formal Privacy Modeling Methodology

This section presents the formal method to model and analyze the Smart Grid system under investigation and its desired privacy properties.

4.1   Data Flow Description Language

Table 1 shows a relevant excerpt of the syntax of the architecture description language of CAPVerDE. An architecture A consists of so-called relations R that model explicit and implicit data flows between the actors (called components C_i). The relation $Has_i(X)$ is the entry point, i.e., it models how data enters the system. The relations can be read as "Component C_i has access to a variable X" for example via a sensor. $Rec_{i,j}(\{X\})$ is the relation that models the passing of data from one actor to another. It can be read as "Component C_i receives the set of variable $\{X\}$ from component C_j." $Comp_i(X = T)$ is the relation that lets actors derive new data from already known data. The natural language description of this relation is "The Component C_i can compute variable X from some term T", where term T consists of already known variables. The language also allows for implicit data flow, that is, calculations that are not intended in the system but possible. Relation $Dep_i(Y, \{X^1, ..., X^n\})$ states that "Component C_i has the computational power to derive variable Y from the set of variables X_i." For example if it is known that $a = b + c$, all actors in the system will have the relation $Dep_i(a, \{b, c\})$. The absence of such a relation denotes the fact that a calculation is not feasible. The addition is not directly reversible, i.e., one cannot derive the summands from the sum alone, therefore the relation $Dep_i(b, \{a\})$ will not exist. It should be noted that, although this type of relation deals with implicit data flow, the relations have to be modeled explicitly, that is, for each equation one has to specify whether it should be reversible. Also, all dependencies of a variable have to be made explicit in this way, as well.

Table 1. Syntax of architecture language

A	$::= \{R\}$	
R	$::= Has_i(X)$	$\mid Rec_{i,j}(\{X\})$
	$\mid Comp_i(X = T)$	$\mid Dep_i(Y, \{ X^1, ..., X^n\})$

A formal software system is defined as a set of relations. To make the description more readable for humans, we will provide a graphical representation of the system. The graphical form shows the components as boxes containing the corresponding relations and arrows between component boxes show the inter-component relations.

The verification process of CAPVerDE works as follows: The modeling of the architecture has to be done by the user. One follows the syntax of the language to describe the data flow. Also, the dependencies between the data has to be expressed. CAPVerDE provides a GUI to aid the modeling process. The tool then automatically checks the architecture for consistency, i.e., whether the data flow is possible. For instance, receiving data from a component that does not possess the data would be inconsistent. If the architecture is consistent, the privacy goals have to be expressed as properties in the provided language. This can also be done using the GUI. The verification of selected properties is done automatically by the tool. It returns "property holds" or "property does not hold" for the given architecture. One can view the verification trace of a property to inspect the applied rules necessary for the verification.

4.2 Privacy Goal Formalization

The only type of property we consider for this paper is the one regarding the access of data. A property $\phi = HasAcc_i(X)$ states that component C_i is able to access variable X. An architecture satisfies this property (denoted by $A \vdash \phi$)

iff the component can use its explicit and implicit data flow to derive X. Also negation of properties is possible. A negated property $\neg\phi$ holds iff the property ϕ does not hold.

Table 2. Rules of inference for the architecture logic in CAPVerDE

$$\mathbf{H1}\,\frac{Has_i(X) \in A}{A \vdash HasAcc_i(X)} \qquad \mathbf{H2}\,\frac{Rec_{i,j}(E) \in A \quad X \in \{E\}}{A \vdash HasAcc_i(X)} \qquad \mathbf{H3}\,\frac{Comp_i(X = T) \in A}{A \vdash HasAcc_i(X)}$$

$$\mathbf{H4}\,\frac{Dep_i(X, \{X^1, ..., X^n\}) \quad \forall l \in [1, n], A \vdash HasAcc_i(X^l)}{A \vdash HasAcc_i(X)}$$

Table 2 shows the rules of inference that are used by the automatic verification process. The first three rules (**H1–H3**) regard the explicit data-flow and hold if the component somehow processes the data. The fourth rule (**H4**) is based on the dependence relation and hence on the computational ability of the component to derive the data.

5   Privacy-Preserving Aggregation

This section presents the integrated concept for managing the aggregation of data in Fog Computing based Smart Grid networks. We first introduce the prerequisites for our scheme, namely a central trusted party which manages the participants' keys. Then we describe the enrollment phase of devices in the network, before we discuss the actual steps the nodes in the network have to perform. We present two protocols: One for disguising the individual readings of a smart meter and another for blinding even the aggregate value to unauthorized aggregators.

Our scheme follows the privacy enhancing architecture of smart metering proposed by Molina-Markham et al [40]. More precisely, we use zero knowledge protocols for communication assume secure communication between the utility service provider and the nodes in the Smart Grid topology. Additionally, we make use of a secret-sharing-based approach as has been proposed multiple times in the past [12,15,35].

Our scheme consists of two procedures. The first procedure, explained in Sect. 5.1, is to hide individual readings from the aggregators. The second procedure is to hide the actual aggregation result from the aggregators themselves, such that only the final recipients, the respective Smart Grid Service Providers, can decrypt the value. This second procedure is described in Sect. 5.2.

5.1   Procedure 1 – Hiding Individual Readings from the Aggregators

We refer to Fig. 2 for a description of the actors. Let each of the n home-level IEDs be IED_n. Each IED_j creates secret-shares of its reading m^j: $m^j = \sum_{i=0}^{n} m_i^j$

and disseminates each share m_i^j to IED_i where $i \neq j$. Each IED_j then accumulates all the shares they have received $x_j = \sum_{i=0}^n m_i^j$ and sends the result on to the data aggregator DA. The DA can calculate $\sum_{j=0}^n x^j$. This is equal to the accumulated readings: $\sum_{j=0}^n m^j$.

This procedure is elegant, because it works locally without a centralized key management authority. It protects the confidentiality of all participating child nodes resp. their contribution. On the other hand, it does not protect the confidentiality of the sum since the aggregator learns the aggregated value. Also, if all child nodes but one collude, they can unveil the measurements of the remaining node. Therefore, we improve the scheme in order to hide both the sum and all the participating nodes.

5.2 Procedure 2 – Hiding the Sum from the Aggregators

We extend the previous protocol by further blinding the values with a secret-share from the intended receiver of the aggregated values. That is, we keep the structure of the participants, but rely on a central key management authority (cf. Sect. 3.2) to generate and distribute keys.

First, the key management authority (KMA) generates a key k and generates shares for each of the n $IEDs$: $k = \sum_{j=0}^n k_j$. Those shares are then sent to each IED_j, which then re-shares that key: $k_j = \sum_{i=0}^n k_j^i$ where $i \neq j$. Each IED_j then blinds the shares of its reading (m_i^j) with the re-shared key, before sending it on to the other $IEDs$: $m_i^j + k_i^j$. Each IED_j accumulates their received shares: $x_j = \sum_{i=0}^n m_i^j + k_i^j$ and sends the result on to the aggregator DA, who then calculates the sum as $\sum_{j=0}^n x^j$. This is equal to the accumulated readings with the blinding: $\sum_{j=0}^n m^j + k_j = k + \sum_{j=0}^n m^j$. Now, only the holder of k can remove the blinding and thus obtain the actual aggregate.

6   Proof of Privacy-Preserving Data Dissemination

In this section we describe the actual proof of privacy preservingness. The high-level security threats as described in Sect. 3.3 are examined and it is discussed how data confidentiality is achieved.

6.1   Procedure 1

Figure 3 shows the architecture of Procedure 1 (cf. Sect. 5.1). Three aggregators for the street-level and one for the district-level are considered. Also for the sake of readability only the rightmost components of each level report to a service provider. The variables m_a, m_b, m_c are measurements of the Intelligent Energy Devices and $value0_a, value0_b, value0_c$ are the aggregated measurements on the smart meter level. $value1_a, value1_b, value1_c$ are the aggregated measurements of the street level and $value2$ is the aggregated measurement of the district level. All other variables are intermediate results and shared secrets between

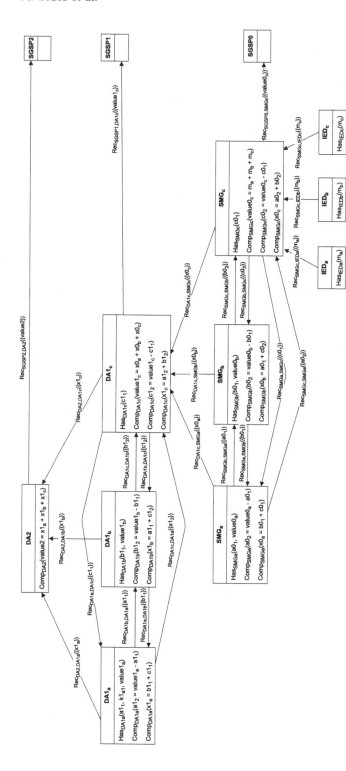

Fig. 3. Graphical representation of the Procedure 1 in the formal description language of CAPVerDE.

the components of one level. $c0_1$ ad $c0_2$, for instance, are the shared secrets of $SMGW_c$, which are distributed between $SMGW_a$ and $SMGW_b$.

The depicted graph describes the explicit data flow of the architecture. As mentioned above, the implicit data flow is described via the dependence relations. For this architecture we assume that all components have the computational power to build sums and differences. Therefore, all components have the same set of dependence relations. All components can perform the explicit calculations done by other components on the system as well as all corresponding equivalent calculations. This is based on the assumption that the protocol is known. For example the set of dependence relations of SMGW A includes the dependence relations $dep_{SMGWa}(c0_2, \{value0_c, c0_1\})$ and also the derived $dep_{SMGWa}(value0_c, \{c0_1, c0_2\})$ and $dep_{SMGWa}(c0_1, \{value0_c, c0_2\})$.

Non-colluding Attackers. In this setting we want to verify that no single actor can access measurements that are not intended for them. To to do so we can verify that components on the same level cannot access each others' values and components on a higher level cannot read individual readings from the lower level. An example of a property of the first type in the syntax of CAPVerDE is $\phi_{1n} = \neg HasAcc_{SMGWa}(value0_c)$. The SMGW A should not be able to read the measurement of SMGW C (same level). An example of a property of the second type is $\phi_{2n} = \neg HasAcc_{AG1c}(value1_c)$. The Aggregator C (street level) should not be able to read the summed measurements of the SMGWs. We refer to Appendix A for the discussion of the verification trace.

Colluding Attackers. Here we consider colluding attackers in the model, that is two components sharing their knowledge to obtain data that both cannot access individually. To model such behavior we have to manually add "attack-relations" to the architecture. To stay with the existing example, we let the SMGWs A and B collude to access the readings of C. Therefore, we add the relation $Rec_{SMGWa,SMGWb}(\{c0_2\})$ to the architecture to model that B shares its secret with A.

The property $\phi_{1c} = \neg HasAcc_{SMGWa}(value0_c)$ fails for the architecture with the additional collusion-relation added. The verification trace looks identical to the one for the non-colluding attacker (depicted in Fig. 5) up to line 37. Rule **H2** for property $HasAcc_{SMGWa}(c0_2)$ now applies, which makes the dependence relation $dep_{SMGWa}(value0_c, \{c0_1, c0_2\})$ possible. Hence, the property $HasAcc_{SMGWa}(value0_c)$ holds and the negation consequently does not. Consequently, the privacy goal is not achieved in this model if one considers colluding attackers.

6.2   Procedure 2

Figure 4 shows the architecture of Procedure 2 (cf. Sect. 5.2). The same simplifications as before apply. As described above, in this version a Key Management Authority distributes the keys. Due to the introduced encryption we now have more variables. The variables $k0_a, k0_b, k0_c$ denote the keys for the smart meters and $k0$ the corresponding key of the service provider of the next level. Accordingly, $k1_a, k1_b, k1_c$ are the keys for the street level aggregators and $k1$ is given to the service provider on the district level. In addition, the variables $acl_a, acl_b, acl_c, ac2$ are introduced for intermediate results.

In this procedure our privacy goal is to guarantee that the aggregators cannot read the aggregated values which are intended for the respective service providers.

Non-colluding Attackers. The property $\phi_{2n} = \neg HasAcc_{AG1c}(value1_c)$ can be verified and produces a long trace. Essentially, the component $AG1c$ has no explicit data flow relations to obtain $value1_c$ and thus can only access it based on dependence relations. The only possible one is $dep_{AG1c}(value1_c, \{acl_c, k0\})$. Rule **H3** applies for the aggregated encrypted sum acl_c. For the service provider key $k0$, however, the component $AG1c$ can only use implicit data flow. Only two dependence relations exist, of which the first is a circle as $dep_{AG1c}(k0, \{acl_c, value1_c\})$ is derived from the same equation as the previously used one. The second one is $dep_{AG1c}(k0, \{k0_c, k0_b, k0_a\})$, which needs the three keys from the SMGWs. $k0_c$ cannot be obtained via explicit data flow and thus $AG1c$ has to use dependence relations, again. Apart from the circle, only $dep_{AG1c}(k0_c, \{k0_c1, k0_c2\})$ is applicable. The only non-circular dependence relation for $k0_c1$ is $dep_{AG1c}(k0_c1, \{c0_1, k0_c2\})$. $dep_{AG1c}(c0_1, \{value0_c, c0_1\})$ is the only applicable implicit relation. However, we have shown above that $HasAcc_{SMGWa}(value0_c)$ does not hold for the architecture of Procedure 1. The same holds for this architecture as no non-circular dependence relation exists that allows $AG1c$ to obtain $value0_c$). Thus, the verification of the property $HasAcc_{AG1c}(value1_c)$ fails and the negation can be successfully verified.

Colluding Attackers. Here we consider an additional collusion relation of the form $Rec_{SMGWa,SMGWb}(\{ck0_2\})$. The property $\phi_{1c} = \neg HasAcc_{SMGWa}(value0_c)$ is again to be verified. We omit the verification steps that are identical to the ones of Procedure 1. We start at dependence relation $dep_{SMGWa}(value0_c, \{c0_1, c0_2\})$. $c0_1$ can only be obtained via $dep_{SMGWa}(c0_1, \{ck0_1, k0_c1\})$. While Rule **H2** applies for $ck0_1$, $k0_c1$ can only be derived via accessing $c0_1$, which we are currently trying to obtain, or $k0_c$. The latter cannot be obtained by $SMGW_a$ without having $k0$ (circle again). Therefore, the verification of $HasAcc_{SMGWa}(value0_c)$ fails and we successfully verify ϕ_{1c}.

The proposed architecture achieves data confidentiality in the presence of honest-but-curious data aggregators as well as non-colluding Nano-Grid neigh-

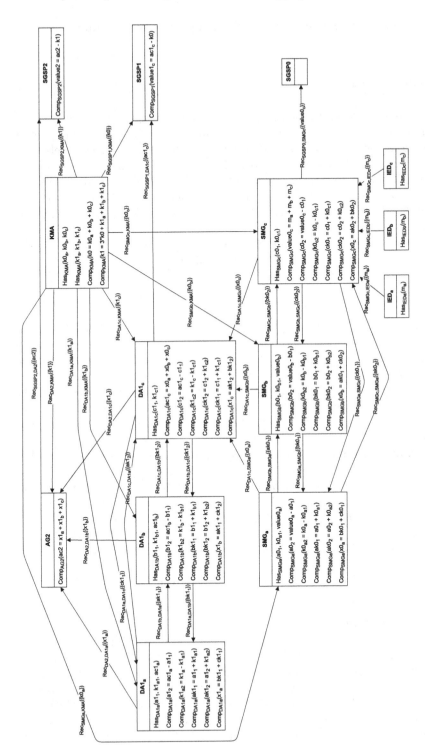

Fig. 4. Graphical representation of the Procedure 2 in the formal description language of CAPVerDE.

bors. It is not possible to deduce individual supply or demand from the aggregated values.

7   Conclusion

The proposed scheme describes an architecture for data aggregation and dissemination in Smart Grids supported by distributed Fog nodes. The architecture is topology-aware in such that a grid-based hierarchy is built. A comprehensive modeling approach has been selected and demonstrated, which aims to enable Smart Grid services to transparently explain and proof their confidentiality. On the infrastructural layer, the scheme describes machine-to-machine communication which assures privacy-preserving aggregation of smart meter readings and dissemination between the SMGWs and possible Smart Grid Service Providers. We model the proposed scheme and show that its integrity and privacy-properties can be validated by CAPVerDE, an automated prover.

7.1   Future Work

In this paper, we have shown that general privacy properties of data flows in the context of Smart Grids can be modeled and proven using automated solvers. As a next step, we elaborate a systematization of aspects that need to be protected from unauthorized access and curious actors. We want to especially look into the protection of meta data and how communication relationships between the different actors can be obfuscated. Examples for such meta data could be the origin of readings, the recipient Smart Grid Service Providers, but also the type of reading (topic) and frequency of transmission.

The proposed scheme is efficient regarding the computational effort, but can still be optimized with respect to the messaging overhead. Anonymity and privacy-respecting data flows always have to evaluate between the price in efficiency and the return in privacy. For future work, we will evaluate other hierarchical aggregation schemes to conduct a systematic network load comparison.

Regarding the key management, for privacy reasons it might be beneficial to investigate distributed schemes instead of using a centralized key management authority. This challenging research field is another follow-up activity in the journey towards the development of truly privacy-respecting Smart Grids.

A   Verification Trace

Figure 5 shows an excerpt of the verification trace of the property ϕ_{1n}. First a negation rule is applied and then the rules **H1** to **H4** are applied in order. Lines 5–10 show that no explicit data flow was found, i.e., component $SMGWa$ does not have the variable $value0_c$. Starting from line 11, CAPVerDE checks whether the component has the ability to compute the variable implicitly. Two matching dependence relations exist that allow deriving $value0_c$:

```
1   Current property to prove: NOT HasAcc_SMG_a(value0_c)
2   Rule I_neg applied for statement:
3   Therefore trying to verify new statement:
4       Current property to prove: HasAcc_SMG_a(value0_c)
5       Trying Rule H1...
6       Rule H1 not applicable
7       Trying Rule H2...
8       Rule H2 not applicable
9       Trying Rule H3...
10      Rule H3 not applicable
11      Trying Rule H4...
12      Found Dep_SMG_a(value0_c,{m_a,m_b,m_c})
13          Current property to prove: HasAcc_SMG_a(m_a)
14          Trying Rule H1...
15          Rule H1 not applicable
16          Trying Rule H2...
17          Rule H2 not applicable
18          Trying Rule H3...
19          Rule H3 not applicable
20          Trying Rule H4...
21          Found Dep_SMG_a(m_a,{value0_c,m_b,m_c})
22              Current property to prove: HasAcc_SMG_a(value0_c)
23              Loop detected
24          Rule H4 not applicable
25          HasAcc_SMG_a(m_a) does not hold
26      Found Dep_SMG_a(value0_c,{c0_1,c0_2})
27          Current property to prove: HasAcc_SMG_a(c0_1)
28          Trying Rule H1...
29          Rule H1 not applicable
30          Trying Rule H2...
31          Rule H2 applied for statement: HasAcc_SMG_a(c0_1)
32          HasAcc_SMG_a(c0_1) holds
33          Current property to prove: HasAcc_SMG_a(c0_2)
34          Trying Rule H1...
35          Rule H1 not applicable
36          Trying Rule H2...
37          Rule H2 not applicable
38          Trying Rule H3...
39          Rule H3 not applicable
40          Trying Rule H4...
41          Found Dep_SMG_a(c0_2,{value0_c,c0_1})
42              Current property to prove: HasAcc_SMG_a(value0_c)
43              Loop detected
44          Rule H4 not applicable
45          HasAcc_SMG_a(c0_2) does not hold
46      Rule H4 not applicable
47      HasAcc_SMG_a(value0_c) does not hold
48  Rule I_neg applied for statement: NOT HasAcc_SMG_a(value0_c)
49
50  Property verification successful!
```

Fig. 5. Verification trace explaining the rule application of CAPVerDE.

$dep_{SMGWa}(value0_c, \{m_a, m_b, m_c\})$ and $dep_{SMGWa}(value0_c, \{c0_1, c0_2\})$. The first is used in lines 12–25 but $SMGWa$ can neither explicitly nor implicitly get access to the variable m_a. Lines 26–45 show the trace of the second dependence relation. The component does have access to the variable $c0_1$ but cannot obtain the also necessary $c0_2$. As there are no more means to obtain variable $value0_c$ left, the property $HasAcc_{SMGWa}(value0_c)$ does not hold, hence the negation does (line 48).

The verification of the property $\phi_{2n} = \neg HasAcc_{AG1c}(value1_c)$, however, fails. Due to the relation $Comp_{AG1c}(value1_c = x0_a + x0_b + x0_c)$ the trace is very short. Rule **H3** applies and consequently $HasAcc_{AG1c}(value1_c)$ holds. Therefore, the negation does not hold and our data protection goal of protecting the aggregated measures against the next level aggregators is not satisfied in this architecture.

References

1. Abeykoon, V., Kankanamdurage, N., Senevirathna, A., Ranaweera, P., Udawalpola, R.: Real time identification of electrical devices through power consumption pattern detection. Perv. Comput. **10**(1), 40–48 (2016)
2. Antignac, T., Le Métayer, D.: Privacy architectures: reasoning about data minimisation and integrity. In: Mauw, S., Jensen, C.D. (eds.) STM 2014. LNCS, vol. 8743, pp. 17–32. Springer, Cham (2014). https://doi.org/10.1007/978-3-319-11851-2_2
3. Antignac, T., Le Métayer, D.: Trust driven strategies for privacy by design. In: Damsgaard Jensen, C., Marsh, S., Dimitrakos, T., Murayama, Y. (eds.) IFIPTM 2015. IAICT, vol. 454, pp. 60–75. Springer, Cham (2015). https://doi.org/10.1007/978-3-319-18491-3_5
4. Antoniadis, I.I., Chatzidimitriou, K.C., Symeonidis, A.L.: Security and privacy for smart meters: a data-driven mapping study. In: 2019 IEEE PES Innovative Smart Grid Technologies Europe (ISGT-Europe), pp. 1–5, September 2019
5. Asghar, M.R., Dán, G., Miorandi, D., Chlamtac, I.: Smart meter data privacy: a survey. IEEE Commun. Surv. Tutorials **19**(4), 2820–2835 (2017)
6. Backes, M., Hritcu, C., Maffei, M.: Automated verification of remote electronic voting protocols in the applied pi-calculus. In: Computer Security Foundations Symposium, pp. 195–209. IEEE (2008)
7. Barth, A., Datta, A., Mitchell, J.C., Nissenbaum, H.: Privacy and contextual integrity: framework and applications. In: Symposium on Security and Privacy, pp. 184–198. IEEE (2006)
8. Barthe, G., Danezis, G., Grégoire, B., Kunz, C., Zanella-Béguelin, S.: Verified computational differential privacy with applications to smart metering. In: 2013 IEEE 26th Computer Security Foundations Symposium, pp. 287–301, June 2013
9. Bavendiek, K., Adams, R., Schupp, S.: Privacy-preserving architectures with probabilistic guaranties. In: 2018 16th Annual Conference on Privacy, Security and Trust (PST), pp. 1–10. IEEE (2018)
10. Bavendiek, K., et al.: Automatically proving purpose limitation in software architectures. In: Dhillon, G., Karlsson, F., Hedström, K., Zúquete, A. (eds.) SEC 2019. IAICT, vol. 562, pp. 345–358. Springer, Cham (2019). https://doi.org/10.1007/978-3-030-22312-0_24
11. Bohli, J.M., Gruschka, N., Jensen, M., Iacono, L.L., Marnau, N.: Security and privacy-enhancing multicloud architectures. IEEE Trans. Dependable Secure Comput. **10**(4), 212–224 (2013)
12. Danezis, G., Fournet, C., Kohlweiss, M., Zanella-Béguelin, S.: Smart meter aggregation via secret-sharing. In: Proceedings of the First ACM Workshop on Smart Energy Grid Security, SEGS 2013, pp. 75–80. Association for Computing Machinery, Berlin, November 2013
13. Delaune, S., Ryan, M., Smyth, B.: Automatic verification of privacy properties in the applied pi calculus. In: Karabulut, Y., Mitchell, J., Herrmann, P., Jensen, C.D. (eds.) IFIPTM 2008. ITIFIP, vol. 263, pp. 263–278. Springer, Boston, MA (2008). https://doi.org/10.1007/978-0-387-09428-1_17
14. Derryberry, J.: Compiling an Honest but Curiuos Protocol (2003). https://ocw.mit.edu/courses/electrical-engineering-and-computer-science/6-876j-advanced-topics-in-cryptography-spring-2003/lecture-notes/lec050703.pdf
15. Dimitriou, T., Awad, M.K.: Secure and scalable aggregation in the smart grid resilient against malicious entities. Ad Hoc Netw. **50**, 58–67 (2016)

16. Diovu, R.C., Agee, J.T.: Enhancing the security of a cloud-based smart grid AMI network by leveraging on the features of quantum key distribution. Trans. Emerg. Telecommun. Technol. **30**(6), e3587 (2019)
17. Efthymiou, C., Kalogridis, G.: Smart grid privacy via anonymization of smart metering data. In: International Conference on Smart Grid Communications (SmartGridComm), pp. 238–243. IEEE (2010)
18. Eibl, G., Engel, D.: Differential privacy for real smart metering data. Comput. Sci. - Res. Dev. **32**(1), 173–182 (2017)
19. Fan, C.I., Huang, S.Y., Lai, Y.L.: Privacy-enhanced data aggregation scheme against internal attackers in smart grid. IEEE Trans. Ind. Inform. **10**(1), 666–675 (2014)
20. Ferrag, M.A., Maglaras, L.A., Janicke, H., Jiang, J., Shu, L.: A systematic review of data protection and privacy preservation schemes for smart grid communications. Sustain. Cities Soc. **38**, 806–835 (2018). http://www.sciencedirect.com/science/article/pii/S2210670717308399
21. Finster, S., Baumgart, I.: Privacy-aware smart metering: a survey. IEEE Commun. Surv. Tutorials **17**(2), 1088–1101 (2015)
22. Fournet, C., Kohlweiss, M., Danezis, G., Luo, Z., et al.: ZQL: a compiler for privacy-preserving data processing. In: USENIX Security Symposium, pp. 163–178 (2013)
23. Gaboardi, M., Haeberlen, A., Hsu, J., Narayan, A., Pierce, B.C.: Linear dependent types for differential privacy. ACM SIGPLAN Not. **48**, 357–370 (2013)
24. Regulation, G.D.P.: Regulation (EU) 2016/679 of the European Parliament and of the Council of 27 April 2016 on the protection of natural persons with regard to the processing of personal data and on the free movement of such data, and repealing Directive 95/46 (GDPR). Official J. Eur. Union (OJ) **59**(1–88), 294 (2016)
25. Greveler, U., Justus, B., Loehr, D.: Multimedia content identification through smart meter power usage profiles. In: Computers, Privacy and Data Protection, p. 8. CPDP, Brussels (2012)
26. Gürses, S., Troncoso, C., Diaz, C.: Engineering privacy by design. Comput. Privacy Data Protect. **14**(3), 25 (2011)
27. Halpern, J.Y., Van Der Meyden, R., Vardi, M.Y.: Complete axiomatizations for reasoning about knowledge and time. SIAM J. Comput. **33**(3), 674–703 (2004)
28. Hoepman, J.-H., Hubbers, E., Jacobs, B., Oostdijk, M., Schreur, R.W.: Crossing borders: security and privacy issues of the European e-Passport. In: Yoshiura, H., Sakurai, K., Rannenberg, K., Murayama, Y., Kawamura, S. (eds.) IWSEC 2006. LNCS, vol. 4266, pp. 152–167. Springer, Heidelberg (2006). https://doi.org/10.1007/11908739_11
29. Jawurek, M., Johns, M., Kerschbaum, F.: Plug-in privacy for smart metering billing. In: Fischer-Hübner, S., Hopper, N. (eds.) PETS 2011. LNCS, vol. 6794, pp. 192–210. Springer, Heidelberg (2011). https://doi.org/10.1007/978-3-642-22263-4_11
30. de Jonge, W., Jacobs, B.: Privacy-friendly electronic traffic pricing via commits. In: Degano, P., Guttman, J., Martinelli, F. (eds.) FAST 2008. LNCS, vol. 5491, pp. 143–161. Springer, Heidelberg (2009). https://doi.org/10.1007/978-3-642-01465-9_10
31. Kalogridis, G., Efthymiou, C., Denic, S.Z., Lewis, T.A., Cepeda, R.: Privacy for smart meters: towards undetectable appliance load signatures. In: 2010 First IEEE International Conference on Smart Grid Communications, pp. 232–237, October 2010

32. Kart, F., Miao, G., Moser, L.E., Melliar-Smith, P.: A distributed e-Healthcare system based on the service oriented architecture. In: International Conference on Services Computing, pp. 652–659. IEEE (2007)

33. Kim, J., Le, T.T.H., Kim, H.: Nonintrusive load monitoring based on advanced deep learning and novel signature. Comput. Intell. Neurosci. **2017**, 22 (2017). https://www.hindawi.com/journals/cin/2017/4216281/

34. Kremer, S., Ryan, M.: Analysis of an electronic voting protocol in the applied pi calculus. In: Sagiv, M. (ed.) ESOP 2005. LNCS, vol. 3444, pp. 186–200. Springer, Heidelberg (2005). https://doi.org/10.1007/978-3-540-31987-0_14

35. Kursawe, K., Danezis, G., Kohlweiss, M.: Privacy-friendly aggregation for the smart-grid. In: Fischer-Hübner, S., Hopper, N. (eds.) PETS 2011. LNCS, vol. 6794, pp. 175–191. Springer, Heidelberg (2011). https://doi.org/10.1007/978-3-642-22263-4_10

36. Li, M., Lou, W., Ren, K.: Data security and privacy in wireless body area networks. IEEE Wirel. Commun. **17**(1), 51–58 (2010)

37. Lodge, T., Crabtree, A., Brown, A.: Developing GDPR compliant apps for the edge. In: Garcia-Alfaro, J., Herrera-Joancomartí, J., Livraga, G., Rios, R. (eds.) DPM/CBT -2018. LNCS, vol. 11025, pp. 313–328. Springer, Cham (2018). https://doi.org/10.1007/978-3-030-00305-0_22

38. Maffei, M., Pecina, K., Reinert, M.: Security and privacy by declarative design. In: Computer Security Foundations Symposium, pp. 81–96. IEEE (2013)

39. Martin-Martínez, F., Sánchez-Miralles, A., Rivier, M.: A literature review of microgrids: a functional layer based classification. Renew. Sustain. Energy Rev. **62**, 1133–1153 (2016)

40. Molina-Markham, A., Shenoy, P., Fu, K., Cecchet, E., Irwin, D.: Private memoirs of a smart meter. In: Proceedings of the 2nd ACM Workshop on Embedded Sensing Systems for Energy-Efficiency in Building, pp. 61–66. BuildSys 2010. Association for Computing Machinery, Zurich, November 2010. https://doi.org/10.1145/1878431.1878446, https://doi.org/10.1145/1878431.1878446

41. Mrabet, Z.E., Kaabouch, N., Ghazi, H.E., Ghazi, H.E.: Cyber-security in smart grid: survey and challenges. Comput. Electr. Eng. **67**, 469–482 (2018). https://doi.org/10.1016/j.compeleceng.2018.01.015, http://www.sciencedirect.com/science/article/pii/S0045790617313423

42. Green, R.C., Wang, L., Alam, M.: High performance computing for electric power systems: applications and trends. In: 2011 IEEE Power and Energy Society General Meeting, pp. 1–8. IEEE, Detroit, July 2011

43. Rehmani, M.H., Davy, A., Jennings, B., Assi, C.: Software defined networks-based smart grid communication: a comprehensive survey. IEEE Commun. Surv. Tutorials **21**(3), 2637–2670 (2019). https://doi.org/10.1109/COMST.2019.2908266

44. Simmhan, Y., et al.: Cloud-based software platform for big data analytics in smart grids. Comput. Sci. Eng. **15**(4), 38–47 (2013)

45. Stübs, M., Ipach, H., Becker, C.: Topology-aware distributed smart grid control using a clustering-based utility maximization approach. In: Proceedings of the 35th Annual ACM Symposium on Applied Computing, pp. 1806–1815 (2020)

46. Stübs, M., Posdorfer, W., Momeni, S.: Blockchain-based multi-tier double-auctions for smart energy distribution grids. In: 2020 IEEE International Conference on Communications Workshops (ICC Workshops). IEEE (2020)

47. Sultan, S.: Privacy-preserving metering in smart grid for billing, operational metering, and incentive-based schemes: a survey. Comput. Secur. **84**, 148–165 (2019). https://doi.org/10.1016/j.cose.2019.03.014, http://www.sciencedirect.com/science/article/pii/S0167404818303675

48. Van Aubel, P., Poll, E.: Smart metering in the Netherlands: what, how, and why. Int. J. Electr. Power Energy Syst. **109**, 719–725 (2019)
49. Wei, L., et al.: Security and privacy for storage and computation in cloud computing. Infor. Sci. **258**, 371–386 (2014)

Non-interactive Private Decision Tree Evaluation

Anselme Tueno[1(✉)], Yordan Boev[1], and Florian Kerschbaum[2]

[1] SAP Security Research, Karlsruhe, Germany
anselme.kemgne.tueno@sap.com
[2] University of Waterloo, Waterloo, Canada

Abstract. In this paper, we address the problem of privately evaluating a decision tree on private data. This scenario consists of a server holding a private decision tree model and a client interested in classifying its private attribute vector using the server's private model. The goal of the computation is to obtain the classification while preserving the privacy of both—the decision tree and the client input. After the computation, the client learns the classification result and nothing else, and the server learns nothing. Existing privacy-preserving protocols that address this problem use or combine different generic secure multiparty computation approaches resulting in several interactions between the client and the server. Our goal is to design and implement a novel client-server protocol that delegates the complete tree evaluation to the server while preserving privacy and reducing the overhead. The idea is to use fully (somewhat) homomorphic encryption and evaluate the tree on ciphertexts encrypted under the client's public key. However, since current somewhat homomorphic encryption schemes have high overhead, we combine efficient data representations with different algorithmic optimizations to keep the computational overhead and the communication cost low. As a result, we are able to provide the first non-interactive protocol, that allows the client to delegate the evaluation to the server by sending an encrypted input and receiving only the encryption of the result. Our scheme has only one round and evaluates a complete tree of depth 10 within seconds.

Keywords: Machine learning · Private decision tree evaluation · Secure multiparty computation · Fully/somewhat homomorphic encryption

1 Introduction

Machine learning (ML) classifiers are valuable tools in many areas such as healthcare, finance, spam filtering, intrusion detection, remote diagnosis, etc. [37]. To perform their task, these classifiers often require access to personal sensitive data such as medical or financial records. Therefore, it is crucial to investigate technologies that preserve the privacy of the data, while benefiting from the advantages of ML. On the one hand, the ML model itself may contain sensitive

© IFIP International Federation for Information Processing 2020
Published by Springer Nature Switzerland AG 2020
A. Singhal and J. Vaidya (Eds.): DBSec 2020, LNCS 12122, pp. 174–194, 2020.
https://doi.org/10.1007/978-3-030-49669-2_10

data. On the other hand, the model may have been built on sensitive data. It is known that white-box and sometimes even black-box access to a ML model allows so-called *model inversion attacks* [18,33,39], which can compromise the privacy of the training data. As a result, making the ML model public could violate the privacy of the training data.

In this paper, we therefore address the problem of private decision tree evaluation (PDTE) on private data. This scenario consists of a server holding a private decision tree model and a client wanting to classify its private attribute vector using the server's private model. The goal of the computation is to obtain the classification while preserving the privacy of both – the decision tree and the client input. After the computation, the classification result is revealed only to the client, and beyond that, nothing further is revealed. The problem can be solved using any generic secure multiparty computation.

Generic secure multiparty computation [16,20] can implement PDTE. There exist frameworks such as ObliVM [27] or CBMC-GC [17], HyCC [8] that are able to automate the transformation of the plaintext decision tree program, written in a high level programming language, into oblivious programs suitable for secure computation. Their straightforward application to decision tree programs does certainly improve performance. However, the size of the resulting oblivious program is still proportional to the size of the tree. As a result generic solution are in general inefficient, in particular when the size of the tree is large.

Specialized protocols [2,4,7,23,24,32,34,38] exploit the domain knowledge of the problem at hand and make use of generic techniques only where it is necessary, resulting in more efficient solutions. Existing protocols for PDTE have several rounds requiring several interactions between the client and the server. Moreover, the communication cost depends on the size of the decision tree, while only a single classification is required by the client. Finally, they also require computational power from the client that depends on the size of the tree.

Our goal is to design and implement a novel client-server protocol that delegates the complete tree evaluation to the server while preserving privacy and keeping the performance acceptable. The idea is to use fully or somewhat homomorphic encryption (FHE/SHE) and evaluate the tree on ciphertexts encrypted under the client's public key. As a result, no intermediate or final computational result is revealed to the evaluating server. However, since current SHE/FHE schemes have high overhead, we combine efficient data representations with different algorithmic optimizations to keep the computational overhead and the communication cost low. At the end, the computational overhead might still be higher than in existing protocols, however the computation task can be parallelized resulting in a reduced computation time. As a result, we are able to provide the first non-interactive protocol, that allows the client to delegate the evaluation to the server by sending an encrypted input and receiving only the encryption of the result. Finally, existing approaches are secure in the semi-honest model (i.e., parties follow the protocol) and can be made *one-sided simulatable* using techniques that may double the computation and communication costs. A one-sided simulatable protocol forces the client to behave semi-honestly and guarantees that a malicious server learns nothing [22]. Our approach is one-sided simulatable by default, as the client does no more than encrypting its input and decrypting the final result of the computation (simulating the client is straightforward), while the server evaluates on ciphertexts encrypted with a semantically secure encryption under the client's public key.

Concrete motivation of our approach are machine learning settings (with applications in areas such as healthcare, finance etc.) where the server is computationally powerful, the client is computationally weak and the network connection is not very fast. Our contributions are as follows:

- We propose a non-interactive protocol for PDTE. Our scheme allows the client to delegate the evaluation to the server by sending an encrypted input and receiving only the encryption of the result.
- We propose PDT-BIN which is an instantiation of the main protocol with binary representation of the input. We combine efficient data representations with different algorithmic optimizations to keep the computational overhead and the communication cost low.
- Finally, we implement and benchmark using HElib [21] and TFHE [11].

The remainder of the paper is structured as follows. We review preliminaries in Sect. 2 before defining correctness and security of our protocol in Sect. 3. The basic construction itself is described in Sect. 4. In Sect. 5, we describe implementation and optimization using a binary representation. We discuss implementation and evaluation details in Sect. 6. We review related work in Sect. 7 before concluding our work in Sect. 8. Due to space constraints, we discuss further details in the appendix.

2   Preliminaries

For ease of exposition, we abstract away the mathematical technicalities behind HE and refer to the literature [1,5,10,19,31]. We start with the notation.

Notation. In this paper, μ denotes the bit length of attribute values, n denotes the dimension of the attribute vector, m denotes the number of decision nodes, d denotes the depth of the decision tree.

Homomorphic Encryption. We focus on (lattice-based) homomorphic encryption (HE) schemes that allow many chained additions and multiplications to be computed on plaintext. In these schemes, the plaintext space is usually a ring $\mathbb{Z}_q[X]/(X^N + 1)$, where q is prime and N might be a power of 2.

A HE consists of the usual algorithms for key generation $(\mathsf{pk}, \mathsf{sk}) \leftarrow \mathsf{KGen}(\lambda)$, encryption $\mathsf{Enc}(\mathsf{pk}, \mathsf{m})$ (we denote $\mathsf{Enc}(\mathsf{pk}, \mathsf{m})$ by $[\![\mathsf{m}]\!]$), decryption $\mathsf{Dec}(\mathsf{sk}, \mathsf{c})$. HE has an additional evaluation algorithm $\mathsf{Eval}(\mathsf{pk}, f, \mathsf{c}_1, \ldots, \mathsf{c}_n)$ that takes pk, an n-ary function f and ciphertexts $\mathsf{c}_1, \ldots \mathsf{c}_n$. It outputs a ciphertext c such that if $\mathsf{c}_i = [\![\mathsf{m}_i]\!]$ then it holds: $\mathsf{Dec}(\mathsf{sk}, \mathsf{Eval}(f, [\![\mathsf{m}_1]\!], \ldots, [\![\mathsf{m}_n]\!])) = \mathsf{Dec}(\mathsf{sk}, [\![f(\mathsf{m}_1, \ldots, \mathsf{m}_n)]\!])$. We require HE to be IND-CPA secure.

The encryption algorithm Enc adds "noise" to the ciphertext which increases during homomorphic evaluation. While addition of ciphertexts increases the noise slightly, the multiplication increases it significantly [5]. If the noise becomes too large then correct decryption is no longer possible. To prevent this from happening, one can either keep the circuit's depth of the function f low enough or use *bootstrapping* procedure which reduces the noise in a ciphertext, i.e., fully HE (FHE). In this paper, we will consider both bootstrapping and the possibility of keeping the circuit's depth low by designing our PDTE using so-called leveled FHE. A leveled FHE has an extra parameter L such that the scheme can evaluate all circuits of depth at most L without bootstrapping.

Homomorphic Operations. We assume a BGV type HE scheme [5]. Plaintexts can be encrypted using an integer representation (an integer x_i is encrypted as $[\![x_i]\!]$) or a binary representation (each bit of the bit representation $x_i^{\mathsf{b}} = x_{i\mu} \ldots x_{i1}$ is encrypted). We describe below HE operations in the binary representation (i.e., arithmetic operations mod 2). They work similarly in the integer representation.

The FHE scheme might support Smart and Vercauteren's ciphertext packing (SVCP) technique [31] to pack many plaintexts in one ciphertext. Using SVCP, a ciphertext consists of a fixed number s of slots, each capable of holding one plaintext, i.e. $[\![\cdot|\cdot|\ldots|\cdot]\!]$. The encryption of a bit b replicates b to all slots, i.e., $[\![b]\!] = [\![b|b|\ldots|b]\!]$. However, we can also pack the bits of x_i^{b} in one ciphertext and will denote it by $[\![\vec{x}_i]\!] = [\![x_{i\mu}|\ldots|x_{i1}|0|\ldots|0]\!]$.

The computation relies on some built-in routines, that allow homomorphic operations on encrypted data. The relevant routines for our scheme are: addition (SHEADD), multiplication (SHEMULT) and comparison (SHECMP). These routines are compatible with the ciphertext packing technique (i.e., operations are replicated on all slots in a SIMD manner).

The routine SHEADD performs a component-wise addition modulo two, i.e., we have: $\text{SHEADD}([\![b_{i1}|\ldots|b_{is}]\!], [\![b_{j1}|\ldots|b_{js}]\!]) = [\![b_{i1} \oplus b_{j1}|\ldots|b_{is} \oplus b_{js}]\!]$. Similarly, SHEMULT performs component-wise multiplication modulo two, i.e., we have: $\text{SHEMULT}([\![b_{i1}|\ldots|b_{is}]\!], [\![b_{j1}|\ldots|b_{js}]\!]) = [\![b_{i1} \cdot b_{j1}|\ldots|b_{is} \cdot b_{js}]\!]$. We will denote addition and multiplication by $\boxplus$ and $\boxdot$, respectively.

Let x_i, x_j be two integers, $b_{ij} = [x_i > x_j]$, $b_{ji} = [x_j > x_i]$, the routine SHECMP takes $[\![x_i^{\mathsf{b}}]\!], [\![x_j^{\mathsf{b}}]\!]$, compares x_i and x_j and returns $[\![b_{ij}]\!]$, $[\![b_{ji}]\!]$: $([\![b_{ij}]\!], [\![b_{ji}]\!]) \leftarrow \text{SHECMP}([\![x_i^{\mathsf{b}}]\!], [\![x_j^{\mathsf{b}}]\!])$. Note that, if the inputs to SHECMP encrypt the same value, then the routine outputs two ciphertexts of 0. This routine implements the comparison circuit described in [9].

If ciphertext packing is enabled, then we also assume that HE supports shift operations. Given a packed ciphertext $[\![b_1|\ldots|b_s]\!]$, the *shift left* operation shifts all slots to the left by a given offset, using zero-fill, i.e., shifting $[\![b_1|\ldots|b_s]\!]$ by i positions returns $[\![b_i|\ldots|b_s|0|\ldots|0]\!]$.

3   Definitions

This section introduces relevant definitions. With $[a, b]$, we denote the set of all integers from a to b. Let $c_0, \ldots, c_{k-1}$ be the classification labels, $k \in \mathbb{N}_{>0}$.

Definition 1 (Decision Tree). *A decision tree (DT) is a function $\mathcal{T} : \mathbb{Z}^n \rightarrow \{c_0, \ldots, c_{k-1}\}$ that maps an* attribute vector $x = (x_0, \ldots, x_{n-1})$ *to a finite set of* classification labels. *A DT consists of* internal *or* decision nodes *containing a* test condition, *and* leaf nodes *containing a* classification label. *A decision tree* model *consists of a DT and the following functions: a function* thr *that assigns to each decision node a* threshold *value,* thr $: [0, m-1] \rightarrow \mathbb{Z}$; *a function* att *that assigns to each decision node an* attribute index, att $: [0, m-1] \rightarrow [0, n-1]$, *and; a labeling function* lab *that assigns to each leaf node a label,* lab $: [m, M-1] \rightarrow \{c_0, \ldots, c_{k-1}\}$. *The decision at each decision node is a "greater-than" comparison between the assigned threshold and attribute values, i.e., the decision at node v is $[x_{\text{att}(v)} \geq \text{thr}(v)]$. We use $\mathcal{M} = (\mathcal{T}, \text{thr}, \text{att})$ to denote a decision tree model.*

Definition 2 (Decision Tree Evaluation). *Given an attribute vector $x = (x_0, \ldots, x_{n-1})$ and $\mathcal{M} = (\mathcal{T}, \text{thr}, \text{att})$, then starting at the root, the* Decision Tree Evaluation *(DTE) evaluates at each reached node v the decision $b \leftarrow [x_{\text{att}(v)} \geq \text{thr}(v)]$ and moves either to the left (if $b = 0$) or right (if $b = 1$) subsequent node. The evaluation returns the label of the reached leaf as result of the computation. We denote this by $\mathcal{T}(x)$.*

Definition 3 (Private DTE). *Given a* client *with a private $x = (x_0, \ldots, x_{n-1})$ and a* server *with a private $\mathcal{M} = (\mathcal{T}, \text{thr}, \text{att})$, a private DTE (PDTE) functionality evaluates the model $\mathcal{M}$ on input x, then reveals to the client the classification label $\mathcal{T}(x)$ and nothing else, while the server learns nothing, i.e., $\mathcal{F}_{\text{PDTE}}(\mathcal{M}, x) \rightarrow (\varepsilon, \mathcal{T}(x))$.*

Definition 4 (Correctness). *Given a* client *with a private $x = (x_0, \ldots, x_{n-1})$ and a* server *with a private $\mathcal{M} = (\mathcal{T}, \text{thr}, \text{att})$, a protocol Π correctly implements a PDTE functionality if after the computation it holds for the result c obtained by the client that $c = \mathcal{T}(x)$.*

Two distributions $\mathcal{D}_1$ and $\mathcal{D}_2$ are *computationally indistinguishable* (denoted $\mathcal{D}_1 \stackrel{c}{\equiv} \mathcal{D}_2$) if no probabilistic polynomial time (PPT) algorithm can distinguish them except with negligible probability. In SMC protocols, the *view* of a party consists of its input and the sequence of messages that it has received during the protocol execution [20].

Definition 5 (PDTE Security). *Given a* client C *with a private* input $x = (x_0, \ldots, x_{n-1})$ *and a server S with a private model $\mathcal{M} = (\mathcal{T}, \text{thr}, \text{att})$, a protocol Π_{PDTE} securely implements the PDTE functionality in the semi-honest model if the following holds: there exists a PPT algorithm $\text{Sim}_S^{\text{pdte}}$ that simulates the server's view $\text{View}_S^{\Pi_{\text{PDTE}}}$ given only $\mathcal{M} = (\mathcal{T}, \text{thr}, \text{att})$, i.e., $\text{Sim}_S^{\text{pdte}}(\mathcal{M}, \varepsilon) \stackrel{c}{\equiv} \text{View}_S^{\Pi_{\text{PDTE}}}(\mathcal{M}, x)$; there exists a PPT algorithm $\text{Sim}_C^{\text{pdte}}$ that simulates the client's view $\text{View}_C^{\Pi_{\text{PDTE}}}$ given only x and $\mathcal{T}(x)$, i.e., $\text{Sim}_C^{\text{pdte}}(x, \mathcal{T}(x)) \stackrel{c}{\equiv} \text{View}_C^{\Pi_{\text{PDTE}}}(\mathcal{M}, x)$.*

A protocol Π_{PDTE} securely implements the PDTE functionality with one-sided simulation if the following conditions hold: For every pair x, x' of different client's inputs, it holds $\text{View}_S^{\Pi_{\text{PDTE}}}(\mathcal{M}, x) \stackrel{c}{\equiv} \text{View}_S^{\Pi_{\text{PDTE}}}(\mathcal{M}, x')$; and Π_{PDTE} is simulatable against every PPT adversary controlling C.

4   The Basic Protocol

We present a modular description of our protocol starting by the data structure.

4.1   Data Structure

We follow the idea of previous protocols [4,12,32] of marking edges of the tree with comparison result. So if the comparison at node v is the bit b then we mark the right edge to v with b and the left edge with $1 - b$. For convenience, we will instead store this information at the child nodes of v and refer to it as cmp.

Definition 6 (Data Structure). *For a decision tree model* $\mathcal{M} = (\mathcal{T}, \text{thr}, \text{att})$, *we let* Node *be a data structure that for each node* v *defines the following fields:* v.threshold *stores the threshold* $\text{thr}(v)$ *of* v; v.aIndex *stores the associated index* $\text{att}(v)$; v.parent *stores the pointer to the parent node (null for the root);* v.left *stores the pointer to the left child node (null for each leaf);* v.right *stores the pointer to the right child node (null for each leaf);* v.cmp *is computed during the tree evaluation and stores the comparison bit* $b \leftarrow [x_{\text{att}(v.\text{parent})} \geq \text{thr}(v.\text{parent})]$ *if* v *is a right node. Otherwise it stores* $1 - b$; v.cLabel *stores the classification label if* v *is a leaf node and the empty string otherwise. We use* $\mathcal{D}$ *to denote the set of all decision nodes and* $\mathcal{L}$ *the set of all leaf nodes of* $\mathcal{M}$. *As a result, we use the equivalent notation* $\mathcal{M} = (\mathcal{T}, \text{thr}, \text{att}) = (\mathcal{D}, \mathcal{L})$.

With the data structure defined above, we now define the classification function.

Definition 7 (Classification Function). *Let* $x = (x_0, \dots, x_{n-1})$ *be the attribute vector and* $\mathcal{M} = (\mathcal{D}, \mathcal{L})$ *be the DT model. We define the* classification function *to be* $f_c(x, \mathcal{M}) = \text{tr}(x, \text{root})$, *where* root *is the root node and* tr *is the* traverse *function define as:*

$$\text{tr}(x, v) = \begin{cases} \text{tr}(x, v.\text{left}) & \text{if } v \in \mathcal{D} \text{ and } x_{v.\text{aIndex}} < v.\text{threshold} \\ \text{tr}(x, v.\text{right}) & \text{if } v \in \mathcal{D} \text{ and } x_{v.\text{aIndex}} \geq v.\text{threshold} \\ v & \text{if } v \in \mathcal{L} \end{cases}$$

Lemma 1. *Let* $x = (x_0, \dots, x_{n-1})$ *be an attribute vector and* $\mathcal{M} = (\mathcal{T}, \text{thr}, \text{att}) = (\mathcal{D}, \mathcal{L})$ *a DT model. We have* $\mathcal{T}(x) = b \cdot \text{tr}(x, \text{root.right}) + (1 - b) \cdot \text{tr}(x, \text{root.left})$, *where* $b = [x_{\text{att}(\text{root})} \geq \text{thr}(\text{root})]$ *is the comparison at the root node.*

Proof. The proof follows by induction on the depth of the tree. In the base case, we have a tree of depth one (i.e., the root and two leaves). In the induction step, we have two trees of depth d and we joint them by adding a new root.

```
1: function EVALPATHS(D, L)          7:    [[v.right.cmp]] ← [[v.right.cmp]] ⊡ [[v.cmp]]
2:   let Q be a queue                8:    if v.left ∈ D then
3:   Q.enqueue(root)                 9:       Q.enqueue(v.left)
4:   while Q.empty() = false do      10:   if v.right ∈ D then
5:     v ← Q.dequeue()               11:      Q.enqueue(v.right)
6:     [[v.left.cmp]] ← [[v.left.cmp]] ⊡ [[v.cmp]]
```

Algorithm 1. Aggregating Decision Bits

4.2 Algorithms

Initialization. The Initialization consists of a one-time key generation. The client generates appropriate pair $(\mathsf{pk}, \mathsf{sk})$ of public and private keys for a HE scheme, and sends pk to the server. For each input classification, the client just encrypts its input and sends it to the server. The size of homomorphic ciphertexts are in general very large. To reduce the communication cost of sending client's input, one can use a trusted randomizer that does not take part in the real protocol and is not allowed to collaborate with the server. The trusted randomizer generates a list of random strings r and sends the encrypted strings $[[r]]$ to server and the list of r's to the client. For an input x, the client then sends $x + r$ to the server in the real protocol. This technique is similar to the commodity based cryptography [3] with the difference that the client can play the role of the randomizer itself and sends the list of $[[r]]$'s (when the network is not too busy) before the protocol's start.

Computing Decision Bits. The server starts by computing for each node $v \in D$ the comparison bit $b \leftarrow [x_{\mathsf{att}(v)} \geq \mathsf{thr}(v)]$ and stores b at the right child node ($v.\mathsf{right.cmp} = b$) and $1 - b$ at the left child node ($v.\mathsf{left.cmp} = 1 - b$). We refer to this algorithm as EVALDNODE($D, [[x]]$).

Aggregating Decision Bits. Then for each leaf node v, the server aggregates the comparison bits along the path from the root to v. We implement it using a queue and traversing the tree in BFS as illustrated in Algorithm 1.

Finalizing. After Aggregating the decision bits along the path to the leaf nodes, each leaf node v stores either $v.\mathsf{cmp} = 0$ or $v.\mathsf{cmp} = 1$. Then, the server aggregates the decision bits at the leaves by computing for each leaf v the value $[[v.\mathsf{cmp}]] \boxdot [[v.\mathsf{cLabel}]]$ and summing all the results. We refer to this algorithm as FINALIZE(L).

Putting It All Together. As illustrated in Protocol 2, the whole computation is performed by the server. It sequentially computes the algorithms described above and sends the resulting ciphertext to the client. The client decrypts and outputs the classification label. The correctness follows from Lemma 1.

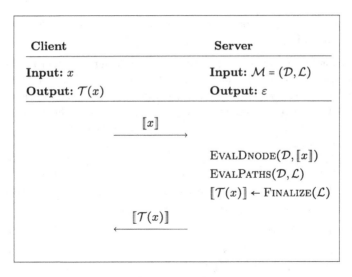

Protocol 2: The Basic Protocol

5   Binary Implementation

In this section, we describe PDT-BIN, an instantiation of the basic scheme that requires encoding the plaintexts using their bit representation. Hence, ciphertexts encrypt bits and arithmetic operations are done mod 2.

5.1   Input Encoding

We encrypt plaintext bitwise. For each plaintext x_i with bit representation $x_i^b = x_{i\mu} \ldots x_{i1}$, we use $[\![x_i^b]\!]$ to denote the vector $([\![x_{i\mu}]\!], \ldots, [\![x_{i1}]\!])$, consisting of encryptions of the bits of x_i. As a result, the client needs to send $n\mu$ ciphertexts for the n attribute values. Unfortunately, homomorphic ciphertexts might be quite large. We can already use the trusted randomizer as explained before to send blinded inputs instead of ciphertexts in this phase. This, however, improves only the online communication. We additionally want to use the SVCP SIMD technique that allows to pack many plaintexts into the same ciphertext and manipulate them together during homomorphic operations.

5.2   Ciphertext Packing

In the binary encoding, ciphertext packing means that each ciphertext encrypts s bits, where s is the number of slots in the ciphertext. Then we can use this property in three different ways. First, one could pack the bit representation of each classification label in a single ciphertext and allow the server to send back a single ciphertext to the client. Second, one could encrypt several attributes together and classify them with a single protocol evaluation. Finally, one could encrypt multiple decision node thresholds that must be compared to the same attribute in the DT model.

Packing Classification Label's Bits. Aggregating the decision bits using Algorithm 1 produces for each leaf $v \in \mathcal{L}$ a decision bit $[\![b_v]\!]$ which encrypts 1 for the classification leaf and 0 otherwise. Moreover, because of SVCP, the bit b_v is replicated to all slots. Now, let k be the number of classification labels (i.e., $|\mathcal{L}| = k$) and its bitlength be $|k|$. For each $v \in \mathcal{L}$, we let c_v denote the classification label $v.\mathsf{cLabel}$ which is $|k|$-bit long and has bit representation $c_v^b = c_{v|k|} \cdots c_{v1}$ with corresponding packed encryption $[\![\vec{c_v}]\!] = [\![c_{v|k|}| \ldots |c_{v1}|0| \ldots |0]\!]$. As a result, computing $[\![b_v]\!] \boxdot [\![\vec{c_v}]\!]$ for each leaf $v \in \mathcal{L}$ and summing over all leaves results in the correct classification label. Note that, this assumes that one is classifying only one vector and not many as in the next case.

Packing Attribute Values. Let $x^{(1)}, \ldots, x^{(s)}$ be s possible attribute vectors with $x^{(l)} = [x_1^{(l)}, \ldots, x_n^{(l)}]$, $1 \le l \le s$. For each $x_i^{(l)}$, let $x_i^{(l)^b} = x_{i\mu}^{(l)}, \ldots, x_{i1}^{(l)}$ be the bit representation. Then, the client generates for each attribute x_i the ciphertexts $[\![cx_{i\mu}]\!], \ldots, [\![cx_{i2}]\!], [\![cx_{i1}]\!]$ as illustrated in Fig. 1a.

To shorten the notation, let y_j denote the threshold of the j-th decision node (i.e., $y_j = v_j.\mathsf{threshold}$) and assume $v_j.\mathsf{aIndex} = i$. The server just encrypts each threshold bitwise which automatically replicates the bit to all slots. This is illustrated in Fig. 1b.

$$[\![cx_{i1}]\!] = [\![x_{i1}^{(1)}| \ldots |x_{i1}^{(s)}]\!] \qquad [\![cy_{j1}]\!] = [\![y_{j1}| \ldots |y_{j1}]\!]$$

$$\ldots \qquad \qquad \ldots$$

$$[\![cx_{i\mu}]\!] = [\![x_{i\mu}^{(1)}| \ldots |x_{i\mu}^{(s)}]\!] \qquad [\![cy_{j\mu}]\!] = [\![y_{j\mu}| \ldots |y_{j\mu}]\!]$$

(a) Packing many x_i (b) Packing y_j

Fig. 1. Packing attribute values

Note that $([\![cy_{j\mu}]\!], \ldots, [\![cy_{j1}]\!]) = [\![y_j^b]\!]$ holds because of SVCP. The above described encoding allows to compare s attribute values together with one threshold. This is possible because the routine SHECMP is compatible with SVCP such that we have: $\mathrm{SHECMP}(([\![cx_{i\mu}]\!], \ldots, [\![cx_{i1}]\!]), [\![y_j^b]\!]) = ([\![b_{ij}^{(1)}| \ldots |b_{ij}^{(s)}]\!], [\![b_{ji}^{(1)}| \ldots |b_{ji}^{(s)}]\!])$, where $b_{ij}^{(l)} = [x_i^{(l)} > y_j]$ and $b_{ji}^{(l)} = [y_j > x_i^{(l)}]$. This results in a single ciphertext such that the l-th slot contains the comparison result between $b_{ij}^{(l)}$.

Aggregating decision bits remains unchanged as described in Algorithm 1. It results in a packed ciphertext $[\![b_v]\!] = [\![b_v^{(1)}| \ldots |b_v^{(s)}]\!]$ for each leaf $v \in \mathcal{L}$, where $b_v^{(l)} = 1$ if $x^{(l)}$ classifies to leaf v and $b_u^{(l)} = 0$ for all other leaf $u \in \mathcal{L} \setminus \{v\}$.

For the classification label c_v of a leaf node $v \in \mathcal{L}$, let $[\![c_v^b]\!] = ([\![c_{v|k|}]\!], \ldots, [\![c_{v1}]\!])$ denote the encryption of the bit representation $c_v^b = c_{v|k|} \cdots c_{v1}$. To select the correct classification label algorithm FINALIZE($\mathcal{L}$) is updated as follows.

We compute $[\![c_{v|k|}]\!] \boxdot [\![b_v]\!], \dots, [\![c_{v1}]\!] \boxdot [\![b_v]\!]$ for each leaf $v \in \mathcal{L}$ and sum them component-wise over all leaves. This results in the encrypted bit representation of the correct classification labels.

Packing Threshold Values. In this case, the client encrypts a single attribute in one ciphertext, while the server encrypts multiple threshold values in a single ciphertext. Hence, for an attribute value x_i, the client generates the ciphertexts similar to in Fig. 1a. Let m_i be the number of decision nodes that compare to the attribute x_i (i.e., $m_i = |\{v_j \in \mathcal{D} : v_j.\mathsf{aIndex} = i\}|$). The server packs all corresponding threshold values in $\lceil \frac{m_i}{s} \rceil$ ciphertext(s).

The packing of threshold values allows to compare one attribute value against multiple threshold values together. Unfortunately, we do not have access to the slots while performing homomorphic operation. Hence, to aggregate the decision bits, we make m_i copies of the resulting packed decision bits and shift left each decision bit to the first slot. Then the aggregation of the decision bits and the finalizing algorithm work as in the previous case with the only difference that only the result in the first slot matters and the remaining can be set to 0.

5.3   Efficient Path Evaluation

Homomorphic multiplication increases the noise significantly [5]. To evaluate paths, we need to keep the multiplication depth small.

Definition 8 (Multiplicative Depth). *Let f be a function, C_f be a boolean circuit that computes f and consists of AND-gates or multiplication (modulo 2) gates and XOR-gates or addition (modulo 2) gates. The circuit depth of C_f is the maximal length of a path from an input gate to an output gate. The multiplicative depth of C_f is the path from an input gate to an output gate with the largest number of multiplication gates.*

Path evaluation requires to homomorphically compute $f([a_1, \dots, a_n]) = \Pi_{i=1}^{n} a_i$, where the a_i are comparison results on the path.

Lemma 2 (Logarithmic Multiplicative Depth). *Let $[a_1, \dots, a_n]$ be an array of n integers and f be the function: $f([a_1, \dots, a_n]) = [a_1', \dots a_{\lceil \frac{n}{2} \rceil}']$, where*

$$a_i' = \begin{cases} a_{2i-1} \cdot a_{2i} & \text{if } (n \bmod 2 = 0) \vee (i < \lceil \frac{n}{2} \rceil), \\ a_n & \text{if } (n \bmod 2 = 1) \wedge (i = \lceil \frac{n}{2} \rceil). \end{cases}$$

Moreover, let f be an iterated function where f^i is the i-th iterate defined as:

$$f^i([a_1, \dots, a_n]) = \begin{cases} [a_1, \dots, a_n] & \text{if } i = 0, \\ f(f^{i-1}([a_1, \dots, a_n])) & \text{if } i \geq 1. \end{cases}$$

The $|n|$-th iterate $f^{|n|}$ of f computes $\Pi_{i=1}^{n} a_i$ and has multiplicative depth $|n| - 1$ if n is a power of two and $|n|$ otherwise, where $|n| = \log n$ is the bitlength of n: $f^{|n|}([a_1, \dots, a_n]) = [\Pi_{i=1}^{n} a_i]$.

Due to space constraints, we provide the algorithm for path evaluation with multiplicative depth in the Appendix (Algorithm 6). This algorithm consists of a main function EVALPATHSE that collects for each leaf v encrypted comparison results on the path from the root to v, and a sub-function EVALMUL which multiplies comparison results according to Lemma 2.

Although highly parallelizable, EVALPATHSE is still not optimal, as each path is considered individually. Since multiple paths in a binary tree share a common prefix (from the root), one would ideally want to handle common prefixes one time and not many times for each leaf. This can be solved using *memoization* technique which is an optimization that stores results of expensive function calls such that they can be used latter if needed. Unfortunately, naive memoization would require a complex synchronization in a multi-threaded environment and linear multiplicative depth. The next section describes a pre-computation on the tree, that would allow us to have the best of both worlds - multiplication with logarithmic depth along the paths, while reusing the result of common prefixes.

5.4   Improving Path Evaluation with Pre-Computation

The idea behind this optimization is to use directed acyclic graph which we want to define first.

Definition 9 (DAG). *A directed acyclic graph (DAG) is a graph with directed edges in which there are no cycles. A vertex v of a DAG is said to be reachable from another vertex u if there exists a non-trivial path that starts at u and ends at v. The reachability relationship is a partial order $\leq$ and we say that two vertices u and v are ordered as $u \leq v$ if there exists a directed path from u to v.*

We require our DAGs to have a unique maximum element. The edges in the DAG define dependency relation between vertices.

Definition 10 (Dependency Graph). *Let h be the function that takes two DAGs G_1, G_2 and returns a DAG G_3 that connects the maxima of G_1 and G_2. We define the function $g([a_1, \ldots, a_n])$ that takes an array of integers and returns:*

- *a graph with a single vertex labeled with a_1 if $n = 1$*
- *$h(g([a_1, \ldots, a_{n'}]), g([a_{n'+1}, \ldots, a_n]))$ if $n > 1$ holds, where $n' = 2^{|n|-1}$ and $|n|$ denotes the bitlength of n.*

We call the DAG G generated by $G = g([a_1, \ldots, a_n])$ a dependency graph. *For each edge (a_i, a_j) in G such that $i < j$, we say that a_j depends on a_i and denote this by adding a_i in the dependency list of a_j. We require that if $L(j) = [a_{i_1}, \ldots, a_{i_{|L(j)|}}]$ is the dependency list of a_j then it holds $i_1 > i_2 > \ldots i_{|L(j)|}$.*

An example of dependency graph generated by the function $g([a_1, \ldots, a_n])$ is illustrated in Fig. 2a for $n = 4$ and $n = 5$.

Lemma 3. *Let $[a_1, \ldots, a_n]$ be an array of n integers. Then $g([a_1, \ldots, a_n])$ as defined above generates a DAG whose maximum element is marked with a_n.*

Lemma 4. *Let $[a_1, \ldots, a_n]$ be an array of n integers, $G = g([a_1, \ldots, a_n])$ be a DAG as above, and $L(j) = [a_{i_1}, \ldots, a_{i_{|L(j)|}}]$ be the dependency list of a_j. Then the algorithm in Fig. 2b computes $\Pi_{i=1}^{n} a_i$ with a multiplicative depth of $\log(n)$.*

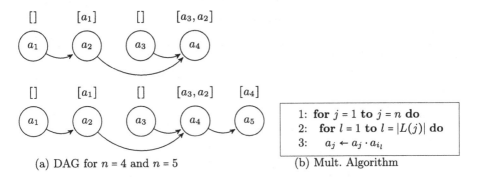

(a) DAG for $n = 4$ and $n = 5$

1: **for** $j = 1$ **to** $j = n$ **do**
2:   **for** $l = 1$ **to** $l = |L(j)|$ **do**
3:     $a_j \leftarrow a_j \cdot a_{i_l}$

(b) Mult. Algorithm

Fig. 2. DAG pre-computation and multiplication algorithm using DAG

The proofs of Lemmas 3 and 4 follow by induction similar to Lemma 2. Before describing the improved path evaluation algorithm, we first extend our Node data structure by adding to it a new field representing a stack denoted dag, that stores the dependency list. Moreover, we group the nodes of the DT by level and use an array denoted level[], such that level[0] stores a pointer to the root and level[i] stores pointers to the child nodes of level[$i-1$] for $i \geq 1$. Now, we are ready to describe the improved path evaluation algorithm which consists of a pre-computation step and an online step.

The pre-computation is a one-time computation that depends only on the structure of the DT and requires no encryption. As described in Algorithm 7, its main function COMPUTEDAG uses the leveled structure of the tree and the dependency graph defined above to compute the dependency list of each node in the tree (i.e., the DAG defined above). The sub-function ADDEDGE is used to actually add nodes to the dependency list of another node (i.e., by adding edges between these nodes in the DAG).

The online step is described in Algorithm 8. It follows the idea of the algorithm in Fig. 2b by multiplying decision bit level-wise depending on the dependency lists. The correctness follows from Lemma 4.

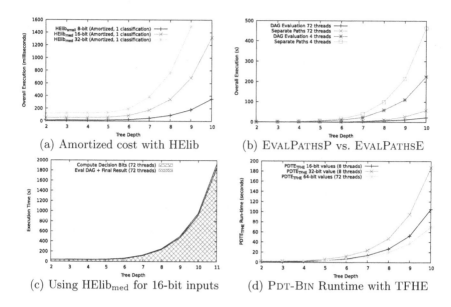

(a) Amortized cost with HElib   (b) EVALPATHSP vs. EVALPATHSE

(c) Using HElib$_{med}$ for 16-bit inputs   (d) PDT-BIN Runtime with TFHE

Fig. 3. PDT-BIN runtime

6   Evaluation

In this section, we discuss some implementation details and evaluate our schemes.

6.1   Implementation Details

We implemented our algorithms using HElib [21] and TFHE [10,11]. We also implemented the main algorithm using an arithmetic circuit based on Lin-Tzeng comparison protocol [26,35]. We refer to this implementation as PDT-INT. HElib is a C++ library that implements FHE. The current version includes an implementation of the BGV scheme [5]. HElib also includes various optimizations that make FHE runs faster, including ciphertext packing (SVCP) techniques [31].

TFHE is a C/C++ library that implements FHE proposed by Chillotti et al. [10]. It allows to evaluate any boolean circuit on encrypted data. The current version implements a very fast gate-by-gate bootstrapping, i.e., bootstrapping is performed after each gate evaluation. Future versions will include leveled FHE and ciphertext packing Chillotti et al. [10]. Dai and Sunar [13,14] propose an implementation of TFHE on CUDA-enabled GPUs that is 26 times faster.

We evaluated our scheme on an AWS instance with Intel(R) Xeon(R) Platinum 8124M CPU @ 3.00 GHz running Ubuntu 18.04.2 LTS; with 36 CPUs, 144 GB Memory and 8 GB SSD. As the bottleneck of our scheme is the overhead of the HE, we focus on the computation done by the server. We describe HE parameters and the performance of basic operations in Appendix A.

6.2 Performance of Pdt-Bin

In this section, we report on our experiment with PDT-BIN on complete trees. Recall that for FHE supporting SIMD, we can use attribute values packing that allows to evaluate many attribute vectors together. We, therefore, focus on attribute packing to show the advantage of SIMD. Figure 3a illustrates the amortized runtime of PDT-BIN with HElib. That is, the time of one PDTE evaluation divided by the number of slots in a ciphertext. As one can expect, the runtime clearly depends on the bitlength of the attribute values and the depth of the tree. The results show a clear advantage of HElib when classifying large data sets. For paths aggregation, we proposed EVALPATHSE (Algorithm 6) and EVALPATHSP (Algorithm 8). Figure 3b illustrates PDT-BIN runtime using these algorithms in a multi-threaded environment and shows a clear advantage of EVALPATHSP which will be used in the remaining experiments with PDT-BIN. Figure 3c illustrates the runtime of PDT-BIN with HElib$_{med}$ showing that the computation cost is dominated by the computation of decision bits which involves homomorphic evaluation of comparison circuits. In Fig. 3d, we report the evaluation of PDT-BIN using TFHE, which shows a clear advantage compared to HElib. For the same experiment with 72 threads, TFHE evaluates a complete tree of depth 10 and 64-bit input in less than 80 s, while HElib takes about 400 s for 16-bit input. Recall that, a CUDA implementation [13,14] of TFHE can further improve the time of PDT-BIN using TFHE.

6.3 Performance on Real Datasets

We also performed experiments on real datasets from the UCI repository [36]. For PDT-BIN, we reported the costs for HElib (single and amortized) and the costs for TFHE. Since TFHE evaluates only boolean circuits, we only have implementation and evaluation of PDT-INT with HElib. We also illustrate in Table 1 the costs of two best previous works that rely only on HE, whereby the figures are taken from the respective papers [28,32]. For one protocol run, PDT-BIN with TFHE is much more faster than PDT-BIN with HElib which is also faster than PDT-INT with HElib. However, because of the large number of slots, the amortized cost of PDT-BIN with HElib is better. For 16-bit inputs, our amortized time with HElib and our time with TFHE outperform XCMP [28] which used 12-bit inputs. For the same input bitlength, XCMP is still much more better than our one run using HElib, since the multiplicative depth is just 3. However, our schemes still have a better communication and PDT-BIN has no leakage. While the scheme of Tai et al. [32] in the semi-honest model has a better time for 64-bit inputs than our schemes for 16-bit inputs, it requires a fast network communication and at least double cost in the malicious model. The efficiency of Tai et al. is in part due to their ECC implementation of the lifted ElGamal, which allows a fast runtime and smaller ciphertexts, but is not secure against a quantum attacker, unlike lattice-based FHE as used in our schemes.

Table 1. Runtime (in seconds) on Real Datasets: λ is the security level. μ is the input bit length. #thd is the number of threads. Column "one" is the time for one protocol run while "am." is the amortized time (e.g., the time for one run divided by s).

		PDT-Bin (TFHE)		PDT-Bin (HElib)		PDT-Int (HElib)	[28] (HElib)	[32] (mcl [29])
λ		128		150		135	128	128
μ		16		16		16	12	64
#thd		16		16		16	16	-
	n, d, m	one	am.	one	am.	one	one	one
Heart-disease	13, 3, 5	0.94	0.05	40.61	0.0073	45.59	0.59	0.25
Housing	13, 13, 92	6.30	0.35	252.38	0.90	428.23	10.27	1.98
Spambase	57, 17, 58	3.66	0.24	174.46	0.72	339.60	6.88	1.80
Artificial	16, 10, 500	22.39	1.81	1303.55	0.75	2207.13	56.37	10.42

Table 2. Comparison of PDTE protocols.

Scheme	Rounds	Tools	Communication	Comparisons	Leakage
[7]	≈ 5	HE+GC	$\mathcal{O}\left(2^d\right)$	d	m, d
[2]	≈ 4	HE+GC	$\mathcal{O}\left(2^d\right)$	d	m, d
[4]	≥ 6	FHE/SHE	$\mathcal{O}\left(2^d\right)$	m	m
[38]	6	HE+OT	$\mathcal{O}\left(2^d\right)$	m	m
[32]	4	HE	$\mathcal{O}\left(2^d\right)$	m	m
[12]	≈ 9	SS	$\mathcal{O}\left(2^d\right)$	m	m, d
[34]	$\mathcal{O}(d)$	GC,OT ORAM	$\mathcal{O}\left(2^d\right)$ $\mathcal{O}\left(d^2\right)$	d	m, d
[28]	1	FHE/SHE	$\mathcal{O}\left(2^d\right)$	m	m
PDT-Bin	1	FHE/SHE	$\mathcal{O}(1), \mathcal{O}(d)$	m	-
PDT-Int	1		$\mathcal{O}\left(2^d/s\right)$		m

7   Related Work

Our work is related to secure multiparty computation (SMC) [16,20], private function evaluation (PFE) [25,30] particularly privacy-preserving DT evaluation [2,4,7,23,24,32,34,38] which we briefly review in this section and refer to the literature for more details. Brikell et al. [7] propose the first protocol for PDTE by combining additively HE and garbled circuits (GC) in a novel way. Although the evaluation time of Brikell et al.'s scheme is sublinear in the tree size, the secure program itself and hence the communication cost is linear and therefore not efficient for large trees. Barni et al. [2] improve the previous scheme by reducing the computation costs by a constant factor. Bost et al. [4] represent the DT as a multivariate polynomial. The parties evaluate this polynomial

Table 3. Comparison of 1-round PDTE protocols.

Scheme	SIMD	Generic	Output-expressive	Multiplicative Depth	Output Length
[28]	No	No	No	3	2^{d+1}
PDT-BIN	Yes	Yes	Yes	$|\mu| + |d| + 2$	1 or d
PDT-INT	Yes	Yes	No	$|\mu| + 1$	$\lceil 2^d/s \rceil$

interactively and encrypted under the client's public key using a fully HE Wu et al. [38] use different techniques that require only additively HE (AHE). They use the DGK protocol [15] for comparison and reveal to the server comparison bits encrypted under the client's public key. Tai et al. [32] use the DGK comparison protocol [15] and AHE as well, but mark the edges with the comparison results at each node. Tueno et al. [34] represent the tree as an array. Then, they traverse the tree interactively and use secure array indexing to select the next node and attribute. Kiss et al. [24] propose a modular design consisting of the sub-functionalities: selection of attributes, integer comparison, and evaluation of paths. De Cock et al. [12] follow the same idea as some previous schemes, but operate in the information theoretic model using secret sharing (SS) based SMC and commodity-based cryptography [3]. Using a polynomial encoding of the inputs and BGV homomorphic scheme [5], Lu et al. [28] propose a non-interactive comparison protocol called XCMP which is *output expressive* (i.e., it preserves additive homomorphism). They implement the scheme of Tai et al. [32] using XCMP. The resulting PDTE is non-interactive and efficient because of the small *multiplicative depth*. However, it is not *generic*, as it primarily works for small inputs and depends explicitly on BGV-type HE scheme. Moreover, it does not support *SIMD* operations and is no longer output expressive as XCMP. Hence, it cannot be extended to a larger protocol (e.g., random forest [6]) while preserving the non-interactive property. Finally, its *output length* (i.e., the number of resulted ciphertexts from server computation) is exponential in the depth d of the tree, while the output length of our binary instantiation PDT-BIN is at most linear in d. A comparison of PDTE protocols is summarized in Tables 2 and 3. A more detailed complexity analysis of our schemes is described in Appendix C.

8   Conclusion

While almost all existing PDTE protocols require many interaction between the client and the server, we designed and implemented novel client-server protocols that delegate the complete evaluation to the server while preserving privacy and keeping the overhead low. Our solutions rely on SHE/FHE and evaluate the tree on ciphertexts encrypted under the client's public key. Since current SHE/FHE schemes have high overhead, we combine efficient data representations with different algorithmic optimizations to keep the computational overhead and the communication cost low.

A   Encryption Parameters and Basic Operations

Recall that FHE schemes – as considered in this paper – are usually defined over a ring $\mathbb{Z}[X]/(X^N + 1)$ and that the encryption scheme might be a leveled FHE with parameter L. For HElib, the parameters N and L determines how to generate encryption keys for a security level λ which is at least 128 in all our experiments. The degree of the ring polynomial in HElib is not necessarily a power of 2. The ring polynomial is chosen among the cyclotomic polynomials. For HElib, we abuse the notation and use N to denote the N-th cyclotomic polynomial. Given the value of L and other parameters, the HElib function FindM$(\cdot)$ computes the N-th cyclotomic polynomial, that guarantees a security level at least equal to a given security parameter λ. Table 4 summarizes the parameters we used for key generation and the resulting sizes for encryption keys and ciphertexts. We refer to it as *homomorphic context* or just *context*. For HElib, one needs to choose L large enough than the depth of the circuit to be evaluated and then computes an appropriate value for N that ensures a security level at least 128. We experimented with tree different contexts (HElib$_{\text{small}}$, HElib$_{\text{med}}$, HElib$_{\text{big}}$) for the binary representation used in PDT-BIN, and HElib$_{\text{int}}$ for the integer representation used in PDT-INT. For TFHE, the default value of N is 1024 and the security level is 128 while L is infinite because of the gate-by-gate bootstrapping. We used the context TFHE$_{128}$ to evaluate PDT-BIN with TFHE. The last two columns of Table 4 reports the average runtime for encryption and decryption over 100 runs.

Table 4. HE Parameters and Results: For HElib, column N is not the degree of the ring polynomial, but the N-th cyclotomic polynomial. It is computed in HElib using a function called FindM$(\cdot)$.

Name	L	N	λ (bits)	Slots	sk (MB)	pk (MB)	Ctxt (MB)	Enc (ms)	Dec (ms)
HElib$_{\text{small}}$	200	13981	151	600	52.2	51.6	1.7	59.21	26.08
HElib$_{\text{med}}$	300	18631	153	720	135.4	134.1	3.7	124.39	54.31
HElib$_{\text{big}}$	500	32109	132	1800	370.1	367.1	8.8	283.49	127.11
HElib$_{\text{int}}$	450	24793	138.161	6198	370.1	367.1	8.8	323.41	88.63
TFHE$_{128}$	∞	1024	128	1	82.1	82.1	0.002	0.04842	0.00129

B   Security Analysis

It is straightforward to see that our protocols are secure. There is no interaction with the client during the computation and a semi-honest server sees only IND-CPA ciphertexts. A semi-honest client only learns the encryption of the result. A malicious server can only return a false classification result. This is inherent to PFE where the function (the DT in our case) is an input to the computation. A malicious client can send a too "noisy" ciphertext, such that after the computation at the server a correct decryption is not possible, leaking some information.

```
Input: leaves set L, decision nodes set D          6:    w ← v
Output: Updated v.cmp for each v ∈ L               7:    while w ≠root do          ▷ path to root
1: function EVALPATHSE(L, D)                        8:      path[l] ← ⟦w.cmp⟧
2:   for each v ∈ L do                              9:      l ← l − 1
3:     let d = #nodes on the path (root → v)       10:      w ← w.parent
4:     let path = empty array of length d          11:    ⟦v.cmp⟧← EVALMUL(1, d, path)
5:     l ← d
```

```
Input: integers from, to; array of nodes path     4:    n ← to − from + 1
Output: Product of elements in path                5:    mid ← 2^{|n−1|−1} + from − 1   ▷ |n| = log₂(n)
1: function EVALMUL(from, to, path)                6:    ⟦left⟧← EVALMUL(from, mid, path)
2:   if from ≥ to then                             7:    ⟦right⟧← EVALMUL(mid + 1, to, path)
3:     return path[from]                           8:    return ⟦left⟧ ⊡ ⟦right⟧
```

Algorithm 6. Paths Evaluation with log Multiplicative Depth

```
Input: integers up and low                         7:    ADDEDGE(v, low, mid)
Output: Computed v.dag for each v ∈ D ∪ L          8:    for i = mid + 1 to low − 1 do          ▷
1: function COMPUTEDAG(up, low)                           non-deepest leaves
2:   if up ≥ low then                              9:      for each v ∈ level[i] ∩ L do
3:     return          ▷ end the recursion        10:        ADDEDGE(v, i, mid)
4:   δ ← low − up + 1                              11:    COMPUTEDAG(up, mid)
5:   mid ← 2^{|δ−1|−1} − 1 + up ▷ |δ| bitlength of δ  12:    COMPUTEDAG(mid + 1, low)
6:   for each v ∈ level[low] do
```

```
Input: Node v, integers currLvl and destLvl       3:    while currLvl > destLvl do
Output: Updated v.dag                              4:      w ← w.parent
1: function ADDEDGE(v, currLvl, destLvl)           5:      currLvl ← currLvl − 1
2:   w ← v                                         6:      v.dag.push(w)          ▷ dag is a stack
```

Algorithm 7. Pre-computation of Multiplication DAG

This attack works only with level FHE and is easy to deal with, namely the computation of a ciphertext capacity is a public function which the server can use to check the ciphertexts before starting the computation. As PDT-BIN returns the bit representation of the resulted classification label whose bitlength is public (i.e., the set of possible classification labels is known to the client), there is no leakage beyond the final output. PDT-INT returns as many ciphertexts as there are leaves and, therefore, leaks the number of decision nodes.

C   Complexity Analysis

We now analyse the complexity of our schemes. We assume that the decision tree is a complete tree with depth d.

Complexity of Pdt-Bin. The SHE comparison circuit has multiplicative depth $|\mu - 1| + 1$ and requires $\mathcal{O}(\mu \cdot |\mu|)$ multiplications [9]. That is, the evaluation of all decision nodes requires $\mathcal{O}\left(2^d \mu \cdot |\mu|\right)$ multiplications. The path evaluation has a multiplicative depth of $|d − 1|$ and requires for all 2^d paths $\mathcal{O}\left(d2^d\right)$ multiplications. The evaluation of the leaves has a multiplicative depth of 1 and requires

Input: nodes stored by level in array level	3:	**for each** $v \in$ level$[i]$ **do**
Output: Updated v.cmp for each $v \in \mathcal{L}$	4:	**while** NOT v.dag.empty() **do** ▷ stack
1: **function** EVALPATHSP	5:	$w \leftarrow v$.dag.pop()
2: **for** $i = 1$ **to** d **do** ▷ top to bottom level	6:	$[\![v.\mathrm{cmp}]\!] \leftarrow [\![v.\mathrm{cmp}]\!] \boxdot [\![w.\mathrm{cmp}]\!]$

Algorithm 8. Aggregate Decision Bits with DAG

in total 2^d multiplications. The total multiplicative depth for PDT-BIN is, therefore, $|\mu - 1| + |d - 1| + 2 \approx |\mu| + |d| + 2$ while the total number of multiplications is $\mathcal{O}\left(2^d \mu \cdot |\mu| + d2^d + 2^d\right) \approx \mathcal{O}\left(d2^d\right)$.

For the label packing, the bit representation of each classification label is packed in one ciphertext. This hold for the final result as well. As a result, if the tree is complete and all classification labels are distinct, then the server sends $\lceil \frac{d}{s} \rceil$ ciphertext(s) to client. In practice, however, $\lceil \frac{d}{s} \rceil = 1$ holds as d is smaller that the number s of slots.

For threshold packing, the decision bit b_v at node v is encrypted as $[\![b_v|0|...|0]\!]$. By encrypting the classification label $c_i = c_{i|k|}...c_{i1}$ as $[\![c_{i|k|}|0|...|0]\!], ..., [\![c_{i1}|0|...|0]\!]$, the final result c_l will be encrypted similarly such that with extra shifts, we can build the ciphertext $[\![c_{l|k|}|...|c_{l1}|0|...|0]\!]$. As a result, the server sends only 1 ciphertext back to the client.

For other cases (e.g., attribute packing, or no packing at all as in the current implementation of TFHE), the bits of a classification label are encrypted separately which holds for the final result as well. As a result the server sends back d ciphertexts to the client.

Complexity of Pdt-Int. The modified Lin-Tzeng comparison circuit has multiplicative $|\mu - 1|$ and requires $\mathcal{O}(\mu - 1)$ multiplications. As a result, the evaluation of all decision node requires $\mathcal{O}\left((\mu - 1)2^d\right)$ multiplications. In PDT-INT, the path evaluation does not requires any multiplication. However, the leave evaluation has a multiplicative depth of 1 and requires in total 2^d multiplications. The total multiplicative depth for PDT-INT is therefore $|\mu - 1| + 1 \approx |\mu| + 1$ while the total number of multiplications is $\mathcal{O}\left((\mu - 1)2^d + 2^d\right) \approx \mathcal{O}\left(2^d\right)$.

For PDT-INT, it is not possible to aggregate the leaves as in PDT-BIN. If the client is classifying many inputs, the server must send 2^d ciphertexts back. If the client is classifying only one input, then the server can use shifts to pack the result in $\lceil \frac{2^d}{s} \rceil$ ciphertext(s).

References

1. Albrecht, M., et al.: Homomorphic encryption security standard. Technical report, HomomorphicEncryption.org, Cambridge MA, March 2018
2. Barni, M., Failla, P., Kolesnikov, V., Lazzeretti, R., Sadeghi, A.-R., Schneider, T.: Secure evaluation of private linear branching programs with medical applications. In: Backes, M., Ning, P. (eds.) ESORICS 2009. LNCS, vol. 5789, pp. 424–439. Springer, Heidelberg (2009). https://doi.org/10.1007/978-3-642-04444-1_26

3. Beaver, D.: Commodity-based cryptography (extended abstract). In: STOC, pp. 446–455. ACM, New York (1997)
4. Bost, R., Popa, R.A., Tu, S., Goldwasser, S.: Machine learning classification over encrypted data. In: NDSS (2015)
5. Brakerski, Z., Gentry, C., Vaikuntanathan, V.: Fully homomorphic encryption without bootstrapping. ECCC **18**, 111 (2011)
6. Breiman, L.: Random forests. Mach. Learn. **45**(1), 5–32 (2001)
7. Brickell, J., Porter, D.E., Shmatikov, V., Witchel, E.: Privacy-preserving remote diagnostics. In: CCS, pp. 498–507. ACM, New York (2007)
8. Büscher, N., Demmler, D., Katzenbeisser, S., Kretzmer, D., Schneider, T.: Hycc: compilation of hybrid protocols for practical secure computation. In: CCS 2018, pp. 847–861 (2018)
9. Cheon, J.H., Kim, M., Kim, M.: Search-and-compute on encrypted data. In: Brenner, M., Christin, N., Johnson, B., Rohloff, K. (eds.) FC 2015. LNCS, vol. 8976, pp. 142–159. Springer, Heidelberg (2015). https://doi.org/10.1007/978-3-662-48051-9_11
10. Chillotti, I., Gama, N., Georgieva, M., Izabachène, M.: TFHE: fast fully homomorphic encryption over the torus. IACR Cryptology ePrint Archive **2018**, 421 (2018)
11. Chillotti, I., Gama, N., Georgieva, M., Izabachène, M.: TFHE: fast fully homomorphic encryption library, August 2016. https://tfhe.github.io/tfhe/
12. Cock, M.D., et al.: Efficient and private scoring of decision trees, support vector machines and logistic regression models based on pre-computation. IEEE Trans. Dependable Sec. Comput. **16**(2), 217–230 (2019)
13. Dai, W., Sunar, B.: cuHE: a homomorphic encryption accelerator library. In: Pasalic, E., Knudsen, L.R. (eds.) BalkanCryptSec 2015. LNCS, vol. 9540, pp. 169–186. Springer, Cham (2016). https://doi.org/10.1007/978-3-319-29172-7_11
14. Dai, W., Sunar, B.: Cuda-accelerated fully homomorphic encryption library, August 2019. https://github.com/vernamlab/cuFHE
15. Damgård, I., Geisler, M., Krøigaard, M.: Efficient and secure comparison for on-line auctions. In: Pieprzyk, J., Ghodosi, H., Dawson, E. (eds.) ACISP 2007. LNCS, vol. 4586, pp. 416–430. Springer, Heidelberg (2007). https://doi.org/10.1007/978-3-540-73458-1_30
16. Damgård, I., Pastro, V., Smart, N., Zakarias, S.: Multiparty computation from somewhat homomorphic encryption. In: Safavi-Naini, R., Canetti, R. (eds.) CRYPTO 2012. LNCS, vol. 7417, pp. 643–662. Springer, Heidelberg (2012). https://doi.org/10.1007/978-3-642-32009-5_38
17. Franz, M., Holzer, A., Katzenbeisser, S., Schallhart, C., Veith, H.: CBMC-GC: an ANSI C compiler for secure two-party computations. In: Cohen, A. (ed.) CC 2014. LNCS, vol. 8409, pp. 244–249. Springer, Heidelberg (2014). https://doi.org/10.1007/978-3-642-54807-9_15
18. Fredrikson, M., Jha, S., Ristenpart, T.: Model inversion attacks that exploit confidence information and basic countermeasures. In: CCS, pp. 1322–1333 (2015)
19. Gentry, C.: Fully homomorphic encryption using ideal lattices. In: STOC, pp. 169–178. ACM, New York (2009)
20. Goldreich, O.: Foundations of Cryptography: Basic Applications, vol. 2. Cambridge University Press, New York (2004)
21. Halevi, S., Shoup, V.: Algorithms in HElib. In: Garay, J.A., Gennaro, R. (eds.) CRYPTO 2014. LNCS, vol. 8616, pp. 554–571. Springer, Heidelberg (2014). https://doi.org/10.1007/978-3-662-44371-2_31

22. Hazay, C., Lindell, Y.: Efficient Secure Two-Party Protocols: Techniques and Constructions, 1st edn. Springer, New York (2010). https://doi.org/10.1007/978-3-642-14303-8

23. Joye, M., Salehi, F.: Private yet efficient decision tree evaluation. In: Kerschbaum, F., Paraboschi, S. (eds.) DBSec 2018. LNCS, vol. 10980, pp. 243–259. Springer, Cham (2018). https://doi.org/10.1007/978-3-319-95729-6_16

24. Kiss, Á., Naderpour, M., Liu, J., Asokan, N., Schneider, T.: SoK: modular and efficient private decision tree evaluation. PoPETs 2019(2), 187–208 (2019)

25. Kiss, Á., Schneider, T.: Valiant's universal circuit is practical. In: Fischlin, M., Coron, J.-S. (eds.) EUROCRYPT 2016. LNCS, vol. 9665, pp. 699–728. Springer, Heidelberg (2016). https://doi.org/10.1007/978-3-662-49890-3_27

26. Lin, H.-Y., Tzeng, W.-G.: An efficient solution to the millionaires' problem based on homomorphic encryption. In: Ioannidis, J., Keromytis, A., Yung, M. (eds.) ACNS 2005. LNCS, vol. 3531, pp. 456–466. Springer, Heidelberg (2005). https://doi.org/10.1007/11496137_31

27. Liu, C., Wang, X.S., Nayak, K., Huang, Y., Shi, E.: ObliVM: a programming framework for secure computation. In: SP, pp. 359–376 (2015)

28. Lu, W.J., Zhou, J.J., Sakuma, J.: Non-interactive and output expressive private comparison from homomorphic encryption. In: ASIACCS 2018, pp. 67–74 (2018)

29. MCL library, September 2019. https://github.com/herumi/mcl/

30. Mohassel, P., Sadeghian, S., Smart, N.P.: Actively secure private function evaluation. In: Sarkar, P., Iwata, T. (eds.) ASIACRYPT 2014. LNCS, vol. 8874, pp. 486–505. Springer, Heidelberg (2014). https://doi.org/10.1007/978-3-662-45608-8_26

31. Smart, N.P., Vercauteren, F.: Fully homomorphic SIMD operations. Des. Codes Cryptogr. 71(1), 57–81 (2014)

32. Tai, R.K.H., Ma, J.P.K., Zhao, Y., Chow, S.S.M.: Privacy-preserving decision trees evaluation via linear functions. In: Foley, S.N., Gollmann, D., Snekkenes, E. (eds.) ESORICS 2017. LNCS, vol. 10493, pp. 494–512. Springer, Cham (2017). https://doi.org/10.1007/978-3-319-66399-9_27

33. Tramèr, F., Zhang, F., Juels, A., Reiter, M.K., Ristenpart, T.: Stealing machine learning models via prediction APIs. In: USENIX, pp. 601–618 (2016)

34. Tueno, A., Kerschbaum, F., Katzenbeisser, S.: Private evaluation of decision trees using sublinear cost. PoPETs 2019, 266–286 (2019)

35. Tueno, A., Kerschbaum, F., Katzenbeisser, S., Boev, Y., Qureshi, M.: Secure computation of the kth-ranked element in a star network. In: FC 2020 (2020)

36. UCI repository (2019). http://archive.ics.uci.edu/ml/index.php

37. Witten, I.H., Frank, E., Hall, M.A.: Data Mining: Practical Machine Learning Tools and Techniques, 3rd edn. Morgan Kaufmann Publishers Inc., San Francisco (2011)

38. Wu, D.J., Feng, T., Naehrig, M., Lauter, K.: Privately evaluating decision trees and random forests. PoPETs 2016(4), 335–355 (2016)

39. Wu, X., Fredrikson, M., Jha, S., Naughton, J.F.: A methodology for formalizing model-inversion attacks. In: CSF, pp. 355–370 (2016)

Privacy-Preserving Anomaly Detection Using Synthetic Data

Rudolf Mayer$^{(\boxtimes)}$ ⓘ, Markus Hittmeir ⓘ, and Andreas Ekelhart ⓘ

SBA Research gGmbH, Floragasse 7, Vienna, Austria
{rmayer,mhittmeir,aekelhart}@sba-research.org

Abstract. With ever increasing capacity for collecting, storing, and processing of data, there is also a high demand for intelligent knowledge discovery and data analysis methods. While there have been impressive advances in machine learning and similar domains in recent years, this also gives rise to concerns regarding the protection of personal and otherwise sensitive data, especially if it is to be analysed by third parties, e.g. in collaborative settings, where it shall be exchanged for the benefit of training more powerful models. One scenario is anomaly detection, which aims at identifying rare items, events or observations, differing from the majority of the data. Such anomalous items, also referred to as outliers, often correspond to problematic cases, e.g. bank fraud, rare medical diseases, or intrusions, e.g. attacks on IT systems.

Besides anonymisation, which becomes difficult to achieve especially with high dimensional data, one approach for privacy-preserving data mining lies in the usage of synthetic data. Synthetic data comes with the promise of protecting the users' data and producing analysis results close to those achieved by using real data. However, since most synthetisation methods aim at preserving rather global properties and not characteristics of individual records to protect sensitive data, this form of data might be inadequate due to a lack of realistic outliers.

In this paper, we therefore analyse a number of different approaches for creating synthetic data. We study the utility of the created datasets for anomaly detection in supervised, semi-supervised and unsupervised settings, and compare it to the baseline of the original data.

Keywords: Synthetic data · Anomaly detection · Machine learning

1 Introduction

The demand for and practice of data sharing and exchange between different data collecting parties is increasing, often because different data sets complement each other, or because the processing and analysis of data is outsourced. Many interesting knowledge discovery tasks are dependent on large, high quality amounts of data being available. However, when data is sensitive, e.g. when it concerns individuals or is business related, there are certain regulatory and

Published by Springer Nature Switzerland AG 2020
A. Singhal and J. Vaidya (Eds.): DBSec 2020, LNCS 12122, pp. 195–207, 2020.
https://doi.org/10.1007/978-3-030-49669-2_11

other barriers for data sharing. Still, collaborative analysis of data can be very beneficial, e.g. when learning from misuse patterns that other parties have been exposed to, such as network intrusions or fraud. Thus, means to enable such data exchange are required. In some cases, anonymisation techniques such as k-anonymity [20] or Differential Privacy [6] can be successfully employed. For a detailed overview on privacy-preserving data publishing methods, see [5]. However, k-anonymity has been shown to be still prone to linkage attacks when adversaries have background knowledge and access to other data sources. Differential privacy, when applied to the model or the output of the model, on the other hand is not applicable for all types of analysis techniques. Both approaches distort the data records to some extend, which, due to the information loss, has potentially negative effects on the utility of the data and the models subsequently trained upon.

Synthetic data is generally considered as data obtained not from direct measurement. In the context of data analysis efforts, it is often considered to be data generated (or synthesised) from a real dataset that, e.g. for privacy considerations, can not be shared. Its aim is to provide a dataset containing records that are similar to the original ones, and that preserve the high-level relationships within the data, without actually disclosing real, single data points. While preserving global properties is often possible, there is generally still a certain loss in data utility, albeit for many settings, this might be acceptable – and potentially be of higher utility than anonymisation techniques.

Approaches can be distinguished on how the model for generating data is obtained. If the original data is not directly used, synthetic data can be generated based on rules and constraints describing the characteristics, requiring an in-depth knowledge on the original data and expert knowledge on the domain. Approaches that can access the original data can learn models from that data, and use these models to generate new data. These methods have the advantage of being applicable to virtually any kind of domain and being scalable to large amounts of attributes. They can also capture correlations that are not easily understood by human experts and for which rule-based methods would fail. The complexity of the employed models for representing the original data is of varying degree, which has implications on how well the synthetic data resembles the original. In this paper, we focus on approaches that utilise the original data.

Another differentiation is whether the dataset is **partially** or **fully** synthetic. The former means that only a subset of the available attributes (or sometimes a subset of the samples), especially those identified to be sensitive, are replaced by synthetically generated ones. For partially synthetic data, data utility is expected to be higher, even though disclosure risks may be higher as well.

Anomaly detection methods typically utilise general outlier detection techniques, but differ when there is a need to distinguish harmless noise from malicious intentions, actions or attacks. Many sub-types of anomaly detection can be distinguished, depending on the type of data, the required output, and whether labels that distinguish between normal and abnormal cases are available [4]. The latter decides whether the detection is to be performed in a supervised, unsupervised or semi-supervised setting. The general settings is that the *anomaly* (or outlier, minority) type of data points are very few compared to the "normal" data points – sometimes well below 1% of the whole dataset.

Anomaly detection can be considered a rather peculiar use case for employing synthetic data, as this approach tries to specifically preserve the global characteristics, but not of single data points – which could result in information leakage. Anomaly detection techniques, however, try to specifically find the unusual data points among a large amount, and the synthetically created dataset is not expected to produce outlier data points similar to the original ones, as they do not represent global properties. In this paper, we thus evaluate the utility of synthetic data for this task. We consider multiple scenarios, utilising three different approaches for generating synthetic data, and address supervised, semi-supervised and unsupervised methods for anomaly detection based on the generated data. We compare the results to a baseline of methods run on the original dataset.

Section 2 describes related work in synthetic data and anomaly detection. Section 3 describes the setup for our experiments, before we present our evaluation in Sect. 4. Finally, we present conclusions and future work in Sect. 5.

2   Related Work

One of the earliest applications of generic synthetic data generation in a data mining context is described by Rubin in [17], where multiple imputation is used to synthetically generate certain columns of datasets. This is thus a setting for partially synthetic data. Specific applications include e.g. the generation of time-series or log data, as they would be encountered for intrusion-detection scenarios [3,11]. More recently, several efforts have been made to generate synthetic images, e.g. in the medical domain for MR images [8].

In general, most approaches to synthetic data generation that are based on existing data, and not (only) on rules, consist of the following steps:

- Learning a representation (**model**) of the original data, with a certain statistical approach (such as estimating a probability density function)
- **Synthesising** the data, i.e. generating new data based on the model
- Optionally, a module to **ensure privacy** of the generated, synthetic data samples, e.g. by means of applying Differential Privacy

A major difference in existing approaches lies in the complexity of the learned model from the data. This can range from relative simple models learning (independent) probability density functions for each attribute, and more sophisticated models that preserve the correlation between attributes e.g. via co-variances, to models that capture very complex correlations e.g. via auto-encoders, or approaches utilising generative adversarial networks (GANs) [7]. In the synthetisation step, some approaches apply further methods for data protection, e.g. by applying Differential Privacy before publishing the synthetic dataset.

While synthetic data has shown to be of utility for multiple data analysis tasks including regression or classification (see e.g. [9]), another major aspect is whether it is actually able to fulfil the promises towards preserving the privacy of the individuals in the original dataset. Regarding disclosure risks for synthetic data, usually a distinction is made between fully and partially synthetic data. Reiter and Mitra [16] proposed identification disclosure risk estimations for partially synthetic data. They also note that the notion of identification disclosure is *not meaningful* for **fully** synthetic data, since fully synthetic records do not relate to original records in terms of a 1-to-1 correspondence. From an intruder's perspective, the approach to gain information by linking certain synthetic records to individuals is thus not promising, as such links generally do not exist, and matches that have been established with real individuals are only spurious, and not real. Other disclosure risks exist, e.g. attribute disclosure, where it is assumed that the intruder knows the values of certain attributes of their victim and wants to learn the value of some sensitive attribute (called the *target* variable). For a detailed discussion of the latter, see e.g. [10].

For our evaluation in this paper, we employ the following three data synthesizers: The *Synthetic Data Vault* (DV) [14] builds a model based on estimates for the distributions of each column. In order to preserve the correlation between attributes, the synthesizer applies a multivariate version of the Gaussian copula and computes the covariance matrix. The *DataSynthesizer* (DS) [15] provides, among simpler techniques, the 'correlated attribute mode', in which dependencies between attributes are represented by a Bayesian network, learned on the original data. The DataSynthesizer further uses the framework of Differential Privacy, and offers the possibility to inject noise in the model and thus the generated data, by a parameter controlling the magnitude. Finally, *synthpop* (SP) [13] uses as the default method a CART (Classification and Regression Trees) algorithm. The user is able to specify a large number of parameters and may apply a built-in function for disclosure control to the resulting synthetic dataset.

When preparing a dataset for publishing via anonymisation, synthetisation or similar approaches, some information at the level of individual records is invariably removed [5] in order to achieve the desired level of protecting the sensitive information that cannot be shared. Utility evaluation of such datasets can generally be done by two methods. One is to measure certain properties on the sanitised dataset and compare it to the original dataset, such as mean or standard deviation or the data distributions. This evaluation has the advantage of being independent of the final task being carried out on the dataset, but is also generally more difficult to put into an application context. Another approach is to measure the utility on a task, e.g. a supervised classification task, or outlier detection. In this approach, the metric measures the differences in effectiveness of the models on the original dataset compared to the sanitised one. In this paper, we focus on the second approach, as it is more suited for anomaly detection.

Anomaly detection typically utilises general outlier detection techniques [2, 21], but differ when there is a need to distinguish harmless noise, fluctuations or various forms of novelty, from malicious intentions, actions or attacks. There are many forms of anomaly detection depending on the nature of the input data, the form of output and the presence or absence of data labels [4]. Point anomalies denote individual data instances that are different from the normal data points. In a contextual anomaly, data instances are anomalous within a specific context, such as temporal or spatial. Collective anomalies identify a collection of instances as anomalous with respect to the entire dataset. In this paper, we focus primarily on point anomalies. Techniques for this type of anomalies are often the building blocks for contextual and collective anomalies, thus some of our conclusions transfer also to these scenarios.

Anomaly detection is used in a wide variety of contexts, such as fraud detection [1], intrusion detection [22], video surveillance systems, or forensic investigations in general. Specific techniques include unsupervised learning to find structures or patterns in data in the absence of any labels. Recent techniques include Generative Adversarial Networks (GANs), such as *f-AnoGAN* [18]. When labels are present only for the "normal" data points, a semi-supervised methods such as a one-class support vector machine (SVM) [19] or autoencoders are employed. Supervised methods require labels for both the normal and the anomaly cases, and can be addressed by utilising standard classification techniques, such as Logistic Regression, Random Forests, or Support Vector Machines.

3   Experiment Setup

In our experiments, we utilise the *"credit card fraud"* dataset by the ML group at ULB, which was provided publicly on Kaggle[1]. It contains data based on real samples from transactions made by credit cards in September 2013 by European cardholders, gathered over two days. Out of the total of 284,807 transactions, only 492 are identified as fraudulent. The dataset is thus highly unbalanced, as frauds account for only 0.172% of all transactions. The dataset contains 30 input variables. Due to confidentiality reasons, most of the original features have been transformed with Principal Component Analysis (PCA). A projection of the dataset to two dimensions can be seen in Fig. 1, created using t-Distributed Stochastic Neighbour Embedding (t-SNE) [12]. It can be observed that some of the anomaly data points are separable, especially the ones seen towards the top-right of the visualisation. However, also a large number of points seem to be mixed with normal (legit) records, and thus likely difficult to separate.

For the generation of synthetic data, we used the Synthetic Data Vault, the DataSynthesizer and the synthpop package (cf. Sect. 2). Our primary goal is an unbiased evaluation, and not an optimisation towards a specific synthesizer or target evaluation, but we performed a limited parameter search starting with the standard settings of each synthesizer. We performed the following procedure in order to synthesise and prepare the data for the utility evaluation.

1. We deleted columns in the context of standard feature cleaning, e.g. purely identifying attributes like the 'Time' column in the original dataset.

---

[1] https://www.kaggle.com/mlg-ulb/creditcardfraud.

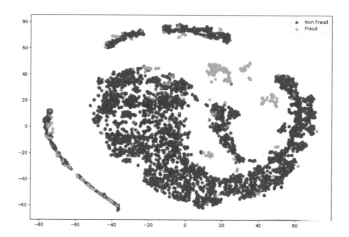

Fig. 1. Projection of the original dataset, generated using t-SNE

2. We performed a holdout method, i.e. we randomly split the data into training and test data, such that the size of the latter is 20% of the original table.
3. On the training data, we applied all three data synthesis methods. As output, we generate new, synthetic training data of equal length.

To investigate different configurations regarding its Differential Privacy settings, the DataSynthesizer is applied twice in Step 3. For each of the splits generated in Step 2, we therefore obtain five data files: (i) the original training data, (ii) the training data synthesised by the Synthetic Data Vault, (iii) the training data synthesised by synthpop, (iv) the training data synthesised by the DataSynthesizer without applying Differential Privacy, and (v) the training data synthesised by the DataSynthesizer applying Differential Privacy with the parameter ε.

With this procedure, we obtain datasets that we utilise for training a supervised anomaly detection system (e.g. a classification algorithm). Moreover, we want to separately investigate the behaviour of semi-supervised and unsupervised methods as well. We simulate semi-supervised data by repeating the above outlined procedure for just the data samples that are present in the training set (i.e. after splitting the data), and are labelled as "normal" cases. Finally, for the unsupervised approach, we simply remove the class label before synthesising the data. We thus obtain another five datasets for each of these cases, as for the supervised case, and therefore utilise in total 15 different synthetic training sets for each of the splits generated in Step 2. In addition, we also utilise the test dataset, which is used to estimate the results of the machine learning models on all the training sets. This dataset is not modified in any way, i.e. the synthetisation is performed only to generate the synthetic training sets. This setup will be used for our experiments for anomaly detection.

In Fig. 2, we show the same projection as in Fig. 1, but for the synthetic data generated by the DataSynthesizer and synthpop. We observe that DataSynthesizer is generating the fraudulent records much closer to the legit ones, while for

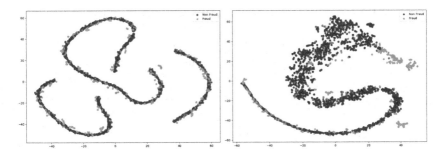

Fig. 2. Projection of the synthetic datasets generated by DataSynthesizer (left) and synthpop (right), generated using t-SNE

synthpop separate clusters of fraudulent data appear. This can be an indication for the utility of the datasets for the anomaly detection task.

For the anomaly detection, we utilise the implementation provided in the Python *scikit-learn* framework[2]. We specifically use these methods, a detailed description of which can be found at the scikit-learn documentation[3]:

- Supervised: Logistic Regression, k-nearest Neighbours, Random Forests, Support Vector Machines (SVMs), Naïve Bayes
- Semi-supervised: One-Class SVMs, Gaussian Mixture Models, Auto Encoder
- Unsupervised: Isolation Forests, Local Outlier Factors

4   Evaluation

Following the generation of synthetic training data, the final step of our experiment is to train machine learning models on the real and the synthesised training datasets and to evaluate these models by comparing their prediction scores on the test data. For a binary task like anomaly detection, which either detects an anomaly or normal behaviour, there can be four different outcomes, depending on the label associated to the data point and the prediction of the machine learning model. Assuming that the fraudulent class is considered the "positive" class, we can distinguish two successful outcomes: *true positives* are data points that are frauds and detected as such, while *true negatives* are data points that are normal (legit) behaviour and identified as such. Two types of errors can occur: *false positives* are legit cases that the model predicts as frauds, while *false negatives* are fraud cases that have not been detected as such, but are considered legit. These are depicted in so-called confusion matrices, which for a binary classification task are 2×2 matrices, where the columns represent the two classes 0 ('legit') and 1 ('fraud'). The first row shows the number of elements in the class that have been predicted to be legit, the second row shows the number of elements that have been predicted to be fraudulent.

---

[2] Specifically, version 0.22, available at https://scikit-learn.org/0.22.

[3] https://scikit-learn.org/stable/modules/outlier_detection.html.

Table 1. Supervised anomaly detection: confusion matrix

	Naïve Bayes	SVM	K-NN	Random forest	Log regression
Real	55626 1224 26 86	56840 10 33 79	56845 5 25 87	56848 2 32 80	56836 14 26 86
SDV	56838 12 100 12	56850 0 112 0	56850 0 112 0	56850 0 112 0	56845 5 102 10
DS	55243 1607 17 95	56848 2 62 50	56848 2 58 54	56843 7 49 63	56776 74 28 84
DSP	56498 352 41 71	56850 0 112 0	56850 0 112 0	56849 1 110 2	56745 105 70 42
SP	55424 1426 24 88	56848 2 51 61	56845 5 39 73	56849 1 41 71	56824 26 26 86

Table 2. Supervised anomaly detection: scores

	Naïve bayes			SVM			K-NN			Random forest			Log regression		
	Pr	Re	F2	Pr	Re	F2	Pr	Re	F2	Pr	Re	F2	Pr	Re	F2
Real	6.6	76.8	24.5	88.8	70.5	73.6	94.6	77.7	80.6	97.6	71.4	75.5	86.0	76.8	78.5
SDV	50.0	10.7	12.7	0.0	0.0	0.0	0.0	0.0	0.0	0.0	0.0	0.0	66.7	8.9	10.8
DS	5.6	84.8	22.1	96.2	44.6	50.0	96.4	48.2	53.6	90.0	56.3	60.8	53.2	75.0	69.3
DSP	16.8	63.4	40.8	0.0	0.0	0.0	0.0	0.0	0.0	66.7	1.8	2.2	28.6	37.5	35.3
SP	5.8	78.6	22.4	96.8	54.5	59.7	93.6	65.2	69.4	98.6	63.4	68.3	76.8	76.8	76.8

Based on this representation, we report the following measures. **Precision** is defined as the ratio of true positives (correctly identified frauds) to all data points predicted as frauds, i.e. how many of the cases the model has *predicted* to be frauds are actually such. **Recall** indicates how many of the frauds have been identified by the model, given as the ratio of the true positives to all cases that have been *labelled* as fraud. Each of these measures alone is not representative, as it is rather easy to optimise one of them, but difficult to have both take high values in conjunction. The **F1 score** provides a unified score, by computing the harmonic mean. The **F2 score** weighs recall higher than precision, which makes it suitable in our application, where it's likely more important to identify most of the anomalies, and a certain amount of false positives can be tolerated. In the following tables, we report these scores in *percent*. It is important to note that classification **accuracy** is less meaningful in our setting. It is defined as the ratio of true positives and true negatives to the size of the dataset. With highly imbalanced data, even models which trivially predict all instances as legit (normal) cases, and do not detect frauds at all, achieve high accuracy scores.

For each of the anomaly detection methods, we performed a random grid search over a number of parameters to optimise the results on the original training set. We then applied these settings, without any further optimisation, also to the models learned on the synthetically created datasets.

Table 1 shows the confusion matrices for the supervised anomaly detection algorithms, the metrics derived thereof are shown in Table 2. We can observe that the anomaly detection is a difficult task already on the original dataset, where Naïve Bayes is achieving a good recall, but has very low precision, and seems thus not usable for that task. The other algorithms perform significantly better, with k-Nearest Neighbours scoring best on precision, recall and F2 score.

On the synthetic datasets, we can see that the Synthetic Data Vault is not able to create datasets that can be learned by the supervised methods. The confusion matrices show that SVMs, k-NN and Random Forest cannot identify any of the anomaly data points, but classify them all as the "non-fraud" class, therefore achieving zero precision, recall, and F2 score. Only a very small number of frauds are correctly identified by Naïve Bayes and Logistic Regression, and while there are relatively few non-fraud cases wrongly predicted as fraud, the overall F2 score stays low – it is in the range of approximately 10%, and thus not useful. We can observe similar patterns for the DataSynthesizer when using Differential Privacy – even though larger values of recall are achieved, the more relevant F2 scores are still rather low, being in the range of 35% to 40%.

The models trained on the data synthesised by the DataSynthesizer without Differential Privacy do a better job at detecting frauds than the models trained on the data synthesised by the Synthetic Data Vault. Precision stays relatively high for most settings, but recall drops compared to the original data. Thus, the overall F2 scores drop by 15% to more than 20%, except for Naïve Bayes, which drops only marginally, but from a very low baseline of 24%. This trend of lower recall is slightly inverted for Logistic Regression, where it drops only marginally, by 1.8%, and thus achieves the best results for this synthetic dataset.

The best results on synthetic data are achieved with synthpop. For Logistic Regression, recall stays the same, and precision drops only marginally, and thus the overall F2 score is very close to the original dataset, lower just by 1.8%. For the other classifiers, the degradation is a bit larger, mostly with a lower recall, which results in an F2 score lower by approximately 10%. In overall, however, the scores are still relatively close to the original dataset.

In Table 3, we can see the confusion matrix for the unsupervised (Isolation Forest, Local Outlier Factor) and semi-supervised (One-Class SVM, Gaussian Mixture Model, Auto Encoder) methods. The scores are given in Table 4. We can observe that the unsupervised task, and to some extent also the semi-supervised task, is a much harder one. The major impact is on precision, where many methods struggle to achieve high values without reducing recall too much.

For the unsupervised methods, the Isolation Forest obtains the best precision values, and also high recall values. Thus, also in regards to the F2 score, Isolation Forest achieves by far the highest scores in the range of around 20%. It is interesting to note that the synthetic datasets are almost on par with the original data for Isolation Forests. Contrary to before, in this setting, the Synthetic Data Vault and DataSynthesizer with Differential Privacy are not much

Table 3. Unsupervised & semi-supervised anomaly detection: confusion matrix

	Isol. Forest	LOF	1-Class SVM	GMM	AutoEncoder
Real	55335 1515 26 86	50756 6094 77 35	53655 3195 19 93	56838 12 32 80	56591 259 50 62
SDV	55268 1582 34 78	51190 5660 13 99	51718 5132 13 99	56759 91 31 81	56582 268 52 60
DS	55185 1665 28 84	51279 5571 25 87	52465 4385 14 98	56309 541 49 63	56533 317 53 59
DSP	55445 1405 33 79	50755 6095 13 99	52126 4724 14 98	56643 207 53 59	56531 319 53 59
SP	55128 1722 29 83	54283 2567 20 92	54110 2740 21 91	56719 131 32 80	56607 243 52 60

different than the other approaches – the latter is even the best of the synthetic datasets, achieving an F2 score of 20.4%. Results for the Local Outlier Factor are generally not satisfying. An interesting observation, however, is that all the synthetic datasets outperform the model on the original dataset – albeit still at a low overall score. Only synthpop is closer to the results of the Isolation Forest.

For the One-Class SVM as a semi-supervised method, the results are in between the two unsupervised other approaches. Interestingly, also for this setting, the synthetic dataset generated by synthpop performs better than the original one. Overall, however, the One-Class SVM shows a low precision. We obtain much better results with the Auto Encoder, which is mostly due to a much lower false-positive rate. The number of actual frauds correctly detected is 62 (55%) on the real data, and only marginally lower on most synthesizers, which achieve 59 or 60 correctly identified fraud cases. Precision and thus F2 score are the highest on the dataset created with synthpop, which is overall very close to the real dataset, with a just 0.4% lower score. Similarly to the unsupervised methods, also on this method the Synthetic Data Vault achieves better results than the DataSynthesizer. Finally, the best results on the semi-supervised task are achieved by the Gaussian Mixture Model. On the original dataset, 71.4% of the fraud cases are identified, with a low false-positive rate of only 12 records. The results on synthpop match the recall, but have a lower precision, thus resulting in an overall rather large drop of F2 score by approximately 14%. Again, the Synthetic Data Vault is the best of the synthesising methods, having actually a marginally higher recall, and a still acceptable precision; thus, the overall F2 score drops only around 9% from 74.1% on the original dataset.

While these are still below the results of the supervised approach, the semi-supervised setting is a more difficult task, as it can rely only on labels for the "normal" cases. It is however a setting of practical application value, as it is generally easier to obtain these labels, and more difficult to label anomaly cases.

Table 4. Unsupervised & semi-supervised anomaly detection: scores

	Isol. Forest			LOF			1-Class SVM			GMM			AutoEncoder		
	Pr	Re	F2	Pr	Re	F2	Pr	Re	F2	Pr	Re	F2	Pr	Re	F2
Real	5.4	76.8	21.0	0.6	31.3	2.7	2.8	83.0	12.4	87.0	71.4	74.1	19.3	55.4	40.3
SDV	4.7	69.6	18.5	1.7	88.4	8.0	1.9	88.4	8.7	47.1	72.3	65.3	18.3	53.6	38.7
DS	4.8	75.0	19.1	1.5	77.7	7.1	2.2	87.5	9.9	10.4	56.3	29.9	15.7	52.7	35.8
DSP	5.3	70.5	20.4	1.6	88.4	7.5	2.0	87.5	9.3	22.2	52.7	41.3	15.6	52.7	35.7
SP	4.6	74.1	18.4	3.5	82.1	14.8	3.2	81.3	13.9	37.9	71.4	60.7	19.8	53.6	39.9

5   Conclusions and Future Work

In this paper, we evaluated the utility of synthetic data for the task of anomaly detection, on the example of fraud detection. We considered the setting where the data required to build the models can not easily be shared with the people responsible for the training due to its sensitive nature. In settings where multiple parties would like to collaborate to obtain a more powerful model, facilitating such exchange can be crucial. Synthetic data can be used to create a counterpart of the data that does not represent individual records, but still preserves important characteristics. Thus, the disclosure of sensitive data can be reduced.

In our evaluation, we considered the cases of supervised, semi-supervised and unsupervised anomaly detection. We have assumed that synthetic data might not be usable for such a task, as anomaly detection deals with outliers, and synthetic data generally preserves global characteristics – thus rather the ones of the legit, normal cases. However, the evaluation showed that while anomaly detection is generally a hard task, in specific settings, synthetic data can reach similar effectiveness as the models trained on the original data. It can thus be a viable alternative when the original data cannot be shared, and other forms of data sanitisation, such as anonymisation via k-anonymity, are not feasible.

Future work will extending our evaluation to additional anomaly detection data sets, e.g. on network intrusion, and will include additional detection methods, especially recent approaches like generative adversarial networks (GANs). Further, we will investigate how well synthetic data compares in terms of utility to datasets that need to be anonymised or otherwise treated before they could be shared. We will investigate further inference attacks on synthetic data, especially in the context of trying to infer information on the outliers.

Acknowledgement. This work was partially funded by the BRIDGE 1 programme (No 871267, "WellFort") of the Austrian Research Promotion Agency (FFG), and the EU Horizon 2020 programme under grant agreement No 732907 ("MyHealth-MyData"). SBA Research (SBA-K1) is funded within the framework of COMET— Competence Centers for Excellent Technologies by BMVIT, BMDW, and the federal state of Vienna, managed by the FFG.

References

1. Abdallah, A., Maarof, M.A., Zainal, A.: Fraud detection system: a survey. J. Netw. Comput. Appl. **68**, 90–113 (2016)
2. Agyemang, M., Barker, K., Alhajj, R.: A comprehensive survey of numeric and symbolic outlier mining techniques. Intell. Data Anal. **10**(6), 521–538 (2006)
3. Barse, E., Kvarnstrom, H., Johnson, E.: Synthesizing test data for fraud detection systems. In: 19th Annual Computer Security Applications Conference, Las Vegas, Nevada, USA. IEEE (2003)
4. Chandola, V., Banerjee, A., Kumar, V.: Anomaly detection: a survey. ACM Comput. Surv. **41**(3), 1–58 (2009)
5. Chen, B.C., Kifer, D., LeFevre, K., Machanavajjhala, A.: Privacy-preserving data publishing. Found. Trends Databases **2**(1–2), 1–167 (2009)
6. Dwork, C.: Differential privacy: a survey of results. In: Agrawal, M., Du, D., Duan, Z., Li, A. (eds.) TAMC 2008. LNCS, vol. 4978, pp. 1–19. Springer, Heidelberg (2008). https://doi.org/10.1007/978-3-540-79228-4_1
7. Goodfellow, I., et al.: Generative adversarial nets. In: Advances in Neural Information Processing Systems, vol. 27. Curran Associates, Inc. (2014)
8. Han, C., et al.: GAN-based synthetic brain MR image generation. In: 15th International Symposium on Biomedical Imaging (ISBI). IEEE, Washington, DC (2018)
9. Hittmeir, M., Ekelhart, A., Mayer, R.: On the utility of synthetic data: an empirical evaluation on machine learning tasks. In: 14th International Conference on Availability, Reliability and Security (ARES), Canterbury, UK. ACM Press (2019)
10. Hittmeir, M., Ekelhart, A., Mayer, R.: A baseline for attribute disclosure risk in synthetic data. In: 10th ACM Conference on Data and Application Security and Privacy (CODASPY), New Orleans, LA, United States (2020)
11. Lundin, E., Kvarnström, H., Jonsson, E.: A synthetic fraud data generation methodology. In: Deng, R., Bao, F., Zhou, J., Qing, S. (eds.) ICICS 2002. LNCS, vol. 2513, pp. 265–277. Springer, Heidelberg (2002). https://doi.org/10.1007/3-540-36159-6_23
12. Maaten, L.V.D., Hinton, G.: Visualizing data using t-SNE. J. Mach. Learn. Res. **9**, 2579–2605 (2008)
13. Nowok, B., Raab, G., Dibben, C.: synthpop: bespoke creation of synthetic data in R. J. Stat. Softw. Art. **74**(11), 1–26 (2016)
14. Patki, N., Wedge, R., Veeramachaneni, K.: The synthetic data vault. In: IEEE International Conference on Data Science and Advanced Analytics (DSAA), Montreal, QC, Canada (2016)
15. Ping, H., Stoyanovich, J., Howe, B.: DataSynthesizer: privacy-preserving synthetic datasets. In: 29th International Conference on Scientific and Statistical Database Management, Chicago, IL, USA (2017)
16. Reiter, J.P., Mitra, R.: Estimating risks of identification disclosure in partially synthetic data. J. Priv. Confidentiality **1**(1), 99–110 (2009)
17. Rubin, D.B.: Multiple Imputation for Nonresponse in Surveys. Wiley, Hoboken (2004)
18. Schlegl, T., Seeböck, P., Waldstein, S.M., Langs, G., Schmidt-Erfurth, U.: f-AnoGAN: fast unsupervised anomaly detection with generative adversarial networks. Med. Image Anal. **54**, 30–44 (2019)
19. Smola, A.J., Schölkopf, B.: A tutorial on support vector regression. Stat. Comput. **14**(3), 199–222 (2004). https://doi.org/10.1023/B:STCO.0000035301.49549.88

20. Sweeney, L.: k-Anonymity: a model for protecting privacy. Int. J. Uncertainty Fuzziness Knowl. Based Syst. **10**(5), 557–570 (2002)
21. Zimek, A., Campello, R.J., Sander, J.: Ensembles for unsupervised outlier detection: challenges and research questions a position paper. ACM SIGKDD Explor. Newsl. **15**(1), 11–22 (2014)
22. Zuech, R., Khoshgoftaar, T.M., Wald, R.: Intrusion detection and Big Heterogeneous Data: a survey. J. Big Data **2**(1), 1–41 (2015). https://doi.org/10.1186/s40537-015-0013-4

Local Differentially Private Matrix Factorization with MoG for Recommendations

Jeyamohan Neera[1]([⊠])(iD), Xiaomin Chen[1](iD), Nauman Aslam[1], and Zhan Shu[2]

[1] Northumbria University, Newcastle upon Tyne, UK
jeyamohan.neera@northumbria.ac.uk
[2] University of Alberta, Edmonton, Canada

Abstract. Unethical data aggregation practices of many recommendation systems have raised privacy concerns among users. Local differential privacy (LDP) based recommendation systems address this problem by perturbing a user's original data locally in their device before sending it to the data aggregator (DA). The DA performs recommendations over perturbed data which causes substantial prediction error. To tackle privacy and utility issues with untrustworthy DA in recommendation systems, we propose a novel LDP matrix factorization (MF) with mixture of Gaussian (MoG). We use a Bounded Laplace mechanism (BLP) to perturb user's original ratings locally. BLP restricts the perturbed ratings to a predefined output domain, thus reducing the level of noise aggregated at DA. The MoG method estimates the noise added to the original ratings, which further improves the prediction accuracy without violating the principles of differential privacy (DP). With Movielens and Jester datasets, we demonstrate that our method offers a higher prediction accuracy under strong privacy protection compared to existing LDP recommendation methods.

Keywords: Local differential privacy · Matrix factorization · Bounded Laplace mechanism · Mixture of Gaussian

1 Introduction

Recommendation systems are often used to help users to find products or services that could interest them. Collaborative Filtering (CF) is a prominent technique used in recommendation systems. CF-based recommendation systems collect and analyse user information to offer better and personalized user experience. However, aggregation and analysis of user information can cause privacy violation. Narayanan et al. [13] demonstrated how analyzing an individual's historical ratings can reveal sensitive information such as user's political preference, medical conditions and even religious disposition. Therefore, it is crucial for recommendation systems to protect the privacy of the users while simultaneously providing high-quality recommendations.

© IFIP International Federation for Information Processing 2020
Published by Springer Nature Switzerland AG 2020
A. Singhal and J. Vaidya (Eds.): DBSec 2020, LNCS 12122, pp. 208–220, 2020.
https://doi.org/10.1007/978-3-030-49669-2_12

Differential privacy (DP) has become a popular tool in various domains to protect the privacy of users even if the adversary possesses a substantial amount of auxiliary information about the aggregated data [5]. Several studies have proposed differential privacy based CF mechanisms [11,14,18] to safeguard against privacy attacks in recommendation systems. However, most of the existing mechanisms imply that the data aggregator (DA) is trusted. Unfortunately, many DAs are inclined to collect more data than required and abuse the privacy of users for their benefits. Due to the concerns over untrusted DAs, many researchers [1,10,15,16] have adopted Local Differential Privacy (LDP) for collaborative filtering. LDP based CF requires each user to locally perturb their data and sends the perturbed data to DA. However, this approach yields low prediction accuracy compared to DP based CF because each user's data is noised locally as opposed to adding noise to aggregates of the user's data. Therefore, it is necessary to design a LDP based recommendation system where each user can protect the privacy of their data from DA and at the same time, DA can perform recommendations with satisfactory prediction accuracy.

Our work aims to design a novel LDP based recommendation system which yields high data utility under strong privacy guarantee. We perturb user's original ratings locally using a Bounded Laplace mechanism (BLP) before sending to the DA. Furthermore, we reduce the prediction error by using MF with MoG at the DA. We estimate the added BLP noise using MoG [4], and Expectation-Maximization (EM) method is used to estimate the parameters of MoG. We demonstrate that our BLP-based recommendation system can provide substantial privacy protection and meanwhile achieve a satisfactory recommendation accuracy. The contribution of our work is as follows:

- We use a Bounded Laplace mechanism (BLP) to perturb each user's ratings locally in their devices. To the best of our knowledge, this is the first work which uses BLP to perturb each user's rating in recommendation systems. BLP ensures that the perturbed ratings fall within a predefined output domain without violating the principles of LDP. Additionally, BLP does not require complex computations to be performed in the user's side contrary to some existing solutions which require users to calculate their latent factors locally in their devices.
- We significantly improve the rating prediction accuracy of LDP based recommendation system. Local rating perturbation induces large error which grows linearly with the number of users and items. However, BLP compared to the Laplace mechanism introduces limited noise to aggregated ratings. Additionally, MoG is used to model the noise before MF to further increase the prediction accuracy. We demonstrate empirically using Movielens and Jester datasets that our proposed method can achieve satisfactory prediction accuracy under strong privacy guarantee and outperforms the works of [1] and [16].
- The communication cost of our proposed method is significantly less compared to other existing solutions, such as [16] as our method only requires users to transmit the perturbed ratings once to the DA, so there is no

additional communication cost is introduced, unlike other methods that involve multiple iterations of information exchanges between a user and the DA.

2   Related Work

LDP is used to protect the user's privacy against untrusted DA in many applications. For example, Google uses LDP to collect each user's chrome usage statistics privately [6]. Likewise, LDP is also used in CF to protect the privacy of users. For instance, [15] introduced an LDP based rating perturbation algorithm which perturbs users' preference within an item category. Even though this mechanism hides a user's preference towards an item from an untrusted data aggregator, it can still reveal users' preferences towards an item category. Hua et al. [10] proposed another LDP based Matrix Factorization for untrusted DA. In their method initially, item profile vectors are learned using a private matrix factorization algorithm. Then these item vectors are sent to the user to derive user profile vectors. As each user's profile vectors do not depend on other users' data, they can easily compute their profile vectors locally instead of centrally. Users send their updated item profile vectors back to DA which then used to update the item profile vectors. The method used an objective function perturbation to achieve differential privacy. However, this method adds additional processing and communication overhead at user side.

Shin et al. [16] also proposed a method similar to [10] which requires the DA to send item profile vectors to each user. However, [16] used a randomized response perturbation mechanism instead of the objective perturbation mechanism and users send back the gradient instead of latent factors to DA. Their method also induces more communication and processing cost as users locally compute their user profile vectors over multiple iterations. Another LDP based rating perturbation mechanism was proposed by [1] where the original ratings are perturbed using Laplace mechanism. However, this proposed method used a clamping method to restrict the out-of-range ratings and used off-shelf optimization problems solvers such as SGD (Stochastic Gradient Descent) and ALS (Alternating Least Squares) in their MF algorithm.

3   Local Differential Privacy Based Recommendation System

In this work, we consider an untrustworthy data aggregator with whom the users are not willing to share any sensitive information. In our proposed system the original ratings are perturbed using Bounded Laplace mechanism and perturbed ratings are aggregated by DA. At DA, we use a MF with MoG for noise estimation and rating predictions. Our proposed rating prediction model will help the DA to reconstruct the original ratings from perturbed ratings without violating the privacy of users. Dwork et al. [5] proved that any mechanism that satisfies

ε-differential privacy is resilient to post-processing. It implies that our perturbed rating from the local differentially private mechanism can be utilised in further processes without producing any additional privacy risk. Figure 1 shows the system architecture for the proposed recommendation system.

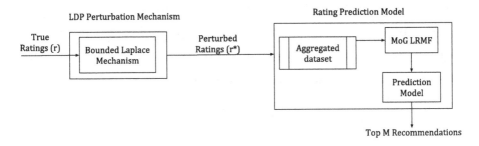

Fig. 1. Local differential privacy based recommendation

3.1 LDP Rating Perturbation

Rating Normalization. As different recommendation systems use distinct rating scales, to produce a generalized theoretical model, we adopt the Min-Max scaling approach to normalize the rating scale between 0 and 1. Given an actual rating of r°, the normalized true rating r can be generated as:

$$r = \frac{r^\circ - r^\circ_{min}}{r^\circ_{max} - r^\circ_{min}} \tag{1}$$

in which r°_{max} is the highest possible rating score on the rating scale, and r°_{min} is the lowest. Local sensitivity is the maximum change rating perturbation mechanism can cause in a rating dataset, which is the difference between the maximum and the minimum rating. In a normalized dataset, the maximum rating is 1 and the minimum rating is 0. Therefore, the local sensitivity of the rating perturbation mechanism is $\Delta r = 1$.

3.2 Bounded Laplace Mechanism

Our system perturbs the user's normalized rating using the BLP mechanism. Bounded Laplace mechanism is used to sanitize the output results of the Laplace mechanism with bounding constraints. BLP satisfies ϵ-DP by ignoring out of bound values and re-samples noise for a given input rating r until a value within the given bound is obtained. BLP mechanism can be defined as follows:

Definition 1 *(Bounded Laplace Mechanism). Given a scale parameter b and a domain rating interval of (l, u), the Bounded Laplace mechanism $M_{BLP} : R \rightarrow R^*$ is given by a conditional probability density function as follows:*

$$f_{r^*|r}(r^*|r) = \begin{cases} \frac{1}{C_r(b)} \frac{1}{2b} exp(-\frac{|r^*-r|}{b}), & if \ r^* \in [l, u] \\ 0, & if \ r^* \notin [l, u] \end{cases} \quad (2)$$

where $C_r(b) = \int_l^u \frac{1}{2b} exp(-\frac{|r^*-r|}{b}) dr^*$ is a normalization constant dependent on input rating r and r^* is the perturbed output.

The normalization constant $C_r(b)$ can be given as:

$$C_r(b) = 1 - \frac{1}{2}\left(exp(-\frac{r-l}{b}) + exp(-\frac{u-r}{b})\right) \quad (3)$$

It can be easily proven that the result of integration will yield Eq. (3). It has been shown in [9] that when local sensitivity $\Delta f = l - u$, BLP mechanism satisfies ε-local differential privacy. Using BLP in our proposed mechanism ensures that the perturbed output range is limited to $[l, u]$. However, the mechanism still guarantees that the adversary is unable to obtain any information about the original data by observing the output and thus preserves the privacy of the user. The privacy budget ε will be determined by the DA and will be shared with user when they register with DA. The BLP mechanism (as given in Algorithm 1) will run every-time a user want to send rating to DA.

Algorithm 1. Bounded Laplace Mechanism

Input: Rating (r) in
Output: Perturbed Rating (r^*) out
  1: Generate a noise sample from the distribution $Lap(0, b)$
  2: Calculate perturbed rating $r^* = r + Lap(0, b)$
  3: **if** $l \leq r^* \leq u$ **then**
  4:    Set the perturbed rating to r^*
  5: **else**
  6:    repeat Step 1
  7: **end if**
  8: **return** Perturbed rating to DA

3.3 Noise Estimation with MoG

Let $R_{m \times n}$ be the original normalized rating matrix and $R^*_{m \times n}$ be the perturbed rating matrix of m users over n items. The perturbed ratings can be decomposed as:

$$R^* = R + E \quad (4)$$

where $E_{m \times n}$ consists of BLP noise. Each element in the noised rating matrix can be represented as:

$$r_{ij}^* = r_{ij} + e_{ij} = (u_i^T)v_j + e_{ij} \tag{5}$$

where u_i is a column vector in user latent factor matrix U and v_j is a column vector in item latent factor matrix V. As any unknown noise distribution can be modelled as a mixture of Gaussian, we assume that noise e_{ij} in Eq. (4) is drawn from MoG distribution [4]:

$$p(e_{ij} \mid \Pi, \Sigma) \sim \sum_{k=1}^{K} \pi_k \mathcal{N}(e_{ij} \mid 0, \sigma_k^2) \tag{6}$$

where $\Pi = (\pi_1, \pi_2, \ldots \pi_k)$, $\Sigma = (\sigma_1, \sigma_2, \ldots \sigma_K)$, σ_k^2 is the variance of Gaussian component k and K is the total number of Gaussian components. π_k is the mixing proportion and $\sum_{k=1}^{K} \pi_k = 1$. Therefore, the probability of each perturbed rating r_{ij}^* of R can be represented as:

$$p(r_{ij}^* \mid u_i, v_j, \Pi, \Sigma) = \sum_{k=1}^{K} \pi_k \mathcal{N}(r_{ij}^* \mid (u_i^T)v_j, \sigma_k^2) \tag{7}$$

The likelihood of R^* can thus be given as:

$$p(R^* \mid U, V, \Pi, \Sigma) = \prod_{i,j \in \Omega} \sum_{k=1}^{K} \pi_k \mathcal{N}(r_{ij}^* \mid (u_i^T)v_j, \sigma_k^2) \tag{8}$$

where Ω is the set of non-missing data points in perturbed rating matrix R^*. Given a dataset R^*, our goal is to compute the parameters U, V, Π and Σ such that the maximum log-likelihood of R^* is achieved.

$$\max_{U, V, \Pi, \Sigma} \ \log p(R^* \mid U, V, \Pi, \Sigma)$$
$$= \sum_{i,j \in \Omega,} \log \sum_{k=1}^{K} \pi_k \mathcal{N}(r_{ij}^* \mid (u_i^T)v_j, \sigma_k^2) \tag{9}$$

3.4 Expectation Maximization for MoG

As maximum log-likelihood function given in Eq. (9) cannot be solved using a closed-form solution, Expectation-Maximization (EM) algorithm is used to estimate model parameters U, V, Π and Σ. The EM algorithm introduced in [4] has two steps, Expectation and Maximization. In E-step we compute posterior responsibility using the current model parameters U, V, Π and Σ for each noise point e_{ij} as:

$$\gamma_{ijk} = \frac{\pi_k \mathcal{N}(r_{ij}^* \mid (u_i^T)v_j, \sigma_k^2)}{\sum_{k=1}^{K} \pi_k \mathcal{N}(r_{ij}^* \mid (u_i^T)v_j, \sigma_k^2)} \tag{10}$$

The posterior responsibility reflects the probability that it is Gaussian component k generates the noise data point e_{ij}. In M-step we re-estimate each model parameter U, V, Π, Σ using the posterior responsibilities such that the maximum log-likelihood Eq. (11) is obtained [12].

$$\max_{U,V,\Pi,\Sigma} \sum_{i,j \in \Omega} \sum_{k=1}^{K} \gamma_{ijk} \left(\log \pi_k - \log \sqrt{2\pi}\sigma_k - \frac{(r_{ij}^* - (u_i^T)v_j)^2}{2\sigma_k^2} \right) \quad (11)$$

To solve the problem given in Eq. (11), we first update Π and Σ:

$$N_k = \sum_{\forall i,j} \gamma_{ijk}$$

$$\pi_k = \frac{N_k}{N}$$

$$\sigma_k^2 = \frac{1}{N_k} \sum_{\forall i,j} \gamma_{ijk}(r_{ij}^* - (u_i^T)v_j)^2 \quad (12)$$

where N_k is the sum of posterior responsibilities for kth Gaussian component and N is the total number of data points. The portion of Eq. (11) related to U and V can be rewritten as:

$$\sum_{i,j \in \Omega} \sum_{k=1}^{K} \gamma_{ijk} \left(-\frac{(r_{ij}^* - (u_i^T)v_j)^2}{2\sigma_k^2} \right)$$

$$= -\sum_{i,j \in \Omega} \left(\sum_{k=1}^{K} \frac{\gamma_{ijk}}{2\sigma_k^2} \right) ((r_{ij}^* - (u_i^T)v_j)^2)$$

$$= -\| W \odot (X - UV^T) \|_{L_2} \quad (13)$$

where W is the weight matrix in which the element w_{ij} is the weight for rating r_{ij} and can be defined as:

$$w_{ij} = \begin{cases} \sqrt{\sum_{k=1}^{K} \frac{\gamma_{ijk}}{2\sigma_k^2}}, & \text{if } i,j \in \Omega \\ 0, & \text{if } i,j \notin \Omega \end{cases} \quad (14)$$

The problem defined by Eq. (13) is equivalent to a weighted L2 low rank matrix factorization problem and any weighted L2-norm solvers such as WPCA [3], WLRA [17] and DN [2] can be used to solve it. We used WPCA in our evaluation. The process of our noise estimation and rating prediction is given in Algorithm 2. The convergence is achieved when the change between two consecutive U latent factor matrices is smaller than a predefined threshold or if the maximum number of iterations is reached.

Algorithm 2. MoG based Noise Estimation and Prediction

Input: Noised Ratings (R^*) in
Output: Predicted Rating out
    Initialization : random initialization of U, V, Π and Σ
1: (E-Step) Estimate posterior responsibility γ_{ijk} using Eq. (10)
2: **for** until convergence occurs **do**
3:    (M-Step for Π and Σ) Estimate MoG parameters Π and Σ using Eq. (12)
4:    (M-Step for U, V) Estimate U and V by solving Eq. (13)
5: **end for**
6: **return** Predict ratings using inner product of user and item latent factor matrices
    U and V

---

4 Evaluation

In this section, we discuss the evaluation of our proposed BLP based MF with MoG approach (BLP-MoG-MF). To demonstrate the effectiveness of our proposed approach, we compare it with the following methods:

- Non-Private Matrix Factorization (Non-Private MF): This is the baseline method we compare our approach with. This method does not perturb any user's ratings and uses SGD based matrix factorization for rating prediction. RMSE value of the baseline method reflects the lower bound for prediction error that can be obtained without any privacy constraints.
- Input Perturbation SGD Method (ISGD) [1]: ISGD method perturb ratings using Laplace mechanism and clamp the resulting perturbed ratings using a clamping parameter locally at the user's device. DA uses MF with SGD method for rating prediction.
- Private Gradient-Matrix Factorization (PG-MF) [16]: In this method initially DA computes item latent factors and sends to each user. Then each user computes their latent factors locally in their device and submits a perturbed gradient to DA. DA updates the item latent factors using the aggregated perturbed gradients from each user.

4.1 Datasets

We used two popular public rating datasets in our evaluation: Movielens [8] and Jester [7]. Among several different version of Movielens dataset, we used the dataset which consists of 100k ratings of 1682 movies rated by 943 users. The minimum rating given is 0.5 and the maximum rating is 5. The Jester dataset consists of 2M ratings of 100 jokes rated by 73,421 users. The minimum rating given in this dataset is -10 and maximum rating given is $+10$.

4.2   Evaluation Metrics

We measure the accuracy of prediction using the metric Root Mean Squared Error (RMSE) given by:

$$RMSE = \sqrt{\frac{\sum_{i=0}^{n-1} (r_i - \hat{r}_i)^2}{n}} \tag{15}$$

in which r_i is the actual rating, $\hat{r}_i$ is the predicted rating and n is the total number of ratings. We use 10-fold cross-validation to train and evaluate our proposed BLP-MoG-MF approach for both Movielens and Jester datasets over various privacy budget ε. The prediction accuracy is dependent on the privacy budget ε, higher values of ε lead to weaker privacy protection levels. As there can be discrepancies while introducing noise through the Bounded Laplace mechanism, the computed RMSE is averaged across multiple runs.

4.3   Results

Bounded Laplace Noise Distribution. In this experiment, we generated noise samples using Laplace and Bounded Laplace mechanisms. We generated 100,000 random noise samples for both mechanisms while setting their privacy budget ϵ to 0.1 and 1 respectively using Movielens dataset. Figure 2(a) and (b) illustrates the frequency of noise under Laplace and Bounded Laplace mechanism. The noise samples generated using Laplace mechanism approximates to a Laplace distribution while the noise samples generated using BLP produces an unknown continuous distribution. As BLP follows a conditional probability density function (see Definition 1), it no more produced noise that can approximate to a Laplace distribution. Hence, MoG is effective in estimating the noise generated by BLP.

Prediction Accuracy over Various Privacy Budget. In this experiment, we compare the prediction accuracy of BLP-MoG-MF with other two LDP based methods. First, we compare the prediction accuracy of our BLP-MoG-MF with PG-MF [16] by varying the privacy budget ε from 0.1 to 1.6 for Movielens dataset. Figure 3 shows the RMSE values for both methods and the baseline method. As expected prediction accuracy of all the methods except the Non-private MF method improves with increase in privacy budget. Because, an increase in privacy budget implies that the magnitude of privacy leakage the mechanism allows is substantial, which in turn, leads to an increase in the utility, i.e. the prediction accuracy.

Secondly, we compare BLP-MoG-MF with ISGD [1] by varying the privacy budget ε from 0.1 to 3 for both Movielens and Jester datasets. Figure 4(a) and (b) illustrate the RMSE values for both methods and Non-Private MF. The RMSE values of Jester dataset are larger than that of Movielens as Jester is sparser than Movielens. Figure 4(a) and (b) shows that the prediction accuracy of BLP-MoG-MF outperforms ISGD for all values of privacy budget ε. The results also show

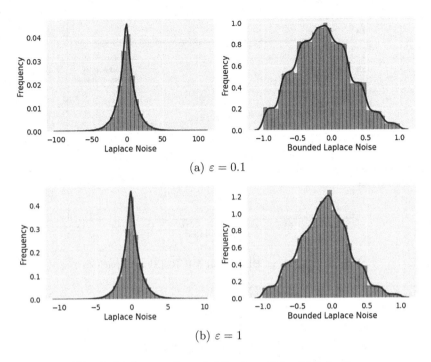

(a) $\varepsilon = 0.1$

(b) $\varepsilon = 1$

Fig. 2. Laplace vs Bounded Laplace Noise Distribution

that BLP-MoG-MG produces a higher increase in prediction accuracy for Jester than Movielens for all the values of privacy budget ε. Jester dataset RMSE values show 35% and 28% of improvement in prediction accuracy when privacy budget ε is 0.1 and 1 respectively. However, the improvement percentage for Movielens dataset is 21% and 16% for the same values of privacy budget ε. This implies that BLP-MoG-MF outperforms ISGD even better when the data is sparse.

Communications Cost. We compare the communication cost of our approach to [16] and [1] in Table 1. In BLP-MoG-MF and ISGD approaches, regardless of the number of items that a user rates, the user always transmits each perturbed rating individually to the DA, once. PG-MF method requires the user to transmit only the perturbed gradient to DA. BLP-MoG-MF and ISGD methods do not require the DA to transmit any information back to the user. However, PG-MF method requires the DA to transmit updated item latent vectors matrix back to the user. The estimated transmission size for PG-MF method is approximately 0.15 MB for Movielens dataset [1], whereas BLP-MoG-MF and ISGD methods will be transmitting approximately 1 byte of data each time user send their data to DA.

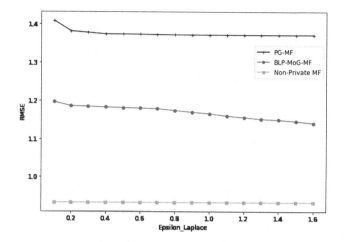

Fig. 3. PG-MF vs BLP-MoG-MF RMSE comparison

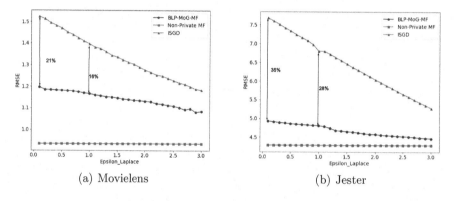

(a) Movielens   (b) Jester

Fig. 4. BLP-MoG-MF vs ISGD RMSE comparison

Table 1. Communication cost comparison

Method	User to DA	DA to user
BLP-MoG-MF	Single perturbed rating	No data
ISGD [1]	Single perturbed rating	No data
PG-MF [16]	Single perturbed gradient	Item latent factor matrix

5   Conclusion

In this work, we propose a local differentially private matrix factorization with mixture of Gaussian (BLP-MoG-MF) method under the consideration of an untrustworthy data aggregator. Our proposed recommendation system guarantees strong user privacy and completely hides a user's preferences over an item from DA. It also pursues better prediction accuracy than the existing LDP based solutions [16] and [1]. Additionally, our method does not incur any additional communication cost to the user side. In future, we intend to explore approaches to improve the robustness of achieved local minima for the non-convex cost function used in MF with MoG.

References

1. Berlioz, A., Friedman, A., Kaafar, M.A., Boreli, R., Berkovsky, S.: Applying differential privacy to matrix factorization. In: Proceedings of the 9th ACM Conference on Recommender Systems, pp. 107–114. ACM (2015)
2. Buchanan, A.M., Fitzgibbon, A.W.: Damped newton algorithms for matrix factorization with missing data. In: 2005 IEEE Computer Society Conference on Computer Vision and Pattern Recognition (CVPR 2005), vol. 2, pp. 316–322. IEEE (2005)
3. De La Torre, F., Black, M.J.: A framework for robust subspace learning. Int. J. Comput. Vis. **54**(1–3), 117–142 (2003)
4. Dempster, A.P., Laird, N.M., Rubin, D.B.: Maximum likelihood from incomplete data via the em algorithm. J. R. Stat. Soc. Ser. B (Methodol.) **39**(1), 1–22 (1977)
5. Dwork, C., Roth, A., et al.: demp. Found. Trends® Theor. Comput. Sci. 9(3–4), 211–407 (2014)
6. Erlingsson, Ú., Pihur, V., Korolova, A.: RAPPOR: randomized aggregatable privacy-preserving ordinal response. In: Proceedings of the 2014 ACM SIGSAC Conference on Computer and Communications Security, pp. 1054–1067. ACM (2014)
7. Goldberg, K., Roeder, T., Gupta, D., Perkins, C.: Eigentaste: a constant time collaborative filtering algorithm. Inf. Retr. **4**(2), 133–151 (2001)
8. Harper, F.M., Konstan, J.A.: The movielens datasets: history and context. ACM Trans. Interact. Intell. Syst. (TiiS) **5**(4), 19 (2016)
9. Holohan, N., Antonatos, S., Braghin, S., Mac Aonghusa, P.: The bounded laplace mechanism in differential privacy. arXiv preprint arXiv:1808.10410 (2018)
10. Hua, J., Xia, C., Zhong, S.: Differentially private matrix factorization. In: Twenty-Fourth International Joint Conference on Artificial Intelligence (2015)
11. McSherry, F., Mironov, I.: Differentially private recommender systems: building privacy into the netflix prize contenders. In: Proceedings of the 15th ACM SIGKDD International Conference on Knowledge Discovery and Data Mining, pp. 627–636. ACM (2009)
12. Meng, D., De La Torre, F.: Robust matrix factorization with unknown noise. In: Proceedings of the IEEE International Conference on Computer Vision, pp. 1337–1344 (2013)
13. Narayanan, A., Shmatikov, V.: Robust de-anonymization of large datasets (how to break anonymity of the netflix prize dataset). University of Texas at Austin (2008)
14. Roy, I., Setty, S.T., Kilzer, A., Shmatikov, V., Witchel, E.: Airavat: security and privacy for MapReduce. NSDI **10**, 297–312 (2010)
15. Shen, Y., Jin, H.: EpicRec: towards practical differentially private framework for personalized recommendation. In: Proceedings of the 2016 ACM SIGSAC Conference on Computer and Communications Security, pp. 180–191. ACM (2016)
16. Shin, H., Kim, S., Shin, J., Xiao, X.: Privacy enhanced matrix factorization for recommendation with local differential privacy. IEEE Trans. Knowl. Data Eng. **30**(9), 1770–1782 (2018)

17. Srebro, N., Jaakkola, T.: Weighted low-rank approximations. In: Proceedings of the 20th International Conference on Machine Learning (ICML 2003), pp. 720–727 (2003)
18. Zhu, T., Li, G., Ren, Y., Zhou, W., Xiong, P.: Differential privacy for neighborhood-based collaborative filtering. In: Proceedings of the 2013 IEEE/ACM International Conference on Advances in Social Networks Analysis and Mining, pp. 752–759. ACM (2013)

Visualization and Analytics for Security

Designing a Decision-Support Visualization for Live Digital Forensic Investigations

Fabian Böhm$^{(\boxtimes)}$ (iD), Ludwig Englbrecht (iD), and Günther Pernul

Universität Regensburg, 93053 Regensburg, Germany
{fabian.boehm,ludwig.englbrecht,guenther.pernul}@ur.de

Abstract. Fileless Malware poses challenges for forensic analysts since the infected system often can't be shut down for a forensic analysis. Turning off the device would destroy forensic artifacts or evidence of the fileless malware. Therefore, a technique called Live Digital Forensics is applied to perform investigations on a running system. During these investigations, domain experts need to carefully decide what tools they want to deploy for their forensic analysis. In this paper we propose a visualization designed to support forensic experts in this decision-making process. Therefore, we follow a design methodology from the visualization domain to come up with a comprehensible design. Following this methodology, we start with identifying and defining the domain problem which the visualization should help to solve. We then translate this domain problem into an abstract description of the available data and user's tasks for the visualization. Finally, we transform these specifications into a visualization design for a Live Digital Forensics decision-support. A use case illustrates the benefits of the proposed method.

Keywords: Digital Forensics · Visual Analytics · Live forensics · Visualization design

1 Introduction

Malware has been around since the early days of computers. While traditional malware relies on malicious executable files, there is one particularly evil type of malware: Fileless Malware (FM). This type is hard to detect as it hides itself in locations that are difficult to analyze [31]. It exists exclusively in memory-based areas like the RAM instead of being written directly on the target's hard drive. This complicates forensic investigations of FM as most traditional Digital Forensic analysis techniques are designed to work on computers after they got turned off [16]. However, as FM solely exists in memory, turning off the target would lead to significant loss of evidence. Although some evidence of FM can be acquired through traditional DF analysis techniques, keeping the potentially infected system running allows the investigator to gather additional evidence

© IFIP International Federation for Information Processing 2020
Published by Springer Nature Switzerland AG 2020
A. Singhal and J. Vaidya (Eds.): DBSec 2020, LNCS 12122, pp. 223–240, 2020.
https://doi.org/10.1007/978-3-030-49669-2_13

occurring during an incident. Moreover, there are mission-critical systems that simply cannot be shut down in order to not disrupt business operations. Therefore, Live Digital Forensics (LDF) is necessary.

LDF allows domain experts to investigate a running system, identify artifacts and collect evidence. This helps to understand FM-based attacks but at the same time requires fast and careful decisions about the LDF tools used to carry out the analysis. A poor choice of the analysis tool could destroy or compromise important artifacts.

In order to support forensic analysts to make faster and better decisions upon which tools should be used during an LDF investigation or upon which indicators might need additional attention, we propose to apply Visual Security Analytics (VSA). VSA allows domain experts to interactively explore the data of the system under investigation. It supports the decision-making process by allowing the forensic investigators to assess the current situation with a tailor-made visualization approach for a specific situation [29]. Therefore, they can lead the attention towards possible indicators for FM and deploy the respective LDF analysis tools like *volatility*[1] or *SysAnalyzer*[2].

This paper shows our process of developing a visual representation aimed to help Digital Forensic experts with directing their attention throughout their analyses. We follow a methodological design approach to bridge the gap between domain (digital forensic) and visualization experts [17,30]. Our main contribution is the methodological design of a visual decision-support system aiding forensic experts to direct their further investigations during a live forensic analysis. We introduce the methodology, derive a design from the requirements and problems within the LDF domain, and evaluate our design by showcasing the identification of a fileless malware's artifacts within a live forensic analysis.

The remainder of this work is structured as follows: Sect. 2 identifies and summarizes related work within the digital forensic analysis domain and existing visualization approaches. We describe the applied methodology to design the visualization in Sect. 3. The first step of our methodology is a characterization of the domain problem in Sect. 4. Section 5 follows the remaining steps of the methodology to design a comprehensible visualization for the characterized domain problem. This design is afterwards evaluated in Sect. 6 by showcasing how artifacts of the fileless malware *Poweliks* can be identified and how this helps to guide further investigations. We conclude our work and point to further possible research in Sect. 7.

2   Related Work

A Live Digital Forensic analysis is performed on a running system during an ongoing incident. The data is collected and analyzed simultaneously. The focus is on the preservation and processing of semi-persistent or volatile traces. This could be the content of the RAM, active network connections or running processes and programs [1]. Since these traces are no longer available after a system

---

[1] https://www.volatilityfoundation.org/.
[2] http://sandsprite.com/iDef/SysAnalyzer/.

restart, they cannot be extracted from a disk image by post-mortem analysis [13]. Live analysis is therefore useful if volatile data is essential for reconstructing an incident. This is the case if the system cannot be shut down for reasons of availability or dependency, or if encrypted data systems can no longer be accessed after a restart, for example when analyzing a fileless malware [11].

A disadvantage of live analysis is that the process can often not be repeated after leaving the location of the seizure [11]. In addition, the analysis takes place in a potentially compromised environment, so that relevant traces can be hidden, for example by using rootkits [1]. Furthermore, in the context of live analysis, a modification of the system by the investigation activities is almost unavoidable [1]. These modifications should be as limited as possible and all activities in the system must be precisely documented [13].

It is challenging to prove in court that the data integrity of the digital evidence has been preserved throughout the entire digital investigation. This may lead to a reduction in the admissibility of the evidence or even to a prohibition of its use. However, there are methods for comprehensible documentation and differentiation between the actions of an Incident Response team and the activities of an active attacker [8]. Providing a profound and tamper-proof documentation of analysis steps reduces the possible impact on the admissibility of volatile evidence and/or its modification. Nevertheless, these methods usually have to be implemented in advance as Digital Forensics Readiness measures.

Additionally, post-mortem and live analysis are not competing approaches, but rather complement each other. Live analysis enables the extraction and processing of additional traces, which can considerably support post-mortem analysis and the reconstruction of the course of events [1].

We identify several related visualization approaches originating from both the Visual Analytics (VA) and the Digital Forensics research domains. Within the VA domain, the designs are often based on user-centered approaches to provide a solution for a specific, relevant task of forensic experts. These visualizations feature a broad variety of use-cases ranging from the forensic investigation of shadow volumes and directories [14,15] to live monitoring of network traffic [3,4]. Tools like EventPad [6] allow the interactive and explorative analysis of large, dynamic data sets to identify malware and its behavior. The KAMAS solution is a tool providing not only innovative automated malware analysis features but also the functionality for malware analysis experts to exchange domain knowledge with the automated analysis methods [28]. Although a variety of related visualization designs exists in the VA domain, none of these visual representations is specifically designed to support the decisions forensic investigators need to make during an ongoing live forensic investigation. The same applies to the VA approaches introduced in the DF research domain. Tools like Timelab [23], LogAnalysis [7], MalViz [22], Vera [26], or Devise [27] allow a visual representation of different types of data for static forensic investigations but are by no means capable to support fast, dynamic decisions for live forensics.

None of the above-described visualization approaches pays special attention to the decision-support required throughout an LDF investigation. Additionally, to the best of our knowledge there is no existing work on bridging the gap between the domains of Live Digital Forensics and Visual Analytics by applying methodologies to develop comprehensive and reproducible visualization designs. Therefore, the knowledge from the Visual Analytics domain is beneficial as it pays attention to design aspects that are being neglected up to now in the LDF domain. We aim to contribute to a transfer of knowledge from the VSA towards the LDF domain in this research as it has been done in other security-related domains within the last years [25].

3   Methodology

This section summarizes the methodology which we follow throughout this work. A methodological approach allows our design decisions to be reproducible and comprehensible. Especially in visualization design this is of utmost importance because even methodologically based decisions remain subjective [18]. Therefore, we follow the Nested Blocks and Guidelines Model (NBGM) which is a well-established methodology for designing visualizations [19]. Another important aspect of the NBGM is that it is aimed to support the collaboration between domain and visualization experts and, therefore helps to close the aforementioned gap in LDF visualization designs [30]. The high-level layers of the NBGM are depicted in Fig. 1 and described in the subsequent sections [19,21].

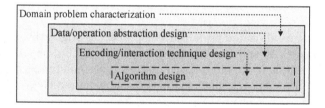

Fig. 1. Nested layers of the NBGM [19,21].

Domain Problem Characterization: The main task in this first layer is the identification of the specific situation and problem for which the visualization should be designed. The tasks and data of the target group are identified including their workflows and processes. Each target domain has its own descriptive vocabulary and it is important within this phase to work with the target users using their familiar vocabulary. This layer of the nested model bridges the gap between visualization experts and domain experts as it allows designers to understand the world the domain experts work in and which problems they face [32].

Data/Operation Abstraction Design: The second level abstracts the domain problem characterization using the vocabulary of the visualization domain. Therefore, it describes visualization tasks and the data relevant to the design. Domain-specific tasks and data descriptions are translated into a visualization-specific vocabulary. This way, visualization designers identify what tasks (e.g. finding outliers, identifying trends) the domain experts have to solve from a visualization point of view. The tasks of the users in visualizations can be derived from a variety of existing task taxonomies [5,28]. Additionally, the data abstraction allows designers to describe data transformations of available data identified within the domain problem characterization into a different format if necessary, for subsequent encoding technique decisions.

Encoding/Interaction Technique Design: This layer describes the visualization (encoding) techniques and the necessary interactions for users. Both, encoding and interactions must be aligned together and are derived from the visualization tasks in combination with the data at hand from the data / operation abstraction design-layer. Encoding and interaction techniques combine the first two nested layers with a design that instantiates the abstract visualization for the domain problem.

Algorithm Design: The innermost layer of the NBGM requires to create appropriate algorithms carrying out the beforehand designed encodings and interactions. We do not consider this step in our current work and focus on the first three layers of the model. The final implementation of the design is part of our further research.

4   Decision-Support for Live Forensics

In the case of an LDF investigation, decisions can be directly linked to the risks involved. Therefore, it is important to make well-considered decisions when choosing the right techniques, tools, and artifacts. In this section, we characterize the domain problem to enable a suitable visualization design helping domain experts facing this domain problem. We emphasize the supporting effect of the visualization for a digital forensic examiner. In particular, the tasks during a live digital forensic investigation are discussed. The goal is to apply the design methods of visualization experts to support better decision-making for a domain expert.

4.1   Live Digital Forensics Process

The collection and analysis of digital evidence should be based on a defined comprehensive process model. A common description of a forensic investigation process is represented by the model of Kent et al. [13]. The investigation process is divided into four phases as depicted in Fig. 2. We have extended the original approach to include an overarching decision-support by an interactive visualization at every stage. The following paragraphs describe the different original stages, which need a decision-support:

Collection: Data related to the criminal activity are identified, labeled, recorded, and secured from all potential sources of relevant data [13]. Possibly relevant additional data sources might be identified, and respective data needs to be collected during an LDF analysis.

Examination: The data collected in the previous phase is evaluated. The aim is to identify and extract relevant data [13]. Since our approach is applied to a live investigation, a visual analysis of the data allows the decision to include additional data sources for the analysis. Consequently, the visual decision-support creates a return to a previous phase.

Analysis: The results of the previous phases are analyzed in depth and interpreted to establish connections between persons, places, objects, and events and to obtain useful information regarding specific questions [13]. Findings from the visual analysis are directly incorporated into the analysis process. Malicious activities can be better understood through a visual representation of the data.

Reporting: The results of the analysis are prepared and presented, including important information. The format and content of the report depend on the type of recipient [13]. Especially, visual representations can contribute considerably to the understanding of the incident. Particularly, if the attack is complex, spikes in network traffic or system performance can provide a good insight on the activities during the incident.

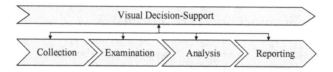

Fig. 2. A high-level process for Live Digital Forensics and Visual Decision-Support.

4.2 Tasks of Domain Experts in Live Digital Forensics

Mistry and Dahiya [20] discuss the volatile memory forensics approach in detail. Using live forensics, real-time data is analyzed and stored based on the system activities. The analysis of the memory (RAM) is very important while considering live computer forensics. The approach of live forensics plays an important role in identifying Indicators of Compromise (IoCs) and recording volatile data, which would be lost after shutting down the system. The authors use *memory forensics* to run through various challenging scenarios and prove their approach based on previously extracted and identified data in real-time. Since their approach provides a good description of the domain experts' workflow and it has been used by the authors in several scenarios, this is further considered. We abstract and extend the original approach as a baseline (see Table 1) to identify the main tasks during an LDF analysis:

Table 1. Summarized expert tasks in LDF.

Task	Details
Data Acquisition	– Identify suspected devices and media
	– Dump RAM, cache, and network traffic
	– Acquire an image of system (if possible)
Establish Intelligence	– Parse memory structure
	– Identify relevant memory segments
	– Identify loaded modules
	– Identify running processes and file accesses
	– Identify established network connections
Memory & Data Analysis	– Search outliers and irrelevant information
	– Extract additional relevant data
	– Verify findings for further decisions
	– Decide the next analysis steps
Documentation	– Document interesting findings
	– Document artifacts and evidence

- **Data Acquisition:** Within this task, investigators need to decide which data they export from the device under investigation. During an LDF analysis, only a limited amount of data can be extracted. An additional limitation for this task is often, that data only can be extracted with a-priori implemented functionalities.
- **Establish Intelligence:** This step is very much based on the present situation and requires that the investigator has a good sense of the specific case. Usually this is due to the prior knowledge of the investigator. It is important that in this step no analysis in the actual sense is carried out, but rather the region for possible purposeful evidence is identified. A graphical processing by means of VSA can contribute significantly to this. Especially decisions about the inclusion of further areas are very time-critical and a visual representation can contribute to a fast identification.
- **Memory & Data Analysis:** In this step, the previously identified data is examined for suspicious features. In addition, the findings are put into context to reconstruct the course of events. By a supporting effect of VSA, outliers and correlations can be better found.
- **Documentation:** The aforementioned tasks are documented during the whole digital forensic investigation to be used in the final report. This is an essential component to make the investigation comprehensible. During an analysis using VSA, findings based on a graphical preparation can be documented in the figures using markers (e.g. at peak values).

4.3   Available Data in Live Digital Forensics

Harichandran et al. [10] formed the term *curated forensic artifact (CuFA)* to specify the scope of forensic artifacts and their supervised attributes. The Artifact Genome Project (AGP), based on CuFA's principles, was launched in 2014 and has received 1099 forensic artifacts within the last few years [9]. It reached an acceptable level of maturity, as registered participants can contribute to this project by uploading artifacts along 19 categories.

Crimes are committed in several ways, and the expedient evidence is accumulated by different forensic artifacts. Depending on the peculiarity of a case, digital evidence either adds more value to an investigation or is completely inappropriate. The ontology of crimes by Kahvedzic et al. [12] provides a specification of past criminal cases and offers the possibility to specify almost every cyber case. We summarize the sub crime cases and focus only on cyber-crime cases.

The violation of the quality of forensic artifacts influences their admissibility at courts. Because of the fast-moving nature of digital evidence, we adopt the legal requirements by Antwi-Boasiako et al. [2] due to their overall completeness and applicability. This framework is appropriate for forensic investigations and reduces the overall scope of common data quality dimensions. These legal requirements cannot be circumvented, as admissibility in court is indispensable. AGP represents an open-source platform based on the CuFA principles. The following forensic artifacts categories have been extracted: Windows registry, memory, file, network packet, process, email message, address, code, disc partition, account, network socket, disk, user account, X509 certificate, user session, windows event log, volume, and Linux packages. These categories are further reduced since our concept focuses on LDF and not all categories are available in this type of investigation. To illustrate the possibilities of our approach, we will focus on the following categories of data sources that can be accessed during a live forensic analysis (without major interference due to the installation and execution of additional applications): *file access, network packets, process-lists, event logs (including PowerShell) and system statistics.*

VSA can support understanding and interpreting the context data in combination with stored data. Therefore, VSA allows experts to make better, context-based decisions for further investigations.

5   A Design for Visual Decision-Support in Live Forensics

Based on the domain problem which arises for forensic experts during a live forensic investigation (see Sect. 4) we derive appropriate visualization tasks, visual encoding and necessary interaction functionalities for a visual decision-support system within this section. Figure 3 depicts an overview over the respective, fully defined NBGM model for this problem domain.

The central contribution of this part of our work is the innovative application of different encoding techniques combined as an interactive, coordinated view where interactions in one view influence the representation in others. This allows a lateral, visual movement in the data enabling forensic analysts to browse

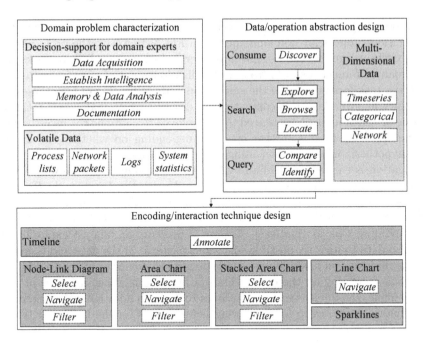

Fig. 3. NBGM applied for LDF covering the results Sects. 4 and 5.

through the data and identify artifacts that need further investigation with specific forensic analysis methods. However, without the visual decision-support they might not even have spotted the artifact. Therefore, we strengthen the necessity of a visual design as proposed by us in the following sections.

5.1   Data/Operation Abstraction Design

This section covers the abstraction of the domain problem characterization above. This step in the NBGM is carried out via designing and identifying data blocks and task blocks that describe the needs, requirements, and problems of the forensic experts. Defining these blocks, subsequently allows a comprehensible decision for specific visual encoding and interaction techniques.

Task Blocks. In Sect. 4.2 we identify several tasks that are important for forensic experts when they are performing an LDF investigation. A visual design for decision-support during these investigations needs to support the experts in these tasks. To be able to transfer the domain problems into a suitable visual design, we identify abstract visualization tasks from the *Why?* part of Brehmer and Munzner's task typology [5]. This typology describes why a specific task is performed in terms of which goal a user is pursuing.

The abstract, process-like overall task of forensic experts is to get an idea or indication where to further direct the ongoing LDF investigation and therefore, which tools they should deploy (see Sect. 4.1). We summarize this high-level task as "Decision-support for domain experts" in Fig. 3. However, the process-based task of decision-support can be split into several abstract visualization tasks. The main goal for forensic experts from a visualization point of view is to *Discover* which is a task formed around the generation and verification of hypotheses. An exemplary hypothesis in this context might describe which malware is acting on a device or which forensic tools need to be deployed to continue the investigation.

The *Discover* task is further specified depending on whether the analyst has a hypothesis in mind when using the visualization or not. When the LDF investigation is carried out to find evidence for a specific malware with known indicators acting on the device, this corresponds with the *Locate* task. *Browsing* outlines actions to search through suspicious indications within the visualization to find out which investigative tool might help to continue the analysis. The remaining task at this level, *Explore*, represents an analyst exploring the displayed data to identify possible suspicious patterns in the data and therefore, to make decisions on possible malware types on the device or at least additional LDF tools to deploy on the device. Once a hypothesis about malware or LDF tools is made, the forensic expert continues to *Identify* additional characteristics of the malware or tries to further strengthen the need for the LDF tool. This is possible by using the visual representation of our design.

Data Blocks. The available volatile data described in Sect. 4.3 is mostly defined as multi-dimensional data from a visualization point of view. However, there are some relevant subcategories of data types and formats which significantly influence the decision for corresponding visual encoding.

All available data that needs to be visualized within the decision-support for LDF is time-based data as it relates to some characteristics or actions of the system at a specific point on time, e.g. the network connections at a specific time or the respective CPU and RAM workload. Additional data categories can be categorical data like the different severity types of collected logs and network data.

5.2   Encoding/Interaction Technique Design

This section connects the different aspects between the problems of the forensic experts and the abstract blocks derived in Sect. 5.1 by introducing the visual encoding and corresponding interaction techniques that are necessary to enable a visual decision-support for LDF investigations. The visual encodings described in the following section are mainly well-known and established visualization techniques. We decided to only use these to ensure easy and fast perception of the design for forensic investigators. The encoding techniques are derived from the available data blocks while the interactions are necessary for the forensic experts to follow their tasks using the visual encoding of the data. The design sketch for the decision-support visualization is shown in Fig. 4. It comprises five interactive main components that are further detailed within this section. In terms of more abstract visualization tasks, the design allows *Navigation, Selection, Filtering,* and *Annotation* [5].

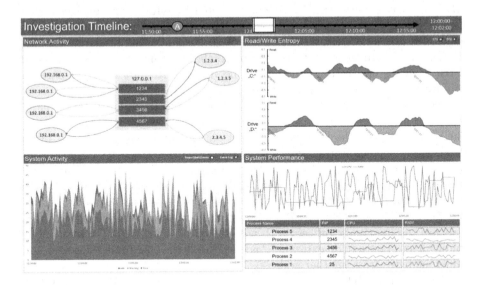

Fig. 4. Resulting design sketch of a decision-support visualization for Live Digital Forensics investigations.

Investigation Timeline. The first component is the overarching *Investigation Timeline*. This component is necessary since most of the data represented within the design is time series data (see Sect. 5.1). Therefore, a timeline allows navigating through different points in time of the collected data and analysts can select a specific time window for their analysis. The selected time window is indicated by the small white box-shaped overlay on the timeline and the time-range on the right side. In the design sketch of Fig. 4 a window of two minutes between 12:00:00 and 12:02:00 is selected. However, the box overlay can be moved across the timeline and can also be resized to allow the selection of different time ranges. The other four components of the visualization design display only data from the selected time window. An additional functionality of the *Investigation Timeline* is the event annotation. Forensic analysts can mark and label specific points in time when they identified possible evidence or interesting artifacts. This allows to come back to these events in a later investigation or even the collaboration of multiple analysts where one can pick up the investigation on a mark added to the timeline by another analyst.

Network Activity. The next component displayed in the upper left corner of Fig. 4 is the *Network Activity*. This view aims to give an overview over the device's external activities regarding the endpoints and IP addresses it communicated with. In the center of this view the device under investigation and process IDs (PIDs) is shown. To keep this representation clearly laid out only PIDs with active connections during the selected time frame are displayed. The connection partners are illustrated with ellipses labeled by IP addresses. The connection targets are clustered by IP address range allowing to distinguish different networks. In the exemplary design sketch, for example, the local network of the device is clustered on the left of the *Network Activity* clearly separated from external connection targets on the right.

We include the connections between a process and its communication partner by adding directed links for both incoming and outgoing communication. The color coding of the links is dependent on the cumulative number of bytes sent through the connection with a scale from blue (i.e. few bytes or "cold connection") to red (i.e. many bytes or "hot connection"). The distinguishable and color-coded links for up-link and down-link connections allow to quickly detect large data flows and to identify the process responsible for this data flow. Examples for possible artifacts needing additional analysis with sophisticated LDF tools are the imaginary process with the PIDs 2345 and 3456. The first one is sending a lot of data to an external IP address while the other one is downloading numerous bytes from another address.

Clicking on a PID highlights the connections of the selected process in this view but also in the *System Performance* and the *Read/Write Entropy* views where the activities of the process are highlighted respectively. This allows a quick indication about a process's overall statistics including its network activity as well as its CPU and RAM activity. Hovering a connection opens a thumbnail with additional information on this specific network communication between a process and an external IP address. This additional information contains the exact number of bytes sent over the connection as well as the port and protocol used to open it. A similar hovering interaction is also provided for the nodes depicting the communication partners of the device under investigation. The thumbnail for these nodes contains the total amount of bytes sent from and to this node as well as ports that were used to connect to. Hovering a node simultaneously also highlights the processes that established a connection with the corresponding IP address.

Read/Write Entropy. In the upper right corner the decision-support visualization design features a *Read/Write Entropy* display. The area charts of this view show the entropy of both read and write operations on mounted drives of the investigated device. The x-axis of the charts encodes the selected time frame from the *Investigation Timeline* while the positive y-axis displays the entropy of the data read from the specific drive at a point in time on a range from 0 to 1 (0% to 100%). Analogously, the negative y-axis represents the same indicators but for data written onto the drive. Therefore, the entropy for write operations is indicated as a negative value in our design. This only serves to clearly distinguish positive and negative y-axis values in the area charts. In addition to indicating the difference of read and write operations by indicating them with different vertical directions, they also are encoded with different colors. In the top right corner of this view, the drives for which the entropy values should be displayed can be selected via check-boxes.

This view allows a zooming interaction, preferably by mouse-wheel, where zooming in narrows down the displayed time window and zooming out analogously widens the time span. If experts zoom into this view, the time window is adjusted respectively for all other views. Possible artifacts that catching an expert's eye in this view are unusually high entropy scores for read or write operations. As an example, serves the increasing entropy scores in the design sketch towards the end of the selected time frame for both drives. This might indicate the writing of a lot of encrypted data on the two drives.

System Activity. The left view in the bottom row of our design is a visual representation is also an area chart, but a stacked version. It provides a visual encoding of *System Activity* by displaying a count of system events (e.g. Windows Event Logs, Powershell Events, Syslogs). The events are colored depending on their type or severity allows experts to detect a rising number of errors or similar indications of artifacts. The check-boxes on the top right of the view allow enabling different event types to be displayed. The x-axes of the area chart are like a timeline while the y-axes indicate the cumulative count of currently displayed event types at a specific point in time. The stacked area chart allows identifying trends and changes in the logged activities of the system.

This chart is also allowing a zoom interaction like the previous *Read/Write Entropy* views. Within this view, an unusually high number of error logs in the Windows Event Log that is constantly appearing throughout the whole two minutes currently under investigation could be an artifact for further analysis.

System Performance. The last view that is part of our visualization design located on the bottom right of Fig. 4. It is split into two smaller views which in combination give an indication of the *System Performance*. The upper part of this view is occupied by a line chart with two different lines. The blue line depicts CPU performance while the second, orange line indicates memory or RAM activity. Both lines are on a relative scale, meaning that the y-axis ranges from 0 to 1. Both lines on the chart are again displayed for the selected window of time. The line chart allows a zoom interaction similar to the interaction described within the *Read/Write Entropy* and the *System Activity* views.

The lower part of the display contains a table with active processes during the time which is currently defined for analysis. The table has four columns for the process name, its PID, and a spark line visualization allowing a fast perception of this process's CPU and RAM activities. A spark line is a special, word-sized type of line chart. They are not displayed with any axes and serve a single purpose: to give an indication about the trend of a single indicator. The table might be longer than the five exemplary rows from our design sketch and therefore, needs to be scrollable. Rows can also be selected leading to a highlighting of the corresponding process in the table and in the *Network Activity* view. Selecting a process also changes the *Read/Write Entropy* view by now only showing the entropy of the read or write operations performed on behalf of this specific process. This enables forensic analysts to conclude on the influence of a process on the systems performance and possible correlations with network activities.

6   Use Case

To show how our visualization design can support forensic experts in their LDF investigations, we go through a short use case featuring a well-known and documented fileless malware attack. We describe how indicators of this malware become apparent within our visual decision-support and how we support the tasks of forensic experts during an LDF investigation identified in Sect. 4.2.

The use case features the fileless-malware *Poweliks* which attacks Windows-based systems. This malware became known as a file-based piece of malicious code but in 2014 it moved to a file-less variant. After computers are infected they are part of a click-fraud botnet where bots request advertisement data from a central Command-and-Control (C&C) server, load the ads and click them to generate revenue [24]. As a side effect, *Poweliks* often acts a door-opener for other malware as it clicks up to 3000 ads per day on a single computer and does not care about whether the ads are malicious or not. Although this malware attracted attention back in 2014, its design is special in two aspects. *Poweliks* acts without leaving a file on the computer's file system. It stores all the data it needs in the registry and memory by injecting code into legitimate processes currently running. Therefore, it is hard to detect once it gained a foothold on the system. The second interesting aspect of *Poweliks* is, that, despite being a fileless malware, restarting the infected device does not remove it as it reboots itself from altered registry keys. This makes *Poweliks* a very special and dangerous type of fileless malware [33]. Because of those characteristics, we choose to describe how indicators for the *Poweliks* malware are visible within our visualization design.

Based on publicly available details and threat hunting details about the ad-fraud variant of *Poweliks*, we describe indicators that can be detected within our design, helping forensic analysts to make decisions where to guide their attention for further analyses. We structure the indicators and their identification according to the different views of our visualization design (see Sect. 5.2).

Network Activity: Regarding the network activity of an infected system, there are several indicators becoming apparent within a visual display. First, *Poweliks* is known to download the Powershell as well as the .NET framework from official Microsoft download pages if not available on the computer. The respective connections might appear in the view as connections of processes to official Microsoft IP addresses and a high payload on the down-link transfer, i.e. the link between the Microsoft IP and the process turns red.

Additionally, as the malware acts as a botnet, it regularly connects to its C&C server. These are only short connections with a very limited payload.

However, as they appear on a very regular basis, they can be identified as an indicator for further analysis why the system is connecting to the respective IPs.

Another suspicious activity to be spotted via the proposed design is the ad-clicking component of *Poweliks*. The behavior of requesting ad data from the C&C server, contacting a search page for the URL of the ad, and clicking the loaded advertisements becomes recognizable as the network activity would show many small-scale connections to a lot of different, external IP addresses. This is all more suspicious when the respective network connections are originating from a single process.

Read/Write Entropy: Overall, activities on the file system is less apparent as *Poweliks* is a file-less malware. However, as the malware can request up to 3000 ads per day on a single computer it is very likely that the malware also "clicks" other malicious ads. The entropy of read and write operations on different drives of a computer shall light on possible ransomware being active due to *Poweliks'* activities. Increasing entropy values in this view indicate the transfer of encrypted data. This highlights the necessity for domain experts to further investigate this malware since it could have features of a ransomware.

System Activity: *Poweliks'* special fileless persistence method uses a watchdog and PowerShell scripts when it is establishing its foothold. It also modifies many key registry entries trying to lower or disable browser security settings to be able to perform the ad-clicking behavior. Both of these actions produce log events (Windows Event Logs, PowerShell Events, etc.) with different severity. However, as the performed behavior is rather uncommon, the *System Activity* view shows several warnings and errors to the domain experts. Therefore, they might for example decide to analyze the changes made to the key registry in depth.

System Performance: Also, the system performance is not too bad during the execution of the *Poweliks* malware. This is because the malware does not want to significantly affect the performance of the infected computer. However, with our concept it can be seen that the CPU and RAM are used when a web page is accessed in the background for a few moments. This is due to the fact that the browser has to interpret and render the website. If the observed computer is not running other programs, this is also a possible indication of the malware. These findings by using a visual display during a live investigation help the forensic examiner to better assess the current situation and to make a well-considered decision for the use of certain tools. Also, the display of the processes and their RAM as well as CPU indicates possible further investigation needs. In the case of *Poweliks* which is hiding in different common processes (e.g. cmmon32.exe, dllhost.exe, logagent.exe), unusual activity of those processes indicates further investigation potential. Especially, when these processes are involved in anomalous network activity as well.

However, the malware *Poweliks* will be detected by current virus scanners but a coming back by a modification of the malicious code or behavior is very likely since file-less techniques evolved in the last few years. Nonetheless, they are relevant artifacts helping forensic experts to guide their further analyses.

7   Conclusion and Future Work

Within this work we made a contribution utilizing Visual Security Analytics as a decision-support approach for Live Digital Forensic investigations. We describe and abstract the problem of forensic investigators which have a wide variety of tools at hand for their analyses but need to decide quickly which of them need to be deployed in the current situation. To support them in this decision-making process we applied a methodology derived from the visualization research domain. Contributing to this domain problem with a tailor-made visualization approach enables forensic investigators to make faster and well informed decisions. We described the proposed visualization design and evaluated the visual representation with a simple use case. Summarizing, we showcased how Visual Security Analytics could help to solve an existing problem on the domain of LDF.

For future work we mainly see two different directions to follow. First of all, we want to apply our visual security analytic approach to a more sophisticated malware using *Process Doppelgänging*[3] where current anti-virus software and forensic tools reach their limits. Process Doppelgänging refers to a file-less code injection that uses a Windows native function and an undocumented implementation of the Windows Process Loader. This technique leaves no traces and is very difficult to detect. Our approach can highlight malicious activities and assist the digital forensics examiner during a live forensics investigation. Furthermore, another path to pursue in future work is the generalization of our approach. This requires to identify inherent characteristics of FMs and their classification based on a subset of those characteristics. A more holistic and modular version of our design approach would allow to have a specific encoding for each malware characteristic. This would support the work of forensic investigators even further as they can define individual dashboards as subsets of the available designs fitting their need to identify known and unknown FM.

References

1. Adelstein, F.: Live forensics: diagnosing your system without killing it first. Commun. ACM **49**(2), 63–66 (2006)
2. Antwi-Boasiako, A., Venter, H.: Implementing the harmonized model for digital evidence admissibility assessment. DigitalForensics 2019. IAICT, vol. 569, pp. 19–36. Springer, Cham (2019). https://doi.org/10.1007/978-3-030-28752-8_2

---

[3] https://www.blackhat.com/docs/eu-17/materials/eu-17-Liberman-Lost-In-Transaction-Process-Doppelganging.pdf.

3. Arendt, D., Best, D., Burtner, R., Lyn Paul, C.: Cyberpetri at CDX 2016: real-time network situation awareness. In: 2016 IEEE Symposium on Visualization for Cyber Security (VizSec), pp. 1–4. IEEE (2016)

4. Boschetti, A., Salgarelli, L., Muelder, C., Ma, K.L.: Tvi: a visual querying system for network monitoring and anomaly detection. In: Proceedings of the 8th International Symposium on Visualization for Cyber Security - VizSec 2011, pp. 1–10. ACM Press, New York (2011)

5. Brehmer, M., Munzner, T.: A multi-level typology of abstract visualization tasks. IEEE Trans. Vis. Comput. Graph. 19(12), 2376–2385 (2013)

6. Cappers, B.C., Meessen, P.N., Etalle, S., van Wijk, J.J.: Eventpad: rapid malware analysis and reverse engineering using visual analytics. In: 2018 IEEE Symposium on Visualization for Cyber Security (VizSec), pp. 1–8. IEEE (2018)

7. Catanese, S.A., Fiumara, G.: A visual tool for forensic analysis of mobile phone traffic. In: Proceedings of the 2nd ACM Workshop on Multimedia in Forensics, Security and Intelligence - MiFor 2010, p. 71. ACM Press, New York (2010)

8. Englbrecht, L., Langner, G., Pernul, G., Quirchmayr, G.: Enhancing credibility of digital evidence through provenance-based incident response handling. In: Proceedings of the 14th International Conference on Availability, Reliability and Security, ARES 2019, pp. 26:1–26:6. ACM (2019)

9. Grajeda, C., Sanchez, L., Baggili, I., Clark, D., Breitinger, F.: Experience constructing the artifact genome project (AGP): managing the domain's knowledge one artifact at a time. Digit. Invest. 26, S47–S58 (2018)

10. Harichandran, V.S., Walnycky, D., Baggili, I., Breitinger, F.: Cufa: a more formal definition for digital forensic artifacts. Digit. Invest. 18, S125–S137 (2016)

11. Hoelz, B., Ralha, C., Mesquita, F.: Case-based reasoning in live forensics. In: Peterson, G., Shenoi, S. (eds.) DigitalForensics 2011. IAICT, vol. 361, pp. 77–88. Springer, Heidelberg (2011). https://doi.org/10.1007/978-3-642-24212-0_6

12. Kahvedzic, D., Kechadi, M.T.: Dialog: a framework for modeling, analysis and reuse of digital forensic knowledge. Digit. Invest. 6, 23–33 (2009)

13. Kent, K., Chevalier, S., Grance, T., Dang, H.: Guide to integrating forensic techniques into incident response. NIST Spec. Publ. 10(14), 800–886 (2006)

14. Leschke, T.R., Nicholas, C.: Change-link 2.0: a digital forensic tool for visualizing changes to shadow volume data. In: Proceedings of the Tenth Workshop on Visualization for Cyber Security - VizSec 2013, pp. 17–24. ACM Press, New York (2013)

15. Leschke, T.R., Sherman, A.T.: Change-link: a digital forensic tool for visualizing changes to directory trees. In: Proceedings of the Ninth International Symposium on Visualization for Cyber Security - VizSec 2012, pp. 48–55. ACM Press, New York (2012)

16. Mansfield-Devine, S.: Fileless attacks: compromising targets without malware. Netw. Secur. 2017(4), 7–11 (2017)

17. Marty, R.: Applied Security Visualization. Safari Tech Books Online. Addison-Wesley, Boston (2009)

18. McCurdy, N., Dykes, J., Meyer, M.: Action design research and visualization design. In: Proceedings of the Beyond Time and Errors on Novel Evaluation Methods for Visualization - BELIV 2016, pp. 10–18. ACM Press, New York (2016)

19. Meyer, M., Sedlmair, M., Quinan, P.S., Munzner, T.: The nested blocks and guidelines model. Inf. Vis. 14(3), 234–249 (2015)

20. Mistry, N.R., Dahiya, M.S.: Signature based volatile memory forensics: a detection based approach for analyzing sophisticated cyber attacks. Int. J. Inf. Technol. 11(3), 583–589 (2018). https://doi.org/10.1007/s41870-018-0263-4

21. Munzner, T.: A nested model for visualization design and validation. IEEE Trans. Vis. Comput. Graph. **15**(6), 921–928 (2009)
22. Nguyen, V.T., Namin, A.S., Dang, T.: Malviz: an interactive visualization tool for tracing malware. In: Proceedings of the 27th ACM SIGSOFT International Symposium on Software Testing and Analysis - ISSTA 2018, pp. 376–379. ACM Press, New York (2018)
23. Olsson, J., Boldt, M.: Computer forensic timeline visualization tool. Digit. Invest. **6**, 78–87 (2009)
24. O'Murchu, L., Gutierrez, F.P.: The evolution of the fileless click-fraud malware poweliks (2015). https://www.symantec.com/content/dam/symantec/docs/security-center/white-papers/evolution-of-fileless-click-fraud-15-en.pdf. Accessed 24 Feb 2020
25. Puchta, A., Böhm, F., Pernul, G.: Contributing to current challenges in identity and access management with visual analytics. In: Foley, S.N. (ed.) DBSec 2019. LNCS, vol. 11559, pp. 221–239. Springer, Cham (2019). https://doi.org/10.1007/978-3-030-22479-0_12
26. Quist, D.A., Liebrock, L.M.: Visualizing compiled executables for malware analysis. In: 2009 6th International Workshop on Visualization for Cyber Security, pp. 27–32. IEEE (2009)
27. Read, H., Xynos, K., Blyth, A.: Presenting devise: data exchange for visualizing security events. IEEE Comput. Graph. Appl. **29**(3), 6–11 (2009)
28. Rind, A., Aigner, W., Wagner, M., Miksch, S., Lammarsch, T.: Task cube: a three-dimensional conceptual space of user tasks in visualization design and evaluation. Inf. Vis. **15**(4), 288–300 (2016)
29. Sacha, D., Stoffel, A., Stoffel, F., Kwon, B.C., Ellis, G., Keim, D.A.: Knowledge generation model for visual analytics. IEEE Trans. Vis. Comput. Graph. **20**(12), 1604–1613 (2014)
30. Simon, S., Mittelstädt, S., Keim, D.A., Sedlmair, M.: Bridging the gap of domain and visualization experts with a liaison. In: Eurographics Conference on Visualization (EuroVis) - Short Papers. The Eurographics Association (2015)
31. Sudhakar, Kumar, S.: An emerging threat fileless malware: a survey and research challenges. Cybersecurity, **3**(1), 1–12 (2020)
32. van Wijk, J.J.: Bridging the gaps. IEEE Comput. Graph. Appl. **26**(6), 6–9 (2006)
33. Wueest, C., Anand, H.: Internet security threat report: living off the land and fileless attack techniques (2017). https://www.symantec.com/content/dam/symantec/docs/security-center/white-papers/istr-living-off-the-land-and-fileless-attack-techniques-en.pdf. Accessed 24 Feb 2020

Predictive Analytics to Prevent Voice over IP International Revenue Sharing Fraud

Yoram J. Meijaard[1(✉)], Bram C. M. Cappers[1,2(✉)], Josh G. M. Mengerink[2(✉)], and Nicola Zannone[1(✉)]

[1] Eindhoven University of Technology, Eindhoven, The Netherlands
y.j.meijaard@student.tue.nl, {b.c.m.cappers,n.zannone}@tue.nl
[2] AnalyzeData, Eindhoven, The Netherlands
{b.cappers,j.mengerink}@analyzedata.com

Abstract. International Revenue Sharing Fraud (IRSF) is the most persistent type of fraud in the telco industry. Hackers try to gain access to an operator's network in order to make expensive unauthorized phone calls on behalf of someone else. This results in massive phone bills that victims have to pay while number owners earn the money. Current anti-fraud solutions enable the detection of IRSF afterwards by detecting deviations in the overall caller's expenses and block phone devices to prevent attack escalation. These solutions suffer from two main drawbacks: *(i)* they act only when financial damage is done and *(ii)* they offer no protection against future attacks. In this paper, we demonstrate how unsupervised machine learning can be used to discover fraudulent calls at the moment of their establishment, thereby preventing IRSF from happening. Specifically, we investigate the use of Isolation Forests for the detection of frauds before calls are initiated and compare the results to an existing industrial post-mortem anti-fraud solution.

1 Introduction

International Revenue Sharing Fraud (also known as Toll fraud) is a multi-billion dollar scheme [17] where fraudsters use telecommunications products or services without the intent to pay. With Voice Over IP (VoIP) enabling devices to communicate over the Internet, VoIP devices and services are a popular target for hackers to abuse. The result is typically phone bills of thousands of euros [28] that victims have to pay. In practice, network operators often covers these expenses either because they were responsible for the vulnerability or they want to maintain customer satisfaction. To minimize this fraud, they often install anti-fraud detection software to detect signs of fraud as quickly as possible. Current anti-fraud solutions typically use pricing information and features such as call duration to determine whether a call was fraudulent. Although such detection turns out to be accurate [4], those features are only available after the call

© IFIP International Federation for Information Processing 2020
Published by Springer Nature Switzerland AG 2020
A. Singhal and J. Vaidya (Eds.): DBSec 2020, LNCS 12122, pp. 241–260, 2020.
https://doi.org/10.1007/978-3-030-49669-2_14

has been made. Since the detection of a fraudulent call does not provide any information about the severity of the next call, operators are often forced to shutdown the phone device or underlying VoIP server (e.g., a Private Branch eXchange) until they are sure that the call was legitimate. The result is that customers can no longer make (regular) phone calls until the fraud has been resolved.

The goal of this work is to explore to what extent fraud can be detected when a call is established, compared to existing industrial (post-mortem) anti-fraud solutions. To this end, we study how we can use unsupervised machine learning solutions and, in particular, Isolation Forests [25] to determine the severity of a phone call using features that are only available at the start of a call. In contrast to traditional anomaly detection algorithms (see [8] for a survey), Isolation Forests enable the detection of anomalies without having to construct profiles of normal behavior. This makes the algorithm particularly suitable for highly dynamic environments where construction of normal profiles can be too resource intensive. In addition, with linear time classification Isolation Forests have also shown to be suitable for the analysis of large data streams [9]. However, in order for machine learning solutions to be applied for fraud detection, the number of false alarms need to be kept to a minimum. This typically requires properly tuning such solutions and underlying parameters, which is a non-trivial task [16].

In this work, we perform a latitudinal study to assess the detection capabilities of Isolation Forests in the context of IRSF detection and to study how different parameter settings and feature spaces affect performance.

Specifically, our main contributions are:

– the application of Isolation Forest anomaly detection for the early-stage detection of IRSF;
– a case study of the approach demonstrating the effect of different parameter settings, feature sets, and the use of derived features to improve detection rates;
– a comparison of the detection with respect to existing post-mortem analysis;
– a number of lessons learned on how to use Isolation Forests for the detection of anomalies in multivariate data.

Our approach offers several benefits compared to existing anti-fraud solutions. In particular, it enables network operators to detect signs of fraudulent calls before they are established, providing operators the opportunity to block the call preemptively rather than blocking a phone device entirely when the fraud has happened.

The remainder of the paper is structured as follows. The next section introduces background on VoIP and related frauds. Section 3 discusses related work. Section 4 presents our methodology and Sect. 5 presents its experimental evaluation. Finally, Sect. 6 discusses the results along with the limitations of the approach and Sect. 7 concludes the paper and provides directions for future work.

2   Background and Motivations

Voice over IP (VoIP) enables users to communicate audio and video over the Internet. Compared to physical phone lines, the Internet provides a cheaper alternative and is widely available. The VoIP infrastructure consists of four main types of components: VoIP devices, Private Branch eXchanges (PBX's), the Public Switched Telephony Network (PSTN), i.e. the legacy phone infrastructure, and VoIP gateways. A VoIP device connects over the Internet to a PBX operated by a network operator, which in turn connects to other PBX's. Over this network, a VoIP device is able to call other VoIP devices. VoIP gateways connect the VoIP network to the PSTN to enable VoIP devices to call legacy phones.

Over the years, several vulnerabilities in VoIP and underpinning network protocols have been discovered. Sahin et al. [32] define a taxonomy of VoIP fraud schemes in which these schemes are categorized with respect to their root causes along with their weaknesses and techniques to exploit them. Given that IRSF has been recognized as the largest class of frauds in practice [17], in this work we focus on the detection of this class.

In IRSF an attacker breaks into the VoIP system of the victim and places numerous calls to a premium phone number, i.e. a number that charges a fee in addition to the regular cost of the call, which is owned by the attacker or a colluding entity. These calls are charged to the victim and the revenue made from this call is shared amongst the attackers. Blacklisting premium numbers is virtually impossible, due to them being ill-defined internationally [32]. Therefore, network operators need methods for the detection of IRSF. Ideally, these methods should be able to detect the fraud when the call is established to prevent it from happening.

Real-time anomaly detection in telco industry, however, is challenging due to the variety and volumes of data [12]. Depending on the type of users, the number of calls can vary from tens to hundreds per month. In addition, data volumes are often too large to analyze all network packets individually. As a result the use of profiling techniques can be too computational intensive.

In order for anomaly detection to be effective in this field, the evaluation of a data point needs to be reliable and efficient. False positives need to be kept to a minimum to avoid operators from being overloaded with false alarms. In particular, the maximum allowable false positive rate should be <2% [23]. The false negative ratio (i.e., the number of missed fraud) is less critical here. We wish to catch as much fraud beforehand as possible, but missed fraud cases could still be detected by a post-mortem detector. In addition, some features such as the call duration and cost are only available after the call has been made. Most data fields in VoIP calls consists of categorical features. In order to enable real-time detection, the evaluation of a new data point and model updating must be efficient [1].

In summary, in order to make the detection of IRSF during call establishment effective, the anomaly detection method should meet several requirements. Specifically, a solution for *online* IRSF detection should:

R1 Be resilient to ill-balanced label distribution (e.g., 99% normal and 1% fraud).

R2 Support the analysis of categorical features.

R3 Enable fast classification of (new) individual calls.

R4 Provide a computational efficient method for training the classification model.

R5 Generate an operationally feasible number of false positives.

R6 Not rely on call features that are only available after the end of a call.

In the next sections we discuss to what extent existing solutions meet the requirements and show how Isolation Forests can be used to solve the detection task.

3   Related Work

Fraud detection is an extensively studied field covering a wide variety of techniques [22]. We first give a broad overview on data analysis techniques used to detect IRSF, followed by a detailed discussion on existing anti-fraud solutions that are based on the analysis of Call Detail Record (CDR) logs. An evaluation of existing solutions with respect to the requirements identified in Sect. 2 is given in Table 1. For a more detailed overview on the use of anomaly detection techniques for the detection of telecom fraud, we refer to [19].

Table 1. Comparison of fraud detection techniques with respect to the requirements for online IRSF detection, as formulated in Sect. 2. In the table, ● means "support", ◑ "partially support", ○ "no support".

Requirements	R1	R2	R3	R4	R5	R6
Wiens et al. [38]	●	●	◑	○	●	○
Kuble [23]	●	●	◑	○	●	○
Olszewski [27]	●	◑	●	○	○	○
Wiens et al. [37]	●	●	◑	○	●	○
Becker et al. [3]	●	●	○	○	○	○

Fraud Detection. Similar to intrusion detection [13], approaches for the detection of (IRSF) fraud can be classified in two main categories, namely *signature-based* detection and *behavioral-based* detection [5]. Signature-based detection uses fixed rules to identify whether a call adheres to predefined patterns. For instance, a suddenly increase in a user's dial expenses compared to his average phone bill provides an indicator for IRSF. For more details on the typical signatures used for fraud detection, we refer to [14]. Although the use of signatures provides an effective approach to fraud detection, it is unable to discover new patterns enabling the detection of IRSF when, for instance, the cost of the call is unknown.

These shortcomings are typically addressed by *behavioral-based* detection techniques. These techniques focus on the (statistical) profiling of entities so that the regularity of new data points can be determined according to a model of expectation derived from historical data. This enables analysts to automatically derive models that are tailored on a per profile basis. In case of IRSF detection, we can identify two main types of behavioral-based techniques, namely *offline* and *online* [7,36]. *Offline* behavioral-based techniques (also referred to as *post-mortem* detection) stores incoming data and do the analysis after all calls have been made. *Online* techniques (a.k.a. (near)-real time analysis) perform the analysis the moment new data arrives (e.g., during call establishment).

Our work can be positioned as online behavioral-based method. In particular, we investigate the possibilities of applying online anomaly detection at the start of a call, enabling the early stage detection of IRSF. This is in contrast to current literature, which mainly focuses on the offline analysis of calls by applying anomaly detection on Call Detail Record (CDR) logs [29]. Next, we review those solutions.

CDR-Based Fraud Analysis. A common approach in the telecommunication domain for offline behavioral-based fraud detection is through the analysis of Call Detail Records (CDR). For instance, Modani et al. [26] use decision trees and logistic regression to predict the churn rate of companies in CDR records whereas Wiens et al. [37,38] apply statistical profiling on user call behavior to detect exploited FRITZ!Boxes in a network. The use of anomaly detection techniques are also shown to be useful for the discovery of unknown patterns in call records. For instance, Becker et al. [3] are one of the first to use unsupervised learning on CDRs to discover cellphone usage patterns. CDRs have also been used to discover relationships between criminals based on the assumption that criminals interact with each other. Specifically, Kumar and colleagues propose a model to construct a CDR database in which these relationships are captured [24].

Kübler et al. [23] analyze toll fraud hindsight by clustering user behavior using unsupervised learning techniques such as k-means clustering and EM mixture models [2]. Instead of using cost-based features, they build user-profiles based on destination number and duration of the call. Although this approach to discover behavioral patterns through feature engineering is similar to ours, it requires the construction of user profiles to determine the severity of a call. In addition, the clustering algorithms proposed in [23] are too computational intensive to be used in online settings. Especially in dynamic environments where users register and leave phone operators on a regular basis, building "normal" profiles can be too resource intensive to be applied in practice. The advantage of using Isolation Forests is that this technique does not require a normal baseline to determine the severity of an anomaly, but aims to isolate "few and different" points from the rest of the data [25].

In summary, current approaches for fraud detection are signature-based or rely on an offline behavioral-based analysis of calls using CDR logs. The absence of offline features such as cost and duration in online detection requires adaptation of existing fraud detection techniques both in terms of the feature space to analyze as well as computational requirements. Our work overcomes these limitations by using Isolation Forests.

4   Methodology

The goal of the methodology is to explore to what extent we are able to detect fraudulent IRSF calls before they are established, giving operators the opportunity to block the call and prevent the fraud from happening.

We enable online IRSF detection through a real-time analysis of the network traffic from and to Private Branch eXchange servers to identify suspicious patterns in the establishment of VoIP calls. The establishment of a VoIP call is achieved by means of a handshake using the Session Initiation Protocol (SIP) [31]. This protocol contains call meta-data similar to Call Detail Records such as call start time, source and destination numbers, and user identifier. In addition, more advanced features can be derived such as the country of origin or in/outside office hours (we refer to Sect. 5.4 for more details). Since the analysis is done during call establishment, we assume that features such as call duration, cost of a call and call end time are unavailable.

Our methodology for online detection of IRSF comprises three steps, as depicted at the top of Fig. 1:

1. From the VoIP data we extract the features to use for training of the isolation forest.
2. We generate an isolation forest from the training data, which assigns an anomaly score to each call.
3. We classify all calls with an anomaly score lower than a given threshold as anomalies. Anomalous records are marked as **fraud** while the other are marked as **normal**.

To validate experimental results, we use an industry post-mortem fraud detector as a baseline. Validation comprises three steps:

5. After the call ended, a CDR record is created by the underpinning PBX server.
6. The industrial anti-fraud detector labels the call records either as **fraud** or **normal**.
7. The evaluation phase compares the labels from our approach with the ones given by the industrial detector and generates a performance report.

In the remainder of the section, we first introduce Isolation Forests after which we discuss the dataset used for our experiments.

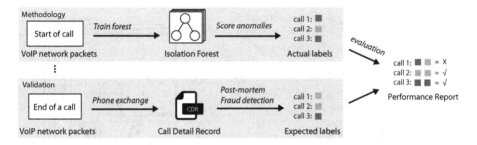

Fig. 1. At the start of a call the isolation forest is trained and anomaly scores are computed on the data points. At the end of a call, the post-mortem anti-fraud detector evaluates the call after which the labels of the isolation forest are compared to the existing solution.

4.1 Isolation Forests

Traditional anomaly detection techniques typically construct a profile of the data that is considered "normal" and evaluate any new data point against that model [8]. Isolation Forests use a different approach as it aims to separate anomalous data points in the dataset without building a distribution or profile. Instead, data is sub-sampled in a tree structure by evaluating data points on randomly chosen features and split on those features. Specifically, if a node contains two or more records, it is split according to a randomly chosen feature. This causes an anomalous data point to reside in their own leaf node. This is also illustrated in Fig. 2. The main idea is that similar data points require more splits before they can be separated from one another while anomalies remain close to the root. Since purely random splits can lead to poor decision trees, data points are evaluated against a collection of generated trees to determine whether they are statistically significantly different from the rest.

The anomaly score of a data point is based on its average depth in all isolation trees. A high score indicates that many splits are required in order to separate a data point from the rest and is therefore considered to be similar to other records. Similarly, if the score is low, only few splits are required to separate the data point and, therefore, it is considered different from the other data points. A user defined threshold is used to determine whether a score is low or high, i.e. whether a data point should be considered anomalous.

In our work, we evaluate the following parameters for the generation of Isolation Forests (illustrated in Fig. 3):

- `nrTrees` represents the number of trees in the forest.
- `sample_size` represents the size of the sample set. The sample size determines the number of records for the construction of a tree in the forest.
- `max_depth` represents the maximum depth for each isolation tree.
- `threshold` is a user-defined threshold that determines the average tree depth that should be exceeded in order for a data point to be considered `normal`.

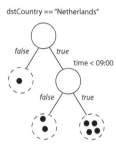

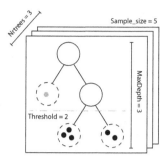

Fig. 2. Example model where seven data points are clustered according to two randomly chosen data splits. Regular data points are assumed to have overlap in values and are therefore harder to separate from one another compared to anomalous data points. Isolation forest uses the path length from the root to determine data points' regularity. Anomalous data points have their own leaf node.

Fig. 3. Parameters in isolation forests manipulate the forest by specifying the number of trees, number of nodes per tree, the maximum depth of generated trees along with the number of samples that must be used for the construction of a tree. The dot in red is anomalous with respect to the chosen threshold. (Color figure online)

– `feature_set` represents the set of features used for the construction of the trees in the forest.

Isolation Forests provide several advantages compared to other machine learning techniques. Compared to black-box techniques such as neural networks, Isolation Forests are transparent. By inspecting the different trees, a VoIP operator is able to provide an explanation on why a data point was considered anomalous, thereby enabling means to judge the quality of a model using domain knowledge. Adaptations of Isolation Forests have been proposed to make them suitable for streaming data [33]. In contrast to other unsupervised learning methods such as k-means and EM-Mixture models [2], the construction of the forest is computationally efficient, since distances between data points are not computed, but features and data splits for the trees are chosen randomly. In addition, the classification of a new data point requires at most $\mathcal{O}(\texttt{max\_depth})$ steps per tree and can be run in parallel for every tree in the forest. Compared to supervised learning techniques such as decision tree classifiers and SVM, Isolation forest do not require labels to identify anomalous data points.

4.2 Data Characteristics

We performed a number of experiments to assess the effectiveness of Isolation Forests for the online detection of IRSF. Our dataset consists of over 10.000 VoIP calls, out of which the industrial anti-fraud solution marked 150 calls as

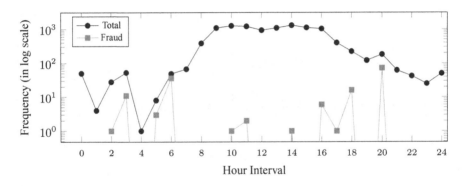

Fig. 4. Distribution of calls over the time of the day in our dataset.

fraudulent. The dataset consists of nine Dutch users where a user can represent a physical person, a server, or an entire phone operator. The data was recorded for a month by mirroring network traffic from a Private Branch eXchange server of a Dutch VoIP provider. Each call is characterized by the following online (i.e., pre-call) features:

- `record_id` is the identifier of the VoIP record.
- `user_id` is the identifier of the user that made the call.
- `srcNr` is an anonymized representation of the source number.
- `srcCtry` represents the country of call source.
- `dstNr` is an anonymized representation of the destination number.
- `dstCtry` represents the country of the call destination.
- `disposition` indicates whether the call was answered, canceled or busy.
- `time` is a timestamp indicating when call took place.

To test the suitability of Isolation Forests for the detection of IRSF in general, we also collected the following offline (i.e., post-call) features:

- `duration` indicates how long the call lasted in seconds.
- `billsec` indicates the cost of the call per second.

We performed an analysis of the dataset to verify that it does not contain any artefacts that could disqualify the experiments. For the sake of space, here we only report our analysis with respect to features `time` and `dstCtry`. As shown in Fig. 4, calls are typically made during work hours whereas fraud cases mainly occur outside of work hours. We can observe in Fig. 5 that the destination of the calls is predominantly to the Netherlands, but there is a wide variety of calls to different countries. The plot also shows that simply blocking calls to certain countries is not a viable solution to fraud prevention, as it would incorrectly block at least as much normal traffic.

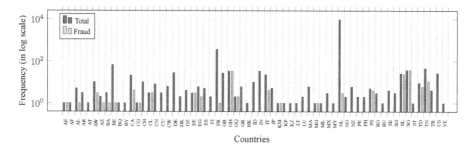

Fig. 5. Distribution of calls over countries (expressed using ISO 3166-1 country codes) in our dataset.

5 Experiments

This work aims to evaluate the effectiveness of Isolation Forests for the detection of IRSF. In particular, we are interested in answering the following research questions:

Q1 Are Isolation Forests suitable for offline and online detection of IRSF ?
Q2 What is the effect of different parameter settings towards detection rates?
Q3 What is the effect of different feature sets towards detection rates?
Q4 To what extent does the use of derived features improve detection rates?

Questions **Q1** and **Q2** validate whether Isolation Forests can be used in general for IRSF detection. **Q3** aims to determine which features in the input data should be taken into account during classification. The naïve usage of features such as `time` or categorical features can significantly blow up the state space in which the algorithm needs to operate and can lead to sub optimal results [10,20]. Similar to Kübler et al. [23], in **Q4** we test the effect of discretizing the `time` feature to see how this influences detection rates.

For the implementation of Isolation Forests we used the h2o framework (version 3.26.0.10) [6]. This framework offers out-of-the-box support for categorical data and is commonly used in academia to study machine learning techniques.

Settings. In our experiments, we tested different configurations for the generation of Isolation Forests by varying the parameters presented in Sect. 4.1. An overview of the parameters for each experiment is given in Table 2. It is worth noting that increasing `nrTrees` does not influence the outcome of the model, since it is statistically unlikely to generate significantly different anomaly scores when averaging over 100 trees given the feature set of VoIP calls. Therefore, the recommended default settings for this parameter is used, i.e. 100. In Experiments 1, 3, and 4 we set parameter `sample_size` to 256, which we deem sufficiently large. This choice is further motivated by Experiment 2 in which we varied this parameter to study its effect on detection rates.

The choice for parameters `max_depth` and `threshold` is based on two observations: Isolation Forests are unable to classify anomalies from normal behaviour

Table 2. Summary of parameter settings used for the experiments described in Sect. 5.

Parameter	Experiment 1	Experiment 2	Experiment 3	Experiment 4
nrTrees	100	100	100	100
sample_size	256	64, 128, 256, 512	256	256
max_depth	$[6, 15] \in \mathbb{N}$	$[6, 15] \in \mathbb{N}$	$[6, 15] \in \mathbb{N}$	$[6, 15] \in \mathbb{N}$
threshold	$[5, 15] \in \mathbb{R}$	$[5, 15] \in \mathbb{R}$	$[5, 15] \in \mathbb{R}$	$[5, 15] \in \mathbb{R}$
feature_set	pre-call, post-call	pre-call	subsets of pre-call	pre-call + derived features

with a small max_depth, e.g., ≤ 5. On the other hand, a large max_depth (e.g., ≥ 15) can result in problematic overfitting, as mentioned in the original paper [25]. Simultaneously, the value of threshold cannot exceed the max_depth value and, therefore, its domain is restricted. Specifically, we varied threshold in the range [5, max_depth], with steps of 0.1.

Evaluation Metrics. In general, the evaluation of an unsupervised learning algorithm is a challenge due to the lack of labeled data or a proper baseline. Inspired by Wang et al. [35] and Dudoit et al. [11], we measure the quality of the resulting model by means of an external index using the labels of the existing anti-fraud solution as the baseline.

The most common evaluation metric to assess the performance of a machine learning algorithm is the Receiver Operating Characteristics (ROC) curve [18]. In this curve the true positive rates and false positive rates are plotted for an algorithm at various thresholds (i.e., the Isolation Forest threshold parameter). In our application domain, the goal is to have a curve where the true positive rate is high and false positive rate is close to 0. The Area Under the Curve (AUC) is an indicator how well the algorithm can discriminate between normal and fraudulent traffic. The AUC can vary between 0.0 and 1.0 and the larger the area, the better the performance.

5.1 Experiment 1: Effectiveness of Isolation Forests for IRSF Detection

In this experiment, we assess whether the classification capabilities of Isolation Forests are suited to fraud detection in VoIP. We test this by applying Isolation Forests to both an online and an offline setting. Specifically, we conduct two tests: one using all data available at the establishment of the call (e.g., pre-call features) and one also including post-call features (cf. Sect. 4.2). Based on **R5**, we require that the false positive rate is less than 2%, while the true positive rate should be sufficient to outweigh operational costs.

The full construction of an isolation forest for the dataset is efficient and takes approximately 1 second (**R4**). Figure 6 reports the ROC curves when using pre-call and post-call features. The figure shows that, at a 2% false positive rate, the true positive rate obtained using pre-call features is insufficient. However, in the post-mortem setting we can detect up to 58% of all fraud cases. At a false positive rate of 5%, we can detect up to 33% of all fraud cases in the pre-call setting, compared to 82% in the post-call setting. The true and false positive rates for the post-call features are comparable to earlier work by Kübler [38] and shows that, with respect to requirements **R1** and **R5**, Isolation Forests have potential for the detection of IRSF. Enabling detection of IRSF using only pre-call features, however, requires additional tuning in order to meet the requirements.

5.2   Experiment 2: Effect of Parameter Settings

This experiments is conducted to evaluate the effect of parameters `max_depth` and `sample_size` on the detection capabilities of Isolation Forests. To this end, we first computed the ROC curves for each value of `max_depth` while varying parameter `threshold` with steps of 0.1 and fixing the `sample_size` parameter to 256. We also computed the ROC curves for each value of `sample_size` while keeping the `max_depth` parameter fixed to $\log(sample\_size)$ and varying the `threshold` with steps of 0.1. For this experiment, we used pre-call features. Figure 7 reports the results of the experiment.

From the plot at the top of Fig. 7, we can observe that, when `max_depth` is lower than 7, the detection rate drops significantly. We believe this is twofold. First, if the `max_depth` becomes smaller than the number of features, there is an increased risk of missing crucial feature splits during the tree generation phase of the algorithm. Second, in Sect. 4.1 we showed that anomalous data points occur alone in the leafs of an isolation tree. With a `max_depth` of 6, at most $2^6 = 64$ anomalous data points can be detected. Given that the dataset includes over 100 cases marked as `fraud`, the size of the tree is insufficient to assign every

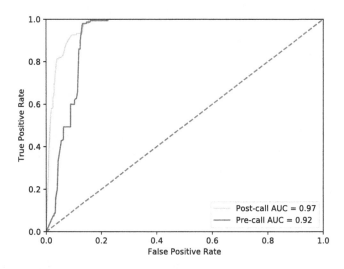

Fig. 6. Comparison of ROC curves for fraud detection using pre-call and post-call features. The dashed line represents the ROC curve for a random classifier.

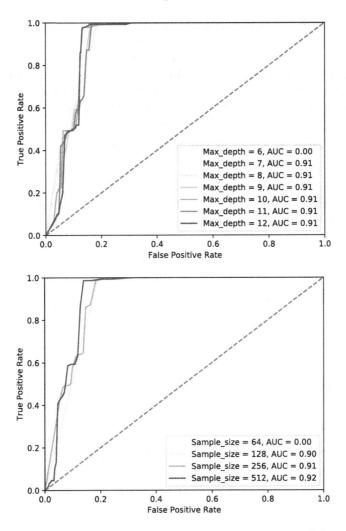

Fig. 7. Comparison of ROC curves for fraud detection using pre-call features at the variations of `max_depth` (top) and `sample_size` (bottom).

anomalous point to an empty leaf node. As a consequence, it is more likely for two inherently different data points to end up in the same leaf node, which leads to an overgeneralization of the resulting model.

A second observation is that increasing the `max_depth` does not significantly affect performance. By default, Liu et al. [25] recommend `max_depth` = $\log_2($`sample_size`$)$ to obtain a balanced tree. In our experiments this recommended value would correspond to $\log_2(256) = 8$. The idea of increasing the depth would be to give the algorithm more slack to add additional splits to better discriminate between normal and fraudulent points. Results show, however, that for `max_depth` $= 8$ the number of splits is already sufficient to identify the anomalies.

The plot at the bottom of Fig. 7 shows that the increase of parameter `sample_size` does not lead to any significant improvement of the performance. This illustrates that taking a sample size of 256 is sufficiently large to obtain a data subset which is representative for the generation of one tree.

5.3 Experiment 3: Effect of Different Features

We conducted this experiment to investigate the impact of including certain features on the effectiveness of Isolation Forests for fraud detection. We compare different sets of features and measure the false positive and true positive rates. In particular, we consider the following feature sets:

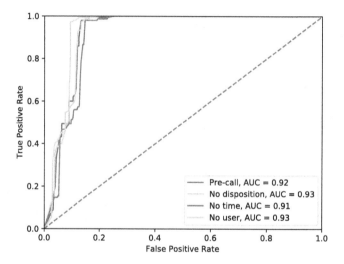

Fig. 8. Comparison of ROC curves for fraud detection using different feature sets. Specifically, the curve obtained using all pre-call features is compared to the curves obtained when either `disposition`, `time` or `user_id` are removed.

1. **Pre-call, no time**: `record_id, user_id, srcNr, srcCtry, dstNr, dstCtry, disposition`, which allows us to study the influence of the time of the call on the detection rate.
2. **Pre-call, no user**: `record_id, srcNr, srcCtry, dstNr, dstCtry, time, disposition`, which allows us to study the influence of the user identity on the detection rate.
3. **Pre-call, no disposition**: `record_id, user_id, srcNr, srcCtry, dstNr, dstCtry, time`, which allows us to study the effect of feature `disposition` on the detection rate.

We use the pre-call ROC curve from Experiment 1 as the baseline for the comparison. If a feature set performs as the pre-call feature set or better, then we conclude that the feature set is effective and the removed feature is not relevant for fraud detection; otherwise the feature set is not effective and the removed feature should be used for the classification of calls.

Figure 8 shows the result of the experiment. The removal of feature disposition has a slightly positive effect on the detection rate, as is the effect of removing user_id. A possible explanation for this could be that both features are not heavily correlated with fraud. Removing time has a negative effect on the detection rate, which coincides with the observation in Sect. 4.2 that the time of the call is a key factor for fraud detection. In the next experiment, we investigate how we can derive additional features from time.

5.4   Experiment 4: Effect of Derived Features

In this experiment we explore how to improve detection rates by deriving additional features from the call's start time field. We extract three kinds of features, namely:

1. **HourOfDay**: 24 Categorical features where every feature corresponds to a one hour interval (24 h notation).
2. **OfficeHours**: A Boolean feature that indicates whether the call has happened between 09:00-17:00.
3. **FocusHourOfDay**: These features are similar to HoursOfDay but in this case only the hours just before 09:00 and just after 17:00 are considered, specifically, in the interval $[5, 9]$ and $[18, 22]$.

These features were introduced to exploit domain knowledge in the classification of calls. From the analysis of the dataset in Sect. 4.2 we observed that most fraud cases occurred outside office hours. We attempted to capture this information is several different ways. Initially, we only tried to capture this in a Boolean feature representing the office hour time-interval, i.e. OfficeHours. We stretched the idea of a Boolean feature per time interval all the way to including such a feature for every hour of a day. Finally, we focused this broad set of features to only including the time-intervals we know are correlated with fraud.

We applied Isolation Forests to the aforementioned feature spaces and compared the results to pre-call results in Fig. 6. Specifically, in each experiment we consider the pre-call data set and replace the time feature with one of the derived features. The time feature is replaced to isolate the effect of including the derived features. The results are given in Fig. 9.

We can observe that the features HourOfDay and FocusHourOfDay significantly improve the detection rates. In particular, with the latter we have a true positive rate of over 45%, at a false positive rate of 2%, which is comparable to the results obtained using post-call features. A possible explanation for this is that by increasing the number of features drastically, the chance of an isolation forest splitting on time increases. Since time is correlated with fraud, this could explain the performance increase.

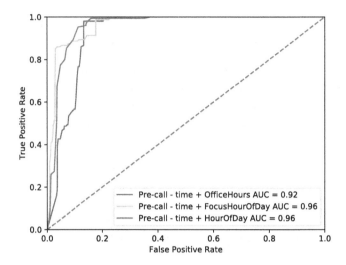

Fig. 9. Comparison of ROC curves for fraud detection using different discretization of feature `time`. Specifically, the curve obtained using all pre-call features is compared to the curves obtained when additionally to the pre-call features, features `OfficeHours`, `HourOfDay` or `FocusHourOfDay` are included.

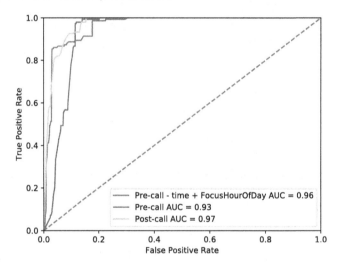

Fig. 10. Summary of the results. Specifically, the ROC curve for fraud detection using all pre-call features is compared to the ROC curve obtained using the feature `FocusHourOfDay`.

6   Discussion and Limitations

The experiments in Sect. 5 show that with careful choice of the parameters and feature space tuning, Isolation Forests provide a reliable tool for fraud detection. Figure 10 shows the false positive and true positive rates of Isolation Forests before and after the proposed optimizations as described in Experiments 1, 2, 3, and 4. Here, we can observe that at least 45% of the fraud can be detected reliably using the pre-call feature set at the cost of a 2% false positive rate and up to 87% at the cost of a 5% false positive rate. Given that the damage of such phone calls can be in the order of thousands of euros per call [15,21,30,34], the discovery of a few fraudulent calls is already sufficient to cover operational expenses.

The introduction of time based derived features improves the detection and coincides with the observation that most of the fraud cases happened outside office hours. Experiment 2 has shown that decreasing max_depth does not yield a significant increase in performance. This is desirable since it gives less branching possible and clusters tend to become larger.

With respect to the requirements presented in Sect. 2, our evaluation shows that Isolation Forests are resilient to ill-balanced label distribution (**R1**) while enabling the support of categorical features with over 50 values per features (**R2**). Isolation Forests have a linear time complexity with a low constant and a low memory requirement which is ideal for high volume datasets (**R3**). Although the training of the forest was a matter of seconds, a larger data sample is needed to test whether requirement **R4** is fully satisfied. Experiments have also shown that, considering only pre-call features (**R6**), we are able to detect almost half of the fraud reliably (**R5**).

Isolation Forest do not limit itself to the analysis of features before call establishment, but can also be used for post-mortem analysis on CDR records. In Experiment 1 we showed that, for post-mortem detection, Isolation Forests shows promising results. However, more future work is required to explore the boundaries of the technique. The computation efficiency of the algorithm enables fast retraining of the model to avoid phenomena such as concept drift [36].

Although Isolation Forests have shown promising results in this application, the approach has some limitations. First, the construction of an isolation forest is done by randomly choosing features and splitting on values. Depending on the domain, however, certain splits might be more favorable than others. Currently, Isolation Forests do not allow enforcing certain splits or influencing the order in which features should be considered. One workaround would be to run the algorithm separately for every data subset of interest (e.g., per user); however, this no longer enables the discovery of any overlapping patterns between the subsets. Another workaround to enforce a data split would be to convert such split into a set of features (like it was done for feature OfficeHours in Experiment 4). This solves the problem only partially, since it is not possible to enforce the split at a certain location in the tree. Another limitation of Isolation Forests is that, like other unsupervised learning methods, this technique does not use labeled data in the training phase; therefore, it cannot leverage this information to learn how to distinguish between normal and fraudulent traffic.

7   Conclusions and Future Work

In this paper, we explored the boundaries of Isolation Forest for online detection of IRSF. We have performed a number of experiments to assess the effectiveness of the approach for both offline and online analysis of VoIP traffic and validated results against an existing industrial fraud detector. The results in Fig. 10 show that Isolation Forest can identify up to 45% of IRSF traffic before the calls have been established. Since the proposed approach makes no underlying assumptions on the data to analyze, it is general and flexible enough to be applied in other domains such as uselogin analysis or clickstream analytics.

An interesting direction for future work is the study of other derived features, for example based on the countries involved. We also plan to perform a performance analysis of Isolation Forests on a larger-scale, e.g., with dozens of calls per second.

References

1. Ahmad, S., Purdy, S.: Real-time anomaly detection for streaming analytics. arXiv preprint arXiv:1607.02480 (2016)
2. Alldrin, N., Smith, A., Turnbull, D.: Clustering with EM and K-means. Technical report, University of San Diego (2003)
3. Becker, R.A., et al.: Clustering anonymized mobile call detail records to find usage groups. In: Workshop on Pervasive and Urban Applications (2011)
4. Becker, R.A., Volinsky, C., Wilks, A.R.: Fraud detection in telecommunications: history and lessons learned. Technometrics **52**(1), 20–33 (2010)
5. Burge, P., Shawe-Taylor, J., et al.: Detecting cellular fraud using adaptive prototypes. In: AI Approaches to Fraud Detection and Risk Management, pp. 9–13 (1997)
6. Candel, A., Parmar, V., LeDell, E., Arora, A.: Deep learning with H2O. H2O. AI Inc. (2016)
7. Cappers, B.: Interactive visualization of event logs for cybersecurity. Ph.D. thesis, Technische Universiteit Eindhoven (2018)
8. Chandola, V., Banerjee, A., Kumar, V.: Anomaly detection: a survey. ACM Comput. Surv. **41**(3), 1–58 (2009)
9. Ding, Z., Fei, M.: An anomaly detection approach based on isolation forest algorithm for streaming data using sliding window. IFAC Proc. Vol. **46**(20), 12–17 (2013)
10. Dong, G., Liu, H.: Feature Engineering for Machine Learning and Data Analytics. CRC Press, Boco Raton (2018)
11. Dudoit, S., Fridlyand, J.: A prediction-based resampling method for estimating the number of clusters in a dataset. Genome Biol. **3**(7) (2002). https://doi.org/10.1186/gb-2002-3-7-research0036
12. Elagib, S.B., Hashim, A.-H.A., Olanrewaju, R.: CDR analysis using big data technology. In: International Conference on Computing, Control, Networking, Electronics and Embedded Systems Engineering, pp. 467–471. IEEE (2015)
13. Etalle, S.: From intrusion detection to software design. In: Foley, S.N., Gollmann, D., Snekkenes, E. (eds.) ESORICS 2017. LNCS, vol. 10492, pp. 1–10. Springer, Cham (2017). https://doi.org/10.1007/978-3-319-66402-6_1

14. Ferreira, P., Alves, R., Belo, O., Cortesão, L.: Establishing fraud detection patterns based on signatures. In: Perner, P. (ed.) ICDM 2006. LNCS (LNAI), vol. 4065, pp. 526–538. Springer, Heidelberg (2006). https://doi.org/10.1007/11790853_41
15. FGSServices: Are you at risk from Toll Fraud? (2017). https://fgsservices.co.uk/fgs-telecoms/systems/systems/toll-fraud/
16. Friedman, M.: There's No Such Thing as a Free Lunch. Open Court LaSalle, Peru (1975)
17. Gibson, C.: Europol Cyber Fraud Intelligence 2019 Report (2019). https://www.europol.europa.eu/sites/default/files/documents/cytel_fraud_intelligence_notification.pdf
18. Hanley, J.A., McNeil, B.J.: The meaning and use of the area under a receiver operating characteristic (ROC) curve. Radiology 143(1), 29–36 (1982)
19. Ighneiwa, I., Mohamed, H.: Bypass fraud detection: artificial intelligence approach. arXiv preprint arXiv:1711.04627 (2017)
20. Indyk, P., Motwani, R.: Approximate nearest neighbors: towards removing the curse of dimensionality. In: Symposium on Theory of Computing, pp. 604–613. ACM (1998)
21. Integrated Solutions: Every business needs to know toll fraud and VoIP (2015). http://www.integratedcom.net/every-business-needs-know-toll-fraud-voip/
22. Kou, Y., Lu, C.-T., Sirwongwattana, S., Huang, Y.-P.: Survey of fraud detection techniques. In: International Conference on Networking, Sensing and Control, vol. 2, pp. 749–754. IEEE (2004)
23. Kübler, S., Massoth, M., Wiens, A., Wiens, T.: Toll fraud detection in voice over IP networks using behavior patterns on unlabeled data. In: International Conference on Networks, pp. 191–197 (2015)
24. Kumar, M., Hanumanthappa, M., Kumar, T.S.: Crime investigation and criminal network analysis using archive call detail records. In: International Conference on Advanced Computing, pp. 46–50. IEEE (2017)
25. Liu, F.T., Ting, K.M., Zhou, Z.: Isolation forest. In: International Conference on Data Mining, pp. 413–422. IEEE (2008)
26. Modani, N., Dey, K., Gupta, R., Godbole, S.: CDR analysis based telco churn prediction and customer behavior insights: a case study. In: Lin, X., Manolopoulos, Y., Srivastava, D., Huang, G. (eds.) WISE 2013. LNCS, vol. 8181, pp. 256–269. Springer, Heidelberg (2013). https://doi.org/10.1007/978-3-642-41154-0_19
27. Olszewski, D., Kacprzyk, J., Zadrożny, S.: Employing self-organizing map for fraud detection. In: Rutkowski, L., Korytkowski, M., Scherer, R., Tadeusiewicz, R., Zadeh, L.A., Zurada, J.M. (eds.) ICAISC 2013. LNCS (LNAI), vol. 7894, pp. 150–161. Springer, Heidelberg (2013). https://doi.org/10.1007/978-3-642-38658-9_14
28. Pelroth, N.: Phone hackers dial and redial to steal billions (2014). https://www.nytimes.com/2014/10/20/technology/dial-and-redial-phone-hackers-stealing-billions-.html
29. Peterson, K.: Business Telecom Systems: A Guide to Choosing the Best Technologies and Services. CRC Press, Boco Raton (2000)
30. Phithakkitnukoon, S., Dantu, R., Baatarjav, E.-A.: VoIP security-attacks and solutions. Inf. Secur. J.: Glob. Perspect. 17(3), 114–123 (2008)
31. Rosenberg, J., et al.: SIP: Session initiation protocol. RFC 3261, IETF (2002)
32. Sahin, M., Francillon, A., Gupta, P., Ahamad, M.: Sok: fraud in telephony networks. In: European Symposium on Security and Privacy, pp. 235–250. IEEE (2017)

33. Tan, S.C., Ting, K.M., Liu, T.F.: Fast anomaly detection for streaming data. In: International Joint Conference on Artificial Intelligence, pp. 1511–1516. AAAI Press (2011)

34. Tech Advance: Business at risk of toll fraud (2018). https://techadvance.co.uk/blog/2018/05/businesses-at-risk-of-toll-fraud/

35. Wang, K., Wang, B., Peng, L.: CVAP: validation for cluster analyses. Data Sci. J. **8**, 88–93 (2009)

36. Widmer, G., Kubat, M.: Learning in the presence of concept drift and hidden contexts. Mach. Learn. **23**(1), 69–101 (1996). https://doi.org/10.1023/A:1018046501280

37. Wiens, A., Kübler, S., Wiens, T., Massoth, M.: Improvement of user profiling, call destination profiling and behavior pattern recognition approaches for telephony toll fraud detection. Int. J. Adv. Secur. **8**(1&2) (2015)

38. Wiens, A., Wiens, T., Massoth, M.: A new unsupervised user profiling approach for detecting toll fraud in VoIP networks. In: Advanced International Conference on Telecommunications, pp. 63–69 (2014)

PUA Detection Based on Bundle Installer Characteristics

Amir Lukach[1(✉)], Ehud Gudes[1,2(✉)], and Asaf Shabtai[3(✉)]

[1] Department of Computer Science, The Open University, Ra'anana, Israel
`amirluckach@gmail.com`
[2] Department of Computer Science, Ben-Gurion University of the Negev,
Be'er Sheva, Israel
`ehud@bgu.ac.il`
[3] Department of Software and Information Systems Engineering,
Ben-Gurion University of the Negev, Be'er Sheva, Israel
`shabtaia@bgu.ac.il`

Abstract. Many applications, such as download managers, antivirus, backup utilities, and Web browsers, are distributed freely via popular download sites in an attempt to increase the application's user base. When such applications also include functionalities which are added as a means of monetizing the applications and may cause inconvenience to the user or compromise the user's privacy, they are referred to as potentially unwanted applications (PUAs). Commonly used methods for detecting malicious software cannot be applied to detect PUAs, since they have a high degree of similarity to benign applications and require user interaction for installation. Previous research aimed at detecting PUAs has relied mainly on the use of a sandbox to monitor the behavior of installed applications, however, the methods suggested had limited accuracy. In this study, we propose a machine learning-based method for detecting PUAs. Our approach can be applied on the target endpoint directly and thus can provide protection against PUAs in real-time.

Keywords: Potentially unwanted applications · Machine learning · Antivirus

1 Introduction

Today, many applications are available for free, via popular download sites. Application distributors employ tactics in order to increase their user base. Examples of such applications include antivirus software, download managers, backup utilities, dictionaries, Web browsers, and other utilities. While these applications are provided free of charge and thus are attractive to many users, there is a cost to the distributors who provide the applications as they must find ways of making a profit, while covering the costs associated with the free applications (e.g., fees for back end servers).

© IFIP International Federation for Information Processing 2020
Published by Springer Nature Switzerland AG 2020
A. Singhal and J. Vaidya (Eds.): DBSec 2020, LNCS 12122, pp. 261–273, 2020.
https://doi.org/10.1007/978-3-030-49669-2_15

Potentially unwanted applications (PUAs) are commonly used to serve as a source of income for distributors of free applications. In addition to their core functionality, PUAs often include functionalities that are difficult to remove and may cause inconvenience to the user (e.g., slow down the computer, compromise the user's privacy, or lure the user into paying for unnecessary services). Such functionalities include advertising, user profiling, changing default settings (e.g., to promote software and services), modifying the system configuration [13], and performing security modifications that can create a security threat [3].

Similar to malware, PUAs also attempt to avoid antivirus software and other detection mechanisms (e.g., Google's Safe Browsing API detection [13]). However, while there has been significant attention on malware detection over the years, there has been little focus on PUAs among the research community. Geniola et al. [3] created a cross-platform detection framework to detect PUAs by launching them in an automated analysis sandbox. Their framework included the simulation of operating system events, in order to click through the PUAs' displayed offers, or user consent forms which are required in order to install PUAs. However, their solution had several limitations: 1) it takes several minutes for each application to be analyzed, and it cannot be applied in real-time, 2) their UI engine could only automate 67% of the tested applications, and 3) in some cases, the proposed solution failed, since the OS event simulation was unsuccessful for some PUAs (e.g., when a simple change to the user interface is applied). In this paper, we propose a practical approach for the accurate detection of PUAs.

The proposed approach can be applied on the endpoints, without the need for external testing in a sandbox environment. Our solution extracts several *bundle installation* features during application installation, including 'running as administrator,' 'number of processes created,' and 'number of folders created,' and applies a machine learning approach, in order to classify the file as a benign application or PUA. Our method can be tuned in such a way that PUA distributors (also known as affiliate networks) will be forced to install fewer applications per installation in order to evade the detection model, thereby reducing their profit and motivation.

To evaluate our proposed method, we collected 771 applications (96 of them are PUAs) from 40 different websites, and monitored their behavior during installation on a Windows 7.0 OS endpoint, on which an antivirus was installed. VirusTotal was used for classifying the applications as benign or PUA. If at least one of VirusTotal's significant engines (e.g., Avast, Symantec) detected the file as a PUA, it was labeled as 'PUA,' otherwise it was labeled as 'benign.' We also implemented a C++ Windows application, which can monitors any running application, to test in real-time if it is a PUA or benign application.

The results show that the rotation forest [10] classifier was capable of detecting all PUA detection based on bundle installer characteristics of the PUAs in our experiment, while maintaining a rate of only 0.5% false positives. The same classifier could detect 79.35% of the PUAs with zero false positives. Based on these results, we conclude that the proposed method can be used to efficiently differentiate a PUA from benign applications during installation and thus can prevent PUA installation by terminating related processes. Furthermore, because of the features that are used for classification, an attempt to evade the proposed solution will result in a significant reduction in the PUA distributor's profit, which is already low [6], since each successfully installed application increases the profit. To summarize, the contributions of this paper are as follows:

1. We propose a machine learning-based method for detecting PUAs. We implement and evaluate our proposed method on a dataset of 96 PUAs and 675 benign samples, and we have made this dataset publicly available to the research community.
2. Unlike previous studies that focused on sandbox-based detection, we focus on real-time detection. We implement an application for detecting PUAs during their installation. When using our application, the installation can be blocked when a PUA is detected, by terminating related processes.

2   Background: Pay Per Install (PPI)

The key players in the PPI business model include (illustrated in Fig. 1):

Application advertiser (1). A person or company that wants to distribute his/her application (e.g., [13]) to a large group of users. Such an application is referred to as the advertiser's component. Note, that while some of the applications distributed are benign (e.g., Opera), others are not and may contain unwanted functionalities such as advertisements (e.g., shoppers) [13]. The requested software, which the user was searching for, is called a carrier, because it 'carries' the components (advertisers' applications) of multiple advertisers, who pay a fee for their distribution.

PPI network (2). PPI networks (e.g., www.payperinstall.com) are the mediators between application advertisers and publishers. PPI networks create the bundle installers which contain several applications from different application advertisers. A bundle installer contains one *carrier application*, which is the main legitimate application that a user will search for and want to install (e.g., Opera). It also contains applications that the user may not be interested in installing. The bundle installers are created based on features extracted from the target machine and user profile, such as geographical location, operating system, or antivirus (AV) installed (extracted in order to enable the bundle installer to evade detection). For example, in the US, applications like Yahoo Toolbar are more likely to be installed, since users in the US are more likely to use Yahoo and are more familiar with its portal. In contrast, in less economically developed countries a common application may be a free AV, like Baidu. PPI networks also provide monitoring and installation statistics based on which the payments to the publisher are calculated and made.

Affiliates (3). Affiliates (also known as publishers) are software application distributors. Affiliates usually conduct marketing campaigns and place advertisements in an attempt to attract potential users and lure them into downloading the free applications advertised. Affiliates pay to run such marketing campaigns and in turn receive a payment from the application advertiser for each successful installation reported.

End user (4). A person who tries to download and install a free application (e.g., Windows OS, as seen in the figure).

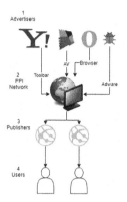

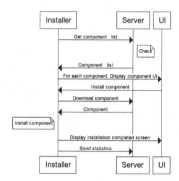

Fig. 1. The key players in the PPI business model.

Fig. 2. PUA installation sequence diagram.

Profit is the motivating factor for the affiliates and PPI networks that spread both benign and unwanted software. A typical PUA installation scenario will start with an end user that wants to download a free software application (see Fig. 1 (4)), like the Opera Web browser.

Usually, the user searches for this application in a search engine, clicks on a sponsored advertisement, which directs him/her to a publisher's website (Fig. 1 (3)), and downloads what he/she believes to be the requested software, but is in fact a PUA (Fig. 1 (2,1)). The download site, often called a landing page, is prepared by the publisher, who pays to advertise his/her landing page, so users will reach it when they search for the Opera Web browser or another application. The affiliate network is the entity that creates the bundle installer and monitors the installation statistics. Upon successful installation, the advertiser makes a payment to the affiliate network, however most of the payment is directed to the publisher who assumes the greatest risk in this scenario, since the publisher must pay for the Web advertisements in advance. The remaining profit goes to the affiliate network. The pay per install model motivates application distributors to bundle several third party applications with their own application in return for a fee, which usually ranges from 0.01 to 1.5 USD, for each application installation. The payment to the PPI network by the advertisers is sometimes made up front, in return for a fixed number of installations. Based on Google Safe Browsing telemetry [13], in 2016, PPI networks resulted in over 60 million download attempts each week (nearly three times that of malware).

While antivirus programs and browsers try to protect users from unwanted software, PPI networks actively interfere with or evade detection [13]. According to the 2019 Quick Heal Threat Report,[1] in the second quarter of 2019 there were 19 million PUA installations. Note that only 24% of the scans mentioned in the Quick Heal Threat Report were performed in real-time (there are other types of scans, e.g., an on-demand scan), and the report does not provide an estimate of the number of PUAs that go undetected. In order to avoid detection by Safe Browsing and other security programs, affiliates churn through domains every few hours or actively cloak against Safe Browsing scans. PUAs require user consent to install additional applications, in order to avoid being marked as malicious by security programs. The PPI model described above is used in Sect. 4 when we discuss our PUA detection methodology.

3   Related Work

In the most relevant paper on PUA detection [7], the author presented several features that can be used with a machine learning PUA classifier, with the aim of creating a set of detailed guidelines to help define PUAs in today's marketplace and inform users about potentially risky applications. Previous work on PUA detection focused primarily on the PPI business model [13] and PUA distribution via download portals [9]. Thomas et al. [13] presented a comprehensive survey of PUA distribution and discussed its economic aspects. The authors demonstrated the deceptive methods used by PPI networks to avoid detection. Kotzias et al. [6] also discussed the economic aspects of PUAs. The authors analyzed several commercial PPI services and addressed issues such as the profitability of commercial PPI services and the operations running them, and the revenue sources of the operations. Their main goal was to evaluate the economics of commercial PPI services used to distribute PUAs, based on their assumption that understanding their economic evolution over time is essential for evaluating the effect of deployed defenses. In this paper we also consider the economics of PUAs and their ecosystem and demonstrate how our solution can decrease a PUA's profit (see Sect. 4). Several papers discussed the detection of PUAs and the challenge of distinguishing them from legitimate applications. Kwon et al. [1] presented a system for detecting silent delivery campaigns for the distribution of malware which do not require user interaction. Such a system is not effective for PUA detection, since a PUA requires user consent for each application it installs. Geniola et al. [3] proposed a sandbox-based architecture for detecting PUAs. Their analysis was based on almost 800 installers, downloaded from eight popular software download portals. In their architecture, the authors used an agent that tries to detect when an installer is waiting for user input and then sends the input event to the installer, which is most likely to advance the installation process. Their solution required the use of a sandbox environment and took a few minutes to analyze each application. Moreover, the proposed solution is not robust, since a PUA's user interface must be known, in order to correctly

---

[1] quickheal2019.

send a windows event to the currently displayed control. Stavova *et al.* [11], conducted a survey of AV beta users to gauge their interest in deploying a PUA detection mechanism based on several warning messages options. Their results indicated that 74.5% of the users would choose to use such a detection mechanism. In a followup paper, the authors conducted another large-scale experiment, in which they used different warning messages designed to encourage users to enable the PUA detection mechanism when installing a security software solution from the Internet [11]. In our study, we use some of the features proposed in [7] (see Sect. 4). Another study discussed the detection of PUAs in a mobile environment [12], mentioning key PUA indicators, such as functionality to root or jailbreak a device, remote monitoring, cracked or repackaged apps, and excessive advertisement packages. Since in our research we focus on desktop computers and the Windows environment, most of the features identified by [12] are not relevant for us.

PUA Detection vs. Malware Detection. In the past decade, there has been significant investment by the research community in developing novel techniques for malware detection. For example, Ding *et al.* [2] presented a deep learning-based method for automatic malware signature generation and classification. The proposed method was based on API calls and their parameters, registry entries used, websites accessed, and ports. Another malware detection method proposed, analyzed the entire executable file [8]. Such malware detection methods are incapable of detecting PUAs, since they don't consider whether the EXE requires admin permissions in order to run, how many folders the EXE creates on the file system, and user interaction, which is critical for a PUA in order to obtain user consent. As we show later in the paper, such features are very useful for PUA detection (see Sect. 5). Moreover, such malware detection methods are based on the API, registry, file system, or port usage, and use a sandbox which can be evaded by a PUA, due to their similarity to benign applications. In addition, many automated malware analysis sandboxes can be detected by taking advantage of the artifacts that affect their virtualization engine [12]. In contrast to techniques commonly used for malware detection, our methodology uses different run-time characteristics (some of which were mentioned in [7]), e.g., whether the process is signed, continuously creates new window pop-ups, or uses Internet Explorer Control to display dynamic Web content.

4   The Methodology

We present a unique, yet practical method that allows users or antivirus software to accurately identify PUAs, without the need for a sandbox. The general idea behind our method is that a PUA is basically a dynamically bundled application. This means that it installs several applications which are selected at run-time based on a user's computer characteristics. In order to perform system changes, during run-time, several processes are created, several folders are created on the file system, and the PUA connects to a server and runs as administrator. In order to evaluate our methodology, we performed a software installation experiment, in which we evaluated the effectiveness of a machine learning classifier, in order to distinguish between PUAs and benign applications (see Sect. 5 for details). Specific PUA behavior is not malicious by nature, but it will allow us to make a distinction between a PUA and benign applications. After creating a machine learning classifier, a monitoring application was used to implement the detection and termination of the PUA installation, using this classifier.

A Machine Learning Classifier Based on Bundle Installer Characteristics. We propose a run-time, machine learning-based classifier for PUA detection. The proposed method utilizes the following set of features (some of which have been used in previous studies [7]):

1. Runs as admin – a Boolean feature, suggested in this research, which checks whether an application runs with administrator privileges. This feature is included, because a PUA needs to run with admin privileges, in order to change system settings and access admin protected folders, such as 'program files', where applications are installed.
2. Number of processes created – a feature, suggested in this research, which indicates the number of processes created by the application. This feature is included, because each application is installed as a separate process; a PUA runs multiple processes in order to detach itself from malicious activity.
3. Number of main folders – an integer feature, suggested in this research, which indicates the number of folders created by the application during installation. This feature is included, because each application installed by a PUA is created in a different folder.
4. Downloads additional installers – an integer feature, suggested in this research, which indicates the number of applications downloaded by an application. This feature is included, because some PUAs dynamically download components according to the user configuration and geographic location.
5. Creates/modifies kernel drivers (.SYS files) – a Boolean feature, suggested in this research, which indicates whether an application creates or modifies existing kernel drivers. This feature is included, because some PUAs use kernel drivers in order to inject advertisements into the websites visited.
6. Uses IE control (uses Internet Explorer Control in an MFC dialog) – a Boolean feature, which indicates if an application uses Internet explorer Control in its user interface. This feature is included, because some PUAs use IE Control to present dynamic offers to users.
7. Imported DLL names include 'oleaut32.dll' – a Boolean feature, suggested in this research. This feature is included, because some PUAs use an OLE (object linking and embedding) library in order to enable a component object model (COM) framework.
8. Number of imported DLLs – an integer feature, suggested in this research. This feature is included, because some PUAs use a limited number of imported DLLs in order to avoid AV detection based on the import table.

Note, that a total of six new features, were introduced in this research. A PUA analyzes the endpoint's characteristics, and then it sends this information to the server. Afterwards, it downloads and installs a list of applications. Note that in some cases a PUA executable can also install applications that are embedded in the setup file itself. Figure 2 presents a diagram of a PUA installation sequence.

Monitor. We created and tested a monitor application for Windows OS, which can be used to terminate a PUA based on the classifier's decision. This monitor contains code which initiates the performance of the following tasks: (1) read EXE signature, (2) check if EXE requests static or run-time admin permissions, (3) read EXE Import table, (4) register shell events (for file system changes notifications) and WMI process creation events to Windows, (5) check if EXE listens to a port, (6) check if EXE uses IE browser control, and (7) call the classifier with the collected features, every k events on feature changes (e.g., number of created processes); if the classifier answers *yes*, terminate EXE, else continue monitoring.

The monitor is a Windows C++ application, which runs in user mode, that the user will drag and drop an executable into. In return, the monitor performs static analysis of the executable; then the monitor runs the executable and performs dynamic analysis, and the file system changes by registering shell events and processes created while it was running on Windows by using WMI (Windows Management Instrumentation) query language notifications. Moreover, the classifier which the monitor is using at real-time, was created by our experiment.

5   Experimental Evaluation

5.1   Dataset

Our dataset contains 771 files (675 benign samples and 96 PUA samples), downloaded from 40 different websites, including the most popular download sites [3]: filehippo.com, cnet.com, and softonic.com. In our experiment, we also tested bundle installers (e.g., Adobe Flash Player, which installs two security products, Avira AV, which is bundled with Opera Web browsers, and other applications we downloaded from commonly used download portals).

Each file was labeled as benign or PUA according to the following process: 1. Scanning in VirusTotal. Our ground truth is that a sample that received one or more positive classifications from significant engines of VirusTotal is a PUA. 2. Manually testing each application. This was done since we saw that in some cases, when downloading a PUA from a dedicated site a second time (two weeks later), we often obtained a clean scan for the newly downloaded PUA in VirusTotal for a PUA which was previously detected.

In addition, each application was downloaded to a Windows 7.0 endpoint, in which an antivirus is installed, using a Chrome browser which checks if the EXE is labeled as malicious/PUA using the Safe Browsing API. We ran each sample on the host computer itself and monitored it using process explorer and our monitor application. Two weeks after scanning each EXE, we scanned them again by downloading them from the same portals and other download sites, to understand the effectiveness of AV for PUA detection.

5.2 Experimental Setup

The applications were downloaded from January to October 2019; during this time, 771 Windows applications were downloaded using Chrome and installed on Windows 7 OS, in which AV was installed. The installed applications included the categories shown in Fig. 3 which shows the frequency of each category.

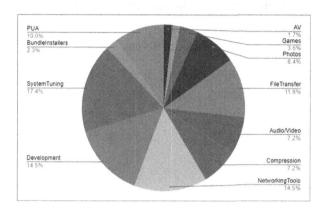

Fig. 3. Categories of installed applications.

AVs and browsers were downloaded from the vendor sites (e.g., Chrome was downloaded from google.com/chrome); the same applies for different utilities, e.g., PDF reader was downloaded from adobe.com. PUAs were downloaded by searching for free products, and they were also downloaded from a list of top ranked freeware websites: cnet.com, filehippo.com and softonic.com [3].

5.3 VirusTotal's PUA Detection

VirusTotal uses 68 different AV engines. Note that when we began the experiment we used VirusTotal scans to determine whether the executable is a PUA or benign file. Two weeks later, we downloaded the PUAs again, and surprisingly 5% of the marked PUA, were not labeled as a PUA anymore (because the EXE file was modified by the hosting site). Some of the websites we used to download PUAs were blocked or the EXE was not found in a related portal. Furthermore, almost all of the PUAs were undetected by most commonly used AV engines. On average, there were 4.7 labels per PUA, with a median of five. Since only one AV is usually installed on a computer, this shows that in many cases, a PUA will not be detected by an AV. This also happened in our experiment, in which the installed AV did not detect any of the PUAs.

5.4 Classifier Detection Rates for PUAs

We evaluated three types of classification algorithms: rotation forest, decision tree, and naive bayes. The results are labeled in Table 1. Our Monitor application, uses the rotation forest classifier to detect if an application is PUA or benign. We used 10-fold cross validations for splitting the samples, to training and test data. The Rotation Forest, which was found to be the best classifier, produced 0.5% false positives for a true positive rate of 100% (i.e., all the PUAs were detected). When set to produce 0.0% false positives, the Rotation Forest classifier detected 79.5% of the PUAs. Detection errors can occur when applications bundle many applications, and one installer, installs multiple applications.

Table 1. Results

Classifier	FPR (TPR = 1.0)	TPR (FPR = 0.0)	AUC
Rotation Forest	0.005	0.795	0.99
Decision Tree	0.005	0.65	0.96
Naive Bayes	0.02	0.2	0.98

5.5   Research Limitations

Our work focuses on PUA executables, which are mainly downloaded from popular download sites [3]. There is a risk that these websites may contain PUAs from a limited number of publishers that they trust. In such a scenario, there might be bias in the classification of the PUAs' features, however these are still the most popular download sites, so the insights from this research are still useful for preventing PUA distribution. Moreover, most PUAs were downloaded from an IP address in Israel (although some were downloaded from an IP address in the US), and Israel is not a country, in which users are used to paying for software, for windows, like the US or UK [6]. Therefore, in US, for example, the classification between PUAs and benign applications would be even more distinct, since more applications would be installed, resulting in more created processes and folders.

6   Conclusions and Future Perspectives

6.1   Adversarial Machine Learning

Machine learning models are known to lack robustness against inputs crafted by an adversary. Such adversarial examples can, for instance, be derived from regular inputs, by introducing minor yet carefully selected perturbations [4]. Behavior-based detection models are currently being investigated as a new methodology for defeating malware. This kind of approach typically relies on system call sequences to model a malicious specification/pattern. There is a new class of attacks, namely shadow attacks, which are used to evade existing behavior-based malware detectors by partitioning one piece of malware into multiple shadow processes. None of the shadow processes contain a recognizable malicious behavior specification known to single process-based malware detectors, yet as a group, these shadow processes can fulfill the original malicious functionality. Attackers are always searching for new attack vectors, and PUAs may serve as means of implementing shadow attacks. Furthermore, we can look at possible ways that adversaries can bypass detection by our method and their possible impact on affiliate network incentives and revenues, and their use of PUA in general. Such ways include:

1. Not running as administrator. This is very challenging, since the 'program files' folder requires administrator permission in order to modify/create files.
2. Reducing the number of processes. This is easy, but it means installing less components, since PUAs only bundle existing components, which by default are installed to different folders; this means that each installation will yield less money, which might affect the profitability of the PPI business model. Moreover, it is possible to create delayed system tasks to install more applications at a later time, however this reduces the chance of success, and it will be difficult to monitor whether the application was installed or not.
3. Reducing the number of folders. This means installing less applications, which will result in a less profitable installation. Furthermore, if the PUA installs several components in a single folder, advertisers will refuse to be associated with such an affiliate network, since such behavior can cause their EXE to be flagged by an AV which will block their installation.

Furthermore, there is another method, that adversaries can use to bypass detection, which is code obfuscation techniques for evading malware detection, suggested by Rozenberg *et al.* [5], which include: modifying the system call parameters; adding no-ops, which means system calls without any effect; and developing equivalent attacks, choosing an alternative system call sequence which will result in the same effect. These will not create a problem, for the proposed solution, since our monitor application monitors file system changes, created processes, and process privileges, and does not monitor or inspect specific system calls or API usage. In short, avoiding our detection model will reduce the potential profit of the affiliate network and reduce the affiliate network's incentive for installing the PUA.

6.2   Summary

Potentially unwanted applications are not viruses, nor do they steal the users' sensitive data directly. They do, however, introduce security risks into the system, decrease the system's efficiency and performance, and disrupt the user experience [7]. Previously suggested methods, includes using sandbox [3]. Alternatively, trying to use sites like Virus Total, is similar to using sandbox, since they require uploading the application to their web site, and running it in an external environment for dynamic analysis, if the PUA has not been scanned by their sites. Therefore, it is not a real-time solution. Our experiment shows that it is possible to create an effective accurate classifier for PUA detection (and thereby prevent their installation), based on machine learning of specific features, including the features of 'running as administrator,' 'number of processes created,' and 'number of folders created.' Such features distinguish PUAs from benign applications. The limitations of this approach are that it may result in possible false positives, misclassifying legitimate bundle applications that install several applications in a single EXE. However, it seems that the users expect no more than one or two such applications per installation, so such cases should be rare. Another issue, is that we are closing the PUA during its installation, so it is possible, that it will install several applications by the time we stop it. Solving this, is out of the scope of this paper, however, since we know when PUA was running, user can return to a safe state, by reverting to a windows restore point, before the PUA was installed. The proposed method can be used in order to reduce the distribution of PUAs and prevent their installation, since even if statistically a PUA is able to avoid detection by our method, our method's detection capabilities can reduce the distribution's profitability and weaken the PUA business model [6]. Our plans for future work include extending the experiment to a larger set of applications and applying similar methods on other operating systems (e.g., macOS).

References

1. Kwon, B.J., Srinivas, V., Deshpande, A., Dumitras, T.: Catching worms, trojan horses and pups: unsupervised detection of silent delivery campaigns. In: Proceedings of NDSS (2017)
2. Yuxin, D., Sheng, C., Jun, X.: Application of deep belief networks for opcode based malware detection. In: Proceedings of 2016 International Joint Conference on Neural Networks (IJCNN), pp. 3901–3908. IEEE (2016)
3. Geniola, A., Antikainen, M., Aura, T.: A large-scale analysis of download portals and freeware installers. In: Lipmaa, H., Mitrokotsa, A., Matulevičius, R. (eds.) NordSec 2017. LNCS, vol. 10674, pp. 209–225. Springer, Cham (2017). https://doi.org/10.1007/978-3-319-70290-2_13
4. Grosse, K., Papernot, N., Manoharan, P., Backes, M., McDaniel, P.: Adversarial examples for malware detection. In: Foley, S.N., Gollmann, D., Snekkenes, E. (eds.) ESORICS 2017. LNCS, vol. 10493, pp. 62–79. Springer, Cham (2017). https://doi.org/10.1007/978-3-319-66399-9_4
5. Rosenberg, I., Gudes, E.: Bypassing system calls-based intrusion detection systems, concurrency and computation. Pract. Exp. **29**, e4023 (2017)
6. Kotzias, P., Caballero, J.: An analysis of pay-per-install economics using entity graphs. WEIS (2017)
7. Mo, J.: How to identify PUA (2016). https://www.infosecurityeurope.com/__novadocuments/86438?v=635670694925570000
8. Raff, E., Barker, J., Sylvester, J., Brandon, R., Catanzaro, B., Nicholas, C.K.: Malware detection by eating a whole exe. In: Workshops at the Thirty-Second AAAI Conference on Artificial Intelligence (2018)
9. Rivera, R., Kotzias, P., Sudhodanan, A., Caballero, J.: Costly freeware: a systematic analysis of abuse in download portals. IET Inf. Secur. **13**(1), 27–35 (2019)
10. Rodríguez, J., Kuncheva, L., Alonso, C.: Rotation forest: a new classifier ensemble method. IEEE Trans. Pattern Anal. Mach. Intell. **28**, 1619–1630 (2006)

11. Stavova, V., Dedkova, L., Matyas, V., Just, M., Smahel, D., Ukrop, M.: Experimental large-scale review of attractors for detection of potentially unwanted applications. Comput. Secur. **76**, 92–100 (2018)
12. Svajcer, V., McDonald, S.: Classifying PUAs in the mobile environment. In: Virus Bulletin Conference (2013)
13. Thomas, K., et al.: Investigating commercial pay-per-install and the distribution of unwanted software. In: 25th USENIX Security Symposium (USENIX Security 2016), pp. 721–739 (2016)

ML-Supported Identification and Prioritization of Threats in the OVVL Threat Modelling Tool

Andreas Schaad[(⊠)] and Dominik Binder

Department of Media and Information, University of Applied Sciences Offenburg, Badstraße 24, 77652 Offenburg, Germany
{andreas.schaad,dbinder}@hs-offenburg.de

Abstract. Threat Modelling is an accepted technique to identify general threats as early as possible in the software development lifecycle. Previous work of ours did present an open-source framework and web-based tool (OVVL) for automating threat analysis on software architectures using STRIDE. However, one open problem is that available threat catalogues are either too general or proprietary with respect to a certain domain (e.g. .Net). Another problem is that a threat analyst should not only be presented (repeatedly) with a list of all possible threats, but already with some automated support for prioritizing these. This paper presents an approach to dynamically generate individual threat catalogues on basis of the established CWE as well as related CVE databases. Roughly 60% of this threat catalogue generation can be done by identifying and matching certain key values. To map the remaining 40% of our data (~50.000 CVE entries) we train a text classification model by using the already mapped 60% of our dataset to perform a supervised machine-learning based text classification. The generated entire dataset allows us to identify possible threats for each individual architectural element and automatically provide an initial prioritization. Our dataset as well as a supporting Jupyter notebook are openly available.

Keywords: Threat analysis · Vulnerability management · Risk assessment

1 Introduction

STRIDE [1] allows to determine possible threats as part of a secure system design activity [2, 3]. It is an accepted industrial-strength technique within the overall secure software development lifecycle [4]. The basic idea of STRIDE is to model a system as a data flow diagram (DFD) and then apply the STRIDE mnemonic on the elements of the DFD. Table 1 summarizes this general mapping. Various tools have been proposed that implement this technique [5–9], including our recently introduced OVVL (https://ovvl.org/) tool [10, 11]. In essence, all of them allow an architect to sketch a data flow diagram of a system and the tools will provide him with a list of possible threats. However, there are several problems with this approach.

A core problem is that the identified threats (the underlying threat catalogue) are often too abstract and vague ("Process could be subject to Tampering") [12] or too

© IFIP International Federation for Information Processing 2020
Published by Springer Nature Switzerland AG 2020
A. Singhal and J. Vaidya (Eds.): DBSec 2020, LNCS 12122, pp. 274–285, 2020.
https://doi.org/10.1007/978-3-030-49669-2_16

domain specific and proprietary to the tool that is used ("An adversary having access to Microsoft Azure Cosmos DB may read sensitive clear-text data") [5].

Table 1. Static mapping of STRIDE threats to DFD elements

	Spoofing	Tampering	Repudiation	Information disclosure	Denial of service	Elevation of privilege
Interactors	X		X			
Processes	X	X	X	X	X	X
Data stores		X		X	X	
Data flows		X		X	X	

Another problem is that a threat analyst will be presented repeatedly with the same information and not with selected subsets of threats individually generated for each architectural element [13].

A third problem is that existing threat modelling tools generate too many "false positives" as they bluntly apply the STRIDE technique over the DFD. Earlier work of ours [6] has reported that an experienced security architect may only deem ~20% of automatically reported threats as relevant enough to push them to an issue management system as part of the later secure software lifecycle.

While many different factors (e.g. professional experience, internal/external guidelines, tacit knowledge) do influence the decisions about automatically reported vs. realistically applicable threats, we believe that a threat modelling tool should provide some support for automated identification and prioritization of "potential" threats as well as individual assignments to each architectural element.

Our approach thus aims at replacing static and proprietary threat catalogues with dynamic threat catalogues that are generated based on additional information about the designed system and information from current external weakness and vulnerability databases such as CWE and CVE. This approach also supports an initial prioritization of identified threats. However, this reconciliation can only be done for ~60% of the CVE entries by means of standard database key matching. For the remaining 40% (~50.000 entries) we suggest a different automated matching technique using machine-learning based text classification.

This paper will thus provide a more detailed discussion of the required technical background regarding STRIDE-based threat modelling automation and our existing OVVL tool (Sect. 2). We then suggest a design and implementation of mapping STRIDE against the established CWE and CVE databases (Sect. 3). In particular, we explain our machine-learning based text classification approach to support a substantial part of this mapping as part of Sect. 4. Section 5 will address integration and usage of the obtained dataset (threat catalogue) in the OVVL framework. Section 6 will provide a summary and discussion about the validity of our approach as well as its limitations. Our dataset as well as a supporting Jupyter notebook are openly available in the OVVL project repository [14].

2   Background Work

2.1   STRIDE-Based Threat Modelling

STRIDE [1] is a method to determine possible threats as part of a secure system design activity. It is an accepted industrial-strength technique within the overall secure software development lifecycle.

Microsoft's Threat Modelling tool [5], though not supported anymore, is an openly available tool that allows a threat analyst to depict a complex system as a set of data flow diagrams. The STRIDE mnemonic is applied on model-elements (compare Table 1) and the analyst is presented with a list of possible threats. However, this toolset is not open-source and the threat catalogue is proprietary with respect to .Net and Microsoft Azure architectures. The OWASP Threat Dragon is another openly available tool [7] that uses STRIDE on DFDs as its primary technique.

Similar commercial tools do exist such as IriusRisk [8] and ThreatModeler [9]. Irius-Risk does promote that threat modelling should have an impact on the later stages of a secure development lifecycle. ThreatModeler is based on the VAST method which explicitly distinguishes between application threat models and operational or infrastructure threat models. We will now discuss how these approaches are addressed in our OVVL tool.

2.2   Weakness and Vulnerability Databases

The core idea of this paper is that we can use existing weakness and vulnerability databases in combination with the STRIDE approach and our OVVL data model to dynamically generate threat catalogues for each model element, including already a system suggested prioritization.

CWE is a community-developed list of common software security weaknesses [15]. It contains 808 common weaknesses and 295 categories (i.e. sets of CWEs that share a common characteristic). As part of the CWE data model, the "Common Consequences" attribute already provides a link to technical impacts that can result from each weakness in CWE. For example, CWE-20: "Improper Input Validation" belongs to the category "Validate Inputs" and one of the possible common consequences may be "Modify Memory; Execute Unauthorized Code or Commands". This common consequence applies to the scope of Confidentiality, Integrity and Availability and is attributed with a generally "High" Impact. CWE-20 then points to more detailed CWEs such as CWE-129 "Improper Validation of Array Index", each with more specific consequences, scope and impact.

CVE is a list of publicly known technical vulnerabilities that exploit weaknesses [16]. CVEs point to none, one or more related CWEs. This allows common static code analysis tools such as [17] to scan code for weakness or vulnerabilities such as the mentioned input validation. Interestingly, only 60% of all existing CVEs will directly map to a unique CWE, i.e. without any indirection via a category. In total, this mapping will yield a subset of 170 CWEs (out of 808). The remaining 40% of all CVEs (~51,489) can not be mapped directly to a unique CWE, however 30% of these (~15,280) will only point to a CWE category instead. This is an important observation as we can only use the "Common Consequences" data structure of a CWE to determine suitable keys for an automated mapping of CWEs to the STRIDE elements. In contrast, a CWE category does not offer any data structure similar to these "Common Consequences" and as such we require a different approach to map CWEs to STRIDE.

An immediate question may now be why we do not just directly map STRIDE to a CWE. The short answer is that we will need to analyse the association between CWEs and CVEs to determine a possible priority of a CWE-based threat when presented to the security architect.

2.3 The OVVL Approach and Tool

As part of our ongoing research we developed a method and supporting tool called OVVL (Open Weakness and Vulnerability Modeler) [4, 5]. Similar to Microsoft's SDL tool [5] and TAM2 [6] that was developed at SAP, we support the graphical definition of data flow diagrams consisting of processes, interactors, data stores and data flows. Once such a diagram has been established, the STRIDE mnemonic is applied over all model elements resulting in a list of possible threats per element. Where deployment information is already known for an element, we support the search for a CPE identifier (a unique serial number for a software component) and can thus already identify all existing CVE entries for that CPE.

3 Design and Technical Approach

Overall, we first build a new database of threats (a threat catalogue) and then use this in combination with information from the system model to identify threats for each architectural element. Our data mapping approach to support the first activity consists of three steps:

1. We build a dataset out of the CVE and CWE database by using the already existing database key that points from a CVE to a CWE (bearing in mind that such a key either does not exist or is not suitable for 40% of the CVEs because it only points to a CWE category).
2. We then map elements of this new dataset against STRIDE using the "Common Consequences" data structure we obtained from the previously mapped CWEs.
3. We use a text classification approach which will eventually allow us to map the remaining 40% of our new dataset to STRIDE. The training set for this is based on the results of the previous step 2.

The remainder of this section will now discuss the preparatory steps 1 and 2, while we will address the problem of machine-learning based text classification as part of the dedicated Sect. 4.

3.1 Step 1: CWE and CVE Mapping

Both datasets, though in parts heavily segmented, are publicly available as JSON (CVE) or XML (CWE) structures. For CVE we worked with all available data (2002–2019) (730 MB size) and for CWE we equally use data up until December 2019 (9 MB size).

In the case of the CVE dataset, this information includes a unique identifier, a description of the vulnerability, which is later used for our text classification process (Sect. 4), and the input values and metrics for the calculation of the CVSS score (Common Vulnerability Scoring System), which will be used for the OVVL framework integration (Sect. 5). Additionally, in most cases, a reference to one or more CWEs is included, indicating the weakness a vulnerability may exploit.

As part of the CWE record, each weakness also contains a unique identifier that matches the identifier of the CVE record so that it can be used to merge the two datasets in form of `pandas DataFrames`. However, since the CVE record can have multiple CWE-IDs per entry, these entries are extended (a CVE entry with two CWE-IDs becomes two entries with one CWE-ID each). From the CWE dataset we also get further information about the circumstances in which a weakness occurs, which are also used in the attribute selection as part of the threat modelling process (Sect. 5). Additionally, the dataset contains the already mentioned "Common Consequences" field, which is used for the STRIDE mapping in the following step (Sect. 3.2).

3.2   Step 2: STRIDE Mapping

Our new dataset contains the "Common Consequences" data structure which consists of a "Scope" and an "Impact". We can use these to map each STRIDE category as shown in Tables 2 and 3.

As some information is redundant, we initially perform our mapping on basis of Table 2 (Scope) and if additionally required using Table 3 (Impact).

The scope indicates which protection target is affected by a certain weakness. As the threats used in the STRIDE methodology are also designed to cover a specific protection target, this allows us to map our dataset directly to the related STRIDE threats based on the given scope.

Table 2. Mapping STRIDE threats based on the Scope

Scope	Affected entries	(STRIDE) threat
Availability	55,240	**D**enial of service
Confidentiality	70,996	**I**nformation disclosure
Non-Repudiation	6,378	**R**epudiation
Authentication	408	**S**poofing
Accountability	76	**R**epudiation
Integrity	62,755	**T**ampering

To additionally assign the values for "Elevation of Privilege" and "Spoofing"-Threats, two impact values were also used, which in contrast to the scope values do not indicate which concrete protection goal is affected, but rather which effects can arise from an attack on that protection goal.

Table 3. Mapping STRIDE threats based on the Impact

Impact	Affected entries	(STRIDE) threat
Gain Privileges or Assume Identity	10,655	Spoofing, Elevation of Privilege
Execute Unauthorized Code or Command	50,333	Spoofing, Elevation of Privilege

However, as we already indicated earlier, this overall mapping exercise can only be used for 60% of our dataset using available keys and the remaining 40% will now be mapped on basis of a text classification approach (compare Fig. 2).

4   Text Classification

To map the remaining 40% of our data we train a text classification model by using the already mapped 60% of our dataset to perform a supervised machine-learning based classification. To accomplish this, we use the available "CVE-Description" for each entry in the dataset, since this field exists for all entries and provides the most information about what threat may potentially give rise to a vulnerability. Since the STRIDE methodology distinguishes six different threats, we create six separate models, each of which performs a binary classification that uses a pre-processed description of a vulnerability to determine if the threat may be enabling that vulnerability. Our dataset as well as a supporting Jupyter notebook allowing to reproduce all steps is available as part of the OVVL project repository [14].

4.1   Pre-processing

We transform the gathered data (CVE-Description) into a machine interpretable format. This activity mainly includes performing a word-tokenization, removing stop words as they have no meaning in our application scenario, perform a lemmatisation and finally vectorize the data.

With the word-tokenization, the textual representation of the CVE description, in the form of a string, is broken down into individual words and converted to lower case.

Stop words are then removed from these individual words, as they contain hardly any useful information for our classification process and are frequently found in natural language. We therefore use a predefined list of 179 words from the python library "Natural Language Tool Kit" (NLTK).

By performing a lemmatization these different inflections are reduced to the lemmata of the word, so that all the inflections are treated equally in the following steps.

To be able to use a set of words for the machine-learning process, they must be transformed into a vector in a suitable form. Therefore, we used the (frequently used) method of "term frequency–inverse document frequency" (tf-idf) vectorization. This allows us to vectorize existing unigrams and bigrams from all vulnerability descriptions by calculating the relation of a term-frequency divided by the document frequency of each term. For the practical implementation the `TfidfVectorizer` of the `scikit-learn` library with a maximum of 5000 features was used.

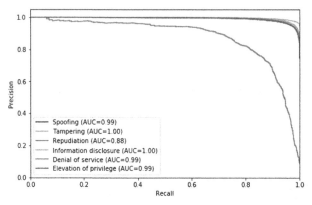

Fig. 1. Precision-Recall-Curve for each threat with corresponding area under the curve (AUC)

4.2 Model Selection

This step involves deciding about which machine-learning model may be most suitable for the intended text classification. Due to the sparseness of the vectorized features, not every type of model is suitable for our classification task. Therefore, we test and evaluate a selection of several models (which are listed in Table 4). For the evaluation it has to be considered that the classes to be calculated are partially heavily unbalanced, which is why an f1-score metric is used for the evaluation. A k-fold cross-validation method with k = 3 is also used for the comparison (Table 4).

Table 4. Model comparison, average f1-score for each threat

Model	S	T	R	I	D	E	Avg.
Naive Bayes	0.932	0.938	0.699	0.966	0.932	0.932	0.9
Logistic Regression	0.952	0.96	0.755	0.978	0.953	0.952	0.925
Decision Tree	0.933	0.946	0.733	0.97	0.935	0.933	0.908
Random Forest	0.954	0.962	0.778	0.979	0.955	0.954	0.93
LightGBM	**0.954**	**0.963**	**0.799**	**0.98**	**0.956**	**0.954**	**0.934**

4.3 Hyper-parameter Optimization

In this step, we sought suitable hyper-parameters to further improve the results of the LightGBM model [18]. For this purpose, a set of parameters were defined from which the best combination was determined by grid-search. To avoid overfitting, the pre-processed data was divided into a training and a validation dataset. The training dataset was again used for a k-fold training process with k = 3. The best parameters were then tested on the validation dataset. Since we use a single model for each threat, this process is run

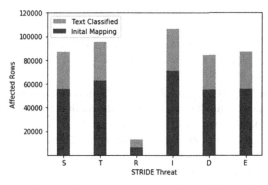

Fig. 2. Complete dataset (60% through key mapping/40% textual classification)

six times separately and the models are stored for further use. However, the achieved optimization appeared to be negligible in our application context.

4.4 Evaluation

In Sect. 4.2, the quality of the model was already measured by calculating the f1-score. In this section, the obtained results will be examined in more detail and based on these evaluations, decisions will be made for practical use, i.e. analysing the PRC curves and determining thresholds by means of the ROC curves (which are excluded for reasons of space but are included in the Jupyter notebook [14]).

Precision-Recall-Curve (PRC). The f1-score (Table 4) is calculated from the precision and the recall score of the model. This calculation takes place independently of the used threshold, which indicates the value at which a calculation (in our case a threat) should be considered positive. However, it is extremely important to observe the threshold, especially in the case of unbalanced data, as in this case. The precision-recall-curve indicates the ratio between precision and recall for the respective threshold. The area under the curve can be used to measure the general quality of the model.

It can be seen from Fig. 1 that our models are highly suitable for identifying the STRIDE threats using the CVE description. The area under the curve for five of the models is nearly (rounded) 1, indicating an extremely effective model. Only the calculation of the "Repudiation" threat performs worse, which we assume is due to the fact that this class is severely underrepresented in the training dataset.

5 OVVL Framework Integration

In order to integrate the obtained mappings into our existing tool we need to decide about suitable attributes that a security architect can select when modelling a system. These attributes will then support the querying of our dataset to generate threat catalogues for each model element. As our dataset is rather large and feeds into a web application, we suggest an approach to pre-compute and reduce threat catalogues based on possible combinations of selected attributes.

5.1   Attribute Selection

In the OVVL Threat Modelling Tool, an analyst can select different attributes and values for each architectural element (e.g. a webserver is "remotely" accessible and requires "user authentication").

The attributes we suggest act as parameters to the queries that yield individual threats for each element in a threat model (i.e. DFD based system description). When choosing suitable attributes, attention was paid to the fact that these are available as completely as possible in our dataset. They should also have a meaningful relation to the threats as well as the environment in which a threat may give rise to vulnerability. Based on these criteria, we were able to identify four suitable attributes (Fig. 3) within our dataset.

The "Access Vector" attribute describes whether a DFD element is accessible either via an external network or locally, which is relevant because certain vulnerabilities and thus weaknesses can only be exploited via one of the two access vectors.

The "Authentication" attribute specifies whether a user must authenticate to access the element and thus also whether the vulnerabilities found can only be exploited by authenticated users

Some more specific weaknesses from the CWE dataset can be traced back to the used programming language. This information is of interest because certain weaknesses are highly dependent on the programming language used. For example, weaknesses that involve memory manipulation are more likely to occur in low-level languages such as C or C++, since the correct memory management must be observed during programming. For our approach, we have assigned individual languages of the CWE dataset to meaningful groups, based on their characteristics. These groups are low level languages (C, C++, Assembly), interpreted languages (Python, Ruby, JavaScript, Perl and other interpreted languages), languages with just-in-time compilation (C#, Java) and languages that are primarily used in web development (PHP, ASP .NET).

The "Technology" Attribute allows differentiation between web and database servers. For both variants, there are several threats that usually only occur with these technologies, such as the frequently occurring sql injection in database systems or a variety of web application related vulnerabilities in web servers. In addition to these two, there are clearly other technologies (e.g. relating to virtualization) or application types (e.g. directly communicating via sockets) which cannot be further specified on the basis of our dataset. For these, as well as for all other attributes, it is possible to indicate that the respective value is unknown, whereby this attribute is not taken into account (compare Sect. 5.2).

5.2   Dataset Reduction

For an efficient practical implementation, a pre-calculation is made based on the previously defined attributes. The entire dataset contains 129,675 entries. For the implementation, however, only all possible combinations of the attribute selection are relevant, including cases in which the value of an attribute is not known and is therefore not specified more precisely. This results in 135 combinations which can be individually applied to each single architectural element.

For each of the possible combinations, the affected entries are determined from the dataset and the values required for the implementation are extracted. This primarily focuses on the weaknesses covered and the relative frequency of these. We assume that weaknesses that occur frequently within the dataset are also likely to occur more frequently in real applications, so we will use this relative frequency as a way to prioritize weaknesses. For all vulnerabilities that are based on a weakness, we also calculate the average values of the CVSSv2 base, impact, and exploitability metrics in order to have another means of prioritization, which is not based on the probability of a vulnerability, but on its impact and the resulting risks. In order to provide a simple measure of these values, the average values were then grouped into the categories low, medium and high.

It should be noted that due to the linear relationship between the attributes and the related threats in this type of implementation, it is possible that for some combinations no entries can be found (as the specified combination does not appear in the dataset). This is even more likely to happen if a large number of attributes of a DFD element are specified. Currently, this restriction is especially present when specifying the used programming language, as the CWE dataset does not necessarily list all affected programming languages in every case.

Fig. 3. Example of attribute selection in OVVL and individually identified threats

6 Summary and Conclusion

A general problem with automated threat modelling tools is to define the underlying threat catalogue [12]. This in turn leads to reported threats being perceived as too general (when just using plain STRIDE) and containing unnecessary duplicates as well as having no means of prioritizing reported threats [13].

Using STRIDE [1, 2] as a mapping technique, we reconciled the CWE and CVE databases to derive a threat catalogue that is used in the OVVL framework to address these concerns. A substantial part of this mapping (40%, ~50.000 records) was done on basis of a supervised machine-learning based text classification. We provided a detailed discussion on text (pre-)processing, model selection (resulting in adoption of LightGBM) as well as evaluation of the trained model. Compared to plain STRIDE-based threat modelling we demonstrated that our approach identifies more specific real-world threats and thus facilitate that more appropriate countermeasures can be defined.

We demonstrated how this derived threat catalogue can be queried on basis of attributes such as access vector or authentication for each single element of a threat model within the OVVL framework. This results in individually reported threats avoiding duplicates as well as the possibility to prioritize these by evaluating the associated impact and exploitability attributes as well as observed frequency of occurrence (i.e. related vulnerability) in the real world.

This approach also complements the already existing feature of OVVL to identify concrete CPEs and CVEs in case it is also known at system design time how a component is realized.

Though we can now automatically prioritize threats this does not necessarily exclude false positives (i.e. reported threats an experienced analyst will rule out on basis of information not captured in the threat model). Future work will thus focus on conducting user studies to understand possible correlations between prioritized threats and whether an analyst will push these as an issue into the project management tool/product backlog. OVVL already exhibits an OpenAPI interface to communicate with such tools in the later stages of the development lifecycle.

We are not aware of other directly related work, though vulnerability information extraction has been discussed in [19]. In [20, 21] a security risk analysis is performed on formalized UML models in combination with OCL rules which is at a much lower level of abstraction than our work. In fact, there is no indication on basis of what dataset risks are identified and the provided examples appear to be manually constructed. Contrary to that, [22] shows how attack trees are generated from vulnerability databases such as CVE. However, this is only done for network related attacks and the authors do not detail how they obtain the required environmental knowledge to analyse the CVE database.

We now want to work on further improving our approach by identifying other additional metadata a threat analyst could augment a system model with. We believe this will provide us with further capabilities to identify relevant threats, as it will allow us to prioritize based on actual software usage rather than the frequency of existing vulnerabilities. We also did already experiment with using data feeds generated by Shodan. Such real-world data also gives us much more information about the environment in use, allowing us to (further) tailor the identification of threats to the specifics of the environment and reconcile this with our DFD-based system model. However, the resulting increased amount of information that goes into modelling would then become too complex to produce a linear relationship between the input values and the threats. We therefore plan to also use machine-learning techniques for this purpose, which we hope will allow our model to establish a much deeper relationship between threats, vulnerabilities and the environment and enabling circumstances in which they may occur.

References

1. Shostack, A.: Threat Modeling: Designing for Security. Wiley, Hoboken (2014)
2. Shevchenko, et al.: Threat modeling: a summary of available methods. Software Engineering Institute, CMU (2018). https://resources.sei.cmu.edu/asset_files/WhitePaper/2018_019_001_524597.pdf. Accessed 25 Feb 2020
3. Khan, et al.: STRIDE-based threat modeling for cyber-physical systems. In: IEEE PES: Innovative Smart Grid Technologies Conference Europe (2017)
4. https://www.microsoft.com/en-us/securityengineering/sdl/threatmodeling. Accessed 25 Feb 2020
5. https://docs.microsoft.com/de-de/azure/security/develop/threat-modeling-tool. Accessed 25 Feb 2020
6. Schaad, A., Borozdin, M.: TAM2: Automated threat analysis. ACM SAC 2012
7. OWASP Threat Dragon. https://threatdragon.org/login. Accessed 25 Feb 2020
8. IriusRisk. https://iriusrisk.com/threat-modeling-tool/. Accessed 25 Feb 2020
9. ThreatModeler. https://threatmodeler.com/. Accessed 25 Feb 2020
10. Schaad, A., Reski, T.: Open weakness and vulnerability modeler (OVVL): an updated approach to threat modeling. In: ICETE (2), pp. 417–424 (2019)
11. Schaad, A.: Project OVVL - Threat Modeling Support for the entire secure development lifecycle. In: Sicherheit 2020, pp. 121–124 (2020)
12. Berger, B.J., Sohr, K., Koschke, R.: Automatically extracting threats from extended data flow diagrams. In: Caballero, J., Bodden, E., Athanasopoulos, E. (eds.) ESSoS 2016. LNCS, vol. 9639, pp. 56–71. Springer, Cham (2016). https://doi.org/10.1007/978-3-319-30806-7_4
13. Sion, et al.: Risk-based design security analysis. In: 1st International Workshop on Security Awareness from Design to Deployment, Sweden (2018)
14. Jupyter Notebook. https://github.com/OVVL-HSO/Threat-Catalogue
15. CWE Database. https://cwe.mitre.org/. Accessed 25 Feb 2020
16. CVE Database. https://cve.mitre.org/. Accessed 25 Feb 2020
17. Sonarqube. https://www.sonarqube.org/. Accessed 25 Feb 2020
18. LightGBM. https://lightgbm.readthedocs.io/en/latest/. Accessed 25 Feb 2020
19. Weerawardhana, S.S., et al.: Automated extraction of vulnerability information for home computer security. In: FPS 2014, pp. 356–366 (2014)
20. Almorsy, M., et al.: Automated software architecture security risk analysis using formalized signatures. In: Proceedings of the 2013 International Conference on Software Engineering, pp. 662–671. IEEE Press (2013)
21. Basin, D., et al.: Automated analysis of security-design models. Inf. Softw. Technol. **51**(5), 815–831 (2009)
22. Birkholz, H., et al.: Efficient automated generation of attack trees from vulnerability databases. In: Working Notes for the 2010 AAAI Workshop on Intelligent Security (SecArt), pp. 47–55 (2010)

Spatial Systems and Crowdsourcing Security

Enhancing the Performance of Spatial Queries on Encrypted Data Through Graph Embedding

Sina Shaham[1], Gabriel Ghinita[2]([⊠]), and Cyrus Shahabi[1]

[1] University of Southern California, Los Angeles, USA
[2] UMass Boston, Boston, USA
gabriel.ghinita@umb.edu

Abstract. Most online mobile services make use of location data to improve customer experience. Mobile users can locate points of interest near them, or can receive recommendations tailored to their whereabouts. However, serious privacy concerns arise when location data is revealed in clear to service providers. Several solutions employ *Searchable Encryption (SE)* to evaluate spatial predicates directly on location ciphertexts. While doing so preserves privacy, the performance overhead incurred is high. We focus on a prominent SE technique in the public-key setting – *Hidden Vector Encryption (HVE)*, and propose a graph embedding technique to encode location data in a way that significantly boosts the performance of processing on ciphertexts. We show that finding the optimal encoding is NP-hard, and provide several heuristics that are fast and obtain significant performance gains. Our extensive experimental evaluation shows that our solutions can improve computational overhead by a factor of two compared to the baseline.

Keywords: Hidden Vector Encryption · Graph embedding

1 Introduction

Location data play an important part in offering customized services to mobile users. Whether they are used to find nearby points of interest, to offer location-based recommendations, or to locate friends situated in proximity to each other, location data significantly enrich the type of interactions between users and their favorite services. However, current service providers collect location data in clear, and often share it with third parties, compromising users' privacy. Movement data can disclose sensitive details about an individual's health status, political orientation, alternative lifestyles, etc. Hence, it is important to support such location-based interactions while protecting privacy.

Our focus is on *secure alert zones*, a type of location-based service where users report their locations in encrypted form to a service provider, and then they

© IFIP International Federation for Information Processing 2020
Published by Springer Nature Switzerland AG 2020
A. Singhal and J. Vaidya (Eds.): DBSec 2020, LNCS 12122, pp. 289–309, 2020.
https://doi.org/10.1007/978-3-030-49669-2_17

receive alerts when an event of interest occurs in their proximity. This operation is very relevant to contact tracing, which is proving to be essential in controlling pandemics, e.g., COVID-19. It is important to determine if a mobile user came in close proximity to an infected person, or to a surface that has been exposed to the virus, but at the same time one must prevent against intrusive surveillance of the population. More applications of alert zones include notifications in the case of other natural disasters, or even commercial applications (e.g., notifying mobile users of nearby sales events).

Searchable Encryption (SE) [3,14,20] is very suitable for implementing secure alert zones. Users encrypt their location before sending it to the service provider, and a special kind of encryption is used, which allows the evaluation of predicates directly on ciphertexts. However, the underlying encryption functions are not specifically designed for geospatial queries, but for arbitrary keyword or range queries. As a result, a data mapping step is typically performed to transform spatial queries to the primitive operations supported on ciphertexts. Due to this translation, the performance overhead can be significant. Some solutions use *Symmetric Searchable Encryption (SSE)* [6,14,20], where a trusted entity knows the secret key of the transformation, and collects the location of all users before encrypting them and sending the ciphertext to the service provider. While the performance of SSE can be quite good, the system model that requires mobile users to share their cleartext locations with a trusted service is not adequate from a privacy perspective, since it still incurs a significant amount of disclosure.

To address the shortcomings of SSE models, the work in [3] introduced the novel concept of *Hidden Vector Encryption (HVE)*, which is an *asymmetric* type of encryption that allows direct evaluation of predicates on top of ciphertext. Each user encrypts her own location using the *public* key of the transformation, and no trusted component that accesses locations in clear is required. This approach has been considered in the location context in [10,16], with encouraging results. However, the performance overhead of HVE in the spatial domain remains high. Motivated by this fact, we study techniques to reduce the computational overhead of HVE. Specifically, we derive special types of spatial data mapping using graph embeddings, which allow us to express spatial queries with predicates that are less computationally-intensive to evaluate.

In existing HVE work for geospatial data [10,16], the data domain is partitioned into a hierarchical data structure, and each node in this structure is assigned a binary string identifier. The binary representation of each node plays an important part in the query encoding, and it influences the amount of computation that needs to be executed when evaluating predicates on ciphertexts. However, the impact of the specific encoding is not evaluated in-depth. Our approach embeds the geospatial data domain to a high-dimensional hypercube, and then it applies graph embedding [4] techniques that directly target the reduction of computation overhead in the predicate evaluation step.

Our specific contributions are:

- We introduce a novel transformation of the spatial data domain based on graph embedding that is able to model accurately the performance overhead incurred when running HVE queries for spatial predicates;

- We transform the problem of minimizing HVE computation to a graph problem, and show that the optimal solution is NP-hard;
- We devise several heuristics that can solve the problem efficiently in the embedded space, while still reducing significantly the computational overhead;
- We perform an extensive experimental evaluation which shows that the proposed approaches are able to halve the performance overhead incurred by HVE when processing spatial queries.

The rest of the paper is organized as follows: Sect. 2 introduces necessary background on the system model (an HVE primer is given in Appendix A). Section 3 provides the details of the proposed graph embedding transformation, and proves that the optimal solution is NP-hard. Section 4 introduces several heuristic algorithms that solve the problem efficiently. Sect. 5 presents an empirical evaluation of the proposed approaches. We survey related work in Sect. 6 and conclude in Sect. 7.

2   Background

2.1   System Model

Consider a $[0,1] \times [0,1]$ spatial data domain divided into n non-overlapping partitions, denoted as $\mathcal{V} = \{v_1, , v_2, ..., v_n\}$. We use the term *cell* to refer to partitions; however, a cell can have an arbitrary size and shape. An example of such a partitioning is provided in Fig. 2a. The system architecture of location-based alert system is represented in Fig. 1, and consists of three types of entities:

1. **Mobile Users** subscribe to the alert system and periodically submit encrypted location updates.
2. The **Trusted Authority (TA)** is a trusted entity that decides which are the alert zones, and creates for each zone a search *token* that allows to check privately if a user location falls within the alert zone or not.
3. The **Server (S)** is the provider of the alert service. It receives encrypted updates from users and search tokens from TA, and performs the predicate evaluation to decide whether encrypted location C_i of user i falls within alert zone j represented by token TK_j. If the predicate holds, the server learns message M_i encrypted by the user, otherwise it learns nothing.

The system supports location-based *alerts*, with the following semantics: a *Trusted Authority (TA)* designates a subset of cells as an *alert zone*, and all the users enclosed by those cells must be notified. The TA can be, for instance, the Center for Disease Control (CDC), who is monitoring cases of a pandemic, and wishes to notify users who may have been affected; or, the TA can be some commercial entity that the users subscribe to, and who notifies users when a sales event occurs at selected locations.

The *privacy requirement* of the system dictates that the server must not learn any information about the user locations, other than what can be derived from

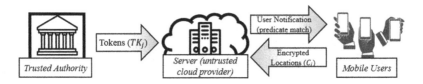

Fig. 1. Location-based alert system.

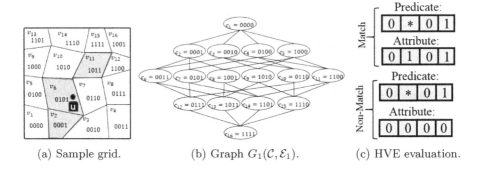

(a) Sample grid.   (b) Graph $G_1(\mathcal{C}, \mathcal{E}_1)$.   (c) HVE evaluation.

Fig. 2. An example of embedding graphs generated based on a sample grid.

the match outcome, i.e., whether the user is in a particular alert zone or not. In case of a successful match, the server S learns that user u is enclosed by zone z. In case of a non-match, the server S learns only that the user is outside the zone z, but no additional location information. Note that, this model is applicable to many real-life scenarios. For instance, users wish to keep their location private most of the time, but they want to be immediately notified if they enter a zone where their personal safety may be threatened. Furthermore, the extent of alert zones is typically small compared to the entire data domain, so the fact that S learns that u is *not* within the set of alert zones does not disclose significant information about u's location. The TA can be an organization such as a city's public emergency department, which is trusted not to compromise user privacy, but at the same time does not have the infrastructure to monitor a large user population, and outsources the service to a cloud provider.

2.2 Problem Statement

Prior work assumed that all cells are equally likely be in an alert zone. However, that is not the case in practice. Some parts of the data domain (e.g., denser areas of a city) are more likely to become alert zones. The cost of encrypted alert zone enclosure evaluation is given by the number of operations required to apply HVE matching at the service provider. As we discuss in our HVE primer in Appendix A, the evaluation cost is directly proportional to the number of non-star bits in the tokens. Armed with knowledge about the likelihood of cells to be part of an alert zone, one can create superior encodings that reduce processing overhead.

Our goal is to find an enhanced encoding that reduces non-star bits for a given set of alert zone tokens. Denote by $p(v_i)$ the probability of cell v_i being part of an alert zone. The *mutual* probability of multiple cells indicates how likely they are to be part of the *same* alert zone. Given individual cell probabilities, the mutual probability of a set of i cells $\mathcal{L} = \{v_1', , v_2', ..., v_i'\}$ is calculated as:

$$p(\mathcal{L}) = \prod_{j=1}^{i} p(v_j').$$
(1)

The problem we study is formally presented as follows:

Problem 1. Find an encoding of the grid that reduces the number of non-star bits in the tokens generated from alert zone cells.

3   Location Domain Mapping Through Graph Embedding

Our approach minimizes the number of non-star bits in alert zone tokens by modeling the data domain partitioning as an embedding problem of a k-cube into a complete graph. We denote a k-cube as $G_1(\mathcal{C}, \mathcal{E}_1)$, where $\mathcal{C} = \{c_1, , c_2, ..., c_n\}$ and $c_i = \{0, 1\}^k$. Figure 2b illustrates a k-cube generated based on the sample partitioning in Fig. 2a. In G_1, two nodes c_i and c_j are connected if their *Hamming distance* is equal to one. We refer to such a bit as *Hamming bit*.

Definition 1 *(Hamming Distance and Bits). The Hamming distance between two indices c_i and c_j in $G_1(\mathcal{C}, \mathcal{E}_1)$ is the minimum number of substitutions required to transform c_i to c_j, denoted by the function $d_h(.)$. We refer to the bits that need to be transformed as the Hamming bits of indices.*

Example 1. *The Hamming distance between indices $c_1 = 0100$ and $c_2 = 0010$ is two $(d_h(c_i, c_j) = 2)$, and the Hamming bits are the second and third most significant bits of the indices.*

The second graph required to formulate the problem of minimizing the number of non-stars is a complete graph generated by all cells in the partitioning, denoted by $G_2(\mathcal{V}, \mathcal{E}_2)$. The set $\mathcal{V}$ represents the nodes corresponding to cells, and an undirected edge connects every two nodes in G_2.

Note that, every token (including those containing stars), can be related to several cycles on the k-cube. For example, token 00** represents four indices 0000, 0001, 0010, 0011, which correspond to cycles (c_1, c_2, c_6, c_3) and (c_1, c_3, c_6, c_2) on the k-cube in Fig. 2b. Unfortunately, there is no one-to-one correspondence between the tokens and the cycles. In particular, for a larger number of stars, there exist several cycles representing the same token. To generate a one-to-one correspondence, we incorporate *Binary-Reflected Gray (BRG)* encoding on the k-cube to create unique cycles corresponding to tokens.

Definition 2 *(BRG path on k-cube). A BRG path between two nodes with nonzero Hamming distance is defined as the path on the k-cube going from one node to another based on BRG coding on Hamming bits.*

As an example, the Hamming bits between 0001 and 1000 are the least and most significant bits, and the BRG path connecting them on the k-cube in Fig. 2b includes indices 0001, 1001, and 1000 in the given order. One can see that as the BRG codes are unique, the BRG path between two indices on the k-cube is also unique. This characteristic of BRG paths is formulated in Lemma 1.

Lemma 1. *A BRG path between two nodes on a k-cube is unique.*

Proof. The uniqueness of the path between two nodes on the k-cube follows from the uniqueness of BRG code, as only one such a path can be constructed.

Definition 3 *(Complete x-bit BRG cycle). Given a k-cube, a complete x-bit BRG cycle is a cyclic BRG path with the length of 2^x, in which only x bits are affected. We denote the set of all possible complete x-bit BRG cycles by $\mathcal{L}_x = \{\bigcup l_i\}$.*

Example 2. *In Fig. 2b, token *0** entails eight indices 0000, 0001, 0011, 0010, 1010, 1011, 1001, 1000. This token maps uniquely to the complete 3-bit BRG cycle on the 4-cube with nodes $(c_1, c_2, c_6, c_3, c_9, c_{13}, c_8, c_5)$ and start point c_1.*

We can uniquely associate a token to a cycle on the k-cube. Consider a token with k bits and x stars. This token is mapped to a complete x-bit BRG cycle on the k-cube, starting from a node in which all the star bits are set to zero. Such a cycle is unique and has a length of 2^x. Based on this mapping, every token is associated with a unique cycle on the k-cube, and every complete x-bit BRG cycle is mapped to a unique token with x-stars. Therefore, there is a one-to-one correspondence between tokens and complete BRG cycles. The formulation of Problem 1 based on graph embedding can be written as follows:

Problem 2. Given two graphs $G_1(\mathcal{C}, \mathcal{E}_1)$ and $G_2(\mathcal{V}, \mathcal{E}_2)$, find a mapping function $\mathcal{F} : G_1 \rightarrow G_2$ with the objective to

$$Maximize\{\sum_{i=1}^{k} p(\mathcal{L}_i)\}. \tag{2}$$

3.1   Gray Optimizer (GO)

The problem of embedding a complete graph within a minimized size k-cube has been shown to be NP-hard [4]. We develop an heuristic algorithm called *Gray Optimizer* that solves Problem 2. Specifically, we determine an optimal embedding with respect to a given node in G_2 with complexity of $\mathcal{O}(n(\log_2 n)^4)$. Consider an initial node of the complete graph $v_r \in \mathcal{V}$, and without loss of generality assume that it is assigned to index[1]c_1. The optimization problem can be formulated as follows.

Problem 3. Given two graphs $G_1(\mathcal{C}, \mathcal{E}_1)$ and $G_2(\mathcal{V}, \mathcal{E}_2)$, and the node $v_r \in \mathcal{V}$ assigned to index c_1, find a mapping function $\mathcal{F} : G_1 \rightarrow G_2$ that

$$Maximize\{\sum_{i=1}^{k} p(\mathcal{L}_i|v_r)\}. \tag{3}$$

Problem 2 requires an assignment of vertices in G_2 to the nodes of G_1 such that the probability of complete BRG cycles is maximized; whereas Problem 3 seeks to maximize the probability of cycles with respect to a particular node, in this case v_r, which is assigned to the index c_1. A reasonable candidate for assignment to c_1 is the cell with the highest probability, as it is most likely to be part of an alert zone. To solve this problem, we propose the heuristic in Algorithm 1. The input of the algorithm is the root index $c_1 \in G_1$, the root node $v_r \in G_2$ (also called seed) and the graphs G_1 and G_2.

Algorithm 1: Gray Optimizer.

   Input : G_1; G_2; c_1; v_r
1 Assign v_r to c_1
2 **for** i in $[1:k]$ **do**
3   Initialize $\mathcal{H}_1, \mathcal{H}_2 = \emptyset$
4     $\mathcal{H}_1 \leftarrow \{\binom{k}{i}$ non-assigned nodes in G_2 with the highest probability$\}$
5   **for** $c_j \in \mathcal{D}_{i|c_1}$ **do**
6   Calculate $p(l_j/c_j) = \prod_{v \in l_j/c_j} p(v)$
7        $\mathcal{H}_2 \leftarrow p(l_j/c_j)$
8   **end**
9   Match vertices in $\mathcal{H}_1$ to $\mathcal{H}_2$ based on Hungarian algorithm.
10 **end**

Denote by $\mathcal{D}_{i|c_1}$ the set of nodes on $\mathcal{C}$ that have a Hamming distance of i from c_1. Note that $\mathcal{D}_{i|c_1}$ includes $\binom{k}{i}$ nodes, each one having a Hamming distance of i from c_1. The overall assignment structure is as follows: first, Algorithm 1 assigns the remaining nodes of $\mathcal{V}$ of the graph G_2 to nodes in $\mathcal{D}_{1|c_1}$. After assignment of all nodes in $\mathcal{D}_{1|c_1}$, the algorithm assigns the nodes in $\mathcal{D}_{2|c_1}$ and follows the same process until all nodes are assigned ($\mathcal{D}_{1|c_1}$ to $\mathcal{D}_{k|c_1}$).

---

[1] We refer to nodes in G_1 interchangeably using their vertex id or binary index.

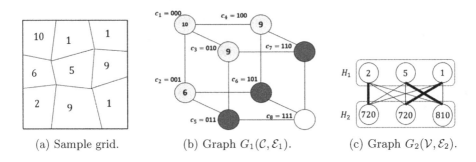

(a) Sample grid.   (b) Graph $G_1(\mathcal{C}, \mathcal{E}_1)$.   (c) Graph $G_2(\mathcal{V}, \mathcal{E}_2)$.

Fig. 3. An example of embedding graphs generated based on a sample grid.

The assignment objective in stage i of the process is to maximize $p(\mathcal{L}_i|v_r)$. Note that (3) can be written as:

$$\sum_{i=1}^{k} Maximize\{p(\mathcal{L}_i|v_r)\}. \tag{4}$$

where $p(\mathcal{L}_i|v_r)$ represents the probability of all complete i-bit BRG cycles that include c_1 ($v_r \rightarrow c_1$). Consider one such a cycle as l. Based on the following lemma, there exists one and only one node c_j in l that has a Hamming distance of i from c_1, which means that $c_j \in \mathcal{D}_{i|c_1}$. Therefore, every complete i-bit BRG cycle given index c_1 includes one node in $\mathcal{D}_{i|c_1}$. On the other hand, every node in $\mathcal{D}_{i|c_1}$ corresponds to a unique complete i-bit BRG cycle passing through c_1, as results from Lemma 1. Therefore, all complete i-bit BRG cycles are considered in stage i and we maximize their probabilities in this stage of the assignment.

Lemma 2. *For each node c_i in a complete x-bit BRG cycle, there exists one and only one node with the Hamming distance of x from c_i.*

Proof. A complete x-bit BRG cycle includes 2^x nodes and only x bits are affected. Therefore, the only index that can exist with the Hamming distance of x from c_i is the one in which all x Hamming bits are opposite.

The assignment process in the stage i of GO creates a bipartite graph, i.e., $(\mathcal{H}_1, \mathcal{H}_2, \mathcal{E}_3)$, where $\mathcal{H}_1$ and $\mathcal{H}_2$ are two set of nodes, and $\mathcal{E}_3$ represents the set of edges. In this stage, the nodes in sets $\mathcal{D}_{1|c_1}, \mathcal{D}_{2|c_1}, ..., \mathcal{D}_{i-1|c_1}$ are already assigned and we aim to find the best assignment for the nodes in $\mathcal{D}_{i|c_1}$ such that $p(\mathcal{L}_i|v_r)$ is maximized. Among the remaining nodes in $\mathcal{V}$, we choose $\binom{k}{i}$ of them that have the highest probabilities, as $|\mathcal{D}_{i|c_1}| = \binom{k}{i}$, and allocate them to $\mathcal{H}_1$.

On the other hand, for each node c_j in $\mathcal{D}_{i|c_1}$, we construct the unique complete i-bit BRG cycle including c_j and c_1. Let us represent this cycle by l_j. Note that all nodes included in l_j are assigned except c_j. The algorithm calculates the probability of the set of nodes in l_j excluding c_j and allocates it to a node in $\mathcal{H}_2$. Based on (1), this probability can be calculated as:

$$p(l_j \setminus \{c_j\}) = \prod_{v \in l_j \setminus \{c_j\}} p(v), \tag{5}$$

The algorithm repeats the process for all nodes in $\mathcal{D}_{i|c_1}$. Next, the best matching is found between these two sets of nodes based on the Hungarian algorithm [12] (Fig. 3).

Lemma 3. *In stage i, GO maximizes $p(\mathcal{L}_i|v_r)$ given the currently assigned nodes $(\mathcal{D}_{1|c_1}, \mathcal{D}_{2|c_1}, ..., \mathcal{D}_{i-1|c_1})$.*

Proof. We prove the lemma based on mathematical induction.
Base case: For $i = 1$, given that the node v_r is assigned to c_1, we aim to prove that GO maximizes $p(\mathcal{L}_1|v_r)$. To start with, GO chooses $\binom{k}{1}$ remaining nodes of $\mathcal{V}$ for the purpose of assignment. The optimal assignment of nodes in $\mathcal{D}_{1|c_1}$ is a permutation of the chosen nodes; otherwise, they could be replaced with a node with a higher probability that would result in a higher value for $p(\mathcal{L}_1|v_r)$. Next, the algorithm generates a bipartite graph $(\mathcal{H}_1, \mathcal{H}_2, \mathcal{E}_3)$. The probability of chosen nodes are allocated to $\mathcal{H}_1$, and the nodes in $\mathcal{H}_2$ represent the probability of complete 1-bit gray cycles constructed from $c_j \in \mathcal{D}_{1|c_1}$ and the node c_1, excluding the probability of c_j itself. As the Hungarian algorithm finds the best match between nodes, GO results in maximal $p(\mathcal{L}_1|v_r)$ given the node c_1.

Induction Step: Let us assume that GO has maximized the probabilities of complete x-bit BRG cycles for $x = 1$ to $i-1$ in stages one to $i-1$. We prove that in stage i, the algorithm maximizes complete i-bit gray cycles, given the previously assigned nodes.

Based on Lemma 2, all complete i-bit BRG cycles are considered in stage i, as each such cycle includes exactly one node in $\mathcal{D}_{i|c_1}$, which has the highest Hamming distance from c_1. GO starts by choosing the cells with the highest probabilities and assigning them to $\mathcal{H}_1$. Same as in the base case, we know that the optimal assignment in this stage includes the chosen set of nodes. Next, the nodes in $\mathcal{H}_2$ are assigned based on finding the probability of complete i-bit BRG cycles for nodes in $\mathcal{D}_{i|c_1}$, excluding the nodes themselves from the probability. As the Hungarian algorithm results in an optimal match, the best permutation of nodes in $\mathcal{H}_1$ is matched to complete i-bit BRG cycles. □

4   Scaling up Gray Optimizer

The time complexity of the Hungarian algorithm is shown to be $\mathcal{O}(n^3)$ [12], which results in the complexity of $\mathcal{O}(n(\log_2 n)^4)$ for GO. The algorithm can lead to significant improvements in the processing of HVE operations; however, there are two major drawbacks once the algorithm is applied to grids with high granularities. *(i)* The complexity of the algorithm creates a processing time bottleneck for its application in HVE; *(ii)* The calculation of probabilities for large complete BRG cycles may result in numerical inaccuracies. To make GO applicable to grids with higher levels of granularity, we propose two variations.

The first proposed algorithm, called *Multiple Seed Gray Optimizer (MSGO)* (Sect. 4.1), generates non-overlapping clusters and applies GO within each one of them. The second algorithm, called Scaled Gray Optimizer (SGO) (Sect. 4.2) takes a *Breadth-First Search (BFS)* [15] approach. The performance of BFS is preferred to its counterpart *Depth-First Search (DFS)* as the nodes closer to the seed have higher probabilities. Thus, it is reasonable to consider those nodes earlier in the process.

4.1 Multiple Seed Gray Optimizer (MSGO)

The starting point of the GO algorithm, which we refer to as *seed*, was chosen as the node in G_2 with the maximum probability. However, the algorithm can work starting with any initial seed, then follow the assignment process for other nodes in ascending order of their Hamming distance from the seed. Furthermore, as BRG cycles become larger, their associated probability becomes smaller. Thus, one way to reduce the complexity of GO is to run the algorithm up to a particular *depth*. Essentially, the algorithm aims at optimizing BRG cycles up to a certain length. We enhance GO by running Algorithm 1 with multiple seeds, and also by limiting the depth of the assignment.

Definition 4 *Depth: For a given seed c_j, the GO algorithm is said to run with a depth of i if it only considers the assignment of nodes in $\mathcal{D}_{1|c_j}, \mathcal{D}_{2|c_j}, ..., \mathcal{D}_{i|c_j}$.*

The pseudocode of the proposed approach is presented in Algorithm 2. The algorithm starts by assigning the node with the highest probability in G_2 to the origin of G_1 or a random index. However, instead of running GO with respect to this index for all depths from one to k, MSGO runs GO with the specified depth as input. The algorithm completes the process of assignment for a cluster of indices in G_1. MSGO then chooses a random index of G_1 among the remaining indices and assigns it to the node in G_2 with maximum probability among remaining nodes. Similarly, this index is used as a seed for GO with the specified depth and generates a new cluster. The cluster-based approach continues until all nodes are assigned to an index. The algorithm supports variable cluster sizes based on the underlying application.

Algorithm 2: Multiple Seed Gray Optimizer (MSGO).

Input : G_1; G_2; *depth*

1 Select a random index on G_1 which is not currently assigned
2 Assign the index with the node that has the maximum probability in G_2
3 Apply Algorithm 1 on the selected index with the specified depth
4 **Repeat** lines 1-3 **until** all indices are assigned

The MSGO algorithm provides a robust solution for grids with higher granularity. The algorithm no longer suffers the drawbacks of GO when the grid size grows, such as numerical inaccuracies in the calculation of the probability of large cycles. The complexity of the algorithm depends on the depth chosen as input, and in low depths, it can be implemented in $\mathcal{O}(n(\log_2 n))$. MSGO can significantly reduce the number of operations required for the implementation of HVE in location-based alert systems, and therefore, making it a practical solution for preserving the privacy of users in location-based alert systems.

4.2   Scaled Gray Optimizer (SGO)

SGO considers overlapping clusters and necessitates that all nodes act as seed during the assignment process. The pseudocode of the proposed approach is presented in Algorithm 3. SGO starts by assigning the node with the highest probability to an index on G_1. However, instead of assigning indices with all depths from one to k with respect to index c_1, the SGO algorithm runs GO with the depth of one. Next, SGO sorts the indices in $\mathcal{D}_{1|c_1}$ based on their assigned probabilities in descending order and runs GO on each one of them. Once the algorithm is applied on all the indices in $\mathcal{D}_{1|c_1}$, the process repeats for indices in $\mathcal{D}_{2|c_1}$, $\mathcal{D}_{3|c_1}$, ..., etc. The algorithm continues until all indices are assigned to a node.

Algorithm 3: Scaled Gray Optimizer (SGO).

Input : G_1; G_2

1 Assign the cell with the highest probability to the origin of G_1, i.e., c_1
2 Apply Algorithm 1 on c_1 with the depth of one
3 **for** $i\, in\, [1:k]$ **do**
4 $\quad$ Sort $\mathcal{D}_{i|c_1}$ in descending order of probabilities assigned to its indices
5 $\quad$ **for** $c_j\, in\, \mathcal{D}_{i|c_1}$ **do**
6 $\quad\quad$ | Apply Algorithm 1 on c_j with the depth of one
7 $\quad$ **end**
8 **end**

Example 3. *Consider a map of a vast rural area in which there is a likelihood of bush fire or security concerns for the residents. Therefore, the alert based notification system is implemented by a service provider to notify the farmers on their request. Due to a large number of cells included in the map, GO and MSGO require a comparably high computation overhead. Hence, the SGO algorithm could be used to improve the time complexity. Starting with the cell that has the highest probability, SGO executes GO with the minimum depth, i.e., one. Then, in a breadth-first-search manner, the algorithm moves to the first neighbors of that node, taking them as seeds of GO, prioritizing the nodes with higher assigned probability. The process continues until all the nodes of the grid are assigned.*

The complexity of the SGO algorithm is $\mathcal{O}(n(\log_2 n))$, which enables GO to be applied on grids with higher granularity. SGO can significantly reduce the number of operations required for the implementation of HVE in location-based alert systems, and therefore, making it a practical solution for preserving the privacy of users in location-based alert systems.

5   Experimental Evaluation

5.1   Experimental Setup

We conduct our experiments on a 3.40 GHz core-i7 Intel processor with 8 GB RAM running 64-bit Windows 7 OS. The code is implemented in Python, and we used the LogicMin Library [7] for binary minimization of token expressions. We compare the proposed approaches (GO, MGSO and SGO) against the hierarchical Gray encoding technique from [10] (labeled *HGE*), the state-of-the-art in location alerts on HVE-encrypted data.

To model the probability of partition cells becoming alert zones, we use the sigmoid function $\mathcal{S}(x) = 1/(1 + \exp^{-b(x-a)})$, where a and b are parameters controlling the function shape. The output value is between zero and one. The sigmoid function is a frequent model used in machine learning, and we choose it because we expect that, in practice, the probability of individual cells becoming part of an alert zone can be computed using such a model built on a regions' map of features (e.g., type of terrain, building designation, point-of-sale information, etc). Parameter a of the sigmoid controls the *inflection* point of the curve, whereas b controls the gradient. Figure 5 plots the logistic function for several different values of a and b which we use in our evaluation.

5.2   Gray Optimizer Evaluation

GO is our core proposed algorithm to reduce the number of HVE operations required to support alert zones. Specifically, by *HVE operations* we refer to the computation executed by the server to determine matches between tokens and encrypted user locations. Recall that, for each non-star item in a token, a number of expensive bilinear map operations are required. GO aims to minimize the number such non-star items in tokens by choosing an appropriate encoding of the domain. Our comparison benchmark is the approach from [10] which uses a hierarchical quadtree structure to partition the data domain. In our experiments, we refer to this approach as *HGE*, and we present our result as an improvement in terms of computation overhead compared with [10].

Improvement in HVE Operations. Figure 4 summarizes the evaluation results of GO for three logistic function parameter settings. The grid size is set to 100 cells (recall from our earlier discussion that GO can only support relatively low granularities). Figure 4 shows the total number of bilinear pairings performed for a ciphertext-token pair. GO clearly outperforms the approach

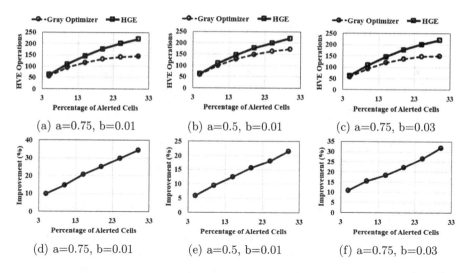

Fig. 4. Evaluation of GO, grid size = 100 cells.

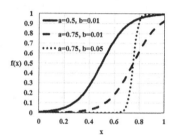

Fig. 5. Sigmoid function shown for parameters used in the experiments.

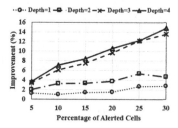

Fig. 6. Performance evaluation of GO for varying depth (100 cells).

from [10]. The relative gain in performance of GO increases when the size of the alert zone increases (i.e., when there are more grid cells covered by the alert zone). This can be explained by the fact that a larger input set gives GO more flexibility to optimize the encoding and decrease the number of non-star entries in a token. In terms of percentage gains, GO can improve performance by up to

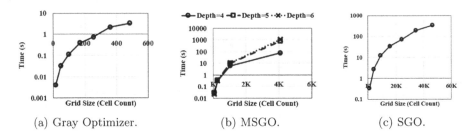

(a) Gray Optimizer.   (b) MSGO.   (c) SGO.

Fig. 7. The execution time performance.

40%, which is quite significant. Also, note that the gains are significant for all parameters of the sigmoid function used. In general, we identified that a higher a value leads to more pronounced gains. This is an encouraging factor, because a higher a corresponds to a more skewed probability case, where a relatively small number of cells are more likely to be included in an alert zone than others. In practice, one would expect that to be the case, since events that trigger alerts also tend to be concentrated over a relatively small area (e.g., very popular hotspots, certain facilities that present higher risks, like a chemical plant, etc.).

Impact of Depth. Recall that the reduction in computation achieved by GO depends on the depth at which the algorithm is run (GO works similar to a depth-first search graph algorithm). In general, running the algorithm with a higher depth will produce better results in terms of performance gain at runtime (i.e., when matching is performed at the server), but it also requires a lot more computational time to compute a good encoding (which is a one-time cost). Figure 6 captures the impact of depth on improvement. In this experiment, GO is executed on a single cell with different depths, and the remaining cells are assigned randomly (the experiment is specifically designed to show the effect of using lower depths on GO). As expected, there is a clear increasing trend, with higher depths resulting in better improvement factors. However, after a sharp initial gain (illustrated by the large distance between the chart graphs corresponding to depths 2 and 3), the improvement stabilizes, and it may no longer be worth increasing the depth of the computation considerably (the gains are stabilizing between depths 3 and 4).

Execution Time. Figure 7a illustrates the execution time of GO. Recall that, the execution time of GO is influenced by the granularity of the grid (finer granularities increase execution time). The results show that GO can complete within a short execution time for smaller grid sizes; however, as the grid granularity increases, there is a sharp increase in execution time. Therefore, GO may not be practical to apply for high granularity grids, and that is the main motivation behind our two variations, MSGO and SGO (which are evaluated next). Moreover, as the grid granularity increases, the length of cycles becomes larger, which will also result in numerical inaccuracies when executing GO. The execution time required by GO for values up to 600 cells is around 10 s. We observed that this value is the maximum number of cells for which GO performs reasonably; beyond this level, the algorithm is not suitable due to increased execution time and numerical inaccuracies associated with the calculation of probabilities for large cycles.

5.3   Evaluation of GO Variations on Higher Granularity Grids

As discussed previously, GO does not perform well when directly applied to high granularity grids. To improve the computational complexity of GO, we proposed two extensions of the algorithm, namely, MSGO and SGO. Next, we evaluate experimentally both these variations.

MSGO. Figure 8 illustrates the performance of MSGO compared to the HGE benchmark scheme from [10]. Unlike the single seed GO, we are able to evaluate the performance of MSGO for grids with much higher granularity (i.e., 1024 cells in this case). There is a similar trend in terms of gain as we have observed with GO, where larger alert zones provide more opportunities for advantageous encodings, and thus overall performance is improved (the percentage of HVE operations eliminated is higher). The relative gain obtained is very close to 50% compared to the benchmark. Also, the absolute amount of improvement is better than for GO in all cases. This occurs due to the fact that MSGO can support higher-granularity grids, and in this setting there is more flexibility in choosing a good encoding (due to the larger number of cells, there are significantly more choices for our algorithm). As expected, increasing the depth of MSGO leads to higher improvement percentage, but the trade-off is a larger computation complexity.

Comparing Figs. 4 and 8, we remark that the MSGO algorithm obtains similar performance gains as the core algorithm GO for low granularity grids, but with a much lower computational overhead. For high granularity grids, GO cannot keep up in terms of computational overhead, whereas MSGO scales reasonably well, and it is able to still obtain significant improvements. One main reason is that MSGO no longer requires the calculation of probabilities of large cycles, avoiding numerical inaccuracies and reducing overall computational overhead. The complexity of the algorithm can be as low as $\mathcal{O}(n(\log_2 n))$ depending on the chosen depth value, which provides a robust and efficient solution for reducing the number of HVE operations.

The execution time of MSGO is illustrated in Fig. 7b. The graph indicates that even for a high level of granularity, such as 4,000, the algorithm requires less than 15 min to encode the grid, depending on the specified depth at the input. As expected, by increasing the depth of the algorithm, better performance can be achieved in terms of HVE operations, at the cost of higher computational overhead. The MSGO algorithm can be extended for an arbitrary number of cells on the grid, and also it may have various cluster sizes depending on the application.

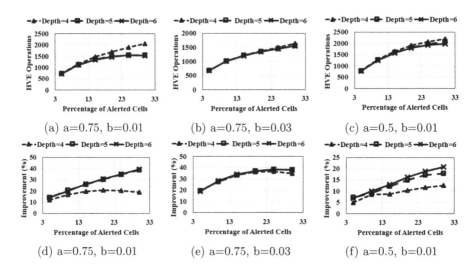

Fig. 8. Performance evaluation of MSGO (grid size = 1024 cells).

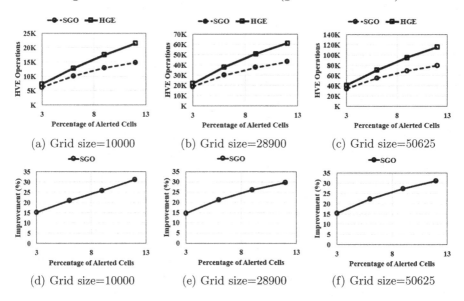

Fig. 9. SGO performance evaluation, varying grid size.

SGO. Figure 9 illustrates the performance gain obtained by SGO. In this experiment, we focused on applying the algorithm to much larger number of cells, up to 50,625 (which is equivalent to a 225 × 225 square grid). Similar to the MSGO algorithm, the improvement achieved by SGO occurs even when the alert zones are small. Since the overall number of cells is larger, the SGO algorithm has even more flexibility in choosing an advantageous encoding, resulting in strong performance gains. For example, at 9% ratio of alert cells, the SGO algorithm results in 25.8, 26, and 27.3% improvements for grid sizes of $10,000$, $28,900$, and $50,625$, respectively.

The execution time of SGO is shown in Fig. 7c. Even for very large grid sizes, such as $50,625$, the algorithm requires less than six minutes to encode the grid. Therefore, the system can be set to regularly update the probabilities and run the algorithm at six-minute intervals, if needed. To compare this time performance with GO, consider the maximum grid size for which the encoding can be computed within 60 s in each case. As shown in Fig. 7a, this number corresponds to a grid size of 1200 for GO, whereas in a similar time, SGO can be applied on the grid size of $22,000$ cells. Therefore, the SGO algorithm requires significantly lower computation overhead to execute compared with GO and even MSGO algorithms, while the performance gain in terms of HVE operations reductions is still solid.

6   Related Work

Location Privacy. Preserving the privacy of users in communication networks and online platforms has been one of the most challenging research problems in the past two decades. In the widely accepted scenario, users provide their location to service providers in exchange for location-based services they offer. The goal is to provide the service without user privacy being compromised by any of the parties involved. Early works to tackle this problem were focused on hiding or obfuscating user locations to achieve a privacy metric termed as k-anonymity. The location of a user is said to be k-anonymous if it is not distinguishable from at least $k - 1$ other queried locations [21].

In [13], the authors aim to provide k-anonymity by hiding the location of user among $k - 1$ fake locations and requesting for desired services for all k locations at the same time. The generation of such dummy locations based on a virtual grid or circle was considered in [18]. The authors in [17] conducted the selection of dummy locations predicated on the number of queries made on the map and aimed at increasing the entropy of k locations in each set. In [5], random regions that enclose the user locations were introduced to bring uncertainty in the authentication of user locations. Unfortunately, fake locations can be revealed particularly in trajectories and with the existence of prior knowledge about the map and users.

Later on, approaches based on *Cloaking Regions (CRs)* proposed by [11] gained momentum in the literature. The principal idea behind this method is to use a trusted anonymizer that clusters k real user locations and query the area they are enclosed by to retrieve points of interest. Doing so, CRs aim to achieve k-anonymity for users and preserve their privacy. This approach is partially effective when snapshots of trajectories are considered, but once users are seen in trajectories, their location privacy would be severely at risk [19]. Even for individual snapshots, it must be noted that a coarse area of real locations is released to the service provider, which could threaten the location privacy of users. Moreover, the CR-based approaches are susceptible to inference attacks predicated on the background knowledge or so-called side information. One such side information is the knowledge about the number of queries made on different locations of the map [17].

More recently, a model for privacy preservation in statistical databases termed as *differential privacy* was developed in [8]. The metric provides a promising prospect for aggregate queries; however, it is not suitable for private retrieval of specific data from datasets. Closer to HVE approach, a private information protocol was proposed in [9]. The PIR technique is based on cryptography and shown to be secure for private retrieval of information. Despite the promising results, there exists an assumption behind PIR approach that the user already knows about the points of interest. Therefore, PIR is not suitable for location-based alert systems as users are not aware of alert zone whereabouts.

Searchable Encryption. Originated from works such as [20], the concept of search encryption was proposed to provide a secure cryptographic search of keywords. Initially, only the exact matches of keywords were supported and later on the approach was extended for comparison queries in [2], and to subset queries and conjunctions of equality in [3]. The authors in [3] also proposed the concept of HVE, used as the underlying tool to provide a secure location-based alert system. This approach and its extension in [1] preserves the privacy of encrypted messages and tokens with the overhead of high computational complexity. The authors in [10] introduced and adopted the HVE for location-based alert systems, conducting the predicate match at a trusted provider, preserving the privacy of encrypted messages as well as tokens. Despite the promising results of the approach for privacy preservation in location-based alert systems, further reduction of computational overhead is necessary to increase the practicality.

7   Conclusion

We proposed a technique to reduce the computational overhead of HVE predicate evaluation in location-based alert systems. Specifically, we used graph embeddings to find advantageous domain space encodings that help reduce the required number of expensive HVE operations. Our heuristic solutions offer an improvement in computation overhead of 50% compared to existing work, and they can scale to domain partitionings of fine granularity. In future work, we will focus on deriving cost models that can estimate the amount of savings in HVE overhead based on the distribution and frequency of alert events. We will also investigate extending the graph embedding approach to other types of searchable encryption, beyond HVE (e.g., Inner Product Evaluation).

Acknowledgment. This research has been funded in part by NSF grants IIS-1910950 and IIS-1909806, the USC Integrated Media Systems Center (IMSC), and unrestricted cash gifts from Microsoft and Google. Any opinions, findings, and conclusions or recommendations expressed in this material are those of the author(s) and do not necessarily reflect the views of any of the sponsors such as the National Science Foundation. Note: Cyrus Shahabi receives consulting income from Google for a different unrelated project.

A   Primer on HVE Encryption

Hidden Vector Encryption (HVE) [3] is a searchable encryption system that supports predicates in the form of conjunctive equality, range and subset queries. Search on ciphertexts can be performed with respect to a number of *index attributes*. HVE represents an attribute as a bit vector (each element has value 0 or 1), and the search predicate as a *pattern* vector where each element can be 0, 1 or '*' that signifies a wildcard (or "don't care") value. Let l denote the HVE *width*, which is the bit length of the attribute, and consequently that of the search predicate. A predicate evaluates to *True* for a ciphertext C if the attribute vector I used to encrypt C has the same values as the pattern vector of the predicate in all positions that are not '*' in the latter. Figure 2c illustrates the two cases of *Match* and *Non-Match* for HVE.

HVE is built on top of a symmetrical bilinear map of composite order [3], which is a function $e : \mathbb{G} \times \mathbb{G} \rightarrow \mathbb{G}_T$ such that $\forall a, b \in \mathbb{G}$ and $\forall u, v \in \mathbb{Z}$ it holds that $e(a^u, b^v) = e(a, b)^{uv}$. $\mathbb{G}$ and $\mathbb{G}_T$ are cyclic multiplicative groups of composite order $N = P \cdot Q$ where P and Q are large primes of equal bit length. We denote by $\mathbb{G}_p$, $\mathbb{G}_q$ the subgroups of $\mathbb{G}$ of orders P and Q, respectively. Let l denote the HVE *width*, which is the bit length of the attribute, and consequently that of the search predicate. HVE consists of the following phases:

Setup. The TA generates the public/secret (PK/SK) key pair and shares PK with the users. SK has the form:

$$SK = (g_q \in \mathbb{G}_q, \quad a \in \mathbb{Z}_p, \quad \forall i \in [1..l] : u_i, h_i, w_i, g, v \in \mathbb{G}_p)$$

To generate PK, the TA first chooses at random elements $R_{u,i}, R_{h,i}, R_{w,i} \in \mathbb{G}_q, \forall i \in [1..l]$ and $R_v \in \mathbb{G}_q$. Next, PK is determined as:

$$PK = (g_q, \quad V = vR_v, \quad A = e(g, v)^a,$$

$$\forall i \in [1..l] : U_i = u_i R_{u,i}, \quad H_i = h_i R_{h,i}, \quad W_i = w_i R_{w,i})$$

Encryption uses PK and takes as parameters index attribute I and message $M \in \mathbb{G}_T$. The following random elements are generated: $Z, Z_{i,1}, Z_{i,2} \in \mathbb{G}_q$ and $s \in \mathbb{Z}_n$. Then, the ciphertext is:

$$C = (C' = MA^s, \quad C_0 = V^s Z,$$

$$\forall i \in [1..l] : C_{i,1} = (U_i^{I_i} H_i)^s Z_{i,1}, \quad C_{i,2} = W_i^s Z_{i,2})$$

Token Generation. Using SK, and given a search predicate encoded as pattern vector I_*, the TA generates a search token TK as follows: let J be the set of all indices i where $I_*[i] \neq *$. TA randomly generates $r_{i,1}$ and $r_{i,2} \in \mathbb{Z}_p, \forall i \in J$. Then

$$TK = (I_*, K_0 = g^a \prod_{i \in J} (u_i^{I_*[i]} h_i)^{r_{i,1}} w_i^{r_{i,2}},$$

$$\forall i \in [1..l] : K_{i,1} = v^{r_i,1}, \quad K_{i,2} = v^{r_i,2})$$

Query is executed at the server, and evaluates if the predicate represented by TK holds for ciphertext C. The server attempts to determine the value of M as

$$M = C'/(e(C_0, K_0)/\prod_{i \in J} e(C_{i,1}, K_{i,1})e(C_{i,2}, K_{i,2}) \tag{6}$$

If the index I based on which C was computed satisfies TK, then the actual value of M is returned, otherwise a special number which is not in the valid message domain (denoted by $\perp$) is obtained.

References

1. Blundo, C., Iovino, V., Persiano, G.: Private-key hidden vector encryption with key confidentiality. In: Garay, J.A., Miyaji, A., Otsuka, A. (eds.) CANS 2009. LNCS, vol. 5888, pp. 259–277. Springer, Heidelberg (2009). https://doi.org/10.1007/978-3-642-10433-6_17

2. Boneh, D., Sahai, A., Waters, B.: Fully collusion resistant traitor tracing with short ciphertexts and private keys. In: Vaudenay, S. (ed.) EUROCRYPT 2006. LNCS, vol. 4004, pp. 573–592. Springer, Heidelberg (2006). https://doi.org/10.1007/11761679_34

3. Boneh, D., Waters, B.: Conjunctive, subset, and range queries on encrypted data. In: Vadhan, S.P. (ed.) TCC 2007. LNCS, vol. 4392, pp. 535–554. Springer, Heidelberg (2007). https://doi.org/10.1007/978-3-540-70936-7_29

4. Chandrasekharam, R., Vinod, V., Subramanian, S.: Genetic algorithm for embedding a complete graph in a hypercube with a VLSI application. Microprocess. Microprogram. **40**(8), 537–552 (1994)

5. Cheng, R., Zhang, Y., Bertino, E., Prabhakar, S.: Preserving user location privacy in mobile data management infrastructures. In: Danezis, G., Golle, P. (eds.) PET 2006. LNCS, vol. 4258, pp. 393–412. Springer, Heidelberg (2006). https://doi.org/10.1007/11957454_23

6. Curtmola, R., Garay, J., Kamara, S., Ostrovsky, R.: Searchable symmetric encryption: improved definitions and efficient constructions. J. Comput. Secur. **19**(5), 895–934 (2011)

7. Drake, C.: Two-level logic minimization (2012). https://pyeda.readthedocs.io/en/latest/2llm.html

8. Dwork, C., McSherry, F., Nissim, K., Smith, A.: Calibrating noise to sensitivity in private data analysis. In: Halevi, S., Rabin, T. (eds.) TCC 2006. LNCS, vol. 3876, pp. 265–284. Springer, Heidelberg (2006). https://doi.org/10.1007/11681878_14

9. Ghinita, G., Kalnis, P., Khoshgozaran, A., Shahabi, C., Tan, K.L.: Private queries in location based services: anonymizers are not necessary. In: Proceedings of the 2008 ACM SIGMOD International Conference on Management of Data, pp. 121–132 (2008)

10. Ghinita, G., Rughinis, R.: An efficient privacy-preserving system for monitoring mobile users: making searchable encryption practical. In: Proceedings of the 4th ACM Conference on Data and Application Security and Privacy, pp. 321–332. ACM (2014)

11. Gruteser, M., Grunwald, D.: Anonymous usage of location-based services through spatial and temporal cloaking. In: Proceedings of the 1st International Conference on Mobile Systems, Applications and Services, pp. 31–42 (2003)
12. Jonker, R., Volgenant, A.: A shortest augmenting path algorithm for dense and sparse linear assignment problems. Computing **38**(4), 325–340 (1987). https://doi.org/10.1007/BF02278710
13. Kido, H., Yanagisawa, Y., Satoh, T.: An anonymous communication technique using dummies for location-based services. In: ICPS 2005, Proceedings, International Conference on Pervasive Services, pp. 88–97. IEEE (2005)
14. Lai, S., et al.: Result pattern hiding searchable encryption for conjunctive queries. In: Proceedings of the 2018 ACM SIGSAC Conference on Computer and Communications Security, pp. 745–762 (2018)
15. Leiserson, C.E., Rivest, R.L., Cormen, T.H., Stein, C.: Introduction to Algorithms, vol. 6. MIT Press, Cambridge (2001)
16. Nguyen, K., Ghinita, G., Naveed, M., Shahabi, C.: A privacy-preserving, accountable and spam-resilient geo-marketplace. In: Proceedings of the 27th ACM SIGSPATIAL International Conference on Advances in Geographic Information Systems, pp. 299–308. ACM (2019)
17. Niu, B., Li, Q., Zhu, X., Cao, G., Li, H.: Achieving k-anonymity in privacy-aware location-based services. In: IEEE INFOCOM 2014-IEEE Conference on Computer Communications, pp. 754–762. IEEE (2014)
18. Niu, B., Zhang, Z., Li, X., Li, H.: Privacy-area aware dummy generation algorithms for location-based services. In: 2014 IEEE International Conference on Communications (ICC), pp. 957–962. IEEE (2014)
19. Shaham, S., Ding, M., Liu, B., Dang, S., Lin, Z., Li, J.: Privacy preserving location data publishing: a machine learning approach. IEEE Trans. Knowl. Data Eng. (2020). https://doi.org/10.1109/TKDE.2020.2964658
20. Song, D.X., Wagner, D., Perrig, A.: Practical techniques for searches on encrypted data. In: Proceedings of 2000 IEEE Symposium on Security and Privacy, S&P 2000, pp. 44–55. IEEE (2000)
21. Sweeney, L.: k-anonymity: a model for protecting privacy. Int. J. Uncertainty, Fuzziness Knowl.-Based Syst. **10**(05), 557–570 (2002)

Crowdsourcing Under Data Poisoning Attacks: A Comparative Study

Farnaz Tahmasebian, Li Xiong$^{(\boxtimes)}$, Mani Sotoodeh, and Vaidy Sunderam

Emory University, Atlanta, GA, USA
{ftahmas,lxiong,msotood,vss}@emory.edu

Abstract. Crowdsourcing is a paradigm that provides a cost-effective solution for obtaining services or data from a large group of users. It is increasingly being used in modern society for data collection in domains such as image annotation or real-time traffic reports. A key component of these crowdsourcing applications is *truth inference* which aims to derive the true answer for a given task from the user-contributed data, e.g. the existence of objects in an image, or true traffic condition of a road. In addition to the variable quality of the contributed data, a potential challenge presented to crowdsourcing applications is *data poisoning attacks* where malicious users may intentionally and strategically report incorrect information in order to mislead the system to infer the wrong truth for all or a targeted set of tasks. In this paper, we propose a comprehensive data poisoning attack taxonomy for truth inference in crowdsourcing and systematically evaluate the state-of-the-art truth inference methods under various data poisoning attacks. We use several evaluation metrics to analyze the robustness or susceptibility of truth inference methods against various attacks, which sheds light on the resilience of existing methods and ultimately helps in building more robust truth inference methods in an open setting.

Keywords: Truth inference · Data poisoning · Crowdsourcing

1 Introduction

Crowdsourcing is a paradigm in which organizations or individuals obtain data or service from a large and relatively open group of users, or *crowd*. It has been increasingly used in modern society for data collection in various domains such as image annotation or real-time traffic reports. Amazon Mechanical Turk (MTurk) [6,20] is one of the most pervasive crowdsourcing marketplaces, in which requesters submit various tasks requiring human intelligence, such as labeling objects in an image or flagging inappropriate content. Another example is Waze [46], a crowd-driven navigation application. Users can report the traffic status at various locations which is then aggregated to update the traffic condition shown on the map.

© IFIP International Federation for Information Processing 2020
Published by Springer Nature Switzerland AG 2020
A. Singhal and J. Vaidya (Eds.): DBSec 2020, LNCS 12122, pp. 310–332, 2020.
https://doi.org/10.1007/978-3-030-49669-2_18

A key component of crowdsourcing applications is *truth inference* which aims to derive the answers for the tasks, e.g. the objects in the image, or true traffic condition of the road, by aggregating the user-provided data. Truth inference [12, 24, 29, 36, 38] is a challenging task due to the open nature of the crowd. First, the number of available ratings per task varies significantly. Second, the reliability of the workers can vary. For example, in the Waze application, it is common for some users to not care to report at all or to carelessly report the traffic condition. So, estimating the level of trust one has in workers' responses and ultimately inferring the correct label for the tasks by aggregating their responses becomes complicated. Finally, the crowdsourcing applications may be subject to *data poisoning attacks* [23, 40] where malicious users purposely and strategically report incorrect responses to mislead the system to infer the wrong label for all or a targeted set of tasks. In the Waze example, attackers might want to take the road with the least traffic by deceiving Waze application to wrongly indicate there is heavy traffic on that specific road. This can be achieved via Sybil attacks [10, 14, 49, 53] where an attacker creates a large number of Sybil workers to strategically report wrong answers.

Traditional Sybil detection in online social networks [1, 45] typically relies on additional features or metadata (e.g., connectivity graph and IP addresses). Recent works have proposed Sybil detection methods for crowdsourcing through defining golden questions and clustering workers [10, 49]. In this paper, we focus on the truth inference methods that only rely on workers' answers, and their robustness against poisoning attacks, which are orthogonal and complementary to Sybil detection methods using additional metadata.

The simplest method in truth inference is *majority voting*, where the inferred truth will be the one chosen by the majority of the assigned workers. Since the reliability of workers is not considered, majority voting may fail in the presence of unreliable or malicious workers. Considerable research has been done on improving the accuracy of truth inference methods, including optimization based methods [22, 28], probabilistic graphical model based methods [11, 25, 33, 44, 56], and neural network based methods [15, 17, 50]. These methods construct models that either explicitly or implicitly consider the credibility of workers, which create some form of defense against unreliable or malicious workers. Zheng et al. [56] evaluated truth inference methods with various worker models, types of tasks, and task models. The evaluation is focused on "normal" settings where workers may have varying reliability, but do not intentionally or strategically manipulate the answers. They concluded that truth inference methods that model worker behavior based on confusion matrix and utilize a probabilistic graphical model (PGM) have the best performances in most settings.

One unanswered question is how robust these inference methods are under intentional and strategic data poisoning attacks that are beyond normal worker behaviors. Adversaries may disguise themselves as normal workers by providing reliable answers for certain tasks to escape the worker's reliability model while providing the wrong answer for other targeted tasks. In the worst case, when adversaries know the truth inference method and other workers' answers, they may optimize theirs to maximizes the error of the truth inference method for all tasks or a subset of tasks [30,31]. Thus, it is important to understand the various types of data poisoning attacks and evaluate how different truth inference methods behave under such attacks to ultimately build robust truth inference methods.

Contributions. We propose a comprehensive data poisoning attack taxonomy for truth inference in crowdsourcing and systematically evaluate the state-of-the-art truth inference methods under various attacks. In summary:

– We present a comprehensive data poisoning attack taxonomy in crowdsourcing. We analyze the attacks along different dimensions, including attack goal (targeted vs untargeted), adversarial knowledge (black-box vs white-box), and attack strategy (heuristic vs optimization based). We also discuss the similarity and differences between data poisoning attacks in crowdsourcing and those in machine learning and other domains.
– We design heuristic and optimization based attacks that can be used on various truth inference methods as part of our evaluation methodology. The heuristic based attacks assume black-box or no adversarial knowledge and model the worker behavior using a confusion matrix [11] and an additional disguise parameter to hide their malicious behavior. The optimization based attacks assume white-box or full adversarial knowledge including the truth inference methods being used and other workers' answers, and are adapted from existing optimization based attacks [30] while making them more generic so they are applicable to broader types of truth inference methods.
– We systematically evaluate the state-of-the-art truth inference methods under both heuristic and optimization based data poisoning attacks. The truth inference methods are selected carefully to represent the different types of methods including majority voting based [22], optimization based [28], probabilistic graphical model based [11,24,25], and neural network based [50]. They also represent different worker behavior models including probability based [28], confusion matrix based [11,24,25], and implicit models [22,28]. Our study includes not only the best performing methods from the experimental study [56], but also additional direct computation [22] and optimization based methods [22,28] and more recent neural network based methods [50].
– We propose several metrics to evaluate the robustness of truth inference methods against data poisoning attacks. We experiment on synthetic and real-world datasets with varying parameters such as percentage of malicious workers, different attack parameters, and sparsity of the crowdsourcing dataset. We summarize the experiment findings and draw conclusions on the robustness, strengths, and weaknesses of the methods. It is our belief that these results help understand the resilience of existing methods and ultimately build more robust truth inference methods against data poisoning attacks.

Section 2 summarizes the existing attacks in related domains. Section 3 formally defines the truth inference problem and presents a categorization of existing truth inference methods and the selected methods for evaluation. Section 4 presents the attack taxonomy. Section 5 describes our evaluation methodology. Section 6 presents the results with discussions and Sect. 7 concludes the paper with key findings and future work.

2   Related Work

Truth inference methods have been studied extensively. We provide a brief description of the methods included in our evaluation in Sect. 3. Here we briefly review the works in data poisoning attacks.

Data poisoning attacks for machine learning (ML) algorithms have been increasingly studied recently [2,5,18,23,37,40,47]. However, data poisoning attacks in ML and crowdsourcing differ in three ways: (1) attacks in ML deal with supervised models and the goal is to degrade the performance of the model on a validation dataset, but crowdsourcing is an unsupervised problem, (2) to carry out the attacks in ML, a certain percentage of records are poisoned, while all the features associated with the poisoned record (e.g. an image) can be altered, but in crowdsourcing, a fraction of workers may be malicious, and (3) ML problems typically have rich features for records while in crowdsourcing for each task only some ratings from workers are available. Hence crowdsourcing systems are more susceptible to data poisoning attacks due to its open and unsupervised nature and lack of rich features for the truth inference problem.

Shilling attack [7,9,16,32,34,55] is a type of data poisoning attacks in recommender systems where intruders attempt to simulate the behavior of a subset of users, leading to strategically manipulated recommendations to other users [16,34]. The main difference between recommender systems and truth discovery is that the true labels of tasks in recommender systems, i.e., users' personal opinions, are subjective, while ground truth for truth discovery is universal.

Other related attacks include spammer [13,19,20,35,48] and sybil [8,26,39, 43,46,51–54] attacks. In a spammer attack, workers (bots) randomly submit answers to tasks [13,19,20]. In sybil attacks, infiltrators create fake identities to affect the performance of the system [53,54]. The attack and defense methods, for example in social media and IoT, typically utilize metadata such as connectivity of graph and relationship between nodes, and IP address. Sybil and spammer attacks mainly focus on the system infiltration part of the attack. The data poisoning attacks considered here assume adversaries have already successfully created or compromised multiple workers and can inject strategic answers.

3   Truth Inference Methods

Truth Inference Problem Definition. We consider a crowdsourcing system comprised of some tasks and a pool of workers. Each task is assigned to a subset of workers. The goal in truth inference is to determine the true answer based on available answers for each task. Tasks in crowdsourcing can be categorized as 1) *decision-making tasks* where workers select a binary answer (e.g. yes or no), 2) *single label tasks* where workers select a single label among multiple candidate labels, and 3) *numeric tasks* where an answer is a number. Moreover, truth inference methods may consider factors such as type of tasks, task difficulty, and task assignment methods [56].

In this paper, we focus on the robustness of truth inference methods under data poisoning attacks for decision-making tasks, i.e. the binary truth inference problem, and do not consider other variations largely orthogonal to our evaluation. Examples of decision-making tasks are labeling the sentiment of sentences as positive or negative or reporting accidents on road. We also assume tasks are equally hard for the average workers and tasks are randomly assigned to a subset of workers following the power-law distribution [41].

Definition 1 *(Truth Inference [36]). Consider a set of M workers $\boldsymbol{W} = \{w_1, .., w_M\}$ and a set of N tasks $\boldsymbol{T} = \{t_1, t_2, ..., t_N\}$ where each task t_j has a truth label $z^*_{t_j} \in \boldsymbol{L} = \{0, 1\}$. Given an answer matrix $\boldsymbol{C}$ where each element $c^{w_i}_{t_j}$ indicates the answer from worker w_i for task t_j, the goal of truth inference is to infer the truth label $\hat{z}_{t_j} \in \boldsymbol{L}$ for each task $t_j \in \boldsymbol{T}$.*

Figure 1 illustrates a crowdsourcing system with 3 workers and 5 tasks and a bipartite task-worker assignment graph. The input of a truth inference method is an answer matrix $\boldsymbol{C}$ provided by the workers. Workers label each task as 0 or 1, while x reflects that the task is not assigned to that worker. The output is $\hat{\boldsymbol{Z}}$ reflecting the inferred answers for the tasks. The ground truth vector $\boldsymbol{Z}^*$ is shown as a reference. Table 1 summarizes notations used throughout the paper.

Truth Inference Methods. There are four main categories of truth inference techniques: 1) direct computation, 2) optimization, 3) probabilistic graphical model (PGM), and 4) neural networks. Direct computation aggregates workers' answers by majority voting while treating workers equally or heuristically assigning weights to them [22]. Optimization based methods [22, 27, 28, 57, 59] treat the estimated labels and worker reliability as unknowns and use an optimization approach to find them. Probabilistic graphical models (PGM) explicitly model workers' reliability to estimate the labels [11, 12, 24, 25, 44, 48]. Optimization and PGM based methods follow an iterative Expectation Maximization (EM)-based approach consisting of: 1) inferring the label of tasks given the estimated workers' reliability, and 2) computing workers' reliability given the current inferred labels of the tasks. Recently, unsupervised neural network based approaches [15, 50] have been proposed that input answers of each task in a neural network and output the inferred label of the task. Other approaches based on tensor augmentation and completion with limited performance have also been suggested [58].

Worker Models. Some truth inference methods do not have an explicit worker model while others model workers by: 1) a single *worker reliability* or *penalty* parameter reflecting their trustworthiness [12, 48], 2) a *confusion matrix* capturing workers' probability of providing a certain label given the true label [11, 25, 44]. The confusion matrix π^{w_i} is an $|L| * |L|$ matrix where element $\pi^{w_i}_{p,q}$ denotes the probability of worker w_i reporting label q given the true label p. Assuming a binary label set $\mathbf{L} = \{0, 1\}$, the matrix is reduced to two variables, α_i and β_i, with $\alpha_i = \mathrm{pr}(c^{w_i}_{t_j} = 1 \mid z^* = 1)$ and $\beta_i = \mathrm{pr}(c^{w_i}_{t_j} = 0 \mid z^* = 0)$, showing the probability of worker w_i correctly reporting a task given true label 1 or 0 respectively.

Table 1. Summary of notations

Symbol	Description
N	Number of tasks
M	Number of workers
T	Set of tasks
W, **W**′	Set of normal, malicious workers
w_i	i-th worker
t_j	j-th task
$\mathbf{T}_{w_i}$	Set of tasks assigned to i-th worker
π^{w_i}	Confusion matrix of i-th worker
C	Answer matrix by all workers
Z*	Ground truth vector
$\hat{\mathbf{Z}}$	Predicted truth vector

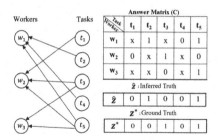

Fig. 1. Example of a crowdsourcing system

Selected Methods. We aim to be comprehensive in representing categories of techniques and worker models to investigate their role in the robustness of inference methods under data poisoning attacks. When possible (e.g. for optimization and PGM based techniques), we leverage the findings of the previous study [56] by selecting the best-performing methods.

For direct computation, MV (majority voting) and its enhanced version, MV-Soft [22], are chosen. For optimization based methods, we include MV-hard [22] which employs a semi-matching optimization for the worker-task bipartite graph and PM [28] which poses an optimization problem on inferred labels and workers' reliability. For PGM based methods, we chose the best-performing D&S [11] and BCC [25] modeling worker reliability by confusion matrix and KOS [24] using a single worker reliability parameter. For neural network based methods, we chose LAA-S [50], the only one applicable to non-complete bipartite graphs. We refer readers to the appendix for a more detailed discussion regarding each method.

4 Data Poisoning Attacks

Due to their open nature, crowdsourcing systems are subject to *data poisoning attacks* [23,40] where malicious workers intentionally and strategically report incorrect labels to mislead the system to infer the wrong answer for all or a targeted set of tasks. This is different from unreliable behavior that is typically non-malicious, unintentional, and non-strategic. We propose a taxonomy for data poisoning attacks in crowdsourcing and review some existing attacks.

4.1 Attack Taxonomy

Attack Goal. Assuming a certain percentage of malicious workers, the answer matrix **C** contains corrupt answers **C**′ contributed by malicious workers. There are two cases:

Untargeted Attack. Adversaries aim to decrease the overall accuracy. Their goal is to mislead the system to infer the wrong label for as many tasks as possible which can be formulated as: $\max_{\mathbf{C}'} \sum_{j=1}^{M} \mathbb{1}(\hat{z_{t_j}} \neq z_{t_j}^{*})$.

Targeted Attack. Adversaries aim to reduce the accuracy for only a targeted subset of tasks $\mathbf{T}_{tar} \subseteq \mathbf{T}$, which can be written as: $\max_{\mathbf{C}'} \sum_{t_j \in \mathbf{T}_{tar}} \mathbb{1}(\hat{z_{t_j}} \neq z_{t_j}^{*})$.

Adversarial Knowledge. Malicious workers can have a varying level of adversarial knowledge.

Black-box Attacks. Adversaries only know their assigned tasks.

White-box Attacks. Adversaries know the inference method and all answers of other workers.

Gray-box Attacks. Adversaries have some knowledge, e.g. part of answers.

Attack Strategy. The attackers can adopt different strategies depending on their level of knowledge.

Heuristic Based Attacks. Attackers can use heuristics, e.g., always reporting the wrong answers for the tasks, or occasionally reporting true answers for some tasks to disguise themselves as honest workers. While this attack may not be as effective as the optimization based one below, it is easy to carry out and does not require strong adversarial knowledge, and hence is applicable to all truth inference algorithms in all black-box and white-box settings.

Optimization Based Attacks. Given the full knowledge, attackers can formulate an optimization problem to provide answers maximizing the number of flipped labels before and after the attack [30,31]. Though more effective, this attack depends on the truth inference algorithm being used and requires full or partial adversarial knowledge, thus it is applicable to white-box or gray-box only.

4.2 Existing Attacks

A few optimization based attacks [30,31] have been studied for representative inference methods, namely D&S [11] and PM [28], assuming attackers' full knowledge of all answers and the inference method used (i.e. white-box setting). Since the adversary does not know the tasks' ground truth, the optimization aims to maximize the number of inferred labels that are flipped from before attack to after attack, while also maximizing the inferred reliability of the attackers by the truth inference method. Intuitively, this helps them to obfuscate their malicious nature and hence succeed in misleading the system.

Let $z_{t_j}^{\hat{a}}$ and $z_{t_j}^{\hat{b}}$ denote the inferred answer for task t_j by the D&S after and before attack respectively. $\hat{\alpha}_{w'}$ and $\hat{\beta}_{w'}$ denote the inferred confusion matrix parameters of the malicious worker w'. The optimization is formulated as Eq. (1) where λ controls the trade-off between the objectives of maximizing the collective reliability of malicious workers and the number of flipped labels.

$$\max_{\mathbf{C}'} \sum_{j=1}^{M} \mathbb{1}(z_{t_j}^{\hat{a}} \neq z_{t_j}^{\hat{b}}) + \lambda \sum_{w' \in \mathbf{W}'} (\hat{\alpha}_{w'} + \hat{\beta}_{w'}) \tag{1}$$

For our evaluation, we design heuristic attack and extend the optimization attack for D&S and PM to all truth inference methods (which we explain in Sect. 5.2).

5 Evaluation Methodology

5.1 Datasets

We use two real datasets of decision making tasks [4, 21] and synthetic datasets with varying parameters for the evaluation. The datasets' properties are summarized in Table 2.

Product Dataset. The task is comparing two products, e.g. "Are iPad Two 16 GB WiFi White and iPad 2nd generation 16 GB WiFi White the same?" [21].

PosSent Dataset. The task is classifying positive/neagtive tweets about the companies' reputation, e.g. "The recent products of Apple is amazing" [4].

Synthetic Dataset. Synthetic datasets are created to evaluate the effect of redundancy, number of tasks, and number of workers on performance. The worker-task assignment graph comes from power-law distribution. The ground truth for tasks comes from a Bernoulli distribution with prior 0.5, i.e a balanced dataset. We experimented changing the prior and observed no significant change and hence only report on 0.5. The workers' reliability α and β come from Beta distribution.

Table 2. Properties of datasets

Dataset	Product	PosSent	Synthetic
N (# of tasks)	8,315	1,000	[200, 40,000]
M (# of workers)	176	85	[100, 500]
V (# of answers)	24,945	20,000	[10,000, 200,000]
Redundancy (# of answers per task)	3	20	[5, 30]
Engagement (# of answers per worker)	141	235	[100, 400]
Skewness (ratio of negative labels)	0.88	0.52	[0.5 0.9]
Avg normal workers' reliability	0.79	0.798	0.85

Table 3. Data poisoning attack parameters

Parameter	Description	Values
$\frac{|W'|}{|W'|+|W|}$	Percentage of malicious workers	[10%, 60%], step $= 10\%$, **30%**
α	Reliability for tasks with truth 1	[0, 1], step $= 0.1$, **1.0**
β	Reliability for tasks with truth 0	[0, 1], step $= 0.1$, **1.0**
α'	Attacker reliability for tasks with truth 1	[0, 1], step $= 0.1$, **0.0**
β'	Attacker reliability for tasks with truth 0	[0, 1], step $= 0.1$, **0.0**
γ	Disguise	[0, 1], step $= 0.1$, **0.0**

5.2   Attack Design

For attacks, we inject a set of malicious workers W', so the faction of malicious workers is $\frac{|W'|}{|W|+|W'|}$. We design both heuristic and optimization attacks for the chosen inference methods in Sect. 3. Both targeted and untargeted attacks are analyzed when feasible. The parameters used in design of attacks are given in Table 3. Default values (highlighted) were used unless specified otherwise.

Heuristic Based Attacks. We design heuristic based attacks applicable in black-box settings.

Untargeted Attacks. With only knowledge of the assigned tasks, the simplest heuristic for attackers is to always report the wrong answer for their tasks. However, this may be easily detected by most truth inference systems (except majority voting) with workers' reliability modeling. Therefore attackers desire to disguise themselves as honest workers by providing correct answers to some tasks to avoid detection and being discounted later. To model such behavior, we use the following enhanced heuristic applicable to all truth inference methods. Each malicious worker behaves as a normal worker modeled by π^w with a disguise probability γ and as a malicious worker modeled by $\pi^{w'}$ with probability $1 - \gamma$. For example, a malicious worker with a moderate level of disguise may be modeled with $\pi^w = \begin{bmatrix} \beta = 1 & 0 \\ 0 & \alpha = 1 \end{bmatrix}$, $\pi^{w'} = \begin{bmatrix} \beta' = 0 & 1 \\ 1 & \alpha' = 0 \end{bmatrix}$, and $\gamma = 0.2$.

Targeted Attacks. For targeted attacks, the best strategy for the malicious workers is to flip the labels for the targeted tasks while acting truthfully for other tasks, building their reliability. Hence we set $(\gamma = 0)$.

Optimization Based Attacks. We design optimization based attacks applicable to white-box settings, i.e., the attacker know the inference method and all others' answers.

Untargeted Attacks. We extend the attack from [30] to all inference methods. For confusion matrix based ones, we use the same formulation as Eq. (1). For methods with a single reliability parameter or no worker model, we set $\lambda = 0$. We varied λ in the interval $[0, 1]$ and observed that a λ value in $[0.9, 1]$ leads to the most successful attack.

Targeted Attacks. Here the aim is to maximize the number of targeted tasks $\mathbf{T}_{tar} \subseteq \mathbf{T}$ whose label is flipped. The optimization is $\max_{\mathbf{C}'} \sum_{t_j \in \mathbf{T}_{tar}} \mathbb{1}(z_{t_j}^{\hat{a}} \neq z_{t_j}^{\hat{b}}) + \lambda \sum_{w' \in \mathbf{W}'}(\hat{\alpha}_{w'} + \hat{\beta}_{w'})$. Similar to untargeted attacks, the second term is considered only for confusion matrix based methods.

5.3   Metrics

We use the following metrics to assess the robustness of inference methods.

Accuracy. Accuracy is the fraction of correctly inferred tasks, formulated as: $\sum_{j=1}^{N} \mathbb{1}(\hat{z}_{t_j} = z_{t_j}^*)/N$, where $\hat{z}_{t_j}$ and $z_{t_j}^*$ are inferred and ground truth of task t_j.

A lower accuracy means a more successful attack. We note that [30] defined the attack success metric as the percentage of inferred labels flipped due to attack, we believe this metric does not truly capture the attackers' success where some inferred labels may be wrong before attack and were flipped to correct due to the attack, i.e., adversaries help the system to correctly infer the label of an otherwise wrongly labeled task. Instead, we use the flipped labels w.r.t. the ground truth, i.e. accuracy, as the metric for attack success. We also report F1 score to account for the skewness of classes in the unbalanced dataset.

Accuracy_Targeted. *Accuracy_Targeted* is the fraction of the targeted tasks $\mathbf{T}_{tar}$ whose truth are inferred correctly, i.e $1 - \sum_{t_j \in \mathbf{T}_{tar}} \mathbb{1}(\hat{z_{t_j}} \neq z_{t_j}^*)/|\mathbf{T}_{tar}|$.

Area Under Curve (AUC). Since the inference methods' accuracy changes over parameters, e.g. percentage of malicious workers, we use AUC to compare the global performance of methods on an interval of parameter values, if feasible.

Recognizability. To assess the adversary detection ability of inference methods with explicit worker models, we define *Recognizability* as the similarity between the simulated (ground truth) worker reliability and the inferred reliability. A higher *Recognizability* means the method is better at detecting malicious workers. The worker behavior is modeled by a normal confusion matrix with α and β, a malicious one with α' and β', and a disguise parameter γ. We aggregate these into a single value $r_{w'}$ showing the expected reliability of a worker and define *Recognizability* as $1 - \frac{1}{|\mathbf{W}'|} \sum_{w' \in \mathbf{W}'} |r_{w'} - \hat{r}_{w'}|$, where $r_{w'}$ and $\hat{r}_{w'}$ are the simulated and inferred reliability of malicious worker w' respectively.

$$r_{w'} = \frac{1}{|\mathbf{T}_{w'}|} \sum_{t_j \in \mathbf{T}_{w'}} (\alpha_{w'} \times \gamma + \alpha'_{w'} \times (1 - \gamma)) \times \mathbb{1}(z_{t_j}^* = 1)$$
$$+ (\beta_{w'} \times \gamma + \beta'_{w'} \times (1 - \gamma)) \times \mathbb{1}(z_{t_j}^* = 0) \tag{2}$$

$$\hat{r}_{w'} = \frac{1}{|\mathbf{T}_{w'}|} \sum_{t_j \in \mathbf{T}_{w'}} \hat{\alpha}_{w'} \times \mathbb{1}(z_{t_j}^* = 1) + \hat{\beta}_{w'} \times \mathbb{1}(z_{t_j}^* = 0) \tag{3}$$

6   Evaluation Results

In this section, we report the robustness of various truth inference methods under heuristic based and optimization based attacks.

6.1   Heuristic Based Attacks: Untargeted

Impact of Percentage of Malicious Workers. The number of normal workers is fixed and the percentage of added malicious workers varies from 0 to 60%. Adversary behavior setting is $\gamma = 0$, $\alpha' = 0$ and $\beta' = 0$.

Accuracy. Figure 2 shows the accuracy of the methods w.r.t. the percentage of malicious workers. We omitted the result for synthetic dataset showing similar

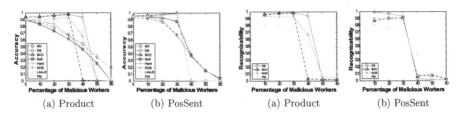

<table>
<tr><td>(a) Product</td><td>(b) PosSent</td><td>(a) Product</td><td>(b) PosSent</td></tr>
</table>

Fig. 2. Untargeted heuristic based attack: accuracy vs. % of malicious workers

Fig. 3. Untargeted heuristic based attack: recognizability vs. % of malicious workers

trends. Increasing the number of malicious workers drops the accuracy of all methods. The direct computation (MV, MV-Soft) and neural network method's (LAA-S) drop is almost linear early on, PGM methods (D&S, BCC, and KOS) and probabilistic method (PM) are more resistant especially with few adversaries and drop to 0 once the percentage goes beyond (40% to 50%). Overall, D&S and LAA-S are the most resilient for this attack. Comparing the datasets, Product dataset is more susceptible to the attack due to its low redundancy. Table 4 shows the AUC of different methods over intervals of [0–30%] of malicious workers as a realistic attack setting, and [0–50%] for more aggressive attacks. Results for Product, confirms the advantage of D&S and LAA-S in their overall performance. While most methods outperform MV, there is no clear winner for PosSent dataset.

Table 4. AUC of methods' accuracy over specified % of malicious workers interval: untargeted heuristic based attack

Dataset (% interval)	MV	D&S	BCC	Soft	Hard	KOS	LAA-S	PM
Product (0–50%)	34.78	**42.9**	33.69	32.2	34.3	38.5	**40.09**	30.92
Product (0–30%)	29.35	**38.2**	33.69	28.58	30.43	**35.31**	34.59	28.9
PosSent (0–50%)	32.88	34.01	34.2	34.99	34.215	33.6	34.062	34.12
PosSent (0–30%)	30.5	33.94	34.2	32.6	31.7	33.6	34.04	33.19

Recognizability. To show adversary detectability in inference methods, we report recognizability of methods with explicit worker modeling, i.e. D&S, BCC, PM, and KOS. We exclude MV and LAA-S as they do not explicitly model reliability. MV-Hard and MV-Soft are excluded too since these methods only remove the least credible worker without explicitly computed reliability.

Figure 3 shows the methods' recognizability w.r.t. varying percentages of malicious workers. D&S and KOS perform better than BCC in adversary detection, while PM performs the worst. This explains the robustness of the accuracy of D&S and KOS we observed earlier. Comparing Fig. 2 and 3, the accuracy and recognizability of D&S and KOS decrease as the percentage of malicious workers increases, i.e. worker modeling with good detection is the key to a robust inference algorithm under attack.

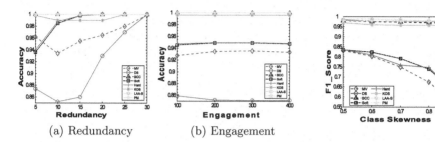

(a) Redundancy   (b) Engagement

Fig. 4. Untargeted heuristic based attack: accuracy vs redundancy and engagement (Synthetic)

Fig. 5. Untargeted heuristic based attack: F1 score vs class skewness

Impact of Redundancy and Engagement. Redundancy is the mean number of workers assigned per task, while worker engagement is the mean number of tasks per worker. Figure 4 shows the accuracy w.r.t. varying redundancy and engagement. As expected, with increased redundancy, it is harder for adversaries to reduce the accuracy (the percentage of attackers is set to 20%). D&S and MV-based models were more sensitive to redundancy in the sparse dataset (Product). Worker engagement had no significant impact, since it does not directly impact their reliability.

Impact of Class Skewness. We show the effect of skewness on F1-score in synthetic data. Figure 5 shows the F1-score w.r.t. varying ratios of the majority class. MV-based methods are vulnerable to imbalance while others are robust.

Impact of Disguise (γ). We show the trend of accuracy and recognizability w.r.t disguise. When in disguise, adversaries' behavior is governed by $\alpha = 1$ and $\beta = 1$ compared to $\alpha' = 0$ and $\beta' = 0$ in pure malicious mode.

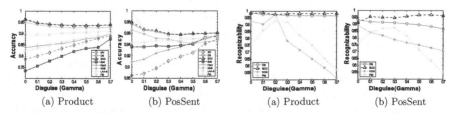

(a) Product   (b) PosSent   (a) Product   (b) PosSent

Fig. 6. Untargeted heuristic based attack: accuracy vs disguise

Fig. 7. Untargeted heuristic based attack: recognizability vs. disguise (γ)

Accuracy. Figure 6 shows the accuracy of methods w.r.t. varying disguise levels. We use a different scale for each dataset's y-axis to highlight their trend. Since increasing disguise after 0.7 resulted in monotonously increasing accuracy for all models, we terminate at 0.7. For methods (e.g. MV) with no inherent attacker recognition, disguising only boosts the accuracy. For more robust methods, as we increase γ slightly, the algorithms fail to identify adversaries leading to the success of the attack. However, as disguise further increases, the accuracy goes back up due to the correct answers by the disguised malicious workers. Hence there's an optimal level of disguise for attackers.

Recognizability. Figure 7 shows the recognizability of methods w.r.t. varying disguise levels on real datasets. Confusion matrix based models, BCC and D&S, are more robust to disguise and model the workers accurately regardless of adversarys' disguise. KOS uses a single reliability value and thus is more sensitive to disguise. Generally, the recognizability of adversaries drops as disguise increases, since their behavior more closely resembles normal workers.

Impact of Malicious Worker Confusion Matrix. We also evaluated the impact of varying worker behavior parameter (α', β'). When varying α', β' is 0, and vice versa. Increasing adversaries' reliability parameters is very similar to increasing disguise. We omit the figures due to space limitations. Simple methods e.g. MV-based, have increasing accuracy due to the adversaries' true answers. In more sophisticated methods, e.g, PGM based, attack can be most successful with an optimal value.

6.2 Heuristic Based Attacks: Targeted

We report the evaluation results for targeted attacks as outlined in Sect. 5.2. We focus on parameters relevant to targeted attacks, the percentage of malicious workers and the proportion of targeted tasks.

Impact of Percentage of Malicious Workers. Figures 8 and 9 show the accuracy of the methods w.r.t. varying percentage of malicious workers on the real datasets. We fixed the fraction of targeted tasks for Product and PosSent dataset to be 0.2 and 0.1, respectively, to ensure: 1) targeted attack is impactful, 2) there is an observable difference among methods' performance. The general trend is that increasing the number of attackers, the overall accuracy of the system increases thanks to the truthful contributions of attackers to non-targeted tasks. However, the accuracy of targeted tasks is decreased by attackers.

Surprisingly, D&S and BCC which are more robust against untargeted attacks are more susceptible to targeted attacks. While they maintain high overall accuracy, their accuracy for the targeted tasks suffers the most due to their failure to differentiate targeted and untargeted tasks when modeling workers' behavior (i.e. being misled by malicious workers based on their true answers to the untargeted tasks). On the other hand, LAA-S is significantly more robust against targeted attacks, even though the overall accuracy is not as high as other methods, explained by the absence of explicit worker modeling. While MV-Soft

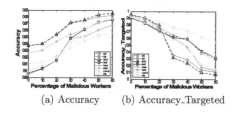

(a) Accuracy   (b) Accuracy_Targeted

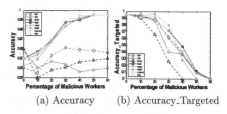

(a) Accuracy   (b) Accuracy_Targeted

Fig. 8. Targeted heuristic based attack: accuracy & accuracy_targeted vs. % of malicious workers (Product dataset)

Fig. 9. Targeted heuristic based attack: accuracy & accuracy_targeted vs. % of malicious workers (PosSent dataset)

performs worse than others in untargeted attacks (Fig. 2), it is the most resilient alongside LAA-S for targeted attacks. MV-Soft's resilience is due to accurate detection and penalization of malicious workers when they are the majority contributing to a task with conflicting answers, which happens more frequently while focusing on limited tasks rather than all tasks.

Impact of Proportion of Targeted Tasks. Figures 10 and 11 show the accuracy of the methods w.r.t. varying percentage of targeted tasks on real datasets. As the ratio of targeted tasks increases, the overall accuracy decrease. However, when the ratio gets sufficiently large, accuracy increase for D&S and BCC. Since malicious workers have to dilute their efforts among a larger set of targeted tasks, they are more discoverable and less effective.

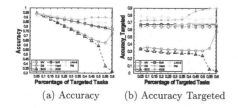

(a) Accuracy   (b) Accuracy Targeted

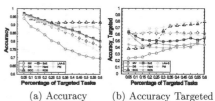

(a) Accuracy   (b) Accuracy Targeted

Fig. 10. Targeted heuristic based attack: accuracy vs. ratio of targeted tasks (Product dataset)

Fig. 11. Targeted heuristic based attack: accuracy vs. ratio of targeted tasks (PosSent dataset)

Comparing the datasets, answer redundancy inversely affect targeted attack's success, similar to untargeted attacks. Given the Product dataset's lower redundancy, this attack is successful even with a high ratio of targeted tasks.

6.3   Optimization Based Attacks: Untargeted

Impact of Percentage of Malicious Workers. We evaluate the optimization based attack in white-box setting, i.e. given the full knowledge of the inference

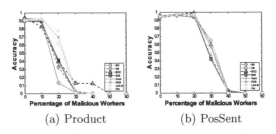

Fig. 12. Untargeted optimization based attack: accuracy vs. % of malicious workers

method used and all other workers' answers. Figure 12 shows the accuracy of the inference methods w.r.t. varying percentage of malicous workers.

All methods' accuracy drops fairly quickly as the percentage of malicious workers increases. Comparing heuristic and optimization based attack (Fig. 2a vs Fig. 12a for Product dataset, Fig. 2b vs Fig. 12b for PosSent dataset), the accuracy under optimization based attack drops to zero at a much lower percentage of malicious workers for all methods. The attackers are indeed more successful when using the optimized scheme given stronger adversarial knowledge. Comparing the different methods, all perform similarly and are susceptible to the attack, since it is optimized for that particular inference method. However, LAA-S has a slight edge over others.

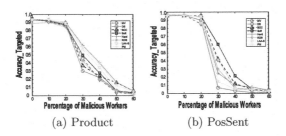

Fig. 13. Targeted optimization based attack: accuracy_targeted vs. % of malicious workers on Product and PosSent dataset

6.4   Optimization Based Attacks: Targeted

Impact of Percentage of Malicious Workers. We set the ratio of targeted tasks to be 0.01 and 0.005 for Product and PosSent datasets respectively. Since optimization based attack is more successful, a lower ratio of targeted tasks is chosen compared to Sect. 6.2. Figure 13 shows accuracy_targeted of the inference methods w.r.t. varying percentage of malicious workers on the real datasets. Overall accuracy is not shown due to space limitations. *Accuracy_Targeted* decreases as percentage of malicious workers increases. Comparing these results to the heuristic based targeted attack (Figs. 8 and 9), the heuristic based attack is more effective in reducing accuracy at a small percentage of malicious workers.

However, with a greater percentage of malicious workers, targeted optimization based attack is more successful. One probable reason is that since a subset of tasks is targeted, the chance of adversary's detection is lower compared to the untargeted setting. So, optimization based attack that trades some accuracy drop in exchange for less detection will lose its edge in attack power over heuristic attack which only focuses on accuracy.

7 Conclusion and Discussion

We summarize our key findings on the performance of leading inference methods under various data poisoning attacks.

Comparison of Methods. Figure 14 shows the overall attack susceptibility of different inference methods along two dimensions (untargeted attacks and targeted attacks) under heuristic and optimization based attacks. Susceptibility is defined as 1 - AUC. A more robust method should have a lower susceptibility across both dimensions. The AUC is the accuracy over an interval of fraction of attackers. Since in reality malicious workers are not the majority, we choose the interval [0–0.5]. The most robust methods should be those dominating others (less vulnerable) in both dimensions, i.e., the pareto optimal methods or skyline. Table 5 shows the top 2 performing methods for each category of attacks. We also discuss the main findings below.

– Among direct computation methods, MV-Soft is more robust than MV, i.e. dominates MV, for all attacks, thanks to its modeling of worker reliability.

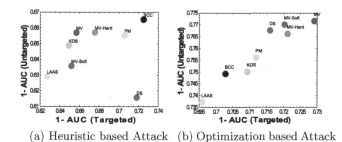

(a) Heuristic based Attack   (b) Optimization based Attack

Fig. 14. Susceptibility of different inference methods

Table 5. Top 2 robust methods under different attacks

Goal	Strategy	
	Heuristic based attack	Optimization based attack
Untargeted	D&S (LAA-S)	LAA-S (KOS)
Targeted	LAA-S (MV-Soft)	LAA-S (BCC)

- Among optimization based methods, MV-Hard is more robust than PM only under targeted heuristic based attack. This can be attributed to its optimal matching algorithm that penalizes or removes malicious workers when they become the majority among the contributing workers for conflicting tasks, which happens when they all give wrong answers to a target set of tasks. On the other hand, PM is more robust than MV-Hard under other attacks.
- Among PGM based methods, for untargeted attacks, D&S dominate BCC under heuristic based attack. However, under optimization attack, BCC dominates D&S. Note that in heuristic attack the responses are designed for each individual worker, while under optimization based attack, the collective effect of malicious workers is considered. Therefore correlation modeling in BCC can counter the possible collusion of malicious workers, reflected in BCC's more resilient behavior under optimization based attack. Overall, D&S is most resilient if only untargeted heuristic based attack is anticipated. However, D&S is vulnerable to all other attacks. Between KOS and BCC, KOS has a slight edge considering all four attacks.
- The neural network based method LAA-S dominates all others in all attacks except having a slightly higher susceptibility than D&S in untargeted heuristic based attack in the low redundancy dataset (Product). We suspect this is due to the sparsity of the task representation vector in contrast to the large number of network parameters combined with the lower quality of malicious answers in heuristic based attack. The superior performance in all other cases can be attributed to its network of parameters, which can be considered as an implicit and sophisticated (non-linear) model of worker reliability.
- Comparing different techniques, besides the best performing neural networks, PGM based methods are generally more robust than optimization based methods and direct computation methods. This is also consistent with the findings in [56] under normal settings with varying worker reliability.
- Comparing different worker models, the confusion matrix based methods generally outperform those with a single reliability model and MV method with no worker model. Neural network based method LAA-S, even though with no explicit worker model, achieves the best performance thanks to its network of parameters, which can be considered as an implicit and more sophisticated (non-linear) model of the reliability associated with each worker.

Comparison of Attacks. From the attack point of view, optimization based attack is more effective compared to heuristic based attack, especially for untargeted attacks. This is not surprising given the adversarial knowledge and optimization based attack strategy. However, optimization based attack can only be carried out in white-box settings given full adversarial knowledge, and may not be a realistic threat to crowdsourcing applications.

For targeted attacks, in a lower percentage of adversaries, heuristic based attack can be more successful compared to optimization based attack. Optimization based attack trades off some accuracy drop in exchange for less adversary detection, hence losing its edge in attack power over heuristic based attack, solely optimizing for accuracy drop. However, there is an optimal level of disguise and percentage of targeted tasks for attackers under heuristic based attack. These may not be easily identifiable as they vary substantially across inference methods and settings.

Comparison of Datasets and Other Factors. The comparison between the datasets reveals that a crowdsourcing system with a higher redundancy of answers is generally more robust. It remains an interesting question for a crowdsourcing system provider to find the best trade-off between redundancy and the overall platform cost to ensure the resiliency of the system. However, worker engagement does not have a major impact on the robustness of the system.

Future Works. The goal of our evaluation is to understand the resilience of existing leading-edge truth inference methods and ultimately build more robust systems. Towards this end, several directions for future work can be explored.

- Attack resistant truth inference: while existing methods provide certain level of resistance to data poisoning attacks, it remains an open question whether we can build more robust systems, e.g. by designing hybrid methods that combine the strength of existing techniques (e.g. LAA-S against optimization based attack and targeted heuristic based attack and D&S against untargeted heuristic based attack) or designing entirely new techniques. A more fundamental question is whether we can have quantifiable guarantees for the robustness of the system against data poisoning attacks.
- Semi-supervised learning: All the truth inference approaches evaluated in this paper assume no access to the ground truth. This unsupervised nature makes the methods inherently susceptible to attacks. A semi-supervised approach [3,42] may help provide resilience to attacks within which ground truth and workers' answers for historical tasks can be used for training the system.
- Dynamic behavior of workers: Our study is focused on a fixed set of workers and tasks. In practice, the workers could join and leave the system as they wish. They could also alter their behaviors dynamically in a strategic way to maximize the attack effect. Understanding the impact of such behaviors and building robust systems in a dynamic setting is also an important direction.

Acknowledgement. This research is supported by Air Force Office of Scientific Research (AFOSR) DDDAS Program under grant FA9550-12-1-0240.

Appendix: Details of Selected Truth Inference Methods

MV-Soft. Majority voting with soft penalty (MV-soft) [22] implicitly models workers' reliability via penalizing unreliable workers. To compute the penalty, the algorithm considers tasks without unanimous answer from all workers, i.e. conflicted tasks. A bipartite graph is created with two set of vertices $\mathbf{W}$ and $\mathbf{T}_{conf}$, where $\mathbf{W}$ and $\mathbf{T}_{conf} \subseteq \mathbf{T}$ are sets of workers and conflicted tasks. Each conflicted task is represented by two nodes, t_j^+ and t_j^-. An edge $\{w_i, t_j^+\}$ or $\{w_i, t_j^-\}$ is added to the graph depending on answer of 1 or 0 provided by worker

w_i ' for task t_j. The penalty for worker w_i is inversely proportional to the number of other workers who have the same answer as w_i, which is measured by the degree of each node in the conflicted task set $\mathbf{T}_{conf}$.

$$Pen_{w_i} = \frac{\sum_{t_j \in \mathbf{T}^{w_i}_{conf}} \frac{1}{deg(t_j^+)} \cdot \mathbb{1}(c^{w_i}_{t_j} = 1) + \frac{1}{deg(t_j^-)} \cdot \mathbb{1}(c^{w_i}_{t_j} = 0)}{|\mathbf{T}^{w_i}_{conf}|} \qquad (4)$$

Here, $\mathbf{T}^{w_i}_{conf}$ is the conflicted tasks assigned to worker w_i and $deg(t_j^+)$, $deg(t_j^-)$ are degrees of task t_j for label 1 and 0 respectively, $c^{w_i}_{t_j}$ shows worker w_i's answer for task t_j and $\mathbb{1}$ is the identifier function which is 1 if the condition holds and 0 otherwise.

MV-Hard. Here an optimal semi-matching for bipartite graph is used to assign penalty [22]. A semi-matching is a matching for the bipartite graph where exactly one worker is chosen among all contributors for each label of each task. The optimal matching minimizes the sum of accumulated degree of all workers, a typical formulation of the semi-matching problem: $\min_{Match} \sum_{w \in \mathbf{W}} \sum_{i=1}^{deg_{Match}(w)} i$, where $deg_{Match}(w)$ is the degree of worker w in matching $Match$. In the optimal semi matching tasks are distributed as evenly as possible among the workers, so one worker cannot dominate others by being the only decision maker for many tasks. Assuming the worker who is the sole contributor for many tasks based on semi matching is more malicious, workers' penalties are their degree in optimal semi-matching. The final label of tasks is the label connected to the worker with the lowest degree or penalty.

PM. Here worker w_i's reliability is modeled using a single value r^{w_i} and the truth inference is posed as optimization problem: $\min_{\mathbf{r}, \hat{\mathbf{z}}} \sum_{w_i \in \mathbf{W}} r^{w_i} \cdot \sum_{t_j \in \mathbf{T}_{w_i}} d(\hat{z}_{t_j}, c^{w_i}_{t_j})$ where $d(\hat{z}_{t_j}, c^{w_i}_{t_j})$ for task t_j, is the distance between the inferred truth and the answer provided by worker w_i and r^{w_i} is worker w_i's reliability [28]. Intuitively, workers with answers deviating from the inferred truth are more malicious. The algorithm iteratively solves the optimization problem updating the truth labels and reliability of workers.

D&S. It is a Probabilistic Graphical Modelling approach showing worker's reliability by confusion matrix. The D&S [11] algorithm uses Expectation Maximization (EM) to solve maximum likelihood estimation (MLE) for the inferred labels $\hat{\mathbf{Z}}$ and the confusion matrices $\pi^{\mathbf{W}}$ iteratively. $\mathbf{W}^{t_j}$ is the workers responding to task t_j. The objective function of this method is: $\max_{\hat{\mathbf{Z}}, \pi \mathbf{w}} \prod_{j=1}^{N} \sum_{l \in \mathbf{L}} pr(\hat{z}_{t_j} = l) \prod_{w_i \in \mathbf{W}^{t_j}} \pi^{w_i}_{l, c^{w_i}_{t_j}}$.

BCC. Bayesian Classifier Combination is also a graphical model approach [25]. For easy tasks, a single shared confusion matrix is used for all workers, whereas for hard tasks, workers have a separate confusion matrix. The inference problem is posed as:

$$\max_{\mathbf{a},\mathbf{b},\hat{\mathbf{Z}},\pi^{\mathbf{w}}} \prod_{j=1}^{N} pr(\hat{\mathbf{Z}} \mid \mathbf{a}) \prod_{i=1}^{M} pr(\pi^{w_i} \mid \mathbf{b}) \prod_{i=1}^{M} pr(c_{t_j}^{w_i} \mid \pi^{w_i}, \hat{\mathbf{Z}}) \qquad (5)$$

There are extensions of the BCC method that take into account the difficulty of tasks and workers collaboration, but we do not consider them in this study.

KOS. The KOS method estimates the worker reliability by maximizing the joint probability distribution [24]. $\max_{\hat{\mathbf{Z}},\pi^{\mathbf{w}}} \prod_{j=1}^{N} \sum_{l \in \mathbf{L}} pr(\hat{z}_{t_j} = l) \prod_{w_i \in \mathbf{W}^{t_j}} \pi_{l,c_{t_j}^{w_i}}^{w_i}$. Since direct estimation of the distribution is intractable, an iterative belief propagation is used to estimate a distribution for the worker reliability. The label of tasks is determined based on the weighted product of estimated worker's reliability and their answers.

LAAS. It is an unsupervised approach where the intuition is learning the latent true label that best represents the original task vector. LAA-S [50] architecture contains two shallow neural networks: 1) an encoder or classifier (q_θ) to convert the task vector (v) into the latent feature (z) showing the true label, and 2) a decoder (p_ϕ) reconstructing a task vector based on the latent feature.

The network is trained on all task vectors by minimizing the reconstruction error between the original and reconstructed task vectors. The training also enforces the latent truth label distribution to resemble the original answer distribution. The objective function is: $\min_{q_\theta, p_\theta} \mathbb{E}_{q_\theta(z|v)} log p_\phi(v|z) - D_{KL}(q_\theta(z|v) \| prior)$.

Here the first term is the reconstruction error and the second term ensures the distribution of inferred labels follows a specific prior using the negative KL divergence D_{KL}. The prior is set based on the fraction of labels in the workers' answers for each task.

References

1. Al-Qurishi, M., Al-Rakhami, M., Alamri, A., Alrubaian, M., Rahman, S.M.M., Hossain, M.S.: Sybil defense techniques in online social networks: a survey. IEEE Access **5**, 1200–1219 (2017)
2. Alsuwat, E., Alsuwat, H., Rose, J., Valtorta, M., Farkas, C.: Detecting adversarial attacks in the context of Bayesian networks. In: Foley, S.N. (ed.) DBSec 2019. LNCS, vol. 11559, pp. 3–22. Springer, Cham (2019). https://doi.org/10.1007/978-3-030-22479-0_1
3. Atarashi, K., Oyama, S., Kurihara, M.: Semi-supervised learning from crowds using deep generative models. In: Thirty-Second AAAI Conference on Artificial Intelligence (2018)
4. Authors, M.: Twitter Sentiment (2018). https://raw.githubusercontent.com/zfz/twitter_corpus/master/full-corpus.csv. Accessed 19 Apr 2018
5. Biggio, B., Nelson, B., Laskov, P.: Poisoning attacks against support vector machines. arXiv preprint arXiv:1206.6389 (2012)

6. Brawley, A.M., Pury, C.L.: Work experiences on MTurk: job satisfaction, turnover, and information sharing. Comput. Hum. Behav. **54**, 531–546 (2016)
7. Bryan, K., O'Mahony, M., Cunningham, P.: Unsupervised retrieval of attack profiles in collaborative recommender systems. In: Proceedings of the 2008 ACM Conference on Recommender Systems, pp. 155–162. ACM (2008)
8. Cao, Q., Yang, X., Yu, J., Palow, C.: Uncovering large groups of active malicious accounts in online social networks. In: Proceedings of the 2014 ACM SIGSAC Conference on Computer and Communications Security, pp. 477–488. ACM (2014)
9. Chirita, P.A., Nejdl, W., Zamfir, C.: Preventing shilling attacks in online recommender systems. In: Proceedings of the 7th Annual ACM International Workshop on Web Information and Data Management, pp. 67–74. ACM (2005)
10. Choi, H., Lee, K., Webb, S.: Detecting malicious campaigns in crowdsourcing platforms. In: Proceedings of the 2016 IEEE/ACM International Conference on Advances in Social Networks Analysis and Mining, pp. 197–202. IEEE Press (2016)
11. Dawid, A.P., Skene, A.M.: Maximum likelihood estimation of observer error-rates using the EM algorithm. Appl. Stat. **28**, 20–28 (1979)
12. Demartini, G., Difallah, D.E., Cudré-Mauroux, P.: ZenCrowd: leveraging probabilistic reasoning and crowdsourcing techniques for large-scale entity linking. In: Proceedings of the 21st International Conference on World Wide Web, pp. 469–478. ACM (2012)
13. Difallah, D.E., Demartini, G., Cudré-Mauroux, P.: Mechanical cheat: spamming schemes and adversarial techniques on crowdsourcing platforms. In: CrowdSearch, pp. 26–30 (2012)
14. Douceur, J.R.: The sybil attack. In: Druschel, P., Kaashoek, F., Rowstron, A. (eds.) IPTPS 2002. LNCS, vol. 2429, pp. 251–260. Springer, Heidelberg (2002). https://doi.org/10.1007/3-540-45748-8_24
15. Gaunt, A., Borsa, D., Bachrach, Y.: Training deep neural nets to aggregate crowdsourced responses. In: Proceedings of the Thirty-Second Conference on Uncertainty in Artificial Intelligence, p. 242251. AUAI Press (2016)
16. Gunes, I., Kaleli, C., Bilge, A., Polat, H.: Shilling attacks against recommender systems: a comprehensive survey. Artif. Intell. Rev. **42**(4), 767–799 (2014)
17. Hong, C., Zhou, Y.: Label aggregation via finding consensus between models. arXiv preprint arXiv:1807.07291 (2018)
18. Huang, L., Joseph, A.D., Nelson, B., Rubinstein, B.I., Tygar, J.: Adversarial machine learning. In: Proceedings of the 4th ACM Workshop on Security and Artificial Intelligence, pp. 43–58. ACM (2011)
19. Hung, N.Q.V., Thang, D.C., Weidlich, M., Aberer, K.: Minimizing efforts in validating crowd answers. In: Proceedings of the 2015 ACM SIGMOD International Conference on Management of Data, pp. 999–1014. ACM (2015)
20. Ipeirotis, P.G., Provost, F., Wang, J.: Quality management on amazon mechanical turk. In: Proceedings of the ACM SIGKDD Workshop on Human Computation, pp. 64–67. ACM (2010)
21. Wang, J., Kraska, T., Franklin, M.J., Feng, J.: Crowdsourcing entity resolution. PVLDB **5**(11), 1483–1494 (2012)
22. Jagabathula, S., Subramanian, L., Venkataraman, A.: Reputation-based worker filtering in crowdsourcing. In: Advances in Neural Information Processing Systems, pp. 2492–2500 (2014)
23. Jagielski, M., Oprea, A., Biggio, B., Liu, C., Nita-Rotaru, C., Li, B.: Manipulating machine learning: poisoning attacks and countermeasures for regression learning. In: 2018 IEEE Symposium on Security and Privacy (SP), pp. 19–35. IEEE (2018)

24. Karger, D.R., Oh, S., Shah, D.: Iterative learning for reliable crowdsourcing systems. In: Advances in Neural Information Processing Systems, pp. 1953–1961 (2011)
25. Kim, H.C., Ghahramani, Z.: Bayesian classifier combination. In: Artificial Intelligence and Statistics, pp. 619–627 (2012)
26. Levine, B.N., Shields, C., Margolin, N.B.: A survey of solutions to the sybil attack. University of Massachusetts Amherst, Amherst, MA, vol. 7, p. 224 (2006)
27. Li, Q., et al.: A confidence-aware approach for truth discovery on long-tail data. Proc. VLDB Endow. 8(4), 425–436 (2014)
28. Li, Q., Li, Y., Gao, J., Zhao, B., Fan, W., Han, J.: Resolving conflicts in heterogeneous data by truth discovery and source reliability estimation. In: Proceedings of the 2014 ACM SIGMOD International Conference on Management of Data, pp. 1187–1198. ACM (2014)
29. Li, Y., et al.: A survey on truth discovery. ACM SIGKDD Explor. Newslett. 17(2), 1–16 (2016)
30. Miao, C., Li, Q., Su, L., Huai, M., Jiang, W., Gao, J.: Attack under disguise: an intelligent data poisoning attack mechanism in crowdsourcing. In: Proceedings of the 2018 World Wide Web Conference on World Wide Web, pp. 13–22. International World Wide Web Conferences Steering Committee (2018)
31. Miao, C., Li, Q., Xiao, H., Jiang, W., Huai, M., Su, L.: Towards data poisoning attacks in crowd sensing systems. In: Proceedings of the Eighteenth ACM International Symposium on Mobile Ad Hoc Networking and Computing, pp. 111–120. ACM (2018)
32. Mobasher, B., Burke, R., Bhaumik, R., Sandvig, J.J.: Attacks and remedies in collaborative recommendation. IEEE Intell. Syst. 22(3), 56–63 (2007)
33. Nguyen, A.T., Wallace, B.C., Lease, M.: A correlated worker model for grouped, imbalanced and multitask data. In: UAI (2016)
34. O'Mahony, M., Hurley, N., Kushmerick, N., Silvestre, G.: Collaborative recommendation: a robustness analysis. ACM Trans. Internet Technol. (TOIT) 4(4), 344–377 (2004)
35. Raykar, V.C., Yu, S.: Eliminating spammers and ranking annotators for crowdsourced labeling tasks. J. Mach. Learn. Res. 13(Feb), 491–518 (2012)
36. Raykar, V.C., et al.: Learning from crowds. J. Mach. Learn. Res. 11(Apr), 1297–1322 (2010)
37. Shafahi, A., et al.: Poison frogs! targeted clean-label poisoning attacks on neural networks. In: Advances in Neural Information Processing Systems, pp. 6106–6116 (2018)
38. Sheng, V.S., Zhang, J.: Machine learning with crowdsourcing: a brief summary of the past research and future directions. In: Proceedings of the AAAI Conference on Artificial Intelligence, vol. 33, pp. 9837–9843 (2019)
39. Stringhini, G., Mourlanne, P., Jacob, G., Egele, M., Kruegel, C., Vigna, G.: Detecting communities of malicious accounts on online services. In: 24th USENIX Security Symposium (USENIX Security 2015), pp. 563–578 (2015)
40. Suciu, O., Marginean, R., Kaya, Y., Daume III, H., Dumitras, T.: When does machine learning fail? Generalized transferability for evasion and poisoning attacks. In: 27th USENIX Security Symposium (USENIX Security 2018), pp. 1299–1316 (2018)
41. Swain, R., Berger, A., Bongard, J., Hines, P.: Participation and contribution in crowdsourced surveys. PLoS ONE 10(4), e0120521 (2015)

42. Tang, W., Lease, M.: Semi-supervised consensus labeling for crowdsourcing. In: SIGIR 2011 Workshop on Crowdsourcing for Information Retrieval (CIR), pp. 1–6 (2011)
43. Vasudeva, A., Sood, M.: Survey on sybil attack defense mechanisms in wireless ad hoc networks. J. Netw. Comput. Appl. **120**, 78–118 (2018)
44. Venanzi, M., Guiver, J., Kazai, G., Kohli, P., Shokouhi, M.: Community-based Bayesian aggregation models for crowdsourcing. In: Proceedings of the 23rd International Conference on World Wide Web, pp. 155–164. ACM (2014)
45. Wang, G., Konolige, T., Wilson, C., Wang, X., Zheng, H., Zhao, B.Y.: You are how you click: clickstream analysis for Sybil detection. Presented as part of the 22nd USENIX Security Symposium (USENIX Security 2013), pp. 241–256 (2013)
46. Wang, G., Wang, B., Wang, T., Nika, A., Zheng, H., Zhao, B.Y.: Defending against Sybil devices in crowdsourced mapping services. In: Proceedings of the 14th Annual International Conference on Mobile Systems, Applications, and Services, pp. 179–191. ACM (2016)
47. Wang, G., Wang, T., Zheng, H., Zhao, B.Y.: Man vs. machine: practical adversarial detection of malicious crowdsourcing workers. In: USENIX Security Symposium, pp. 239–254 (2014)
48. Whitehill, J., Wu, T.F., Bergsma, J., Movellan, J.R., Ruvolo, P.L.: Whose vote should count more: optimal integration of labels from labelers of unknown expertise. In: Advances in Neural Information Processing Systems, pp. 2035–2043 (2009)
49. Yang, Z., Wilson, C., Wang, X., Gao, T., Zhao, B.Y., Dai, Y.: Uncovering social network Sybils in the wild. ACM Trans. Knowl. Discov. Data (TKDD) **8**(1), 2 (2014)
50. Yin, L., Han, J., Zhang, W., Yu, Y.: Aggregating crowd wisdoms with label-aware autoencoders. In: Proceedings of the 26th International Joint Conference on Artificial Intelligence, pp. 1325–1331. AAAI Press (2017)
51. Yu, H., Kaminsky, M., Gibbons, P.B., Flaxman, A.: Sybilguard: defending against Sybil attacks via social networks. ACM SIGCOMM Comput. Commun. Rev. **36**(4), 267–278 (2006)
52. Yu, H., Shi, C., Kaminsky, M., Gibbons, P.B., Xiao, F.: DSybil: optimal Sybil-resistance for recommendation systems. In: 2009 30th IEEE Symposium on Security and Privacy, pp. 283–298. IEEE (2009)
53. Yuan, D., Li, G., Li, Q., Zheng, Y.: Sybil defense in crowdsourcing platforms. In: Proceedings of the 2017 ACM on Conference on Information and Knowledge Management, pp. 1529–1538. ACM (2017)
54. Zhang, K., Liang, X., Lu, R., Shen, X.: Sybil attacks and their defenses in the Internet of Things. IEEE Internet Things J. **1**(5), 372–383 (2014)
55. Zhang, Y., Tan, Y., Zhang, M., Liu, Y., Chua, T.S., Ma, S.: Catch the black sheep: unified framework for shilling attack detection based on fraudulent action propagation. In: Twenty-Fourth International Joint Conference on Artificial Intelligence (2015)
56. Zheng, Y., Li, G., Li, Y., Shan, C., Cheng, R.: Truth inference in crowdsourcing: is the problem solved? Proc. VLDB Endow. **10**(5), 541–552 (2017)
57. Zhou, D., Basu, S., Mao, Y., Platt, J.C.: Learning from the wisdom of crowds by minimax entropy. In: Advances in Neural Information Processing Systems, pp. 2195–2203 (2012)
58. Zhou, Y., He, J.: Crowdsourcing via tensor augmentation and completion. In: IJCAI, pp. 2435–2441 (2016)
59. Zhou, Y., Ying, L., He, J.: MultiC2: an optimization framework for learning from task and worker dual heterogeneity. In: Proceedings of the 2017 SIAM International Conference on Data Mining, pp. 579–587. SIAM (2017)

Self-enhancing GPS-Based Authentication Using Corresponding Address

Tran Phuong Thao$^{(\boxtimes)}$, Mhd Irvan, Ryosuke Kobayashi,
Rie Shigetomi Yamaguchi, and Toshiyuki Nakata

Graduate School of Information Science and Technology, The University of Tokyo,
Bunkyo, Japan
{tpthao,irvan}@yamagula.ic.i.u-tokyo.ac.jp,
{kobayashi.ryousuke,nakata.toshiyuki}@sict.i.u-tokyo.ac.jp,
yamaguchi.rie@i.u-tokyo.ac.jp

Abstract. Behavioral-based authentication is a new research approach for user authentication. A promising idea for this approach is to use location history as the behavioral features for the user classification because location history is relatively unique even when there are many people living in the same area and even when the people have occasional travel, it does not vary from day to day. For Global Positioning System (GPS) location data, most of the previous work used longitude and latitude values. In this paper, we investigate the advantage of metadata extracted from the longitude and latitude themselves without the need to require any other information other than the longitude and latitude. That is the location identification name (i.e., the address). Our idea is based on the fact that given a pair of longitude and latitude, there is a corresponding address. This is why we use the term *self-enhancing* in the title. We then applied text mining on the address and combined the extracted text features with the longitude and latitude for the features of the classification. The result showed that the combination approach outperforms the GPS approach using Adaptive Boosting and Gradient Boosting algorithms.

Keywords: Location-based authentication · Lifestyle authentication · Global Positioning System (GPS) · Text mining · Reverse geocoding

1 Introduction

Japan aims to become the first country in the world to achieve Society 5.0 (after Society 1.0 (the hunting society), Society 2.0 (agricultural society), Society 3.0 (industrial society), and Society 4.0 (information society)) which is defined as: "A human-centered society that balances economic advancement with the resolution of social problems by a system that highly integrates cyberspace (virtual space) and physical space (real space)" according to the Government of Japan [1]. It sets a blueprint for a super-smart society with the support of Artificial Intelligent

© IFIP International Federation for Information Processing 2020
Published by Springer Nature Switzerland AG 2020
A. Singhal and J. Vaidya (Eds.): DBSec 2020, LNCS 12122, pp. 333–344, 2020.
https://doi.org/10.1007/978-3-030-49669-2_19

(AI) and cutting-edge technology. Let's consider an example of the payment system. In 1946, John Biggins invented a credit card which can be used to replace paper money. In 2011, Google was the first company to launch a project of mobile wallet which can be used to replace physical cash and even credit cards. Nowadays, the cashless payment system becomes a recent trend and many digital wallet services appeared such as Apple Pay (from 2014), Google Pay (from 2015 as Android Pay and from 2018 as Google Pay), Rakuten Pay (from 2016), etc. The biggest challenge for such payment systems is how to authenticate (verify) the users. The current approach is to rely on the authentication of the mobile phones using PIN code, biometrics information (i.e., fingerprinting, iris, palm vein, etc), or multi-factor method.

Motivation. Toward the construction for a smarter mobile-based authentication system, we have several research questions. First, several studies found that a large number of users do not lock their smartphones such as 33% by B. Dirk et al. [20], 29% by S. Egelman et al. [21], 48% by L. Fridman et al. [12], or even 57% by M. Harbach et al. [22]. So we ask the question: *Is there an additional mobile-based authentication method that can support the conventional method like using PIN code or biometrics information?*. Second, in the current cashless payment system, even though the users do not need to bring their credit cards, they have to bring their phones. So, we ask another question: *Is it "human-centered" enough? Whether a new authentication system can be done via smaller wearable devices such as smartwatches, RFID chips, or satellite sensors rather than the smartphone?*. Third, imaging the scenario that a person is on the way going to a coffee shop. Before he/she arrives, the coffee shop can predict that he/she will arrive 10 min later with a high probability, and prepares in advance his/her usual order, and will automatically subtract the charge from his account. The person then does not need to wait time for the order and payment process. So, the final question is: *Is it possible to authenticate and predict the location (for example, the coffee shop) that the users are likely going to?*

An idea that can answer these questions is using behavioral (or habit)-based information. There are very few studies focusing on it due to the challenge of how to decide behavioral information for authentication. Inspirited from L. Fridman et al. [12], GPS location history is the most promising approach because "It is relatively unique to each individual even for people living in the same area of a city. Also, outside of occasional travel, it does not vary significantly from day to day. Human beings are creatures of habit, and in as much as location is a measure of habit". If we can construct a payment system in which the users do not need to bring anything even small wearable devices such as smartwatches or RFID chips (e.g., the data can be collected via satellite sensors) and which can replace the conventional biometrics authentication, it is a successful achievement for the Society 5.0 goal.

Contribution. Most of the previous papers utilized longitude and latitude of GPS as the features in the classification machine learning models for the user authentication. In this paper, we propose an idea of extracting metadata of the

GPS itself without the need to request any other information besides the GPS. That is the location identification name (i.e., the address) which can be inferred from the longitude and latitude. We then applied text mining on the address and combined the extracted text features with the longitude and latitude for the learning features. We made an experiment to see how the combination approach is compared with the approach using only the GPS.

Considering it reasonability, it may raise the discussion that since the address can be inferred from a pair of longitude and latitude (i.e., using reverse geocoding), so whether the entropy of the address is the same as that of the GPS (in other words, whether the address gives no additional information to the GPS). However, we should remark that, for machine learning, a pair of two float numbers (i.e., longitude and latitude) and a string of text (i.e., address) are totally different and independent. Therefore, we hypothesized that the combination approach may add a certain amount of information to the approach using only GPS. Furthermore, the model using GPS and address, of course, can be improved if they can combine with other factors such as date times, indoor location history like wifi information, web browser log, etc. However, the goal in this paper is to make clear whether information (i.e., the GPS) along with the metadata extracted from that information itself (i.e., the address) can be helpful for the better classification model. We thus excluded other factors to make the comparison clean.

To evaluate how the feasibility of our hypothesis is, concretely, we collected 14,655 GPS records from 50 users. We extracted the corresponding address using reverse geocoding. We applied text mining on the address and obtained 3,803 text features using the term frequency-inverse document frequency. We performed multi-class classification using different ensemble algorithms on total of 3,805 scaled features including longitude, latitude, and text features. The result showed that the combination approach outperforms the approach using only the GPS with the Adaptive Boosting and Gradient Boosting ensemble algorithms.

Roadmap. The rest of this paper is organized as follows. The related work is described in Sect. 2. The proposed idea is presented in Sect. 3. The experiment is given in Sect. 4. The discussion is mentioned in Sect. 5. Finally, the conclusion is drawn in Sect. 6.

2   Related Work

2.1   Multimodal Location-Based Authentication

The term *multi-modal* (not multi-model) is used in biometrics authentication to indicate multiple biometric data; it is opposite with *unimodal* that uses only a single biometric data. L. Fridman et al. [12] collected behavioral data of four modalities collected from active mobile devices including text stylometry typed on a soft keyboard, application usage patterns, web browsing behavior, and physical location of the device from GPS and Wifi. The authors proposed a location-based classification method and showed that its performance is applicable to an actual authentication system. W. Shi et al. [14] proposed an authentication framework that enables continuous and implicit user identification service for a smartphone. The data is collected from four sensor modalities including voice, GPS location, multitouch, and locomotion. A. Alejandro et al. [15] analyzed their behavior-based signals obtained from the smartphone sensors including touch dynamics (gestures and keystroking), accelerometer, gyroscope, WiFi, GPS location and app usage. They proposed two authentication models including the one-time approach that uses all the channel information available during one session, and the active approach that uses behavioral data from multiple sessions by updating a confidence score. B. Aaron et al. [16] proposed a wallet repository that can store biometric data using multiple layers: biometric layer, a genomic layer, a health layer, a privacy layer, and a processing layer. The processing layer can be used to determine and track the user location, the speed when the user is moving using GPS data. R. Valentin et al. [17] presented the context of multimodal sensing modalities with mobile devices when the GPS, accelerometer, and audio signals are utilized for human recognition. They then discussed several challenges for modality fusion such as imbalance distribution when the GPS samples have to be correlated to accelerometer readings.

2.2   Learning from Metadata

We introduce related work that utilize metadata extracted from the main information to gain additional knowledge or the accuracy like our paper. T. Thao et al. [11] proposed a classification method of landing and distribution webpages from drive-by-download attack. A landing webpage is the original webpage that the victim visits while a distribution webpage is the final webpage that exploits malware in the redirection chain of the attack. While most of the previous papers analyze the characteristics around the landing and distribution webpages themselves (e.g., the HTML content, the pattern of the URL, etc.), this paper found the benefits when using the metadata from the webpages. Concretely, they extracted the registration information from the domain of the webpages called Whois. Whois contains registration name, organization, registration date, update date, expiration date, address, email, etc. They then applied text mining to the Whois documents and proved that the method can increase the classification accuracy. Similarly, Whois was also used to distinguish whether a homograph domain is registered by brand companies or by attackers [23]. A Castiglione et al. [18] analyzed the format extracted from a plain-text document using digital forensics and found that such kind of evidence in the forensic environment can provide a lot of valuable hidden information such as author name, organizational information of users involved, previously deleted text, and machine-related information. B. Duy et el. [19] proposed a classification method to extract the data from a PDF document. Besides using the information from the documents itself such as title, abstract, body-text, and semi-structure, the authors used metadata surround the document including publication information (i.e., authorship, affiliation, bibliography), journal name, header and footer, and references. Their method can improve 9.7% of accuracy from the best performing algorithm.

3   Our Method

3.1   Data Collection

The data is collected from 50 Internet users who installed a smartphone navigation application (named MITHRA (Multi-factor Identification/auTHentication ReseArch)) created by a project of the University of Tokyo. The application runs in the background and collects the GPS data including the longitude and latitude. The application works for both Android and iOS versions. The data is collected for four months from January 11th to April 26th in 2017. Although the GPS was collected from smartphones in this project, nowadays, GPS can be collected from smaller devices such as smartwatch or smartband.

The privacy agreement is showed during the installation process. The application installation is only done if the users accept the agreement. Even after the installation is finished, the users can choose to start participating or stop using the application anytime during the experimental period. The project was reviewed by the Ethics Review Committee of the Graduate School of Information Science and Technology, the University of Tokyo. No personal information such as age, name, race, ethnicity, income, education, etc. is collected. Only the email address is used as the user identity in the collected data. Finally, all 50 users agreed to participate in our project.

The total number of samples (i.e., GPS records including pairs of longitude and latitude) from the 50 users is 14,655. Each user has a different number of samples that range from 67 to 999. The distribution curve and distribution summary of the number of samples are described in Fig. 1. The Kurtosis and Skewness scores are computed as 1.864 and 1.537, respectively. Both of the scores lie in the range $[-2, +2]$ which are acceptable for normal distribution [2,4,5].

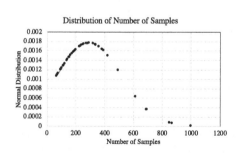

Metric	Value
Mean	293.100
Standard Error	31.899
Median	237.000
Standard Deviation	225.561
Kurtosis	1.864
Skewness	1.537
Range	932.000
Min	67.000
Max	999.000
Confidence Level (95.0 %)	64.104

Fig. 1. Distribution curve and distribution summary of the number of samples

3.2   Feature Selection

All the samples are unique for each user. Each GPS sample is a pair of a longitude and a latitude represented by two float numbers with 6 decimal digits, and can be positive or negative values.

Address Extraction. Reverse geocoding is the process of reverse coding of a pair of latitude and longitude to a corresponding address. There are several reverse geocoding methods but we use Google's reverse geocoding [3] since it is the most reliable, fast, and stable. Especially, different from other services, Google's reverse geocoding can provide pinpoint addresses. For each request containing a pair of longitude and latitude, the service returns the addresses and the corresponding tags with the following values: *rooftop* (the most precise geocode), *range interpolated* (the address is interpolated between two precise points like intersections), *geometric center* (such as a polyline (street) or polygon (region)), and *approximate* (the approximated address). Since it is possible that multiple addresses with different tags are returned, we sorted each tag in the descending order of precision scale (rooftop → range interpolated → geometric center → approximate) and selected the first one (the most precise one).

Address Text Mining. Given the address texts, the word tokenization is perform to build a dictionary of features. The texts are then transformed to feature vectors. N-grams of words which are the sequences of N consecutive characters from the given words are counted. Let $T = \{t_1, t_2, \cdots, t_n\}$ denote the set of n texts t_i for $i = [1, n]$. Given a word w, the *Term Frequency* (tf) of w in t_i and the *Inverse Document Frequency* (idf) used for measuring how much information that w provides or whether w is common or rare in all the texts T are computed as: $tf(w, t_i) = \frac{occ(w, t_i)}{|corpus(t_i)|}$ and $idf(w, T) = log(\frac{1+n}{1+df(w,T)}) + 1$ where $corpus(t_i)$ denotes the set of all tokenized unique words in t_i. $|corpus(t_i)|$ denotes its length. $occ(w, t_i)$ denotes the occurrence count of w in t_i. $df(w, T)$ denotes the number of text $t_i \in T$ that contains w. The *Term Frequency Inverse Document Frequency* ($tf\text{-}idf$) is then computed to downscale weights of w that may occur in many texts: $tf\text{-}idf(w, t_i) = tf(w, t_i) \cdot idf(w, T)$. Finally, each word tokenized from the texts is used as a feature with its $tf\text{-}idf$.

Feature Scaling. While the longitude and the latitude range from $[-180, +180]$ and from $[-90, +90]$ respectively, the text features mostly range from $(0, 1]$. We thus use *Standard* (*Z-score*) scaling to normalize the features. For a given original feature f_x, the new standard for f_x is computed as: $f'_x = \frac{f_x - \mu}{\sigma}$ where μ and σ denote the mean and the standard deviation of the training samples, respectively. Standard scaling rescales the features by subtracting the mean and scaling the features to unit variance (the data distribution is centered around 0 and a standard deviation of 1).

3.3   Training

There are multiple users and each user has a different set of data. The conventional solution is the one-class classification in which each label corresponds to each user. However, when the number of users is large, the authentication performance can be low. Furthermore, if there is a new user participating in the system, it is not scalable since the classification should be trained again. Therefore, the one-class classification is transformed into a more lightweight approach known as the multi-class classification. Each user has a different classifier with binary classes representing whether or not a new sample belongs to that user.

One-vs-rest Multi-class Classification. We use *One-vs-rest* strategy that consists in fitting one classifier per class (the samples belonging to the considered class are labelled as positive and the other samples of the other classes are marked as negatives). Suppose there are q classifiers c_i where $i \in \{1, \cdots, q\}$. Given a new sample x, the one-vs-rest approach classifies x into the label k such that: $\hat{y} = \text{argmax } c_k(x)$ where $k \in \{1, \cdots, q\}$ and all the classifiers are applied to x and predict k which has the highest confidence score. $\hat{y}$ represents the approximate score. Besides the computational efficiency and scalability when there is a new class, an advantage of this approach is the interpretability. The learner can gain knowledge about the class by inspecting its corresponding classifier.

Ensemble Algorithms for One-vs-rest. Since our data contains a large number of samples (14,655) with a large number of features (3,805), instead of using traditional algorithms we use advanced *ensemble techniques*. The ensemble technique combines base estimators to produce one optimal predictive estimator with better performance using two approaches: boosting and averaging. In boosting approach, the base estimators are built sequentially. Each base estimator is used to correct and reduce the bias of its predecessor. We use two algorithms AdaBoost [6] (Adaptive Boost) and Gradient Boost [7]. In averaging approach, the estimators are built independently and their predictions are then averaged based on the aggregated results. The combined estimator reduces the variance. We use three algorithms: ExtraTrees [8], Bagging [9] (Bootstrap Aggregating), and Random Rorest [10].

3.4   Validation

Stratified KFold. First, the data is shuffled. The numbers of samples of the classes are imbalanced, ranging from 66 to 999 (0.45% to 6.82% of 14,655 samples). Using normal k-fold cross validation can lead to the problem that there may exist a class such that all the samples from the class belong to the test set, and the training set does not contain any of them. The classifier then cannot learn about the class. We thus used *Stratified k-fold* to deal with such imbalanced data. It splits the data in the train and the test sets and returns stratified folds made by preserving the percentage of samples for each class.

Metrics. To evaluate the model, we measure the accuracy (acc), precision (pre), recal (rec), and F1 score ($F1$) with the following formulas: $acc = \frac{tp+tn}{tp+fp+fn+tn}$, $pre = \frac{tp}{tp+fp}$, $rec = \frac{tp}{tp+fn}$, $F1 = 2 \times \frac{rec \times pre}{rec+pre}$ where tp, tn, fp, fn denote the true positive, true negative, false positive, and false negative values obtained from the confusion matrix, respectively. Accuracy is a good metric when the class distribution is similar; but for imbalanced classes F1-score is a better metric.

4 Experiment

We use Python 3.7.4 on a MacBook Pro 2.8 GHz Intel Core i7, RAM 16 GB. The addresses are extracted using Google reverse geocoding [3]. The machine learning algorithms are executed using *scikit-learn* 0.22 [13].

4.1 Parameter Setting and Data Pre-processing

Our experiment is designed with three different plans. Let #class, n, λ, η denote the number of classes, the number of samples, the number of text features, and the number of combined features. The first plan is #class $= 10$, $n = 2,671$, $\lambda = 836$, $\eta = 838$. The second plan is #class $= 30$, $n = 9,068$, $\lambda = 2,514$, $\eta = 2,516$. The third plan is #class $= 50$, $n = 14,655$, $\lambda = 3,803$, $\eta = 3,805$. All the five ensemble algorithms are performed with three approaches (using the GPS only, using the address only, and using the combined GPS and address). For each algorithm, the number of base estimators is set to $n\_estimators = 100$. The feature scaling is necessary for the third approach. Since all the addresses are fortunately returned with the rooftop tags, we can obtain the most precise address. k in the stratified k-fold is set to $k = 2$. Since the labels of the classes are independent categories represented in string type (i.e., 'user1', 'user2', etc.), we transformed the categorical labels to numerical values using *label encoding* which is the most lightweight and uses less disk space (compared with ordinal encoding or one-hot encoding). Since the data is imbalanced, to avoid the situation that F1 cannot be between precision and recall, we calculate the precision, recall, and F1 score for each label and find their average weight by the number of true instances of each class using the parameter $average = $ 'weighted' in the *sklearn.metrics*. For the accuracy, this parameter is not necessary.

4.2 Result

The result is shown in Table 1. All the scores are reduced when the number of classes is increased. It is common for most of the multi-class classifications. The result shows that using the address only cannot beat using the GPS only. Let $\triangle$ denote the difference of F1 score between the combination approach and using only the GPS. The magnitude $|\triangle|$ is increased when the number of classes is increased. $\triangle$ is negative for ExtraTrees, Random Forest, and Bagging but is positive for AdaBoost and GradientBoost. It indicates that the combination approach outperforms the GPS approach using the ensemble boosting algorithms. Therefore, we suggest using the boosting algorithms for our approach.

Table 1. GPS-based, address-based, and combination approaches

Alg.	Score (%)	#Classes = 10				#Classes = 30				#Classes = 50			
		LL	A	LLA	△	LL	A	LLA	△	LL	A	LLA	△
AdaBoost	Acc	99.36	99.21	99.40		96.79	96.44	97.29		95.09	95.04	95.67	
	Pre	99.43	99.28	99.45		96.86	96.54	97.32		95.26	95.25	95.80	
	Rec	99.36	99.21	99.40		96.79	96.44	97.29		95.09	95.04	95.67	
	F1	99.37	99.23	99.41	+0.04	96.78	96.44	97.28	+0.50	95.11	95.07	95.70	+0.59
GradientBoost	Acc	99.74	99.51	99.81		97.24	97.07	97.35		95.55	95.36	95.91	
	Pre	99.74	99.52	99.82		97.29	97.11	97.39		95.63	95.46	96.05	
	Rec	99.74	99.51	99.81		97.24	97.07	97.35		95.55	95.36	95.91	
	F1	99.74	99.51	99.81	+0.07	97.21	97.06	97.35	+0.14	95.55	95.36	95.94	+0.39
ExtraTrees	Acc	99.59	99.18	99.14		98.14	97.14	97.35		97.78	96.02	96.28	
	Pre	99.60	99.19	99.15		98.16	97.17	97.37		97.80	96.05	96.31	
	Rec	99.59	99.18	99.14		98.14	97.14	97.35		97.78	96.02	96.28	
	F1	99.59	99.17	99.13	−0.46	98.13	97.10	97.33	−0.80	97.78	96.01	96.28	−1.50
Random Forest	Acc	99.70	99.14	99.44		97.93	96.85	97.06		97.33	95.58	95.79	
	Pre	99.71	99.16	99.45		97.95	96.85	97.08		97.37	95.60	95.87	
	Rec	99.70	99.14	99.44		97.93	96.85	97.06		97.33	95.58	95.79	
	F1	99.70	99.12	99.44	−0.26	97.92	96.81	97.03	−0.89	97.33	95.56	95.79	−1.54
Bagging	Acc	99.59	99.44	99.55		97.81	97.03	97.44		97.07	95.61	96.23	
	Pre	99.60	99.45	99.57		97.82	97.11	97.49		97.13	95.65	96.27	
	Rec	99.59	99.44	99.55		97.81	97.03	97.44		97.07	95.61	96.23	
	F1	99.59	99.44	99.55	−0.04	97.78	97.03	97.43	−0.35	97.07	95.59	96.22	−0.85

(LL): the GPS approach, (A): the address approach, (LLA): the combination approach Acc: accuracy, Pre: precision, Rec: recall

4.3 Analysis

We analyze how well the data points fit the data mean in boosting and averaging algorithms by measuring the variance and the bias. Let y and $\hat{y}$ denote the true samples and the predicted samples. The variance is calculated as: $var(\hat{y}) = \frac{\sum(x_i - \bar{x})}{n-1}$ where x_i, $\bar{x}$, and n denote the sample in the dataset, the sample mean, and the number of samples. The bias is calculated as: $bias(\hat{y}) = mean((mean(\hat{y}) - y)^2) - var(\hat{y}) - 0.01$ where $mean((mean(\hat{y}) - y)^2)$ is the sum of squared errors. We set the number of estimators varying $\{1, 2, \cdots, 10\}$. We choose the second plan ($\#class = 30$, $n = 9,068$) for the analysis. The graphs of variance and bias are showed in Figs. 2 and 3. Ten curves GPS(Ada), Com(Ada), GPS(Gra), Com(Gra), GPs(Ext), Com(Ext), GPS(Ran), Com(Ran), GPS(Bag), and Com(Bag) represent the GPS approach or the combination approach using the five algorithms with the first 3 letters as the abbreviations.

In Fig. 2, the variances are separated into two different groups. The first group that has higher variance score includes only the combination approach regardless of which algorithm is used. The other group includes the remaining curves which are only the GPS approach regardless of which algorithm is used. This indicates that the text features make the data samples spread out from the mean and from one another rather than the GPS. In both the groups, the averaging algorithms give a higher variance than the boosting algorithms for the first estimator. After a number of estimators, the variances become convergent and constant in each group. Considering the bias in Fig. 3, there is no separation like the variance.

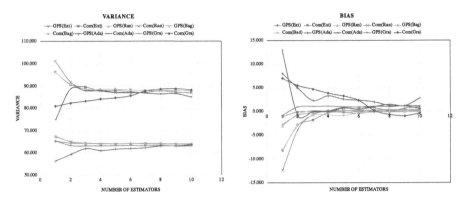

Fig. 2. Variance   **Fig. 3.** Bias

Also, the boosting algorithms give higher bias than the averaging algorithms for both the GPS and combination approaches. After a number of estimators, the bias becomes convergent to zero. It is reasonable when there is a trade-off between the variance and bias. In summary, while the GPS approach give low bias and lower variance, the combination approach gives low bias and higher variance since text features may contain more noise. Higher variance does not mean lower accuracy or F1. It just explains how the data samples spread out from the mean and from one another.

5   Discussion

In this section, we present our plans for future work and the threat model.

Feature Improvement. First, the addresses were extracted in English. Since most of the collected GPS records are in Japan, applying semantic text mining on Japanese addresses may have some other meanings. For example, "Minato-ku" means the name of a ward in Tokyo, but in Japanese Kanji, it also means a port; and in fact, Minato ward is near to a port. It is possible since the Google reverse geocoding supports the Japanese language. Second, we used (tf-idf) as the text features in the current experiment. tf-idf is used when the lengths of every text are too different, so it is possible that a word may occur much more times in long texts than shorter texts. However, the addresses have almost the same length, the word occurrence count or tf may be enough for the text features. Third, the standard scaling was used for normalizing the features. Combining it with other feature scalings (e.g., Robust scaling) may give some extra information. Four, the number of features extracted from the addresses is large, e.g., 3,805 features for 50 users. To improve the accuracy, the number of features can be reduced by selecting only the most important features. A threshold ϕ can be determined, then only the top features with tf-$idf \geq \phi$ are chosen. A large ϕ is not necessary since all the algorithms are compared in the same dataset and parameter setting, so it is fair.

Threat Model and Other Behavioral Data. In such authentication system, the threat model deals with insider attack in which an authorized user tries to obtain the authentication from the other authorized users. Collusion attack (the authorized users in the system share their data together) and outsider attack (i.e., network eavesdropping, device hacking, etc.) are assumed in the model. Mitigating the attack can be done via improving the authentication accuracy. Proposing new approaches to achieve a high accuracy with a low false positive rate is the main goal in such authentication system. Besides extending the GPS collection, we launched a project to collect other behavioral data, i.e., calorie burning, distance, heart rate, ladders, sleep, speed, steps using wearable devices like smartwatch. A first result from this project can be found in [24]. Integrating different behavioral data for authentication is a future work.

6   Conclusion

In this paper, we proved that the GPS-based authentication can improve itself using its metadata. The address can be inferred from the GPS without the need to extract any other information. We collected 14,655 GPS records from 50 users. We extracted the address using the reverse geocoding. We applied text mining on the addresses and selected 3,803 text features using the tf-idf. Ensemble boosting and averaging algorithms are applied to the multi-class classification. The result showed that the combining approach outperforms the GPS approach using AdaBoost and GradientBoost.

References

1. Cabinet Office, the Government of Japan, Society 5.0. https://www8.cao.go.jp/cstp/english/society5_0/index.html
2. George, D., Mallery, P.: SPSS for Windows Step by Step: A Simple Guide and Reference (17.0 Update). Allyn and Bacon, Boston (2010)
3. Google Geocoding and Reverse Geocoding. https://developers.google.com/maps/documentation/geocoding/intro
4. Thao, T.P., et al.: Influences of human demographics, brand familiarity and security backgrounds on homograph recognition. arXiv:1904.10595 (2020)
5. Thao, T., et al.: Human factors in homograph attack recognition. In: 18th International Conference on Applied Cryptography and Network Security (ACNS 2020) (2020)
6. Zhu, J., Hui, Z., Saharon, R., Thevor, H.: Multi-class AdaBoost. Stat. Interface **2**, 349–360 (2009)
7. Friedman, J.: Greedy function approximation: a gradient boosting machine. Ann. Stat. **29**(5), 1189–1232 (2001)
8. Geurts, P., Damien, E., Wehenkel, L.: Extremely randomized trees. Mach. Learn. **63**(1), 3–42 (2006)
9. Louppe, G., Geurts, P.: Ensembles on random patches. In: Flach, P.A., De Bie, T., Cristianini, N. (eds.) ECML PKDD 2012. LNCS (LNAI), vol. 7523, pp. 346–361. Springer, Heidelberg (2012). https://doi.org/10.1007/978-3-642-33460-3_28

10. Breiman, L.: Random forests. Mach. Learn. **45**(1), 5–32 (2001)
11. Thao, T., Yamada, A., Murakami, K., Urakawa, J., Sawaya, Y., Kubota, A.: Classification of landing and distribution domains using Whois's text mining. In: 16th IEEE Conference on Trust, Security and Privacy in Computing and Communications (IEEE TrustCom-17), pp. 1–8 (2017)
12. Fridman, L., Steven, W., Rachel, G., Moshe, K.: Active authentication on mobile devices via stylometry, application usage, web browsing, and GPS location. IEEE Syst. J. **11**(2), 513–521 (2016)
13. Scikit-learn. scikit-learn.org
14. Shi, W., Yang, J., Jiang, Y., Yang, F., Xiong, Y.: SenGuard: passive user identification on smartphones using multiple sensors. In: IEEE 7th Conference on Wireless and Mobile Computing, Networking and Communications (WiMob 2011), pp 141–148 (2011)
15. Alejandro, A., Aythami, M., Vera-Rodriguez, R., Julian, F., Ruben, T.: MultiLock: mobile active authentication based on multiple biometric and behavioral patterns. In: Multimodal Understanding and Learning for Embodied Applications (MULEA 2019), pp. 53–59 (2019)
16. Aaron, B., Christopher, D., Barry, G., David, K.: System and method for real world biometric analytics through the use of a multimodal biometric analytic wallet. US patent, US20180276362A1 (2018)
17. Radu, V., et al.: Multimodal deep learning for activity and context recognition. In: Interactive, Mobile, Wearable and Ubiquitous Technologies (IMWUT 2018), Article no. 157 (2018)
18. Castiglione, A., Santis, A., Soriente, C.: Taking advantages of a disadvantage: digital forensics and steganography using document metadata. J. Syst. Softw. **80**(5), 750–764 (2007)
19. Duy, B., Guilherme, F., Siddhartha, J.: PDF text classification to leverage information extraction from publication reports. J. Biomed. Inform. **61**, 141–148 (2016)
20. Dirk, B., Shu, L., Mitch, K., Aaron, S., Charles, C., John, D.: Modifying smartphone user locking behavior. In: 9th SOUPS 2013 Symposium, article no. 10, pp. 1–14 (2013)
21. Egelman, S., Jain, S., Portnoff, R., Liao, K., Consolvo, S., Wagner, D.: Are you ready to lock? In: ACM Conference on Computer and Communications Security (CCS 2014), pp. 750–761 (2014)
22. Harbach, M., Zezschwitz, E., Fichtner, A., Luca, A., Smith, M.: It's a hard lock life: a field study of smartphone (un)locking behavior and risk perception. In: 10th USENIX Conference on Usable Privacy and Security (SOUP 2014), pp. 213–230 (2014)
23. Thao, T., Sawaya, Y., Nguyen-Son, H., Yamada, A., Omote, K., Kubota, A.: Hunting brand domain forgery: a scalable classification for homograph attack. In: 34th International Information Security and Privacy Conference (IFIP Sec 2019), pp. 3–18 (2019)
24. Thao, T., Takahashi, M., Shigeta, N., Irvan, M., Nakata, T., Yamaguchi, R.: Human factors in exhaustion and stress of Japanese nursery teachers: evidence from regression model on a novel dataset. In: 13th International Conference on Advances in Computer-Human Interactions (ACHI 2020) (2020)

Secure Outsourcing and Privacy

GOOSE: A Secure Framework for Graph Outsourcing and SPARQL Evaluation

Radu Ciucanu[1]([⊠]) and Pascal Lafourcade[2]

[1] INSA Centre Val de Loire, Univ. Orléans, LIFO EA 4022, Orléans, France
`radu.ciucanu@insa-cvl.fr`
[2] Université Clermont Auvergne, LIMOS CNRS UMR 6158, Clermont-Ferrand,
France
`pascal.lafourcade@uca.fr`

Abstract. We address the security concerns that occur when outsourcing graph data and query evaluation to an *honest-but-curious* cloud i.e., that executes tasks dutifully, but tries to gain as much information as possible. We present GOOSE, a secure framework for Graph OutsOurcing and SPARQL Evaluation. GOOSE relies on cryptographic schemes and secure multi-party computation to achieve desirable security properties: (i) no cloud node can learn the graph, (ii) no cloud node can learn at the same time the query and the query answers, and (iii) an external network observer cannot learn the graph, the query, or the query answers. As query language, GOOSE supports *Unions of Conjunctions of Regular Path Queries* (UCRPQ) that are at the core of the W3C's SPARQL 1.1, including recursive queries. We show that the overhead due to cryptographic schemes is linear in the input's and output's size. We empirically show the scalability of GOOSE via a large-scale experimental study.

Keywords: Unions of Conjunctions of Regular Path Queries · Secure SPARQL evaluation · Secure graph outsourcing · Honest-but-curious cloud

1 Introduction

Outsourcing data and computations to a public cloud gained increasing popularity over the last years. Many cloud providers offer an important amount of data storage and computation power at a reasonable price e.g., Google Cloud Platform, Amazon Web Services, Microsoft Azure. However, cloud providers do not usually address the fundamental problem of protecting data security. The outsourced data can be communicated over some network and processed on some machines where malicious cloud admins could learn and leak sensitive data. We address the data security issues that occur when outsourcing an RDF graph database to a public cloud and querying the outsourced graph with SPARQL.

We depict the considered scenario in Fig. 1, where a *data owner* outsources a graph to the cloud, then a *user* is allowed to query the graph by submitting

© IFIP International Federation for Information Processing 2020
Published by Springer Nature Switzerland AG 2020
A. Singhal and J. Vaidya (Eds.): DBSec 2020, LNCS 12122, pp. 347–366, 2020.
https://doi.org/10.1007/978-3-030-49669-2_20

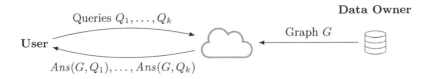

Fig. 1. Outsourcing data and computations.

queries to the cloud, which computes and returns the queries' answers to the user. Our scenario is inspired by the *database as a service* cloud computing service model, which usually considers relational databases, and security is well-known as a major concern [8]: "*A significant barrier to deploying databases in the cloud is the perceived lack of privacy, which in turn reduces the degree of trust users are willing to place in the system.*" A typical solution to this concern (developed in systems such as CryptDB [18]) is to outsource encrypted data and use SQL-aware encryption schemes to answer queries directly on encrypted data.

Although SQL and SPARQL share some common functionalities, adapting a system such as CryptDB to securely answer SPARQL queries on outsourced graphs is not trivial because SPARQL allows to naturally express classes of queries that are cumbersome to express in SQL. This is the case for the recursive queries, which can be easily expressed using the Kleene star in the property paths of SPARQL 1.1[1]. To express such recursive queries in SQL, one needs to define recursive views. After analyzing the source code of the SQL parser inside CryptDB[2], we concluded that such queries are beyond the scope of CryptDB and it is unclear how hard it is to extend their system to support recursive queries.

We propose GOOSE, a framework for Graph OutsOurcing and SPARQL Evaluation, which allows the data owner to securely outsource to the cloud a graph that can be then queried by the user. We assume that the cloud is *honest-but-curious* i.e., executes tasks dutifully, but tries to gain as much information as possible. Similarly to CryptDB, GOOSE evaluates queries on encrypted data without any change to the query engine, which in our case is the standard Apache Jena for evaluating SPARQL queries. As query language, GOOSE supports *Unions of Conjunctions of Regular Path Queries* (UCRPQ) that are at the core of the W3C's SPARQL 1.1, including recursive queries via the Kleene star.

The key ingredients of GOOSE are: (i) *secure multi-party computation* i.e., the graph storage is distributed among 3 cloud participants, which can jointly compute the query answers for each submitted query, but none of the cloud participants can learn the graph, and none of the cloud participants can learn at the same time the query and the answers of the query on the graph, and (ii) *cryptographic schemes* i.e., all messages exchanged between GOOSE participants are encrypted with AES-CBC [1,5] such that an external network observer cannot learn the graph, the query, or the answers of the query on the graph.

---

[1] https://www.w3.org/TR/sparql11-property-paths/.
[2] https://css.csail.mit.edu/cryptdb/#Software.

Related Work. GOOSE follows a recent line of research on tackling the security concerns related to RDF graph data storage and querying [10–12, 14–16].

The state-of-the-art system for query evaluation on encrypted graphs is HDT_{crypt} [11], which focuses on (non-recursive) SPARQL queries defined as triple patterns. HDT_{crypt} combines HDT (a compression technique useful for reducing RDF storage space) and encryption (to hide particular subgraphs from unauthorized users). Our work is complementary to this related research direction since we assume that query evaluation is outsourced to the cloud and our security goals are different from theirs: we want to avoid that the cloud nodes and network observer learn the entire graph, queries or query answers, whereas their goal is to allow multiple users with different access rights to query the graph. A common idea between HDT compression and our GOOSE is to map nodes and edge labels to integers, but for different goals. For HDT_{crypt}, the goal is to reduce storage and bandwidth usage. For GOOSE, the combination of this technique with secure multi-party computation is particularly useful for achieving security since the actual mapping functions are not shared with the node responsible for query evaluation, which is able to evaluate UCRPQ without knowing which are the true nodes and edge labels that it manipulates.

If one chooses to store RDF graphs in a relational database and query them with SQL, then one can choose CryptDB [18] to run queries directly in the encrypted domain. As already mentioned, CryptDB does not currently support recursive queries, and such queries are anywise cumbersome to express in SQL as they require recursive views. CryptDB has been extended as CryptGraphDB [2] to run Neo4j queries on encrypted graphs, but again without considering recursive queries. GOOSE is complementary to these systems since our goal is to propose a system that is able to run UCRPQ while enjoying similar security properties. We choose to rely on UCRPQ because this class of queries is at the core of the W3C's SPARQL 1.1 property paths, including recursive queries via the Kleene star. A recent large-scale analytical study of SPARQL query logs [7] includes more than a million such recursive queries, which suggests that a secure protocol for evaluating recursive graph queries would be also useful in practice. To the best of our knowledge, GOOSE is the first provably-secure system that is able to run UCRPQ on outsourced graphs, without doing any change to the standard SPARQL engine.

Our work is also related to query-based linked data anonymization [9], where the idea is that the data owner, before publishing a graph, adds some noise, specified declaratively using $SPARQL_L$. Then, a user is able to download the anonymized graph and query it. However, their hypothesis and ours are different as we assume that the bulk of computations is outsourced to the cloud and our user does not need to do any computation effort other than decrypting the query answers received from the cloud. For us, the challenge is to design a distributed protocol that guarantees that the cloud cannot learn the graph, queries, and query answers, while minimizing the overhead due to cryptographic primitives. On the other hand, their challenge is to anonymize the graph before publishing, while finding a good compromise between privacy and utility.

Summary of Contributions and Paper Organization. In Sect. 2, we introduce some basic notions: graph data and queries, and cryptographic tools. Then, Sect. 3 is the core of our contribution:

- We propose the GOOSE framework for secure graph outsourcing and SPARQL evaluation.
- We formally prove that GOOSE satisfies desirable security properties that we precisely characterize:
  1. No cloud node can learn the graph.
  2. No cloud node can learn at the same time the query and the answers of the query on the graph.
  3. An external network observer cannot learn the graph, the query, or the answers of the query on the graph.
- We analyze the theoretical complexity of GOOSE, by quantifying the number of calls of cryptographic primitives: GOOSE uses a number of AES-CBC encryptions/decryptions that is linear in the input's and output's size.

In Sect. 4, we report on a large-scale empirical evaluation that confirms the theoretical complexity, and shows the scalability of GOOSE. Finally, we conclude our paper and outline directions for future work in Sect. 5.

2 Preliminaries

In Sect. 2.1 we define graph data and queries. In Sect. 2.2 we introduce the AES-CBC symmetric encryption scheme and the notion of IND-CPA security that is useful for proving our protocol's security.

2.1 Graph Data and Queries

Graph Data. An RDF (Resource Description Framework[3]) graph database is a set of triples (s, p, o) where s is the *subject*, p is the *predicate*, and o is the *object*. According to the specification, $s \in \mathcal{I} \cup \mathcal{B}, p \in \mathcal{I}, o \in \mathcal{I} \cup \mathcal{B} \cup \mathcal{L}$, where $\mathcal{I}, \mathcal{B}, \mathcal{L}$ are three disjoint sets of Internationalized Resource Identifiers (IRIs), blank nodes, and literals, respectively. For the goal of this paper, the distinction between IRIs, blank nodes, and literals is not important. Therefore, we simply assume that a graph database $G = (V, E)$ is a *directed, edge-labeled graph*, where V is a set of nodes and $E \subseteq V \times \Sigma \times V$ is a set of directed edges between nodes of V and with labels from an *alphabet* Σ. For example, the graph in Fig. 2 has:

- Set of nodes $V = \{\text{Alice, Bob, Charlie, David, Milan, Paris}\}$. The first four nodes correspond to persons and the last two correspond to cities.
- Alphabet $\Sigma = \{\text{Follows, ReadsAbout, TravelsTo}\}$. The first label occurs between two persons and defines the follower relation as in a social network e.g., Twitter. The other two labels occur between a person and a city.

---

[3] https://www.w3.org/TR/rdf11-concepts/.

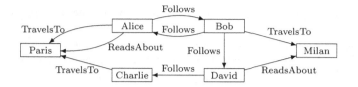

Fig. 2. Example of graph database.

- Set of edges E such as (Alice, Follows, Bob), (Alice, TravelsTo, Paris), etc. There are 9 edges in total, corresponding to the 9 arrows in Fig. 2.

Graph Queries. We focus on *Unions of Conjunctions of Regular Path Queries* (UCRPQ), which are at the core of the W3C's SPARQL 1.1[4]. Recall that Σ is an alphabet and let $\Sigma^+ = \{a, a^- \mid a \in \Sigma\}$, where a^- denotes the *inverse* of the edge label a. Let $V = \{?x, ?y, \dots\}$ be a set of variables and $n > 0$. A *query rule* is an expression of the form *head* ← *body*, more precisely:

$$(\overline{?v}) \leftarrow (?x_1, r_1, ?y_1), \dots, (?x_n, r_n, ?y_n)$$

where: for each $1 \leq i \leq n$, it is the case that $?x_i, ?y_i$ are variables from V and $\overline{?v}$ is a vector of zero or more of these variables, the length of which is called the *arity* of the rule. For each $1 \leq i \leq n$, it is the case that r_i is a regular expression over Σ^+ using $\{\cdot, +, *\}$ (i.e., *concatenation, disjunction,* and *Kleene star*). A query $Q \in$ UCRPQ is a finite non-empty set of query rules of the same arity. By $Ans(G, Q)$ we denote the answers of query Q over a graph G, using standard SPARQL semantics. For example, the UCRPQ query

$$(?x, ?z) \leftarrow (?x, \text{Follows}^+, ?y), (?y, \text{TravelsTo}, ?z)$$

selects nodes $?x, ?z$ such that there exists node $?y$ such that one can go from $?x$ to $?y$ with a path in the language of "Follows$^+$" and can go from $?y$ to $?z$ with a path in the language of "TravelsTo". The answers of this query on the graph from Fig. 2 are (Alice, Milan), (Alice, Paris), (Bob, Milan), (Bob, Paris), (David, Paris). For example, the tuple (Alice, Paris) is an answer because of paths Alice $\overrightarrow{\text{Follows}}$ Bob $\overrightarrow{\text{Follows}}$ David $\overrightarrow{\text{Follows}}$ Charlie and Charlie $\overrightarrow{\text{TravelsTo}}$ Paris, where $?x, ?y, ?z$ are mapped to Alice, Charlie, Paris, respectively.

2.2 Cryptographic Tools

We next introduce AES-CBC symmetric encryption and IND-CPA security.

AES-CBC Symmetric Encryption. AES [1] is a NIST standard for symmetric encryption that encrypts messages of 128 bits. AES is used as a block cipher, for instance using CBC mode (Cipher Block Chaining). The AES-CBC cryptosystem is a symmetric encryption scheme defined by a triple of polynomial-time algorithms (KeyGen, Enc, Dec) and a security parameter λ such that:

---

[4] https://www.w3.org/TR/sparql11-query/.

- KeyGen(λ) generates Key, a uniformly random symmetric key whose size depends on λ.
- Enc(Key, m, IV) splits m in blocks of 128 bits $m_0, \ldots, m_n$ (padding bits may be added if m_n is smaller than 128 bits). Enc computes $c_0 = \mathsf{E}(\mathsf{Key}, m_0 \oplus IV)$, where E is the AES encryption [1] and IV is a random 128-bits number. By $x \oplus y$ we denote the standard bit-wise xor operation between two bit strings x and y. Then, Enc computes $c_i = \mathsf{E}(\mathsf{Key}, c_{i-1} \oplus m_i)$ for $1 \leq i \leq n$ and returns the tuple $((c_0, \ldots, c_n), IV)$.
- Dec(Key, c, IV) splits c in blocks of 128 bits $c_0, \ldots, c_n$ and computes $m_0 = \mathsf{D}(\mathsf{Key}, c_0) \oplus IV$, where D is the AES decryption [1]. Similarly, Dec computes $m_i = \mathsf{D}(\mathsf{Key}, c_i) \oplus c_{i-1}$ for $1 \leq i \leq n$ and returns $m_0, \ldots, m_n$.

IND-CPA [5] (INDistinguishability under Chosen-Plaintext Attack). Let $\Pi = $ (KeyGen, Enc, Dec) be a cryptographic scheme. The *probabilistic polynomial-time (PPT) adversary* $\mathcal{A}$ tries to break the security of Π. The IND-CPA game, denoted by $\mathrm{EXP}(\mathcal{A})$, works as follows: the adversary $\mathcal{A}$ chooses two messages (m_0, m_1) and receives a challenge $c = \mathsf{Enc}(LR_b(m_0, m_1))$ from the *challenger* who selects a bit $b \in \{0, 1\}$ uniformly at random, and where $LR_b(m_0, m_1)$ is equal to m_0 if $b = 0$, and m_1 otherwise. The adversary, knowing m_0, m_1 and c, is allowed to perform any number of polynomial computations or encryptions of any messages, using the encryption oracle, in order to output a guess b' of the encrypted message in c chosen by the challenger. Intuitively, Π is IND-CPA if there is no PPT adversary that can guess b with a probability significantly better than $\frac{1}{2}$. By $\alpha = \Pr[b' \leftarrow \mathrm{EXP}(\mathcal{A}); b = b']$, we denote the probability that $\mathcal{A}$ correctly outputs her guessed bit b' when the bit chosen by the challenger in the experiment is b. A scheme is IND-CPA secure if $\alpha - \frac{1}{2}$ is negligible function in λ, where a function γ is negligible in λ, denoted $negl(\lambda)$, if for every positive polynomial $p(\cdot)$ and sufficiently large λ, $\gamma(\lambda) < 1/p(\lambda)$. In particular, if f and g are negligible in λ, then $f(\lambda) + g(\lambda)$ is also negligible in λ.

AES-CBC is IND-CPA under the standard assumption that AES is a pseudorandom permutation [5]. We also point out that all theoretical security properties of our protocol also hold if we choose any other IND-CPA symmetric scheme instead of AES-CBC. Our choice to rely on AES-CBC is due to practical reasons since AES-CBC is a NIST standard, and moreover, is very efficient in practice and implemented in standard libraries for modern programming languages.

3   Secure Graph Outsourcing and SPARQL Evaluation

We define the security model and the desired security properties in Sect. 3.1. Then, we propose our secure protocol GOOSE (Sect. 3.2), and we analyze its correctness (Sect. 3.3), security properties (Sect. 3.4), and complexity (Sect. 3.5).

3.1   Security Model

We assume that the cloud is *honest-but-curious* i.e., it executes tasks dutifully, but tries to extract as much information as possible from the data that it sees.

Our model follows the classical formulation in [13] (Ch. 7.5, where *honest-but-curious* is denoted *semi-honest*), in particular (i) each cloud node is trusted: it correctly does the required computations, it does not sniff the network and it does not collude with other nodes, and (ii) an external observer has access to all messages exchanged over the network. The aforementioned security model is of practical interest in a real-world cloud environment. In particular, to satisfy all our theoretical security properties while achieving the no-collusion hypothesis, it suffice to host each cloud node of our protocol by a different cloud provider. This should be feasible as our protocol requires only three cloud nodes.

As already outlined in the introduction and in Fig. 1, we assume that the data (i.e., the graph) and the computations (i.e., the query evaluation algorithm) are outsourced. More precisely, the data owner outsources the graph G to the cloud once at the beginning. Then, the user sends query Q_1 to the cloud and receives $Ans(G, Q_1)$, then the user sends query Q_2 to the cloud and receives $Ans(G, Q_2)$, etc. The user does not have to do any query evaluation on her side. We expect the following *security properties*:

1. No cloud node can learn the graph G.
2. No cloud node can learn at the same time a query Q submitted by the user and the answers $Ans(G, Q)$ of the query Q on the graph G.
3. By analyzing network messages, an external observer cannot learn the graph G, cannot learn any query Q, and cannot learn any $Ans(G, Q)$.

Next, we propose GOOSE, a distributed protocol that satisfies these properties. Intuitively, we achieve the aforementioned properties by exchanging only encrypted messages, and moreover, by distributing the computations among several cloud node participants, each of them having access only to the specific data that it needs for performing its task and nothing else. The challenge is to efficiently distribute tasks among as few cloud participants as possible, while minimizing the time needed for cryptographic primitives.

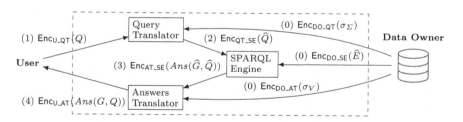

Fig. 3. Architecture of GOOSE. The dashed rectangle is the cloud. Graph outsourcing (step 0) is done only once at the beginning. Query evaluation (steps 1–4) is done for each submitted query. The hat on some data means that the data is hidden using functions σ_V, σ_Σ, or both (depends on step, see GOOSE description for details).

3.2   Overview of GOOSE

In Fig. 3, we depict the architecture of GOOSE, which has 5 participants: *data owner* (DO), who owns the graph that it outsources to the cloud in order to be queried, *user* (U), who submits graph queries to the cloud and receives query answers, and 3 cloud participants: *query translator* (QT), *SPARQL engine* (SE) and *answers translator* (AT). We next explain each step via a running example.

By Enc_{A_B} or Enc_{B_A} we denote symmetric AES-CBC encryption using the key shared between participants A and B. We have 7 such shared keys because there are 7 combinations of participants exchanging messages, hence 7 arrows in Fig. 3. We assume that the sharing of AES keys has been done before starting the actual protocol and there are many classical key exchange protocols in the literature for doing this.

Step 0. The *graph outsourcing* (i.e., the 3 outgoing arrows from DO in Fig. 3) is done only once at the beginning by DO. Intuitively, DO sends to each cloud participant a piece of the graph such that each participant can perform its task during query evaluation but no participant can reconstruct the entire graph. As shown in the pseudocode of DO in Fig. 4(a), DO generates two random bijections: σ_Σ and σ_V, one for the edge labels and another one for the graph nodes, respectively. By σ^{-1} we denote the inverse of σ (this is needed later on at the end of query evaluation). For our example graph in Fig. 2, DO may generate:

$$\sigma_V = \{\text{Alice} \rightarrow 5, \text{Bob} \rightarrow 3, \text{Charlie} \rightarrow 0, \text{David} \rightarrow 1, \text{Milan} \rightarrow 2, \text{Paris} \rightarrow 4\}$$
$$\sigma_\Sigma = \{\text{Follows} \rightarrow 1, \text{ReadsAbout} \rightarrow 2, \text{TravelsTo} \rightarrow 0\}.$$

Then, DO uses these two functions to hide the graph edges. As shown in Fig. 4(a), by $\widehat{E}$ we denote the hidden set of edges generated from E, where the nodes are replaced using σ_V, and the edge labels are replaced using σ_Σ. On our example graph in Fig. 2, edge (Alice, Follows, Bob) becomes (5, 1, 3), edge (Alice, ReadsAbout, Paris) becomes (5, 2, 4), etc., and finally:

$$\widehat{E} = \{(5,1,3),(5,2,4),(5,0,4),(3,1,5),(3,1,1),(3,0,2),(0,0,4),(1,1,0),(1,2,2)\}.$$

As shown in Figs. 3 and 4(a), DO sends σ_Σ, σ_V, and $\widehat{E}$ to cloud nodes QT, AT, and SE, respectively. Each message sent over the network is encrypted with the key shared between DO and the corresponding cloud participant, which can decrypt the message upon reception. Messages are encrypted to avoid that an external observer that sees them in clear is able to learn the graph G, thus violating one of the desirable security properties stated in Sect. 3.1. Moreover, the distribution of graph storage among cloud participants makes that none of them can learn the graph G, which is also a desirable security property cf. Sect. 3.1.

We next discuss *query evaluation* i.e., steps 1–4 cf. Fig. 3, done for each query submitted by U. Similarly to graph outsourcing, each message exchanged over the network during query evaluation is encrypted with the key shared between corresponding participants, such that an external observer cannot learn the query and its answers to satisfy another desirable security property cf. Sect. 3.1.

Let σ_Σ = random bijection : $\Sigma \rightarrow \{0, \ldots, |\Sigma|-1\}$
Let σ_V = random bijection : $V \rightarrow \{0, \ldots, |V|-1\}$
Let $\widehat{E} = \{(\sigma_V(s), \sigma_\Sigma(p), \sigma_V(o)) \mid (s,p,o) \in E\}$
Send $\mathsf{Enc}_{\mathsf{DO\_QT}}(\sigma_\Sigma)$ to QT
Send $\mathsf{Enc}_{\mathsf{DO\_AT}}(\sigma_V)$ to AT
Send $\mathsf{Enc}_{\mathsf{DO\_SE}}(\widehat{E})$ to SE

(a) Pseudocode of outsourcing graph $G = (V, E)$ by DO (step 0).

Generate query $\widehat{Q}$ from Q by replacing each occurrence of a label p with $\sigma_\Sigma(p)$
Send $\mathsf{Enc}_{\mathsf{QT\_SE}}(\widehat{Q})$ to SE

(b) Pseudocode of QT during query evaluation (step 2).

Let $\widehat{G} = (\bigcup_{(\widehat{s},\widehat{p},\widehat{o}) \in \widehat{E}} \{\widehat{s}, \widehat{o}\}, \widehat{E})$
Let $Ans(\widehat{G}, \widehat{Q})$ be the answers of $\widehat{Q}$ on $\widehat{G}$, computed with some SPARQL engine
Send $\mathsf{Enc}_{\mathsf{AT\_SE}}(Ans(\widehat{G}, \widehat{Q}))$ to AT

(c) Pseudocode of SE during query evaluation (step 3).

Let $Ans(G, Q) = \{(\sigma_V^{-1}(v_1), \ldots, \sigma_V^{-1}(v_n)) \mid (v_1, \ldots, v_n) \in Ans(\widehat{G}, \widehat{Q})\}$
Send $\mathsf{Enc}_{\mathsf{U\_AT}}(Ans(G, Q))$ to U

(d) Pseudocode of AT during query evaluation (step 4).

Fig. 4. Pseudocode of the non-trivial steps of GOOSE cf. Fig. 3.

Step 1. U submits query Q to QT. For example, recall the query $(?x, ?z) \leftarrow (?x, \mathrm{Follows}^+, ?y), (?y, \mathrm{TravelsTo}, ?z)$ from Sect. 2.

Step 2. QT translates the received query Q by replacing all labels used in Q using the function σ_Σ received from DO, as shown in Fig. 4(b). By $\widehat{Q}$ we denote the query Q translated using σ_Σ. On our running example, the query from step 1 becomes $(?x, ?z) \leftarrow (?x, 1^+, ?y), (?y, 0, ?z)$.

Step 3. As shown in Fig. 4(c), SE evaluates translated query $\widehat{Q}$ received from QT at step 2 on the graph with hidden nodes and edge labels as defined by $\widehat{E}$ received from DO during step 0. To do so, SE simply uses some standard SPARQL engine as a black-box, without any change to the query engine. We denote the result of SE by $Ans(\widehat{G}, \widehat{Q})$, where the true answers $Ans(G, Q)$ are still hidden using function σ_V. On our running example, $Ans(\widehat{G}, \widehat{Q}) = \{(5,2), (5,4), (3,2), (3,4), (1,4)\}$.

Step 4. AT uses the function $\sigma_{V^{-1}}$ to translate the received hidden query answers $Ans(\widehat{G}, \widehat{Q})$ into the true query answers, as shown in Fig. 4(d). On our running example, AT recovers $Ans(G, Q) = \{(\mathrm{Alice}, \mathrm{Milan}), (\mathrm{Alice}, \mathrm{Paris}), (\mathrm{Bob}, \mathrm{Milan}), (\mathrm{Bob}, \mathrm{Paris}), (\mathrm{David}, \mathrm{Paris})\}$ that AT sends to U.

3.3   Correctness of **GOOSE**

To show the correctness, we point out a reduction from GOOSE to the standard
SPARQL evaluation engine used as a black-box in SE. Take a graph G outsourced
by DO and a query Q submitted by U. If we remove all encryptions/decryptions
of GOOSE, hence all messages are communicated in clear between participants,
then we obtain protocol GOOSE$'$ that yields exactly the same result as GOOSE.
This happens because of the consistency property of AES-CBC i.e., if we encrypt
message M using Enc to obtain ciphertext C, then if we decrypt C using Dec
we obtain exactly M. Next, take the SE participant of GOOSE$'$, which evaluates
query $\widehat{Q}$ (cf. Fig. 4(b)) over graph $\widehat{G}$ (cf. Fig. 4(c)). Since DO and QT use the
same function σ_Σ for hiding edge labels, then $Ans(\widehat{G}, \widehat{Q}) = Ans(\widehat{G}', Q)$, where
$\widehat{G}' = (\{0, \ldots, |V| - 1\}, \{(\sigma_V(s), p, \sigma_V(o)) \mid (s, p, o) \in E\})$. Then, AT inverses the
function σ_V on each value of each tuple of $Ans(\widehat{G}, \widehat{Q})$ cf. Fig. 4(d) and generates
exactly $Ans(G, Q)$ because AT uses the same function σ_V that is used in $\widehat{G}'$. In
conclusion, U receives the correct answers $Ans(G, Q)$.

3.4   Security of **GOOSE**

We next show that GOOSE satisfies the desirable properties outlined in Sect. 3.1,
proven as Theorems 1, 2, and 3. In the sequel, by $data_A$, we denote the data to
which A has access, where A can be a cloud participant (QT, SE, AT) or an
external network observer (ext). We first characterize $data$ for all participants.
Given a graph $G = (V, E)$ and a workload of k queries $Q_1, \ldots, Q_k$:

$$data_{\mathsf{QT}} = \{\sigma_\Sigma\} \cup \bigcup_{1 \leq i \leq k} \{Q_i\},$$

$$data_{\mathsf{SE}} = \{\widehat{E}\} \cup \bigcup_{1 \leq i \leq k} \{\widehat{Q}_i, \ Ans(\widehat{G}, \widehat{Q}_i)\},$$

$$data_{\mathsf{AT}} = \{\sigma_V\} \cup \bigcup_{1 \leq i \leq k} \{Ans(G, Q_i)\},$$

$$data_{ext} = \{\mathsf{Enc}_{\mathsf{DO\_QT}}(\sigma_\Sigma), \mathsf{Enc}_{\mathsf{DO\_SE}}(\widehat{E}), \mathsf{Enc}_{\mathsf{DO\_AT}}(\sigma_V)\} \cup \bigcup_{1 \leq i \leq k} \{\mathsf{Enc}_{\mathsf{U\_QT}}(Q_i),$$

$$\mathsf{Enc}_{\mathsf{QT\_SE}}(\widehat{Q}_i), \mathsf{Enc}_{\mathsf{AT\_SE}}(Ans(\widehat{G}, \widehat{Q}_i)), \mathsf{Enc}_{\mathsf{U\_AT}}(Ans(G, Q_i))\}.$$

We next show that GOOSE satisfies Property 1 from Sect. 3.1.

Theorem 1. *For each cloud participant $A \in \{\mathsf{QT}, \mathsf{SE}, \mathsf{AT}\}$, A cannot guess
from $data_A$ the graph $G = (V, E)$ with probability better than random under
the assumption that bijections σ_Σ and σ_V are pseudorandom.*

Proof. • QT. By construction, $data_{\mathsf{QT}}$ does not include information on the
nodes of G. In particular, QT does not know V or even $|V|$. Moreover,
although $data_{\mathsf{QT}}$ include σ_Σ from which QT can infer Σ, there is no other
information available on E, not even $|E|$. Hence, if QT wants to guess G, its

best strategy is random i.e., pick random set of nodes V' and edges (s, p, o), with $s, o \in V'$ and $p \in \Sigma$.

- SE. By construction, SE can learn, from $data_{SE}$, a graph $\widehat{G}$ (cf. Fig. 4(c)) isomorphic to G. If SE can learn G from $\widehat{G}$, this implies that SE can learn the two pseudorandom bijections σ_Σ and σ_V. This cannot be done with probability better than random because $data_{SE}$ does not include information on the nodes and edges of G hence SE sees no information on the domains of σ_Σ and σ_V.

- AT. By construction, $\sigma_V \in data_{AT}$ thus AT can infer V. However, $data_{AT}$ does not include information on the edges of G, not even $|E|$ or $|\Sigma|$. Hence, if AT wants to guess G, its best strategy is random i.e., pick random alphabet Σ' and random edges (s, p, o), with $s, o \in V$ and $p \in \Sigma'$. $\qquad\Box$

We next show that GOOSE satisfies Property 2 from Sect. 3.1.

Theorem 2. *For each cloud participant $A \in \{QT, SE, AT\}$, A cannot guess from $data_A$, at the same time, a query Q and its answers $Ans(G, Q)$ with probability better than random under the assumption that bijections σ_Σ and σ_V are pseudorandom.*

Proof. • QT. By construction, QT knows the query Q, but does not see any information on $Ans(G, Q)$. Its best strategy to guess $Ans(G, Q)$ is random i.e., pick a random set of nodes V' and output a random set of tuples of the same arity as Q using nodes of V'.

- SE. By construction, SE knows the number of answers $|Ans(G, Q))|$, without knowing to which true nodes the answers correspond and what is query Q. The best strategy of SE for guessing $Ans(G, Q)$ is random, similar to the QT case.

- AT. By construction, AT knows the query result $Ans(G, Q)$, but does not see any information on Q or on alphabet Σ. Hence, if AT wants to guess Q, its best strategy is random i.e., pick a random alphabet Σ' and output a random query over Σ' that has the same arity as $Ans(G, Q)$. $\qquad\Box$

We next prove the security of an external observer, more precisely we show that GOOSE satisfies Property 3 from Sect. 3.1.

Theorem 3. *Given $data_{ext}$, then the graph $G = (V, E)$, any query Q, and any query answers $Ans(G, Q)$ are indistinguishable of random for an external network observer of GOOSE under the assumption that the symmetric encryption used is IND-CPA.*

Proof. This proof relies on the notion of IND-CPA security as defined in Sect. 2. Before proving the theorem, we first need to introduce some notation:

- By $\mathcal{A}^{pb}(data_{ext})$ we denote the guess of a Probabilistic Polynomial Time (PPT) adversary $\mathcal{A}$ that knows $data_{ext}$ and tries to solve problem pb among: $guessE$ (that returns the $\mathcal{A}$'s guess of some graph edge in E), $guessQ$ (that returns the $\mathcal{A}$'s guess of some query Q in the workload), *guessAns* (that returns the $\mathcal{A}$'s guess of the answers $Ans(G, Q)$ of some query Q in the workload).

- By construction of $data_{ext}$, we infer that ext can learn, based on $data_{ext}$, size estimates of the graph components $|E|, |V|, |\Sigma|$ (from the messages exchanged at step 0), and size estimates $|Q|$ for each query and $|Ans(G, Q)|$ for its query answers (from the messages exchanged at steps 1–4). By $p_E(data_{ext})$, $p_Q(data_{ext})$, $p_{Ans}(data_{ext})$, we denote the probability that ext randomly outputs, based on $data_{ext}$, a correct graph edge, a correct query, or a correct query answers set, respectively.

Hence, to prove the theorem, we need to prove that, for a graph $G = (V, E)$ and a query workload $\bigcup_{1 \le i \le k} \{Q_i\}$, for all PPT adversaries $\mathcal{A}$,

$$|\Pr[\mathcal{A}^{guessE}(data_{ext}) \in E] - p_E(data_{ext})| \qquad \text{is negligible in } \lambda,$$

$$|\Pr[\mathcal{A}^{guessQ}(data_{ext}) \in \bigcup_{1 \le i \le k} \{Q_i\}] - p_Q(data_{ext})| \qquad \text{is negligible in } \lambda,$$

$$|\Pr[\mathcal{A}^{guessAns}(data_{ext}) \in \bigcup_{1 \le i \le k} \{Ans(G, Q_i)\}] - p_{Ans}(data_{ext})| \quad \text{is negligible in } \lambda.$$

Each of the 3 statements can be proven separately by contradiction. We prove here only the first statement, the other two proofs being similar and omitted here due to space constraints, but available in Appendix A.

We assume, toward a contradiction, that there exists a PPT adversary $\mathcal{A}$ able from $data_{ext}$ to find a correct edge in E with a non-negligible advantage x:

$$|\Pr[\mathcal{A}^{guessE}(data_{ext}) \in E] - p_E(data_{ext})| = x + negl(\lambda).$$

If $data_{ext}$ does not correspond to an actual collection of encrypted messages as ext sees during an execution of GOOSE, then the advantage for such an input is naturally negligible.

We show that by using the adversary $\mathcal{A}$, we can construct an adversary $\mathcal{B}$ able to break the IND-CPA property of AES-CBC [1,5]. We build an IND-CPA game, in which $\mathcal{B}$ chooses two values m_0, m_1, and sends them to the challenger. The challenger randomly selects $b \in \{0, 1\}$ and answers with $\mathsf{Enc}_{\mathsf{DO\_QT}}(m_b)$. Adversary $\mathcal{B}$ wins the IND-CPA game if $\mathcal{B}$ guesses b with a non-negligible advantage.

To do so, $\mathcal{B}$ simulates a GOOSE execution i.e., $\mathcal{B}$ chooses a graph (over alphabet $\Sigma = \{a_1, \ldots, a_n\}$), a query workload, and the functions (σ_Σ and σ_V) used by DO during graph outsourcing; $\mathcal{B}$ does not know the keys shared among the participants of GOOSE. Let $data_\mathcal{B}$ be the set of encrypted messages exchanged during the GOOSE simulation (including $\mathsf{Enc}_{\mathsf{DO\_QT}}(\sigma_\Sigma)$, among others). As input for the IND-CPA game, $\mathcal{B}$ chooses $m_1 = \sigma_\Sigma$ and $m_0 = \sigma'_\Sigma$, where for $a \in \Sigma$, if $\sigma_\Sigma(a) \ne 0$, then $\sigma'_\Sigma(a) = \sigma_\Sigma(a)$, else $\sigma'_\Sigma(a) = -1$. Then, $\mathcal{B}$ sends m_0, m_1 to the challenger, and receives $\mathsf{Enc}_{\mathsf{DO\_QT}}(m_b)$. Next, $\mathcal{B}$ calls $\mathcal{A}^{guessE}(data_\mathcal{B} \setminus \{\mathsf{Enc}_{\mathsf{DO\_QT}}(\sigma_\Sigma)\} \cup \{\mathsf{Enc}_{\mathsf{DO\_QT}}(m_b)\})$. The strategy of $\mathcal{B}$ is as follows: if $\mathcal{A}$ returns a true edge having the label a for which $\sigma_\Sigma(a) = 0$, then $\mathcal{B}$ answers 1. Otherwise, $\mathcal{B}$ answers randomly. We next derive the probability of a correct answer by $\mathcal{B}$:

- If $b = 0$ (probability $\frac{1}{2}$), then $\mathcal{A}$ does not receive a correct simulation because the functions used during graph outsourcing to compute the pieces sent to QT and SE are not the same. According to our assumption, $\mathcal{A}$ does not give any advantage. $\mathcal{B}$ answers randomly and is right with probability $\frac{1}{2}$, hence the probability of success of this branch is $\frac{1}{4}$.
- If $b = 1$ (probability $\frac{1}{2}$), then $\mathcal{B}$ can leverage the advantage given by $\mathcal{A}$.
    - If $\mathcal{A}$ returns a true edge having the label a for which $\sigma_\Sigma(a) = 0$ (probability $p_E(data_\mathcal{B}) + x + negl(\lambda)$), then $\mathcal{B}$ correctly answers 1. The probability of success of this branch is $\frac{1}{2}(p_E(data_\mathcal{B}) + x + negl(\lambda))$.
    - Otherwise, (probability $1 - p_E(data_\mathcal{B}) - x - negl(\lambda)$), $\mathcal{B}$ answers randomly and is correct with probability $\frac{1}{2}$. This branch yields a probability of success of $\frac{1}{2}(1 - p_E(data_\mathcal{B}) - x - negl(\lambda))\frac{1}{2}$.

By aggregating these cases, the probability α of success of $\mathcal{B}$ is:

$$
\begin{aligned}
\alpha &= \frac{1}{4} + \frac{1}{2}(p_E(data_\mathcal{B}) + x + negl(\lambda)) + \frac{1}{2}(1 - p_E(data_\mathcal{B}) - x - negl(\lambda))\frac{1}{2} \\
&= \frac{1}{4} + \frac{p_E(data_\mathcal{B})}{2} + \frac{x}{2} + \frac{1}{4} - \frac{p_E(data_\mathcal{B})}{4} - \frac{x}{4} + negl(\lambda) \\
&= \frac{1}{2} + \frac{p_E(data_\mathcal{B})}{4} + \frac{x}{4} + negl(\lambda)
\end{aligned}
$$

Note that $p_E(data_\mathcal{B}) \geq 0$ (since it is a probability) and recall that x is non-negligible (by hypothesis). Hence, $\mathcal{B}$ has a non-negligible advantage of $\frac{p_E(data_\mathcal{B})}{4} + \frac{x}{4}$ in the IND-CPA game, which contradicts the fact that AES-CBC is IND-CPA secure. Hence, we conclude that there does not exist any PPT adversary $\mathcal{A}$ that violates the property stated in the theorem.   □

3.5   Complexity of GOOSE

The number of cryptographic operations used by GOOSE is linear in the input's and output's size:

Theorem 4. *Given a graph $G = (V, E)$ over an alphabet Σ and a workload of k queries $Q_1, \ldots, Q_k$, the total size that GOOSE encrypts, as well as the total size that it decrypts, is*

$$
|\Sigma| + |V| + |E| + 2 \sum_{1 \leq i \leq k} (|Q_i| + |Ans(G, Q_i)|).
$$

Proof. This follows from the construction of GOOSE. During graph outsourcing, the size of encrypted data by DO is $|\Sigma| + |V| + |E|$, which is also the size of data decrypted by the cloud participants. For evaluating query $1 \leq i \leq k$ in the workload, the size of encrypted data is $|Q_i| + |Q_i| + |Ans(G, Q_i)| + |Ans(G, Q_i)|$, done sequentially by U, QT, SE, AT, and the size of decrypted data is the same, done sequentially by QT, SE, AT, U. By summing up the size for all queries in the workload, we obtain exactly the formula in the theorem statement.   □

4   Experiments

We present a large-scale empirical evaluation devoted to showing the practical feasibility and scalability of GOOSE, for both graph outsourcing and query evaluation. We also compare GOOSE query evaluation with standard SPARQL evaluation and we zoom on the running time shares of each GOOSE participant.

Implementation. We implemented GOOSE in Python 3. For AES-CBC we used keys of 256 bits with the *PyCryptodome* library[5]. As SPARQL engine, we used Apache Jena[6]. We carried out our experiments on a system with CPU Intel Xeon of 3 GHz and 755 GB of RAM, running CentOS Linux 7.

Open-Source Code. For reproducibility reasons, we make available on a public GitHub repository[7] our source code, together with scripts that install needed libraries, run the large-scale experiment, and generate the plots. This experiment took 8 days on our system and generated 46 GB of data (total size for graphs, queries, and query answers).

Datasets. We relied on gMark[8] [3,4], a schema-driven benchmark that allows generating synthetic graphs and queries with finely-tuned constraints. gMark provided us a large quantity of diverse data and queries to stress-test GOOSE as we used all 4 use cases that we found on the gMark repository: *uniprot* (biological data where proteins interact with other proteins, are encoded on genes, etc.), *shop* (online shop selling different types of products to users, etc.), *social-network* (social network where persons know other persons, work in companies, etc.), and *bib* (bibliographical data about researchers that author papers published in journals or conferences, etc.). Each use case encodes different types of constraints, which make the generated graphs and queries have different characteristics, that we detail when necessary to explain experimental results.

Scalability of Graph Outsourcing. For each of the 4 use cases, we consider 5 scaling factors, from 10^3 to 10^7, where a scaling factor n means that gMark should generate a graph with n nodes. For each combination (use case, scaling factor), we report the GOOSE graph outsourcing time, averaged over 10 graphs, each of them outsourced 3 times. We show the result of this experiment in Fig. 5(a), where we observe a smooth, linear-time behavior. We next explain the running times difference between the use cases by detailing their characteristics. In particular, the number of generated nodes for a scaling factor depends on how large is n and what constraints are specified in the use case. This is why, to help understanding the behavior in Fig. 5(a), we also plot in Fig. 5(b) the size (# of nodes vs # of edges) for the generated graphs. To simulate realistic graph constraints, each use case specifies how the number of nodes of some type increases: there are types of nodes whose number increases when the graph size

---

[5] https://pycryptodome.readthedocs.io/en/latest/src/cipher/classic.html.
[6] https://jena.apache.org/.
[7] https://github.com/radul/goose.
[8] https://github.com/graphMark/gmark.

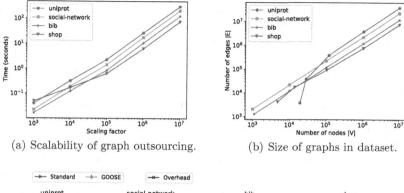

(a) Scalability of graph outsourcing.   (b) Size of graphs in dataset.

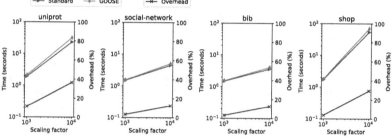

(c) Scalability of query evaluation, and comparison standard vs GOOSE.

(d) Zoom on end-to-end solution i.e., graph outsourcing and query evaluation for a workload of 5 queries, for graphs of fixed scaling factor 10^4. The shares of participants DO, U, and QT are barely visible.

Fig. 5. Experimental results.

increases (e.g., users and purchases in *shop*), and types of nodes whose number is constant for all graph sizes (e.g., cities and countries in *shop*). When we take a small scaling factor and a use case with strong constraints on the types with constant number of occurrences, gMark may have to add nodes beyond the size specified by the scaling factor to satisfy the number of nodes for each type. This explains the behavior for small scaling factors in Fig. 5(b) for *shop* (12 types of constant node types), and *uniprot* (3 types of constant node types, among which one with 15K occurrences, hence for the scaling factor 10^3, the generated graphs have at least 15 times more nodes). For large scaling factors ($10^5, 10^6, 10^7$), the number of constant node types is dominated by the nodes with types that increase with the graph size, hence the hierarchy of the use cases in terms of size is clear and determined by the number of edges that should be generated in each use case. We conclude this experiment by observing that the GOOSE graph outsourcing time is strongly correlated to the graph size: if you take any two graphs A and B, if A has more edges than B (cf. Y axis in Fig. 5(b)), then the time to outsource A is larger than the time to outsource B (cf. Y axis in Fig. 5(a)). This is particularly visible for large scaling factors, where the hierarchy of the generated graph sizes (in terms of # of edges) is strictly followed by the hierarchy of use cases in terms of graph outsourcing times.

Scalability of Query Evaluation. For each of the 4 use cases, for each of the scaling factors 10^3 and 10^4, we generate with gMark 200 graphs and a workload of 5 queries coupled to each graph. Hence, we have run a total number of 8000 queries, having diverse properties specified in the gMark use cases. In particular, for each use case the generated queries are unary/binary, recursive/non-recursive (i.e., contain Kleene stars or not), linear/constant (i.e., return a number of answers that depend or not on the size of the graph), and have various shapes (chain, star, cycle, star-chain). Although we were able to easily scale the GOOSE graph outsourcing up to scaling factor 10^7, for the query evaluation experiment we evaluated queries only up to 10^4 because the bottleneck of this experiment is the standard SPARQL engine. Indeed, if we simply evaluate a generated query on a generated graph of scaling factor 10^4, it may happen that this takes already up to a minute, without any GOOSE security. This limitation of current SPARQL engines, in particular for evaluating recursive queries, has been already pointed out in the literature e.g., in [4]. Hence, we were able to benchmark GOOSE query evaluation vs standard query evaluation only on scaling factors 10^3 and 10^4, and we run 3 times each query with each system before averaging. We show our results in Fig. 5(c). We observe that the running times depend on the use case in the sense that if a graph has more nodes, it is more likely that a query has more results hence it may take more time to enumerate all results. This is why *uniprot* and *shop* take more time than the others. If we compare the relative performance of standard SPARQL evaluation vs GOOSE query evaluation, we observe that the overhead due to cryptographic primitives in GOOSE is dominated by the time taken by the GOOSE SPARQL engine. We also plot the relative overhead, which obviously increases when there are more query answers to encrypt and decrypt during steps 3 and 4 in GOOSE. Hence, a large overhead in this experiment is correlated to a large share of the answers translator in the next one.

Zoom of End-to-End Solution. In this last experiment, we see GOOSE as an end-to-end solution consisting of outsourcing a graph and then evaluating several queries on it. In Fig. 5(d), we show the time shares taken by each GOOSE participant, for each of the 4 use cases, for fixed scaling factor 10^4, after summing up the times needed for graph outsourcing (cf. the first experiment) and for evaluating all 5 queries in the workload (cf. the second experiment). As expected, the SPARQL engine takes the lion's share. Moreover, the next most visible participant is the answers translator, which has to decrypt hidden answers received from the SPARQL engine, translate the answers, and re-encrypt the true answers before sending them to the user. Without surprise, the time shares taken by the two participants outside the cloud (data owner and user) are negligible, the bulk of the computation being outsourced to the cloud.

5   Conclusions and Future Work

We presented the design and implementation of the GOOSE secure framework for outsourcing graphs and querying them with SPARQL queries defined by UCRPQ. We formally proved that GOOSE enjoys desirable security properties and that its overhead due to cryptographic primitives is linear in the input's and output's size. Our large-scale experimental study confirms the scalability of GOOSE. As future work, we plan to extend GOOSE to support other practical SPARQL features such as aggregates and comparisons, for which we need to use cryptographic schemes such as Paillier [17] and order-preserving encryption [6].

A   Appendix: Proof of Theorem 3 (Continued)

Recall that Theorem 3 states: *Given* $data_{ext}$, *then the graph* $G = (V, E)$, *any query* Q, *and any query answers* $Ans(G, Q)$ *are indistinguishable of random for an external network observer of* GOOSE *under the assumption that the symmetric encryption used is IND-CPA.*

In the main body of the paper (Sect. 3.4), we started the proof of Theorem 3, where we have first shown that proving the theorem boils down to proving that for a graph $G = (V, E)$ and a query workload $\bigcup_{1 \le i \le k} \{Q_i\}$, for all PPT adversaries $\mathcal{A}$,

$$|\Pr[\mathcal{A}^{guessE}(data_{ext}) \in E] - p_E(data_{ext})| \qquad \text{is negligible in } \lambda,$$

$$\left|\Pr[\mathcal{A}^{guessQ}(data_{ext}) \in \bigcup_{1 \le i \le k} \{Q_i\}] - p_Q(data_{ext})\right| \qquad \text{is negligible in } \lambda,$$

$$\left|\Pr[\mathcal{A}^{guessAns}(data_{ext}) \in \bigcup_{1 \le i \le k} \{Ans(G, Q_i)\}] - p_{Ans}(data_{ext})\right| \quad \text{is negligible in } \lambda.$$

In the main body of the paper (Sect. 3.4), we have proven the first of the aforementioned statements, and we omitted the other two due to space constraints. We prove here the other two statements.

We assume, toward a contradiction, that there exists a PPT adversary $\mathcal{A}$ able from $data_{ext}$ to find a correct query Q_i with a non-negligible advantage x:

$$\left|\Pr[\mathcal{A}^{guessQ}(data_{ext}) \in \bigcup_{1 \le i \le k} \{Q_i\}] - p_Q(data_{ext})\right| = x + negl(\lambda).$$

If $data_{ext}$ does not correspond to an actual collection of encrypted messages as ext sees during an execution of GOOSE, then the advantage for such an input is naturally negligible.

We next show that by using the adversary $\mathcal{A}$, we can construct an adversary $\mathcal{B}$ able to break the IND-CPA property of AES-CBC [1,5]. We build an IND-CPA game, in which $\mathcal{B}$ chooses two values m_0, m_1, and sends them to the challenger. The challenger randomly selects $b \in \{0, 1\}$ and answers with $\mathsf{Enc}_{\mathsf{U\_QT}}(m_b)$. Adversary $\mathcal{B}$ wins the IND-CPA game if $\mathcal{B}$ guesses b with a non-negligible advantage.

To do so, $\mathcal{B}$ simulates a GOOSE execution i.e., $\mathcal{B}$ chooses a graph, a query workload consisting of a single query Q_1 that is $?x \leftarrow (?x, a+, ?y)$, such that $Ans(G, Q_1) \neq \emptyset$, and the functions used by DO during graph outsourcing; $\mathcal{B}$ does not know the keys shared among the participants of GOOSE. Let $data_{\mathcal{B}}$ be the set of encrypted messages seen by an external observer of the simulation of GOOSE done by $\mathcal{B}$, which includes, among others, $\mathsf{Enc}_{\mathsf{U\_QT}}(Q_1)$.

As input for the IND-CPA game, $\mathcal{B}$ chooses $m_1 = Q_1$ and $m_0 = Q_1'$ obtained by replacing a in Q_1 by a fresh label $a' \notin \Sigma$. Then, $\mathcal{B}$ sends m_0, m_1 to the challenger, and receives $\mathsf{Enc}_{\mathsf{U\_QT}}(m_b)$. Next, $\mathcal{B}$ calls $\mathcal{A}^{guessQ}(data_{\mathcal{B}} \setminus \{\mathsf{Enc}_{\mathsf{U\_QT}}(Q_1)\} \cup \{\mathsf{Enc}_{\mathsf{U\_QT}}(m_b)\})$. The strategy of $\mathcal{B}$ is as follows: if $\mathcal{A}$ returns Q_1, then $\mathcal{B}$ answers 1. Otherwise, $\mathcal{B}$ answers randomly. We next derive the probability of a correct answer by $\mathcal{B}$:

- If $b = 0$ (probability $\frac{1}{2}$), then $\mathcal{A}$ does not receive a correct simulation because $a' \notin \Sigma$, hence $Ans(G, Q_1') = \emptyset$ that is different from $Ans(G, Q_1) \neq \emptyset$ that also belongs to $data_{ext}$. According to our assumption, in such a case $\mathcal{A}$ does not give any advantage. $\mathcal{B}$ answers randomly and is right with probability $\frac{1}{2}$, hence the probability of success of this branch is $\frac{1}{4}$.
- If $b = 1$ (probability $\frac{1}{2}$), then $\mathcal{B}$ can leverage the advantage given by $\mathcal{A}$.
  - If $\mathcal{A}$ returns Q_1 (probability $p_Q(data_{\mathcal{B}}) + x + negl(\lambda)$), then $\mathcal{B}$ correctly answers 1. The probability of success of this branch is $\frac{1}{2}(p_Q(data_{\mathcal{B}}) + x + negl(\lambda))$.
  - Otherwise, (probability $1 - p_Q(data_{\mathcal{B}}) - x - negl(\lambda)$), $\mathcal{B}$ answers randomly and is correct with probability $\frac{1}{2}$. This branch yields a probability of success of $\frac{1}{2}(1 - p_Q(data_{\mathcal{B}}) - x - negl(\lambda))\frac{1}{2}$.

By aggregating these cases, the probability α of success of $\mathcal{B}$ is:

$$\alpha = \frac{1}{4} + \frac{1}{2}(p_Q(data_{\mathcal{B}}) + x + negl(\lambda)) + \frac{1}{2}(1 - p_Q(data_{\mathcal{B}}) - x - negl(\lambda))\frac{1}{2}$$

$$= \frac{1}{4} + \frac{p_Q(data_{\mathcal{B}})}{2} + \frac{x}{2} + \frac{1}{4} - \frac{p_Q(data_{\mathcal{B}})}{4} - \frac{x}{4} + negl(\lambda)$$

$$= \frac{1}{2} + \frac{p_Q(data_{\mathcal{B}})}{4} + \frac{x}{4} + negl(\lambda)$$

Note that $p_E(data_{\mathcal{B}}) \geq 0$ (since it is a probability) and recall that x is non-negligible (by hypothesis). Hence, $\mathcal{B}$ has a non-negligible advantage of $\frac{p_Q(data_{\mathcal{B}})}{4} + \frac{x}{4}$ in the IND-CPA game, which contradicts the fact that AES-CBC is IND-CPA secure. Hence, we conclude that there does not exist any PPT adversary $\mathcal{A}$ that violates the property stated in the theorem.

Next, we assume, toward a contradiction, that there exists a PPT adversary $\mathcal{A}$ able from $data_{ext}$ to find correct query answers $Ans(G, Q_i)$ with a non-negligible advantage x:

$$|\Pr[\mathcal{A}^{guessAns}(data_{ext}) \in \bigcup_{1 \leq i \leq k} \{Ans(G, Q_i)\}] - p_{Ans}(data_{ext})| = x + negl(\lambda).$$

Similarly to the previous statement, if $data_{ext}$ does not correspond to an actual collection of encrypted messages as ext sees during an execution of GOOSE, then the advantage for such an input is naturally negligible.

We next show that by using the adversary $\mathcal{A}$, we can construct an adversary $\mathcal{B}$ able to break the IND-CPA property of AES-CBC [1,5]. We build an IND-CPA game, in which $\mathcal{B}$ chooses two values m_0, m_1, and sends them to the challenger. The challenger randomly selects $b \in \{0,1\}$ and answers with $Enc_{U\_AT}(m_b)$. Adversary $\mathcal{B}$ wins the IND-CPA game if $\mathcal{B}$ guesses b with a non-negligible advantage.

To do so, $\mathcal{B}$ simulates a GOOSE execution i.e., $\mathcal{B}$ chooses a graph G, a query workload consisting of a single query Q_1 such that $Ans(G, Q_1) = \{(v_1)\}$, and the functions used by DO during graph outsourcing; $\mathcal{B}$ does not know the keys shared among the participants of GOOSE. Let $data_\mathcal{B}$ be the set of encrypted messages seen by an external observer of the simulation of GOOSE done by $\mathcal{B}$, which includes, among others, $Enc_{U\_AT}(Ans(G, Q_1))$.

As input for the IND-CPA game, $\mathcal{B}$ chooses $m_1 = Ans(G, Q_1)$ and $m_0 = \{(v_1')\}$, where v_1' is a fresh node $\notin V$. Then, $\mathcal{B}$ sends m_0, m_1 to the challenger, and receives $Enc_{U\_AT}(m_b)$. Next, $\mathcal{B}$ calls $\mathcal{A}^{guessAns}(data_\mathcal{B} \setminus \{Enc_{U\_AT}(Ans(G, Q_1))\} \cup \{Enc_{U\_AT}(m_b)\})$. The strategy of $\mathcal{B}$ is as follows: if $\mathcal{A}$ returns $Ans(G, Q_1)$, then $\mathcal{B}$ answers 1. Otherwise, $\mathcal{B}$ answers randomly. We next derive the probability of a correct answer by $\mathcal{B}$:

- If $b = 0$ (probability $\frac{1}{2}$), then $\mathcal{A}$ does not receive a correct simulation because $v' \notin V$, hence v' could not belong to the answer set of a query from the workload. According to our assumption, in such a case $\mathcal{A}$ does not give any advantage. $\mathcal{B}$ answers randomly and is right with probability $\frac{1}{2}$, hence the probability of success of this branch is $\frac{1}{4}$.
- If $b = 1$ (probability $\frac{1}{2}$), then $\mathcal{B}$ can leverage the advantage given by $\mathcal{A}$.
  - If $\mathcal{A}$ returns $Ans(G, Q_1)$ (probability $p_{Ans}(data_\mathcal{B}) + x + negl(\lambda)$), then $\mathcal{B}$ correctly answers 1. The probability of success of this branch is $\frac{1}{2}(p_{Ans}(data_\mathcal{B}) + x + negl(\lambda))$.
  - Otherwise, (probability $1 - p_{Ans}(data_\mathcal{B}) - x - negl(\lambda)$), $\mathcal{B}$ answers randomly and is correct with probability $\frac{1}{2}$. This branch yields a probability of success of $\frac{1}{2}(1 - p_{Ans}(data_\mathcal{B}) - x - negl(\lambda))\frac{1}{2}$.

By aggregating these cases, the probability α of success of $\mathcal{B}$ is:

$$\alpha = \frac{1}{4} + \frac{1}{2}(p_{Ans}(data_\mathcal{B}) + x + negl(\lambda)) + \frac{1}{2}(1 - p_{Ans}(data_\mathcal{B}) - x - negl(\lambda))\frac{1}{2}$$

$$= \frac{1}{4} + \frac{p_{Ans}(data_\mathcal{B})}{2} + \frac{x}{2} + \frac{1}{4} - \frac{p_{Ans}(data_\mathcal{B})}{4} - \frac{x}{4} + negl(\lambda)$$

$$= \frac{1}{2} + \frac{p_{Ans}(data_\mathcal{B})}{4} + \frac{x}{4} + negl(\lambda)$$

Note that $p_E(data_\mathcal{B}) \geq 0$ (since it is a probability) and recall that x is non-negligible (by hypothesis). Hence, $\mathcal{B}$ has a non-negligible advantage of $\frac{p_{Ans}(data_\mathcal{B})}{4} + \frac{x}{4}$ in the IND-CPA game, which contradicts the fact that AES-CBC is IND-CPA secure. Hence, we conclude that there does not exist any PPT adversary $\mathcal{A}$ that violates the property stated in the theorem. $\qquad \square$

References

1. Advanced Encryption Standard (AES), FIPS Publication 197 (2001). https://nvlpubs.nist.gov/nistpubs/FIPS/NIST.FIPS.197.pdf
2. Aburawi, N., Lisitsa, A., Coenen, F.: Querying encrypted graph databases. In: ICISSP, pp. 447–451 (2018)
3. Bagan, G., Bonifati, A., Ciucanu, R., Fletcher, G.H.L., Lemay, A., Advokaat, N.: Generating flexible workloads for graph databases. PVLDB **9**(13), 1457–1460 (2016)
4. Bagan, G., Bonifati, A., Ciucanu, R., Fletcher, G.H.L., Lemay, A., Advokaat, N.: gMark: schema-driven generation of graphs and queries. IEEE TKDE **29**(4), 856–869 (2017)
5. Bellare, M., Desai, A., Jokipii, E., Rogaway, P.: A concrete security treatment of symmetric encryption. In: FOCS, pp. 394–403 (1997)
6. Boldyreva, A., Chenette, N., Lee, Y., O'Neill, A.: Order-preserving symmetric encryption. In: Joux, A. (ed.) EUROCRYPT 2009. LNCS, vol. 5479, pp. 224–241. Springer, Heidelberg (2009). https://doi.org/10.1007/978-3-642-01001-9_13
7. Bonifati, A., Martens, W., Timm, T.: An analytical study of large SPARQL query logs. VLDB J. **29**(2), 655–679 (2020)
8. Curino, C., et al.: Relational cloud: a database service for the cloud. In: CIDR, pp. 235–240 (2011)
9. Delanaux, R., Bonifati, A., Rousset, M.-C., Thion, R.: Query-based linked data anonymization. In: Vrandečić, D., et al. (eds.) ISWC 2018. LNCS, vol. 11136, pp. 530–546. Springer, Cham (2018). https://doi.org/10.1007/978-3-030-00671-6_31
10. Fernández, J.D., Kirrane, S., Polleres, A., Steyskal, S.: Self-enforcing access control for encrypted RDF. In: Blomqvist, E., Maynard, D., Gangemi, A., Hoekstra, R., Hitzler, P., Hartig, O. (eds.) ESWC 2017. LNCS, vol. 10249, pp. 607–622. Springer, Cham (2017). https://doi.org/10.1007/978-3-319-58068-5_37
11. Fernández, J., Kirrane, S., Polleres, A., Steyskal, S.: HDT$_{crypt}$: compression and encryption of RDF datasets. Semant. Web J. (2018)
12. Giereth, M.: On partial encryption of RDF-graphs. In: Gil, Y., Motta, E., Benjamins, V.R., Musen, M.A. (eds.) ISWC 2005. LNCS, vol. 3729, pp. 308–322. Springer, Heidelberg (2005). https://doi.org/10.1007/11574620_24
13. Goldreich, O.: The Foundations of Cryptography - Volume 2: Basic Applications. Cambridge University Press, Cambridge (2004)
14. Kasten, A., Scherp, A., Armknecht, F., Krause, M.: Towards search on encrypted graph data. In: PrivOn@ISWC (2013)
15. Kirrane, S., Abdelrahman, A., Mileo, A., Decker, S.: Secure manipulation of linked data. In: Alani, H., et al. (eds.) ISWC 2013. LNCS, vol. 8218, pp. 248–263. Springer, Heidelberg (2013). https://doi.org/10.1007/978-3-642-41335-3_16
16. Kirrane, S., Villata, S., d'Aquin, M.: Privacy, security and policies: a review of problems and solutions with semantic web technologies. Semant. Web **9**(2), 153–161 (2018)
17. Paillier, P.: Public-key cryptosystems based on composite degree residuosity classes. In: Stern, J. (ed.) EUROCRYPT 1999. LNCS, vol. 1592, pp. 223–238. Springer, Heidelberg (1999). https://doi.org/10.1007/3-540-48910-X_16
18. Popa, R.A., Redfield, C.M.S., Zeldovich, N., Balakrishnan, H.: CryptDB: protecting confidentiality with encrypted query processing. In: SOSP, pp. 85–100 (2011)

SGX-IR: Secure Information Retrieval with Trusted Processors

Fahad Shaon[✉] and Murat Kantarcioglu

The University of Texas at Dallas, Richardson, TX 75070, USA
{fahad.shaon,muratk}@utdallas.edu

Abstract. To preserve the security and the privacy of the data need for cloud applications, encrypting the data before outsourcing has emerged as an important tool. Furthermore, to enable efficient processing over the encrypted data stored in the cloud, utilizing efficient searchable symmetric encryption (SSE) schemes became popular. Usually, SSE schemes require an encrypted index to be built for efficient query processing. If the data owner has limited power, building this encrypted index before data is outsourced to the cloud could become a computational bottleneck. At the same time, secure outsourcing of encrypted index building using techniques such as homomorphic encryption is too costly for large data. Instead, in this work, we use a trusted processor, e.g, Intel Software Guard eXtension (SGX), to build a secure information retrieval system that provides better security guarantee and performance improvements. Unlike other related works, we focus on securely building the encrypted index in the cloud computing environment using the SGX, and show that the encrypted index could be used for executing keyword queries over text documents and face recognition detection in image documents. Finally, we show the effectiveness of our system via extensive empirical evaluation.

Keywords: Encrypted index building · Trusted processor · Secure search

1 Introduction

One of the reliable and proven approaches to keep data secure in the cloud environment is to encrypt data before uploading it to the cloud. As a result, searching and selectively retrieving encrypted data efficiently without significant information leakage has attracted a lot of attention recently. The most prominent solution is searchable symmetric encryption (SSE), where users create an encrypted index, outsource the index to cloud service provider and later find a subset of documents using carefully crafted trapdoors for query keywords. However, typical practical SSE systems trade-off some aspects of security for performance. Because providing complete security in the SSE setup has large overhead.

© IFIP International Federation for Information Processing 2020
Published by Springer Nature Switzerland AG 2020
A. Singhal and J. Vaidya (Eds.): DBSec 2020, LNCS 12122, pp. 367–387, 2020.
https://doi.org/10.1007/978-3-030-49669-2_21

On the other hand, we can build significantly secure encrypted applications for outsourced environments using trusted hardware, which allows a user to execute programs securely. Previously we needed specialized hardware to set up such a system. Now, Intel has included a security module named *Software Guard eXtension (SGX)* in 6th generation and afterward CPU. In short, SGX allows users to create secure isolated compartments (called *enclave*) inside the process. We can perform secure computation in the enclave that can not be altered without detection by the operating systems or hypervisor or other system-level processes. In addition, data stored inside the enclave is not *directly* observable.

Due to omnipresence and practicality, a lot of systems have been built using SGX including accessing the encrypted index. For instance, in Oblix [23], the authors propose few ways to access an inverted index obliviously inside the enclave. In HardIDX [13], authors propose building a secure B+ index, which can later be used to build other applications. In Rearguard [35] authors proposed a system to retrieve the list of documents obliviously from the encrypted index. However, in these works authors assume that the inverted index is already available and only focused on accessing the encrypted index securely. In contrast, we focus on building the index securely using SGX. Because building an inverted index might be trivial but it is very memory consuming computation. An inverted index is traditionally defined as a function that returns the list of documents associated with an input token. So, to build such an index by reading a set of input documents, we need to maintain a hash map (or equivalent data structure) of the token to document lists. For a memory constraint system, such as a smartphone, this computation might be infeasible. So in our design, we push as much computation to the SGX enclave as possible.

Furthermore, the existing works mainly focus on building systems targeting the text index. In our work, we also build a secure index for text and image search. Once we built the inverted index we can utilize existing index accessing systems to efficiently retrieve data.

Securely building an index entirely inside the SGX enclave has its challenges. First, SGX memory access can be observed by host operating system and memory access reviles a lot of information as shown in [17,24]. To protect against such attacks, we need to build data oblivious algorithms, i.e. we do not perform data specific branching so that an attacker that observes memory accesses can not learn any sensitive information. Second, SGX is a very memory-constrained environment one can effectively allocate about 90 MB of dynamic memory inside the enclave natively. So we need an efficient blocking and caching mechanism to process large datasets. To that end, we adopted SGX-BigMatrix [34] mechanism and we represent our internal data structures in BigMatrix.

We proposed a secure encrypted index building for text and image data. We build text index to support TF-IDF and different variants [9], such as log, augmented, boolean term frequency with cosine normalization. To do that efficiently, we first do document level summarization and create a stream of tuples of token id, document id, and count. Next, we encrypt and send it to the server. In the server, we compute different TF-IDF values. For face recognition, we encrypt the face images and send them to the server. In the server, we scale all the face images to the same size and calculate eigenfaces [36] of the input images. We adopt Jacobi's eigenvector calculation algorithm to compute the eigenfaces.

Our contributions in this work can be summarized as follows:

- We propose data oblivious algorithms for building an encrypted search index for text data that supports TF-IDF based ranked information retrieval.
- We propose data oblivious algorithm for computing eigenvectors for a given matrix and show how to use it for face recognition on encrypted image data.
- We build a prototype of the system and show its practical effectiveness.

2   Background

In this section, we provide background on Intel SGX, Data Obliviousness, and Secure Searchable Encryption to better explain our system.

2.1   Intel SGX

Intel SGX is a set of CPU instructions for executing secure code in Intel processors [5]. Using these instructions a program can create secure compartments in the CPU called an *enclave*. SGX uses systems main memory to store the code and data of enclave in an encrypted format and only decrypts inside the CPU. So, the operating system, hypervisor, and other privileged processes of the system can not *directly* observe computation inside the enclave. To leverage the security benefit we need partition the code into trusted and untrusted components. The trusted code is encrypted and integrity protected, but the untrusted code is directly observable by the operating system. During the program execution, the untrusted component creates an enclave with the trusted code. We can verify that the intended code is loaded and securely provision the code with secret keys using the *attestation* process. The trusted and untrusted components communicate with each other using programmer-defined entry points. Entry points defined in trusted code is called *ECalls*, which can be called by untrusted part once the enclave is loaded. Similarly, entry points defined in untrusted code is called *OCalls*, which can be called by the trusted part. More details about the SGX execution model are described in [10,26].

2.2   Data Oblivious Execution

A data oblivious program executes the same code path for all data inputs. We build our program to be data oblivious because we assume that, an adversary in an SGX environment can observe memory accesses, time to execute, OCalls, and any resource usages from OCalls [20]. However, an adversary in SGX cannot observe the content of the internal CPU registers. So, we remove data specific branching to reduce access pattern leakage, which has been shown to reveal information about data in [17,24].

Data arithmetic assembly instructions, such as add, mult, etc., are by definition data oblivious because the instruction performs the same task irrespective of any input data. However, conditional branching instructions are *not* data oblivious. For example, all jcc (jump if condition is met) family instructions, are not data oblivious because these instructions execute different parts of the code based on input data. To implement programs that require such conditional operations, we first assign values from all possible code paths, to different registers, then set a flag based on the condition that we want to test, swap according to the flag, and finally, return the contents of a fixed register. Such techniques are used in previous works (e.g., [25,32]).

2.3 Searchable Symmetric Encryption

Searchable Symmetric Encryption (SSE) is one of the prominent mechanisms to search encrypted files in a cloud computing environment. To achieve that we built and upload an encrypted index with the encrypted data. Traditionally SSE consists of five algorithms - Gen, Enc, Trpdr, Search, and Dec. Given a security parameter Gen generates a master symmetric key, Enc generates the encrypted inverted index and encrypted data sets from the input dataset, Trpdr algorithm takes keywords as input and outputs the trapdoor, which is used by the Search algorithm to find a list of documents associated with input keywords. Finally, the Dec algorithm decrypts the encrypted document given the id and the proper key. We refer the reader to [11] for further discussion of SSE. Traditionally Gen, Enc, Trpdr, and Dec are performed in a client device and the Search algorithm is performed in a cloud server. In these work we focus on preforming core part of the index building in the cloud server securely using trusted processors.

3 System

In this section, we outline our system details including setup and core building blocks. Our system has two components: client and server. We briefly discuss these components and the threat model below:

Client. To organize and properly utilize our server, we need a client program that runs in users device. It is capable of encrypting user data and send it to server for further computation. We also assume that computational capability of our users' systems are significantly limited. Our primary motivation is to off-load the index creation step for encrypted search to cloud. So that users with smaller capability machines can perform very large privacy preserving computation using secure server.

Server. Our server has hardware based trusted execution environment (i.e. Intel SGX) and services that manages and monitors secure enclave life-cycle.

Threat Model. We follow standard threat model of trusted processor base systems. Specifically, we are considering a scenario, where a user has large number of documents on which she wants to build search index in a secure cloud server. Our user do not trust the server completely. User expects that server will follow the given protocol but server will want to infer information form the data. User only trusts the trusted component of the server, e.g. Intel SGX. Apart for the trusted component, all other components of the server, such as, hypervisor, operating system, main memory, etc., are not trusted by the user. We are assuming that user can verify that server is executing proper code using proper attestation mechanism. In addition, we assume that communication between client and server is done over secure channel (TLS/SSL).

3.1 Storage

We adopted techniques outlined in SGX-BigMatrix [34] to store large dataset in our system. In short we break a large matrix into smaller blocks and load only blocks that are required to perform the intended operation. Once done we remove the block and encrypt the block again with session key and store in disk. We use least recently used (LRU) technique to manage the block caching. In addition, we also keep the IV and MAC of all the blocks into a header file, which is integrity protected.

3.2 Notation

We represent all of our data in two dimensional matrices. In some cases, we also define column names of matrices. We use $A[i]$ to denote i^{th} row of a 2D matrix or table, $A[i].col\_name$ to denote value of the column col_name on i^{th} row.

3.3 Oblivious Text Indexing in Server

To define the oblivious algorithm we need to avoid conditional branching, instead we perform flag based conditional move. We first define a secure building block *obliviousSelect*, which obliviously selects between two integer values based on comparison variables.

obliviousSelect(a, b, x, y): Let, a and b are two integers to select from, x and y be two comparison variables. We return a if $x == y$, otherwise return b. We show the most important lines of the implementation in the following code listing. We start by copying value of x and y to eax and ebx registers, then perform xor, in line 5. As a result, if x and y are equal then the zero flag is set. Next, we copy value of a and b into ecx and edx. Now we conditionally move values (based on zero flag) between ecx and edx registers, in line 9. So, if zero flag is set then edx will have the value of eax otherwise the value will remain unchanged. Finally, we return the value of edx register. In our setup, the adversary can only observe the sequence of operations but can not know exactly which value was selected.

```
1   oblivousSelect (a, b, x, y):
2   ...
3   mov %[x],%%eax
4   mov %[y],%%ebx
5   xor %%eax, %%ebx
6   ...
7   mov %[a],%%ecx
8   mov %[b],%%edx
9   cmovz %%ecx,%%edx
10  ...
11  mov %%edx, %[out]
```

Now, we define the oblivious text index building schema. We start by creating token and document pair and encrypting them in the client side. We perform initial tokenization in the client to achieve privacy (i.e., cloud only sees the encrypted data). In addition, we can perform tokenization using traditional algorithms, such as, Porter stemming [29], in one pass over the data. So we tokenize before data encryption. In addition, our client has limited memory so we use hash function to generate token id from lexical token. Let, $\mathcal{D} = \{d_1, d_2, ..., d_n\}$ be a set of input documents, $id(d_i)$ be the document id, Θ_d be set of tokens in document d, $\mathcal{H}$ be a collision resistant deterministic hash function that generates token-id from lexical, $tf_{t,d}$ be the number of times token t occurred in document d. We start by extracting tokens from all the documents. We build matrix I with three columns - $token\_id$, doc_id, and $frequency$. For all t in Θ_d we add $\langle \mathcal{H}(t), id(d), tf_{t,d} \rangle$ to I. We can perform this step easily on client, because in most of cases, text datasets consists of a lot of small files. Furthermore, if we need to process a large document we can split it into smaller files then process as usual. Next, we encrypt I and send it to server.

In the server, we start by decrypting I inside the enclave. Next, we obliviously sort I in ascending order of token id and assign the result to I', as listed in Algorithm 1 in line 3. We utilize bitonic sorting algorithm for oblivious sorting, more on our sorting implementation in Sect. 3.4. Next, We define two matrices $\mathcal{U}(token\_id, count, sum)$ to store the number of documents that a token occurred and summation of total occurrences of all tokens. We iterate sequentially over I, calculate token boundary condition $c \leftarrow I'[i].token\_id \neq I'[i-1].token\_id$, in line 8. If c is true, this implies that we are now reading a new token's information otherwise we are reading current token's information. Based on c we obliviously fill $count$ and sum column of $\mathcal{U}$ with the count and summation of the token or a dummy value, in lines 9 to 13. We sort $\mathcal{U}$ based on $token\_id$, to move the dummy values to end, in line 15. At this stage, in $\mathcal{U}$, i^{th} row has the count and sum of $(i-1)^{th}$ token. So, we shift the count and sum one row in lines 15 and 16. To access a token's information obliviously, we need to create an equal length block for all the tokens. One approach can be, find the maximum count of any token and allocate the maximum number of elements per token. However, based on the experimental results, we observe that token frequencies

---

Algorithm 1. Text index building

1: **Require:** $I = n \times 3$ input matrix
2: **Output:** $\mathcal{T} =$ Index $p \times 3$ and $DF = p \times 2$ matrices
3: $I' \leftarrow obliviousSort(I, token\_id)$
4: $\# \leftarrow -1$ ▷ dummy value
5: $sum \leftarrow 0, count \leftarrow 0$
6: $\mathcal{U}[0] \leftarrow \langle I'[0].token\_id, 0, 0 \rangle$
7: **for** i = 1 **to** $I'.length$ **do**
8:     $c \leftarrow I'[i].token\_id \neq I'[i-1].tok\_id$
9:     $\mathcal{U}[i].token\_id \leftarrow obliviousSelect(I[i].tok\_id, \#, 1, c)$
10:     $\mathcal{U}[i].count \leftarrow obliviousSelect(count, \#, 1, c)$
11:     $\mathcal{U}[i].sum \leftarrow obliviousSelect(sum, \#, 1, c)$
12:     $count \leftarrow obliviousSelect(count, 0, 1, c) + 1$
13:     $sum \leftarrow obliviousSelect(sum, 0, 1, c) + I[i].frequency$
14: **end for**
15: $\mathcal{U}' \leftarrow obliviousSort(\mathcal{U}, token\_id)$
16: $\mathcal{U}'[i].count = \mathcal{U}'[i+1].count$
17: $\mathcal{U}'[i].sum = \mathcal{U}'[i+1].sum$
18: Remove rows with $\#$
19: Generate inverse document frequency from $\mathcal{U}'$
20: $b \leftarrow optimizeBlockSize(\mathcal{U}.count)$
21: $count \leftarrow 0$
22: **for** i = 0 **to** $I'.length$ **do**
23:     $J[i].token\_id \leftarrow \sigma(I'[i].token\_id, \lfloor \frac{count}{b} \rfloor)$
24:     $count \leftarrow obliviousSelect(count + 1, 0, 1, count < b)$
25: **end for**
26: **for** i = 0 **to** $numToken$ **do**
27:     **for** j = b − 1 **to** 0 **do**
28:         $c \leftarrow \mathcal{U}'[i].count\%b < j$
29:         $t \leftarrow \sigma(\mathcal{U}'[i].token\_id, \lfloor \frac{\mathcal{U}'[i].count}{b} \rfloor)$
30:         $X[i*b+j].token\_id \leftarrow obliviousSelect(t, \#, 1, c)$
31:     **end for**
32: **end for**
33: $\mathcal{T} \leftarrow mergeAndSort(J, X, doc\_id)$

---

follow Pareto distribution or power law, i.e., a large number of tokens will appear in a relatively small number of documents. So if we block based on the maximum token count, we will have a lot of dummy entries. To reduce the storage overhead, we split large token into smaller blocks. We use optimization strategies outlined in [33] to find the optimal size of b. We adopt this specific technique because it assumes a distribution of frequencies rather than relying on real data. In our scenario, the block size will be revealed to the adversary, so such an approach will help us reduce the information leakage. Next, we define a deterministic collision-resistant hash function σ that returns a new *token_id* given *token_id* and relative block number. For all the entries in I', we apply σ on token id and generate J matrix with *token_id'*, *doc_id*, and *frequency*, in lines 21 to 25. Next, for all the tokens in $\mathcal{U}'$ we add $\mathcal{U}[i]'.count\%b$ dummy entries into X obliviously,

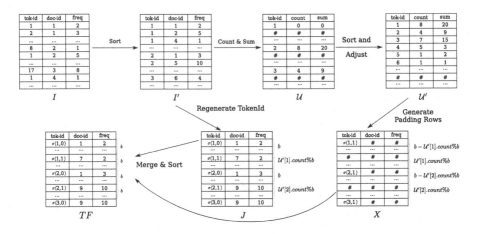

Fig. 1. Text indexing example

in lines 26 to 32. Also, we merge X with J and sort the resulting matrix. Finally, we remove the rows with only dummy entries. So that $\mathcal{T}$ contain m rows per token. Now we push m rows into *any* standard ORAM if we want to access specific token information obliviously in sub-linear time. Otherwise, we can read a token's information obliviously by reading the entire $\mathcal{T}$ matrix once. Figure 1 illustrates an example of secure text indexing.

3.4 Oblivious Arbitrary Length Bitonic Sort

We use bitonic sort [6] for sorting in the server, because in bitonic sort we perform exactly the same comparisons irrespective of input data value. Specifically we use the arbitrary length version to save time and space. In our empirical analysis, we have observe that total number to rows in matrices I, J, etc. can go up to 2^{26} or more. So to utilize traditional bitonic sort, we need to pad the matrices with dummy entries to 2^{27} number of rows. In practice, we observe that this adds upto 40% overhead. In addition, we implement an iterative variant of the bitonic sort of arbitrary length. We avoid recursion to save stack space, since SGX is a memory constraint environment. In Algorithm 2 we define our iterative implementation. We utilize existing definition of iterative bitonic sort defined in [8,38] for length 2^k. The core idea behind this implementation is that any number can be expressed as summation of one or more 2^k format numbers, such as, $N = 2^{x_1} + ... + 2^{x_m}$. For given N element array/matrix, we consider it as block of $2^{x_1}, ..., 2^{x_{m-1}}$ rows. We sort first $(m-1)$ blocks in descending order and sort the final block m ascending order using existing definition of non-recursive bitonic sort. Next we merge last two blocks m and $(m-1)$ in ascending order. We iteratively continue to merge the result with previous block. So, finally we get a sorted array/matrix in ascending order. In addition, we also make the exchange step oblivious. So the adversary will not get any additional information from sequence of comparisons and successful swaps.

Algorithm 2. Non-recursive non-trivial bitonic sort for arbitrary length

```
 1: for  d = 0 to ⌈log₂(N)⌉  do
 2:     if  ((N >> d)&1) ≠ 0 then
 3:         start ← (−1 << (d + 1))&N
 4:         size ← 1 << d
 5:         dir ← (size&N& − N) == (N& − N)
 6:         bitonicSort2K(start, size, dir)
 7:         if !dir then
 8:             bitonicMerge(start, N − start, 1)
 9:         end if
10:     end if
11: end for
```

3.5 Image Indexing for Face Recognition

For face recognition we adopt *Eigenface* [36]. It is a very well studied, effective yet simple technique for face recognition using static 2D face image. We first discuss Eigenface technique then outline the oblivious version of it. This face recognition technique consists of three major operations - finding eigenvectors of faces, finding weights of each faces, and finally recognition.

Finding Eigenvectors. We start with M face centered upright frontal images that are represented as $N \times N$ square matrices. Let, $\{\Gamma_1, ..., \Gamma_M\}$ are $N^2 \times 1$ vector representation of these square matrices, $\Psi = \frac{1}{M} \sum_{i=1}^{M} \Gamma_i$ is the average of these vectors, and $\Phi_i = \Gamma_i - \Psi$ is computed by subtracting average Ψ from ith image vector.

Now eigenvectors u_i of co-variance matrix $C = AA^T$, where $A = [\Phi_1 \ \Phi_2 ... \Phi_M]$, can be used to approximate the faces. However, there are N^2 eigenvectors for C. In practice N^2 can be a very large number, thus computing eigenvectors of C can be very difficult. So instead of AA^T matrix we compute eigenvectors of $A^T A$ and take top K vectors for approximating eigenvectors u_i, where $\|u_i\| = 1$.

Finding Weights. We can represent Φ_i as a linear combination of these eigenvectors, $\Phi_i = \sum_{j=1}^{K} w_j u_j$ and weights are $w_j = u_j^T \Phi_i$. Each normalized image is represented in this basis as a vector $\Omega_i = \begin{bmatrix} w_1 & w_2 & ... & w_k \end{bmatrix}^T$ for $i = 1, 2, ... M$. This is essentially projecting face images into new eigenspace (the collection of eigenvectors).

Recognition. Given a probe image Γ, we first normalize $\Phi = \Gamma - \Psi$ then project into eigenspace such that $\Omega = \begin{bmatrix} w_1 & w_2 & ... & w_K \end{bmatrix}^T$, where $w_i = u_i^T \Phi$. Now we need to find out nearest faces in this eigenspace by $e_r = min \|\Omega - \Omega_i\|$. If $e_r <$ a threshold chosen heuristically, then we can say that the probe image is recognized as the image with which it gives the lowest score.

In summary, we consider face images as a point in a high dimensional space (the eigenspace). We compute the eigenspace by finding few significant eigen vectors of the co-variance matrix. Now during recognition phase we project the face into this eigenspace and compute distance between all the training faces. If any training image is bellow the predetermined threshold the we report it as a match.

Oblivious Eigenface. To make the entire process data oblivious, we need oblivious eigen vector calculation and oblivious comparison of projected test image. We discuss oblivious eigen vector calculation in a separate subsection. For oblivious distance calculation, we compute the distance function for all input training faces. We create $M \times 2$ matrix $\mathcal{F}$, where first column is face id and second column contains 1 if that face's distance is bellow the threshold and 0 otherwise. Finally, we sort $\mathcal{F}$ based on second column in descending order to get the matching face id.

3.6 Oblivious Eigen Vector Calculation

We adopted Jacobi method [14] of eigen vector computation for oblivious calculation. In Jacobi eigenvalue method, we start with finding maximum value and index of maximum value (k, l) in input symmetric matrix. Next we compute few values based on max, $A_{k,l}$, $A_{l,k}$ Next, we assign zero to $A_{k,l}$ and $A_{l,k}$, and compute $A_{k,k}$ and $A_{l,l}$. Then, we perform rotations on k^{th} column and l^{th} column. However, since this is a symmetric matrix we can perform same computation only on upper triangular matrix. We also perform the same rotation on eigen matrix E, which is initialized with identity matrix We repeat the process until the input matrix becomes diagonal. The values in the main diagonal approximates the eigen values and normalized version of the eigen matrix E consists of all the eigen vectors of matrix A. In practice, for eigenface, we need top n largest eigen vectors. To extract top n eigen vectors we sort the eigen vectors based on eigen values. In Appendix A we outline an implementation of Jacobi method.

Now, to build an oblivious version, we need to read and write the matrix obliviously. So, we define a few additional oblivious functions, which we use later in the oblivious eigenvector calculation algorithm.

obliviousValueExtract(U, k): Given an array U and an index k, we extract the value of U_x obliviously. We initialize $v \leftarrow U_0$ then we iterate over all the elements in the array and run *obliviousSelect(v, U_i, i, k)* and assign the return value to v. As a result, when i is equal to k the return value will be U_k, otherwise it will always return existing value of v. Similarly we define *obliviousValueAssign(U, k, a)*, where we assign value a to k^{th} location of input array U.

obliviousColumnExtract(A, k): Given a 2D matrix A and a column index k, we extract k^{th} column of matrix A. We utilized previously defined oblivious select. For a given row, r, we iterate over all the columns c and assign U_r to output of *obliviousSelect($A_{r,c}, U_r, r, k$)*. As a result, when r is equal to k then we get the value of $A_{r,c}$ in U_r, otherwise value of U_r remains the same. Similarly, we define *obliviousColumnAssign()* and *obliviousRowAssign()*, where we assign the input column in a specific column or row of input matrix. In addition, we also define *obliviousConditionalColumnAssign()* and *obliviousConditionalRowAssign()*, with one more boolean parameter, where we perform the assignment if and only if the boolean parameter is true.

obliviousMaxIndex(&m, e, &mR, &mC, eR, eC): Let, &m be the reference of current maximum value, e be current element value, &mR and &mC be the reference of row and column of current maximum element, eR and eC be the row and column of element. We update the value of m with e, mR with eR, and mC with eC, if $m < e$, otherwise we keep the values of &m, &mR, and &mC.

We start by copying the current element and current maximum into floating-point stacks in st(1) and st(0). Next, we perform floating-point comparison, as shown in line 3 in the following code listing, which sets zero flag, carry flag, and parity flag accordingly. Next, we perform fcmovb conditional move operation that swaps values in the floating-point stack if the carry flag is set, in line 4. As a result, the maximum value will be at the top of the floating-point stack, which we assign back to the maximum variable.

Next, we move row of maximum and current element into two registers, eax and ebx respectively, in lines 6 and 7. Then we again conditionally swap these two registers and the flag was set during the initial float comparison, in line 8. So, the index of the largest value will be in eax, which read back to mR variable. Similarly, we also perform a conditional move for maximum column index in lines 10, 11, and 12.

```
 1   obliviousMaxIndex(&m, e, &mR, &mC, eR, eC):
 2   ...
 3   fucomi %%st(1), %%st
 4   fcmovb %%st(1), %%st
 5   ...
 6   mov %[mR],%%eax
 7   mov %[eR],%%ebx
 8   cmovb %%ebx, %%eax
 9   ...
10   mov %[mC],%%eax
11   mov %[eC],%%ebx
12   cmovb %%ebx, %%eax
13   ...
```

Algorithm 3. Oblivious Eigen vector with Jacobi method

1: **Require:** $A = n \times n$ diagonal matrix
2: **Output:** $E =$ eigen vectors, $V =$ eigen values
3: $E \leftarrow identity(n)$
4: $\epsilon_1 \leftarrow 10^{-12}, \epsilon_2 \leftarrow 10^{-36}$
5: **for** it $= 0$ **to** n^2 **do**
6:     $max, k, l \leftarrow obliviousMaxIndex(A)$
7:     $\mathcal{C} \leftarrow max < \epsilon_1$
8:     $U \leftarrow obliviousColumnExtract(A, k)$
9:     $V \leftarrow obliviousColumnExtract(A, l)$
10:     $kk \leftarrow obliviousValueExtract(U, k)$
11:     $ll \leftarrow obliviousValueExtract(V, l)$
12:     $d \leftarrow ll - kk$
13:     $m \leftarrow |max| < \epsilon_2|d|$
14:     $p \leftarrow \frac{d}{2 \times max}$
15:     $t_1 \leftarrow \frac{max}{d}, t_2 \leftarrow |\frac{1}{|p|+\sqrt{p^2+1}}|$
16:     $t \leftarrow obliviousSelect(t_1, t_2, m, 1)$
17:     $c \leftarrow \frac{1}{\sqrt{t^2+1}}, s \leftarrow t \times c, \tau \leftarrow \frac{s}{1+c}$
18:     $\mathcal{R} \leftarrow s. \begin{bmatrix} -\tau & -1 \\ 1 & -\tau \end{bmatrix}$
19:     $\begin{bmatrix} U \\ V \end{bmatrix} + = \mathcal{R} \times \begin{bmatrix} U \\ V \end{bmatrix}$
20:     $kk \leftarrow kk - t \times max, ll \leftarrow ll + t \times max$
21:     $obliviousValueAssign(U, k, kk)$
22:     $obliviousValueAssign(V, l, ll)$
23:     $obliviousValueAssign(U, l, 0)$
24:     $obliviousValueAssign(V, k, 0)$
25:     $obliviousConditionalColumnAssign(A, U, k, !\mathcal{C})$
26:     $obliviousConditionalColumnAssign(A, V, l, !\mathcal{C})$
27:     $obliviousConditionalRowAssign(A, U, k, !\mathcal{C})$
28:     $obliviousConditionalRowAssign(A, V, l, !\mathcal{C})$
29:     $U \leftarrow obliviousColumnExtract(E, k)$
30:     $V \leftarrow obliviousColumnExtract(E, l)$
31:     $\begin{bmatrix} U \\ V \end{bmatrix} + = \mathcal{R} \times \begin{bmatrix} U \\ V \end{bmatrix}$
32:     $obliviousConditionalColumnAssign(E, U, k, !\mathcal{C})$
33:     $obliviousConditionalColumnAssign(E, V, l, !\mathcal{C})$
34: **end for**
35: $V_i \leftarrow A_{i,i}, \forall i \in 0$ to n
36: $normalize(E)$
37: $sort(E)$ based on V

Now, we create the data oblivious version of Jacobi's eigenvalue calculation, as listed in Algorithm 3. First, we fix the number of iterations and do not return early based on convergence. As a result, the adversary can not learn information about data based on the iteration count. Next for finding the maximum, max and index of maximum elements (k, l) using $obliviousMaxIndex$ operation in line 6.

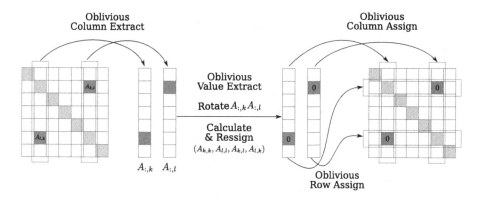

Fig. 2. Oblivious eigen matrix calculation

We extract k^{th} and l^{th} columns, U and V using *obliviousColumnExtract*, in lines 8 and 9. Next, we extract values of kk and ll using *obliviousValueExtract* operation in lines 10 and 11. Next, we calculate value τ, t, s in lines from 12 to 17. For t we first calculate both $\frac{max}{d}$ and $|\frac{1}{|p|+\sqrt{p^2+1}}|$ then we obliviously choose correct version using *obliviousSelect*. Next, we perform the rotation on extracted column and assign k^{th} and l^{th} value of U and V appropriately in lines 18 to 24. Then, we assign the column back to A if the algorithm is not converged, in lines 25 to 28. We also illustrate these operations in Fig. 2. We determine convergence condition $\mathcal{C}$ in line 7 by check whether the current maximum is smaller than a predefined small value. We perform similar rotation on matrix E, in lines 29 to 33. We iterate the entire process fix number of times. Finally, we normalize and sort the eigen matrix based on eigenvalues in lines 35 to 37. The normalization process is naturally data oblivious, i.e. we execute same instructions irrespective of input data. For sorting we use our previously defined bitonic sort.

4   Experimental Evaluations

In this section, we discuss the performance of our proposed system. We develop a prototype of the proposed system SGX-IR, using *Intel Software Extensions SDK 2.6* for Linux. We write most of the code in $C++$ with the exception of the *oblivious* blocks, which we write in assembly. We also have implemented numerous unit tests to ensure the correctness of the oblivious blocks. Since our building blocks are data oblivious, the final prototype is data oblivious as well. We perform the experiments on a *Intel LR1304SPCFSGX1* server with *Intel®* *Xeon® CPU E3-1270 @ 3.80* GHz CPU, *64* GB main memory, *128* MB enclave memory, and running *Ubuntu Server 18.04*.

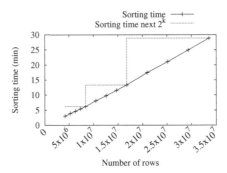

Fig. 3. Bitonic sort time

4.1 Bitonic Sort

We first briefly discuss the impact of arbitrary length bitonic sort. In Fig. 3 we show that sort time of the different size matrices with 3 columns. The solid line represents sorting duration and the dotted line represents sorting duration for the next 2^k element matrix. With the arbitrary length algorithm, the growth of the required time is linear. On the other hand, the required time of the 2^k version is a step function. In extreme cases, it has close to 50% overhead.

4.2 Text Indexing

Dataset. We use Enron dataset [18] for text indexing experiments. We randomly select sub-set of files from the Enron dataset. Then we parse the data in the client end. We tokenize, stem [29], and build document token pairs. Next, we encrypt and send the data to server. In server we follow the algorithm outlined in Sect. 3.3 to sort and generate index.

Performance. In Fig. 4(a) we show the performance of client-side index pre-processing. We show time to build the input matrix using different types of cryptographic and non-cryptographic hashing functions and keeping an in-memory map for token id generation. We observe that incrementation token id generation is the most expensive and non-cryptographic hash, i.e., MurMur Hash, is the least expensive. In addition, we show the time required for only encrypting the data without performing any tokenization and token id generation, which shows the overhead of read-write and encryption. The gap between encryption only and a hashing token id generation signifies the overhead of our tokenization and matrix generation. Finally, in all theses cases we observe the growth is linear.

In Fig. 4(b) we show server-side index processing cost. We compare our results with a non-oblivious version of a similar index building. For non-oblivious implementation, we sort the input matrix based on token id then build a separate matrix that is equivalent to $\mathcal{T}$ by iterating the sorted matrix. We observe that

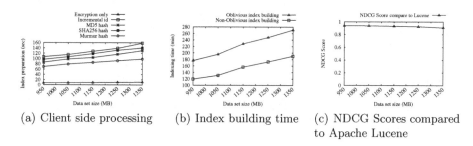

(a) Client side processing   (b) Index building time   (c) NDCG Scores compared
to Apache Lucene

Fig. 4. Enron experiment

the obliviousness implementation is about 1.49 times more expensive. Finally, to show the effectiveness, of our information retrieval system we compare ranked results with Apache Lucene [1] library result. Apache Lucene library is the de-facto standard of information retrieval library and is used in numerous commercial and open-source search engine software, such as Apache Solr [2], Elasticsearch [3]. We adopt normalized discounted cumulative gain (NDCG) score [9] to compare the ranked results of the information retrieval systems. In Fig. 4(c) we report the NDCG score of our system compared to Apache Lucene for randomly selected 1,000 tokens. We observe that our scores are about 0.92. In other words, our model works relatively well compared to the industry-standard information retrieval system. In addition, we allow different types of frequency normalizations. So users of the system can tune the normalization functions to improve the results as needed.

4.3 Face Recognition

Dataset. We use *Color FERET* [27,28] dataset for testing face recognition. *Color FERET* dataset contains a total of 11338 facial images, which were collected by photographing 994 subjects at various angles. The dataset images contain face images in front of different background often containing other objects. So, wrote a face detection program using OpenCV implementation of haar cascade classifier [21,37] for frontal face. We extract frontal face images with `fa` suffix from the dataset. We found that there are total 1364 such images. Our face detection system successfully detected 1235 images, yielding 90.33% accuracy. Here, most of the failed cases has glass or similar face obstructing additions. We extract the frontal faces and scale to 100×100 faces. Then we randomly selected sub-set of images and build our face recognition dataset.

Performance. In Fig. 5(a), we show the performance of face image preparation and in Fig. 5(c) face finding overhead. Both of these operations are standard matrix operations. So overheads are very minimal under a minute. In Fig. 5(b) we show the required time for building the eigenface index, which is dominated by the overhead of in eigenvector calculation. We compare our results with a non-oblivious version of the algorithm. For the non-oblivious version, we implement

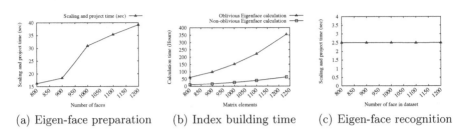

(a) Eigen-face preparation   (b) Index building time   (c) Eigen-face recognition

Fig. 5. Oblivious eigen-face experiment

the Jacobi algorithm without accessing the matrix values obliviously. We observe that both the cases the required times are quite large because of the large number required iteration for the Jacobi algorithm to converge. We observe that, the obliviousness adds around 5 times more overhead. We incur such large overheads because we read the entire matrix to extract and assign the required rows and columns.

5 Related Work

System Using Intel SGX. Because of the availability and sound security guarantees, Intel SGX is already used in many studies to build secure systems. For instance, Ohrimenko et al. [25] proposed algorithms to perform machine learning in multi-party settings obliviously using SGX. Here authors also has shown the effectiveness of oblivious primitives to achieve data obliviousness. In [34] authors built oblivious system to analyze large datasets using SGX, which we adopted for our data storage. In [41], the authors proposed a package for Apache Spark SQL named Opaque, which enables SQL query processing in a distributed manner. Opaque offers data encryption and access pattern hiding using Intel SGX. EnclaveDB [30], ObliDB [12], and StealthDB [15] also proposed secure database functionality with Intel SGX. Part of the text indexing processing in Sect. 3.3 can be expressed with some non-traditional relational algebra, which can be expressed with techniques described in this works. However, for completeness and efficiency reason we describe our own version.

Intel SGX Based Search Index. In Rearguard [35] authors build search indexes for different types of keyword searches. However, authors assumed to have an initial inverted index built in client end. In HardIDX [13] authors proposed building secure B+ index and used it to build encrypted databases and searchable encryption schema. However, proposed algorithms are not made oblivious as a result leaks a lot of information via a side channel. In Oblix [23] authors proposed building different type of oblivious data structures using oblivious ram (ORAM) techniques. In [16], authors used Oblix data structures to build large scale search systems. However, authors build the index in client side. We consider our work as a complement to these works one can build index using our techniques and use these systems later to access the inverted index. Finally, in [4] Intel maintains a somewhat extensive categorized list of academic research publications related to SGX.

Searchable Encryption Systems. SSE has been studied extensively as shown in an extensive survey of provably secure searchable encryption by Bösch at el. in [7]. One of the relevant SSE schemas is defined by Kuzu at el. in [19], where authors used locality sensitive hashing to convert similarity search into equality search. In [33] authors proposed SSE schema for image data and complex queries, such as, face recognition, image similarity, using simple server storage. In addition, there has been several works to build content based secure image retrieval in [22,31,39]. In [40] authors proposed secure image retrieval using SGX as well. However, in their construction authors are building the index in client side and the system is not oblivious.

6 Conclusion

In this work, we propose a secure information retrieval system for text and image data. Unlike other existing works, we focus on building the encrypted index in the cloud securely using trusted processors, such as Intel SGX. We address the information leakage due to memory access pattern issue by proposing data oblivious indexing algorithms. We build a text index to support ranked document retrieval using TF-IDF scoring mechanisms. Also, we build an image index to support the face recognition query. In addition, we also propose a non-recursive version of the bitonic sort algorithm for arbitrary input length.

Acknowledgments. We thank the anonymous reviewers for their insightful comments. The research reported herein was supported in part by NIH award 1R01HG006844, NSF awards CICI-1547324, IIS-1633331, CNS-1837627, OAC-1828467 and ARO award W911NF-17-1-0356.

A Jacobi Method Implementation

In this section we provide an implementation of Jacobi algorithm. In this particular implementation we change only upper triangular elements.

Algorithm 4. Eigen vector with Jacobi method

1: **Require:** $A = n \times n$ diagonal matrix
2: **Output:** E = eigen vectors, V = eigen values
3: $E \leftarrow identity(n)$
4: $\epsilon_1 \leftarrow 10^{-12}$, $\epsilon_2 \leftarrow 10^{-36}$
5: **for** it $= 0$ **to** n^2 **do**
6:     $max \leftarrow max(A)$ in off-diagonal upper triangle
7:     $(k, l) \leftarrow maxIndex(A)$
8:     **if** $max < \epsilon_1$ **then**
9:         $V_i \leftarrow A_{i,i}, \forall i \in 0$ to n
10:         $normalize(E)$
11:         **return**
12:     **end if**
13:     $d \leftarrow A_{l,l} - A_{k,k}$
14:     **if** $|A_{k,l}| < \epsilon_2 |d|$ **then**
15:         $t \leftarrow \frac{A_{k,l}}{d}$
16:     **else**
17:         $p \leftarrow \frac{d}{2A_{k,l}}$
18:         $t \leftarrow |\frac{1}{|p|+\sqrt{p^2+1}}|$
19:     **end if**
20:     $c \leftarrow \frac{1}{\sqrt{t^2+1}}$, $s \leftarrow t \times c$, $\tau \leftarrow \frac{s}{1+c}$
21:     $A_{k,k} \leftarrow A_{k,k} - t \times A_{k,l}$, $A_{l,l} \leftarrow A_{l,l} + t \times A_{k,l}$, $A_{k,l} \leftarrow 0$
22:     $\mathcal{R} \leftarrow s.\begin{bmatrix} -\tau & -1 \\ 1 & -\tau \end{bmatrix}$
23:     **for** $i = 0$ **to** $k - 1$ **do**
24:         $\begin{bmatrix} A_{i,k} \\ A_{i,l} \end{bmatrix} += \mathcal{R} \times \begin{bmatrix} A_{i,k} \\ A_{i,l} \end{bmatrix}$
25:     **end for**
26:     **for** $i = k + 1$ **to** $l - 1$ **do**
27:         $\begin{bmatrix} A_{k,i} \\ A_{i,l} \end{bmatrix} += \mathcal{R} \times \begin{bmatrix} A_{k,i} \\ A_{i,l} \end{bmatrix}$
28:     **end for**
29:     **for** $i = l + 1$ **to** $n - 1$ **do**
30:         $\begin{bmatrix} A_{k,i} \\ A_{l,i} \end{bmatrix} += \mathcal{R} \times \begin{bmatrix} A_{k,i} \\ A_{l,i} \end{bmatrix}$
31:     **end for**
32:     **for** $i = 0$ **to** $n - 1$ **do**
33:         $\begin{bmatrix} E_{i,k} \\ E_{i,l} \end{bmatrix} += \mathcal{R} \times \begin{bmatrix} E_{i,k} \\ E_{i,l} \end{bmatrix}$
34:     **end for**
35: **end for**

References

1. Apache Lucene. https://lucene.apache.org/. Accessed 20 Apr 2020
2. Apache Solor. https://lucene.apache.org/solr/. Accessed 20 Apr 2020
3. Elasticsearch. https://www.elastic.co/. Accessed 20 Apr 2020

4. Intel software guard extension - academic research. https://software.intel.com/en-us/sgx/documentation/academic-research. Accessed 20 Apr 2020

5. Anati, I., Gueron, S., Johnson, S., Scarlata, V.: Innovative technology for CPU based attestation and sealing. In: Proceedings of the 2nd International Workshop on Hardware and Architectural Support for Security and Privacy, vol. 13 (2013)

6. Batcher, K.E.: Sorting networks and their applications. In: Proceedings of the April 30–May 2, 1968, Spring Joint Computer Conference, pp. 307–314. ACM (1968)

7. Bösch, C., Hartel, P., Jonker, W., Peter, A.: A survey of provably secure searchable encryption. ACM Comput. Surv. (CSUR) **47**(2), 18 (2015)

8. Christopher, T.W.: Bitonic sort. https://www.tools-of-computing.com/tc/CS/Sorts/bitonic_sort.htm. Accessed 20 Apr 2020

9. Manning, C.D., Raghavan, P., Schütze, H.: Introduction to Information Retrieval. Cambridge University Press, Cambridge (2008)

10. Costan, V., Devadas, S.: Intel SGX explained. IACR Cryptology ePrint Archive 2016(086), 1–118 (2016)

11. Curtmola, R., Garay, J., Kamara, S., Ostrovsky, R.: Searchable symmetric encryption: improved definitions and efficient constructions. In: Proceedings of the 13th ACM Conference on Computer and Communications Security, pp. 79–88. ACM (2006)

12. Eskandarian, S., Zaharia, M.: ObliDB: oblivious query processing using hardware enclaves. arXiv preprint arXiv:1710.00458 (2017)

13. Fuhry, B., Bahmani, R., Brasser, F., Hahn, F., Kerschbaum, F., Sadeghi, A.-R.: HardIDX: practical and secure index with SGX. In: Livraga, G., Zhu, S. (eds.) DBSec 2017. LNCS, vol. 10359, pp. 386–408. Springer, Cham (2017). https://doi.org/10.1007/978-3-319-61176-1_22

14. Golub, G.H., Van der Vorst, H.A.: Eigenvalue computation in the 20th century. In: Numerical Analysis: Historical Developments in the 20th Century, pp. 209–239. Elsevier (2001)

15. Gribov, A., Vinayagamurthy, D., Gorbunov, S.: StealthDB: a scalable encrypted database with full SQL query support. arXiv preprint arXiv:1711.02279 (2017)

16. Hoang, T., Ozmen, M.O., Jang, Y., Yavuz, A.A.: Hardware-supported oram in effect: practical oblivious search and update on very large dataset. Proc. Priv. Enhanc. Technol. **2019**(1), 172–191 (2019)

17. Islam, M.S., Kuzu, M., Kantarcioglu, M.: Access pattern disclosure on searchable encryption: ramification, attack and mitigation. In: NDSS, vol. 20, p. 12 (2012)

18. Klimt, B., Yang, Y.: The Enron corpus: a new dataset for email classification research. In: Boulicaut, J.-F., Esposito, F., Giannotti, F., Pedreschi, D. (eds.) ECML 2004. LNCS (LNAI), vol. 3201, pp. 217–226. Springer, Heidelberg (2004). https://doi.org/10.1007/978-3-540-30115-8_22

19. Kuzu, M., Islam, M.S., Kantarcioglu, M.: Efficient similarity search over encrypted data. In: 2012 IEEE 28th International Conference on Data Engineering (ICDE), pp. 1156–1167. IEEE (2012)

20. Lee, S., Shih, M.W., Gera, P., Kim, T., Kim, H., Peinado, M.: Inferring fine-grained control flow inside {SGX} enclaves with branch shadowing. In: 26th {USENIX} Security Symposium ({USENIX} Security 2017), pp. 557–574 (2017)

21. Lienhart, R., Maydt, J.: An extended set of Haar-like features for rapid object detection. In: 2002 Proceedings of the International Conference on Image Processing, vol. 1, pp. I-900. IEEE (2002)

22. Lu, W., Swaminathan, A., Varna, A.L., Wu, M.: Enabling search over encrypted multimedia databases. In: IS&T/SPIE Electronic Imaging, p. 725418. International Society for Optics and Photonics (2009)

23. Mishra, P., Poddar, R., Chen, J., Chiesa, A., Popa, R.A.: Oblix: an efficient oblivious search index. In: 2018 IEEE Symposium on Security and Privacy (SP), pp. 279–296. IEEE (2018)

24. Naveed, M., Kamara, S., Wright, C.V.: Inference attacks on property-preserving encrypted databases. In: Proceedings of the 22nd ACM SIGSAC Conference on Computer and Communications Security, pp. 644–655. ACM (2015)

25. Ohrimenko, O., et al.: Oblivious multi-party machine learning on trusted processors. In: 25th USENIX Security Symposium (USENIX Security 2016), pp. 619–636. USENIX Association, Austin (2016)

26. Pass, R., Shi, E., Tramèr, F.: Formal abstractions for attested execution secure processors. In: Coron, J.-S., Nielsen, J.B. (eds.) EUROCRYPT 2017. LNCS, vol. 10210, pp. 260–289. Springer, Cham (2017). https://doi.org/10.1007/978-3-319-56620-7_10

27. Phillips, P.J., Moon, H., Rizvi, S., Rauss, P.J., et al.: The FERET evaluation methodology for face-recognition algorithms. IEEE Trans. Pattern Anal. Mach. Intell. **22**(10), 1090–1104 (2000)

28. Phillips, P.J., Wechsler, H., Huang, J., Rauss, P.J.: The FERET database and evaluation procedure for face-recognition algorithms. Image Vis. Comput. **16**(5), 295–306 (1998)

29. Porter, M.F.: An algorithm for suffix stripping. Program (2006)

30. Priebe, C., Vaswani, K., Costa, M.: EnclaveDB: a secure database using SGX. IEEE (2018)

31. Qin, Z., Yan, J., Ren, K., Chen, C.W., Wang, C.: Towards efficient privacy-preserving image feature extraction in cloud computing. In: Proceedings of the ACM International Conference on Multimedia, pp. 497–506. ACM (2014)

32. Rane, A., Lin, C., Tiwari, M.: Raccoon: closing digital side-channels through obfuscated execution. In: 24th USENIX Security Symposium (USENIX Security 2015), pp. 431–446 (2015)

33. Shaon, F., Kantarcioglu, M.: A practical framework for executing complex queries over encrypted multimedia data. In: Ranise, S., Swarup, V. (eds.) DBSec 2016. LNCS, vol. 9766, pp. 179–195. Springer, Cham (2016). https://doi.org/10.1007/978-3-319-41483-6_14

34. Shaon, F., Kantarcioglu, M., Lin, Z., Khan, L.: SGX-BigMatrix: a practical encrypted data analytic framework with trusted processors. In: Proceedings of the 2017 ACM SIGSAC Conference on Computer and Communications Security, pp. 1211–1228. ACM (2017)

35. Sun, W., Zhang, R., Lou, W., Hou, Y.T.: Rearguard: secure keyword search using trusted hardware. In: IEEE INFORM (2018)

36. Turk, M., Pentland, A.: Eigenfaces for recognition. J. Cogn. Neurosci. **3**(1), 71–86 (1991)

37. Viola, P., Jones, M.: Rapid object detection using a boosted cascade of simple features. In: Proceedings of the 2001 IEEE Computer Society Conference on Computer Vision and Pattern Recognition, CVPR 2001, vol. 1, pp. I–511. IEEE (2001)

38. Wikipedia contributors: Bitonic sorter – Wikipedia, the free encyclopedia. https://en.wikipedia.org/w/index.php?title=Bitonic_sorter&oldid=908641033. Accessed 20 Apr 2020

39. Xia, Z., Zhu, Y., Sun, X., Wang, J.: A similarity search scheme over encrypted cloud images based on secure transformation. Int. J. Future Gener. Commun. Netw. **6**(6), 71–80 (2013)

40. Yan, H., Chen, Z., Jia, C.: SSIR Secure similarity image retrieval in IoTD. Inf. Sci. **479**, 153–163 (2019)

41. Zheng, W., Dave, A., Beekman, J., Popa, R.A., Gonzalez, J., Stoica, I.: Opaque: a data analytics platform with strong security. In: 14th USENIX Symposium on Networked Systems Design and Implementation (NSDI 2017). USENIX Association, Boston (2017)

Readability of Privacy Policies

Barbara Krumay$^{(\boxtimes)}$ [ORCID] and Jennifer Klar

Johannes Kepler University Linz, Linz, Austria
barbara.krumay@jku.at

Abstract. Privacy policies have become an important tool to communicate with users on the website of companies and inform them about how, what and what for private data is collected. In these privacy policies, social, legal and technical aspects have to be explained in a clear and understandable way. However, as legal and technical issues often require specific expert language, organizations have to find a solution to transfer the information in a way that the users are able to comprehend it. To measure readability, several approaches have been available for quite a long time. Whereas qualitative parameters try to assess a text, approaches to measure readability in a more quantitative way to calculate a score or grade compared to an education scheme. We investigated seven quantitative approaches to measure readability by applying them to the privacy policies of companies. The results slightly differed, depending on the granularity and measurement approach. However, we conclude that by combining different approaches, companies may receive information regarding the readability of their privacy policies. Based on the results, we describe an approach to measure the readability of privacy statements.

Keywords: Readability · Privacy policies · Cookies · Comprehensibility

1 Introduction

Privacy policies are a vital instrument for communicating with customers about how and why sensitive data (personal data revealing, for example, racial or ethnic origin, political opinions, religious or philosophical beliefs) is collected [1]. It has been shown, that about 90% of all websites in the US collect data from users during their visit [2]. Companies, in particular, those doing business on the internet are forced by laws and regulations to explain reasons, amount and handling of personal data collected. However, these statements are often full of expert language, on technological or legal issues [3]. The language used is therefore hard to understand for most people without technical or legal education. Some regulations like the GDPR [4, 5], force companies to focus on the use of clear and understandable language in privacy statements, yet do not further elaborate on it. Some studies already addressed the influence of readability (e.g. [3, 6]) on users' behaviour [7, 8]. Although general measures for assessing the readability of text do exist, their applicability for privacy policies has rarely been tested (e.g. [6]). In this study we therefore investigate seven common approaches to assess the readability by applying them on selected privacy statements of fifteen companies. The goal of this

© IFIP International Federation for Information Processing 2020
Published by Springer Nature Switzerland AG 2020
A. Singhal and J. Vaidya (Eds.): DBSec 2020, LNCS 12122, pp. 388–399, 2020.
https://doi.org/10.1007/978-3-030-49669-2_22

research consequently is to show, how existing approaches can be applied to assess the readability of privacy policies. Thus, we aim at closing the gap between current research and possibilities to measure readability of privacy policies. As a result, we aim at suggesting an approach on how to measure readability of privacy policies. The remainder of the paper is structured as follows. First, we give a brief overview of related research followed by a description of our approach and research design. We, in brief, describe seven different approaches, followed by results from applying these approaches to measure readability. In addition, we exposed the text to consumers of different grade levels, asking them to assess the text in terms of readability. Next, we discuss the results and provide recommendations based on the insights gained. Finally, we show limitations and provide some insights into further research.

2 Related Research

Privacy can be understood as a "claim of individuals, groups and institutions to determine for themselves, when, how and to what extent information about them is communicated to others" [9]. This offers the individual the possibility to decide which of its private data is transferred to someone else [10]. As companies need user data to stay competitive [1, 11], a conflict between customers' right to privacy and organizations' need to know about their customers to enable targeted marketing is necessary [12, 13] evolves. The increasing reluctance to providing private [10] and sensitive data (Personally Identifiable Information – PII) [14] has been investigated widely. On the other hand, it has been shown that most people disclose a lot more data than they think, often referred to as privacy paradox [13, 16]. Research suggests that people make informed considerations, even calculate the pros and cons before transferring PII [15]. To communicate with users and overcome their concerns [17], organizations use privacy policies to inform about how, which and when data is collected and stored [3]. This is a common way of communicating data collection activities and establish an agreement [18] or informed consent [19] between organization and user. The role of privacy policies in e-commerce has already been discussed intensively, for being necessary to establish a relationship [6] and trust [15, 20, 21] as well as influencing customers' purchase behaviour [22]. Privacy policies in general consist of information mainly regarding legal [25, 26] and technical issues or technology applied [3, 27], but also social issues [18, 23, 24]. The language used to explain and describe legal issues and technical activities is often rather complex and has been found to protect the organization not explaining the rights of users [23, 28]. Complex and hard to assess privacy statements influence the balance of power between users and organizations [29].

Not only research claimed, that readability of privacy statements has to be improved to enable all customers and users to understand privacy statements [8]. Policymakers have found this to be important resulting in the General Data Protection Regulation (GDPR), which came into force on May, 25th 2018 [5]. However, in the last twenty years, it was evidenced that privacy statements are not written in plain and clear language [3, 7, 30]. By contrast, privacy policies often require a high level of reading ability and vocabulary above the average [3, 30, 31], distracting the users from reading them [6]. Readability has been defined as the "sum total (including the interactions) of all those elements within a given piece of printed material that affects the success that a group of readers have with it" [32]. In the early 1960s, Klare defined that readability is "the ease of understanding or comprehension due to the style of writing" [33], focusing on writing style but not text structure. Later in the same century, McLaughlin defined readability as "the degree to which a given class of people find certain reading matter compelling and comprehensible" [34], identifying classes of people as determining factor for readability of a text. In particular for young people, it was found that simple language, paragraph organization, avoidance of redundant information spread in the text as well as highlighting important information would improve readability [27]. And even more, organization and structure (see [32]) or design [27] of the text influence readability. Readability is also influenced by the readers' general ability to read and how interested they are in the text [32]. Other authors identified more quantitative characteristics of text as influential, such as length (i.e., word count and words per sentence), negative words (negativity rating), immediacy, vagueness or subordinating conjunctions [29]. Such measurable variables qualify for calculating scores, making readability of text comparable [29]. Different approaches for calculating scores are at hand [35, 36], such as the Flesch-Kincaid Grade Level (respectively Flesch Reading Ease) [37–39], the Gunning Fog Index Readability Formula [40], the SMOG Grading by McLaughlin [34], the Coleman-Liau Index [41], and the Automated Readability Index [42]. Other scoring schemes like the Dale-Chall Index [32, 43] and the Fry Graph Readability Formula [44] are also important. It is important to notice, these approaches have been developed for and applied on books, websites, medical, military or official documents.

3   Research Design

To show how existing approaches can be applied to assess the readability of privacy policies, we applied the scales on a sample of privacy statements of 15 companies listed in the Forbes Magazine. To allow comparability and control over biasing factors, only a very specific part existing in every privacy statement was used as the basis for assessment and calculation. All privacy statements were downloaded in spring 2019 and preprocessed (i.e., converted into machine-readable text). The analysis of the privacy statements was supported by software The analysis was conducted by two researchers independently. In general, the process started with an in-depth literature review to identify approaches to assess readability. Next, we identified privacy policies and decided which part of them should be assessed for readability. We applied qualitative analysis first, relying on qualities of text influencing readability, on these parts. Next, we applied the quantitative approaches and exposed the sample to people on different grade levels.

3.1   Approaches to Assess Readability

Approaches to measure the readability of different types of English text (e.g. military or medical context) have been developed already in the last century and are still the basis for current computer-based readability assessment [45, 46]. Based on prior studies [35, 36, 45, 47], we selected seven scales (Dale-Chall Index [32, 43], Automated Readability Index Gunning Fog Index Readability Formula [40], SMOG Grading [34], Fry Graph

Readability Formula [44], Flesch-Kincaid Grade Level [37–39], Coleman-Liau Index [41]) with low standard errors. They have been discussed extensively in the literature and are among the most used readability scales [45, 46]. In general, the approaches use different variables derived from the text (e.g., word count, sentence length) and combine the numbers with constants to adjust the weight of the variables.

The Dale-Chall Index [32, 43] (DCI) relies on the average sentence length (ASL) and the percentage of unfamiliar words (out of a list of 3,000 commonly used words) [32, 43]. Calculated are the Dale score (ratio of familiar and unfamiliar words as a percentage and the raw score (RS), which is converted into grades based on a correction table. The Automated Readability Index (ARI) [42], uses sentence length (words per sentence - SL) and word length (number of characters or letters per word - WL). It has been developed to overcome flaws in other approaches [38, 43]. The Gunning Fog Index Readability Formula (FOG Index) [40] uses average sentence length (ASL) and the number of complex words of a text of approximately 100 words [48]. Complexity of words is related to length represented by syllables of a word, whereby for example three or more syllables in general qualify for a complex or long word. The number of complex words is divided by the number of overall words, leading to a percentage of hard words (PHW). The results correspond to the US grade levels. The SMOG Grading [34] is related to the FOG Index as it uses the idea of complex words, expressed in syllables. In addition, it has some rules to split the text and count polysyllable (with three or more syllables) words (PSW). It relies on 30 sentences only, hence, some improved formulas have been developed [35, 49]. The Fry Graph Readability Formula [44], relies on three different parts at the beginning, middle and end of the text of 100 words each (resulting in 300 words). The average number of sentences as well as the average number of syllables are calculated. The values are applied to the so-called Fry Graph [44], where word length (short words – long words) is on one axes and sentence length (short sentence – long sentence) is on the other. By allocating the results to according sections, the grade level can be derived from it [44]. The Flesch Reading Ease (FRE), which focuses on the relationship of average sentence length (ASL) compared to the average number of syllables per word (ASW) or syllables per 100 words (ASW/100). The Flesch-Kincaid Grade Level [29, 37] (FKGL) extends the FRE, but focuses more on the length of sentences due to constants used in the formula. Finally, the Coleman-Liau Index (CLI) [41] focuses on a readability formula that can be applied by computer programs. The variables are the average sentence length (ASL) represented by the average number of sentences per 100 words and the average number of characters per 100 words (AC). Table 1 briefly summarizes variables, formulas and results of the seven approaches.

3.2 Selection and Analysis of Privacy Statements

Our study focuses on companies operating in Europe to reflect the GDPR [5] forcing companies to aim at understandability of privacy policies. As sensitive data is mainly an issue for end consumers, B2B-companies were not selected, leading to fifteen companies (Allianz, Axa Group, Banco Santander, BMW Group, BNP Paribas, Daimler, Gazprom, HSBC Holding, ING Group, Nestle, Sberbank, Shell, Siemens, Total, Volkswagen – links to the privacy statements are provided upon request). We pre-screened the privacy statements to identify particular parts which are appropriate (e.g., in terms of length)

Table 1. Approaches Chosen – Overview (incl. formulas)

Approach	Based on (Variables)	Results
Dale-Chall Index [32, 43] (1948)	Average sentence length; percentage of unfamiliar words	Index (Grade levels)
RS = (ASL * 0.496) + Dale score * 0.1579 + 3.6365 [32, 43]		
Automated Readability Index [42] (1967)	Words per sentence; characters per word	Index (Grade levels)
GL = (4.71 * WL) + (0.5 * SL) – 21.43 [42] / ARI = WL + (9 * SL) [42]		
Gunning Fog Index Readability Formula [40] (1968)	Sentence length; complex words	Grade levels
FOG Index = 0.4 * (ASL + PHW) [40]		
SMOG Grading [34] (1969)	Number of polysyllable words	Grade levels
SMOG Grading = $\sqrt[2]{PSW}$ + 3 [34]		
Fry Graph Readability Formula [44] (1968)	Average number of sentences; average number of syllables per word	(Grade levels)
FRE = 206,835 – (1.015 * ASL) – (84.6 * ASW) [38]		
Flesch-Kincaid Grade Level [37–39] (1975)	Average sentence length; average number of syllables per word	Grade levels
FKGL = (0.39 * ASL) + (11.8 * ASW) – 15.59 [39]		
Coleman-Liau Index [41] (1975)	Average sentence length; average number of characters per word	Index (Grade levels)
CLI = (0.0588 * AC) – (0.296 * ASL) – 15.8 [35, 41]		

for analysis. By comparing the privacy statements, we identified the part describing 'cookie policy' (further referred to as the sample) as most appropriate. First, this part was present in every document. Second, it is a rather technical part which is not so easy to comprehend without further knowledge. Third, in all statements, this part was long enough for applying all seven approaches.

To set a baseline, we analyzed the text parts based on qualitative parameters such as simple language, paragraph organization, avoidance of redundant information spread in the text as well as highlighting important information (to improve readability) [27]. In addition, we assessed, organization and structure (see [32]) respectively design [27]. We developed a coding sheet and to control for bias, two researchers independently analyzed them but compared and discussed the results after having finished their analysis. The coding sheet included the qualitative parameters and scores from 'fulfilled' to 'not fulfilled' in five grades (ordinal scale). We calculated inter-coder and intra-coder reliability based on Holsti [50], resulting in score of 0.97 and 0.95 (intracoder reliability) and 0.81 (intercoder reliability). We used MAXQDA, which is a tool for analyzing text in a semi-automated way, to count text length, sentences, words, syllables and characters based on the according rules. In addition, we used the software for quantifying readability parameters such as negativity rate or vagueness and qualification [29]. Further rules had to be established due to some specific words in cookie policies (e.g., the name of the company, contact details or and tables). We applied all seven approaches to the sample and documented the results. In a final step to verify the quantitative results, we exposed the sample to 15 people on five different grade levels in accordance with the Dale-Chal approach (i.e., 7–8, 9–10, 11–12, 13–15, above 16 – three people per grade level). The participants were selected from students of an international school (with English as their first language, age 13–18 years) and an international study program (age 19–24 years). Based on variables used in the selected scales, we developed a validation scheme of five questions (5-point liker scales): length of text (short – long), length of sentences (short – long), complex sentences (some – many), unfamiliar words (some – many) and general readability (very easy – very hard) and documented reading speed (expressed in minutes per 1 500 words). However, we only assessed their impression, not how well they understood the text.

4 Results

Although quantitative approaches to measure readability are in the focus of this study, we first summarize the results from the qualitative analysis. Regarding the simple language used in the sample, we found some parts easy to read ('fulfilled'), whereas others require a rather deep knowledge technical knowledge ('hardly fulfilled' or 'not fulfilled'). Parameters like paragraph organization, avoidance of redundant information spread in the text as well as highlighting important information [27] has been found in most of the documents ('partly fulfilled' or 'fulfilled'). The same applies to the structure [32] and design [27], which has been 'partly fulfilled' or 'fulfilled' in all but one text of the sample. Regarding quantifiable parameters, we first want to give an overview regarding word count (WC), sentence count (SC), average sentence length in words (ASL), average syllables per word (ASW), letters per word (LW), negativity rating (NR), vagueness and qualification (V&Q) [29] (see Table 2). The word count (WC) on average is approximately 849 words, whereas the sentence count (SC) is 41. A rather wide variation can be found in the average sentence length (ASL), varying from 18.06 to 40.26. The longest text has 1518 words and 75 sentences (BMW Group), whereas the shortest text of the sample has only 303 words (Allianz) respectively 19 sentences (Banco Santander), which shows also the longest average sentence length (40.26) in the text. Average syllables per word (ASW) are rather stable between 1.6 and 1.8, whereas the average characters per word (AC) vary from 4.7 to 5.1. The rather low variation in ASW and AC can be explained by the limited variety of words in the text. Regarding negativity rating, a range below 1% of the words being negative is seen as not being too complex [29]. In five cases, the result is above 1, but still rather low. In the same manner, vagueness and qualification is in the range (below 2%), which is considered acceptable for comprehensibility [29]. Table 2 summarizes the results.

Next, all seven approaches were applied and compared to each other. We do not report on the Dale-Chall Index (as the results were not conclusive, probably biased by the Dales list of familiar words) and the FRE, which is part as the FKGL. In general, considering

Table 2. Quantifiable Parameters of the Sample - Legend: word count (WC), sentence count (SC), average sentence length in words (ASL), average syllables per word (ASW), average characters per word (AC), negativity rating (NR), vagueness and qualification (V&Q)

	WC	SC	ASL	ASW	AC	NR	V&Q
Allianz	303	49	21.64	1.7	5.0	0.33%	1.65%
AXA Group	560	31	18.06	1.6	5.0	1.07%	0.89%
Banco Santander	765	19	40.26	1.6	4.7	0.39%	1.31%
BMW Group	1518	75	20.24	1.7	5.0	1.25%	0.13%
BNP Paribas	788	30	26.27	1.6	4.7	0.13%	0.76%
Daimler	813	44	18.48	1.6	4.8	0.62%	0.37%
Gazprom	1237	52	23.79	1.7	5.0	1.37%	1.37%
HSBC Holding	941	41	22.95	1.6	4.7	0.64%	0.53%
ING Group	781	41	19.05	1.7	5.0	0.90%	0.77%
Nestle	1144	51	22.43	1.6	4.7	0.52%	0.87%
Sberbank	689	27	25.52	1.8	5.0	0.29%	0.29%
Shell	878	43	20.42	1.6	4.8	1.14%	0.80%
Siemens	1261	59	21.37	1.7	5.1	1.11%	0.48%
Total	566	27	20.96	1.6	4.8	0.71%	0.35%
Volkswagen	492	24	20.50	1.6	4.7	0.81%	0.41%

all results, the sample seems to require at least grade 10. As we can see, the Coleman-Liau Index (CLI) and the Flesch-Kincaid Grade Level (FKGL) are often slightly lower, compared to other scores. However, some scores are not in-line, for example, the CLI related to the text from Banco Santander pretty much average, whereas the other scores (ARI, FOG, SMOG, FKGL) are rather high and so is the average of all scores for this text. This is interesting since the text from Banco Santander has already been identified as the one with the longest average sentence length and the lowest number of sentences. The scores from the text from Daimler, interestingly, are rather low (average 11.16, all scores below 12). Another low average score (11.31) has been calculated from the scores for the cookie policy of Daimler, however, the FOG is above 12. A summary of the results of six approaches, including an average (excluding Fry), is given in Table 3.

By exposing the sample to fifteen consumers, we gained more insights for the interpretation of the results. The text with the highest average score (17.75 - Banco Santander, Table 3) was experienced by all participants as the longest, most complex and hard to understand. However, the text experienced as holding many unfamiliar words was from Gazprom. Interestingly, fast readers (5 min per 1 500 words) and slow readers (12 min per 1 500 words) were found on all grade levels. In general, text experienced by all participants as very easy or easy to read (ETR) showed average scores below 12. By contrast, text experienced as hard to read (HTR) by all participants showed average scores above 14. Averages score between 12 and 14 showed an expected result: hard to

Table 3. Results of Approaches - Scores per Approach and Assessment of Participants (Exp. = Experience, HTR = Hard to read for all participants/ETR = Easy to read for all participants/M = mixed results

	ARI	FOG	SMOG	FKGL	CLI	*Avg.*	Fry	Exp.
Allianz	12.94	13.67	13.24	11.73	12.03	*12.72*	College	M
AXA Group	11.15	11.87	12.00	10.34	11.74	*11.42*	12	ETR
Banco Santander	20.84	20.08	17.59	18.99	11.25	*17.75*	College	HTR
BMW Group	12.24	13.00	13.00	12.36	12.07	*12.53*	College	M
BNP Paribas	13.84	15.28	14.00	13.53	10.87	*13.50*	12	M
Daimler	10.42	12.26	12.00	10.50	10.60	*11.16*	12	ETR
Gazprom	14.01	14.85	15.00	13.75	12.38	*13.99*	College	HTR
HSBC Holding	12.18	13.52	13.00	12.24	10.61	*12.31*	11	M
ING Group	11.64	13.41	13.00	11.90	11.96	*12.38*	College	M
Nestle	11.92	12.85	12.00	12.04	10.56	*11.87*	11	ETR
Sberbank	14.88	16.42	15.59	15.60	12.65	*15.03*	College	HTR
Shell	11.39	12.13	12.00	11.25	10.92	*11.54*	11	ETR
Siemens	13.28	14.67	14.00	12.81	12.66	*13.48*	College	M
Total	11.66	12.20	12.44	11.47	11.11	*11.78*	12	ETR
Volkswagen	10.96	11.78	11.94	11.29	10.58	*11.31*	11	ETR
Average	*12.89*	*13.87*	*13.39*	*12.65*	*11.47*	*12.85*	–	M

read for participants falling into grade level below 12, easy or very easy to read for grade levels above 12. Text from Daimler and Volkswagen were assessed as being very easy to read by all participants.

5   Discussion

As discussed already, due to the drawbacks of qualitative assessment of readability (e.g. requiring trained individuals, subjective assessment, low bias control) automated approaches gain importance [46]. In this study, we investigated how quantitative approaches to measure readability as the basis for computer-based approaches can be applied to privacy statements, in particular cookie policies. The selected approaches use similar variables (e.g., average sentence length, average word length) and combine them [45, 47], to generate easy-to-assess results. The approaches provide scores or grades (related to the US education scheme), indicating the minimum requirement for being able to understand the text. Due to this easy-to-assess result, these approaches have gained some importance for organizations, aiming at improving the readability of their privacy policies due to the variables used and grade scores. This study consequently contributes to both, research, by providing evidence of an ongoing issue, since readability of privacy statements has been addressed in research [7, 8] without providing tools to measure it. For companies, some interesting insights and hints for improving privacy statements' readability may be derived.

Besides similarities, the approaches investigated differ significantly in terms of variables, rules and sample size. Whereas some approaches can be applied on small text parts (e.g., FRE and FKGL 100 words), others require for example 300 words from a longer text (e.g., Fry Graph Readability Formula). Regarding variables used, sentence length seems to be an accurate measure, however, the average number of syllables per word is not a good parameter for readability assessment [36]. This is interesting, as in our study the approaches using syllables (Fry Graph Readability Formula, Flesch-Kincaid Grade Level and SMOG Grading) are not specifically different from the other approaches. However, privacy statements (as text type) differ from traditional text types (e.g., in textbooks), sharing some characteristics with web pages, on which the application of readability measures has been questioned [36]. In addition, for specific text types, such as cookie policies, the existing rules may not fit. Hence, defining rules for new terms (e.g., email addresses) is necessary. A list of familiar words (like in the Dale-Chall formula [43]) would have to be adopted to the specific context (i.e., privacy statements on web pages) and updated frequently.

These quantitative approaches to measure readability, ignore abilities of the readers which are not reflected by grade levels (e.g., vocabulary knowledge in the specific field) [3]. Traditional readability metrics do not consider people with intellectual disabilities [52]. As the approaches are not designed to measure how well a single person would comprehend the content of the written text since they exclude the reader's attitude towards the text [51]. For example, a person on grade level 8, interested in computers and online games, may have more specific required vocabulary knowledge compared to a person on 16th grade with no interest in computers at all. Even more, as semantic complexity is measured, additional factors influencing readability (e.g., writing style, negativity rating) are not considered [3]. However, our additional assessment by exposing the sample to fifteen participants more or less supported the results of the quantitative approaches. We do not want to overemphasize the results, but there seems to be a borderline marking a text as being in general easy to read or hard to read regardless of grade levels. However, to overcome the problems of traditional readability measures [3], statistical language models [36] or cloze procedures [53, 54] have been discussed. Combining lexical and syntactical traits of tests [52] as well as integrate content in the formula [36] seems to be a valid solution. Further research is necessary in order to test, whether this approach would lead to significantly different results, in particular when applied to privacy statements. Cloze procedures [53, 54] integrate the know-how of the readers by involving people from the target group of the text to assess readability. In a rather complex procedure, participants are asked to replicate certain passages, by filling in removed words [3].

Companies, interested in improving the readability of privacy statements, could combine different scales, as already discussed in the literature [35], avoiding over- and underestimating the scores. Although not specifically mentioned in the GDPR, a grade level of 9–10 seems to be appropriate to provide privacy statements readable for the public in general. Based on our insights gained from this study, we suggest using combing approaches which are syllable- and word-based, to not favour the one over the other. Due to cost and time constraints, companies would not apply all seven approaches. With our sample, we tested different combinations related to the average score. Resulting in a combination of FOG, SMOG and CLI on average changes the results by 0.05 grades. Only the average score of the text from Banco Santander changed by -1.4 (average grade level 16). We suggest combining the three approaches, enriched by specific rules and related to privacy policies (e.g., for contact email), with vagueness and negativity rating (weighted). Two different scenarios to improve the readability of privacy statements are proposed. First, comparing different versions of privacy statements, to identify the one with best readability score or permanently rewriting and measuring privacy policies until the readability formulas generate a certain grade level (e.g., 9–10).

6 Conclusion, Limitations and Further Research

As we have shown in our research, existing approaches to measure readability can be applied to privacy policies, but require some additional rules. The results can be used as a basis for decision making, but do not explicitly suggest, what to change. A combination of different scales and adding some of the qualitative parameters might be a solution. This study for sure has some limitations, as we investigated only the parts or privacy statements, explaining cookies and how they are handled. However, we think that this is not only one of the most recognized parts, but also loaded with technical terms. Another limitation owes to the fact that most measures are only reliable for text in English. Further extending the study to other parts and other companies may reveal different results, in terms of additional rules or ways to improve the measurement. As we have only started this research, we plan further elaborating on it, in particular, we would like to compare scores with more in-depth users' assessment. And even more, since readability does not mean comprehensibility, some more research has to be done on the link of actual privacy statements, readability and comprehensibility.

References

1. Castells, M.: The Rise of the Network Society. Wiley, Chichester (2010). https://doi.org/10.1002/9781444319514
2. Adkinson, W.F., Eisenach, J.A., Lenard, T.M.: Privacy online: a report on the information practices and policies of commercial web sites. Progress and Freedom Foundation, Washington DC (2002)
3. Singh, R.I., Sumeeth, M., Miller, J.: Evaluating the readability of privacy policies in mobile environments. Int. J. Mobile Hum. Comput. Interact. (IJMHCI) **3**, 55–78 (2011)
4. Voss, W.G.: Looking at European Union data protection law reform through a different prism: the proposed EU General Data Protection Regulation two years later. J. Internet Law **17** (2014)
5. European Commission: Regulation (EU) 2016/679 of the European Parliament and of the Council
6. Milne, G.R., Culnan, M.J., Greene, H.: A longitudinal assessment of online privacy notice readability. J. Public Policy Market. **25**, 238–249 (2006). https://doi.org/10.1509/jppm.25.2.238
7. Ermakova, T., Krasnova, H., Fabian, B.: Exploring the impact of readability of privacy polices on users' trust. In: ECIS 2016 Proceedings, Istanbul, Turkey, p. 17 (2016)

8. Ermakova, T., Baumann, A., Fabian, B., Krasnova, H.: Privacy policies and users' trust: does readability matter? In: Proceedings of the Twentieth Americas Conference on Information Systems, Savannah, p. 12 (2014)

9. Westin, A.F.: Privacy and freedom. Washington Lee Law Rev. **25**, 166 (1968)

10. Acquisti, A., Brandimarte, L., Loewenstein, G.: Privacy and human behavior in the age of information. Science **347**, 509–514 (2015)

11. Flavián, C., Guinalíu, M.: Consumer trust, perceived security and privacy policy: three basic elements of loyalty to a web site I Emerald Insight. Ind. Manage. Data Syst. **106**, 601–620 (2006)

12. Goldfarb, A., Tucker, C.E.: Privacy regulation and online advertising. Manage. Sci. **57**, 57–71 (2011)

13. Awad, K.: The personalization privacy paradox: an empirical evaluation of information transparency and the willingness to be profiled online for personalization. MIS Q. **30**, 13 (2006). https://doi.org/10.2307/25148715

14. Bélanger, F., Hiller, J.S., Smith, W.J.: Trustworthiness in electronic commerce: the role of privacy, security, and site attributes. J. Strateg. Inf. Syst. **11**, 245–270 (2002). https://doi.org/10.1016/S0963-8687(02)00018-5

15. Dinev, T., Hart, P.: An extended privacy calculus model for e-commerce transactions. Inf. Syst. Res. **17**, 61–80 (2006). https://doi.org/10.1287/isre.1060.0080

16. Norberg, P.A., Horne, D.R., Horne, D.A.: The privacy paradox: personal information disclosure intentions versus behaviors. J. Consum. Aff. **41**, 100–126 (2007)

17. Udo, G.J.: Privacy and security concerns as major barriers for e-commerce: a survey study. Inform. Manage. Comput. Secur. **9**(4), 165–174 (2001)

18. Jensen, C., Potts, C.: Privacy policies as decision-making tools: an evaluation of online privacy notices. In: Proceedings of the SIGCHI Conference on Human Factors in Computing Systems, pp. 471–478 (2004). https://doi.org/10.1145/985692.985752

19. Pollach, I.: A typology of communicative strategies in online privacy policies: ethics, power and informed consent. J. Bus. Ethics **62**, 221 (2005)

20. Pan, Y., Zinkhan, G.M.: Exploring the impact of online privacy disclosures on consumer trust. J. Retail. **82**, 331–338 (2006)

21. Wu, K.-W., Huang, S.Y., Yen, D.C., Popova, I.: The effect of online privacy policy on consumer privacy concern and trust. Comput. Hum. Behav. **28**, 889–897 (2012)

22. Tsai, J.Y., Egelman, S., Cranor, L., Acquisti, A.: The effect of online privacy information on purchasing behavior: an experimental study. Inf. Syst. Res. **22**, 254–268 (2011). https://doi.org/10.1287/isre.1090.0260

23. Earp, J., Anton, A., Jarvinen, O.: A social, technical, and legal framework for privacy management and policies. In: AMCIS 2002 Proceedings, Dallas, Texas, pp. 605–612 (2002)

24. Papacharissi, Z., Fernback, J.: Online privacy and consumer protection: an analysis of portal privacy statements. J. Broadcast. Electron. Media **49**, 259–281 (2005). https://doi.org/10.1207/s15506878jobem4903_1

25. Caudill, E.M., Murphy, P.E.: Consumer online privacy: legal and ethical issues. J. Public Policy Market. **19**, 7–19 (2000)

26. Fernback, J., Papacharissi, Z.: Online privacy as legal safeguard: the relationship among consumer, online portal, and privacy policies. New Media Soc. **9**, 715–734 (2007)

27. Micheti, A., Burkell, J., Steeves, V.: Fixing broken doors: strategies for drafting privacy policies young people can understand. Bull. Sci. Technol. Soc. **30**, 130–143 (2010). https://doi.org/10.1177/0270467610365355

28. Earp, J.B., Antón, A.I., Aiman-Smith, L., Stufflebeam, W.H.: Examining Internet privacy policies within the context of user privacy values. IEEE Trans. Eng. Manage. **52**, 227–237 (2005)

29. Cadogan, R.A.: An imbalance of power: the readability of internet privacy policies. J. Bus. Econ. Res. (JBER) **2** (2004)
30. Anton, A., Earp, J.B., Bolchini, D., He, Q., Jensen, C., Stufflebeam, W.: The Lack of Clarity in Financial Privacy Policies and the Need for Standardization. North Carolina State University Technical Report# TR-2 (2003)
31. McDonald, A.M., Reeder, R.W., Kelley, P.G., Cranor, L.F.: A comparative study of online privacy policies and formats. In: Goldberg, I., Atallah, M.J. (eds.) PETS 2009. LNCS, vol. 5672, pp. 37–55. Springer, Heidelberg (2009). https://doi.org/10.1007/978-3-642-03168-7_3
32. Dale, E., Chall, J.S.: The concept of readability. Elem. Eng. **26**, 19–26 (1949)
33. Klare, G.R.: Assessing readability. Read. Res. Q. **10**, 62–102 (1974). https://doi.org/10.2307/747086
34. McLaughlin, G.H.: SMOG grading-a new readability formula. J. Read. **12**, 639–646 (1969)
35. Karmakar, S., Zhu, Y.: Visualizing multiple text readability indexes. In: 2010 International Conference on Education and Management Technology, pp. 133–137. IEEE (2010)
36. Si, L., Callan, J.: A statistical model for scientific readability. In: Proceedings of the Tenth International Conference on Information and Knowledge Management, pp. 574–576 (2001)
37. Flesch, R., Gould, A.J.: The Art of Readable Writing. Harper, New York (1949)
38. Flesch, R.: A new readability yardstick. J. Appl. Psychol. **32**, 221 (1948)
39. Kincaid, J.P., Fishburne Jr., R.P., Rogers, R.L., Chissom, B.S.: Derivation of new readability formulas (automated readability index, fog count and flesch reading ease formula) for navy enlisted personnel. University of Central Florida (1975)
40. Gunning, R.: Technique of Clear Writing. McGraw-Hill, New York (1952)
41. Coleman, M., Liau, T.L.: A computer readability formula designed for machine scoring. J. Appl. Psychol. **60**, 283 (1975)
42. Senter, R.J., Smith, E.A.: Automated Readability Index. Aerospace Medical Research Laboratories, Ohio (1967)
43. Dale, D.: The Dale-Chall formula for predicting readability. Educ. Res. Bull. **27**, 11–20 (1948)
44. Fry, E.: A readability formula that saves time. J. Read. **11**, 513–578 (1968)
45. McCallum, D.R., Peterson, J.L.: Computer-based readability indexes. In: Proceedings of the ACM 1982 Conference, pp. 44–48 (1982)
46. Atcherson, S.R., DeLaune, A.E., Hadden, K., Zraick, R.I., Kelly-Campbell, R.J., Minaya, C.P.: A computer-based readability analysis of consumer materials on the American Speech-Language-Hearing Association website. Contemp. Issues Commun. Sci. Disord. **41**, 12–23 (2014)
47. Meyer, B.J.: Text coherence and readability. Top. Lang. Disord. **23**, 204–224 (2003)
48. Vervalin, C.H.: Checked your fog index lately? IEEE Trans. Prof. Commun., 87–88 (1980). https://doi.org/10.1109/TPC.1980.6501857
49. Olsen, S.: Instruments for clinical health-care research. Jones & Bartlett Learning (2004)
50. Neuendorf, K.A.: The Content Analysis Guidebook. SAGE Publications, Inc., Thousand Oaks (2017). https://doi.org/10.4135/9781071802878
51. Rowan, M., Dehlinger, J.: A privacy policy comparison of health and fitness related mobile applications. Proc. Comput. Sci. **37**, 348–355 (2014)
52. Feng, L., Elhadad, N., Huenerfauth, M.: Cognitively motivated features for readability assessment. In: Proceedings of the 12th Conference of the European Chapter of the ACL (EACL 2009), pp. 229–237 (2009)
53. Bormuth, J.R.: The cloze readability procedure. Elem. Eng. **45**, 429–436 (1968)
54. Taylor, W.L.: "Cloze procedure": a new tool for measuring readability. J. Q. **30**, 415–433 (1953). https://doi.org/10.1177/107769905303000401

Author Index

Printed in the United States
By Bookmasters